THE LITERARY 100,
REVISED EDITION

THE LITERARY 100,
REVISED EDITION

A Ranking of the Most Influential Novelists,
Playwrights, and Poets of All Time

Daniel S. Burt

An imprint of Infobase Publishing

The Literary 100, Revised Edition: A Ranking of the Most Influential Novelists, Playwrights, and Poets of All Time

Copyright © 2009 by Daniel S. Burt

Facts On File, Inc.
An imprint of Infobase Publishing
132 West 31st Street
New York NY 10001

The poems of W. H. Auden are reprinted by permission of Random House, Inc.,
   from *Collected Poems*.
The poems of Robert Frost are reprinted by permission of Henry Holt and Co. from
   The Poetry of Robert Frost.
The poems of Wallace Stevens are reprinted by permission of Alfred A. Knopf, Inc.,
   from *Collected Poems*, copyright © 1923, renewed 1951 by Wallace Stevens.
The poems of W. B. Yeats are reprinted with the permission of Scribner, a division of
   Simon & Schuster, from *The Collected Poems of W. B. Yeats*, Revised Second Edition,
   edited by Richard J. Finneran (New York: Scribner, 1996).

Library of Congress Cataloging-in-Publication Data

Burt, Daniel S.
  The literary 100 : a ranking of the most influential novelists, playwrights, and poets of all time / Daniel S. Burt. — Rev. ed.
      p. cm.
  Includes bibliographical references and index.
  ISBN-13: 978-0-8160-6267-6 (hc : alk. paper)
  1. Authors—Biography. 2. Literature—History and criticism. I. Title.
  PN451.B87 2008
  809—dc22
  [B]   2008010066

Text design by Joan M. Toro

Printed in the United States of America

MP ML 10 9 8 7 6 5 4 3 2 1

Grateful acknowledgment is made to the following sources for permission to reproduce photographs:

Chinua Achebe: Brigitte Lacombe

Emily Dickinson: Amherst College Library

Christopher Marlowe (Putative Portrait): Masters and Fellows of Corpus Christi College, Cambridge

Robert Musil: Austrian Cultural Institute

Bertolt Brecht (Jörg Kolbe), Ralph Ellison, Seamus Heaney (Christopher Felser), Kawabata Yasunari, Doris Lessing (Christopher Felser), Vladimir Nabokov, Flannery O'Connor, George Orwell, Harold Pinter (Hulton Deutsch), Rainer Maria Rilke, and Wallace Stevens: © Bettman/ CORBIS

E. M. Forster, Federico García Lorca, Marcel Proust, and Virginia Woolf: Culver Pictures, Inc.

Günter Grass and Franz Kafka: German Information Center

Samuel Beckett: Grove Press (Jerry Bauer)

Jorge Luis Borges, Du Fu, Zeami Motokiyo, Jun'ichirō Tanizaki, Cao Xueqin: Harvard University Archives, Harvard-Yenching Library

W. H. Auden, Jane Austen, Charlotte Brontë, Feodor Dostoevsky, Theodore Dreiser, George Eliot, William Faulkner, F. Scott Fitzgerald, Gustave Flaubert, Robert Frost, Nikolai Gogol, Nathaniel Hawthorne, Heinrich Heine, Ernest Hemingway, Arthur Miller, Luigi Pirandello, Edgar Allan Poe, Gertrude Stein, Mark Twain, Walt Whitman, Oscar Wilde, Tennessee Williams, Richard Wright: Library of Congress

Aeschylus, Aristophanes, Honoré de Balzac, Charles Baudelaire, William Blake, Giovanni Boccaccio, Emily Brontë, Robert Browning, Lord Byron, Catullus, Miguel de Cervantes Saavedra, Geoffrey Chaucer, Anton Chekov, Joseph Conrad, Dante Alighieri, Daniel Defoe, Charles Dickens, John Donne, Euripides, Henry Fielding, Du Fu, Johann Wolfgang von Goethe, Thomas Hardy, Homer, Victor Hugo, Henrik Ibsen, Henry James, James Joyce, John Keats, D. H. Lawrence, John Milton, Molière, Ovid, Francesco Petrarch, Alexander Pope, Alexander Pushkin, François Rabelais, Jean Racine, Walter Scott, William Shakespeare, Percy Bysshe Shelley, Sophocles, Stendhal, Laurence Sterne, August Strindberg, Jonathan Swift, Alfred, Lord Tennyson, William Makepeace Thackeray, Leo Tolstoy, Anthony Trollope, Virgil, Voltaire, and William Wordsworth: New York Public Library Picture Collection

Albert Camus, T. S. Eliot, Gabriel García Márquez, Thomas Mann, Toni Morrison, Pablo Neruda, Eugene O'Neill, George Bernard Shaw, Isaac Bashevis Singer, Rabindranath Tagore, and William Butler Yeats: Nobel Foundation

CONTENTS

ACKNOWLEDGMENTS

I am extremely grateful for the advice and assistance I received during the preparation of this book. Although I am indebted to a number of faculty members at Wesleyan University for their sensible guidance in the earliest stages of the ranking, I alone am responsible for any criticism my choices receive. Thanks to Carla M. Antonaccio, associate professor of classical studies; Anthony H. Chambers, professor of Asian languages and literatures; Antonio Gonzalez, professor of Romance languages and literatures; Indira Karamcheti, associate professor of English; Leo A. Lensing, professor of German studies; Joyce O. Lowrie, professor of Romance languages and literatures; Priscilla Meyer, professor of Russian language and literature; William Pinch, assistant professor of history; Roger A. Sanchez-Berroa, director of the language laboratory; Diana Sorensen, professor of Romance languages and literatures; Khachig Tololyan, professor of English; Ellen B. Widmer, professor of Asian languages and literatures.

Thanks as well to Justina Gregory, professor of classical studies at Smith College. I owe a particularly large debt to Krishna R. Winston, professor of German studies at Wesleyan University, for her support and friendship. I am grateful to my students at Wesleyan University, particularly to my class in the Graduate Liberal Studies Program during the fall of 1997, who shared their thoughts with me. I am grateful as well to the staffs at Wesleyan University's Olin Memorial Library, the New York Public Library Picture Collection, the Prints and Photographs Division of the Library of Congress, and the Harvard-Yenching Library for their many courtesies. I want particularly to thank Taylor Loeb for her skill and dedication in helping with the illustrations to this book; Donald J. Davidson for his patience and assistance, and most especially Jim Ellison, who, over a series of pleasant and stimulating conversations, helped me focus on essential questions. Lastly, I owe the greatest debt to my wife, Deborah G. Felder.

PREFACE TO NEW EDITION

Few writers get the opportunity of a "do over," as I have with this expanded version of my previous book, *The Literary 100*. Since it was published in 2001, I have often been asked about the 100 I selected as part of the honorable mentions list, a second grouping of worthy writers more than deserving of recognition for their considerable achievement. Readers have wondered, as with the main ranking, why these and not others? Now I have the opportunity to respond, at least in part, by expanding the main ranking by an additional 25. Rather than simply promoting 25 bench players to the starting lineup and adding them to the bottom of the batting order, I have taken the opportunity in this new edition to reexamine and reformulate the entire ranking. I have indeed promoted some and proposed new names, while integrating the 25 fully into the ranking where it made the most sense to do so, based on a comparative and fresh assessment.

Taking a fresh look at the entire enterprise—the selection and ranking of the greatest poets, dramatists, and fiction writers of all time—after several years is inevitable. Considerable time has passed since I made my initial selections and rankings. The list alters over time because I have changed. I often tell my students that the greatest works of literature demand to be reread every five years or so, not because they alter, but because you do. Every few years you bring a different perspective, informed by different experiences, to bear on the texts, and suddenly what was familiar seems strange, while formerly unnoticed aspects of the work assume a new prominence and urgency. Most of us begin by identifying with Hamlet but wind up with Lear! Reading Joyce's great novel *Ulysses* first as a student, I sympathized with the alienated and isolated Stephen Dedalus, my undergraduate soul mate; in maturity, I, like Joyce himself, have shifted my allegiance to the middle-aged striver and survivor Leopold Bloom. Time and experience alter everything, including literary monuments; they, of course, similarly affect rankings of literary greatness.

Since 2001, when *The Literary 100* appeared, I have been actively teaching many of the writers on the original list, as well as others. Works that I thought I knew, I now know, if not better, differently. Other writers have forced upon me new perspectives and challenges to established views. I have also spent much of my time since 2001 completing two additional volumes prompted by the success of *The Literary 100—The Novel 100*, rankings of the greatest novels of all time, and *The Drama 100*, the greatest plays of all time. Each book took about three years to complete, an absorption into the ways and means of novelists and playwrights that I am sure has found its way into the revised *Literary 100*. From the vantage point of time and experience, if not wisdom, I have returned to the original questions posed by *The Literary 100* in its introduction: "What makes a literary artist great? How can we measure and compare that greatness?" By inviting an additional 25 to the table, the seating arrangement had to change. Some of the alterations to the ranking seem, from my perspective on my former self, corrections in the mode of "What on Earth was I thinking?" Others have allowed me to redress some perceived imbalances in various categories of genre, gender, nationality, and historical coverage. Ultimately, I believe that *The Literary 100, Revised Edition*, is a much stronger book by having to accommodate 25 additional writers. The debate over questions of literary importance can only be enhanced by additional representatives.

Here, then, again, is one reader's attempt to frame a consideration of literary greatness. I look forward to seeing how it all looks in another seven years.

INTRODUCTION

Compiling a ranking of the most influential literary artists of all time is not a task for the faint of heart. Although I have heeded the caution that fools rush in where scholars fear to tread, I also have been energized by an undertaking that seems a rarity nowadays, as the study of literature has been given over largely to specialists who seldom venture beyond their chosen, narrow territory into a tremendously rich and diverse field of study. The attempt to look at literature as a whole, comparatively, across cultural and historical divisions, certainly invites charges of superficiality and bias, but the effort remains a worthy one if it serves to stimulate thinking about literature from the broadest possible perspective. What makes a literary artist great? How can we measure and compare that greatness? What follows is one possible set of answers to these questions. In this ranking, I have tried to determine which novelists, playwrights, and poets have asserted the greatest influence, and which writers opened up the boundaries of the imagination in the most significant ways.

If my choices invite criticism and different conclusions, so much the better, because controversy should lead to further thought and discussion of literary values. I hope that my perspective will stimulate your own. Although I have taught the works of many of the writers in this ranking for more than 25 years, I make no special claims to comprehensive expertise in the full range of world literature over the centuries. Rather, I have approached the task in the spirit of a general reader who is forced to choose, based on literary tradition, critical history, and personal preference, the best that has been written. I have tried not to let any one of these elements assert too much weight in the process. Nor have I ignored a subjective component in this ranking. I have, as best as I could, made choices that reflect some consensus beyond personal taste or a narrow cultural bias.

Influence, in particular, is a tricky concept, and popularity alone is an insufficient measure for literary greatness. There are numerous examples in literary history of authors ignored by their contemporaries but revered by later generations, as well as enormously popular writers whom posterity has forgotten. Should a literary work, therefore, be evaluated for its impact on its own time or on ours, and particularly in non-Western literature, on its own culture or through translation within Western culture? My ranking of the best novelists, playwrights, and poets of all time tries to balance these issues while recognizing that another writer, from a different time or culture as well as my own, determined to attempt an elusive level of objectivity, would have provided a different list.

In a sense, this book is a variant on the perennially fascinating question of what one should take to a desert island, with a limit of 125 of the best possible expressions of literary imagination. I posed this problem to a number of my academic colleagues and students to test my own choices and to learn from theirs, with revealing results. Among scholars it was not surprising that the writers with whom each specialized ranked highly; in many cases, the figures on one scholar's list were left off another's list entirely. Many scholars also were reluctant even to state an opinion on the relative merits of authors beyond their area of study. My students were the least intimidated by the question of literary greatness and were often far more willing to challenge conventional wisdom for the pleasure principle that many scholars resisted. Perhaps the best advice I received, from one of my students in Wesleyan University's Graduate Liberal Studies Program, was the sensible suggestion that the greatest writer of all time must surely be Anonymous—that highly eclectic and prodigious author of the Bible, the Icelandic sagas, *Beowulf, The Thousand and One Arabian Nights, The Tale of Heike*, and more—but I had to reject this advice in favor of known authors for the purpose of my ranking. Consensus among all whom I queried was impossible, but the majority of the authors in the final selection consistently appeared on everyone's list. After I learned a great deal from the choices of both scholars and students, the final selection was mine alone.

At various points, I would have liked to have had either a much shorter list or a much longer one in order to include more of the writers consigned here to the honorable mention list. To make the final cut, I have been guided by my sense of which authors have exerted the greatest influence over time in fundamentally establishing or altering the way we see the world through literature. The degree to which each writer shaped his or her literary tradition through the imagination and genius helped determine the ranking. As the literary critic Barbara Hardy has observed, "Good artists work within their chosen genre, great artists transform it." Innovation seems indispensable to literary influence over the centuries, and I confess a bias in favor of authors whose daring conceptions broke with the past and radically reconceptualized the world. To a greater or lesser degree, all of the writers in this ranking helped redefine literature, establishing a standard with which succeeding generations of writers and readers have had to contend.

Once the list was assembled, I considered each writer's merits and impact relatively, in a mental exercise akin to lining up the 125 greatest literary figures of all time to receive an honorary degree. The thrill derived from the juxtaposition of such diverse talents is, I hope, the appeal of this book. I have always taken a secret delight in the randomness of my book collection, in which I have resisted the practicality of alphabetization for the pleasure of accidental proximity. Hardy stands next to Shaw, Woolf next to Beckett, Fielding next to Poe, and so on. Each pairing suggests a dialogue of intentions and achievement that this ranking also attempts.

   In each profile I have tried to distill the essence of each writer's career and character to help prompt the reader's consideration of literary merit and relationships. I hope my efforts will encourage readers to greater appreciation of the achievement each writer so richly demonstrates, and to stimulate their own valuation of literary excellence—in Matthew Arnold's phrase, "to learn and propagate the best that is known and thought in the world."

WILLIAM SHAKESPEARE

1564–1616

The striking feature of Shakespeare's mind was its generic quality, its power of communi-
cation with all other minds,—so that it contained a universe of thought and feeling within
itself, and had no one particular bias, or exclusive excellence more than another. He was
just like any other man, but that he was like all other men. He was the least of an egotist
that it was possible to be. He was nothing in himself, but he was all that others were, or
that they could become.

—William Hazlitt, *On Shakespeare and Milton*

It should come as no surprise to see William Shakespeare placed at the head of
a ranking of the most influential literary artists of all time. At literature's most
basic and elemental level of language, form, and vision, Shakespeare's power
is unequaled. If the mark of a writer's greatness is the creation of the largest
imaginary universe populated by believable characters and the reflection of
the widest human experience, surely Shakespeare is alone in the magnitude
of his achievement. Acknowledged as the greatest English writer, unrivaled
in popular and critical acclaim, Shakespeare is also the recognized international master whose universality communicates across cultural divides. Shortly
after Shakespeare's death, BEN JONSON [66] wrote in tribute to Shakespeare's
greatness:

Thou art a Moniment, without a tombe,
An art alive still, while thy Booke doth live,
And we have wits to read, and praise to give . . .
Triumph, my *Britaine*, thou has one to showe,
To whom all Scenes of *Europe* homage owe.
He was not of an age, but for all time!

Jonson's sentiment has held sway as each generation since Shakespeare's has discovered new relevance and significance in his plays and poems. No other writer has so completely established literature's boundaries and excellence in the creation of fully realized characters, in the genius of his dramatic storytelling, and, most magnificently, in his supreme mastery of language as an expressive, poetic medium.

The little we know about Shakespeare's life and artistic development has contributed both to the myth of the playwright as a natural, instinctual artist rather than a conscious craftsman, and also to the search for alternative sources of his creations in other authors, such as Francis Bacon or Edward de Vere, whose education and experiences seem a better fit to explain the genius of the playwright. The essence of the man who produced such a glittering array of masterpieces has eluded and confounded his critics. "Shakespeare is in the singularly fortunate position," W. H. AUDEN [103] once remarked, "of being to all intents and purposes, anonymous." Ralph Waldo Emerson rightly argued that "Shakespeare is the only biographer of Shakespeare." What continually perplexes us is Shakespeare's defiance of customary artistic limitations, his unmatched objectivity, and his freedom from the personal bias that confines most artists. Shakespeare's art is one of remarkable inclusiveness that captures the full range of human experience, in which most traces of inspiration and the personality of its creator have been fully absorbed in the works themselves.

What we know for sure of Shakespeare's life comes from a few scanty records that fix his birth, marriage, the baptism of his three children, and his later theatrical successes as an actor and playwright. Shakespeare was born in Stratford-upon-Avon in the geographical center of England, a rural community of fewer than 2,000. His father was a prosperous and prominent tradesman, bailiff, and alderman, who suffered a decline in fortune and prestige. It is likely that Shakespeare was educated at the local grammar school, where he was exposed to the Latin classics, of which OVID [26] was a particular favorite. At the age of 18 he married a farmer's daughter, Anne Hathaway, who bore him three children: Susanna in 1583 and the twins Hamnet and Judith in 1585. What Shakespeare did or experienced in the next seven years, before records locate him in London as a successful playwright and actor, remains a mystery. By 1594 records show that he was a shareholder in London's most celebrated stage company under the patronage of the Lord Chamberlain. Besides his early plays—the comedies, *Comedy of Errors* (1592), *Two Gentlemen of Verona* (1594), *Love's Labour's Lost* (1594), and *A Midsummer Night's Dream* (1595); historical chronicles, *Henry VI* (1590), *Richard III* (1592), and *Richard II* (1595); and the early tragedies, *Titus Andronicus* (1593) and *Romeo and Juliet* (1594)—Shakespeare achieved literary distinction as a poet with *Venus and Adonis* (1593) and *The Rape of Lucrece* (1594). He would continue his nondramatic writing with a masterful sonnet cycle that circulated among his friends and was published in 1609. The achievement evident in the sonnets alone would have secured Shakespeare a significant place in English literary history.

By the late 1590s, Shakespeare's prominence and success allowed him to purchase a large home, New Place, in Stratford, and to secure the rank of a gentleman with the recognition of his family's coat of arms in 1596. He shared in the expenses for the construction of the Globe in 1598, a large playhouse on the south bank of the Thames, where his masterpieces were performed. They include the great comedies, *As You Like It* (1599) and *Twelfth Night* (1599); the historical cycle of *Henry IV* (1597) and *Henry V* (1598); the great tragedies, *Hamlet* (1600), *Othello* (1604), *King Lear* (1605), and *Macbeth* (1605); and the Roman plays, *Julius Caesar* (1599) and *Antony and Cleopatra* (1606). Around 1610 Shakespeare retired to Stratford, although he continued to write a series of romances or tragicomedies that include *Cymbeline* (1609), *The Winter's Tale* (1610), and *The Tempest* (1611) before his death in 1616 at the age of 52.

It is impossible to write briefly of Shakespeare's achievement in a literary canon that includes more than 30 plays, the majority of which are crucial to an understanding of literary history and resist reduction even to the conventional categories of comedies, tragedies, and histories. It is possible here only to point to some of the central qualities that define Shakespeare's genius. One place to start is with the dramatic tradition that Shakespeare inherited and revolutionized. As with all of literature's greatest figures, Shakespeare's work is derived from a complex blend of time, place, and particular genius.

Shakespeare is fundamentally a great assimilator of the popular dramatic tradition, joined with the humanist energies released by the Renaissance and the expansive freedom of expression and form that the Elizabethan stage allowed. Prior to the Elizabethan dramatists, the English theater offered mainly religious and allegorical themes. Shakespeare, preeminently, instead used drama to explore secular human experience and reflect the actual life of English and world history, shaped by a remarkable grasp of the commonplace and the subtlety of behavior and psychology. He established the link with Aeschylus [27], Sophocles [13], and Euripides [22] in reviving drama as a medium for the most profound exploration of human existence. Extending the rules of classical drama, he created an expressive dramatic form that would serve as a romantic alternative to the classical norm of order and balance, and helped establish the tension between classicism and romanticism that defines modernism.

Shakespeare divided his efforts fairly equally among the four major categories available to him in drama—tragedies, comedies, histories, and romances—and turned the potential limitations of the Elizabethan theater, with its bare, open stage, into a great strength, as his expressive language compensated for limited stage effects. From king to clown, Shakespeare is able to capture the high heroism of a character like Hotspur in *Henry IV* and his opposite in Falstaff; the tortured melancholy of youth in *Hamlet* and the anguish of age in *King Lear*; and the delightful follies of love in his comedies, as well as love's corruption in *Othello* and *Macbeth*. Expressed in his remarkable expressive language, as Thomas Carlyle observed, "woven all of sheet-lightning and sunbeams," Shakespeare exploited the widest vocabulary of any English creative writer and fashioned an unsurpassed pattern of dazzling and functional imagery. Yet Shakespeare's greatness rests not principally on either his daunting range or virtuosity, but instead in his power to communicate, to reveal our selves in the mirror of his art.

DANTE ALIGHIERI

2

1265–1321

. . . And she delivered of a son, whom by common consent with his father, they called by the name Dante [the Giver]; and rightly so, because, as will be seen in the sequel, the issue was most perfectly consonant with this name. This was that Dante of whom is the present discourse. This was that Dante granted by the special grace of God to our age. This was the Dante, who was first to open the way for the return of the Muses, banished from Italy. 'Twas he that brought under the rule of due numbers every beauty of the vernacular speech. 'Twas he who may be truly said to have brought back dead poesy to life. The which things, when duly considered, will show that he could not rightly have borne any name but Dante.

—Giovanni Boccaccio, *The Early Lives of Dante*

The greatest artists dominate and define their age, even as they are defined by it. Dante is such an artist. He towers over the Middle Ages as its consummate literary figure, creating out of medieval beliefs poetry that has claimed our attention ever since. Even as Dante's faith and theology may fail the modern reader, the sheer majesty of Dante's vision and the coalescence of human thought and experience into visionary poetry continues to delight and inspire. With Dante, hyperbole is inevitable. He remains a touchstone for Western civilization, and *The Divine Comedy* is one of the most revered and influential literary works in history, perhaps the greatest single poem that has ever been written. According to T. S. Eliot [19], Dante's style is "the perfection of a common language," and after Shakespeare [1] and Dante, "there is no third." With this ranking, I obviously contradict Eliot's assertion with 123 candidates for consideration beyond Shakespeare and Dante, although I concur with Eliot's placement of the initial pair. With Dante one has the sense of the literature of Homer, the epic of a culture's values, restored in the vernacular Italian that Dante legitimized in the poetic legacy he passed along to Shakespeare and the Renaissance. No modern writer seems as central to his age as Dante is to the Middle Ages. He is the essential visionary and conscience of his era.

Although Dante's greatest poetic works concern the private life of the soul and the world of the afterlife, an understanding of his age and the forces that shaped his thoughts is essential in tracing his development and uniqueness. At the center of Dante's public life was the political turmoil of his native city of Florence: the factional conflict between its status as an independent, republican city-state and the power of the Holy Roman Empire and the papacy. In the *Inferno*, Dante reports that his ancestors were among the first Romans to colonize Florence, and he was educated to play an important role in Florence's public and cultural life. In his early biography of Dante, Boccaccio [68] states that as a young man, Dante studied poetry, painting, and music. His early poems indicate that he was influenced by French Provençal poetry, the classics known at the time, and by Italian vernacular poetry, just beginning to flourish. After military service, Dante held a series of increasingly prominent political offices, becoming one of the chief magistrates of Florence in 1300. Two years later, while he was in Rome on a diplomatic mission, he was unjustly accused of graft, fined, and banished for two years. When he refused to pay the fine, he faced a sentence of execution at the stake, and never saw Florence again. He spent his remaining years on the move, dependent on a series of patrons in various Italian cities, hoping for a political regeneration that never came. Although his poetry is intensely private, concerned with the self and the soul's redemption, the political struggle of his time is reflected in his art and sets the basic framework for the urgency of his meditations on moral and spiritual issues.

On a personal level, the defining moment of Dante's life was his encounter at the age of nine with Beatrice Portinari, for whom he conceived a lifelong idealistic passion. Though his contacts with Beatrice were few, her death in 1290 provided him with the inspiration to write *La Vita Nuova* (The New Life), a psychological and spiritual autobiography that blends sonnets and odes with prose commentary to trace the development of his love for Beatrice. The work is unique in medieval literature, combining the lyrical and the philosophical into a narrative of the poet's growth. Dante's other important works include the philosophical *Convivio* (Banquet), significant for its use of Italian prose instead of Latin for serious reflection; *De Vulgari Eloquentia* (Eloquence in the Vernacular Tongue), which set forth the goals and means for achieving a vernacular literature; and *De Monarchia* (Monarchy), his political theories on good government, which radically suggest the separation of church and state.

Dante became one of the most learned men in Europe, whose reflections about his world and scholarship were synthesized in his monumental *Commedia*, written between 1308 and 1321 (*Divina* was added to its title in the 16th century). The scope of Dante's plan was unprecedented: to dramatize in intensely personal terms, in a single poem, the Christian cosmology and doctrines that shaped the medieval worldview. His work is called a comedy, reflecting both the process of the poem from sin to redemption and Dante's style, which differed from the formal grandeur of the epic and tragedy. Written in direct and colloquial language, the poem is expansive enough to include all aspects of human experience—the tragic and the comic—in a manner that redefines the epic as the inward, spiritual journey toward full understanding of God and the universe.

Although the *Commedia* can be read as both an allegorical and theological treatise, its principal power derives from the personal narrative of Dante the pilgrim lost in a dark forest in search of the straight path. His journey takes him through the three regions of the Christian afterlife—hell, purgatory, and heaven—in a story that is at once a great adventure tale and the inner journey of a soul's struggle toward redemption. What separates the *Commedia* from other religious meditations is the clarity of Dante's vision, populated by actual historical figures. Their stories, narrated sympathetically with humor as well as awe, establish the *Commedia*'s humanity and social themes that are joined to the inner drama of the poet's progression toward enlightenment. In arguing that Dante should rightly be regarded as the father of all modern literature, Erich Auerbach writes:

> Dante was the first to configure what classical antiquity had configured very differently and the Middle Ages not at all: man, not as a remote legendary hero, not as an abstract or anecdotal representative of an ethical type, but man as we know him in his living historical reality, the concrete individual in his unity and wholeness; and in that he has been followed by all subsequent portrayers of man, regardless of whether they treated a historical or mythical or a religious subject, for after Dante myth and legend also became history. Even in portraying saints, writers have striven for truth to life, for historical concreteness, as though saints too were part of the historical process. . . . Christian legend came to be treated as an immanent historical reality; the arts have striven to represent a more perfect unity of spirit and body, spun into the fabric of man's destiny, and despite changes of taste and differences in artistic technique, this striving has endured, through many perils and darkenings, down to our day.

Despite the allegorical tendency to see Dante in the poem as an every-man, his linking of the spiritual and the divine to the recognizable world is the source of the poem's great power. On his journey, led first by the spirit of VIRGIL [9] and then by Beatrice, Dante confronts the essential moral and human issues of sin and belief in a larger power that orders human destiny, beyond that of the individual. The *Commedia* extends itself to the limit of artistic imagination captured in poetry that is in turns clear, precise, serious, and sublime.

Dante's structural genius, his development of a flexible poetic style capable of a great range of effects, and his placement of human experience at the center of his poem while contemplating the essential questions of existence, have exerted their influence on all subsequent literature in the West. He was, as Boccaccio rightly points out, well named the Giver.

HOMER

fl. c. 750(?) B.C.

In grave amazement he understood. In this night too, in this night of his mortal eyes into which he was now descending, love and danger were again waiting. Ares and Aphrodite, for already he divined (already it encircled him) a murmur of glory and hexameters, a murmur of men defending a temple the gods will not save, and of black vessels searching the sea for a beloved isle, the murmur of Odysseys and Iliads it was his destiny to sing and leave echoing concavely in the memory of man.

—Jorge Luis Borges, *Dreamtigers*

Merely to assert that Homer is the first literary artist and arguably the greatest does not begin to do justice to his remarkable achievement. In a fundamental sense, literature originates with Homer. As the progenitor of epic poetry, Homer in the *Iliad* and the *Odyssey* defined the monumental work of literary art that captures an entire culture, synthesizing beliefs, customs, and tradition into a serious and popular form that has been the aspiration of writers ever since. His only rivals to have a comparable impact on Western culture are the Bible, SHAKESPEARE [1], and DANTE [2], and no single author has carried such uninterrupted influence for so long. Although Homer follows Shakespeare and Dante in my ranking, strong argument could easily alter this arrangement. Only the passing of the heroic age that Homer chronicled so magnificently, more remote in its values to the modern reader than the medieval world of

Dante and the Renaissance of Shakespeare, has determined his placement below both.

Homer's achievement is clouded in scholarly controversy, beginning with the central question of whether there was a historical Homer at all. Did a single poet create the *Iliad* and the *Odyssey*, or were they the work of several individuals, the gradual accretion of collective voices out of the oral tradition from which they originated? If a single poet wrote both, how is the author of the *Iliad* also the creator of the very different *Odyssey*? Recent textual analysis points strongly to the likelihood that the *Iliad* is indeed the work of one poet, but on both sides of the argument there is doubt that the same poet is also the author of the *Odyssey*, though the evidence is insufficient to overturn the conventional belief that Homer is the creator of both poems. Adding to the mystery, we know virtually nothing about Homer, except that he was likely a bard in the eighth century B.C. whose homeland was in Ionia, south of Troy in Asia Minor (now modern Turkey). He traditionally is thought to have been blind. What is incontestable is the considerable value the Greeks placed on the Homeric poems from their inception. Aristotle considered Homer's work to represent the ideal of heroic poetry, and knowledge of Homer's verses was part of every Greek's education. Homer's prestige remained uncontested by the Romans and reasserted its influence in Europe during the Renaissance with the widespread dissemination of classical learning.

In appreciating Homer's achievement, it is crucial to recognize that the poems were oral creations, not literary ones. Homer made his poems in performance, borrowing and adapting stories, ideas, and phrases from the oral tradition of a preliterate culture. Each performance in effect produced a new poem. The texts that we now read are later transcriptions, standardized from various written versions by scholars and librarians from the fifth to the second century B.C. Composed in Greek dactylic hexameter (12 syllable lines with a meter of one stressed syllable followed by two unstressed ones) Homer's epics were originally sung or recited to the accompaniment of a lyre, and were based on the poet's memory and skill at improvisation. The poems' formulaic phrases—"fleet-footed Achilles," "rosy-fingered dawn," "bronze-shirted Achaians"—and repetition are all evidence of oral performance, aiding the audience's understanding and helping the poet fit his language to the metric structure.

Given the traditional qualities of Homer's epics, in which he borrowed from a storehouse of stories and phrases, what makes his work so unique are the overall excellence of his verse, his perceptiveness, and the sheer magnitude of his conception. Individual oral compositions are thought to have been between 500 and 600 lines in length, able to hold the attention of an audience on a single occasion—for example, following an evening meal—as seen in the *Odyssey's* Book Eight in the performance of the bard Demodocus. This is the length of just a single book of a total of 24 in both the *Iliad* and the *Odyssey*.

Homer is considered unique in his monumental expansion of oral poetry into a much grander dramatic unity, shaping traditional stories and methods into a whole of unprecedented range. To achieve the dramatic unity and coherence of his epics without the possibility of revision or the deliberate forethought and planning we associate with writing, is almost unthinkable and a testimony to Homer's unmatched skill as a poet and storyteller.

Homer's greatness is evident even through a superficial look at his epics. In the *Iliad,* his subject is war and the various examples of heroism it represents under the threat of death. Tradition dictated that heroic poetry must deal with past events and figures of great renown and distinction, and Homer selects the 10-year Trojan War at its climax. The *Iliad* describes the events leading up to the fatal and decisive combat between Achilles, the Greeks' greatest warrior, and the Trojan champion Hector in a battle that ensures Troy's fall. Homer's poem begins with Achilles' withdrawal from the battlefield as a result of the slight to his honor by Agamemnon, the commander of the Greeks. This allows the Trojans a momentary triumph and results in the slaying of Achilles' closest friend Patroclus by Hector. Only the absolute obligation of blood vengeance is sufficient to overcome the slight to Achilles' honor, and he meets and kills Hector. The poem ends with Achilles' change of heart from vengeance to pity and the ending of his wrath, which culminates in his agreement to return Hector's body to his family for proper burial.

The *Iliad* works on a number of levels, but primarily it is an exciting story that Homer narrates skillfully with godlike objectivity and focus on the telling detail. Although all of Homer's characters are remarkable in their qualities and accomplishments, which are well beyond the reach of ordinary men and women, each acts according to his or her personality and temperament. Collectively, the characters and events describe the values of a heroic world in which honor is the highest virtue and violent death is almost certain.

In the *Odyssey,* Homer reimagines the tragic heroism of the *Iliad* as heroic comedy. Following the fall of Troy, Odysseus struggles for 10 years to return home to Ithaca and restore the life he led before the conflict. The dramatic unity of the *Iliad* is replaced by the extended episodes of Odysseus's journey and the multiple stories of his son Telemachus and his wife Penelope, afflicted by a collection of rapacious suitors who must be vanquished in the story's climax. Odysseus's heroism is also markedly different from that of Achilles. Odysseus is the consummate survivor who is shown as more human, with a more complex blend of skills and weaknesses, than the unrelenting demigod and warrior Achilles.

Although there is no mistaking the heroic worldview of both Homeric poems, the *Odyssey* locates its values more closely in the world of Homer's audience. It also redirects his art to essential themes of home and domestic love, and the eventual prize and goal of the hero in recapturing both, even in a story that involves a visit to the underworld and encounters with mythical creatures. If the *Iliad* portrays a heroic world and values that were waning, archaic even to Homer's first audiences, the *Odyssey* points heroic art in a new direction, toward ordinary life of mixed character. It is not surprising that JAMES JOYCE [7], in looking for a structuring principle for his modern epic *Ulysses*, should select Homer's *Odyssey*. For Joyce, Odysseus was the only completely well-rounded character presented by any writer, and as he observed, "The most beautiful, all-embracing theme is that of the *Odyssey*. It is greater, more human, than that of *Hamlet, Don Quixote*, Dante, *Faust* . . . I find the subject of Ulysses the most human in world literature. . . . After Troy there is no further talk of Achilles, Menelaus, Agamemnon. Only one man is not done with; his heroic career has hardly begun: Ulysses."

In the *Iliad* and the *Odyssey*, Homer shows his mastery of the experience of war and peace in themes that are both serious and profoundly human. With Homer, the epic, wide-ranging enough to capture the values of an entire culture, evolves as a form and sets a standard that later writers would try to master as the highest aspiration of literary art. By succeeding, a writer can be described as the Homer of his age, a tribute to the power and possibility of art that Homer established.

LEO TOLSTOY

4

1828–1910

Of course you have read Tolstoi's War and Peace *and* Anna Karenina. *I never had that exquisite felicity before the summer, and now I feel as if I knew the perfection in the representation of human life. Life indeed seems less real than his tale of it. Such infallible veracity! The impression haunts me as nothing literary ever haunted me before.*
— William James, letter to Henry James, 1872

Paradox and contradiction surround the gigantic figure of Tolstoy. The author of two of the greatest novels ever written, Tolstoy repudiated both, as well as the works of SHAKESPEARE [1], as "bad art," unworthy of the moral teaching that his later life demanded. A member of Russia's aristocracy, Tolstoy transformed himself from an idle and dissolute creature of his class into a supreme novelist with unrivaled imaginative powers, and then became a prophetic sage who tried to conform to a comprehensive vision of primitive Christian simplicity. In a sense, Tolstoy's determined search for meaning, which forms the core of his books, is the one constant in an otherwise tangled life. Few authors have embodied their discoveries as relentlessly as Tolstoy, but it is Tolstoy the artist, not Tolstoy the holy man, who continues to speak to us. As John Bayley, in his critical study *Tolstoy and the Novel*, observed, "No one who is not interested in himself can be interested in a great novel, and in Tolstoy we experience in greater measure than in any other novelist the recognition of ourselves that leads to increased self-knowledge."

Tolstoy was born in 1828 into a wealthy, noble family and grew up on the Tolstoy estate of Yasnaya Polyana, south of Moscow. Both his parents died while he was a child, and he was reared by relatives and educated by private tutors. After three years as a student at Kazan University, he returned home to manage the estate and to live an aimless and pleasure-seeking life among upper-class circles in St. Petersburg and Moscow. At the age of 23, Tolstoy entered the army as an artillery officer and campaigned against the Caucasian hill tribes and helped defend Sevastopol during the Crimean War. While in the army, he developed an addiction to gambling as well as a determination to become a writer. His first works reflect his war experiences and his recollections of childhood. Published in Russian magazines, Tolstoy's early fiction announced the arrival of promising liter-ary talent, part of the extraordinary flowering of Russian fiction in the 19th century, whose masters included Turgenev and Dostoevsky [14]. Tolstoy traveled in Europe before marrying in 1862, then settled down to raise a family of 13 children. He reorganized his estate to reflect the principles of peasantry reform, including land ownership and improved education for his serfs, which interested him.

Between 1863 and 1877, Tolstoy wrote his two great masterpieces, *War and Peace* (1869) and *Anna Karenina* (1877). The first is a grand Russian epic that depicts the events of Napoleon's invasion through the affairs of several Russian families. *War and Peace* particularly concerns the search by two men, Prince Andrey Bolkonsky and Pierre Bezuhov, for significance and meaning in their lives. The second novel, one of the great love stories in world literature, traces the adulterous affair of Anna Karenina and Count Alexey Vronsky to Anna's destruction when she refuses to conform to the hypocritical values of upper-class morality. Anna's tragedy is paralleled by a search for an alternative to society's values by Levin, who finds his answers domestically among the peasants on his estate.

The conflict Tolstoy explored in both novels between self-fulfillment and society, as well as history's grip on the individual, produced a personal crisis and the beginning of a quest for answers that he discovered in a unique blend of primitive Christianity, faith in simple peasant values derived from a close relationship to the land, and the renunciation of government, private prop-erty, and organized religion. He spent the rest of his life attempting to live according to his precepts and writing books that embodied his philosophy. Although Tolstoy the moralist predominates over Tolstoy the artist during this period, with his great gift for capturing the vitality and variety of life and human experience, some of his works after his conversion are among his fin-est, particularly "The Death of Ivan Ilych" (1886) and "The Kreutzer Sonata" (1891). Tolstoy's mysticism and asceticism attracted devoted followers but largely alienated him from his wife and family. He caught a chill and died in the house of a stationmaster while attempting to escape their control on a journey to a monastery.

A fascination with Tolstoy's remarkable life and philosophy has dominated the appreciation of his work. The genius that created such massive portraits of lived experience seems to dwarf and make irrelevant any consideration of his artistry and the means he used to create his novels. GUSTAVE FLAUBERT [30], in offering his opinion of *War and Peace*, provides a typical judgment. Complaining of the weakness of the novel's conclusion, Flaubert observed: "The first two volumes are sublime, but the third goes downhill dreadfully. He repeats himself. And he philosophizes. In a word here one sees the gentleman, the author, and the Russian, whereas hitherto one had seen only Nature and Humanity." At his best, Tolstoy possessed an unprecedented capacity for entering the life around him to such an imaginative degree that the art that produces his effects dissolves, and the reader seems to directly perceive life itself.

The standard that Tolstoy set, like that of Shakespeare, seems impossibly high. Additionally, in most instances Tolstoy's novels defy the structural logic of other European novels with their aesthetic of tight control and authorial distancing. HENRY JAMES [38] called Tolstoy's kind of novels "loose, baggy monsters," and Tolstoy seems much closer stylistically to CHARLES DICKENS [6], whom Tolstoy greatly admired, than to Flaubert and James himself. Tolstoy's novels are expansive, pushing outward toward the panoramic; they are novels of the social group, large enough to accommodate the widest possible vision of society and human experience.

We come to know Tolstoy's characters as intimates, far more real to us than most of the people we know in life. Isaiah Berlin has written that "no author who has ever lived has shown such a power of insight into the variety of life—the differences, the contrasts, the collisions of persons and things and situations, each apprehended in its absolute uniqueness and conveyed with a degree of directness and a precision of concrete imagery to be found in no other writer." Perhaps fellow Russian writer Isaac Babel put it best when he asserted, "If the world could write by itself, it would write like Tolstoy."

If his novels contain multitudes, Tolstoy is no less adept at pushing the local and the temporal into universal relevance. With *War and Peace*, Tolstoy reconfigures the history of Russia's patriotic resistance to Napoleon into a national epic that was embraced even by the Soviet regime, although Soviet leaders privately considered Tolstoy's work to be counterrevolutionary. During World War II and the Nazi invasion, Tolstoy was the most published author in Russia, and relevant sections of *War and Peace* were posted on Moscow's streets for inspiration. Although both *War and Peace* and *Anna Karenina* are firmly rooted in their time and place, neither are restricted by them, as Tolstoy pursues larger truths of history and human nature.

In the end, Tolstoy's pursuit of truth led him beyond fiction and illusion to realize a version of his revelations about humanity and spirituality in his own life. As Vladimir Nabokov observed:

> What one would like to do, would be to kick the glorified soapbox from under his sandalled feet and then lock him up in a stone house on a desert island with gallons of ink and reams of paper—far away from the things, ethical and pedagogical, that diverted his attention from observing the way the dark hair curled above Anna's white neck. But the thing cannot be done: Tolstoy is homogeneous. . . . Tolstoy was striving, in spite of all the obstacles, to get at the truth. As the author of *Anna Karenina*, he used one method of discovering truth; in his sermons, he used another; but somehow, no matter how subtle his art was and no matter how dull some of his other attitudes were, truth which he was ponderously groping for or magically finding just around the corner, was always the same truth— this truth was he and this he was an art.

Most will agree with Nabokov that it is Tolstoy the artist rather than Tolstoy the mystic philosopher who compels our attention, and that his sublime framing of the expansive questions of life satisfy more than the narrower answers for which he eventually settled.

GEOFFREY CHAUCER

c. 1340–1400

Chaucer was one of the most original men who ever lived. There had never been anything like the lively realism of the ride to Canterbury done or dreamed of in our literature before. He is not only the father of all our poets, but the grandfather of all our hundred million novelists. It is rather a responsibility for him. But anyhow, nothing can be more original than an origin.

—G. K. Chesterton, *Chaucer*

Chaucer's greatness as a poet derives not only from his pride of place as England's first major writer and his pioneering mastery of the expressive power of the English vernacular, but also from his fundamental redefinition of the possibility of poetic expression. That the English literary tradition starts with Chaucer is not simply a matter of history—the accidental conjunction of an artistic genius and a time and place. It also stems from the more essential recognition that with Chaucer, English literature became profoundly different from what it had been before. By redefining the literary canon, Chaucer affected the course of literature in fundamental ways. Only a handful of writers exerted this kind of gravitational pull, subsuming the past and altering the future of literature. Soon after Chaucer's death, Thomas Hoccleve appropriately observed that he was "the first findere of our faire langage."

We know far more about Chaucer than we do about HOMER [3] or SHAKE-SPEARE [1]. At the center of the English court for most of his life, Chaucer survives in 493 documentary records that trace his career as a page, soldier, squire of the royal household, and governmental and civil servant. There is far less evidence about his life as a poet. Only one of his works, *The Book of the Duchess*, can be dated with any degree of certainty. The disjunction between what is known about Chaucer's public life and what is unknown about his writing life has contributed to the tradition of seeing him as a kind of rough diamond, an accidental progenitor of English literature, whose works say more about the era that produced them than the genius that defined his age. Yet Chaucer, like all great artists, is best seen in the complex relationship between the age that fashioned him and his art, which reshaped his world.

Chaucer was the son of a well-to-do London wine merchant, a member of the increasingly important middle class. His father's wealth provided him with an education and access to the world of the nobility and royalty. He served as a page in the household of Lionel of Antwerp, the second son of the monarch Edward III; later he became a member of the king's household and formed a lifelong relationship with another of the king's sons, John of Gaunt. From then on, Chaucer's fortunes would be inextricably linked with those of England's royals, including Edward's nephew Richard II, who succeeded to the throne in 1377, and John of Gaunt's son, Henry Bolingbroke, who seized the throne in 1399.

Chaucer was a participant in and observer of the great events of the 14th century. As a child he survived the first and most lethal outbreak of the plague, from 1348 to 1349, in which 1.5 to 2 million of England's population of 4–5 million died, most within eight months. When Chaucer was born, Edward III had reopened the war with France that would continue for the next century. The great English victories at Crécy and Poitiers occurred during Chaucer's lifetime, and as a soldier he was captured by the French and ransomed by the king (for a lesser sum than the king was forced to pay for his favorite horse). Finally, the dynastic struggle that eventually cost Richard II his throne helped alter the absolute power of the monarch and shook the foundations of the medieval hierarchy. If there are few direct allusions to specific events in Chaucer's poetry, the concerns of the age and Chaucer's depiction of the life around him are at the center of his art. As a soldier, courtier, diplomat, government agent, and member of Parliament, Chaucer was well placed to convert his broad range of experience into poetry.

Chaucer's poetry also represents a unique fusion of personal genius with the historical moment. During his lifetime, English was to emerge as the national language, replacing the French of the Norman conquerors as the language of culture and commerce, and codified in the Midland dialect of the important trading center, London. Chaucer's poetic language is the first great flowering of an English vernacular that he helped shape into an expressive artistic form. That Chaucer was a layman, not a cleric, and that his poetry was performed before a court audience, are also important factors in the poetry he produced.

The stages of Chaucer's poetic development have been traditionally divided into three periods. His poetic apprenticeship during the 1360s shows him influenced by French forms. During this period, he produced a translation of the *Roman de la Rose* and *The Book of the Duchess*, an elegy for John of Gaunt's wife, Blanche. In 1372, while on a trading mission for the crown, Chaucer visited Italy. There he encountered the works of DANTE [2], BOCCACCIO [68], and PETRARCH [51], whose influence is seen in his *House of Fame, Parliament of Fowls*, and *Troilus and Criseide*. The final stage represents the work of his full maturity, beginning in 1386 with the distinctly English voice of *The Canterbury Tales*. A view that posits the synthesis of Chaucer's native English expression from the influences of French and Italian sources is somewhat misleading. A high degree of originality, along with the reworking of borrowed sources, is present at every stage of Chaucer's career. His achievement comes not from the absence of derived forms but from his remarkable animation of traditional elements into a fresh and unique artistic vision. His greatness as a poet is demonstrated most clearly in his masterpieces *Troilus and Criseide* and *The Canterbury Tales*.

Troilus and Criseide, the greatest of Chaucer's completed works, would have secured his place as one of the giants of English literature even if he never had written *The Canterbury Tales*. The poem, set during the Trojan War, has been described by Chaucerian scholar George Lyman Kittredge as "the first novel, in the modern sense, that ever was written in the world." It tells the story of the "double sorwe of Troilus," son of King Priam, first in loving Criseide, and then in losing her when Criseide, in a prisoner exchange, is taken by the Greeks and proves unfaithful. Chaucer's principal source is Boccaccio's *Il Filostrato* (The Love-Stricken), a shorter, cynical tale of frustrated passion that Chaucer expands into a psychologically rich exploration of the nature of love and its human costs set against the background of war, the conflict between private values and communal responsibility, and the opposition of will and destiny. His great innovation is in investing his characters with a naturalism that justifies Kittredge's assessment. The poem also displays Chaucer's virtuosity as a storyteller and demonstrates his readiness and skill to produce the vast human comedy that would become his most popular and enduring work.

Everything about *The Canterbury Tales* is monumental, beginning with Chaucer's original conception of a series of tales told by a group of 30 pilgrims journeying to Canterbury. Of the 120 tales originally projected for the series (two for each pilgrim on the way to Canterbury and two more from each on the way back), Chaucer actually completed only 22. He probably began *The Canterbury Tales* in 1386 and devoted the last 14 years of his life to the project. Collections of stories linked by a framing device were not original; early in the 14th century Boccaccio had arranged the 100 tales of his *Decameron*, delivered by 10 characters. What was original was the relationship established between the tellers and their tales and the intricate byplay among the pilgrims that establishes a comic and ironic context for many of the stories, as when the Miller's silly and cuckolded carpenter offends the Reeve, who retaliates with his own story, using a miller as his comic target. The effect is a delightful double fiction, with multiple dramatic and literary effects.

Through the agency of the pilgrimage, Chaucer not only produced a masterful literary compendium of medieval story genres—romance, fabliau, saint's tale, beast story, and sermon—but also managed to collect a cross section of medieval society. Chaucer brings his characters to life through a series of colorful portraits in the General Prologue, then has them reveal themselves in all their delightful human frailty during their journey. As John Dryden aptly pointed out, "here is God's plenty."

Chaucer's greatness as a poet is most completely demonstrated in his skillful details, which create a complex and ironic texture to his verbal painting. In *The Canterbury Tales*, the static and the stylized elements of medieval literature are replaced by dynamic, living portraits of complex individuals—such as the Prioress, the Pardoner, and especially the Wife of Bath—who command our attention not for their high rank or deeds but for their humanity. Chaucer succeeds in creating a new realistic standard in poetry that redefined the subject and treatment of literature. The human behavior of ordinary individuals claims full artistic treatment for the first time, as Chaucer expands the range of poetic expression to embrace all aspects of life and experience.

CHARLES DICKENS

6

1812–1870

But Dickens is significant for more than the sheer intensity with which he reflects experience. His is a penetrating vision of modern life. The unifying thread of his entire career was a critical analysis of nineteenth-century society unsurpassed by any novelist in grasp and scope.

—Edgar Johnson, preface to *Charles Dickens: His Tragedy and Triumph*

Directly following CHAUCER [5], I have selected Charles Dickens, who, like the author of *The Canterbury Tales*, magnificently "numbered the classes of men." Literary critic Edmund Wilson has called Dickens "the greatest dramatic writer that the English had had since Shakespeare who created the largest and most varied world." Dickens's enormous stature as a writer was acknowledged by his fellow Victorians, by TOLSTOY [4] and DOSTOEVSKY [14], and by such modern writers as GEORGE BERNARD SHAW [44] and GEORGE ORWELL [118]. With the exception of SHAKESPEARE [1], no writer in English literature has enjoyed a comparable degree of popular and critical acclaim. Dickens is simply England's greatest novelist and deserves to be ranked with the top literary artists of all time.

Despite such high praise, an appreciation of Dickens is not free from criticism. It is possible to charge him with sentimentality, of tugging too insistently at our heartstrings, and of reducing experience to idealized and overly melodramatic patterns. His power and singularity as a novelist more than compensate for his defects, however. His range and depth are enormous, while his imaginative power, energy, and intensity as a writer earn him a comparison with Shakespeare. Through the power of his imagination and skill, Dickens offers a unique view of the world, rich in comedy, horror, and pathos, and we live in a world that still can be described as Dickensian in many important ways.

The trajectory of Dickens's career is a spectacular rise from what he considered the unspeakable degradation his family experienced in his youth. The second child and eldest son of John and Elizabeth Dickens, the novelist was born in Portsmouth, England, where his father worked as a clerk in the navy pay office. Both his parents came from lower-middle-class backgrounds of domestic service and clerical work. John Dickens, the inspiration for his son's portrait of the tragicomic spendthrift Wilkins Micawber in *David Copperfield*, could barely manage a respectable household, and Dickens's childhood was disrupted by a series of moves to increasingly less genteel addresses, first in Chatham on the east coast of England and later in London.

Charles was a slight, unathletic child who was extremely sensitive and a voracious reader. His early upbringing and imaginative habits explain much about his writing, particularly his love of theatrical blood-and-thunder scenes, with their dramatic confrontations between good and evil, the weak and the powerful. His earliest memories were the tales told by his nurse about a huge black cat that hunted small children and of "Captain Murderer," who, like Sweeney Todd, converted his victims into meat pies. Remembering these stories, Dickens stated, "I suspect we should find our nurses responsible for most of the dark corners we are forced to go back to, against our wills." One of his favorite toys was a miniature theater in which he could act out his favorite stories. The theater, therefore, was the backdrop for his initial imaginary creations, and his lifelong dramatic interest helps explain his later statement that "every writer of fiction in effect writes for the stage."

Dickens's developing imagination received a traumatic jolt when his father was arrested for debt and sent to debtor's prison. Two days after his 12th birthday, separated from his family, who accompanied John Dickens to prison in the custom of the time, Charles was sent to work as a boy apprentice in a blacking factory, pasting labels on pots of dye for 12 hours a day in a rat-infested warehouse. Having been encouraged in his intellectual accomplishments and claims to gentility, Dickens felt as if he had fallen through the social hierarchy to the lowest depths of the laboring class, "utterly neglected and hopeless." After four months he was rescued by his father and allowed to resume his education, but the humiliating stigma cast a permanent shadow on his psyche. Years later, when breaking the silence of this deep secret by preparing to reexperience it in *David Copperfield*, Dickens recalled, "My father said I should go back no more, and should go to school. I do not write resentfully or angrily; for I know how all these things have worked together to make me what I am: but I never afterwards forgot, I never shall forget, I never can forget, that my mother was warm for my being sent back." It is possible to view Dickens's frantic assault on success and some of his darkest themes, particularly the victimization of children, as a response to the pain caused by this early experience.

Critical estimation of Dickens's career generally divides his novels into two groups: the early novels, from his debut with *The Pickwick Papers* (1836–37) to *David Copperfield* (1849–50), and his later novels, beginning with *Bleak House* (1852–53). Admirers of all that is commonly meant by the term *Dickensian*—the novelist's irrepressible vitality and inexhaustible supply of eccentrics, comic situations, sentiment, and humor—locate Dickens's greatness in this first period. Modern critics, beginning with George Bernard Shaw, generally tend to emphasize the complexity, psychological subtlety, and profound social exploration of the later novels as the primary source of Dickens's genius. Regardless of reader preference, Dickens's entire canon shows amazing technical and artistic development.

Dickens began his career as a novelist almost by accident, when he was hired to write narrative connectives for a series of illustrations of Cockney sporting scenes that became *The Pickwick Papers*, but he quickly took control of the project, shifting his story to the primary interest, and *Pickwick* became one of the 19th century's phenomenal best-sellers. Dickens's early books were mostly written in the serialized installment form that *The Pickwick Papers* first popularized, a "detached and desultory form of publication," as he described it in his 1837 preface, in which "no artfully interwoven or ingeniously complicated plot can with reason be expected."

Improvised and with little preplanning or attendance to a larger theme, Dickens's early novels, such as *Oliver Twist*, *Nicholas Nickleby*, *Barnaby Rudge*, *The Old Curiosity Shop*, and *Martin Chuzzlewit*, show him working toward a more complex structure of characters who cause the drama rather than having it imposed on them, and much more elaborate and massive portraits of society supported by the most demanding narrative method of all, that of mystery and suspense. Dickens's later novels—*Bleak House, Hard Times, Little Dorrit, A Tale of Two Cities, Great Expectations, Our Mutual Friend*, and the unfinished *The Mystery of Edwin Drood*—are all cut to the pattern of intrigue and detection that joins a vast network of relationships and social and psychological themes in a unified whole.

Unlike most modern novelists, Dickens is a traditional storyteller who employs such theatrical techniques as secrets, surprises, and coincidences to heighten suspense and uncover universal patterns beneath the surface of things. His fictional formula, expressed in his preface to *Bleak House*, is to show the "romantic side of familiar things." His novels are built on conflict, with dramatic action replacing authorial analysis and commentary. "My notion always is," Dickens observed, "that when I have made the people to play out the play, it is, as it were, their business to do it, and not mine." In the arranged collision of characters, Dickens reaches his desired illumination of increasingly more complex psychological and social themes. Through the combination of realism and symbolism, evident particularly in his later novels, Dickens anticipates the central dynamic of the modern novel, linking his work with later novelists such as THOMAS HARDY [43], JAMES JOYCE [7], FRANZ KAFKA [31], and WILLIAM FAULKNER [15].

While working at a frenzied pace, Dickens still managed a full social and personal life. In 1836, he married Catherine Hogarth, who gave birth to 10 children. Although secure in his literary and financial success, Dickens remained restless and dissatisfied. He visited America, hoping to find an ideal democracy but discovering instead moral and political anarchy that helped confirm his own Englishness and increasing distrust of political solutions to social ills. Traveling and living abroad, busy as an editor of his own periodicals, acting in amateur theatricals and in dramatic readings from his books, Dickens channeled his restless energy into continual, often manic, activity. His later career was marked by domestic unhappiness, in which he separated from his wife and had an affair with Ellen Ternan, an actress 20 years his junior. In 1870, after a second tour of America and an exhausting series of public readings, and while at work on his last book, Dickens had a stroke and died in the grand house he had seen years before as a boy, with his father, as a symbol of material accomplishment impossibly beyond his reach.

Dickens's life is an amazing story of the power of the imagination to produce a seemingly inexhaustible supply of unforgettable characters—Pickwick, Sam and Tony Weller, Fagin, Bumble, Quilp, Scrooge, Pecksniff, Sairey Gamp, Micawber, Lady Dedlock, Mr. F's Aunt, Miss Havisham, to name just a few—in an imaginary yet recognizable universe animated by the novelist's great powers of visualization. Dickens remains the novelist nonpareil, capable of probing at the deepest level the light and dark elements of his mind and world.

JAMES JOYCE

1882–1941

Joyce radicalized literature, so that it would never recover. He reconstructed narrative, both external and internal; he changed our conception of daytime consciousness and of night-time unconsciousness. He made us reconsider language as the product and the prompter of unconscious imaginings. These did not come to him as experiments or as innovations; he did not regard himself as an experimenter. Rather they were solutions to the literary and intellectual problems he set himself.
—Richard Ellmann, "James Joyce In and Out of Art," from *Four Dubliners*

James Joyce is as essential to an understanding of modern fiction as T. S. ELIOT [19] and W. B. YEATS [17] are to modern poetry and Pablo Picasso is to modern art. His achievement is nothing less than a great artistic explosion in which we are still sifting through the debris and dealing with the fallout. We are still learning how to read him, and novelists continue to show his influence, as the history of the novel can be divided with only slight exaggeration into two periods: before and after Joyce. Some writers in despair of ever surpassing him have lamented that Joyce took the novel as far as it can go, as SHAKESPEARE [1] took drama. Others have complained that Joyce stretched the form of fiction past a breaking point, and the aftermath is a chaos of meaning that many feel was Joyce's principal legacy.

Joyce's collected works are few: two collections of poetry, a play, a volume of short stories, and three novels. Although hardly an innovative or preeminent poet or dramatist, his achievement in fiction was to effect a revolution at literature's core. *Dubliners* sets the pattern and technique for the modern short story. With *A Portrait of the Artist As a Young Man*, Joyce took on the solidly traditional novel of education and development and reimagined it in an absolutely new manner that has caused other treatments of this theme to seem shallow and routine. With *Ulysses*, Joyce created a modern epic out of the commonplace events of a single day in the life of Dublin with a modern Odysseus, Leopold Bloom, a Jew and a cuckold, as his hero. In *Finnegans Wake*, a novel shaped by dream logic and the destruction of the barriers of time and space, Joyce developed an entirely new literary language to write a universal history based on the life and times of a pub owner, Humphrey Chimpden Earwicker. Each step in Joyce's artistic development challenged previous assumptions and perfected new techniques to capture consciousness and the complexity of experience. To my mind, among the world's novelists, only TOLSTOY [4] and DICKENS [6] have fashioned a richer imaginative world.

Born on February 2, 1882, Joyce was the eldest of 10 children. His parents, who came from an upper-middle-class background, declined, due to the improvidence of Joyce's father, into shabby gentility and eventually worse during Joyce's youth. Between 1882 and 1902, when Joyce first left Ireland, he had resided at 14 different addresses, each one step lower on the ladder of respectability. Joyce's father is captured in Stephen Dedalus's catalogue of his father, Simon, in *Portrait*: "a medical student, an oarsman, a tenor, an amateur actor, a shouting politician, a small landlord, something in a distillery, a tax-gatherer, a bankrupt, and at present a praiser of his own past." For Joyce, the forces opposing his growth and artistic development were a succession of fathers: his own, his fatherland Ireland, and God the father, represented by the Catholic Church. In his art, Joyce would confront and attempt to master each.

At the age of six and a half Joyce was sent to a Jesuit boarding school, Clongowes Wood, where he was the youngest boy at the school. His experiences there are reflected in *Portrait*, in which Stephen Dedalus's glasses are broken, and he is subsequently beaten, or "pandied," for neglecting his schoolwork. There are obvious differences between the young Joyce and his fictional reflection, however. Joyce's nickname at school was "Sunny Jim." He excelled at sports, and unlike the dour and isolated Stephen Dedalus, he was well liked and generally fun-loving. When his father's financial distress led to his withdrawal from Clongowes, he eventually continued his studies at a Jesuit school in Dublin. As Joyce later remarked, "You allude to me as Catholic. Now for the sake of precision and to get the correct contour of me, you ought to allude to me as a Jesuit." Like Stephen in *Portrait*, Joyce followed a similar cycle of religious devotion, followed by a decline in religious faith, and a growth of faith in art.

As a student at University College, Dublin, Joyce studied languages and began to acquire a literary reputation when, as an early proponent of HENRIK IBSEN [36], he published a review of the Norwegian playwright's work in an English magazine. In 1902, Joyce departed Ireland intent on becoming a doctor, but with the rather exotic notion of studying medicine in Paris. He returned after a few months because of the death of his mother and remained in Dublin until 1904. Joyce taught for a short time, began an autobiographical novel, *Stephen Hero*, and wrote short stories for an Irish farmers' magazine. His first date with a Galway-born chambermaid, Nora Barnacle, on June 16, 1904, would be forever memorialized as "Bloomsday," the day that encompasses the action of *Ulysses*. The couple left Dublin together in October 1904 to begin a life together in exile from their homeland, about which Joyce never stopped writing. They lived in Trieste, Rome, Paris, and Zurich, supported by Joyce's occasional language teaching, infrequent earnings from his writings, and support from a variety of patrons. The couple raised two children and were finally married in 1931.

Joyce began his writing career with lyrical poetry. He also collected what he called *silhouettes*: brief prose sketches of scenes, conversations, and incidents of observed Dublin life. From these Joyce developed his literary technique of the epiphany, the sudden "revelation of the whatness of a thing" in which the "soul of the commonest object . . . seems to be radiant."

Transformation, therefore, is the key function of the epiphany, and for Joyce the artist is "a priest of eternal imagination, transmuting the daily bread of experience into the radiant body of everliving life." The technique of the epiphany, the foundation of Joyce's art, shows him working out the central problem for the novelist in the 20th century, expressed in the choice between realism and symbolism. On the one hand, the novel was opening up new territory of reality rarely examined in fiction before; on the other, writers were searching for a way of penetrating reality to express its essential truths in symbolic patterns. Joyce is at the center of these tendencies. No realist has offered a more exhaustive and unsparing depiction of the immediacies of commonplace life; no symbolist has spun a more subtle or complicated network of meanings.

At their best, Joyce's stories and novels work simultaneously on both levels, culminating in the extraordinary accomplishment of *Ulysses*, which attempts nothing less than a complete reconstruction of a day in the life of Dublin, underlaid with a correspondence of myth and symbol borrowed from HOMER [3]. Leopold Bloom is the modern Odysseus and everyman, defined by his ordinariness, whose spiritual son is the romantic and self-absorbed Stephen Dedalus. The novel arranges a conjunction of their experience into a grand and epic totality. Experience is fragmented and elusive, captured in the flow of consciousness of Joyce's characters, in which sensory data form patterns of meaning shaped by the invisible but controlling vision of the novelist.

Ulysses was published on Joyce's 40th birthday in 1922 to a storm of controversy that surrounded virtually all of his published works. Banned in England and America as obscene for more than 10 years, the book asserted its influence in smuggled copies printed in France. Joyce devoted the rest of his life to the production of his "night" book, *Finnegans Wake*, a dream sequence of Earwicker's unconscious associations through the course of one night, as a complement to the "day" book, *Ulysses*, the story of a typical Dublin day. With its dream logic, portmanteau words, and punning from multiple languages, *Finnegans Wake* is even more experimental than the daring innovation of Joyce's previous work, and to unlock its considerable riches in comedy and linguistic virtuosity, it requires far more labor than most readers are willing to devote. To the end, through two world wars, the mental breakdown of his daughter, and his own failing eyesight, as one of the greatest innovators in world literature, Joyce persisted in shaping a radical redefinition of fictional form, technique, and language to capture modern experience.

8

JOHN MILTON

1608–1674

The characteristick quality of his poem is sublimity. He sometimes descends to the elegant, but his element is the great. He can occasionally invest himself with grace, but his natural port is gigantick loftiness. He can please when pleasure is required, but it is his peculiar power to astonish.

—Samuel Johnson, *Lives of the Poets*

Towering seems the term best reserved for John Milton. In English poetry, no writers except SHAKESPEARE [1] and CHAUCER [5] have exerted such a lasting and powerful influence. In *Lycidas*, Milton wrote what many assert is the greatest English lyrical poem; *Samson Agonistes* has been judged the English poetic drama closest to the tragic greatness of the ancient Greeks; and in *Paradise Lost* Milton created the defining English epic.

In a sense, Milton is the great hinge figure, joining the Renaissance with the modern world of increasing uncertainty, which was ushered in during the political and spiritual turmoil of his lifetime. Having read and absorbed virtually everything that had been written in the past, Milton synthesized his scholarship of classical forms into a great contemporary epic, consciously rivaling the achievements of HOMER [3], VIRGIL [9], and DANTE [2], and he helped redefine the epic tradition from the heroic to the spiritual, shifting the epic's emphasis to the questions of the nature of good and evil. *Paradise Lost*, like the *Iliad* and the *Odyssey*, the *Aeneid*, and *The Divine Comedy*, is one of the touchstone documents of Western civilization. Milton's sublime verse and the depth and grandeur of his poetic vision have few rivals.

Milton's preparation for his great achievement began with the best possible education. His father was a successful London businessman who provided his son with private tutors and schooling in London and Cambridge. At the university, Milton was nicknamed the Lady of Christ's College for his good looks and seriousness. He received his B.A. degree in 1629 and his M.A. degree in 1632, then followed his formal schooling with five years of study on his father's estate near Windsor. Milton was fluent in Latin, Greek, Italian, and Hebrew, and he committed the Bible to memory. Before age 30, Milton had written *L'Allegro* and *Il Penseroso* (companion poetic meditations on the active and the contemplative life), the masques *Arcades* and *Comus*, and the pastoral elegy *Lycidas*. In 1638 Milton left England for a 15-month tour of the continent, during which he visited Florence, Rome, and Naples, and met such important figures as Galileo and the Dutch jurist and humanist Hugo Grotius. He returned to England as the conflict over royal authority pushed the nation into civil war.

For the next 20 years Milton aligned himself with the Puritan radicals and played a key role in the fortunes of the parliamentary forces opposed to Charles I. He was at the center of his age's political debates and controversies, writing treatises that opposed the bishops' control of the church, favored freedom of the press, and urged the sanctioning of divorce on grounds of incompatibility. (The first of his three marriages, to Mary Powell in 1642, led to an estrangement after six weeks, although she later returned to him and gave birth to three daughters.) Under Oliver Cromwell's rule, Milton served as Latin secretary to the Council of State, with responsibility to justify the government's actions at home and abroad. With the Restoration, Milton's prospects and life were threatened. He was briefly imprisoned, lost the greater part of his fortune, and he retired to resume the literary aspirations that had been postponed during his years of public service. By 1651 his eyesight had deteriorated into total blindness, and he depended on his daughters to assist him in his writing and reading.

Milton unfairly has been tarred as a Puritan apologist and associated with inflexible fanaticism and prejudice. He is better seen as a radical freethinker whose attempt to define Christian orthodoxy is both original and controversial. Beginning with the romantics, a revisionist view of Milton has dominated criticism, in which his artistic genius is seen at war with his intentions. In a famous pronouncement, WILLIAM BLAKE [29] declared that "the reason Milton wrote in fetters when he wrote of Angels and God, and at liberty when of Devils and Hell, is because he was a true Poet and of the Devil's party without knowing it." SHELLEY [77], recasting Milton and *Paradise Lost* in his own rebellious image, goes even further by asserting that Satan is the true hero of the poem. "Milton has so far violated the popular creed (if this shall be judged a violation)," Shelley argued, "as to have alleged no superiority of moral value to his God over his Devil. And this bold neglect of direct moral purpose is the most decisive proof of Milton's genius." That such a skewed reading of Milton is possible at all is a testament to his artistry, which expressed his intention in *Paradise Lost* to "justify the ways of God to men" in a fair fight between the forces of good and evil. He also explored in profound ways the eternal conflict in human nature between faith and belief, and the assertion of self against unavoidable limitation.

Paradise Lost originally was conceived as a tragedy, but the theme of mankind's fall and redemption needed an epic of a very different kind from the classical models. In Milton's poem, the heroic values of Homer and the nationalistic ideals of Virgil are subordinated to the grander theme of the Christian myth. In Book IX Milton defines his subject and his argument:

> Not less but more heroic than the wrath
> Of stern Achilles on his foe pursued
> Thrice fugitive about Troy wall; or rage
> Of Turnus for Lavinia disespoused;
> Or Neptune's ire, or Juno's, that so long
> Perplexed the Greek, and Cytherea's son:
> If answerable style I can obtain
> Of my celestial Patroness, who deigns
> Her nightly visitation unimplored,
> And dictates to me slumbering, or inspires
> Easy my unpremeditated verse,
> Since first this subject for heroic song
> Pleased me, long choosing and beginning late,
> Not sedulous by nature to indite
> Wars, hitherto the only argument
> Heroic deemed, chief mastery to dissect
> With long and tedious havoc fabled knights
> In battles feigned (the better fortitude
> Of patience and heroic martyrdom
> Unsung), or to describe races and games,
> Or tilting furniture, emblazoned shields,
> Impresses quaint, caparisons and steeds,
> Bases and tinsel trappings, gorgeous knights
> At joust and tournament; then marshaled feast
> Served up in hall with sewers and seneschals:
> The skill of artifice or office mean;
> Not that which justly gives heroic name
> To person or to poem.

(Book IX, 14–41)

With its staggering range of classical reference, its long, packed, and complexly subordinated sentences, Milton's epic, though imitative of the grand style and dignity of his classical predecessors, aims at a different message: man's fall and God's divine plan of order and redemption. In Milton's scheme, Satan is the model for the classical hero whose ego denies the divine and plunges humankind into evil and separation from the wholeness that God represents. In one of the greatest portraits of villainy ever created, the poem traces Satan's battle with God for the souls of Adam and Eve. Although Satan's evil is rendered with tempting conviction, there should be no mistaking whose side Milton is on, as the Christian myth is developed in a richly patterned mosaic of allusions, associations, and structural parallels. In his study of Milton's life and poetry, Douglas Bush observed: "In its texture and structure, in all its imaginative variety and power, *Paradise Lost* is an inexhaustible source of aesthetic pleasure of a kind unique in English poetry. And, whatever theological elements some readers may choose to ignore, the essential myth, the picture of the grandeur and misery of man, remains 'true,' and infinitely more noble and beautiful than anything modern literature has been able to provide. The question is not how far the poem is worthy of our attention, but how far we can make ourselves worthy of it."

For 200 years following the publication of *Paradise Lost*, Milton's talent and presence dominated literature, with his masterpiece regarded as the pinnacle of what could be achieved in writing. It would take the romantic movement and the modernists, led by T. S. ELIOT [19], to break Milton's control over poetic language and offer an alternative epic vision. Samuel Taylor Coleridge provides a fitting judgment of Milton's contribution to the world's culture: "Finding it impossible to realize his own aspirations, either in religion or politics, or society, he gave up his heart to the living spirit and light within him, and avenged himself on the world by enriching it with this record of his own transcendent ideal."

VIRGIL

9

70–19 B.C.

Thou that seest Universal
* Nature moved by Universal Mind;*
Thou majestic in thy sadness
* at the doubtful doom of human kind;*
      . . .
Light among the vanish'd ages;
* star that gildest yet this phantom shore;*
Golden branch amid the shadows,
* kings and realms that pass to rise no more;*
      . . .
I salute thee, Mantovano,
* I that loved thee since my day began,*
Wielder of the stateliest measure
* ever moulded by the lips of man.*

—Alfred, Lord Tennyson, from "To Virgil"

Virgil, the supreme Latin poet, produced in the *Aeneid* an epic that has been
one of the most revered and influential works of art in Western cultural history. Only HOMER [3], whose heroic poetry Virgil absorbed and transformed,
has exerted a comparable, continual influence in Western thought and art.

Virgil also set the prototype for the artist for whom poetry is both a way of life and a means for the deepest personal, cultural, and religious inquiry.

Like CATULLUS [82], Publius Vergilius Maro was a native of Cisalpine Gaul in northern Italy, and from a rural district not far from Mantua. His father was a landowner and farmer, prominent enough to provide Virgil with a solid education in Cremona, Milan, and finally Rome, where he arrived at the age of 17. Initially Virgil pursued a career in law, but he gave it up for the life of a professional poet and scholar. Shy and studious, Virgil took no part in public life, despite contact with prominent figures of his day, including Caesar Augustus, but the political background of his times is central to an understanding of his poetry. During his lifetime, as a result of the scramble for autocratic power between Pompey and Julius Caesar, and the civil war that followed Caesar's assassination, the Roman Republic broke apart. Augustus was to emerge from the chaos with a political and cultural mission to restore order and the Roman values that had gained Rome its great empire. Virgil's role as an apologist for the Augustan regime should be seen in the context of his fear of the violence and lawlessness that preceded Augustus's reign. In his art, Virgil accepted his part in establishing a bulwark against the forces antithetical to Roman values and their principal contribution to civilization, law, and government. His poetry has, therefore, a strong didactic and nationalistic quality, though his sheer poetic brilliance and moral complexity transcend and expand these aims.

Virgil's poetic achievement is expressed in three monumental works. His earliest is the *Eclogues*, written 42–37 B.C., in which he set out to become the Roman Theocritus (the great Greek pastoral poet of the third century B.C.) by reviving the pastoral form. His celebration of idyllic rustic life, though in one sense escapist, is rooted in reality, with references to historical figures and current topics, and is clearly meant to contrast the present with the natural and the simple life. In the *Georgics* (36 to 29), considered by many his finest work, Virgil provides a Roman version of Hesiod's *Works and Days*, a description of the agricultural life, in a didactic poem that is both a practical handbook on husbandry and a patriotic paean expressing his love of the land and the enduring wisdom of rural values. Virgil read the poem to Augustus on his return to Italy in 29 B.C., and it must have resonated with the new emperor, whose political and cultural goals coincided with the poem's message. The *Georgics* is widely regarded as technically the most perfect of all Latin poems. Both poems show Virgil working toward the expansion of the epic, national and moral purposes of the *Aeneid*, which he composed during his last 10 years. The poem, one of the greatest verse narratives in world literature, follows the adventures of the Trojan Aeneas after the fall of Troy through his affair with Dido, queen of Carthage, and his descent into the underworld, to his arrival in Italy, where he defeats in combat the warrior Turnus and establishes the beginning of the Roman state. Virgil died before completing revisions and instructed that the poem should be destroyed. It is believed that Augustus himself overruled Virgil's final wish and saved the *Aeneid* for posterity.

It was natural for Virgil to turn to Homer when looking for a model for the great poem he aspired to write. The Homeric epics represented, for the Romans as well as for the Greeks, the highest poetic achievement and the appropriate form for a serious, monumental work. Unlike Homer, Virgil was a literary artist, not an oral performer, and he transformed the epic by both his unique genius and the opportunity that written composition represented. Although his meter (dactylic hexameter), structure (the first half of the Aeneid corresponds to the *Odyssey* and the second to the *Iliad*), elements like similes, catalogues, and phrases, and entire episodes, such as the visit to the underworld, are borrowed from Homer, Virgil achieves a great deal more in the *Aeneid* than a convincing imitation. The *Aeneid* fundamentally alters the Homeric worldview and shifts the purpose of the epic into a new direction that would have important implications for later writers like DANTE [2] and MILTON [8], who would take up the epic form again.

In looking back to the heroic world of Homer, Virgil began to trace the possibilities of a grand, nationalistic poem for his own day. To celebrate Roman greatness, he located the origin of that greatness in the legendary journey of the Trojan prince Aeneas after the fall of Troy to found Lavinium, in Latium, which would eventually become Rome. The Homeric past therefore becomes a means for Virgil to explore his own present, offering an explanation of how the present was shaped by the past and suggesting the heroic elements that define the Roman character.

Aeneas, the prototype of the Roman leader, is a different kind of hero than either Achilles or Odysseus, and one of the poem's radical concepts is a fundamental redefinition of the essential qualities of heroism and its cost in self-sacrifice. Aeneas accepts his divine mission to found the Roman state, and his adventures are lessons in suffering as well as tests in the values necessary to become a true leader. Achilles exerts his skills as a warrior for his own glory and honor; Odysseus struggles to reestablish himself in Ithaca. The adventures of Aeneas, however, point to a much larger purpose, one that goes beyond personal fulfillment. His virtues of duty and responsibility run counter to the often self-centered preoccupations of Homer's heroes.

Aeneas has been called a puppet, a "shadow of a man," and most memorably by Charles James Fox, as "always either insipid or odious," but such interpretations miss Virgil's intention in the *Aeneid*, which was his willingness to sacrifice Aeneas's individuality and to place him in the context of Rome's destiny. One of the signs of the poem's greatness is Virgil's recognition of the cost of leadership and the degree to which a proper hero must sacrifice self-fulfillment for the greater good. In Aeneas's tragic affair with Dido, queen of Carthage, Virgil raises the stakes impossibly high. It would have been far easier for Virgil to turn Dido, once the queen of Rome's bitterest enemy, into a far more resistible adversary for Aeneas. Dido is one of the most memorable and sympathetic character portraits in all classical literature, evidence of Virgil's honesty and the complex moral tone of the *Aeneid*.

In the *Aeneid*, Virgil achieves an epic that is both nationalistic in purpose and deeply subjective in its probing of the inner meaning of heroism and man's fate. For later generations, the poem served, like the Bible, as an important source for wisdom and guidance. The fact that readers would select passages at random for inspiration is a testimony to the multilayered tone and nuances of Virgil's poetry, which reaches well beyond his patriotic nationalism to deeper reflections of human experience. The *Aeneid* is suffused with Virgil's presence and persistent melancholy, which Matthew Arnold recognized as "the haunting, the irresistible self-dissatisfaction of his heart." That the dramatic and objective epic form of Homer could be remade into a personal as well as a political poem of great sweep and depth is due to Virgil's great genius. Later writers who took up the epic would have to contend with a second master of its form.

JOHANN WOLFGANG von GOETHE

10

1749–1832

Goethe's profound, imperturbable naturalism is absolutely fatal to all routine thinking; he puts the standard, once for all, inside every man instead of outside him; when he is told, such a thing must be so, there is immense authority and custom in favour of its being so, it has been held to be so for a thousand years, he answers with Olympian politeness, "But is it so? is it so to me?" Nothing could be more really subversive of the foundations on which the old European order rested; and it may be remarked that no persons are so radically detached from this order, no persons so thoroughly modern, as those who have felt Goethe's influence most deeply.

—Matthew Arnold, "Heinrich Heine"

Goethe, the preeminent literary artist in Germany, is, in many ways, the last fully integrated literary figure for whom literature, art, science, scholarship, and public life came together over a long career as a writer, minister of state, man of science, theater director, and critic. A powerful influence on world literature, Goethe dominated his period as only a few others, such as DANTE [2], MILTON [8], and VOLTAIRE [69], have done. He achieved greatness in virtually every literary genre: lyrical poetry, drama, and fiction. In doing so, Goethe helped to define the romantic age in his groundbreaking novel, *The Sorrows of Young Werther*, while in *Faust* he produced one of world literature's greatest mythic fables that has, like Dante's *The Divine Comedy* and CERVANTES's

[11] *Don Quixote*, fundamentally shaped our imaginative understanding of the human condition. A legend in his lifetime, Goethe is, in the critic Harold Bloom's terminology, the archetypal "strong poet" who provides points of reference and a source of imitation and refutation to the generations that followed him.

Born in Frankfurt, Goethe studied law, first at the University of Leipzig and, after an interruption from illness, at Strasbourg, where he received a law degree in 1771. His friendship with J. G. Herder, the principal exponent of the *Sturm und Drang* (Storm and Stress) literary movement, an early flowering of German romanticism and reaction to neoclassical thought and art, was a significant influence on Goethe's first major work, *Götz von Berlichingen* (1773), a historical drama. A year later, the publication of *The Sorrows of Young Werther* produced a furor of controversy and gave Goethe an international reputation.

It is difficult to imagine another single book that has had the comparable impact and influence as Goethe's epistolary confessions of the radically subjective Werther, whose deep feelings and disappointments lead to release in suicide. A victim of a hopeless love and a dangerously refined sensitivity, Werther is unable to escape his own torment, and Goethe records the progression of Werther's world-weary suffering, a new subject for the novel. As Karl Viëtor has argued:

> Among European novels Werther is the first in which an inward life, a spiritual process and nothing else, is represented, and hence it is the first psychological novel—though naturally not the first in which the inner life in general is seriously dealt with. The conflict between an immoderately burgeoning passion and the ordered world of society is here described, as it were, "from within." The scene is the soul of the hero. All events and figures are regarded only in the light of the significance they have for Werther's emotion. All that happens serves but to nourish the absolution of Werther's emotions—a fatal propensity which swells to a demonic possession and engulfs all other inward forces and possibilities.

The novel, which has a strong basis in Goethe's own experiences, diagnoses his generation's romantic self-obsession with no social outlets in which to channel spiritual energies. "I am weary of bewailing the fate of our generation of human beings," Goethe wrote, "but I will so depict them that they may understand themselves, if that is possible, as I have understood them." As Goethe warned, "the end of this disease is death! The goal of such sentimental enthusiasm is suicide!" Despite his warning, the novel exposed a style and attitude of self-absorption that Goethe had detected as latent in his generation. In imitation of Werther's world-weariness, young men began to dress like Goethe's protagonist in blue cutaways and yellow vest and breeches, to adopt his attitudes, and, indeed, to take their own lives. Goethe felt the need to add to the second edition of the novel Werther's own admonition, "Be a man, do not follow me." The novel is remarkable for Goethe's skill in presenting Werther's tortured psychology and reflecting the milieu that produced him. Werther also set the pattern for the melancholy and striving romantic hero that would be echoed most noticeably in the lives and works of BYRON [83] and SHELLEY [77].

In 1775, Goethe accepted an invitation from an admirer, Duke Karl August of Saxe-Weimar, to serve at court in Weimar. He became a cabinet minister of agriculture, finance, and mines, and was for 10 years the duke's chief minister. In 1786, Goethe left Germany for a two-year stay in Italy, where he deepened his appreciation of classical art. His earlier romantic attitudes of individualism and freedom matured and led to a heightened awareness of the importance of discipline and universality. This creative tension is balanced in his mature work, including the novel *Wilhelm Meister's Apprenticeship* (1796) and its sequel *Wilhelm Meister's Travels* (1829), which set the model for the bildungsroman, the novel of growth and development; the drama *Iphigenie auf Tauris* (1788); and *Faust* (part one was published in 1808; part two after Goethe's death in 1832).

Besides his continual creative work, including some of the finest lyrical poetry in German literature, Goethe was the director of the state theater for more than 20 years; conducted scientific research in evolutionary botany, anatomy, and the theory of color; and undertook a serious study of non-Western literature. A polymath of extraordinary ability, Goethe was recognized during his lifetime as a sage. A host of visitors, including Napoleon, came to Weimar to pay their respects and to learn from the master. Admiration for Goethe and his works throughout Europe and America contributed greatly to the spread of German ideas and culture worldwide, with profound effects on scholarship, education, and philosophy, as well as literature, throughout the 19th century.

Goethe's greatest achievement, however, is the poetic drama *Faust*, the conception and composition of which occupied him from his early 20s to the year before he died, when he finally completed the second part of the work. *Faust* provides a synthesis of all of his works and skills as a poet. Adapting the medieval legend of the man of intellect who trades his soul for knowledge and power, Goethe turns man's boundless yearning into the potentially damning but ultimately redeeming factor that earns his salvation, and he creates in the character of Faust a central romantic hero, like Werther, Shelley's Prometheus, and Byron's Manfred. Faust represents the individual's aspiration for transcendence in defiance of all limits.

In Goethe's version, Faust's demonic bargain, in which Mephistopheles can claim Faust's soul at the moment of his contentment, turns on the realization that no single experience will be finally satisfying, that aspiration and striving will alone sustain Faust. Goethe further tests Faust's assertion of the individual's dominating will with the counterclaim of love in his relationship with Gretchen.

Part one of *Faust* ends with the protagonist suspended between the seemingly irreconcilable poles of the need of self and the importance of the other. In part two of the drama, the tone shifts to the more directly allegorical and philosophical as Goethe attempts to find a way out of the dilemma and a synthesis between romantic and classical attitudes, between freedom and restraint, liberty and order. Faust discovers his eventual contentment in the continual aspiration of social improvement, in which the individual will finds a worthy object in the world to which to devote its striving energy. Because the improvements Faust desires are always in the process of becoming. Mephistopheles finally loses his bargain to possess Faust's soul. Such a bald summary of Goethe's masterpiece only sketches the barest outline of a work that Goethe created with genius through the complexity of his thinking and the mastery of his poetic expression.

Goethe's greatness as a writer stems from his ability to question his own assumptions and those of his age, and to recast them imaginatively into forms of inquiry. As William James summarized, "He was alive at every pore of his skin, and received every impression in a sort of undistracted leisure; which makes the movement of his mental machinery one of the most extraordinary exhibitions which this planet can ever have witnessed."

MIGUEL DE CERVANTES SAAVEDRA

11

1547–1616

To crown him with an adjective of his own choosing, Cervantes continues to be the exemplary novelist. It is a truism, of course, that he set the example for all other novelists to follow. The paradox is that, by exemplifying the effects of fantasy on the mind, he pointed the one way for fiction to attain the effect of truth.

—Harry Levin, "The Example of Cervantes" in *Contexts of Criticism*

Perhaps no modern myth has been as persistent as that created by Cervantes in *Don Quixote*. With this book, Cervantes synthesized the epic and dramatic genres into a new form that became the modern novel, and the characters that he fashioned, along with their obsessions, have entered the deepest level of our culture. Those who have never read Cervantes recognize at once the absurdly visionary Don Quixote along with his practical companion Sancho Panza, and the novel's central situation is embedded, rightly or wrongly, in the terms and phrases "quixotic," "tilting at windmills," and "to dream the impossible dream."

Artistically, the tradition and development of the novel, as well as its central concerns of human psychology and social satire, the question of human identity, and the interplay of the artist between the real and the imagined, can all be traced directly to Cervantes. The 19th-century French literary historian Sainte-Beuve described Cervantes's masterpiece as the "Bible of Humanity,"

41

and the 20th-century critic Lionel Trilling observed that "all prose fiction is a variation of the theme of *Don Quixote*." *Don Quixote* was a popular and critical sensation from the start, and its power has not diminished after nearly 400 years.

Cervantes's life corresponds to the blend of high adventure and grim reality that shaped his masterpiece. He was born in Alcalá de Henares, not far from Madrid, during the reign of Charles V and the beginning of Spain's golden age. His father was an impoverished apothecary and surgeon, and Cervantes's early life was spent on the move from Valladolid, Córdoba, and Seville, to Madrid, as his father relocated his family one step ahead of his creditors. Cervantes was educated at an elementary school in Córdoba and the Jesuit college in Seville, in which, as he later recalled, "I led the life of a student, without hunger and without the itch." A voracious reader, Cervantes was also enthralled by the theater. When his family moved to Madrid in 1566, Cervantes probably continued his studies there, but his activities are shadowy except for his departure in 1569 to Italy. It has been speculated, partially based on Cervantes's own confession of a "youthful imprudence" and through court records, that he was involved in a duel and fled Spain to avoid a royal sentence that called for the loss of his right hand and ten years exile.

Instead, Cervantes began a 12-year absence from Spain that eventually cost him his left hand. He first served in Rome in the retinue of Cardinal Acquaviva, and later as a soldier in the Spanish forces of the Holy League, who fought the Turks for control of the Mediterranean. In 1571, Cervantes was severely wounded during the sea battle of Lepanto—his left hand was shattered, and he lost use of it permanently. He spent four more years on other military campaigns, and in 1575, on his way back to Spain, was captured by pirates and endured five years in captivity as a slave in Algiers. He led four unsuccessful attempts to organize an uprising of the Christian slaves there before being ransomed in 1580. Returning to Spain at the age of 33, partially crippled and with no prospects, Cervantes spent the next 25 years desperately struggling to earn a living. Writing was one way, and Cervantes tried his hand at pastoral romance and drama, the popular genres of the time, but found little success with either. He secured positions as a commissary, buying supplies for the Armada as it prepared for its invasion of England, and as a tax collector. He fathered a daughter in an affair with an actress who deserted him, and married Catalina de Salazar y Palacios in 1584, taking on the financial responsibility for an extended family that included his mother and two sisters, his daughter, and widowed mother-in-law. He was imprisoned several times for shortcomings in his accounts, and tradition asserts that while he was in prison in Seville he began work on *Don Quixote*, the first part of which appeared in 1605, with its sequel published in 1615, shortly before his death. In one of the most remarkable coincidences of literary history, Cervantes published his tale of his mad knight in the same year that SHAKESPEARE [1] saw his play about his mad king, *King Lear*, first performed. Both writers died on the same date, April 23, 1616, though there was a 10-day difference between the English and the Spanish calendars.

Cervantes's *The Ingenious Gentleman Don Quixote de la Mancha* began with a narrow target—the comic, satiric puncturing of the popular indulgence in tales of chivalry—that grew to embrace much wider and more profound themes. Given the desultory nature of the book's creation and plan, the novel has been viewed as a kind of literary miracle—an accidental, spontaneous combustion of a character into an archetype and a joke into a multilevel masterpiece. In a sense, Cervantes's creation has been wrestled away from him, and his intentions as well as the evidence of what he wrote often have been ignored in pursuit of themes that fit the reader's preoccupations.

Like all great masterpieces, the novel has served as an illuminating mirror for each age that picks it up. When the novel first appeared, the picaresque adventures of the mad Quixote, who confuses the world of chivalry with the ordinary and the mundane, primarily inspired riotous laughter at the misidentification of reality and the ensuing slapstick humor. In the rationalistic 18th century, *Don Quixote* was viewed as an epic of reason in which the Don's mad refusal to accept things as they are and adapt to society's norms causes his repeated and just punishment. By the 19th century, *Don Quixote* no longer was viewed as a comic novel but instead as a philosophical one devoted to uncovering the nature of human identity in the battle between self and society. The novel's pathos toward the Don's insistence on his illusions, despite the inevitable victory of reality, seemed to be Cervantes's greatest insight. His comedy was wide enough to embrace its opposite in tragedy, and the Don's "impossible dream" summons as many tears as laughter.

Despite shifts in interpretation over the years, Cervantes's masterpiece is neither an accident nor a contradiction. Beginning with his central conceit to relocate the values of chivalry in the terms of ordinary, contemporary life, Cervantes discovered a rich vein of comedy and pathos. In following the novel through its progression, not in simply extracting certain passages, it is evident that Cervantes's themes and characterization grow in richness and ambiguity. If Don Quixote was to be only a figure of mockery, why grant his illusions such nobility and invest his insistence on them with such heroism? If the novel concludes with the victory of reason and fact over fancy and idealism, why does the world seem so diminished in this victory? By pairing the idealistic Don with the commonsensical Sancho Panza, Cervantes does not simply join opposites but instead shows how each shares elements of the other. By the novel's end, Don Quixote stands firmly on the side of the real, while Sancho urges the continuing pursuit of the ideal. Cervantes's greatness in *Don Quixote* lies in staging a fair battle between appearance and reality, the implication of which goes to the heart of the creative process and human nature, which has dominated the novel and novelists ever since.

MURASAKI SHIKIBU

c. 978–1030

When romancers of the tenth century attempt characterization, and it is of a rudimental sort, they write fairy stories, and when they write of such matters as court intrigues, the characterization is so flat that it can hardly be called characterization at all. The diaries of the tenth century may perhaps have been something of an inspiration for Murasaki Shikibu, but the awareness that an imagined predicament can be made more real than a real one required a great leap of the imagination, and Murasaki Shikibu made it herself.

—Edward G. Seidensticker, introduction to the Vintage edition
of *The Tale of Genji*

The Tale of Genji, by Murasaki Shikibu, a lady of the 11th-century Japanese court, is one of the masterworks of world literature and the best-known example of premodern Japanese literature. Drawing on the tradition of Chinese historical writing and Chinese and Japanese lyrical poetry, Lady Murasaki produced something new and unique, a prose romance filled with believable characters in real situations that anticipated the development of the novel in the West by nearly 800 years. *The Tale of Genji* is, however, more than a significant literary precursor. It remains one of the greatest works of the imagination ever written. An essential component of any serious Japanese education, it is the most influential literary work to reach the Western world in translation and has extended its impact beyond the domain of the scholar and Japanese specialist.

We know very little about the author of *The Tale of Genji*. Her father was a provincial governor and a not-very-prominent member of the ruling Fujiwara clan. Although her family was not powerful, it was distinguished by literary achievement. Murasaki Shikibu's great-grandfather played a role in the compilation of the first imperial anthology of Japanese verse, and her father was a poet and a scholar of Chinese classics, an essential prerequisite for bureaucratic success in the male-dominated public life of the time. Lady Murasaki's early literary skills were evident but underappreciated. As she records in her diary, "When my brother . . . was a young boy learning the Chinese classics, I was in the habit of listening to him and I became unusually proficient at understanding those passages which he found too difficult to grasp. Father, a most learned man, was always regretting the fact: 'Just my luck!' he would say. 'What a pity she was not born a man!'"

Around 998, Murasaki Shikibu was married to her cousin, a member of the imperial guard, and in 1011 she was widowed. It was at this point that she began writing her great work. *The Tale of Genji* was completed over many years, and her manuscripts in the form of handwritten notebooks were passed around, read, and copied. Chapters may have been read at court, and she came to the attention of the regent, Michinaga, who brought her to court as the companion and tutor for his daughter Soshi, the imperial consort. She was then afforded the opportunity to observe closely the court world that she incorporated in many of *The Tale of Genji*'s scenes and characters. During her court period, Lady Murasaki recorded the events of two years of her service in her diary, the best surviving window on imperial life at the time. She remained at court until about 1013. What happened afterward and the details of her death are not known.

Despite the circumscribed and cloistered life of women during the period—most had no public function and their names were rarely recorded—it is not surprising that a woman did produce a Japanese literary masterpiece. If Chinese art and culture were the exclusive province of males, the Japanese vernacular was largely left to women, and the literature of the period is dominated by women writers as they devised an indigenous literary style. Murasaki Shikibu's literary talent was no doubt a major asset in her court service, and she had the time and leisure to create, which she used to full advantage in producing her epic.

The Tale of Genji is a massive work of 1,000 pages that covers 75 years in the careers of the nobleman Genji and his two offspring. Genji, the son of the emperor, is in many ways a paragon of manly virtues, possessing wit, sophistication, and great physical attraction. In the novel's opening chapter, he is prevented from succeeding his father and thereby begins a lifelong quest to achieve some other compensation for his loss of rank. This takes the form of a search to find the perfect woman and redemption through love. Over the years, Genji's early idealism is tested in a series of encounters with women, culminating in his disastrous affair with his father's consort, which causes his exile and eventually allows him insights into his own shortcomings. What makes the novel unique is that instead of the expected romance of marvelous events and idealized characters, Genji's story is dramatized with psychological penetration and a clear sense of reality. As Lady Murasaki writes in the book, "Anything whatsoever may become the subject of a novel provided only that it happens in mundane life and not in some fairyland beyond our human experience." Genji, who begins his career as a near-perfect hero, ends it as a complex human blend of positive and negative attributes. Lady Murasaki frames her protagonist's story with dozens of character portraits, all firmly rooted in a time and place that is for the Western reader both exotic and familiar. Throughout, Murasaki Shikibu manages what all great novels attempt: a shock of recognition as the various aspects of love and human needs are brought to the surface in a style that is simultaneously exact and full of nuance and poetic intensity.

It would take more than 800 years for other writers to attempt what Lady Murasaki accomplished in *The Tale of Genji*. Arguably the first novelist, Lady Murasaki is certainly one of history's most influential. *The Tale of Genji* represents, in the words of Nobel Prize–winning author KAWABATA YASUNARI [109], "the highest pinnacle of Japanese literature."

SOPHOCLES

13

496–406 B.C.

. . . But be his
My special thanks, whose even-balanced soul,
From first youth tested up to extreme old age,
Business could not make dull, nor passion wild;

Who saw life steadily, and saw it whole;
The mellow glory of the Attic stage,
Singer of sweet Colonus, and its child.

—Matthew Arnold, "To a Friend"

In analyzing the role and importance of the three great Greek tragedians, Aeschylus [27] is most often seen as the great originator, Euripides [22] the great outsider and iconoclast, and Sophocles the technical master of the classic tragic form. Sophocles synthesized the ethical and religious concerns of Aeschylus with the psychological penetration of Euripides into consummate artistry. For Aristotle, Sophocles' plays exemplified the ideal expression of Attic tragedy and provided Aristotle's model for understanding the tragic process examined in his *Poetics*. The modern concept of tragic drama, centered on the dilemma of a single central character, begins with Sophocles, and is exemplified by his *Oedipus Rex*, arguably the most influential play ever written.

Besides his dramatic achievement and innovation, Sophocles is further distinguished as the representative figure of his age in a lifetime that coincided with the rise and fall of Athens as a political and cultural power in the fifth century B.C. Sophocles was born in 496 B.C. in Colonus, near Athens. At the age of 16, already an accomplished dancer and lyre player, he was selected to lead the celebration of the victory over the Persians at the battle of Salamis, the event that ushered in the golden age of Athens. He died in 406 B.C., two years before the fall of Athens to Sparta, which ended nearly a century of Athenian supremacy and cultural achievement. Very much at the center of Athenian public life, Sophocles served as an imperial treasurer and diplomat, and was twice elected general. In 413, when he was more than 80 years old, Sophocles was appointed a special commissioner to investigate an Athenian military disaster in Sicily. A lay priest in the cult of a local deity, Sophocles also founded a literary association and was an intimate of such prominent men of letters as Ion of Chios, Herodotus, and Archelaus. Urbane, garrulous, and witty, Sophocles was remembered fondly by his contemporaries as possessing all the admired qualities of balance and serenity. Nicknamed the Bee for his "honeyed" style of flowing eloquence, the highest compliment the Greeks could bestow on a poet or speaker, Sophocles was regarded as the tragic Homer.

In marked contrast to his secure and stable public role and private life, Sophocles' plays orchestrate a disturbing challenge to assurance and certainty, questioning in fundamental ways frail human nature pitted against the forces of destiny. His works are informed by a central observation that human strength and achievement must be balanced by a total vulnerability to circumstance. Sophocles began his career as a playwright in 468 with a first-prize victory over Aeschylus in the Great Dionysia, the annual Athenian play competition. During the next 60 years he produced more than 120 plays (only seven have survived intact), winning first prize at the Dionysia 24 times and never earning less than second place, making him unquestionably the most successful and popular playwright of his time. To Attic drama, which previously consisted of a pair of mask actors and a chorus, Sophocles introduced a third actor, creating the possibility for more complex dramatic situations and deepened psychological penetration through personal relationships and dialogue among the characters. Sophocles replaced the connected trilogies of Aeschylus with separate plays on different subjects establishing the norm that has continued in Western drama, with an emphasis on the intensity and unity of dramatic action. If Aeschylus is credited with discovering the poetic and emotional possibilities of tragedy, it is Sophocles whose refinements and technical mastery provide the standards by which the form has been judged since the fifth century B.C.

Because so few of his plays have survived and they can be only imprecisely dated, it is impossible to trace Sophocles' artistic development with certainty.

It is possible, however, to offer some general comments on the central themes and characteristics that distinguish his art and vision. At the center of all of his plays—*Ajax, Antigone, Trachiniae, Oedipus Rex, Electra, Philoctetes,* and *Oedipus at Colonus*—is the dramatic conflict of strong central characters achieving a level of truth and awareness through suffering. As the classical scholar Bernard Knox has observed, "Sophocles presents us for the first time with what we recognize as a 'tragic hero': one who, unsupported by the gods and in the face of human opposition, makes a decision which springs from the deepest layer of his individual nature, his *physis,* and then blindly, ferociously, heroically maintains that decision even to the point of self-destruction."

At their core, Sophocles' tragedies are essentially moral and religious dramas that pit the tragic hero against unalterable fate and the divine will of the gods. In his masterpiece *Oedipus Rex,* Oedipus is the model leader whose very strengths, conjoined with his human fallibility, set in motion the revelation that he has violated social and divine order through patricide and incest. The play dramatizes in intensely human terms Oedipus's painful journey toward self-understanding—evoking, in Aristotle's terms, the pity and fear of tragedy as the audience is made to bear witness to a deepened understanding of human nature and its implications. By the end of the play, Oedipus has achieved truth, but he is blind and an outcast. The chorus summarizes the harsh lesson that the play dramatizes:

> Look and learn all Theban people and this Oedipus behold,
> This, that read the famous riddle, and we hailed him chief of men,
> And his glory and his fortune was no Theban but admired—
> Now upon his head the billows of disaster dire are poured.
> Therefore, waiting still and watching for that final day of all,
> On no mortal man the verdict "He is happy" we pronounce,
> Till his goal of life he passes, clear of sorrow to its close.

In all of his tragedies, Sophocles poses an essential moral or religious problem as his characters confront fundamental issues, testing each in a cycle of consequence and responsibility. In *Antigone,* the play turns on the question of whether the traitor Polynices, Antigone's brother, can be buried. Antigone's family loyalty is set in conflict with the Theban king Creon's civic responsibility and pride. In the end, Antigone, one of the great literary examples of resistance to authority, is proven right in her opposition to Creon, but at tremendous cost. Creon's realization of Antigone's higher family duty comes too late to save her, and his own family is destroyed by his actions. The chorus again offers a summary of what the drama has vividly enacted: "The mighty words of the proud are paid in full with mighty blows of fate, and at long last those blows will teach us wisdom."

Sophocles was the first playwright to achieve in art such a profound examination of the nature of the universe and the human capacity to cope with its ambiguities. By testing his characters so severely, Sophocles orchestrated adversity into revelations that continue to evoke an audience's capacity for wonder and compassion.

FEODOR DOSTOEVSKY

14

1821–1881

Four facets may be distinguished in the rich personality of Dostoevsky: the creative artist, the neurotic, the moralist and the sinner. How is one to find one's way in this bewildering complexity?

—Sigmund Freud, "Dostoevsky and Parricide"

It is a critical commonplace to contrast Dostoevsky with his Russian contemporary, TOLSTOY [4]. Tolstoy's Moscow can be set against Dostoevsky's St. Petersburg; Tolstoy's light and epic expansion compared with Dostoevsky's dark tragedy and fragmentation of the alienated and divided self. Such contrasts overstate differences and ignore points of similarity, the greatest of which is their remarkable penetrating imaginations, which produced landmark novels in the history of world literature. Like DICKENS [6] and THACKERAY [94], Dostoevsky and Tolstoy are forever linked as competing artists whose different masterpieces and approach establish a kind of imaginative boundary for the novel. Dostoevsky's creations—the Underground Man, Raskolnikov, Prince Myshkin, and the Karamazovs—have entered literary culture, as have his obsessions and angle of vision that describe a peculiar tone and state of mind as Dostoevskian. Dostoevsky's vision is so resonant and suggestive that it encourages different philosophical and artistic camps to claim him as a partisan. His power stems from his ability to dramatize insights into the human condition that continue to exert a modern relevance.

Dostoevsky has been seen as a precursor of existentialism, as well as a mystic and a religious and political prophet—both a revolutionary and a reactionary—and, in the view of THOMAS MANN [35], a "Sinner and Saint in one." That particular personality complex, detected by Sigmund Freud, and Dostoevsky's various themes, evident in his writing, have a biographical basis.

Dostoevsky was born in a Moscow hospital for the poor, where his father was a resident physician. A violent, domineering alcoholic, Dostoevsky's father was eventually murdered in 1839 on his small estate by serfs in retaliation for their mistreatment, and Dostoevsky's fascination with crime and tyranny clearly can be traced back to his early associations with his father. In 1843, Dostoevsky graduated from a military engineering school but resigned his commission to embark on a writing career. During the 1840s, he published two novels, *Poor People*, a realistic proletarian work, and *The Double*, the story of a paranoid civil servant who meets a man who could be his identical twin. *The Double* established Dostoevsky's characteristic interest in divided psychological states.

In 1849, Dostoevsky was arrested as a member of the Petrashevsky Circle, a utopian, socialist discussion group, and sentenced to be executed. Although the conspirators' sentence was commuted to exile in a Siberian labor camp, the czarist police first staged a sham execution, lining them up in front of the firing squad before announcing their reprieve. Dostoevsky endured 10 years of exile, four at a labor camp working in chains in a log house, and six as a common soldier at a Siberian frontier post near the Mongolian border. The agonies Dostoevsky experienced are described in *The House of the Dead* (1862), which he equated to being buried alive with his identity obliterated, a condition that Dostoevsky would return to again and again in his novels in portraits of alienation and the psychological makeup of the criminal. The experience aggravated an epileptic condition that would persist throughout his life, and ended his search for a socialist solution to Russia's problems. Instead, Dostoevsky was to develop a radical conservative philosophy based on the theory of humanity's innate depravity, the decay of the West, and a faith in Russian nationalism and simple Christianity.

In 1859, Dostoevsky was permitted to resign from the army and return to St. Petersburg, where he attempted to reestablish his literary career. He had married Maria Isaeva while in Siberia, but their relationship was unhappy, and she died of tuberculosis in 1864. Despite domestic troubles, a tempestuous love affair, chronic debt, and an addiction to gambling, Dostoevsky published *Crime and Punishment* in 1866, to critical acclaim. *The Idiot* followed in 1868. Dostoevsky fell in love with Anna Grigorevna, the stenographer he had hired to copy *The Gambler*, which he wrote in 26 days to satisfy a publisher's claim.

She provided Dostoevsky with stability during his last decade, during which he wrote *The Possessed* (1873), *A Raw Youth* (1876), and his masterpiece, *The Brothers Karamazov* (1880). The novelist died from emphysema a few months after he delivered a rousing speech commemorating the spirit of ALEXANDER PUSHKIN [18] as an example of the means to achieve peace and brotherhood, for which Dostoevsky was heralded as a prophet.

An emphasis on the biographical basis of Dostoevsky's fiction can lead to the undervaluing of his power and control as an artist. Although there are certain correspondences between Dostoevsky's background and the situations and characters in his novels that do suggest he drew heavily on his self-analysis and circumstances, his essential strengths are not confessional but instead dramatic. Like Dickens, Dostoevsky was drawn to the sensational to reach a revelation of character closed by other means. His four great novels—*Crime and Punishment, The Idiot, The Possessed,* and *The Brothers Karamazov*—turn on crimes that form a dramatic basis for his exploration of the psychology of adversity and the clash of ideas that interested him: good and evil, free will and authority, faith and disbelief. In *Crime and Punishment*, the intellectual Raskolnikov carries out his murder of the pawnbroker and her sister from complex motives that the novel gradually exposes. Therefore, the novel provides philosophical and psychological insights fully visualized in scenes and settings that simultaneously function as particular and universal. Raskolnikov is both a completely realized individual and emblematic of the condition Dostoevsky explored most extensively in the tour-de-force monologue *Notes From the Underground* (1864), in which the speaker is self-divided: forced to try to connect with his world, but unable to sustain integration. Philip Rahv has written:

> Dostoevsky is the first novelist to have fully accepted and dramatized the principle of uncertainty or indeterminacy in the presentation of character. In terms of novelistic technique this principle manifests itself as a kind of hyperbolic suspense—suspense no longer generated merely by the traditional means and devices of fiction, though these are skillfully brought into play, but as it were by the very structure of human reality. To take this hyperbolic suspense as a literary invention pure and simple is to fail in comprehending it; it originates rather in Dostoevsky's acute awareness (self-awareness at bottom) of the problematic nature of the modern personality and of its tortuous efforts to stem the disintegration threatening it.

As Rahv makes clear, all of Dostoevsky's protagonists are marked by a sense of "spiritual and mental self-division and self-contradiction," in which the criminal becomes an archetype of a peculiarly modern psychological condition of alienation and self-destruction.

Alternatives to his damned and self-divided characters are glimpsed in such characters as Prince Lev Myshkin, Dostoevsky's idiot, an ideal of humility and compassion, who, though his innocence is crushed and his sanity is lost by the end of the novel, is still a powerful moral force. In the symphonic arrangement of *The Brothers Karamazov*, Dmitri, Ivan, and Alyosha come to represent three different responses to their inner conflict—the sensual, intellectual, and the religious—and it is only the last that provides a satisfactory answer in the end.

Dostoevsky's answers to some of life's most persistent and vexing questions are muted and ambiguous, and Dostoevsky the novelist is more important as the visualizer of dilemmas than as a philosopher with solutions. His strengths as a novelist rest with his vivid and dramatic probing of the human heart, mind, and soul.

WILLIAM FAULKNER

15

1897–1962

The truth is that Faulkner unites in his work two of the dominant trends in American literature from the beginning: that of the psychological horror story as developed by Haw-thorne, Poe, and Stephen Crane, among others; and that of realistic frontier humor, with Mark Twain as its best example. If you imagine Huckleberry Finn living in the House of Usher and telling uproarious stories while the walls crumble about him, that will give you the double quality of Faulkner's work at its best.
　　　　　　　—Malcolm Cowley, "Some Uses of Folk Humor by Faulkner,"
　　　　　　　　　　in *William Faulkner, Four Decades of Criticism*

Only Edgar Allan Poe [53] and Herman Melville [24] have had as compa-rable a rise to prominence in American literature as William Faulkner. The novelist was more ignored than acclaimed through much of his writing career. By the mid-1940s, his best books behind him and all his novels out of print, the selection of his work published as *The Portable Faulkner* (1946) started a reassessment and appreciation. Today, Faulkner's status is secure as one of America's greatest writers and without peer in modern literature.

　　This most American of writers has become one of the giants of world literature whose influence extends to Latin America, Russia, France, China, and elsewhere around the globe. For the sheer range of his vision and the originality of his expression, I have selected Faulkner to lead the American delegation in this ranking. Few other writers of any nationality have created an imaginary world so rich and complex or have achieved a comparable balance of the local and regional that is at the same time an expression of a culture and a history, as well as a reflection of universal and mythical themes. "I like to think of the world I created," Faulkner observed, "as being a kind of keystone in the universe; that, small as the keystone is, if it were taken away the universe itself would collapse." Rooted in the vernacular and the American folk tradition, Faulkner combined those elements with literary modernism and the most daring European experiments in symbolism and stream of consciousness to produce his enduring masterpieces.

Born William Cuthbert Falkner (he added the *u* to his family's name in 1924 with his first book) in New Albany, Mississippi, the eldest of four sons, the novelist grew up in Oxford, home of the University of Mississippi. Faulkner was named for his great-grandfather Colonel William C. Falkner, who fought in the Civil War, made the family's fortune in the railroad business, and was a popular romantic novelist. Faulkner's namesake loomed large in his descendant's imagination as the source of stories of the Southern past and the Civil War, as well as the Faulkner family's own grand history, though in Faulkner's time its fortune was considerably diminished. After the family railroad was sold, Faulkner's father ran a livery stable and hardware store in Oxford, and eventually became the university's business manager.

Although an avid reader, William Faulkner dropped out of high school after two years to work as a bookkeeper in his grandfather's bank. Encouraged in his reading and writing by an older friend, Faulkner was introduced to the works of BALZAC [40] and the French symbolist poets. The latters' influence is reflected in his first published work, *The Marble Faun* (1924), a private edition of his poetry. In 1918, when his sweetheart Estelle Oldham married another, Faulkner joined the Canadian Royal Air Force as a quick route to World War I. The war ended, however, before he had completed basic training. After returning to Oxford, Faulkner enrolled as a special student at the university and worked in a New York bookstore, one of a succession of miscellaneous jobs, which included a three-year appointment as the university's postmaster. The most decisive experience during Faulkner's literary apprenticeship was a six-month stay in New Orleans in 1925, when he met the writer Sherwood Anderson and mingled with a coterie of the city's literary types. Anderson assisted Faulkner in getting his first novel, *Soldiers' Pay* (1926), published and encouraged him to exploit his Southern background. Faulkner instead took a freighter to Europe, where he bicycled through Italy and France. On his return he completed a second novel, *Mosquitoes* (1927), a satire on the New Orleans literary scene. His third novel, *Flags in the Dust*, was rejected, but Faulkner revised it into *Sartoris* (1929), the first novel in the expansive saga of Yoknapatawpha County, his imagined version of his native Lincoln County with, as he wrote on a map of his fictional world, "William Faulkner, sole owner and proprietor."

In imitation of Balzac's *Human Comedy*, Faulkner launched a fictional recreation of a place and its history in a series of novels with repeated characters and a cumulatively revealed pattern that reflects the rise and fall of the South, from the displacement of the Indians to the rise of a plantation society and its attendant code of chivalry and honor, to its fall through the tragedy of slavery and replacement by modern values of the mercantile, acquisitive North. Faulkner dramatizes his cycle of a paradise lost through human limitations and uncontrollable passions in the story of various characters and their family histories which form chapters in the chronicle of a region and a past. Faulkner raises these stories to the level of the mythic and universal in the comedy and tragedy of his Sartorises, Compsons, McCaslins, Bundrens, Snopeses, and others. Their stories are often refracted by multiple narrative perspectives, nonlinear time sequences, and a highly opaque, suggestive, and sinuous prose style. *The Sound and the Fury* (1929), for example, the story of the decay of the Compson family, is told from four different perspectives, with the most challenging that of the mentally disturbed Benjy. Clearly influenced by HENRY JAMES [38] and JAMES JOYCE [7], Faulkner builds his story out of the progressive revelation to be won from an intense engagement with several consciousnesses.

Launched in 1929 as a novelist with his dominant subject and method already in place, Faulkner married the once divorced Estelle Oldham and settled in a rundown antebellum house outside Oxford. Over a 12-year period, from 1930 to 1942, he produced his greatest novels: *As I Lay Dying* (1930), *Sanctuary* (1931), *Light in August* (1932), *Absalom, Absalom!* (1936), *The Unvanquished* (1938), *The Wild Palms* (1939), *The Hamlet* (1940), and *Go Down, Moses* (1942). Despite a considerable reputation in France and among a small circle of writers, Faulkner initially did not reach a wider audience, except with *Sanctuary*, his intentional assault on commercial success. The novel's brutality and lurid subject, the rape and prostitution of a schoolgirl, created a stir, and the novel was made into a movie. The experience led Faulkner to work in Hollywood as a scriptwriter and "film doctor" of others' scripts before his later fame culminated in the Nobel Prize for literature in 1949. Faulkner's final work includes *Intruder in the Dust* (1948); his collected stories, issued in 1950; *A Fable* (1954); the completion of his Snopes trilogy with *A Town* (1957) and *The Mansion* (1959); and his last novel, the comic *The Reivers* (1962). A writer in residence at the University of Virginia, Faulkner closed his career somewhat abashed by his accomplishments, often assuming the pose of the simple country farmer rather than the international literary celebrity he had become.

More profoundly than any of his contemporaries, Faulkner reveals with forceful originality the dark and disturbing textures of American experience, establishing the South as the central symbolic landscape for their expression, to which a succession of talented writers such as FLANNERY O'CONNOR [108], Thomas Wolfe, Katherine Anne Porter, and Eudora Welty have also given voice. None, however, has achieved the epic and mythical tonalities of William Faulkner. His genius lies in his ability to capture a place and time and join them to a wider conception that transcends both.

MARCEL PROUST

16

1871–1922

He has most of the other qualities for which we praise the greatest of novelists. In range, he cannot rank with Dickens, Balzac, and Dostoevski. In naturalness, Tolstoy outshines him. But his deep penetration both into reality and into man's emotions and thoughts is hardly equaled anywhere.
　　—Henri Peyre, "The Legacy of Proust," from *The Contemporary French Novel*

In his remarkable series of novels that *Remembrance of Things Past (À la recherche du temps perdu)* comprises, Proust created one of the most influential masterpieces of 20th-century literature. Along with *Ulysses*, by JAMES JOYCE [7], Proust's sequence of novels fundamentally changed the form and altered many of fiction's operative principles. Proust replaced conventional plot and characterization with a complex and intimate uncovering of an individual's identity, the cumulative development of a lifetime of relationships and long-buried experiences. As José Ortega y Gasset asserted, "He stands as the inventor of a new distance between things and ourselves. . . . The whole of the novel that preceded him suddenly appears like a bird's eye literature, crudely panoramic, when compared to that delightfully near-sighted genius." In Proust's hands childhood, memory, the complexity of society, and sensibility gain a new subtlety that makes previous treatment primitive in comparison. Those who have never read any of his masterpieces still understand references to the "Proustian moment" and "involuntary memory" because the terms have entered 20th-century culture, as has the image of Proust, the massive egotist and hypochondriac, shut up in his cork-lined bedroom above Paris's Boulevard Haussmann, composing himself and his memories.

It seems both unlikely and inevitable that someone like Proust could write such a work as *Remembrance of Things Past*. He was the eldest of two sons of a distinguished Paris doctor and professor of medicine. His father was Catholic, his mother Jewish. At the age of nine, Proust was stricken with severe asthma, a physical affliction that would be complicated by a variety of neurotic symptoms for the rest of his life. In childhood Proust sought relief at a seaside resort in Normandy that served as the model for the fictional Balbec of his novels. Despite the limitations of his illness, he received his baccalaureate degree in 1889, completed a year of military service, and studied at the École des Sciences Politiques and at the Sorbonne, where he attended lectures by the philosopher Henri Bergson, whose theory of time would have a profound influence on him.

With little expected of him because of his condition and his family's means, Proust indulged in fashionable idleness at the various salons of the noble and genteel of the Faubourg St. Germain. He also wrote occasional pieces and a translation of John Ruskin that is very much the work of a literary raconteur and dabbler. Assisted by his devoted mother, Proust established a routine of sleeping during the day and working and socializing at night. His physical condition was aggravated by guilt over his homosexuality, which caused him to haunt servant quarters and male brothels as well as the salons of the rich and influential. During the 1890s, Proust seemed much like one of the snobs that his novels would later expose as shallow and self-absorbed, elaborately courting the favors of the fashionable.

In 1905, the death of his mother resulted in a period of long and painful mourning and the growing realization that his self-indulgence contributed to his mother's death, in which his needs caused him to ignore his mother's. In 1909, Proust experienced the famous epiphany celebrated in *Remembrance*, when a cup of tea and a bit of toast triggered a sensory illumination of the past with memory the means to restore it. Proust felt he now possessed the key to the mysteries of his childhood and development that he had struggled to record in an earlier, unfinished novel, *Jean Santeuil*, as well as the pattern for the series of novels that he would labor to complete for 13 years, up to his death in 1922.

Remembrance of Things Past expanded into a series of seven parts, published in French in 15 volumes between 1913 and 1927. The complete work reached 4,000 pages of about a million and a half words. The scope of the novel covers the period from about 1840 to 1915 and concerns the growth and development of the narrator, Marcel, from childhood to maturity, and his eventual discovery of his role as a novelist. Marcel is and is not Proust himself.

Although the basis of the novel is indeed autobiographical, confession is very much controlled in the elaborately shaped imagination of the novelist. The novel resists categorization as a strictly linear *Künstlerroman*, the story of the growth of the artist, but shifts backward and forward in time and expands its focus to include a cast of some 200 characters. As Proust revealed in an interview:

> As you know we have both plane and solid geometry—geometry in two-dimensional and in three-dimensional space. Well, for me the novel means not just plane (or plain) psychology but psychology in time. It is this invisible substance of time that I have tried to isolate, and it meant that the experiment had to last over a long period. I hope that at the end of my book certain unimportant social events, like the marriage between two characters who in the first volume belonged to totally different social worlds, will imply that time has passed and will take on the kind of beauty and patina you can see on the statues at Versailles which time has gradually coated with an emerald sheath.

At its core, the novel explores the way in which time can be recovered, and how the past, aided by involuntary memory, can be regained and preserved in art. Central to Proust's innovations in the novel is the way in which characters are not fixed entities but are fluid and revealed only gradually, shaped by context and perception. In this way, the novel proceeds to paint an intimate portrait of the past with a poetic intimacy that the form had never attempted to such a degree. Readers attuned to the simpler progression of conventional novels must readjust their expectations and perceptions under Proust's allusive, highly metaphorical manner and digressive style. As Proust observed: "Style has nothing to do with embellishment, as some people think; it's not even a matter of technique. Like the color sense in some painters, it's a quality of vision, the revelation of a particular universe that each of us sees and that no one else sees. The pleasure an artist offers us is to convey another universe to us."

The universe Proust conveys is both the intensely private domestic world of the narrator and a massive panorama of Parisian society at the turn of the century in a series of nuanced portraits of scenes and characters. As the English critic Raymond Mortimer observed, "No novelist has made his characters more real to us than Proust, and we know much more about them than about any other figure in fiction. For this reason alone, I believe him to be incomparably the greatest writer who has flourished in my lifetime." Proust's social and psychological portraits are revealed not in a flash of illumination, nor in a dramatic collision, but slowly and gradually, as sensibility, reflecting a complex of inner and outer stimuli, processes experience into a revealing totality.

Proust's powerful example of depicting a life that breaks down the barriers of time and space into a fuller artistic whole has been one of the most transformative influences in 20th-century art. His personal dedication in relentlessly and obsessively conveying his vision has also defined the modern role of the literary artist.

WILLIAM BUTLER YEATS

17

1865–1939

Early and late he has the simple, indispensable gift of enchanting the ear. . . . It was not this gift alone which made Yeats the poet he was, though without it no poet can be great. He was also the poet who, while very much of his own day in Ireland, spoke best to the people of all countries. And though he plunged deep into arcane studies, his themes are most clearly the general ones of life and death, love and hate, man's condition and history's meanings. He began as a sometimes effete post-Romantic, heir to the pre-Raphaelites, and then, quite naturally, became a leading British Symbolist; but he grew at last into the boldest, most vigorous voice of this century.

—M. L. Rosenthal, *The Poetry of Yeats*

T. S. ELIOT [19], who merits consideration as the 20th century's preeminent poet, gave that title to Yeats, whom he regarded as "the greatest poet of our time—certainly the greatest in this language, and as far as I am able to judge in any language." In a remarkable career that spanned the Victorian and modern worlds, Yeats showed how a truly great poet can reflect the various concerns of his age while maintaining a distinctive individual voice.

Beginning under the influence of the aesthetes of the 1890s, whose dreamy, sensuous style and advocacy of the primacy of beauty attracted him, Yeats developed a tougher and simpler poetic diction in verse that is personal and public, richly suggestive, visually sharp, and musically rich. His development and achievement represent, in a sense, the history of English poetry in the 50 years between 1890 and 1940. For all of his uniqueness and peculiar genius, Yeats also is the least formally experimental of the great modern poets. Avoiding free verse and the elliptical methods of others, Yeats instead endeavored to reinvigorate the poetic tradition that he inherited from the romantics. "All my life," Yeats observed, "I have tried to get rid of modern subjectivity by insisting on construction and contemporary words and syntax." His resulting achievement is as richly complex and varied as his personality, a mixed blend of a private and public man, the ethereal dreamer and the activist.

Yeats was born in Dublin to an Anglo-Irish family. His father, John Butler Yeats, gave up a law career to become a portrait painter. His mother came from an Irish merchant family with deep roots in County Sligo, where Yeats spent his summers and school holidays, and was exposed to the beauty of the Irish countryside and Irish folklore. Yeats's father, a free-thinker and religious skeptic, took over his son's education upon the discovery that at the age of eight the boy still could not read. Under the influence of Darwin and others who toppled Victorian faith, John Yeats passed on ideas to his son that Yeats's early poetry would later reject. Like many in his generation, Yeats felt caught between skepticism and the need for belief, between reason and the imagination, with no way to bridge the gap. The oscillation between the ideal world of art, beauty, and the spiritual, and the opposing pull of the real would shape his thinking and his poetry throughout his career.

Yeats's early poetry shows a tendency toward aesthetic escape. "I am very religious," Yeats later recalled, "and deprived by Huxley and Tyndall, whom I detested, of the simple-minded religion of my childhood, I had made a new religion, almost an infallible church of poetic tradition." His search for a compensating religious tradition led him first to romantic literature and the French symbolists, and then to mysticism of one kind or another: folklore, theosophy, spiritualism, Neoplatonism, and finally to his own symbolic system, an increasing elaborate vocabulary of archetypes and correspondences borrowed from various sources to give pattern and coherence to the expression of his thoughts and need for belief.

The dreamy and ethereal quality of his earliest poems eventually gave way to poetry grounded in the details of Irish life. It was Ireland that saved Yeats from becoming a derivative aesthete. In the folklore that he learned from his grandparents' servants he found fresh subject matter, and in the peasant speech of Irish country people he absorbed a diction and rhythm that, while still poetic, were fresh and vigorous. It became clear to Yeats that only be defining his relation to his native country, by putting the symbols of Ireland in order, could he achieve the kind of poetic system that joined the real and the ideal.

In 1896, Yeats met Lady Augusta Gregory, the Irish nationalist with whom he founded the Irish Literary Theatre, which in 1904 became the

Abbey Theatre. One of the world's great stage companies, the Abbey was a main source of the great flowering of the Irish literary renaissance, with Yeats as one of its central figures. His principal contribution to the Irish nationalist movement was his play *Cathleen ni Houlihan* (1902), in which his title character personified Ireland and became a rallying figure in the independence movement.

Yeats's role in Irish politics and the revitalization of Irish consciousness led to the poet's disillusionment and increasing isolation, expressed in the poem "September 1913," with its reference to John O'Leary, the Irish patriot who first called for an Irish national literature and despaired over Ireland's nonheroic provincialism:

> For men were born to pray and save:
> Romantic Ireland's dead and gone,
> It's with O'Leary in the grave.

Out of Yeats's bitterness emerged a sharper, realistic poetic style forged from the poet's interpretation of his own experience. His short, sardonic poem "A Coat" conveys the shift in style and subject matter:

> I have made my song a coat
> Covered with embroideries
> Out of old mythologies
> From heel to throat;
> But the fools caught it,
> Wore it in the world's eyes
> As though they'd wrought it.
> Song, let them take it,
> For there's more enterprise
> In walking naked.

Yeats's greatest achievements followed his determination to capture life, not escape from it, in the interaction between the private self and public events. In such poems as "Easter, 1916," "Meditations in Time of Civil War," and "The Tower," Yeats explores the pressures of history in shaping consciousness. Although he derived great power from confronting the real, Yeats continued to search for a means to express the spiritual world and patterns of history, evolving from multiple sources, including his wife's psychic ability, a system of cosmic order that he outlined in *A Vision* (1925). His fascination with the occult and his private mythology are important not as a systematic philosophy but instead as a storehouse of images and symbols for his poetry; one does not need to master the arcana of Yeats's system to appreciate his poetry. Perhaps the best example of this is the poem "The Second Coming," which depends on his notion of history as inherently cyclical. The power of the poem's dark prophecy, with its messianic "rough beast" that "Slouches towards Bethlehem to be born," is derived not so much from the poet's notions but from the effectiveness of his language, which distills his observation in a tight but irreducible universal complex of imagery:

> Turning and turning in the widening gyre
> The falcon cannot hear the falconer;
> Things fall apart; the centre cannot hold;
> Mere anarchy is loosed upon the world,
> The blood-dimmed tide is loosed, and everywhere
> The ceremony of innocence is drowned;
> The best lack all conviction, while the worst
> Are full of passionate intensity.

Here, as in countless other works, Yeats's remarkable, spare epigrammatic language, imagery, and symbols, drawn from different sources, show a poet of the highest quality engaged with both local and universal questions. Yeats remains the poetic fountainhead of modern literature, an emblematic figure in the artistic quest to incorporate experience in expressive forms of meaning.

ALEXANDER PUSHKIN

18

1799–1837

Pushkin grew with the years. Every other writer claimed descent from him. Inexplicably, the whole of Russian literature proceeded from his genius. Poetry, novels, short stories, history, theater, criticism—he had opened up the whole gamut of literary endeavor to his countrymen. He was first in time, and first in quality. He was the source. Neither Gogol nor Tolstoy could have existed without him, for he made the Russian language; he prepared the ground for the growth of every genre.

—Henri Troyat, *Pushkin*

Russia's national poet and literary fountainhead, Pushkin has been served least well in translation of all his country's great writers. Although an icon in Russia—the source for children's lessons in the Russian language, the subject of monuments and street names all over the country—Pushkin elsewhere is perhaps the least read significant figure in world literature. He served as his nation's first great European influence, who shaped Russian history and culture into artistic form. Only such giants as DANTE [2], SHAKESPEARE [1], CERVANTES [11], and GOETHE [10] have exerted a comparable impact on their national language by defining the very possibilities of a country's literature. Pushkin is, however, a prisoner of his language, whose genius awaits a skilled translator to approximate his great gifts for a non-Russian reading audience. Without the means to appreciate his remarkable talent fully, non-Russian readers are left with occasional hints of his poetic achievement and the testimony of virtually all of his countrymen, who attest to his centrality in establishing the literary language of Russia.

Pushkin's impact on Russian art and culture stems equally from his brilliance and from the historical moment of the early 19th century, when Russia emerged as a significant European power. Pushkin initiated a remarkable flowering of Russian literary achievement, synthesizing European and indigenous Russian forms and themes. His ancestry, which he could trace back 600 years, was aristocratic, though the family's fortune had declined. His father was a minor literary figure whose library of French classics and friendship with prominent literary figures of the day exposed Pushkin to a literary tradition and climate. His mother was the granddaughter of Abram Hannibal, an Abyssinian slave whom Peter the Great acquired in Constantinople and helped to become a prominent member of his court. Like most Russian aristocrats of his day, Pushkin wrote and read French and absorbed French culture far more than Russian, but he acquired a store of Russian stories and folk tales from his maternal grandmother and nurse. At the Imperial Lyceum at Tsarskoye Selo, a boarding school for highborn boys training for a government career, Pushkin was nicknamed the Frenchman for his literary skills. He first published his poetry at the age of 15, and by the time he graduated from the lyceum three years later, he had begun to earn a literary reputation.

After his schooling, Pushkin received a nominal position in the foreign office and led a dissolute life in St. Petersburg, drifting into liberal politics. His 1820 "Ode to Freedom" attacked tyrannical government and resulted in his exile from St. Petersburg to a remote southern province under the supervision of its military commander. Pushkin's "southern exile" coincided with his publication of his first major work, *Ruslan and Lyudmila*, a comic epic in the tradition of Alexander Pope's *Rape of the Lock*, but with material from Russian folk tradition and fairy tales, concerning the abduction of a young bride by an evil magician. In the debate over the fate of the Russian language and art, Pushkin was a dedicated "Westerner," adapting European models and influences to portray Russian subjects and themes. One of his foremost influences was BYRON [83], whose verse narrative form and romantic imagination dominated Pushkin's works during the 1820s, including *The Prisoner of the Caucasus* (1822), *The Robber Brothers* (1822), and *The Fountain of Bakchisaray* (1823). These works made Pushkin the most famous poet in Russia and the principal figure of Russian romanticism.

In 1824, suspicions of Pushkin's atheism and his courting of his superior officer's wife in Odessa led to his dismissal from government service and internal exile to his mother's estate under the supervision of his father. After Alexander I's death in 1825, Pushkin petitioned the new czar, Nicholas I, to end his exile. Nicholas allowed Pushkin to return to Moscow and agreed to serve as his censor. Pushkin's years in exile and his subsequent life in Moscow and St. Petersburg during the 1830s were his most productive in a variety of poetic, dramatic, and narrative forms. In 1825, Pushkin's verse drama *Boris Godunov* appeared, in which the influence of Shakespeare helped him move Russian drama away from the French neoclassical models of RACINE [62] to a freer, more expansive form derived from the events of Russian history.

In 1833, Pushkin completed his eight-year labor on his masterpiece, *Eugene Onegin*. Subtitled a "novel in verse," it is considered Russia's first novel and the foundation document of Russian realism. The story of the complex hero Onegin, an intelligent young aristocrat and dandy, and Tatyana's tragic love for him, unfolds in the context of contemporary life and includes a meticulous portrait of the social customs and attitudes of the time. The narrative poem features a variety of subtle portraits clearly derived from Pushkin's emotional and philosophical self-analysis, and masterfully combines the lyrical with the social.

In the 1830s, Pushkin also wrote his four "little tragedies," experiments in compressed psychological dramas—*The Covetous Knight, Mozart and Salieri, The Stone Guest*, and *The Feast before the Plague*—and the five short stories comprising The Tales of the Late I. P. Belkin, most notably the brilliant "The Queen of Spades," known outside Russia as perhaps his most famous work. The story, again with a realistic setting of contemporary life, is suffused with suggestive elements of Russian folk tradition that create a haunting atmosphere of manipulation and corruption. The story influenced DOSTOEVSKY [14], who modeled his character Raskolnikov in *Crime and Punishment* on Hermann, Pushkin's enigmatic central character. Pushkin's final nonlyrical works include *A Small House in Kolomna*, a comic poem of lower-class life; the narrative poem *The Bronze Horseman*; and the historical novel *The Captain's Daughter*. Each in their way solidified Pushkin's ability to produce native versions of literary genres that serve as his primary legacy for later generations of Russian writers.

In 1831, Pushkin married the young beauty Natalia Nikolaevna Goncharova, but he was not the sole object of her affection. Her flirtatiousness even extended to the czar himself, who appointed Pushkin a gentleman of the bedchamber to serve him to keep his wife a close attendant at court. In the end, however, Pushkin's ultimate rival was not the czar but instead Georges Anthès, the adopted son of the Russian ambassador from the Netherlands. His affair with Pushkin's wife prompted a duel that mortally wounded Pushkin at the age of 37.

At the news of Pushkin's death, the 16-year-old Dostoevsky went into mourning as if a member of his own family had died. In Italy, NIKOLAI GOGOL [93] reflected that "no worse news could have come from Russia. With him goes the greatest joy of my life." In 1880, when the writer's statue on Pushkin Square in Moscow was unveiled with impassioned speeches in his memory by Dostoevsky and Turgenev, Pushkin's reputation in Russia reached apotheosis, and his title of Russia's national poet continued through the years of the Soviet Union. He remains the principal shaper of the Russian language into an expressive imaginative form: his spare and intense reworking of European forms to reflect deeply personal and Russian themes set the standard for all Russian literature that followed.

T. S. ELIOT

19

1888–1965

When the news of Eliot's death came through, commercial television had just presented an abridgement of Middleton's The Changeling. *Watching it, I thought that this could never have happened if Eliot hadn't opened our eyes to the greatness of the Jacobeans. Spike Milligan, on a comic TV show, could say, "Not with a banger but a wimpy," and most of the audience caught the reference. Weather forecasters would joke about April being the cruellest month. Demagogues would quote John Donne and novelists make titles out of Donne's poems or religious meditations. . . . And, though not everyone could follow Eliot to the final austerities of Anglicanism, Royalism and Classicism, his affirmation of the importance of tradition was accepted even by the avant-garde. For, with Eliot, the past was not a dull and venerable ancestor but a living force which modified the present and was in turn modified by it. Time was not an army of unalterable law; time was a kind of ectoplasm.*

—Anthony Burgess, *Urgent Copy*

Perhaps more than any other single figure of the 20th century, except possibly JAMES JOYCE [7], T. S. Eliot dominated the literary world in the period between the wars and produced a revolution in poetic and critical taste. The publication of *Prufrock and Other Observations* in 1917 has been compared to the appearance in 1798 of WORDSWORTH [23] and Coleridge's *Lyrical Ballads.* Both events signaled the arrival of a new poetic era. In *The Waste Land,* called by fellow poet William Carlos Williams, "the atomic bomb of poetry," Eliot captured the spirit of his age, defining its disillusionment and search for moral and spiritual values, and the need for a new tradition to replace the cultural barrenness left after the Great War. Eliot's career shows his attempt to define that tradition, and if his answers fail to satisfy, his diagnosis of the problem and his method of capturing the complexity and ambiguity of modern experience continue to exert their influence. Like Joyce in the 20th-century novel, Eliot is the primary modern poet whose works best capture the contemporary moment.

Eliot, who would eventually define himself as a "classicist in literature, royalist in politics, and Anglo-Catholic in religion," was born in St. Louis, Missouri. His grandfather had come west from Harvard Divinity School to found St. Louis's first Unitarian church and Washington University. Eliot's father was a prosperous brick manufacturer, and his mother was a woman of literary tastes. The family spent summers on the Massachusetts coast, and Eliot returned to the East for college, graduating from Harvard in only three years. He stayed on as a graduate student in philosophy, going to Europe on a travel grant, where he sat in on lectures by Henri Bergson at the Sorbonne and went to Oxford to complete his dissertation on the philosopher F. H. Bradley. Eliot completed his thesis but never received his degree, rejecting an expected academic career for life in England as a writer. In 1915, Eliot married Vivien Haigh-Wood, a woman prone to mental illness, and their 17-year marriage was marked by emotional and physical strain. Eliot supported himself by teaching in an English grammar school, lecturing and writing reviews and criticism, and holding a position in Lloyd's Bank for eight years. Friends, led by the poet Ezra Pound, tried to find funds to extricate him from Lloyd's, which Eliot resisted. He liked the work, which, although punishing given the demands of his writing, provided a secure routine that helped him cope with his chaotic domestic life and his struggles with his poetry. Fastidious and reserved, Eliot suffered a mental breakdown in 1921 and was treated in Lausanne, Switzerland. In 1922 he published his landmark poem, *The Waste Land*, which baffled critics but created a sensation—particularly among the young, who regarded Eliot as the avatar of the modern age, a literary icon whose poetic technique, vision, and artistic sensibility were profoundly influential. With characteristic diffidence, he dismissed the role thrust upon him as the age's spokesman.

In 1925, he left Lloyd's to be an editor at Faber and Faber, a position he held for the rest of his life. He also became a British subject and converted to Anglicanism. His creative efforts turned from poetry to drama. In his plays, most notably *Murder in the Cathedral* (1935), *The Family Reunion* (1939), and *The Cocktail Party* (1950), he fashioned a new kind of poetic drama infused with the search for spiritual meaning evident in his poetry. In criticism, Eliot exerted an enormous influence in redefining literary taste, reasserting the power of metaphysical poets such as JOHN DONNE [33], and refashioning a critical framework for a new modern classicism to replace the vagueness and moralizing of the Victorians. His final important work of poetry, *Four Quartets*, appeared from 1934 to 1943, and is regarded by many as Eliot's greatest poetic statement. The poems are meditations on the power of memory and private experience to reach a form of transcendence that all of Eliot's works explored.

The state of English poetry in Eliot's time was largely exhausted and moribund. The romantics' innovation of personal exploration had atrophied in the stately cadences and moralizing of the Victorians; it had become little more than a pose drained of significance and a set of Western traditions invalidated by the experience of the Great War. English poetry would be reinvigorated by an Irishman, W. B. YEATS [17], and two American expatriates, Ezra Pound and T. S. Eliot. At the core of Eliot's poetics was the search to invest language with a new means to capture modern experience. In his essay "The Metaphysical Poets," Eliot provides a clue to his intentions: "Our civilization comprehends great variety and complexity, and this variety and complexity, playing upon a refined sensibility, must produce various and complex results. The poet must become more and more comprehensive, more allusive, more indirect, in order to force, to dislocate if necessary, language into meaning."

To wrestle meaning out of complexity, Eliot pursued a strategy, derived from the French symbolists and the imagists, of dislocation and disunity, with the image as the basic element, or what Eliot called the "objective correlative," a concrete detail to evoke thought and feeling. Eliot's first major poem, "The Love Song of J. Alfred Prufrock," written in 1910 but not published until 1915, set his poetic method and characteristic concerns. Confronting all the vulgarity and sordidness of modern life while plumbing the depths of private emotion and feeling, Eliot creates a dramatic monologue in which Prufrock reveals his consciousness in a series of startling images of a disconnected mind trapped by its own inadequacies. Eliot's technique is cinematic, surveying the landscape of Prufrock's neuroses not through analysis but through images that expose his deepest fears, such as Prufrock measuring his life "with coffee spoons" and his regressive vision of himself as "a pair of ragged claws/Scuttling across the floors of silent seas."

The Waste Land both widens and deepens Eliot's approach. Again, the core is dramatic, exploiting Eliot's skill at mimicry, and fragmentary, as bits and pieces of allusions and cultural references are associated to contrast the barrenness of modern experience with the earlier heroic tradition of sustaining myths and values. The effect is a symphony of voices, scenes, and images that surround the central question of what one can believe when the possibility of belief is absent. With Ezra Pound's assistance, Eliot removed much of the connective tissue of a linear narrative and proceeded directly to a series of moments of greatest intensity in which it is the reader's responsibility to reassemble the "heap of broken images" and the "fragments shored against my ruins" into a meaningful pattern. In *The Waste Land,* Eliot achieves the combined power of lyrical intensity and the wider, social implications of the epic.

Eliot's *Waste Land* is one of the central literary landmarks of the 20th century, a foundation that later poets have continued to build upon. Like James Joyce's *Ulysses, The Waste Land* has exerted such a powerful influence that we continue to wait for the next Joyce or Eliot to provide the next important shift of artistic consciousness.

JANE AUSTEN

20

1775–1817

Oh! Mrs Bennet! Mrs Norris too!
While memory survives we'll dream of you.
And Mr Woodhouse, whose abstemious lip
Must thin, but not too thin, his gruel sip.
Miss Bates, our idol, though the village bore;
And Mrs Elton, ardent to explore.
While the clear style flows on without pretence,
With unsustained purity and unmatched sense:
Or, if a sister e'er approached the throne,
She called the rich "inheritance" her own.

—Lord Morpeth, "Keepsake"

Jane Austen is the first great woman writer in English and, arguably, England's first great novelist. Such a valuation is remarkable when applied to a writer whose range was consciously limited to what she knew best—two or three families in a country village—and who characterized herself as "the most unlearned and uninformed female who ever dared to be an authoress." Jane Austen described her artistry with characteristic modesty as "the little bit (two inches wide) of Ivory on which I work with so fine a brush, as produces little effect after much labour."

Critics of Austen have attacked her restricted view and her acceptance of the world as she found it. CHARLOTTE BRONTË [60] argued that Jane Austen "ruffles her reader by nothing vehement, disturbs him by nothing profound." Ralph Waldo Emerson characterized her novels as "vulgar in tone, sterile in artistic invention, imprisoned in the wretched conventions of English society." Some critics, echoing Jane Austen's own self-deprecating assessment, have labeled her a skilled miniaturist rather than a profound artist in search of a grand vision. Such views, however, miss the point of Austen's intentions and accomplishments. A supremely comic writer and moralist, Austen redefined the novel as a delicate instrument to reveal human nature. Her novels demonstrate that commonplace, everyday experience can be the source of great and enduring art.

Jane Austen was born into the English gentry class, whose customs are her novels' exclusive concern. The youngest daughter of the eight children of George Austen, the rector of Steventon in Hampshire, and Cassandra Leigh Austen, Austen spent her life at the center of a large family circle whose circumference extended only to a few English counties, as well as Bath, Southampton, and London. She shared a room for her entire life with her older sister Cassandra and had no personal acquaintance with any other important writer. Although all her books concern the central domestic drama of matrimony, Austen never married, though biographers suspect several affairs of the heart and know of at least one rejected marriage proposal. Instead of imitating her heroines and securing a husband and a household of her own, Austen embarked on the riskier endeavor of succeeding as a novelist.

Austen protected her anonymity as a writer with an almost obsessive diligence. Only a few outside her family circle knew that she was a novelist at all, since none of her books published during her lifetime revealed her identity. Her first published novel, *Sense and Sensibility,* indicated on its title page only that it was written by "a Lady." Subsequent books identified her only as the author of her previous novels. Although her books were read with interest, they were by no means best-sellers. Her reputation as one of the seminal novelists of all time was late in coming, even though her contemporary, Walter Scott, the most respected writer of the age, recognized her "exquisite touch, which renders ordinary commonplace things and characters interesting, from the truth of the description and the sentiment." By the Victorian period, the critic George Henry Lewes called Austen a "prose Shakespeare," and her stature has grown ever since. Today, as A. Walton Litz has observed, "of all English and American novelists Jane Austen is perhaps the most secure in her reputation."

Jane Austen's writing career is divided into two distinct periods. Her earliest work, written in Steventon during the 1790s, includes fragments, satires, literary burlesques, and the first drafts of what would become *Pride and Prejudice, Sense and Sensibility,* and *Northanger Abbey.* A 12-year period followed in which the Austen family moved to Bath, and, after the death of George Austen, to Southampton, during which Jane Austen wrote little. In 1809, she returned to the Hampshire countryside and Chawton Cottage with her mother and sister. There, at the age of 34, with no further hope of marriage, she concentrated on her role as a novelist, publishing *Sense and Sensibility* (1811) and *Pride and Prejudice* (1813) and writing three other novels: *Mansfield Park* (1814), *Emma* (1815), and *Persuasion* (1818). The latter, along with the earlier *Northanger Abbey* (begun in 1798), were published posthumously.

Hers was, on the surface at least, an uneventful life. Although the great events of the period—the French Revolution and the wars with France— intruded on the affairs of her family, particularly through the naval careers of her youngest brothers, they rarely had a direct influence on her writing. Instead, her novels are concerned with the drama of ordinary life and the customs of English country families. Excluded by the novelist's exacting standard of truthfulness is everything that Jane Austen did not know intimately. For example, in all of her books there are virtually no scenes of men speaking with each other alone. Yet within her narrow frame of reference, her novels are neither undramatic nor unimportant in presenting profound issues. Each book provides a moral education for its central heroine as she learns to see the world and herself clearly and to adjust her behavior and beliefs under the pressure of social values. Different from the novels of gothic terror and sentiment that Austen read and enjoyed lampooning, her novels ask the reader to respond to a different kind of literary experience. A contemporary reviewer noted that in Jane Austen's novels there are "no dark passages; no secret chambers; no wind-howlings in long galleries; no drops of blood upon a rusty dagger—things that should now be left to ladies' maids and sentimental washerwomen." In place of the artificial and the exaggerated, Jane Austen offers the recognizable and the ordinary as the subjects of the writer's most intense moral and psychological exploration.

At the dramatic core of all of Austen's books is the complicated maneuvering that leads to marriage. Austen treats marriage not as a simple sentimental climax, but instead as a complex moral and social negotiation that reveals much about human nature and frailty. In *Sense and Sensibility*, Austen attempts to work out the complicated calculus between the demands of heart and head. In *Pride and Prejudice*, Elizabeth Bennet must adjust her moral vision: she is forced to realize how appearances deceive, and learns that seeing clearly depends on recognizing the prejudices of the viewer. In *Emma*, the novel's heroine learns painful lessons about self-deception and the drive for mastery and control. In all her novels, Austen instructs her heroines and her readers in the complicated matter of living, substituting common sense and clarity for self-deception and idealization. No novelist before Austen, and few since, have dramatized truth wrung from the ordinary details of daily life so effectively and entertainingly.

GEORGE ELIOT

21

1819–1880

You see, it was really George Eliot who started it all. . . . And how wild they were with her for doing it. It was she who started putting all the action inside.

—D. H. Lawrence, quoted in Jessie Chambers,
D. H. Lawrence: A Personal Record

If JANE AUSTEN [20] was the first to tap the realistic potential of the novel, George Eliot won respectability for the novel as a serious art form and for the novelist as more than an entertainer. She brought to her work the intellectual gifts of a first-rate thinker and transformed fiction into a serious criticism of life, as well as an instrument for profound social and psychological inquiry. While most novels by women in the Victorian period could be grouped, as she wrote in a famous review, as "Silly Novels by Lady Novelists," George Eliot earned respect for her sex as capable of the deepest artistic and intellectual penetration. After George Eliot, it was not necessary for a woman novelist to hide behind a male pseudonym to be taken seriously.

George Eliot was born Mary Ann Evans in Warwickshire in the English Midlands. She was the youngest of the five children of Robert Evans, an estate manager. Mary Ann was a serious and studious child who read widely. While attending boarding school, she came under the influence of the charismatic, evangelical clergyman John Edmund Jones. To a precocious and thoughtful young girl like Mary Ann, Jones's dramatic preaching and message of personal salvation through faith and religious self-sacrifice struck a sympathetic cord. In 1841, she moved with her retired father to Coventry, where her family, worried about her religious zeal, encouraged her friendship with the local progressive freethinkers, Charles and Caroline Bray, in the hope that Mary Ann would moderate her almost fanatical piety. Instead, the philosophical rationalism to which she was exposed caused her not only to renounce her evangelical devotion but also to lose her religious faith entirely. In a confrontation with her family that became a paradigm for similar scenes in her novels—conflicts between independence and duty, self and community—Mary Ann refused to attend church any longer. She eventually compromised, agreeing to go to church but refusing to give up her conviction that a personal morality, not based on the authority of religious faith, must prevail. In her final years at home she ran her father's household, read extensively, and translated Spinoza and David Strauss's iconoclastic *Life of Jesus*, the story of Christ shorn of all supernatural elements, which was published in 1846.

When Eliot's father died in 1849, she was free to enter a wider circle better suited to her considerable intellectual gifts. This meant going to London, where she worked as an assistant editor of the progressive *Westminster Review*. She wrote numerous book reviews and mingled with the literary and somewhat bohemian circle surrounding the magazine, which included critic and author George Henry Lewes. Eliot fell in love with Lewes, who was estranged from his wife but, under the restrictive divorce laws of the time, could not divorce and legally remarry. The situation prompted the second and greatest personal crisis in Eliot's life. Defying conventions and strong family disapproval, Eliot and Lewes established a home together, managing a happy, if secluded, life in London, ideal for their literary work. It was Lewes who first encouraged Eliot to write fiction.

George Eliot always had been an insightful thinker, but as she began to write fiction she faced the challenge of animating her thoughts and creating believable human characters and situations. She also set out to alter the basic formula of Victorian fiction from idealization and melodrama to a careful analysis of commonplace experience. Eliot met these challenges by relying on her memories of childhood in provincial Warwickshire. *Scenes of Clerical Life*, her first work of fiction, comprises three short stories in which she attempted, in her words, "to do what has never yet been done in our literature . . . representing the clergy like any other class with the humours, sorrows, and troubles of other men." The book set the pattern for her subsequent novels: it insisted that ordinary life is the proper domain of fiction, showed tolerance and sympathy toward the characters, and dramatized lessons of human behavior through what Eliot called "aesthetic teaching." As she declared, "Art must be either real and concrete or ideal and eclectic. Both are good and true in their way, but my stories are of the former kind. I undertake to exhibit nothing as it should be; I only try to exhibit some things as they have been or are."

Scenes of Clerical Life established Eliot's characteristics as a writer, but her first novel, *Adam Bede* (1859) brought her acclaim and success. Widely regarded as the finest pastoral novel in English, *Adam Bede* announced the arrival of a major writing talent. As critic and Eliot biographer Gordon Haight has observed, "No book had made such an impression since *Uncle Tom's Cabin* swept the world." The story of the village carpenter Adam Bede and his love for the pretty, vain Hetty Sorrel, who is seduced by the young squire Arthur Donnithorne, set a new realistic standard in the English novel with its social, historical, and psychological precision. George Eliot quickly followed its success with two other novels, *The Mill on the Floss* (1860), the story of impulsive and individualistic Maggie Tulliver's conflict with conventional values that divides her from her community and her adored brother, and *Silas Marner* (1861), a tale of an outcast and miser redeemed by his love for a young child. Both owe much of their power and appeal to George Eliot's sympathetic reconstruction of her memories of Warwickshire.

When these sources began to run thin, Eliot attempted a departure in *Romola* (1863), a historical novel of 15th-century Florence. To research the novel, she traveled to Italy and studied the customs and values of a different culture with the eye of a social scientist. With *Romola*, she learned to go beyond her own memories and see an entire society as a complex whole.

This experience deepened and widened her scope as a novelist when she returned to more familiar English scenes for her last three novels: *Felix Holt* (1866), *Middlemarch* (1872), and *Daniel Deronda* (1876). All three are massive novels in which she attempts to show the complex relationship among the environment, the individual, and society. Rightly regarded as one of the first sociological novelists, Eliot dramatized the "natural history of our social classes, especially of the small shopkeepers, artisans, and peasantry, and the degree in which they are influenced by local conditions, their maxims and habits, the point of view from which they regard their religious teachers, [and] the interactions of the various classes on each other."

Middlemarch, George Eliot's masterpiece, is regarded by many critics as the greatest English novel, and is, according to VIRGINIA WOOLF [48], "one of the few English novels written for adult people." In it Eliot creates a detailed depiction of life in a provincial English town. The story principally concerns the ardent Dorothea Brooke, whose dream of a fulfilled life is disappointed by her marriage to the elderly pedant Mr. Casaubon, and the equally disappointing experiences of the idealistic young doctor Lydgate, whose marriage compromises his hopes. Around these two central characters are dozens of other fully realized characters, all carefully rendered through regional details, historical elements, and psychological perceptions. There are no real villains and few stirring events beyond the everyday transactions of the community, yet in the underlying pattern, which Eliot describes in the novel as the "suppressed transitions that unite all contrasts," the correlation of history, class, and personality brings her characters and their world to life. Her plot grows out of her characters' interactions and their complex blend of temperament and motivation. Other novelists had revealed the internal forces that drive behavior, but no novelist had done so as extensively. Eliot distinguished herself as the first truly psychological novelist on the grand scale.

By the 1870s, Eliot had achieved social respectability despite her unconventional life with Lewes and was recognized as the most eminent novelist of her day. With George Eliot, the novel earned its place beside the epic and the tragedy as one of the preeminent art forms suited to a wide and profound examination of life. George Eliot's depth of learning and her sense that the novel could contain the skills of the sociologist, psychologist, and cultural historian set a new standard for the art of fiction.

EURIPIDES

22

c. 480–406 B.C.

Sophocles said he drew men as they ought to be, and Euripides as they were.

—Aristotle, *Poetics*

With Euripides, the youngest of the three great Athenian tragedians of the fifth century B.C., Attic drama takes on a familiarly modern tone. Although Aristotle regarded Euripides as "the most tragic of the tragic poets," such critics as Friedrich von Schlegel and Friedrich Nietzsche blamed him for the death of tragedy and the end of the cohesion of Attic drama. A more balanced view is that Euripides fulfilled drama's capacity to expand its range, combining elements of tragedy and comedy, realism and fantasy, as well as extending spiritual, moral, and psychological explorations to the realm of ordinary life. It was Euripides, not AESCHYLUS [27] or SOPHOCLES [13], who depicted on stage the various intellectual controversies of his day and captured the growing anxiety and doubt that beset Athenian society at the end of fifth century. Through his techniques and themes, Euripides became the true progenitor of drama and it is not too far-fetched to suggest that the world after Athens's golden age became Euripidean, as did the drama that reflected it.

Euripides wrote 92 plays, of which 18 have survived. This is by far the largest number of surviving plays among the great Athenian playwrights, a testimony both to the accidents of literary survival and of high regard for

82

Euripides by succeeding generations. An iconoclast in his life and art, Euripides is the prototype for the modern alienated artist. Euripides played no role in public life. An intellectual who wrote in isolation (according to tradition, in a cave in his native Salamis), he won first prize for his plays at the annual Great Dionysia only four times, far fewer than did Aeschylus or Sophocles, and his critics, particularly ARISTOPHANES [34], who treated Euripides as a frequent comic target, were severe. According to Aristophanes, Euripides persuaded men that the gods did not exist, debunked the heroic, and taught the moral degeneration that transformed Athenians into "marketplace loungers, tricksters, and scoundrels." The last years of Euripides' life were spent away from Athens in Macedonia, although the reason for his departure is unknown. His immense popularity came only after his death, when, in the fourth century and after, his plays eclipsed in popularity those of all of the other great Athenian playwrights.

As his life redefined the status and place of the artist in society, his plays provided challenges to established dramatic technique and the tragic vision of Aeschylus and Sophocles. Since so many examples of his work have survived and can be accurately dated, it is possible to trace Euripides' artistic development to a greater degree than the other Attic playwrights. His early plays (*Medea*, *Hippolytus*) show his achievement in heroic tragedy. In the opening years of the Peloponnesian War, Euripides wrote patriotic plays (*Heraclidae*, *Suppliants*), followed by plays expressing disapproval of the war (*Hecuba*, *The Trojan Women*). His later plays show him turning away from tragedy to romantic intrigue (*Ion*, *Iphigenia in Taurus*, *Helen*), in the process developing a new theatrical genre that has come to be labeled tragicomedy. He then returned to tragedy in a more violent and despairing mode (*Orestes*, *Phoenissae*, *The Bacchae*).

Euripides' remarkable range includes many contradictions. His skepticism concerning divine will and purpose earned him the title of "the poet of the Greek enlightenment," yet he is also the preeminent explorer of human nature's passionate and irrational side. The first playwright to put women at the center of the action, Euripides has been labeled both a feminist and a misogynist for portraying his female characters in believable yet unflattering ways. Finally, Euripides has been seen as drama's first great realist, the playwright who relocated tragic action in everyday life and portrayed gods and heroes with recognizable human and psychological traits. Yet his realism shares the stage with supernatural elements, exotic settings, and a reliance on the deus ex machina, the fortuitous arrival of a god to provide a climactic resolution to the play's complex dilemmas.

The essential component, however, of all Euripides' plays is a challenging reexamination of orthodoxy and conventional beliefs. In the works of Aeschylus and Sophocles, the ways of men may be hard to fathom, but the will and purpose of the gods are assumed, if not always accepted. For Euripides, the

ability of the gods to provide certainty and order is as doubtful as an individual's preference for the good. In Euripides gods resemble those of Homer, full
of pride, passion, vindictiveness, and irrational characteristics that resemble
those of humans. Divine will and order are replaced by an indifferent fate,
and the tragic hero is the victim of forces beyond his control. The playwright
reinterprets the myths to emphasize their human relevance, and, as Sophocles
observed, men are shown as they are, full of contradictions and mixed qualities of strengths and weaknesses. Contrary to the generic types and mono-
lithic characters of Sophocles, for whom consistency is primary, Euripides'
characters are marked by their changeability and contradictions. Medea, for
example, changes her mind so often that the effect is dizzying yet believable.
Because Euripides' characters offer us so many different sides and are haunted
by both the rational and the irrational, the playwright earns the distinction of
being the first great psychological artist in the modern sense, in an awareness
of complex motives and contradictions that make up identity and determine
actions.

Euripides also was revolutionary in the way he extended drama's range.
His plays dramatize subjects and perspectives never depicted before on stage.
The Trojan Women, for example, shows war from the point of view of its casualties, not its combatants. Eric Havelock has summarized the Euripidean revolution as "putting on stage rooms never seen before." Instead of the throne
room, Euripides takes his audience into the living room and presents the
drama of characters who resemble the audience members instead of heroic
paragons. As Aristophanes correctly pointed out, Euripides brought to the
stage "familiar affairs" and "household things." He allowed drama to explore
central questions of the day in education, politics, and religion.

Euripides' drama also takes the audience to the limits of endurance by
portraying suffering in the absence of any consolation and without the promise of order and reconciliation. In his masterpiece *The Bacchae*, Pentheus, the
young Theban ruler who refuses to acknowledge the power of Dionysus, god
of wine and ecstasy, is literally torn apart through the agency of Dionysus's
destructiveness and his own revealed irrationality. Pentheus's experiences
reflect the process of Euripides' drama to shatter illusion and force the audience to confront the chaotic nature of human existence. The existential tone
of Euripidean drama became an integral feature of drama in the West, from
SHAKESPEARE [1] through HENRIK IBSEN [36], AUGUST STRINDBERG [56], and
EUGENE O'NEILL [59].

WILLIAM WORDSWORTH

23

1770–1850

I needed to be made to feel that there was real, permanent happiness in tranquil contemplation. Wordsworth taught me this not only without turning away from, but with a greatly increased interest in the common feelings and common destiny of human beings.
—John Stuart Mill, *Autobiography*

An honest evaluation of Wordsworth's sizable contribution to literature must first deal with the long shadow of his declining powers as a poet, and his transformation from his early greatness as an original and rebellious thinker to his later mediocrity as a pious conformist and occasional poet. Some critics have argued that Wordsworth ceased to produce important poetry as early as 1805, yet he continued to write for another 45 years, disavowing his former challenging stances and becoming the public spokesman of the establishment that he attacked in his youth. For ROBERT BROWNING [58], Wordsworth was "the Lost Leader," about whom he writes:

> Just for a handful of silver he left us,
>   Just for a riband to stick in his coat—
> Found the one gift of which fortune bereft us,
>   Lost all the others she lets us devote; . . .
> We that had loved him so, followed him, honoured him,

Lived in his mild and magnificent eye,
Learned his great language, caught his clear accents,
   Made him our pattern to live and to die!
Shakespeare was of us, Milton was of us,
   Burns, Shelley, were with us,—they watch from their graves!
He alone breaks from the van and the freemen,
   He alone sinks to the rear and the slaves!

Yet the diminishment of Wordsworth's power and originality should not obscure the heights of his achievement. The publication of *Lyrical Ballads* in 1798 is perhaps the most influential single event in English literary history. Wordsworth, in collaboration with Coleridge, staged a literary revolution that revitalized literature and set it on its modern course.

If, as Wordsworth asserted, "The child is father of the man," his early experiences provide a key to his development. Born in Cockermouth in England's Lake District, Wordsworth lost both his parents at an early age: his mother when he was eight, and his father, the business agent of a noble-man, when he was 13. After their death, the five Wordsworth children were separated, producing for Wordsworth a painful split from his beloved sister Dorothy. He was educated at a school in rustic Hawkshead, where the natural surroundings helped the future poet form an important bond with nature and common country life. After his studies at Cambridge, it was expected that Wordsworth would become a clergyman, a profession that he resisted. In 1791, he lived in France for a year, observing firsthand the events of the revolution which, at least initially, and contrary to many of his English con-temporaries, he enthusiastically supported. During this period he had an affair with a French woman, Annette Vallon, with whom he had a daughter, a deeply buried secret that became public knowledge only in the 20th century. Lack of money forced him to return to England, and the ensuing war with France separated the pair for 10 years. They never married, as they had planned to do. Wordsworth's growing disillusionment with the course of the French revolu-tion and his increasing skepticism under the influence of such London radical thinkers as William Godwin produced a near-collapse. He recovered after an unexpected legacy from a friend, whom Wordsworth had helped nurse during his final illness, allowed him to secure a home with Dorothy, who would live with the poet for the rest of his life.

In 1797 Wordsworth began his intimacy with Coleridge, a friendship that proved to be one of the most productive in literary history. Together they con-ceived the means to revitalize English literature with a new poetic language whose purpose was to restore poetry as an instrument of truth. In the preface to *Lyrical Ballads*, regarded as the principal manifesto of English romanticism, Wordsworth announces his challenge to the stale and artificial manner of 18th-century poetry. The poet, he writes, should be "a man speaking to men" in ordinary language of commonplace things. Forsaking grandeur and "gaudiness and inane phraseology," the poet should create interest in the essential qualities of human experience, with "storm and sunshine, with the revolution of the seasons, with cold and heat, with loss of friends and kindred, with injuries and resentment, gratitude and hope, with fear and sorrow. These, and the like, are the sensations and objects which the Poet describes, as they are the sensations of other men, and the objects which interest them."

The poems comprising *Lyrical Ballads* extended the range and subject matter of poetry to capture experience directly and honestly. In the simple ballads, like *The Idiot Boy* and *We Are Seven*, and the lyrical meditation of *Tintern Abbey*, Wordsworth achieves an interplay between nature and the imagination that explores both the external world of sensory experience and the internal workings of the mind in contemplation. Wordsworth substitutes direct experience in his depiction of nature for the artificial quality of earlier treatments. In his best work in such poems as *The Ruined Cottage, Michael, Ode: Intimations of Immortality*, and *The Solitary Reaper*, Wordsworth combines intense introspection with a vivid descriptive power enriched by regional details, achieving a depth and truthfulness that poetry rarely had achieved before.

A year after the appearance of the first edition of *Lyrical Ballads* (a longer second edition was published in 1800), Wordsworth and his sister moved back to the Lake District, where they remained for the rest of their lives. There, Wordsworth married a childhood friend, Mary Hutchinson, with whom he had five children. There was little drama in the rest of Wordsworth's life, but he experienced a steady rise of public appreciation—culminating in 1843 when he was named poet laureate—and the equally steady decline of his poetic talent. Wordsworth's greatest poetic achievement, however, remained unpublished during his lifetime. Following the publication of *Lyrical Ballads*, be began to conceive a massive philosophical poem that synthesized all his thoughts on man, nature, and society. Only *The Excursion* (1814) was published, but the highly personal portion that became *The Prelude* was completed in 1805 and revised throughout the rest of his life. Its subtitle, "The Growth of a Poet's Mind," suggests Wordsworth's intention to trace, autobiographically, the stages of his development from infancy to the period of the *Lyrical Ballads*. *The Prelude* is unique in English poetry in that it resembles a modern psychological novel in verse with aspirations to be a kind of modern epic of inner consciousness. In the poem, Wordsworth imaginatively re-creates the various concrete and specific moments and memories that formed him. His emphasis on the importance of childhood and his notion of the working of the unconscious suggest an integrated theory of the mind in advance of Freud. In the poem, Wordsworth traces the source of poetic awareness:

> There are in our existence spots of time,
> That with distinct pre-eminence retain

A renovating virtue, whence, depressed
By false opion and contentious thought,
Or aught of heavier or more deadly weight,
In trivial occupations, and the round
Of ordinary intercourse, our minds
Are nourished and invisibly repaired,
A virtue, by which pleasure is enhanced,
That penetrates, enables us to mount
When high, more high, and lifts us up when fallen.

In such moments of revelation, Wordsworth realized that the power of the imagination could transform dull perception and redeem experience. His greatness as a poet stems from this realization, opening up the full range of human experience to enlighten and save an otherwise impoverished and barren world. Despite the steady decline of Wordworth's genius, on his death in 1850 Matthew Arnold, in "Memorial Verses," considered the loss immense, and Wordsworth fit to be included in a select pantheon with GOETHE [10] and BYRON [83] as poetry's greatest voices:

Ah! since dark days still bring to light
Man's prudence and man's fiery might,
Time may restore us in his course
Goethe's sage mind and Byron's force;
But where will Europe's later hour
Again find Wordsworth's healing power?
Others will teach us how to dare,
And against fear our breast to steel;
Others will strengthen us to bear—
But who, ah! who, will make us feel?

HERMAN MELVILLE

1819–1891

He can neither believe, nor be comfortable in his unbelief; and he is too honest and coura-
geous not to try to do one or the other. If he were a religious man, he would be one of the
most truly religious and reverential; he has a very high and noble nature, and better worth
immortality than most of us.

—Nathaniel Hawthorne, *Notebooks*

No other American writer so typifies an artist's aspirations and anxieties as
Herman Melville. The author of an undisputed masterpiece of American and
world literature, *Moby-Dick*, Melville was a critical and commercial failure during his lifetime. He was so long forgotten at the time of his death that, as one
of his obituaries noted, "even his own generation has long thought him dead,
so quiet have been the later years of his life." The rehabilitation of Melville's
critical reputation did not begin until the 1920s, when he was acclaimed in
the same terms he had used to praise his friend and mentor NATHANIEL HAW-
THORNE [72], as one who "dives," a great literary explorer. Today, Melville is
ranked with the pantheon of American writers who, during the 1850s, created
the greatest decade in American literary history. Works such as *Moby-Dick*,
Ralph Waldo Emerson's *Representative Men*, Hawthorne's *The Scarlet Letter*,
Thoreau's *Walden*, and Whitman's *Leaves of Grass* helped define an indigenous
American literature that later generations have continued to absorb, modify,

and expand. Pride of place, however, at least in terms of grandiosity of design in fiction, in this impressive list belongs to Melville's *Moby-Dick*, which continues to set the standard as *the* great American novel.

Herman Melville was born in New York City, the second son of parents descended from prominent Dutch and English colonial ancestors. When he was 12, his father died bankrupt, and his mother relocated the family near Albany. Melville's schooling ended at 15, when he went to work as a clerk in his brother's store and in a bank. He tried teaching for a time and studied surveying, but, after an initial voyage to Liverpool as a cabin boy, he decided upon a life at sea. In 1841, he shipped out on the whaler *Acushnet*, bound for the Pacific.

Like Ishmael, his narrator in *Moby-Dick*, Melville could justifiably declare that "a whale-ship was my Yale College and my Harvard." His life aboard the *Acushnet* lasted 18 months, until he deserted at Nukuhiva in the Marquesas Islands with a friend. For at least a month, Melville lived among the Marquesan Taipis, a cannibal tribe, before leaving the island aboard an Australian whaler. The crew mutinied, and he was imprisoned for a time in Tahiti for his part in the rebellion. He went next to Hawaii aboard a Nantucket whaler and finally enlisted for service in the American navy aboard the frigate *United States* for the duration of its 14-month voyage home to Boston. During his four years before the mast and in exotic locales of the South Pacific, Melville gained a wealth of experience that he would mine in his literary work for the next decade.

Melville set about converting his adventures into fiction with a determination and concentration that shocked his family, who were accustomed to his previous restless energy and lack of both focus and ambition. In the next 11 years, Melville would compose 10 major works. *Typee* (1846), the first modern novel of South Seas adventure, is a fictionalized version of Melville's Marquesan experiences. *Omoo* (1847) continues the story of Melville's voyage through the mutiny and his imprisonment in Tahiti. Both books earned Melville critical attention and some commercial success. His next book, *Mardi* (1849), baffled his audience by mixing the travel-romance genre with heavy political and religious allegory. Melville followed *Mardi* with two more conventional sea stories: *Redburn* (1849), which tells of his first voyage to Liverpool, and *White-Jacket* (1850), based on his voyage home on the *United States*. The latter novel capitalized on contemporary interest in the cruel life of enlisted men in naval service.

Melville's first five novels give little indication that his next book, *Moby-Dick*, would be his masterpiece. Elements from his earlier novels—realistic portraiture in *Typee* and *Omoo*, allegory and metaphysical exploration in *Mardi*, and symbolism in *Redburn* and *White-Jacket*—would be orchestrated into a new artistic whole. The theme of all five—the quest by a youthful protagonist for meaning and community—would be recast in a sea story dominated by a monomaniacal captain who vents his despair on a malevolent universe in the form of vengeance on a white whale. In the process of composing *Moby-Dick*, Melville transformed his artistry and achieved for the only time in his career artistic expression commensurate with his deepening vision of human nature and the universe.

The transformation of Melville into an artist of the first order is attributable in part to his famous friendship with Nathaniel Hawthorne, which began in 1850. Melville married in 1847 and later moved to a farm in Pittsfield, Massachusetts, near Hawthorne's home. The 46-year-old Hawthorne was the author of *The Scarlet Letter* and the greatest writer America had yet produced. Melville acknowledged Hawthorne's greatness, calling him an "American Shakespeare," and it is likely that Melville recast the first draft of *Moby-Dick* from a realistic, documentary whaling story to the richer, darker, and more symbolically suggestive final version under Hawthorne's influence. Melville admired Hawthorne's ability to deal with questions of evil, to say in Melville-phrase, "No in thunder," and Melville incorporates much of the same tone in his own "wicked book," which he called "broiled in hell fire."

Moby-Dick blends narrative, metaphysical, dramatic, and documentary elements into what a contemporary reviewer called a "salamagundi of fact, fiction, and philosophy." The whole is modulated by two outcasts: the novel's narrator, Ishmael, who has turned to the sea to relieve the "damp, drizzly November in my soul," and Captain Ahab, whose demonic obsession with the whale Moby-Dick will damn the crew of the whaling ship *Pequod*. The novel's central symbol, the endlessly suggestive white whale, represents God, the universe, evil, meaninglessness, and more. Moby-Dick functions like a mirror in which Ahab, the crewmen of the *Pequod*, and the reader see their darkest fears and desires.

The failure of *Moby-Dick* to find an appreciative audience when it was published embittered Melville, and his subsequent writing reflects his increasing alienation and isolation. Alternately intensely private and scathingly satirical, Melville's later work offers occasional glimpses of his genius as he continued to explore the dark themes that haunted him. *Pierre* (1852), a domestic romance, is deeply psychological and troubled by a central theme of incest. A slight historical novel, *Israel Potter,* appeared in 1855, and Melville's last novel, *The Confidence Man*, an acid tale of deception aboard a Mississippi riverboat, was published in 1857. Melville also collected a number of shorter works in *The Piazza Tales* (1856), the best of which is the story "Bartleby the Scrivener," a black comedy about an outcast who wills his disengagement from life with the repeated refrain that he "would prefer not to."

In 1866, Melville took a position as a deputy customs inspector in New York, a post he held for the next 19 years as he largely withdrew from public and literary life. What writing he did was mainly poetry. *Battle-Pieces and Aspects of the War,* a collection of Civil War poetry, was published in 1866, and

Clarel, a book-length symbolic poem based on his tour of the Mediterranean and Palestine, appeared in 1876. Melville resigned his position in 1885 and died six years later, leaving in manuscript a novella, *Billy Budd*. Some critics see this story of an innocent seaman provoked to destruction by the evil Claggert as Melville's final resignation and acceptance of Christian consolation, as Billy reaches a level of apotheosis in the triumph of good against implacable evil.

Such a view seems too simplistic, an attempt to contain and categorize Melville, whose entire career challenged the conventional. Melville's genius rests in his confronting the deepest questions of human nature. If the story of Melville's career is a cautionary one to future authors in search of an understanding and appreciative audience, it is also the bold story of genius locked in a profound struggle to wrestle meaning and artistic form out of the most profound human dilemmas. Few authors before or since have dived so deeply.

JOHN KEATS

1795–1821

Keats earned his place in the tradition of English poetry by his courage to take the great dare of self-creation, his willingness to accept failure and move beyond it, his patience in learning his craft from those who could teach him. His sober prophecy as he started Hyperion—"I think I shall be among the English Poets after my death"—has been fulfilled; as Matthew Arnold confirmed it, sixty years later, "He is—he is with Shakespeare."

—Aileen Ward, *John Keats: The Making of a Poet*

Inevitably, as with EMILY DICKINSON [52], the story of the poet competes with the view of the poetry. We are moved as much by Keats's sad end at the age of 25 as by his remarkable progress as a poet, which promised even more than he was able to create. Assisted by SHELLEY [77] in his elegiac *Adonais*, myth has surrounded Keats since his death.

> O, weep for Adonais! though our tears
> Thaw not the frost which binds so dear a head!
> And thou, sad Hour, selected from all years
> To mourn our loss, rouse thy obscure compeers,
> And teach them thine own sorrow, say: with me
> Died Adonais: till the Future dares

Forget the Past, his fate and fame shall be
An echo and a light unto eternity!

The more arch lines of BYRON [83] in *Don Juan*, blame Keats's death on the critics:

John Keats, who was kill'd off by one critique,
  Just as he really promised something great,
If not intelligible, without Greek
  Contrived to talk about the Gods of late,
Much as they might have been supposed to speak.
  Poor fellow! His was an untoward fate;
'Tis strange the mind, that very fiery particle,
  Should let itself be snuff'd out by an article.

Both views have partially obscured the truth of Keats's story, which is far more moving when dealt with honestly. But it is also important to add that our interest in Keats stems not from the pathos of his unfulfilled promise but from his actual accomplishment. He has been called Shakespearean in his sympathetic objectivity, honesty, and attempt to comprehend the wholeness of experience. OSCAR WILDE [92] declared, "It is in Keats that one observes the beginning of the artistic renaissance of England. Byron was a rebel, and Shelley a dreamer; but in the calmness and clearness of his vision, his self-control, his unerring sense of beauty, and his recognition of a separate realm for the imagination, Keats was the pure and serene artist." No English poet except MILTON [8] has had such a profound influence on later poets as Keats. The youngest of the romantics, Keats brings to a culmination the ideas that marked the romantic revolution and pointed poetry away from self-centeredness toward an engagement with experience, concreteness, and a richer expressiveness.

Keats's life concentrates artistic development and achievement in a remarkably short span, measured in months rather than other poets' years. His father was a hostler at a London inn who was killed in an accident when Keats was eight years old. His mother's remarriage left him as a virtual surrogate parent to his three younger siblings. He went to a good school but showed little talent or much interest in literature. He dreamed of becoming a great military hero. Instead, at 16 he began training to become an apothecary and surgeon, but abandoned medicine to pursue poetry. He began an intense apprenticeship in which he absorbed a variety of literary influences, most notably from SPENSER [71], Milton, WORDSWORTH [23], and SHAKESPEARE [1] in an effort to find his own poetic voice. Keats came to the attention of Leigh Hunt, a political radical, poet, and critic, through whom he met Shelley, William Hazlitt, and Charles Lamb. He absorbed Hunt's interest in mythology and his version of poetry as luxurious escape, which marred Keats's early poetic promise.

Keats's determination to move beyond the merely decorous or self-obsessed to embrace deeper themes of tragic experience was greatly influenced by the death of his brother Tom from tuberculosis and his tormented love for Fanny Brawne, to whom he became engaged in 1819. In one year, from 1818 to 1819, Keats had one of the most astonishingly productive periods that any poet has ever had. During this time Keats wrote all of his major poems, including his great odes, which established his place in literature. In total mastery of poetic control and a variety of poetic forms, Keats had found his mature voice and achieved balance between self-analysis and a deeper confrontation with the external world. In 1820, diagnosed with tuberculosis, Keats traveled to Rome, where he died. On his tomb is the epitaph that he composed:

> This grave contains all that was mortal of a young English poet, who, on his death bed, in the bitterness of his heart at the malicious power of his enemies, desired these words to be graven on his tombstone, "Here lies one whose name was writ in water."

In his letters, which T. S. ELIOT [19] called "the most important ever written by any English poet," Keats emerges in his full stature: his honesty about himself and his experience made possible his growth as a poet. In a letter to his brothers written in 1818, he provides insight into his poetic intentions. "The excellence of every Art," he writes, "is its intensity, capable of making all disagreeables evaporate, from their being in close relationship with Beauty and Truth." For Keats the means to this end rested in what he called negative capability, which he defined as "when man is capable of being in uncertainties, Mysteries, doubts, without any irritable reaching after fact and reason." In his greatest poems, "Ode on a Grecian Urn," "Ode to a Nightingale," "Ode to Melancholy," and "To Autumn," which according to critic and biographer Walter Jackson Bate "may be said to begin the modern lyric of symbolic debate," Keats dramatically confronts bewildering, even numbing experience through the interplay between the imagination and a sharply sensual identification. The experience is not so much resolved as revealed in its complexity through the oppositions of the self and the other, the eternal and the temporal, transcendence and limitation, suspended in a poetic wholeness. Keats displays such symbols as the nightingale and the urn with infinite suggestiveness in meditations that are as sensuous as they are thoughtful. For Keats, the poet's obligation is to reach an intense level of insight that comprehends the most profound oppositions, such as that between melancholy and beauty in "Ode on Melancholy":

> She dwells with Beauty—Beauty that must die;
>   And Joy, whose hand is ever at his lips
> Bidding adieu; and aching Pleasure nigh,

Turning to Poison while the bee-mouth sips:
Ay, in the very temple of Delight
Veil'd Melancholy has her sovran shrine,
Though seen of none save him whose strenuous tongue
Can burst Joy's grape against his palate fine;
His soul shall taste the sadness of her might,
And be among her cloudy trophies hung.

In Keats's musical and sensuous verse, the poet's mind, in conflict with itself, attempts to reach the limit of its great capacity for the deepest feeling and thought. In the process, Keats affirms poetry's central mission as a force for beauty and truth.

OVID

26

43 B.C.—A.D. 17

He took the one thing that was to him emotionally real—the love that unites and destroys men and women—and made an epic of it. . . . The Metamorphoses remains unique: it is the only epic of love.

—Brooks Otis, *Ovid As an Epic Poet*

Few writers burst on the literary scene so audaciously or as powerfully as Ovid. BYRON [83] alone comes to mind, with a comparable meteoric rise and instant celebrity. Like Byron, Ovid awoke to find himself famous, with only the great VIRGIL [9] as his poetic peer. Also, like Byron, Ovid's career exploded into controversy and exile. Through all his notoriety and adversity, Ovid managed to write one of the seminal works of Western literature, the *Metamorphoses*, which, along with the *Iliad*, *Odyssey*, and the *Aeneid*, is one of the most influential works of the classical period.

Publius Ovidius Naso was born into a prominent family one year after the assassination of Julius Caesar. When he was 12, he came to Rome to become a lawyer at the time of Augustus's defeat of Marc Antony and Cleopatra at the decisive battle of Actium. Unlike the older Virgil, Ovid reached manhood during the peace and prosperity that Augustus's victory and consolidation of power secured, which may help to explain his contrary attitudes compared to the serious and essentially conservative Virgil. After working in the Roman civil service and traveling to Greece, Ovid abandoned the law to become a professional poet. His debut, *Amores*, followed by *Ars Amatoria*, were both daring and technically astonishing. He injected originality and vitality into the established form of the love elegy. Urbane, witty, at times subversive and amoral, Ovid's fresh take on love and manners must have shocked and delighted the Romans, while almost certainly setting the poet on a collision course with the more austere, old Roman values that Augustus was determined to revive.

In A.D. 8, at the height of his poetic career, Ovid was summoned before Augustus, summarily tried, and exiled to the town of Tomis, in what is now Romania, at the farthest edge of the Roman empire and the civilized Western world. The exact reason for his banishment is not known, although he confessed to an indiscretion and admitted that Augustus's action was justified. Gossip suggests the possibility of his involvement in a scandal surrounding Augustus's daughter, Julia. It is also possible that Ovid's offense was primarily a literary one and that Augustus was attempting to silence the poet, whose cynical love verses brought his regime offense and embarrassment. Whatever the cause, Ovid found himself cut off from civilization and must have regarded his exile as a death sentence. He remained in Tomis for the rest of his life, writing a series of poems, *Tristia* (The Sorrows), intended to gain a pardon that never came.

At the time of his exile, Ovid had just completed his masterpiece, the *Metamorphoses*, one of the greatest and most entertaining narrative poems ever written. It is a storehouse of poetic inspiration that has asserted its influence through the Middle Ages and the Renaissance into the modern period as a source of enduring stories and a veritable handbook of poetic techniques. An epic of a different kind than those of HOMER [3] and Virgil, the *Metamorphoses* is a seriocomic poem that attempts nothing less than a mythological history from creation to the assassination and apotheosis of Julius Caesar. The scale and scope of the poem are unprecedented: an anthology of Greek and Roman myths and legends reimagined and reshaped by Ovid's wit, invention, and the expressive power of his verse. Its larger significance and intention beyond amusement, however, have been debated since the poem first appeared. Much critical effort has been spent in deciphering the poem's structural and thematic unity, and many solutions, particularly the attempt in the Middle Ages to read it as a Christian allegory, are ingenious but ultimately fanciful, and far more rigid and reductive than Ovid must have intended.

Ovid's expansive structure, ranging in time from, in the poet's words, "the world's beginning to our own days," through legendary and human history, allows the poet the freedom to explore human and divine nature under the transforming power of love and abnormal psychological states produced by passion. The stories are linked by the central theme of metamorphoses or variations on the subject of miraculous transformations, but the poem's principal unity derives from Ovid's unique treatment of traditional tales. Different from Virgil's epic of history, Ovid's poem is essentially an epic of the emotions, as the human side of myths and legends are plumbed for their meaning. In Ovid's cosmogony, the gods and humans are victims of their passions, and each story, from the creation of the world through accounts of such figures in Greek and Roman mythology as Orpheus and Eurydice, Apollo and Hyacinthus, Pygmalion, and Venus and Adonis, shows Ovid's exploration of the volatility of the emotions and the unceasing dynamic of natural, supernatural, and human change. In contrast to the classical standard of order and balance, Ovid offers the more modern sense of a world in continual flux, whose multiplicity and vitality are life's highest attributes. The *Metamorphoses*, itself an example of artistic transformation, shows the power of the imagination to reshape the world and its sustaining myths into magically entertaining sources of truth and pleasure.

Only a handful of artistic creations—Homer's epics, the *Aeneid*, *The Divine Comedy*, *Don Quixote*—share with the *Metamorphoses* as high a place as one of the most influential literary works ever produced. Writers from CHAUCER [5] and SHAKESPEARE [1] to KAFKA [31] have mined Ovid's poem as a source of stories, poetic technique, and inspiration, while Ovid remains secure as a mediator between the ancient world and our own, a poet whose great achievement was to recognize the infinite variety of human experience to be transformed into the permanence of art.

AESCHYLUS

27

c. 525–456 B.C.

Aeschylus may have found some of his starting-points in contemporary events but he looked far beyond them to the lasting principles which they illustrated and which could best be presented in a mythical form without any distracting local or ephemeral details. If Pindar illuminates the events of his own time by myths, Aeschylus goes further and makes myths illustrate matters which pass far beyond the present and are often everlasting principles behind the changing scene.

—C. M. Bowra, *Landmarks in Greek Literature*

The origins of tragedy are obscure, but most authorities point to the religious ceremonies of the Greeks in the sixth century B.C. and the religious celebrations of the cult of Dionysus. Aristotle believed that tragedy originated from the speeches of "those who led the dithyramb," the choral hymn to Dionysus. Tradition credits the Athenian Thespis (none of whose plays survive) with first combining the choral song and dances with the speeches of a mask actor who took the part of a god or hero in a dramatic narrative and engaged the chorus in dialogue. It is the Greek playwright Aeschylus, however, from whom the Western theatrical tradition derives its first great dramas. Called the Creator of Tragedy, Aeschylus's innovations initiated the remarkable flourishing of a century of Athenian dramatic art that still defines the conventions of tragedy.

Aeschylus was born in Eleusis, near Athens, around 525 B.C., the son of Euphorion, a eupatrid, or one of the hereditary aristocrats of ancient Greece. The known facts of his life are few. He fought in the wars against the Persians in the battle of Marathon in 490, where his brother Cynegeirus was killed. His eyewitness account of the battle of Salamis in his play *The Persians*, the only surviving Greek drama based on a contemporary historical event, suggests that he also participated in that battle. We know that Aeschylus visited Sicily at least twice. Between 472 and 468 he was at the court of Hieron I at Syracuse, and in 456 he had traveled again to Sicily, where he died at Gela. Although scholars disagree on his role in Athenian politics and his political sympathies, it is incontestable that in his plays Aeschylus promoted many of the central values of the Greeks during the period of political and cultural achievement that followed the defeat of the Persians and the emergence of Athens to supremacy in the Greek world.

Aeschylus wrote, acted in, and produced between 80 and 90 plays, of which only seven—the earliest documents in the history of the Western theater—survive. The theatrical conventions that Aeschylus inherited and would transform grew out of now obscure religious rituals involving songs performed and danced by a chorus. The Greek word *tragidia*, from which tragedy is derived, means "goat-song," and the members of the tragic chorus were "goat-singers," possibly because a goat was the prize for the best song, or because a goat was sacrificed during the singing, or to suggest the connection to the vegetation deity, Dionysus, in whose honor the songs were sung at his annual celebration. Sometime in the late sixth century B.C. Athenians turned the cult of Dionysus into a citywide theatrical contest in which choruses competed for prizes in a festival that lasted for several days. During the annual spring Great Dionysia, performed in an open-air theater that held an audience of 15,000 or more, business was suspended and prisoners were released on bail for the duration of the festival. The first day was devoted to traditional choral hymns followed by the competition, in which a dramatist's cycle of three tragedies and a comic "satyr" play were performed on each of the remaining days. The songs of the chorus were joined with the spoken words of male actors, whose masks and costumes allowed them to assume a variety of roles. Aeschylus is credited with adding a second actor to the innovation of Thespis and thereby widening the dramatic possibilities of the performance, with multiple characters on stage at the same time. The dramatized stories were based on myths previously celebrated by epic or lyric poets in a work of 1,100 to 1,500 lines that could be performed in two hours. According to Aristotle, it was also Aeschylus who reduced the choral element and "gave the leading role to the spoken word." He is also credited with developing the conventions of tragedy's grand diction, rich costuming, and spectacular dramatic effects.

It is unclear, however, how much credit to give Aeschylus's genius and innovation for the development of tragedy because we know so little about his predecessors or contemporaries. It is also not possible to trace his artistic development with certainty because so little of his work has survived, and what remains cannot be dated with precision. He won his first victory at the Great Dionysia in 484 B.C., which was followed by 13 or in some accounts 28 subsequent victories, although the higher total could indicate victories won after his death or because he was allowed to perform his plays in subsequent competitions. Even the lower number, however, indicates his great acclaim and preeminence as a dramatist. His surviving plays include *The Persians*, *Seven against Thebes*, *The Suppliants*, and *Prometheus Bound*. Each is a third of a trilogy whose companion plays have been lost, making it difficult to interpret accurately his overall design and intention. With the *Oresteia*, however, we have the only surviving tragic trilogy, a form that Aeschylus either invented or mastered, and which became the rule in the Athenian competition. Though the three plays could be unrelated to one another, Aeschylus was a master of the linked theme and is considered the first dramatist to explore the wider implications of the same myth, thus extending the range of tragedy to a truly epic scale.

The Oresteian trilogy (*Agamemnon*, *The Libation Bearers*, and *The Eumenides*), based on HOMER [3], combines themes from both the *Iliad* and the *Odyssey* and concerns the fall of the House of Atreus in a series of retributive murders over three generations. Agamemnon, who has killed his own daughter to insure success against the Trojans, returns home and is in turn killed by his wife, Clytemnestra, and her lover, Aegisthus. Agamemnon's murder must be avenged by his son Orestes, setting in motion the moral and ethical dilemma of whether justice can be attained if it violates the important blood relationship between mother and child. Orestes is pursued by the Furies, serpent-haired female avengers, first to Delphi, where Apollo is unable to protect him, and then to Athens, where Athena, the patroness of the city, arranges Orestes' trial. Orestes is acquitted, and the Furies are persuaded to become Athens's protectors. Such a bald summary does little justice to the magnificent scope and range of Aeschylus's achievement in the *Oresteia*, a work that explores political and religious themes in a manner that never loses touch with essential human questions. Aeschylus searches for nothing less than the meaning of human suffering and justice as civilization replaces the old order of blood vengeance.

Aeschylus's daring works include scenes of magnificent poetic expression and spectacle. Ancient critics indicated that his method was to aim at "astonishment," and it is said that the first appearance of the Furies in *The Eumenides* caused children in the audience to faint and pregnant women to miscarry. The force and intensity of Aeschylus's dramatic conception are joined to his grand style of language and a pattern of imagery and symbol that gives his drama a thematic unity. The works stand comparison to the achievement of DANTE [2] in *The Divine Comedy* and the great tragedies of SHAKESPEARE [1]. Aeschylus remains one of the greatest playwrights of the Western world, who succeeded in uniting the profound exploration of universal, human themes with emotionally intense and riveting poetic drama.

DU FU

28

712–770

Tu Fu was the master stylist of regulated verse, the poet of social protest, the confessional poet, the playful and casual wit, the panegyricist of the imperial order, the poet of everyday life, the poet of the visionary imagination. He was the poet who used colloquial and informal expressions with greater freedom than any of his contemporaries; he was the poet who experimented most boldly with densely artificial poetic diction; he was the most learned poet in recondite allusion and a sense of the historicity of language. One function of literary history is to account for a poet's identity; Tu Fu's poetry defies such reduction: the only aspect that can be emphasized without distorting his work as a whole is the very fact of its multiplicity.

—Stephen Owen, *The Great Age of Chinese Poetry*

The poetry of China's Tang dynasty (618–907) represents a watershed of poetic development that has continued to nourish Chinese literature ever since. During the seventh century, poetry was the elite language of social discourse and diversion in court circles. By the end of the eighth century, poetry had been transformed into a conscious art form practiced by a much wider range of the population as a serious instrument for exploring private, social, and cultural values. Regarded by many as China's greatest poet, Du Fu (or, according to the alternate Wade-Giles transliteration system, Tu Fu) is the Tang poet who best exploited the possibility of a deeper and richer poetic art.

Like SHAKESPEARE [1] in the West, Du Fu is a measure for artistic greatness, the standard by which all subsequent Chinese poetry has been compared. The poetic tendencies and emphases of later periods have their precedents in Du Fu's artistry.

Du Fu achieved recognition for his poetic achievement only after his death. His poems' multiplicity of forms and complex, shifting attitudes, different from the uniformity of tone and approach of his poetic contemporaries, so valued by future generations in China, were too daring and unconventional to be appreciated during his lifetime. Marked by failure and disappointment, Du Fu's literary career was compensated only by the quality of the poetry that he managed to write about his own checkered life.

Du Fu was the grandson of Du Shenyan, one of the most distinguished court poets of the early eighth century. We know little of Du Fu's youth, except that he later recalled he was a prodigy whose precociousness was recognized by his elders. He failed, however, in his first examination to secure a government position, and his attempts to gain a respectable posting dominated his efforts throughout much of his life. In 751, poems sent to the emperor found favor and resulted in a special examination that Du Fu passed, although no appointment came until several years later, when he obtained the lowest county post appointed by the central government. In 755 the rebellion of the northeastern armies under An Lushan broke out. When the rebels seized the capital, causing the emperor to flee to the west, Du Fu was captured by rebel forces. After escaping through the rebel lines to the temporary capital, he secured service to a minister, but, after the ultimate imperial victory over the rebels, he was demoted to a low provincial post in Huazhou. Du Fu resigned the hated appointment in 759 and set off for Qinzhou in Northwest China, where he remained for the last 11 years of his life.

Although by his own account Du Fu wrote prolifically during his early years, only a few of these poems survive. Those that do show a fully mature poet and a consummate craftsman with a command of the Chinese literary tradition that his genius would push to new poetic possibilities. Du Fu transformed the artificial diction and highly stylized form into a richer, more expressive medium for self-analysis and reflection. His so-called shifting style, expressing multiple moods in a single poem, was a radical break with tradition that turned his poems into complex structures of many dimensions. Du Fu's poetry can be read as an autobiographical chronicle of his life and career in which he brilliantly records his experiences as well as the events of his times. Prior to Du Fu, Chinese poetry rarely mirrored the larger world and the rush of historical events. Accordingly, Du Fu has been called the "poet historian." In a poem such as "Song of Pengya," he records the flight of his family during the An Lushan Rebellion, providing a naturalistic reflection of the scene that is unprecedented in Chinese poetry. His style is colloquial and direct, and the poem gathers its strength from a precise rendering of actual details. His poem "Homeless" displays his characteristic blend of intense introspection, simple and direct diction, and a reflection of the personal and historical moment:

> Years and years and years of war!
> The houses, the gardens, are turned to tall grass.
> In my village, only one hundred homes,
> Under the arrows people pass,
> Most of them are I think now dead.
>
> I alone come back to the old homestead,
> On all sides homes empty, empty streets,
> Even the sun has grown paler, and thin.
> Only foxes and wolves wandering one meets.
> They prick up their ears. They howl and grin.
> . . .
> No one cares now what I do!
> I have only my body to carry through.
>
> If they drive me away it is just the same,
> There was no home for me when I came.
>
> I cry for my mother!
>
> She died when they drove me forth as a slave.
> She made me become her murderer.
> This grief will follow me to my grave.
> But who will live long enough to follow me when I go there?

Du Fu's poetry ranges widely in mood and attitude, with consummate craft and astonishing variety. The poet's introspection and engagement with his world, unprecedented in Chinese poetry, set a new standard that has been absorbed by Chinese poets ever since. In "Meditation," Du Fu bitterly considers his failure to achieve distinction as a poet and laments his passing into silence, "weary and worn" like a "a lonely bird adrift." Posterity has granted him a much greater legacy.

WILLIAM BLAKE

29

1757–1827

Blake, in the hierarchy of the inspired, stands very high indeed. If one could strike an average among poets, it would probably be true to say that, as far as inspiration is concerned, Blake is to the average poet, as the average poet is to the man in the street. All poetry, to be poetry at all, must have the power of making one, now and then, involuntarily ejaculate: 'What made him think of that?' With Blake, one is asking the question all the time.
—Lytton Strachey, *Books and Characters*

Of all the major figures of English romanticism, Blake was almost unknown and ignored in his day and rejected by succeeding generations as a demented mystic and writer of impenetrable and incoherent works. In the modern period, however, he has finally emerged as perhaps the greatest and most influential of the romantics. The revitalizing power of his imagination provides an alternative to the nihilism of much modern thought. Blake unabashedly pursued the role of the poet as prophet who attempted a transformation of thought and perception through his visionary power. Blake, therefore, stands today as the English DANTE [2], whose poetic imagination embraces the widest reaches of the mind to comprehend all of the human condition, joining the human and the divine.

Like the other English romantic poets, Blake's development as an artist can be understood fully only in the context of the various political, social, and religious forces that shaped him. A product of the revolutionary thinking that would transform 18th-century concepts of order, political and religious hierarchies, and faith in reason and empiricism, Blake's reference point was London, where he lived for all but three years of his life. He was the son of a London shopkeeper and self-educated. His powerful spiritual awareness, heavily influenced by the evangelical movement's recognition of a defining personal inner life, was joined with an extraordinary capacity for visualization that produced many visionary experiences. Alexander Gilchrist's 19th-century account of Blake's life records that

> while quite a child, of eight or ten perhaps, he had his "first vision." Saun-tering along, the boy looks up and sees a tree filled with angels, bright angelic wings bespangling every bough like stars. Returned home he relates the incident, and only through his mother's intercession escapes a thrashing from his honest father, for telling a lie. Another time, one summer morn, he sees the haymakers at work, and amid them angelic figures walking.

Blake's perception of the world of spirit existing alongside the ordinary formed his imagination from this beginning, and it would define all of his future artistic and literary work. Politically, Blake sympathized with the revolutionary spirit that freed America from Britain and swept through France, and he opposed the repression through which England tried to maintain its orthodox and authoritarian powers. Yet his accidental participation in the mob violence that stormed Newgate Prison in 1780 during the anti-Catholic riots also contributed to his distrust of simple assertions of populist freedom and the destructive power of political revolution disconnected from the deeper, more fundamental human reform. Without such reform, according to Blake, victims simply became the new masters, and one form of slavery was exchanged for another. For Blake, political and religious solutions were joined with the transformative power of the imagination that his art and poetry attempted to reveal.

At the age of 10, Blake began to train in drawing, and when he was 21 he had completed a seven-year apprenticeship as an engraver, the profession that supported him fitfully during his lifetime. In 1782, he married Catherine Boucher, the illiterate daughter of a Battersea market-gardener. Blake taught her to write, and she became an important collaborator in his artistic work. Although he studied at the Royal Academy of Art, he chafed under the criticism of its president, Sir Joshua Reynolds. As Gilchrist recounts, Reynolds urged Blake to discipline his art "with less extravagance and more simplicity, and to correct his drawing. This Blake seemed to regard as an affront never to be forgotten." For Blake, Reynolds remained the paradigm of neoclassical rigidity, for whom art is made to "Serve Nobility and Fashionable Taste."

Instead, Blake was determined to go his own way, willing to sacrifice popular taste and success for his personal vision.

Blake's earliest poems were lyrics for songs to music of his own composition, and the musical element shapes the meter of his later lyrics. In 1783, *Poetical Sketches*, his only conventionally printed book, appeared. In 1789, he began *Songs of Innocence* with the illuminated printing method that he would use for all his subsequent work, combining the art of printmaking and verse. The method, Blake asserted, was revealed to him by his dead artist brother Robert in a dream. Blake wrote his lines of poetry and then drew the accompanying illustration on a copper plate, using acid to etch the areas of each plate surrounding his lettering and the lines of his drawing. After printing, Blake hand-colored each drawing. The process was laborious and impossible to reproduce in quantity at a low cost, and although facsimiles have been published in limited, expensive editions, most of Blake's readers have never seen his full conception of the relationship between text and design, which is unique in literary history.

The sequence of deceptively simple lyrics in *Songs of Innocence* was combined with the corresponding *Songs of Experience* in 1794, Blake's most familiar poems, which developed his characteristic theme of lost innocence corrupted by forces of repression. The one dramatic event of Blake's life brought him directly in contact with the age's authoritarian forces. In 1802, his attempt to expel a soldier from his garden resulted in a charge of sedition for which he was eventually acquitted. "London," Blake's most famous prophetic lyric, distills the age's tensions and their cost:

> I wander thro' each charter'd street,
> Near where the charter'd Thames does flow,
> And mark in every face I meet
> Marks of weakness, marks of woe.
>
> In every cry of every Man,
> In every Infant's cry of fear,
> In every voice, in every ban,
> The mind-forg'd manacles I hear
>
> How the Chimney-sweeper's cry
> Every blackning Church appalls;
> And the hapless Soldier's sigh,
> Runs in blood down Palace walls.
>
> But most thro' midnight streets I hear
> How the youthful Harlot's curse
> Blasts the new-born Infant's tear,
> And blights with plagues the Marriage hearse.

All of Blake's poetry can be related to his analysis of the cause and cure of man's "mind-forg'd manacles." For Blake, the key was to go beyond simple perception limited by the senses to a deeper understanding through the aid of the imagination. All of his poetry is fundamentally allegorical, unlocking the universal and eternal correspondences that reside beneath the surface of things. His shorter and longer epic and prophetic works, such as *The Marriage of Heaven and Hell, America, Europe, Urizen, The Four Zoas, Milton,* and *Jerusalem,* explore the tension between individual liberation and the political, historical, and psychological factors that diminish human possibilities. Often obscure and confusing because of Blake's private system of archetypes and mythological correspondences, the poems nonetheless offer a remarkable program for imaginative revitalization and rebirth. As the first of the English romantics, Blake shares with them the energies of artistic liberation and the redirection of poetry to fundamental questions of how we perceive the world and how to transcend its limits.

30

GUSTAVE FLAUBERT

1821–1880

Ponder most carefully the following fact: a master of Flaubert's artistic power manages to transform what he has conceived as a sordid world inhabited by frauds and philistines and mediocrities and brutes and wayward ladies into one of the most perfect pieces of poetical fiction known, and this he achieves by bringing all the parts into harmony, by the inner force of style, by all such devices of form as the counter-point of transition from one theme to another, of foreshadowing and echoes. Without Flaubert there would have been no Marcel Proust in France, no James Joyce in Ireland. Chekhov in Russia would not have been quite Chekhov. So much for Flaubert's literary influence.
        —Vladimir Nabokov, "Madame Bovary" in *Lectures on Literature*

Flaubert has been held responsible for creating the modern novel and defining the role of novelist as artist, as well as for diminishing the form with an aesthetic philosophy so refined that the life of the novel is secondary to its static, though beautiful, design. Both views of Flaubert's literary contribution have validity, but the former—Flaubert's role as the originator of a new kind of fiction—clearly predominates. His novel *Madame Bovary* (1856) is a landmark work in the history of fiction that set the novel on a new course. It earned Flaubert the accolade from Henry James [38] of the "novelist's novelist," and gave the novel the respectability and seriousness in France formerly reserved for poetry, tragedy, and the epic.

Flaubert evolved his high standard for the novel, which included his advocacy of realism and strict artistic control over his material, in a hard-fought struggle with his own divided temperament. Flaubert oscillated between a desire for romantic escape and a sharp awareness of a world that he often found disappointing and appalling. Flaubert's battle to shape both contradictory elements, romance and realism, into art is one of the great heroic stories of literature.

Born in Rouen, Flaubert came from the bourgeois background that he analyzed so meticulously and found so limited and stultifying. His father was the chief surgeon at the Hôtel-Dieu hospital; his mother was the daughter of a small-town doctor. Possessing a precocious literary talent, Flaubert began writing romantic stories at the age of 16. His family, however, was determined that he should become a lawyer, and Flaubert spent a year at the University of Paris, where he studied little and failed his examinations. A nervous collapse brought him back to the family estate at Croisset, near Rouen, where, after the death of his father in 1846, he lived with his mother and niece for the rest of his life, devoting his time exclusively to writing.

The origin of his masterpiece, *Madame Bovary*, began with friends' negative reaction to the romantic excesses of an early version of the novel that would later become *The Temptation of Saint Anthony* (1874). They suggested Flaubert discipline his imagination with a tale of ordinary life, suggesting as a possible topic the actual incident of the wife of a country doctor in Normandy who died after she deceived and ruined her husband. Despite the sordid subject and its philistine atmosphere, which he found so distasteful, Flaubert began a five-year labor to re-create small-town French life and to enter the lives of his characters imaginatively.

The story describes the married life of Charles and Emma Bovary. He is a plodding country doctor; she is in search of the romantic escape glimpsed in her reading. Emma's dream is translated into two shallow and tawdry affairs, mounting debt, and her eventual suicide. Central to the domestic drama is the surrounding atmosphere of bourgeois pettiness and hypocrisy that permeates the novel. Flaubert's creative attempt, described in his extraordinary correspondence, to capture his characters and their milieu evolved into a new kind of literary realism and craftsmanship. In Flaubert's work, the author does not direct the reader's interpretation of the characters and story. Flaubert asserted, "The author, in his work, must be like God in the Universe, present everywhere and visible nowhere." As densely patterned as an alternative, imagined universe, Flaubert's novel achieves a remarkable fidelity to reality while searching for the perfect expression (*le mot juste*) to connect language with meaning, achieving beauty and truth even over the most mundane and trivial. His agonies of composition, which involved spending entire days on finding the right phrase and vomiting in a chamber pot after describing Emma Bovary's death by poison, suggest the novelist's attempt to subsume his entire personality in the artistic process, which more than justifies his later explanation of his central character's origin: *"Madame Bovary, c'est moi."*

Madame Bovary was an immediate succès de scandale in which Flaubert was tried and narrowly acquitted for "outraging public morals and religion." He followed with the lushly exotic *Salammbô* (1862), a historical novel set in ancient Carthage for which he traveled to Tunisia to gather background material. His next novel, again showing oscillation between romance and realism, is the large-scale social panorama of *A Sentimental Education* (1869), the story of Frédéric Moreau's passion for the older wife of a businessman. This was followed by a final version of the early work, *The Temptation of Saint Anthony* and *Three Tales* (1877), linked stories that described saints' lives. One of the stories, "A Simple Heart," which Ezra Pound said "contains all that anyone knows about writing," has been regarded as a model of technique for short fiction. Flaubert died suddenly from a stroke, leaving unfinished the satiric novel, *Bouvard and Pécuchet*.

If the novel once had the unsavory reputation of light entertainment with the expectation, in ANTHONY TROLLOPE's [107] phrase, of "sugarplums for their conclusions," Flaubert helped change that in both his subject and his style. Affected by the romantic age's notion of *l'art pour l'art* (art for art's sake), he created a new artistic standard for the novel in which consistency and unity of design predominate over a reader's conventional expectations. He replaced the episodic, desultory structure of earlier novels with a method of construction borrowed from poetry, of counterpoint and an elaborate pattern of associations that develop the novel's meaning. Critics have attacked Flaubert's clinical detachment and his clear distaste for the life he so scrupulously revealed. His statements—such as "Life is something so hideous . . . that the only way to endure it is to escape it. And one escapes by living in art" and "the only truth in this world is in a well-made sentence"—seem to corroborate the view that he shifted the novel away from engagement with life, replacing its clutter and vitality with the admirable, though admittedly limited, art of the exquisite miniature.

Such a reduction of art to artifice is more the risk of Flaubert's method than his actual accomplishment. No one could confuse *Madame Bovary* with the art of the miniature. Flaubert's tortured composition, however, as well as his feelings of inadequacy and failure, color his achievement and help establish the archetype of the alienated novelist. Even Flaubert the master stylist admitted that "[great men] do not have to go in for style; they are strong in spite of their failings and because of them. But we little men find our value only in the perfect execution of our work. . . . Very great men often write very badly, and so much the better for them. It is not in their work that we must seek the art of form, but among the second-raters." Despite his bitter analysis of his own inadequacies, Flaubert's achievement is secure: he derived artistic excellence by harnessing romance and realism. The creative tensions that Flaubert dramatized so completely in himself are those the modern novelist continues to battle.

FRANZ KAFKA

31

1883–1924

The world that Kafka was "condemned to see with such blinding clarity that he found unbearable" is our post-Auschwitz universe, on the brink of extinction. His work is subversive, not because he found the truth but because, being human and therefore having failed to find it, he refused to settle for half-truths and compromise solution. In visions wrested from his innermost self, and in language of crystalline purity, he gave shape to the anguish of being human.

—Ernst Pavel, *The Nightmare of Reason*

No writer has probed 20th-century trauma and neurosis with more penetration than Franz Kafka. It would not be an exaggeration to describe much of the century's political and social history as Kafkaesque, an adjective that Kafka's disturbing, nightmarish stories and novels have implanted in the modern psyche. The dislocation of sensibility, alienation, and victimization of his dreams and fears have proven to be not just prescient but prophetic. Although Kafka died before the Holocaust, all the surviving members of his family were killed in Nazi concentration camps, giving the horrors that Kafka presented as literature a terrible reality.

Kafka's vision is firmly established in the details of his background and development. As a Jew in Catholic Prague whose German-speaking father identified with the oppressors of Czech independence, Kafka's peculiar displacement and alienation were deeply rooted. He was the oldest child of Hermann and Julie Kafka. His father was a former itinerant peddler from southern Bohemia who became a prosperous merchant and ignored or bullied his sensitive son. Kafka's nightmare world of tyrants and victims is based in large measure on his relationship with his father. "It seemed as if the world was divided into three parts," Kafka confessed to his father. "In one part I lived as a slave, subject to laws which had been specially devised for me, and which for some unknown reason I could never completely satisfy. The second world, infinitely removed from my own, was the one in which you lived, occupied with running the business, issuing orders—and getting angry when they were not carried out. The third world was the one where everyone else lived happy lives, in which the giving and taking of orders played no part." Hermann Kafka's inability to provide his son with love and support set the dominant themes in Kafka's fiction and was the private source of the traumas in his writing. "My writing was about you," Kafka told his father. "All I was bewailing in it was what I could not weep about on your shoulder."

After attending a strict German grammar school, Kafka studied law at the German University in Prague, achieving his doctorate at the age of 23. Law offered the possibility of a safe career among the few then open to Jews, but Kafka had no illusions that the work would be fulfilling. "Even as a small child," he wrote, "I had a pretty clear notion of what all my studying and choosing a career would amount to: I expected no salvation from that quarter." He secured a position at the Workers Accident Insurance Institute, where he dealt with accident claims and managed the business of a large bureaucracy for 14 years. After work, he devoted himself to his writing, which he approached as an inevitability: "God doesn't want me to be a writer. But I have no choice."

Although Kafka struggled under the oppressive yoke of his father and family, he lacked the means and self-confidence to free himself. Despite a number of romantic liaisons and the tortured courtship of Felice Bauer that continued for five years, Kafka never married. Instead, he devoted himself to his writing and the job that he alternately loathed and depended upon "like an eiderdown, heavy and warm. If I crawled out from underneath it I should immediately run the risk of catching a cold: they don't heat the outside world." His family, his relationships, and his bureaucratic position provided him with material that he transformed in his writing to the exclusion of everything else. "I am a clear case," he wrote, "of somebody whose powers have been channeled in the direction of writing. When my body realized that writing was to be my most productive bent, all my strength flowed into the activity and ceased to nourish whatever capacity I may have had for enjoying sex, food, drink, philosophical reflection, and above all music. My taste for all these things began to atrophy."

Kafka's artistic breakthrough occurred in 1912, when he wrote "The Judgment," an Oedipal fantasy clearly based on his relationship with Hermann Kafka, in which a father condemns his son to death by drowning and the son lovingly carries out his sentence. The process of tapping into his dream obsessions had, in Kafka's words, "come out of me like a birth" and signaled a radical departure in his writing. By describing his fantasies, Kafka reached levels of the unconscious closed to more conventional approaches. All of his best writing is intimately self-analytical, based on a relentless probing of himself and his preoccupations. His stories and novels are shaped by a dream logic of the fantastic, involving archetypes as characters but captured with the realistic details of ordinary life.

Kafka's most famous story, "The Metamorphosis," begins with one of the most shocking and celebrated opening sentences in modern literature: "As Gregor Samsa awoke one morning from uneasy dreams he found himself transformed in his bed into a gigantic insect." Gregor, a put-upon traveling salesman who feels treated like an insect, becomes one, and the story explores the family dynamic that the fantastical transformation brings about. What is most bizarre in the story is not the initial situation but the terrifying *ordinariness* that proceeds from it, as the Samsa family makes its adjustments. The nightmare is joined to the commonplace in ways that complement both elements and provide a symbolic expansion of Kafka's initial fantasy.

In most of Kafka's stories and novels a baffling and unexpected situation, like that in a dream, confronts the protagonist, who struggles to make sense of it and to maintain his individuality in the face of forces determined to control or limit his behavior. In *The Trial* (1925), the hero is charged with unspecified crimes and is eventually executed. In *The Castle* (1926), a land surveyor tries to communicate unsuccessfully with his employer and receives a series of incomprehensible messages instead. The protagonists struggle to discover a rational explanation in a system that is fundamentally absurd and to maintain a sense of self in a world determined to destroy autonomy. Kafka's vision reveals the modern landscape as barren of the possibility of fulfillment as *The Waste Land* of T. S. ELIOT [19], suggesting a cycle of victimization that is both systematic and, in the words of WILLIAM BLAKE [29], "mind-forg'd."

Few of Kafka's works were published during his lifetime. When he died in 1924, short of his 41st birthday, of tuberculosis first diagnosed in 1917, he instructed that his manuscripts be destroyed and his published work not be reprinted. His friend and executor, Max Brod, ignored his final request and helped spread Kafka's reputation as one of the great masters of 20th-century literature. Kafka's style and vision have become part of the landscape of modern literature, essential components of such diverse writers as Jean-Paul Sartre, SAMUEL BECKETT [47], HAROLD PINTER [115], and GABRIEL GARCÍA MÁRQUEZ [76]. Kafka's nightmares continue to haunt us.

MOLIÈRE

32

1622–1673

By his presence, by his example, by his personal devotion, the art of the theater changes in meaning, nature and scope. It rediscovers a principle of life, it becomes a true art in which the spirit of creation and the means of realization are intimately mingled and in which the principles of the craft are as one with the inspiration of the creative artist.
—Jacques Copeau, "Discours au public pour le trois centième anniversaire de la naissance de Molière"

Molière and ARISTOPHANES [34] are the great innovators of comic drama. Together the pair mark out the boundaries for comedy. Molière revived comedy in the 17th century as a serious reflection of human nature and experience, and perfected theatrical conventions that have maintained their powers in the hands of such different artists as SAMUEL BECKETT [47], Eugene Ionesco, and Charlie Chaplin. One also must credit Molière for the legitimatization of comic theater in the West, the establishment of a classical repertory and, largely in his honor, a national theater, the Comédie-Française. After more than 300 years, Molière, like SHAKESPEARE [1], continues to dominate the theater that he helped to create.

Molière was born Jean-Baptiste Poquelin into a prosperous, bourgeois Parisian family. His father was an upholsterer whose clients included the king, and it was expected that Molière would continue in the family business. He received a fine education under the Jesuits at the Collège de Clermont in Paris and studied law. To the horror of his family, be gave up his prospects for a life in the theater in 1644, a far from respectable profession that may explain his adopting the stage name of Molière to avoid family embarrassment. Love as much as a passion for the stage may have played a part in his becoming an actor. The allure of Madeleine Béjart, an experienced actress six years his senior, compelled him to join forces with the Béjart family to form L'Illustre Théâtre company, which he eventually headed. In Paris at the time there were only two legitimate theaters, and performances were arranged in unused, enclosed tennis courts—long, narrow spaces fitted with a proscenium stage at one end. The company performed sporadically and incurred debts for which Molière was imprisoned and rescued by his father. In 1645, Molière's reconstituted company left Paris for a 12-year tour of the provinces, during which time he wrote plays to exploit his own and his company's skill in comedy.

Molière's talents as an actor were modest. In the view of one contemporary, "Nature, which had been so generous to him in the realm of intellectual gifts, had refused him those outward talents so necessary for the stage, particularly for tragic roles. A muffled voice, harsh inflections, and a hurried speech which made him declaim too quickly, all rendered him far inferior to the actors of the Hôtel de Bourgogne [his rivals]."

If Molière did not possess the talent to succeed in tragedy, his gifts were appropriate for comedy, augmented by his considerable genius for adapting conventional comic forms for new and provocative uses. The comedy of Molière's day was largely the creation of the Italian commedia dell'arte, to which Molière was extensively exposed on his troupe's tour of the southern provinces. Based on set comic routines, the commedia depended on stock roles familiar to the audience and witty improvisations by the actors, which included topical references. In the long apprenticeship of the provincial tour, Molière mastered the farcical base upon which he began to build a new kind of comedy, while elevating the form to the serious aspirations of tragedy. If comedy before Molière was composed exclusively of rough-and-tumble entertainment and low humor, he would help transform it into a critique of life. His early plays show him gradually expanding the range of the knockabout farce and stock characters to encompass social satire and the reflection of the real life and experience of his audience. In 1658, Molière's company returned to Paris, where he enjoyed the undependable support of Louis XIV. Controversy and personal attack greeted most of his mature work, which he wrote during his last 15 years. In 1662, Molière married Armande Béjart, the younger sister or possibly the daughter of Madeleine Béjart, and produced *The School for Wives,* a landmark in the history of drama, comparable to the birth of romantic drama with the opening of *Hernani* by VICTOR HUGO [105], in 1830. In Molière's comic war of the sexes the farcical masks of conventional comedy become mirrors in which the audience can see themselves. The play seemed subversive to Molière's critics, suggesting that theater's entertainment might also disturb. As critic Jacques Guicharnaud observed:

> Essentially unrealistic, like all poetic works, Molière's major plays of that period show that everyone's life is a romance, a farce, a disgrace. Their effect might be compared to what would happen if, in a Mack Sennett movie, when a clown throws a cream pie, that pie—by some miracle of film technique—should splash on the faces of all the spectators. The devout, the well-born, the lovers, the husbands become indignant: they have just been told that they are hypocritical or stupid, ridiculous or cuckolded. Unreality invades reality. The spectator doubts himself—or rather, he is led into a state of bad faith to avoid doubting himself.

Molière had succeeded in devising out of farcical and folk elements a high comedy of ideas and a serious, though humorous, reflection of human nature. *The School for Wives* began a remarkable series of literary masterpieces that included *Tartuffe, Don Juan, The Misanthrope,* and *The Miser.* All show Molière's skill in adapting traditional comic conventions to the new uses of character comedy, in which he exposes the vice and folly embodied in the excesses of his characters. In *Tartuffe,* Molière's target is religious hypocrisy and the contradictions between appearance and reality, the basic resource of comedy. Molière's religious target proved far too controversial, and the play was banned in Paris for five years as Molière struggled to obtain the authorization to produce it.

In 1673, while acting the role of the hypochondriac Argan in *The Imaginary Invalid,* Molière collapsed onstage and, although he managed to finish the performance, died a few hours later. Parish priests refused him the last rites, and the intervention of the king was required for burial at night to avoid scandal. After his death, Molière became the guiding spirit of the Comèdie-Française, created by the merger of Molière's company with a rival company by the king in 1680. Molière's plays have remained a staple of the company's classical repertory, the pinnacle of neoclassical comedy, as RACINE's [62] plays are the high point of neoclassical tragedy.

In his widening of theatrical forms to incorporate serious themes, Molière is one of the major innovators of modern drama. Most subsequent innovations, such as the spectacle of romantic drama and the symbolic antirealistic techniques of modern drama, can be traced to Molière. The comic vision of Molière, the discrepancy between how we would like to be seen and who we truly are, sets the tone of much modern literature, from the antiheroic to the absurd, in which the sanity of Molière's exposed truths is the essential consolation.

JOHN DONNE

1572–1631

He was the one English love poet who was not afraid to acknowledge that he was composed of body, soul, and mind, and who faithfully recorded all the pitched battles, alarms, treaties, sieges, and fanfares of that extraordinary triangular warfare.

—Rupert Brooke, *John Donne*

Donne's life and career as courtier, poet, and churchman mirror the quality of his verse and his most celebrated technique, the conceit—in which, as Samuel Johnson explains, "the most heterogeneous ideas are yoked by violence together." The heterogeneous Donne's very identity seems spliced. He was a man in whom the earthly was joined with the spiritual, the profane with the sacred, the rake and sensualist with the religious man of faith and devotion. The range of his writing is no less varied and contrary. His *Songs and Sonets* is one of the finest collection of love lyrics in English literature; his *Holy Sonnets* represents some of the greatest spiritual poems ever written. In between these two poles, Donne wrote satires, elegies, epigrams, epithalamiums, controversial prose, and sermons. All feature a unique voice and display a lively mind that seemed to absorb everything around it, which Donne struggled to fashion into a meaningful whole.

John Donne's early life reveals the stages of a young man who aspired to make a name and career for himself in the Elizabethan court. His father was a successful London ironmonger. His family was Catholic, which would be an important factor in Donne's assault on secular success and his eventual religious career. In his early biography of the poet, Izaak Walton recorded that Donne "had his first breeding in his father's house, where a private Tutor had the care of him, until the tenth year of his age." He matriculated at Oxford and possibly at Cambridge, but as a Catholic could not receive a degree. It is thought that he traveled to Italy and Spain and was a military volunteer on the Essex expeditions to Cadiz in 1596 and to the Azores in 1597. After studying law at the Inns of Court, Donne had fulfilled all the standard requirements of a gentleman—university education, continental travel, military service, and legal training—to become a courtier. He was appointed as one of the secretaries of Sir Thomas Egerton, Lord Keeper of the Great Seal. He became a member of parliament and a landowner, securing gentry status, and his witty poetry, mostly circulated privately among his colleagues at the Inns of Court, marked him as an ambitious rising talent.

In 1601, however, Donne secretly married the 16-year-old niece of Lady Egerton, Ann More. The affair, viewed as a betrayal of his patron's confidence, was ruinous to Donne's hope for success at court, as he ruefully and succinctly wrote in a letter to his wife when he was dismissed from Sir Thomas Egerton's service: "John Donne, Ann Donne, Un-done." There followed a 14-year period of unsuccessful attempts to regain his lost opportunities while struggling to survive economically with an ever-growing family. Donne's writing during this period reflects the darkening of his possibilities and the tortuous struggle of conscience that eventually led to his leaving the Catholic Church and his ordination in the Church of England in 1615.

Critics have viewed Donne's transformation either as crass opportunism, in which he turned to the church for career advancement when the secular route was closed, or, as Izaak Walton claims, a conversion that rivaled that of St. Augustine. The truth is somewhere in between, and more complex than either position suggests. Donne's poetry points not to a radical break between Jack Donne, sensualist, and Dr. Donne, spiritualist, but to a more gradual development. His themes, which reflect a darker analysis of life's possibilities and a concern about death and ultimate meaning, are as much a product of age and maturity as his lack of prospects. Reading any of Donne's religious poems written during the period leading up to his Anglican conversion, it is difficult not to credit the sincerity of his deeply personal exploration and passionate engagement. Donne's Holy Sonnet XIV, one of his most famous poems, shows him redirecting the intense, sensual language of his love lyrics to a religious purpose:

> Batter my heart, three-personed God; for You
> As yet but knock, breathe, shine, and seek to mend;
> That I may rise and stand, o'erthrow me, and bend

Your force to break, blow, burn, and make me new.
I, like an usurped town, to another due,
Labor to admit You, but O, to no end;
Reason, Your viceroy in me, me should defend,
But is captured, and proves weak or untrue.
Yet dearly I love You, and would be loved fain,
But am betrothed unto Your enemy.
Divorce me, untie or break that knot again;
Take me to You, imprison me, for I,
Except You enthrall me, never shall be free,
Nor ever chaste, except You ravish me.

With his spiritual reservations resolved, Donne entered the final public phase of his life, which would include his duties as a rector and one of the most esteemed and powerful preachers of his time. With the support of James I, Donne was appointed dean of St. Paul's in 1621, a position he held until his death.

Donne was not a professional poet at any point in his career. He published little of his work, sharing it instead among his friends and with people who mattered in his advancement. At the time, to make one's living as a poet was not only difficult but also contrary to his aspiration to be considered a gentleman. Prior to his marriage, Donne's poems show him taking on the various roles of the Elizabethan wit and man of the world, and the expected poses of a talented young man anxious to display his skills in love and verse. "The Indifferent" captures Donne's witty vitality, in which nothing is sacred either in love or the poetic tradition:

I can love both fair and brown,
Her whom abundance melts, and her whom want betrays,
Her who loves loneness best, and her who masks and plays,
Her whom the country formed, and whom the town,
Her who believes, and her who tries,
Her who still weeps with spongy eyes,
And her who is dry cork, and never cries;
I can love her, and her, and you, and you,
I can love any, so she be not true.

Donne shows his mastery of a poetic voice informed by a colloquial style and an exuberance that seems to lift off the page. His display of wit for his sophisticated audience helps explain his use of elaborate and startling images and associations borrowed from folklore, science, geography, law, theology, and everyday life. In one of his wittiest seduction poems, "The Flea," Donne uses the occasion of a flea crawling on his beloved to justify their love with a logic that is both scholastic and devilish. His most famous conceit occurs in "A Valediction: Forbidding Mourning," in which he attempts to persuade his wife not to doubt his devotion to her in his absence, with references to metallurgy and an instrument of geography, the compass:

> Our two souls therefore, which are one,
>   Though I must go, endure not yet
> A breach, but an expansion,
>   Like gold to airy thinness beat.
>
> If they be two, they are two so
>   As stiff twin compasses are two;
> Thy soul, the fixed foot, makes no show
>   To move, but doth, if th' other do.
>
> And though it in the center sit,
>   Yet when the other far doth roam,
> It leans and hearkens after it,
>   And grows erect, as that comes home.
>
> Such wilt thou be to me, who must
>   Like th' other foot, obliquely run;
> Thy firmness makes my circle just,
>   And makes me end where I begun.

Until relatively recently, Donne's unconventional style kept him from being considered one of English literature's greatest poets. His irregularities of meter and unconventional blending of thought and feeling were seen as a liability. The 17th-century poet John Dryden complained that "he affects metaphysics, not only in his satires, but in his amorous verses where nature only should reign; and perplexes the minds of the fair sex with nice speculations of philosophy, when he should engage their hearts and entertain them with the softness of love." Dryden continues, "I may safely say it of this present age, that if we are not so great wits as Donne, yet certainly we are better poets."

Donne's stature rose considerably in the 20th century as readers grew to appreciate all of the elements Dryden disparaged. T. S. ELIOT [19] in particular helped Donne's reputation in one of his most famous pronouncements:

> Tennyson and Browning are poets, and they think; but they do not feel their thought as immediately as the odour of a rose. A thought to Donne was an experience; it modified his sensibility. When a poet's mind is perfectly equipped for its work, it is constantly amalgamating disparate

experience; the ordinary man's experience is chaotic, irregular, fragmentary. The latter falls in love, or reads Spinoza, and these two experiences have nothing to do with each other, or with the noise of the typewriter or the smell of cooking; in the mind of the poet these experiences are always forming new wholes.

Donne's reputation is now secure as one of English literature's greatest poets, the epitome of the poet whose range and method comprehend the widest examination of human experience.

ARISTOPHANES

34

c. 450–c. 385 B.C.

Like Aeschylus, Aristophanes rarely philosophizes, rarely explains: philosophy and explanation vibrate in the actions and words themselves. In both artists, the polished intellectuality and elegant pattern-making of Sophocles or Euripides are replaced by rawness, illogicality, feeling itself. Our interest focuses not so much on the forces at work on man as on man himself: protean, creative, unpredictable.

—Kenneth McLeish, *The Theatre of Aristophanes*

If Aristophanes did not invent comedy, he is its earliest skilled practitioner. His plays provide the only examples of Greek Old Comedy, the raucous, profane, and intellectually daring form that, along with poetic tragedy, was the great achievement of Attic drama during the fifth century B.C. In Aristophanes, comic drama finds its greatest progenitor and most influential proponent.

We know little of Aristophanes' life and personality, but a great deal about his times is reflected in his plays (11 of the 40 he wrote have survived). A native Athenian, Aristophanes was at the center of his city's life, a political and intellectual gadfly whose plays offer some of the best reflections of the period's controversies and preoccupations. It is said that when Dionysius, the tyrant of Syracuse, wanted to learn about the people and the institutions of Athens, Plato advised him to read the comedies of Aristophanes. He was born in the years when Pericles was initiating the reforms that created the golden age of

Athenian democracy, and he lived through the period of Athens's growth as an empire and as a center of intellectual and cultural achievement. Nine of his plays, however, concern the tragic consequences of the long Peloponnesian War with Sparta, which culminated in Athens's defeat and rapid decline. The last surviving great fifth-century B.C. playwright, Aristophanes with his death brought to an end a century of dramatic achievement. His final years were spent in a milieu hostile to the freewheeling, irreverent openness upon which his comedies depended. The Old Comedy of Aristophanes was to be replaced by the more realistic New Comedy of the fourth century—the narrower, less outrageous and fantastical, comedy of manners written by Menander, which, in the adaptations by the Romans Plautus and Terence, formed the main model for comic drama in Western literature. Aristophanes' comedy, however, should be regarded as far more significant than a dead end and a cultural curiosity. His genius, both as a poet and a playwright, contains the germs of comedy's greatest resources as a form. His plays offer a serious reflection of the world while encouraging our ability to laugh at its absurdity, excesses, and pretensions.

The origins of Greek comedy are as obscure as those of tragedy. Both spring from the communal and ritual celebration of the Greek god Dionysus. The Greek word *kômoidia*, from which the term comedy is derived, means the "song of a band of revelers," and the *komos* was a procession of revelers who sang and danced through town, often dressed as and impersonating animals, to celebrate nature and fertility. Their raucous performances, filled with obscenity, scatology, and the direct taunts to the onlookers, were designed to disrupt order and provide an emotional and sexual release. The *komos* formed the prototype of the comedy that Greek playwrights in the fifth century B.C. adapted into a chorus, with actors taking the parts of characters in a plot in which obstacles are surmounted, often in fantastical manner, to end with a celebration and affirmation.

The method and outcome of comedy are, therefore, the opposite of tragedy, which evokes pity and fear in a dramatization of a hero's limitations. In comedy, laughter comes from the breaking of boundaries, the shattering of illusions, and an emotionally satisfying transcendence over the ordinary or the preordained. While tragedy dealt with familiar mythological subjects and heroes, Attic comedy was original and based on the details of ordinary life, with characters as flawed and as recognizable as anyone in the audience. Issues of the day, such as politics, literature, and philosophy, were fair game. Aristophanes' comedies also make use of actual figures, such as Socrates, EURIPIDES [22], AESCHYLUS [27], and the Athenian political leader, Cleon. During a performance of *Clouds*, it is said that Socrates stood up in the audience to show how well done his likeness was on the mask of the actor who played him. In his heyday, Aristophanes had the freedom to take up seemingly any topic and treat it as outrageously as his inventive imagination could muster.

Aristophanes' comic targets included such sacred cows as Athenian democracy and the Athenian jury system. Both revered institutions and their representatives are exposed as falling short of the ideal. In *Knights*, two actual Athenian generals are made the slaves of an old man, and Cleon is bested and humiliated by an offal seller. Two adventurers in *Birds* create an alternative heavenly state that proves to be as imperialist and corrupt as the one they left behind on the ground. In *Wasps*, an uproarious plot in which a dog is put on trial for stealing a Sicilian cheese exposes the Athenians' litigiousness as corrupted by a desire for monetary gain, with justice sacrificed to self-interest. The philosophy of the Sophists and their principal advocate, Socrates, draws Aristophanes' fire in *Clouds*, and two of his other plays ridicule Euripides. In *Thesmophoriazusae*, Aristophanes arranges Euripides' ultimate escape from women who wish to punish him for giving them a bad name, but not before the playwright lampoons Euripides' personality, poetry, and philosophy. In *Frogs*, Dionysus goes down to Hades to fetch Euripides, who has just died, back to Athens to fill the poetic void he has left. There, Dionysus must judge between Euripides and Aeschylus in a contest to determine who should reign as the preeminent poet of the underworld. On every score Euripides is bested, as Aristophanes' farce underscores a serious debate on the worth of poetry and its place in Athenian life.

Almost all of Aristophanes' surviving plays were produced during the Peloponnesian War, which the playwright daringly condemns as unjust and morally reprehensible. In *Acharnians*, Dicaeopolis makes a separate peace with the Spartans and must get the better of a hard-line general whose patriotism is exposed as a destructive fraud. In *Peace*, the Goddess of Peace must be rescued from the pit in which she is imprisoned by Trygaeus, who ascends to heaven on a dung beetle. *Lysistrata* presents the provocative fantasy that the war can be stopped by the women on both sides, who agree to deny sex to the combatants until peace is secured.

Politics, philosophy, war and peace, the battle of the sexes, and the generational conflict between the old and the young provide Aristophanes with his subjects, which his wit and inventiveness shape into hilarious comedy. He has remained a rich comic source to be reworked and refashioned, and echoes of his style are readily found in the epic theater of BERTOLT BRECHT [73] and the intellectual high jinks of Tom Stoppard. If later comic drama is less exuberant and more dignified than Aristophanes' plays, the essential elements in his works—irreverence, celebration of human nature's foibles and multiplicity, and the exhilarating acts of liberation from repression and pretensions—established comedy's core values and strategies.

THOMAS MANN

35

1875–1955

Temperamentally unsuited to be either a martyr or a hero, he came close to playing a heroic role in keeping German culture alive after Germany had surrendered to the dark forces of Nazism and France had surrendered to Germany. "Thomas Mann is Europe," said Albert Guerard. . . . He was the last great European man of letters.

—Ronald Hayman, Thomas Mann

At the conclusion of Thomas Mann's 20th-century masterpiece *The Magic Mountain* (1925), Mann's protagonist Hans Castorp ends his seven years of isolation in a mountaintop tuberculosis sanatorium to commit himself to a world gripped by the destruction of the World War I. The story of his emotional and intellectual development has been told in the preceding chapters, many of which are devoted to the battle of worldviews represented by the humanist Settembrini and the cynical Naphta. Mann uses his sanatorium, with its international gathering of patients, as a microcosm to show Europe's spiritual disease. This far-ranging philosophical novel is constructed with such artistry that the characters and ideas are concretely realized, and every detail accrues a strong symbolic resonance. In *The Magic Mountain*, Mann develops his characteristic themes and favorite polarities—art and life, reason and feeling, self and society—which he sees as inherent in the human condition. The delicacy and subtlety of his ironic diagnosis of the human condition mark the novelist as one of the giants of modern literature.

Second only to GOETHE [10] among German writers, Thomas Mann spent much of his long, distinguished career attempting to play a responsible role as social critic and defender of humane values. Through the experiences of two world wars and the debacle of modern German history, Mann remained a chronicler of his time, an observer and participant in the spiritual and cultural crisis of Europe. Unlike other modernist artists, for whom art is the only solution, Mann remained ever conscious of the artist's dual potential to create and uncover significant patterns of experience on the one hand, and to falsify experience and drift into a decadent self-preoccupation on the other. His willingness to take on the widest and the deepest issues in his writing and public activity made him an international figure and one of the century's most respected thinkers. Yet the pervasive irony in his work reveals his uneasiness in such a role, an uneasiness born of the recognition that the pursuit of artistic form can lead one into an amoral realm.

Thomas Mann came from the pragmatic bourgeois background that he alternately celebrated and criticized. Born in the Baltic seaport of Lübeck in northern Germany, Mann was a member of a prominent merchant family in decline. His father was a grain dealer and head of the family firm; his mother, from a German-Brazilian family, provided Mann with his lifelong passion for music. After his father died, when Mann was 16, the firm was dissolved, and the family moved to Munich. There Mann attended the university, but did not earn a degree. He worked briefly in an insurance office while testing his calling as a writer. From 1896 to 1898 he lived in Italy with his brother Heinrich, also destined to become a noted writer. There he began his first major work, *Buddenbrooks* (1901). This massive work chronicles the history of the Buddenbrook clan over three generations. Clearly autobiographical, the novel invokes developments in 19th-century Germany as well as the larger theme of the decay of the bourgeois and the trials of the artistic consciousness. The novel sets forth the conflict that is characteristic of much of Mann's work in the opposing tendencies that hurtle his protagonists between intellect and passion, engagement and detachment, citizenship and art.

One of Mann's great strengths as a novelist and thinker is his ability to grant equal attention to both sides in this struggle, an even-handedness perhaps best expressed in his novella *Tonio Kröger* (1903), which expresses the need of the artist to acknowledge the equal claims of the imagination and the external world. The consequences for failing to do so form the theme in Mann's best-known work, *Death in Venice* (1912). In it the highly disciplined writer Gustav von Aschenbach succumbs to long-denied Dionysian forces when he becomes enamored of the youth, Tadzio. His personal decline reveals the power of the imagination either to create or to destroy, with Venice, at once voluptuous and deadly, as an emblem of Europe in decline. The strands of Mann's provocative and intellectually challenging story are woven with consummate skill, employing the characteristic leitmotiv technique he borrowed from Wagner's music: repeated image patterns that create meaning in multiple dimensions. With *Death in Venice*, as in other Mann works, ideas, images, and emotions are joined in a remarkable fusion with multiple reverberations.

When World War I broke out, Mann first embraced the German cause and defended his country's authoritarian nationalism. After Germany's defeat, amid the ensuing chaos and extremism of the postwar period, he became an outspoken proponent of democracy and, inevitably, an opponent of the Nazis. *The Magic Mountain*, which helped earn him the Nobel Prize in 1929, captures the antinomies with which he had been struggling—freedom versus authority, life versus death, love versus hate. When Hitler came to power, Mann went into exile in Switzerland and later the United States. Stripped of his German citizenship by the Nazis, he became an American citizen in 1944 and refused an invitation to return to Germany to live after the war.

In America, Mann completed the tetralogy *Joseph and His Brothers* (1933–45), a reinterpretation of the biblical story with contemporary thematic echoes. Joseph's exile reflects Mann's own experience with a world gone awry and his search for a meaningful response. Mann's last great masterpiece is *Doctor Faustus* (1947), the story of the composer Adrian Leverkühn, a modern Faust whose story reflects many of the experiences and attitudes of the philosopher Friedrich Nietzsche. The novel conveys Mann's searing analysis of Nazism, which, by means of an elaborate narrative construction, he links with the corruption of the artistic temperament in its drive to achieve mastery. Leverkühn, like Faust, enters into a pact with the devil in exchange for intensification of artistic experience. The devil's condition: "Thou shalt not love!" traps Leverkühn in an isolation from human concerns and involvement that Mann recognized as the tragic side of the artistic temperament, which needs distance and detachment to create form.

In all of his work, Mann exposed the tension within the traditions of Western culture. In the face of that culture's imminent collapse he sought to reassert the values in art and life that constituted culture's supreme achievement. His stature as a writer stems from his ability to capture, with exquisite irony, the conflicting forces in human behavior and thought that give life its fullest meaning and at the same time constitute its greatest peril. Only the very greatest writers, such as DOSTOEVSKY [14], TOLSTOY [4], and KAFKA [31], have taken their readers as far to ponder such essential questions of human nature and existence. Mann's legacy is the joining of thought and feeling to halt the drift toward nihilism and the reestablishment in the 20th century of the writer's role as the core interpreter of the world—in SHELLEY's [77] phrase, as the "unacknowledged legislator of the world." As Hans Castorp learns, the temptation of death and various forms of self-extinction are too inviting. Mann's achievement rests in his ability to assess the consequences and dramatize alternatives.

HENRIK IBSEN

36

1828–1906

The drama was born of old from the union of two desires: the desire to have a dance and the desire to hear story. The dance became a rant; the story became a situation. When Ibsen began to make plays, the art of the dramatist had shrunk into the art of contriving a situation. And it was held that the stranger the situation, the more interesting the play. Shakespear[e] had put ourselves on the stage but not our situations. . . . Ibsen supplies the want left by Shakespear[e]. He gives us not only ourselves, but ourselves in our situations. . . . his plays . . . are capable of both hurting us cruelly and of filling us with excited hope of escape from idealistic tyrannies, and with visions of intenser life in the future.
—George Bernard Shaw, *The Quintessence of Ibsenism*

It is a critical commonplace to assert that modern drama originates with Henrik Ibsen, even to mark the exact moment when the modern theater began: December 4, 1879, with the publication of Ibsen's *A Doll's House*. Although the complexity and many crosscurrents of modern drama make the idea of a single source difficult to support, it is incontestable that Ibsen set in motion a revolution on the stage as distinctive in the history of the theater as that in fifth-century B.C. Athens or Elizabethan London. Like SHAKESPEARE [1] and the great Athenian dramatists, Ibsen fundamentally redefined the drama and set a standard that later dramatists have had to absorb or challenge. The stage that he inherited had largely ceased to function as a serious medium. After

133

Ibsen, drama was restored as an important vehicle for a comprehensive criticism of life. The momentum that propelled his artistic revolt was sustained primarily from his outsider status, as an exile both at home and abroad. His last word was "*Tvertimod!*" (On the contrary!), which serves as a fitting epitaph and description of his artistic stance.

Born in Skien, Norway, a logging town southwest of Oslo, Ibsen endured a lonely and impoverished childhood, particularly after the bankruptcy of his businessman father when Ibsen was eight. At 15, he was sent to Grimstad as an apothecary's apprentice, where he lived for six years in an attic room on meager pay, sustained by romantic poetry, sagas, and folk ballads. He later recalled feeling "on a war footing with the little community where I felt I was being suppressed by my situation and by circumstances in general." His first play, *Cataline*, a historical drama featuring a revolutionary hero, reflects his own alienation. "*Cataline* was written," Ibsen later recalled, "in a little provincial town, where it was impossible for me to give expression to all that fermented in me except by mad, riotous pranks, which brought down upon me the ill will of all the respectable citizens who could not enter into that world which I was wrestling with alone."

Largely self-educated, Ibsen failed the university entrance examination to pursue medical training and instead set out for a career in the theater. In 1851, he began a 13-year apprenticeship in the theater in Bergen and Oslo, doing everything from sweeping the stage to directing, stage managing, and writing mostly verse dramas based on Norwegian legends and historical subjects. The experience gave him a solid knowledge of the stage conventions of the day, particularly of the so-called "well-made play" of Augustin Eugène Scribe and his French successors, with its emphasis on a complicated, artificial plot based on secrets, suspense, and surprises. Ibsen would transform the conventions of the "well-made play" into the problem play, exploring controversial social and human questions including women's rights, fanaticism, incest, and euthanasia. Although his stage experience in Norway was marked chiefly by failure, Ibsen's apprenticeship was an important period in which he perfected his craft and developed skills to mount the assault on theatrical conventions in his mature work.

In 1864, Ibsen began a self-imposed exile from Norway that would last for 27 years. He traveled first to Italy, where he was joined by his wife Susannah, whom he married in 1858, and his son, and the family divided their time between Italy and Germany. The experience was liberating for Ibsen; he felt he had "escaped from darkness into light," releasing the productive energy with which he composed the succession of plays that brought him worldwide fame. His first important works, *Brand* (1866) and *Peer Gynt* (1867), were poetic dramas in the romantic mode addressing the individual's conflict with experience and the gap between heroic assertion and accomplishment, between reality and blind idealism. *Pillars of Society* (1877) shows him experimenting with ways of exploring his diagnosis of the ills of modern life, the first of a series of realistic dramas that redefined the conventions and subjects of the modern theater. In such plays as *A Doll's House* (1879), *Ghosts* (1881), *The Wild Duck* (1884), *An Enemy of the People* (1886), *Rosmersholm* (1886), *The Lady from the Sea* (1888), and *Hedda Gabler* (1890), Ibsen replaced an idealistic vision of life as it should be with a realistic method in which the spectator is made to feel "as if he were actually sitting, listening, and looking at events happening in real life." The plays reworked artificial conventions of the stage to focus on ordinary individuals whose dramas were based on the details and circumstances of recognizable middle-class life in contemporary society.

A Doll's House explores the socially respectable, pampered wife Nora Helmer as she becomes aware of her isolation and repression in her cagelike home and eventually recognizes the entrapment of her marriage, in which her prosperity has been purchased by the denial of her true identity. Her liberation, in which she sacrifices her husband and her children for her duty to self, still has the ability to shock in its assault on conventional values; in 1879 its power must have been truly electrifying. Heralded as an early advocate of women's liberation, Ibsen, with characteristic contrariness, dismissed his contribution by suggesting that his play was concerned not with a women's theme but "a problem of mankind in general." *A Doll's House* provides a model for Ibsen's mature work, in which the problems of identity and self-definition are placed in the context of social customs and habits of thought and behavior that restrict and cripple the individual.

Increasingly, Ibsen's plays explored extreme character types whose dilemmas emerge in neurotic behavior, orchestrated by means of symbolism as a dramatic agent. In *The Wild Duck*, for example, the killing of the bird in the play comes to symbolize the escape from reality that makes Ibsen's thematic point, in dramatizing the disintegration of the Ekdal family, that only illusion, or the "life-lie," makes most existences bearable. His final four plays—*The Master Builder* (1892), *Little Eyolf* (1894), *John Gabriel Borkman* (1896), and *When We Dead Awaken* (1899)—study the insufficiency of the individual's will and imagination in a series of portraits of strong males whose misuse of others and their own great needs are dramatized through elements of dream and fantasy very different from Ibsen's earlier "slice of life" realism.

In Ibsen's tremendous artistic range he achieved a remarkable dramatic conception of human experience while establishing the foundation for modern drama in both its realism and symbolism. Although many of his plays begin with an examination of contemporary social issues, such as the narrowness of small-town life, the consuming force of commercialism, and the inadequacy of religious beliefs, they are rarely bound by these issues or restricted to a narrow social analysis. Instead, Ibsen's social depiction becomes an occasion for a deeper penetration, from symptoms to causes that reside in human nature itself. In Ibsen's fierce rejection of conventional patterns of behavior, which are shown as inadequate and limiting, he reveals a pioneering modern vision. "Ibsen was a true agonist," Ezra Pound declared, "struggling with very real problems. 'Life is a combat with the phantoms of the mind'—he was always in combat for himself and for the rest of mankind. More than any one man, it is he who has made us 'our world,' that is to say, 'our modernity.'"

ANTON CHEKHOV

37

1860–1904

An artist must pass judgment only on what he understands; his range is limited as that of any other specialist—what I keep repeating and insisting upon. Anyone who says that the artist's field is all answers and no questions has never done any writing or had any dealings with imagery. An artist observes, selects, guesses and synthesizes.
—Anton Chekhov in a letter to A. S. Suvorin, 1888

Of all the principal shapers of modern drama—IBSEN [36], SHAW [44], O'NEILL [59], BRECHT [73], and BECKETT [47]—Chekhov's reputation was the slowest to be recognized outside of his native country. He is Russia's greatest dramatist, who fundamentally changed the theater as a vehicle to express a particularly modern conception of human experience and social possibilities. As a writer, Chekhov achieved distinction not only in his work for the stage but also as one of the world's greatest short story writers, whose reshaping of narrative is a pioneering legacy for fiction in the 20th century. In both his plays and his stories, Chekhov rejected the standard arrangement of plot and presentation of character for a subtler method of rendering the conscious and unconscious forces resting beneath surface appearance. With characteristic modesty, Chekhov diminished his own achievement, except as an innovator. "Everything I have written," he remarked, "will be forgotten in five or ten years; but the paths I have cut out will be safe and sound—my only service lies in this."

Of all the considerable literary geniuses in 19th-century Russia, it was Chekhov whom Tolstoy [4] saw as his closest rival. "Chekhov is an incomparable artist," Tolstoy observed, "yes, yes: just incomparable. . . . An artist of life . . . Chekhov created new forms of writing, completely new, in my opinion, to the entire world, the like of which I have encountered nowhere. . . . And already it is impossible to compare Chekhov, as an artist, with earlier Russian writers—with Turgenev, with Dostoevsky, or with me. Chekhov has his own special form, like the impressionists."

Chekhov's development into a groundbreaking literary artist began in the Taganrog, a dreary southern Russian port on the Sea of Azov. His father was a former serf who rose to become a grocer but whose artistic interests as a choirmaster, violinist, and occasional painter kept him from practical considerations. When Chekhov was 16, his father became bankrupt and relocated his family to a Moscow slum to avoid his creditors. Chekhov remained behind to finish his education at the local gymnasium, supporting himself by tutoring younger students. When he was 19, Chekhov came to Moscow and assumed financial responsibility for his family while enrolled in the five-year medical program at Moscow University. He paid for his education by writing comic sketches and short stories for humorous magazines. When he became a doctor, in 1884, he continued writing stories and one-act satirical farces based on many of them, while torn between his medical career ("my lawful spouse") and writing ("my mistress"). During the years between 1885 and 1887 he published more than 300 stories and treated thousands of patients.

In 1888, Chekhov began to experiment with more serious literary forms. His long story "The Steppe" is an account of a journey through the Ukraine seen through the eyes of a child. The play *Ivanov* (1887) displays a new realism of characterization and depiction of the mood of the period. The experimental play *The Wood Demon* was rejected for production, which caused Chekhov to abandon the theater for seven years. Before resuming his theatrical work, he made an extended journey across Siberia to the Russian penal settlement on Sakhalin Island and participated in the relief programs during the famine of 1891 to 1892. On his return to Moscow, he bought the small Melikhovo estate, where he moved with his family and participated in local affairs while serving as a country doctor. There, in 1895, Chekhov wrote his second full-length play, *The Seagull*, which he described as "a comedy, three female parts, six male, four acts, landscape (view of a lake); lots of talk about literature, little action, five tons of love." The play consciously broke most of the stage conventions of the time: it located major action offstage, asserting an earlier Chekhovian ideal in which every character, or no character, is the protagonist, and employed fragmentary speech, gesture, and soliloquy to reach unconscious self-revelation. The first production in St. Petersburg in 1896 was a disaster, but its revival two years later as one of the first productions of the newly created Moscow Art Theater under the direction of Stanislavsky became a landmark in the history of the modern theater. So central was the play to the new method of acting and performance pioneered by the Moscow Art Theater that a stylized seagull became the company's logo.

In 1896, Chekhov experienced the first symptoms of tuberculosis, which necessitated his removal to Yalta on the Crimean coast. There he followed up the success of *The Seagull* with *Uncle Vanya* (1899), a reworking of his earlier *The Wood Demon; The Three Sisters* (1901); and his masterpiece, *The Cherry Orchard* (1904). Because of ill health, Chekhov was unable to attend the Moscow performances of either *The Seagull* or *Uncle Vanya*, but he had attended a rehearsal for *The Seagull* and fell in love with the actress, Olga Knipper, who played Nina. They were married in 1901 and had a happy life together, with Chekhov confined to Yalta and Olga in Moscow during the theatrical season. Chekhov attended the Moscow opening of *The Cherry Orchard*, the occasion for an emotional tribute to his contribution to the stage. He died six months later in the German resort town of Badenweiler.

Chekhov's art features an essential truthfulness and realism. "A play should be written," he argued, "in which people arrive, go away, have dinner, talk about the weather, and play cards. Life must be exactly as it is, and people as they are—not on stilts. . . . Let everything on the stage be just as complicated, and at the same time just as simple as it is in life." Underlying the surface realism is a consummate artistry that connects every stage element to the play's overall design. As Chekhov remarked to a young playwright in a famous piece of advice: "If a gun is hanging on the wall in the first act, it must be fired in the last."

Stripped of the usual narrative or dramatic action, Chekhov's stories and plays locate their interest in the gradual revelation of characters "in all the grayness of their everyday life." Major events occur offstage, and even the expected dramatic conflicts derived from dialogue focus on the inner voices of the characters, who do not so much communicate with one another as reveal themselves in isolation with the depth of their character often only suggested indirectly by gesture and nuance. At their core, Chekhov's plays reach a shattering tragic vision in an atmosphere of futility and stagnation. In his world, community and the fully-integrated personality move toward breakup and disintegration, with little evident consolation except the universal principles of love and work. In *The Cherry Orchard*, for example, Chekhov uses the fate of a Russian family's property to dramatize the passing of an era and the failure of the Russian gentry to maintain its values and responsibilities, exploring a powerful social theme while probing the human and psychological consequences of a society that has lost its way. Like THOMAS HARDY [43], Chekhov expresses a deeply pessimistic view stripped of comforting illusions. His always disturbing and often unbearable truths are sustained by the basic sanity of his vision, without reliance on ideological or political solutions to reduce the essential elements of life to a simplistic formula.

HENRY JAMES

38

1843–1916

In Heaven there'll be no algebra,
No learning dates and names,
But only playing golden harps
And reading Henry James.

      —Anonymous, quoted in Edward Stone, *The Battle and the Books:*
Some Aspects of Henry James

In the magisterial hands of Henry James, the novel reached a level of refinement as an instrument of truth unimagined when he was born. The expansive novels of DICKENS [6] and TOLSTOY [4], in James's famous dismissal, "loose, baggy monsters," find a shape and sophistication in James that raise the novelist's art to an ultimate psychological and moral complexity and formal expressiveness. Demanding in his writing style, James challenges his readers to reach his level of sensibility, with the attendant pleasure of seeing the world at its most complex and nuanced. Few other writers have played so great a role in establishing the art of the novel or the role of the novelist as artist. An American by birth, James was international in temperament. By absorbing the lessons of his masters—BALZAC [40], Turgenev, and FLAUBERT [30]—he brought the European novel into the mainstream of English fiction. In the role of the clinical observer of life, borrowed from the naturalists such as ZOLA

[65], James sifted his observations into increasingly convoluted structures. In his psychological and symbolic expressiveness, he anticipated the main current of modern fiction that shaped the writing of JOSEPH CONRAD [55], D. H. LAWRENCE [57], Ford Madox Ford, Edith Wharton, JAMES JOYCE [7], VIRGINIA WOOLF [48], WILLIAM FAULKNER [15], and others. Few novelists who followed Henry James have been able to ignore his technical accomplishments or the standard he set in fiction.

James's father was a wealthy philosopher and Swedenborgian theologian, a friend of Ralph Waldo Emerson and Thomas Carlyle, who raised Henry and his brother William, the future philosopher, with the widest possible exposure to civilization and culture. He also helped foster a basic rootlessness in both of them. Born in New York City, James was taken abroad before he could speak, and later returned to Europe for a three-year educational experiment in Geneva, London, Paris, and Boulogne. In America, the James family divided their time between New York, Albany, and Newport, Rhode Island. James's only exposure to conventional education was his matriculation at the age of 19 at Harvard Law School. An injury prevented him from participating in the American Civil War, and he embarked on a career as a writer, publishing stories, sketches, and critical reviews before departing in 1869 for Europe, where he would reside, except for occasional visits to America, until his death. Although he made his home in England, Paris and Italy were important in his development. In Paris he met Turgenev and Flaubert, from whom he learned the art of the novel. In Italy he found a rich source of themes, particularly the claims of the past on the emotions, and a setting for many of his stories and novels. James, who never married, sacrificed intimacy to the exacting demands of his art, and he set out quite consciously to interpose his vision of form and order in his books as an alternative to the chaos of life.

James's long and varied career can be organized into phases. The first climaxes with his great masterpiece *The Portrait of a Lady* (1881). His other important books of this early period include *Roderick Hudson* (1876), *The American* (1877), and *Daisy Miller* (1879). All demonstrate his characteristic theme of the confrontation between Americans and the subtle and often corrupting influence of European society and conventions. For James, American life was too unformed, without a past or precedent; it lacked the clear lines of European culture and hierarchy desirable to a novelist interested in the intricate drama of manners. By transporting the vitality and unshaped moral earnestness of his Americans to Europe, where his protagonists mature through exposure to European conventions, James found the ideal source for his moral exploration of personal and social values. The works of his early career are accomplished comedies of manners that brought him his greatest popular successes. He would steadily lose his audience as he developed a more mannered and increasingly complex technique to capture the moral dramas that fascinated him.

James's second phase was a period of experimentation and failed attempts to succeed as a dramatist. The experience led to the creative fulfillment that produced *The Aspern Papers* (1888), *The Turn of the Screw* (1898), and his three greatest novels, *The Wings of the Dove* (1902), *The Ambassadors* (1903), and *The Golden Bowl* (1904). In these three books in particular the lineaments of the "James novel" are most evident. To create the proper illusion of the novel's truth-telling, James eliminates the omniscient, intrusive author's viewpoint and filters the story through the consciousness of one or more of his characters. Though very little seems to happen in James's novels, which are stripped of most artificial plot devices, dramatic action occurs in speech and gesture that the reader, instructed in nuance by the observing narrative consciousness, gradually detects with greater clarity. What is revealed is a subtle moral drama that pits opposing notions of the world and human possibilities against one another. *The Ambassadors* is perhaps the best example of James's characteristic theme and formal technique. In the story, Lambert Strether is sent to retrieve from Paris the expatriate son of a New England widow who fears his corruption. The trip is intended to rescue him from European influence, but Strether instead is liberated by his contact with a richer, cultivated world and changes places with the widow's son. Strether's previous sense of his life is unalterably changed, and because his shift of perception is brilliantly described from his vantage point, the reader reaches a similar heightening of vision. The confrontation of Americans with Europe remains central, but in James's later novels this confrontation evokes a deeper, more fundamental moral and psychological exploration, as well as a social one.

James's final phase began with his first trip to America in 20 years. His negative assessment is *The American Scene* (1907) which laments "the large and noble sanities that I see around are" converted to "crudities, to invalidities, hideous and unashamed." During this phase James also produced several volumes of memoirs, critical introductions to his novels, and two unfinished experimental novels, *The Ivory Tower* and *The Sense of the Past*. By his end, James had become an acknowledged, if under-read, fictional master whose true literary apotheosis occurred only after his death. Recognized for his artistic integrity and determination, James also was criticized for writing "more and more about less and less," of excluding too much of life and human experience from his novels. In this view James is too detached, too refined to deal with life directly, offering instead the cool perfection of his form and good taste rather than any appetite. E. M. FORSTER [121] echoes this perspective by observing that "many readers cannot get interested in James, although they can follow what he says (his difficulty has been much exaggerated), and can appreciate his effects. They cannot grant his premise, which is that most of human life has to disappear before he can do us a novel." Ezra Pound, however, provides an opposite interpretation: "When he died one felt there was no one to ask about anything. Up to then one felt someone knew."

   With the outbreak of World War I and the destruction of culture that his books had forewarned, James, in the year before his death, in solidarity with the British war effort and in despair over America's refusal to join it, became a British subject. Over a remarkable career, Henry James impresses with the quantity as well as the quality of his achievement as the novel's great practitioner and theoretician.

WALT WHITMAN

39

1819–1892

He was the poet of the self's motion downwards into the abysses of darkness and guilt and pain and isolation, upwards to the creative act in which darkness was transmuted into beauty. When the self became lost to the world, Whitman was lost for poetry. But before that happened, Whitman had, in his own example, made poetry possible in America.
                    —R. W. B. Lewis, "Walt Whitman" in *Major Writers of America*

When Walt Whitman's *Leaves of Grass* appeared in 1855, it signaled a poetic revolution with a new native voice as fresh and daring as the young country. The persona he created to embody a distinctive American voice is as brash and oversized as the nation. Truly American poetry that is not derivative of European models begins with Whitman. To express a nation, Whitman created an open and flexible poetic form and broadened poetry's subject to include the common life and sexuality, which have been some of the greatest influences in shaping poetry in the 20th century. Ezra Pound, whose own rallying cry to "make it new" echoes Whitman, grudgingly acknowledged the other's greatness:

> He *is* America. His crudity is an exceeding great stench, but it is America. He is the hollow place in the rock that echoes with his time. He *does* "chant the crucial stage" and he is the "voice triumphant." He is

disgusting. He is an exceedingly nauseating pill, but he accomplishes his mission. . . . He is content to be what he is, and he is his time and his people.

Complex, contradictory, possessed of a boundless ego coupled with a limitless capacity to enter the world around him imaginatively, Whitman insisted on being regarded as the American epic poet, who recorded, in his own words, an "aggregated, inseparable, unprecedented, vast, composite, electric *Democratic Nationality*."

Whitman's background provided the ideal preparation for his eventual calling to memorialize the American experience. He was born on Long Island, New York. His father was a farmer and carpenter who moved his family to nearby Brooklyn, then a small city, when Walt was not quite five. Whitman's youth, therefore, embraced both the city and the country, rural and urban life. He left school when he was 11 to work as an office boy before becoming an apprentice to a printer. By the age of 17, he was a compositor, and also worked occasionally as a country schoolmaster. Printing work led to journalism, and Whitman, until the age of 31, held a number of positions as a reporter, editorial writer, and editor on New York newspapers, serving as the editor of Brooklyn's *Daily Eagle* from 1846 to 1848. A fervent free-soil Democrat, Whitman lost his job in a dispute over the paper's politics and embarked on a three-month trip to New Orleans. During this period, Whitman, discouraged by America's involvement in war with Mexico and the widening division between free and slave states, began to conceive of a great poetic work to celebrate the ideals of American democracy and the American experience. He also began to assume the physical persona of the American bard and prophet he desired to become, growing a full beard and wearing workingman's clothes.

Leaves of Grass, which he published himself, broke all the rules of poetry in form and content. Whitman abandoned traditional meter for a rhythmical free verse, as flexible as the spoken voice and structured by parallelism, repetition, association, and imagery. Its center was a protean sensibility that refracted and absorbed teeming American life, as he writes in "Song of Myself":

> The blab of the pave, the tires of carts, sluff of boot-soles, talk of the
>   promenaders,
> The heavy omnibus, the driver with his interrogating thumb, the
>   clank of the shod horses on the granite floor,
> The snow-sleighs, clinking, shouted jokes, pelts of snow-balls,
> The hurrahs of popular favorites, the fury of rous'd mobs,
> The flap of the curtain'd litter, a sick man inside borne to the hospital,
> The meeting of enemies, the sudden oath, the blows and fall,
> The excited crowd, the policeman with his star quickly working his
>   passage to the centre of the crowd,

The impassive stones that receive and return so many echoes,
What groans of over-fed or half-starv'd who fall sunstruck or in fits,
What exclamations of women taken suddenly who hurry home and
     give birth to babes,
What living and buried speech is always vibrating here, what howls
     restrain'd by decorum,
Arrests of criminals, slights, adulterous offers made,
     acceptances, rejections with convex lips,
I mind them or the show or resonance of them—I come and I depart.

Whitman's unconventional form, unpoetic subject, and overt sensuality insured hostile critical reaction and popular neglect. Yet *Leaves of Grass* was embraced and appreciated by such figures as Henry David Thoreau and Ralph Waldo Emerson, who wrote Whitman the famous message: "I greet you at the beginning of a great career."

For the rest of his life Whitman expanded and revised the poems of *Leaves of Grass* (there were nine subsequent editions) into a single all-encompassing poetic sequence, incorporating his early optimism at America's democratic prospects with the increasing tragic tone from his experiences in the Civil War. When he learned his brother had been wounded, he left for the war front. Although his brother's injuries were not severe, Whitman stayed on in Washington, volunteering as a nurse in military hospitals. After the war, Whitman worked in government offices before suffering a paralyzing stroke that required him to live the rest of his life at his brother's home in Camden, New Jersey. He was able to give occasional readings and lectures, receive admirers—who regarded him as a prophet, seer, and "the good, gray poet"—and even manage a long-anticipated transcontinental journey west as far as Nevada. He died after overseeing the final edition of *Leaves of Grass*.

Whitman's remarkable poetic achievement rests both in the excellence of individual lyrics, such as "Song of Myself," "Crossing Brooklyn Ferry," "When Lilacs Last in the Dooryard Bloom'd," and "Out of the Cradle Endlessly Rocking," and the overall symphonic arrangement of lyrical parts to form a vast, single epic poem. He redefined the form and the method of the traditional epic so that it became a narrative not of the exploits of a traditional hero, but instead of a heroic sensibility uncovering meaning and value closest to hand, which Whitman saw embedded in the American experience. That experience, filled with both vitality and promise, and incorporating America's central tragedy of the Civil War, is Whitman's particular subject. The poetic possibility of the American experience would become a major resource for later poets, such as Hart Crane in *The Bridge* and William Carlos Williams in *Paterson*. As Williams observed in *Leaves of Grass One Hundred Years After* (1955):

Leaves of Grass! It was a good title for a book of poems, especially for a new book of American poems. It was a challenge to the entire concept of the poetic idea, and from a new viewpoint, a rebel viewpoint, an American viewpoint. In a word and at the beginning it enunciated a shocking truth, that the common ground is of itself a poetic source. There had been inklings before this that such was the case in the works of Robert Burns and the poet Wordsworth, but in this instance the very forms of the writing had been altered: it had gone over to the style of the words as they appeared on the page. Whitman's so-called "free verse" was an assault on the very citadel of the poem itself; it constituted a direct challenge to all living poets to show cause why they should not do likewise. It is a challenge that still holds good after a century of vigorous life during which it has been practically continuously under fire but never defeated.

Whitman's courage and vision created a new epoch for poetry. He placed the poet at the center of an expansive, contradictory world and challenged the imagination to capture experience in a fresh and muscular poetic language. Finally, as with all great poets, Whitman is irreducible and boundlessly suggestive, as the closing lines of "Song of Myself" reflect:

> I too am not a bit tamed. I too am untranslatable,
> I sound my barbaric yawp over the roofs of the world.
>
> The last scud of day holds back for me,
> It flings my likeness after the rest and true as any on the shadow'd
>   wilds,
> It coaxes me to the vapor and the dusk.
>
> I depart as air, I shake my white locks at the runaway sun,
> I effuse my flesh in eddies, and drift it in lacy jags.
>
> I bequeath myself to the dirt to grow from the grass I love,
> If you want me again look for me under your boot-soles.
>
> You will hardly know who I am or what I mean,
> But I shall be good health to you nevertheless,
> And filter and fibre your blood.
>
> Failing to fetch me at first keep encouraged,
> Missing me one place search another,
> I stop somewhere waiting for you.

HONORÉ DE BALZAC

40

1799–1850

Quantity and intensity are at once and together his sign.

—Henry James, *The Lesson of Balzac*

Known as the father of the modern novel, Balzac provides the foremost example of the novelist who attempts to comprehend everything in his fiction. Compared to the direction in much modern fiction toward the narrow intensity of private experience, Balzac extends the novel outward to embrace imaginatively all that surrounded him in a feat of creativity as prodigious and gargantuan as his own oversized lifestyle and appetites. From his first novel, written under his own name and published in 1829, to his death 21 years later, Balzac published nearly 100 novels and collections of tales, filling more than 40 volumes and describing more than 2,000 characters. No novelist wrote as many good novels as Balzac. If his frenetic pace, shortcomings of literary style, and tendency toward melodrama and moralizing deny him admission to the highest rank of the world's greatest novelists, his amazing example of what the novel and the novelist could do to capture human and social experience in all its complexity, along with the force, variety, and vitality of his writing, make him one of the most influential figures in fiction's history.

Balzac was born in Tours in the last month of the Directorate and lived through Napoleon's rise and fall, the Restoration, the July Revolution of

1830, and the violent revolution of 1848. He experienced some of the most important years of French history, which would see the emergence of modern urban society and the triumph of the middle class, whose values and customs Balzac would be the first to chronicle in depth. Friedrich Engels remarked, "I have learned more [from Balzac] than from all the professional historians, economists and statisticians put together." Inspired by the example of WALTER SCOTT [87], who turned the novel toward history, Balzac discovered the panorama of the present as history.

Balzac's father rose from a peasant background to respectability as a civil servant during the tumult of the French Revolution and Napoleon's empire. Balzac added the aristocratic preposition "de" to his name, a gesture designed to reflect his family's aspirations. He was a poor student but a prodigious reader, gifted with a phenomenal memory. When his family moved to Paris in 1814, Balzac studied law and worked in a law office for three years before embarking on a career as a writer. His first literary effort was a tragedy, *Cromwell*, modeled on the French playwright Corneille. After reading it to his bored family and receiving negative criticism from a literary expert to whom the play was shown, the ever-resilient Balzac declared, "All it does is to show I am not good at writing tragedies." He turned to the novel, and during the 1820s wrote and collaborated on a series of trashy potboilers, imitative of English gothic thrillers, historical novels, novels of terror, and supernatural fantasies, while churning out popular articles. He failed in the publishing and printing businesses, though his experience, or lack thereof, with the world of finance would be mined productively in his later novels. Balzac was one of the first novelists to diagnose the money ethic of his society, in which the pursuit of fortune had replaced religion or a moral code as the key adhesive of the social system.

In 1829, Balzac published his first books under his own name and began the massive work that would become *The Human Comedy*. He achieved fame and success through his iron will and self-discipline, writing continually, despite overindulgence in food, possessions, and passionate liaisons. His writing method, which he retained throughout his career, was to go to bed around eight in the evening and rise at midnight, put on a monk's robe of white cashmere belted by a gold chain, and begin his daily labors. He wrote until dawn, sustained by numerous cups of coffee (it is estimated that during his lifetime he drank some 50,000 cups). After resting for an hour in a hot bath, he began revising printer's proofs. Despite his amazing fecundity and invention (it has been said that he could write as fast as he could talk), he was a notorious reviser who preferred the expensive method of laboriously rewriting and recasting his novels from printer's proofs. After a light lunch, he returned to his revising and letter writing until five, followed by visits with friends, dinner, and bed, when the cycle would be repeated.

Balzac's regimen bespeaks a boundless creative imagination and an obsessive drive to capture his entire world in his fiction. In 1833, Balzac revealed to his sister his ambitious plan for *The Human Comedy* by announcing, "I am about to become a genius." He imagined a sequence of novels in which he later summarized, "I have undertaken the history of a whole society. I have often described my plan in this one sentence: 'A generation is a drama with four or five thousand outstanding characters.' That drama is my book." In his massive undertaking his novels, first called *Studies of Manners* (*Études des Moeurs*) and later renamed *The Human Comedy* to contrast with DANTE's [2] *Divine Comedy*, would collectively form a structure that Balzac called his Madeleine, after the Paris church then under construction:

> They will portray all aspects of society, so that not a single situation of life, not a face, not the characters of any man or woman, not a way of life, not a profession, not a social group, will be missing. Not an aspect of childhood, maturity, old age, politics, justice, war, will be left out. On this foundation I shall examine every thread of the human heart, every social factor and it will be real.
>
> On the second storey I shall place the philosophical stories, for after portraying effects, I shall deal with what has caused them. . . . Finally I shall turn to an analysis of principles. . . . *Les Moeurs* are the play, the causes go behind the scenes and the principle—he's the novelist him- self. . . . The whole will be an *Arabian Nights* of the West.

Nothing so grand or comprehensive had ever been attempted in any art form. Balzac planned to redefine the scope and the structure of the novel so that individual books would become chapters in an ever-expanding fictional universe connected by his diagnoses of human experience and society. Charac- ters would be studied at various stages of their careers; secondary characters or those merely passing through one book would dominate the action in another. The effect and Balzac's achievement in *The Human Comedy* is a study of his society and his times that is both wide and deep. For Balzac, the center of his colossal panorama was Paris, which he called "mud studded with diamonds." He was one of the first novelists to examine comprehensively the effects of the modern city and the ways in which the various classes connected. His canvas stretched from the salons of the aristocrats to the world of the parvenu, from the financiers of the Bourse, tradesmen, merchants, craftsmen, and artisans, to the substrata of the criminals and the demimonde. The world of Paris that Balzac minutely detailed both in its external features and its internal attitudes and preoccupation extended outward as well, into the provinces, where greed, delusion, virtue, and vice also resided.

In all of his novels, particularly in his masterpieces—*Louis Lambert* (1832), *Eugénie Grandet* (1833), *The Quest of the Absolute* (1834), *Père Goriot* (1835), *Lost Illusions* (1837), *César Birotteau* (1837), *Cousin Bette* (1847), and *Cousin Pons* (1847)—Balzac shows the rare ability to identify with his characters and their milieu, bringing both to vivid life. BAUDELAIRE [46] praised Balzac's "prodigious taste for detail," and Balzac's documentation of the particular solidly roots his characters and their stories in everyday life. The stories, if lacking the introspection of other novelists and veering toward the bold coloring of melodrama, nonetheless grip readers as few writers have done, in a sympathetic understanding of personality and motive.

The Human Comedy eventually reached 40 volumes although Balzac failed to complete his grand scheme, which called for 144 studies in all. It is no exaggeration to say that he wrote himself to death. His final accomplishment, besides the individual successes of the parts of his monumental design, rests in the daring of his vision and his creating in the novel a massive criticism of life.

JONATHAN SWIFT

1667–1745

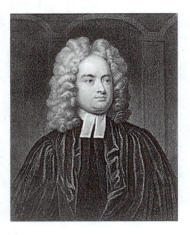

*Swift was anima Rabelaisii habitans in sicco—the soul of Rabelais dwelling in a
dry place.*

—Samuel Taylor Coleridge, *Table Talk*

Few writers have so haunted the imagination as Jonathan Swift. His life and
work continue to disturb, and have resisted reduction to simple and comfortable formulation. Is he the great sanity principle of his age, or a madman
whose so-called excremental vision and lacerating satire distort rather than
illuminate? Swift has maintained his status as one of literature's most paradoxical and controversial figures, the power of whose satire continues to find
its target. How else to explain the intemperate tone of WILLIAM THACKERAY
[94], himself accustomed to exposing the weaknesses to which humankind is
prey, in his rejection of the fourth book of *Gulliver's Travels*, urging his audience not to read this "monster gibbering shrieks and gnashing imprecations
against mankind—tearing down all shreds of modesty, past all sense of manli-
ness and shame; filthy in word, filthy in thought, furious, raging, obscene." In
an age of optimism, Swift provided a darker vision, opposed to the notion of
civilization's progress and man's perfectibility. In an age of great satire, Swift's
was its most remarkable satirical voice, offering disturbing truths with wit and
inventiveness that delight even as they sting.

Despite the radical force of Swift's satire, it is important not to view him divorced from his era, as later generations have done, or as a Jeremiah whose distorted vision can only be explained by madness. Swift's age, which followed the turbulence of the 17th century, was fundamentally conservative, valuing order and control, concerned with stability and harnessing the energies released by the Elizabethans. In this context, Swift represents his age through his concern with man as a social and reasonable creature, and as a classicist in the debate between ancient restraint and modern self-expression. One of the greatest prose stylists in English, Swift defines good style as "proper words in proper places," which suggests his allegiance to clarity and simplicity, the predominant literary tastes of his day. His political journalism put him at the center of England's shifting political battles between the Whigs and the Tories over the power of Parliament and the crown, and Swift allied himself first with the former and then the latter.

Clearly a product of his age's attitudes and concerns, Swift nonetheless is most accurately seen not in his conformity but in his dissent. His voice of opposition to the prevailing mood of his time is explained in part by his outsider status. Born in Ireland of English parents, he was in a way a man without a country: too Irish for success in England, too English to be happy in Ireland. His conflicts with his era have a strong basis in personal and professional disappointments. Both helped to produce the reevaluation of the age's fundamental values that shaped his work.

After schooling at Trinity College, Dublin, Swift went to England in 1689 as the secretary to Sir William Temple, a retired diplomat. After receiving his master's degree from Oxford in 1692, he reluctantly decided on a career in the church and was ordained in 1695. At about the same time, he began his career as a political journalist and satirist. In 1704, Swift published his first important books. *A Tale of a Tub*, addresses religious and scientific corruption. *The Battle of the Books*, a mock epic on the conflict between classical and modern literary forms, compares the moderns to spiders and the ancients to bees, whose production of honey and wax is a source of sweetness and light.

Swift eventually shifted his political stance away from the Whigs' opposition to the power of the church and the crown to become one of the greatest Tory apologists, from whom he expected advancement to an English bishopric. Instead, he was appointed dean of St. Patrick's Cathedral in Ireland in 1713. A year later, on the death of Queen Anne and the rise of the Whigs, Swift's hopes for English preferment ended, and he remained, except for two brief visits to England, as he described it, in "wretched Dublin in miserable Ireland" for the rest of his life. He was an effective ecclesiastical administrator, and with the publication of *The Drapier's Letters* (1724) he became a champion of Irish freedom against English neglect and oppression. His most famous satiric attack on the Irish question is "A Modest Proposal" (1729), which offers, with the calculating logic of the social scientist, the conversion of Irish children into a ready food source as the solution to Irish overpopulation and misery.

In 1726, at the age of 59, Swift published his satiric masterpiece, *Gulliver's Travels*, anonymously. The tale, framed by the appeal of voyages to exotic and unknown lands, is remarkable in its imaginative inventiveness and clarity, and has remained a perennial children's classic. As Maynard Mack has argued, however, its relegation "to the nursery can be explained in part by the fact that most adults are unwilling to face the truth about themselves." *Gulliver's Travels* is, in short, one of the most devastating assaults on human pretenses and pride ever written. Swift summarizes his strategies as follows:

> The chief end of all my labors is to vex the world rather than divert it. . . . I have ever hated all nations, professions, and communities, and all my love is toward individuals. . . . I hate and detest the animal called man, although I heartily love John, Peter, Thomas, and so forth. . . . I have got materials towards a treatise proving the falsity of that definition *animal rationale*, and to show it should only be *rationis capax*. Upon this great foundation of misanthropy . . . the whole building of my *Travels* is erected.

Swift's imaginative treatise begins with the rather simple process of altering the perspectives with which we normally see the world. By creating the imaginary kingdom of Lilliput at one-twelfth the scale of our world, Swift is able to point out our own pettiness and triviality as we begin to see ourselves reflected in the absurd pretensions of the miniature Lilliputians. Government service is determined by how well the ministers jump over a stick and walk a tightrope; religious warfare is generated by which end of an egg to break. By Swift's implied comparison, our world is gradually shrunk to Lilliput's size in the resemblances we are meant to notice. Gulliver begins to see pride as a great defect, the source of political and religious corruption, and as we leave we are meant to ask how much of Lilliput is to be found in our full-scale world.

In Gulliver's second voyage to Brobdingnag he finds himself a Lilliputian in comparison to the giant Brobdingnagians. Our pettiness and pretensions are now made explicit, as Gulliver finds the giants enlightened and morally as well as physically great. He tries to rival them by bragging about the great benefits and superior customs of the English and mankind. After learning English history, the Brobdingnagians are not impressed and conclude that the English must be "the most pernicious race of little vermin that nature ever suffered to crawl upon the surface of the earth."

By Gulliver's fourth voyage, he faces the ultimate lesson and Swift's final crushing indictment. Up to this point, by combining wit, fantasy, and satire, Swift makes us laugh even while lashing us. The satire of the earlier voyages deals with human flaws and defects of man's actions; with the fourth voyage Swift targets human nature itself. Instead of altering the proportions, Swift splits human nature in two. Man's unrestrained and selfish appetites are characteristics of the brutish Yahoos, while man's rationality is the exclusive province of the horselike Houyhnhnms. Gulliver comes to see himself as a Yahoo and is expelled from the seemingly benign but ultimately limited Houyhnhnm world of pure reason. On his return home, Gulliver is disgusted by the Yahoo-like world he inhabits and tries to become a horse. He has missed Swift's point, but the reader should not: Man is neither a Yahoo nor a Houyhnhnm but combines the qualities of both. He is neither pure appetite nor pure reason, but capable of reason and thus able to transcend the pride and flaws that Swift's satire exposes.

The final words on Swifts remarkable career and vision should best be his, from "Verses on the Death of Dr. Swift":

> Perhaps I may allow the Dean
> Had too much satire in his vein,
> And seemed determined not to starve it,
> Because no age could more deserve it.
> Yet malice never was his aim;
> He lashed the vice but spared the name;
> No individual could resent,
> Where thousands equally were meant;
> His satire points at no defect,
> But what all mortals may correct . . .

STENDHAL

1783–1842

Stendhal is above all a psychologist. M. Taine accurately defined the scope of his work when he said that Beyle was exclusively interested in the life of the soul. . . . In sum Stendhal is the one true link in the chain which connects the novel of today with the novel of the eighteenth century. . . . Like Balzac he is a father to all of us, he brought the art of analysis to the novel.

—Émile Zola, *Naturalist Novelists*

Among the many contenders to the title of originator of the modern novel, including BALZAC [40], GEORGE ELIOT [21], and FLAUBERT [30], Stendhal's claim for consideration is one of the strongest. Although his novels are at places marred by romantic excess and melodramatic effects, it is his tone and overall style that appear so modern. Before Stendhal, the novel rarely possessed his degree of psychological realism and penetration. He presents a world that is socially fragmented and at odds with his heroes, who are self-willed and self-defined outsiders and who typify the modern condition. His influence is evident in the works of TOLSTOY [4], who claimed Stendhal was the novelist who affected him the most, DOSTOEVSKY [14], and CAMUS [99]. Stendhal began the process of turning the novel inward toward an intimate presentation of private consciousness.

Stendhal's originality as a novelist is traceable to his nonconformity and provocative nature. Born Marie-Henri Beyle to a father he loathed in provincial Grenoble, whose bourgeois character and royalist sympathies he despised, Stendhal lived through the French Revolution, Napoleon's rise and fall, and the Restoration, with the turmoil of each era as a constant in his formation and development. Desiring to obliterate his bourgeois background, he was determined to be regarded as aristocratic and Parisian, though he grew to find both corrupt and shallow. Though a Frenchman, Stendhal later saw himself as an Italian and asked that his tombstone should read "Arrigo Beyle, Milanese." In Stendhal's biography there is a sense of constant restlessness and movement, shifting and almost always disappointing relationships, and a permanent outsider status. He resembles nothing so much as a party of one in perpetual opposition.

After studies in Grenoble, Stendhal arrived in Paris at his earliest opportunity, and through a relative secured an army commission that took him for the first time to Italy during Napoleon's campaign there. Shortly after resigning his commission, Stendhal returned to Paris convinced that his destiny was not as a military hero, like Napoleon, whom he admired, but in literature. "What is my aim?" he wrote in 1803. "To be the greatest poet possible. For this I must know man perfectly." While completing his study, Stendhal, again through his family connections, served in a series of administrative posts in the army and the civil service in Germany, Austria, and, during Napoleon's campaign, in Russia, where he participated in the disastrous retreat from Moscow.

After Napoleon's fall, Stendhal settled until 1820 mainly in Milan, where he began his literary career, publishing *Lives of Haydn, Mozart and Métastase* (1815), *History of Painting in Italy*, and *Rome, Naples, and Florence* (1817). He found an interested audience for his works in England, where he visited on several occasions, publishing social commentary there. Other notable early writings include *De l'amour* (1822), a psychological analysis of love, and *Racine and Shakespeare* (1825). In the latter work Stendhal joined the debate between classicism and romanticism, which he framed as the contrast between Racine's [62] adherence to neoclassical forms and the unbounded imagination of Shakespeare [1]. Characteristically, he championed Shakespeare and the freedom and liberation of the romantics, but resisted any affiliation with the movement, particularly out of his dislike for Victor Hugo [105]. Stendhal came to the novel late after writing criticism and biography. He published his first novel, *Armance*, in 1822, a failure in which most critics were unable to recognize his daring if ineffective psychological character study implying that the novel's tragedy was the result of the protagonist's impotence.

With the accession of Louis Philippe in 1830, Stendhal secured an appointment as consul to Trieste but was forced to shift to the consulship of Civitavecchia, outside Rome, when Metternich objected to his books and

liberal attitudes. Also that year Stendhal published the first of his two masterpieces, *The Red and the Black. The Charterhouse of Parma* followed in 1839.
During the 1830s, Stendhal wrote constantly, producing two autobiographical studies and an unfinished novel, *Lucien Leuwen*, which were all published
posthumously. Perhaps no writer has left so much documentation about his
daily life and thoughts recorded in extensive journals and correspondence, yet
still no writer seems as enigmatic as Stendhal, justifying a description of him
as a "displaced man." The basis of his art, however, stems from his rigorous
self-analysis and the internal and external conflicts that he embodied in his
novels.

The story of Julien Sorel, the provincial parvenu whose father was a carpenter, and his assault on prestige and power in *The Red and the Black*, has an
obvious correspondence with Stendhal's own history. Sorel is one of fiction's
first great antiheroes, a supreme egoist who mastered *Tartuffe*, by MOLIÈRE
[32] as a blueprint for gaining his way through calculation and exploitation,
playing on the illusions and weaknesses of others. The title of Stendhal's novel
refers to the two courses available for a man on the make: the red of the military and the black of the church. Sorel's dilemma is that he is a Napoleon-like
figure in the black world of the Restoration, in which the egoist is expected to
conform, and to observe rank and hierarchy. Sorel's conflict and complexity
mark him as a new type of fictional character. As Irving Howe suggests:

> The modern hero, the man who forces society to accept him as its agent—
> the hero by will rather than birth—now appears for the first time: and he
> carries with him the disease of ambition, which flourishes among those
> who are most committed to the doctrine of equality and spreads all the
> deeper as the restored Bourbons try to suppress that doctrine. Before the
> revolution men had been concerned with privileges, not expectations;
> now they dream of success, that is, of a self-willed effort to lift oneself,
> through industry or chicanery, to a higher social level. Life becomes an
> experiment in strategy, an adventure in plan, ruse, and combat; the hero
> is not merely ambitious but sensitive to the point of paranoia, discovering
> and imagining a constant assault upon his dignity; and Stendhal carries
> this outlook to its extreme limit, perhaps even to caricature, by applying
> it to the affairs of love.

With breathtaking frankness, Stendhal treats love and ambition with the
same analytical skill. His exposure of conventionality and delusion more than
justifies the repeated claim that he is the originator of realism in the novel.

The Charterhouse of Parma, which many critics consider Stendhal's greatest
novel, offers its contemporary social critique obliquely from the vantage point
of the autocratic region of Parma, Italy. The novel features another psychological portrait of ambition, following Fabrizio del Dongo onto the battlefield

of Waterloo, and features one of the greatest modern treatments of war, seen from the confused perspective of a single individual. Fabrizio's progress in the church and political intrigue in Italy are joined with his various experiences of love, notably in his affair with his aunt, Gina, duchess of Sansèvèrina. The novel, which Balzac considered, because of its lack of illusions in the ways of the world, a modern version of Machiavelli's *The Prince*, and HENRY JAMES [38] regarded "among the dozen finest novels we possess," is Stendhal's most masterful synthesis of psychological penetration and social insight, which makes earlier attempts at both in the novel seem crude and naive.

Stendhal predicted that his work would not be fully appreciated until 1880 or later, and he was essentially correct. ÉMILE ZOLA [65] and the naturalists claimed Stendhal as their realistic forebear, and Stendhal's psychological introspection and sense of social corruption, as well as his diagnosis of the individual's alienation, have remained an important legacy for the novel in the 20th century.

THOMAS HARDY

43

1840–1928

No one has written worse English than Mr Hardy in some of his novels—cumbrous, stilted, ugly, and inexpressive—yes, but at the same time so strangely expressive of something attractive to us in Mr Hardy himself that we would not change it for the perfection of Sterne at his best. It becomes coloured by its surroundings; it becomes literature.
—Virginia Woolf, *The Moment*

What initially amazes the reader of Thomas Hardy is his life span. Born in 1840, Hardy lived long enough to watch one of his novels made into a film. Perhaps more than any other English writer, he influenced the transition from Victorianism to modernism in both fiction and poetry. The last major Victorian novelist, Hardy is also the first major modern English novelist, whose work is a hybrid of 19th-century methods and modern ideas and concerns. Like FAULKNER [15], Hardy's achievement derives from his creation of an imaginary world richly textured from local customs and regional elements but also profoundly universal, with some of the starkest views of human existence ever recorded outside of the plays of SHAKESPEARE [1] and the tragedies of the ancient Greeks. His vision tested the limits of censorship and the commercial restrictions of the novel form. At mid-career, tired of the struggle, Hardy abandoned the novel entirely for poetry and launched a second and equally impressive career as a poet. In common with only the greatest writers, Hardy has caused us to see the world through his unique and characteristic perspective that is easily recognizable as Hardyean.

Hardy was the eldest child of Thomas and Jemima Hardy of Higher Brockhampton, Dorset, in southwest England. His ancestors were French in origin, an old family of spent social energy and importance. His father was a builder and country musician and ballad singer who took his young son to village weddings and festivities, one of the sources of the strong rural and regional textures in Hardy's work. Frail and precocious, Hardy was kept home until the age of eight, when he was sent to school in nearby Dorchester. At the age of 16 he was apprenticed to an architect and church restorer. Thereafter, he would read and study on his own. In 1862, Hardy moved to London and was employed in an architect's office. There he read Darwin and went through a process of intellectual development and doubt similar to that of GEORGE ELIOT [21], but without her strong religious faith. An agnostic from an early age, Hardy was greatly influenced by John Stuart Mill's *On Liberty*, which became the source for Hardy's exploration of the conflict between the individual and society in his novels. Hardy also began to write poetry, which would remain his first love.

In 1867, in poor health, Hardy returned to Dorset and began work on a novel, *The Poor Man and the Lady*. With the subtitle "A Novel with No Plot," his satire on upper-class life was rejected but, encouraged by the publisher's reader, the novelist George Meredith, to add more dramatic interest, he next produced a novel, *Desperate Remedies* (1871), with little else than a sensational plot. Published anonymously, the novel launched Hardy's writing career with his characteristic reliance on fictional melodrama and sensation to stimulate interest. In 1870 Hardy was sent to Cornwall to work on a church restoration and met Emma Lavinia Gifford, a spinster of inflated social pretensions and literary aspirations. A four-year courtship followed until her father finally agreed to the match. During the 1870s, Hardy produced a succession of conventional romances with rural settings—*Under the Greenwood Tree* (1872), *A Pair of Blue Eyes* (1873), and *The Hand of Ethelberta* (1876). With *Far from the Madding Crowd* (1874) and *The Return of the Native* (1878) Hardy shifted from the comic to the tragic mode with his invention of Wessex, a fictional equivalent of England's six southwest counties that formed a partly real and partly imagined landscape. By 1883, Hardy had moved permanently to Dorchester. Though marked by marital discord that involved Emma's jealousy over his literary success, as well as conflict between her conventionality and his heterodoxical views, this was the period of Hardy's greatest masterpieces—*The Mayor of Casterbridge* (1886), *Tess of the D'Urbervilles* (1891), and *Jude the Obscure* (1896). The furor over *Tess*, fueled by its subtitle, "A Pure Woman," in which Hardy asserted his character's essential virtue despite her seduction, the birth of her illegitimate child, and her murder of her seducer, prompted Hardy to consider giving up fiction for poetry, which he did after a final blistering attack on conventional morality in *Jude*.

During the 1890s the divergence between Hardy and his wife had grown from forbearance to indifference. Emma's death in 1912, however, prompted Hardy to reexamine his past with her, and these thoughts became the source of some of his greatest lyrical poetry. Much of his imaginative labor was devoted to *The Dynasts* (1908), his epic devoted to the Napoleonic era, with Napoleon as the central tragic figure. In 1914, Hardy married his secretary, Florence Dugdale, who published a biography of the writer, actually written by Hardy himself. Honored in later years for having survived so long, Hardy was buried in Poet's Corner in London's Westminster Cathedral, though Hardy insisted that his heart should be interred in Emma's grave in Stinsford Churchyard in the Dorset countryside.

An understanding of Hardy's theory of fiction, which also was a shaping force in his poetry, should begin with his avowed role as a storyteller. Through his father, Hardy absorbed the rustic, oral storytelling tradition that shaped his works with a ballad structure and an emphasis on action, usually of tragic events arranged into a highly contrived plot (appropriate for Hardy the architect). Action is not only frequent but unusual and exceptional enough to seize the reader's attention. "We tale-tellers are all Ancient Mariners," Hardy observed, "and none of us is warranted in stopping Wedding Guests (in other words, the hurrying public) unless he has something more unusual to relate than ordinary experience of every average man and woman." For Hardy, unlike JANE AUSTEN [20] or George Eliot, the value of art was not its representation of reality, but its exploration of its surface to reveal a deeper, universal significance. "Art is disproportioning," Hardy asserted, "(i.e., distorting, throwing out of proportion) of realities, which if merely copied or reported inventorily, might possibly be overlooked. Hence realism is not Art."

Thus, in Hardy we find the intentional coincidence, extraordinary turns of plot, and formal counterpointing of characters and details to produce a symbolic or deeper meaning. The truths uncovered show his characters caught in the grip of forces beyond their control in a universe ruled by "hap" (happenstance) in Hardy's word, or blind chance. Heroism and dignity are possible in their existential dramas through strength of character and resistance. The darkness of his vision has caused him to be labeled a pessimist, but he insisted that he was a "meliorist," convinced that the world might be made bearable by human effort and self-knowledge. The power of his work, however, stems not from the answer to the problem of the human condition but from his continual questions about meaning and his testing of inadequate responses.

In Hardy's Wessex, rural England is in decline and decay. The fixed and stable tradition has broken down, and a modern age of rootless alienation and dehumanized labor has begun in a world with no sustaining values. Hardy's works probe the "ache of modernism." They assert the writer's mission to face the reality that there are no easy answers, no helpful supports for the agony of life, in which humanity has evolved only far enough to insure our awareness of misery. No other writer has so honestly or as persistently considered the full implications of these revelations as Thomas Hardy, one of the greatest shapers of modern consciousness.

GEORGE BERNARD SHAW

44

1856–1950

He is a daring pilgrim who set out from the grave to find the cradle. He started from points of view which no one else was clever enough to discover, and he is at last discovering points of view which no one else was ever stupid enough to ignore.

—G. K. Chesterton, "Shaw the Puritan," *Essays*

George Bernard Shaw, the most influential 20th-century playwright, unquestionably can claim the distinction as the greatest English dramatist since SHAKESPEARE [1]. Over a lifetime that began in the High Victorian period and spanned two world wars, over a career that exceeded 70 years as a published author, Shaw actively confronted the largest moral and philosophical questions, refusing the solipsism of "art for art's sake" for the wider relevance of reforming and persuading through a comic vision. Critical opinions on Shaw's achievement and his personality have varied from extreme admiration to equally extreme contempt, and Shaw has been the occasion for a collection of quips that attempt to take the measure of the man. The writer Benjamin de Casseres declared, "His brain is a half-inch layer of champagne poured over a bucket of Methodist near-beer"; OSCAR WILDE [92] asserted that "he hasn't an enemy in the world, and none of his friends like him"; even YEATS [17], who admired Shaw, referred to him as a perpetually smiling sewing machine. Shaw's multiplicity and quirkiness, his love of paradox and contrariness, and his many years of brilliant opposition insured a mixed reception for his ideas and works. Few who dismiss his theories can avoid his impact, however. Shaw played a central role in revitalizing modern drama, giving the problem plays of IBSEN [36] an English home and establishing a modern theater of ideas. Perhaps one of the best appreciations of Shaw's power comes from BERTOLT BRECHT [73], whose plays and ideas show the influence of Shaw. "It should be clear by now," Brecht writes, "that Shaw is a terrorist. The Shavian terror is an unusual one, and he employs an unusual weapon—that of humor."

Shaw's contribution to the theater came late in his career, though early in a lifetime of 94 years, and almost accidentally. He grew up in Dublin with Anglo-Irish Protestant parents. His father was a drunkard, and his talented but aloof mother moved to London to pursue a career as an opera singer and voice coach. Shaw remained with his father until the age of 20. After schooling in Dublin, in which Shaw asserted he learned nothing except that schools are prisons, he worked for a time in an office. As he later recalled, "I made good in spite of myself, and found, to my dismay, that Business, instead of expelling me as the worthless impostor I was, was fastening upon me with no intention of letting me go. Behold me, therefore, in my twentieth year, with a business training, in an occupation which I detested as cordially as any sane person lets himself detest anything he cannot escape from. In March 1876 I broke loose." Shaw left Dublin for London to work as a novelist and a critic of music, art, and drama. Remembering this time, he said:

> My office training had left me with a habit of doing something regularly every day as a fundamental condition of industry as distinguished from idleness. I knew I was making no headway unless I was doing this, and that I should never produce a book in any other fashion. I bought a sup-ply of white paper, demy size, by sixpence-worths at a time; folded it in quarto; and condemned myself to fill five pages of it a day, rain or shine, dull or inspired. I had so much of the schoolboy and the clerk still in me that if my five pages ended in the middle of a sentence I did not finish it until the next day. On the other hand, if I missed a day, I made up for it by doing a double task on the morrow. On this plan, I produced five novels in five years. It was my professional apprenticeship.

He found no success with his novels, however, and supported himself as a reviewer who set about to improve his audiences' taste and performers' stan-dards. He championed Wagner and Mozart in music and Ibsen in drama. He also rejected the aesthetic movement's doctrine of the essential uselessness of art for one in which art must play a role in moral and social reform.

During the 1880s, Shaw developed his political theories by absorbing and refining the tenets of socialism. In 1885, Shaw and William Archer, an influential drama critic and fellow advocate of Ibsen, collaborated on a play in which Archer supplied the plot and Shaw the dialogue. The result was *Widowers' Houses*, in which Shaw first displayed his dramatic genius. Shaw transformed the play, borrowed from the conventions of the French dramatist Augustin Eugène Scribe's well-made play in which plot is paramount, into a vehicle to express his political theories of modern capitalism. The events are made to serve Shaw's ideas and are driven by his characters, who are not the conventional passengers of the typical well-made play hurried along by plot contrivance. Shaw followed *Widowers' Houses* with a succession of plays, including *Mrs. Warren's Profession, Arms and the Man*, and *Candida*. None were theatrical successes, but Shaw attempted to reach his audience by publishing the plays with detailed stage directions and the famous Shavian prefaces that outlined his intentions. In 1898, his first seven plays were published as *Plays Pleasant and Unpleasant*, demonstrating his extraordinary versatility and delightful debunking of expected norms of behavior and thought. In 1901, Shaw published *Plays for Puritans*, a collection that included *The Devil's Disciple* and *Caesar and Cleopatra*, in which he perfected his characteristic technique of employing an educator who offers instruction in the truth of the world to a reluctant student. "I avoid plots like the plague," Shaw observed about his dramatic technique. "My procedure is to imagine characters and let them rip."

In most of his plays, Shaw reverses the method of MOLIÈRE [32], in which a deviant from the norm is exposed and ridiculed. Shaw instead injects a provacateur, in the guise of a particular character or point of view, to disrupt the conventional; the norm itself is suspect and found wanting from the standards that the playwright advocates. All of Shaw's plays show his considerable wit and delight in confounding expectations. His brilliance is perhaps best expressed in his play *Major Barbara*, in which a passionate Salvation Army visionary, Barbara, sets out to save the soul of the capitalist arms manufacturer Undersbaft, and is made to reexamine her own assumptions about war, peace, charity, love, and human relations. The play's daring ingenuity is designed to keep discussion active after the curtain has fallen, accomplishing Shaw's desired goal of breaking habits of thought and unearned intellectual responses.

Shaw's masterpiece and synthesis of both his dramatic method and ideas is *Man and Superman* (written between 1901 and 1903). In it Shaw offers a modern version of Mozart's *Don Giovanni* that begins as a satiric look at the relationship between the sexes and reaches what one critic has called "the most searching conversation on philosophy and religion in modern English." John Tanner, a wealthy intellectual and revolutionary, and a model for Shaw's typical educator, is himself educated in the deeper relevance of the Life Force beyond mere political and social questions by Ann Whitfield in a series of witty clashes. The immovable Tanner tries to preserve his social commitments and intellectual detachment against Ann's equally irresistible sexual powers. In the experimental "Don Juan in Hell" dream sequence of the play's third act, a comic battle of the sexes receives full allegorical, philosophical treatment, meriting the play's subtitle, "A Comedy and a Philosophy." Jack, now as his legendary ancestor Don Juan, and Ann as Doña Ana meet with the devil in hell to discuss the meaning of love, marriage, good and evil. Jack eventually accepts the inevitability of marriage as the unavoidable culmination of the Life Force in accomplishing humankind's "creative evolution." Bristling with wit and intellectual challenge, *Man and Superman* breaks all the bounds of theatrical conventions and defies classification. It is both a play bursting with ideas and ideas in the form of a play.

During the first decade of the 20th century, Shaw's plays brought him great success and worldwide renown. During World War I, Shaw's outspoken criticism of the war met with denunciations, but he persisted with his attacks in a sequence of increasingly symbolic plays, the first of which is *Heartbreak House*—one of the greatest monitory lessons for a century given over to self-destruction as it ignored the principles which Shaw's plays tried to teach. Until his death, Shaw wrote vigorously and mischievously; his plays generated controversy even as he was being recognized as a modern sage and eccentric. In a sense, his greatest contribution was to make the theater large enough to contain the considerable reach and multiplicity of his genius.

MARK TWAIN

45

1835–1910

I am persuaded that the future historian of America will find your works as indispensable to him as a French historian finds the political tracts of Voltaire.
  —George Bernard Shaw, in a letter to Mark Twain

The remark by ERNEST HEMINGWAY [63] that all American literature derives from Mark Twain's novel *The Adventures of Huckleberry Finn* is an extravagant overgeneralization, but it has more than a kernel of truth. Perhaps more than any other American writer, Mark Twain (Samuel Langhorne Clemens) discovered the literary power and possibility of America and its vernacular. Twain is America's greatest humorist, and one of the greatest chroniclers of the American experience. With Huck and Jim's voyage down the Mississippi River, the center of the nation, and their symbolic voyage through its tragic central conflict Twain opened up the boundaries of American literature. If Twain's art never again equaled the achievement of *Huckleberry Finn*, this novel alone justifies William Dean Howells's contention that Twain was "the Lincoln of our literature."

Twain's success in capturing American life stems both from his history and his experience. Born in the center of the country during the antebellum years of nation building, Twain lived through America's central tragedy of the Civil War and its emergence as a world power. He was equally familiar with the customs of the Western frontier and the mores of sophisticated Eastern drawing rooms and boardrooms. A self-made proponent of the American Dream, Twain also was one of its sternest critics, comically exposing the gap between appearance and reality, between American illusion and what the nation had become. As an artist, Twain tapped the great vernacular sources of folk and oral traditions and set the prototype of the American literary artist as celebrity and showman, visionary and commercial entertainer.

Samuel Langhorne Clemens was born in the village of Florida, Missouri. His father was a Virginian, a local magistrate and merchant who moved his family in 1839 to Hannibal, Missouri, a river town of nearly 500 on the west bank of the Mississippi. His mother was descended from the early settlers of Kentucky who had followed Daniel Boone west. Twain's mother's strong Presbyterian faith contrasted with his father's agnosticism, producing Twain's blend of free-thinking with a solid core of conscience. Hannibal was, as Twain recalled, the source of his greatest inspiration and "a heavenly place for a boy," filled with colorful riverfront life and boundless adventures. At the age of 12, after his father's death, Twain ended his formal schooling to work as an apprentice in a printer's shop. There, he discovered a book about Joan of Arc and was for the first time thrilled by what he read. Shortly thereafter, he began to write humorous sketches for the local newspaper. In 1853, Twain left Hannibal for New York and Philadelphia, sending home travel pieces. By 1857, he had set off to New Orleans with the notion of continuing on to the Amazon, but instead became a steamboat pilot. His two years on the Mississippi River provided him with a rich collection of American types and stories. "When I find a well-drawn character in fiction or biography," he later recalled, "I generally take a warm personal interest in him, for the reason that I have known him before—met him on the river."

The outbreak of the Civil War ended Twain's river career, as he impulsively joined a Confederate militia band that quickly broke up. Twain next accompanied his Unionist brother, Orion, on a trip west to Nevada, where Orion was appointed secretary of the territory. The account of their trip and Twain's subsequent mining adventures and work on a Virginia City newspaper are described in *Roughing It* (1872). Twain's journalism took him to San Francisco and the Sandwich Islands (Hawaii). In 1863, Twain met the famous humorist Artemus Ward and credited him with teaching him the art of storytelling. Twain's first important story, "The Celebrated Jumping Frog of Calaveras County," was published in 1865 under his pseudonym, a term for a riverboat measure of safe water. His first volume of comic sketches appeared in 1867, and his excursion to Europe and the Middle East was chronicled in *The Innocents Abroad* (1869). "When I began to lecture," Twain recalled, "and in my earlier writings, my sole idea was to make comic capital out of everything I saw and heard." Drawing from his considerable experience of American life and customs, Twain launched his writing career while creating the persona of the wild American frontiersman, in marked contrast to the New England literary establishment and his own more sensitive nature.

Twain's contradictions are perhaps best expressed in his marriage to Olivia Langdon, the semi-invalid daughter of the richest businessman in Elmira, New York, with whom he started a family in Hartford, Connecticut, in 1871. Much critical controversy has surrounded their relationship and the effect of his conventional and orthodox wife on his writing. Whether she was responsible for taming Twain's genius or whether he was equally willing to be censored by her, Twain accepted the challenge created by his growing family and respectable lifestyle to translate his writing into commercially viable forms. His first novel, *The Gilded Age* (1873), in collaboration with Charles Dudley Warner, is a satirical look at the post–Civil War age of excess that the book first named. The novel's perspective has been called a combination of JONATHAN SWIFT [41] and Horatio Alger, and the novel's divided theme of the attraction and repulsion of American wealth and power marks in fundamental ways Twain's own contradictions between satire and the pursuit of get-rich schemes, between exposing the falsity of the American dream and celebrating it.

Twain's greatest achievements resulted from his literary return to the world of his childhood that produced his major books, *The Adventures of Tom Sawyer* (1876), *Life on the Mississippi* (1883), and *The Adventures of Huckleberry Finn* (1885). The last is a masterpiece of American and world literature. Told in dialect by Huck himself, Huck's adventures aboard a raft with the fugitive slave Jim are a vehicle for Twain's most inspired social satire, connected to the central core question of race and America's tragic flaw of slavery. Their voyage also becomes a rite of passage for Huck, in which his decision to "go to Hell" on behalf of Jim's humanity and claim to dignity and freedom raises the novel to the level of genuine American myth.

Twain never reached a comparable level in his later books, which increasingly took the more distant past for their inspiration, although *A Connecticut Yankee in King Arthur's Court* (1889) has many worthy passages and an ingenious plan to subvert old world values with Yankee ingenuity. Twain's artistic vision steadily darkened in his later career, suggesting the progressive imbalance between his celebration of life's vitality and a more cynical rejection of human possibility. In *The Tragedy of Pudd'nhead Wilson* (1894), Twain explores miscegenation with an increasingly bitter tone. In his posthumously published story *The Mysterious Stranger.* (1916)—written in despair at a beloved daughter's death, another daughter's incurable epilepsy, his wife's invalidism, and his own toil to pay off creditors—Twain reaches a tragic awareness of life's fundamental absurdity. The story's supernatural visitor teaches a lesson of unrelieved despair:

It is true, that which I have revealed to you; there is no God, no universe, no human race, no earthly life, no heaven, no hell. It is all a dream—a grotesque and foolish dream. Nothing exists but you. And you are but a *thought*—a vagrant thought, a useless thought, a homeless thought, wandering forlorn among the empty eternities!

By the end of his career, Twain's comedy had soured. At his best, however, Mark Twain is the source of America's comic tradition in the way he combines both the exuberant possibilities and the shortcomings of American life.

CHARLES BAUDELAIRE

46

1821–1867

Baudelaire was a great poet of a decadence. In other words, he was a great modern poet; for the decadence which shaped him by compelling him to revolt against it was the "civilization of industrial progress" which has endured from his day to our own. Baudelaire confronted the reality like the hero he strove to be; he had the courage both of his attitude and his art, and the result of his unremitting exercise of will in transforming his keen emotions is a poetic achievement that makes a single and profound impression on our minds. Baudelaire, true to the practice of the great poet, had crystallized his experience; he had accumulated a weight of conviction to endorse his emotions.
—John Middleton Murry, "Baudelaire," from Countries of the Mind

The greatest of the French symbolists who exerted a profound influence on the course of poetry in the 20th century, Charles Baudelaire has been called the "first modern poet" and remains the most read French poet around the world. T. S. ELIOT [19] went so far as to assert that Baudelaire was "the greatest exemplar in *modern* poetry in any language." Such high praise is even more remarkable considering his complete works consist only of a single volume of poetry, a book of prose poems, criticism, and three volumes of translations of the works of EDGAR ALLAN POE [53]. There is, however, an imaginative unity in Baudelaire's work that defines a unique poetic voice. Baudelaire established as well the role of the poet whose primary goal is to shock his audience into a reassessment of accepted values, through an unflinching analysis of his own torment and life at moments of both transcendence and revulsion.

Baudelaire came to maturity during the great flowering of French romanticism under the influence of Lamartine, VICTOR HUGO [105], Musset, and Vigny, and his poetic career was shaped by his desire to compete with and surpass these romantic masters. In a departure from the romantics' fascination with nature and the pastoral, Baudelaire, born in Paris, is preeminently a poet of the city, captivated by its teeming vitality and the proximity of beauty and ugliness, triumph and despair. His father died when he was six, and he rebelled under the strict discipline of his stepfather. When he turned 21, his family, concerned about his unconventional behavior and debts, obtained a court order to supervise his finances, and he lived for the rest of his life on an allowance. The turning point of his artistic career was the chance discovery around 1846 of the works of Edgar Allan Poe, with whom Baudelaire felt not simply a kinship but a complete identification. As Baudelaire recalled, "The first time I opened one of his books I saw, to my amazement and delight, not simply certain subjects which I had dreamed of, but *sentences* which I had thought out, written by him twenty years before." Baudelaire searched out editions of Poe's works and, through his translations and advocacy, helped secure Poe's worldwide reputation. Poe's conception of the unity of poetical effects and the pursuit of beauty, stripped of didacticism or moralism, led Baudelaire's ideas and art away from the imprecision of the romantics and toward the new poetic method of the symbolists. Influenced by Poe's attraction to the darker reaches of psychology and emotions, Baudelaire helped turn poetry from the picturesque to confront his personal torment, and depict shocking images from modern urban life that fascinated him.

Baudelaire, consciously determined to reject the strengths of the romantics, set out to create a sensation. "Illustrious poets," he observed, "have long divided the richest provinces of the poetical domain among themselves. Consequently, I shall do something else. . . ." Baudelaire's assault on the poetic conventions took the form of his landmark volume, *Les Fleurs du Mal* (*The Flowers of Evil*), which appeared in 1857. Like GUSTAVE FLAUBERT's [30] novel *Madame Bovary*, published the previous year, the volume redefines the artist's control over his material and portrays experience in a frank and honest style unmitigated by supportive illusions. Both Flaubert and Baudelaire were prosecuted for corrupting public morals. Compared to Flaubert's aloof relationship with his audience, however, Baudelaire directly challenged his readers to confront the disturbing qualities of his work and to reject their inaction or indifference, which Baudelaire calls boredom. His opening poem, "To the Reader," catalogues in a series of taunts and shocking images the subjects and themes that the poems will explore: infatuation, sadism, lust, and avarice. Baudelaire announces a still greater wickedness:

There is one uglier, crueler, fouler, worse!
Although he stirs not, nor grumbles where he sits,
But he would crush this world of ours to bits
And in a yawn devour the universe;
It's BOREDOM—impotent and sniveling ghoul.
He chain-smokes and dreams of bloody knives.
You, my Reader, know this monster of a thousand lives,

Oh, hypocrite Reader—my soul, my brother!

Baudelaire asserts at the outset his connection with his reader and their equal share in the dark and destructive forces his poetry will expose.

His daring language and musical effects encompass a range of experience and emotions never before displayed in poetry. Central to Baudelaire's vision is the pursuit of transcendence that never loses sight of the forces in opposition—the spirit trapped by time and decay. In one of his most disturbing poems, "A Carcass," Baudelaire juxtaposes the Petrarchan theme of the ennobling power of love with the lovers' chance encounter with death and corruption:

With legs spread like a wanton whore,
    A baked and reeking mass
Of poison, cynically displayed.
    Its belly filled with gas.

The conventional lesson that love is mortal and will decay is drawn with an overpowering intensity from the force of his images, concluding with the bitter vision that joins in a heightened awareness of love, beauty, and their destruction:

—Yet you too will be as that corruption foul,
    That thing, with horror rife,
Star of my eye and sun within my soul,
    Oh thou, my love, my life!

Yes, you will be as this, oh queen of grace,
    When the last mass is said,
Underneath the grass and flowers, flower-face,
    To mould among corpses dead.

Then, oh my beauty, cry unto the worms
    Whose kiss shall nibble thee,

> That in this scroll I've kept love's soul and form,
>   Though love decays, and we!

Baudelaire provided the foundation for the explosion of poetic expression in France by such writers as Verlaine, Rimbaud, Mallarmé, Laforgue, and Valéry, who observed, "There may be French poets greater and more powerfully endowed than Baudelaire, there is none more *important*." His importance is established in reinvigorating the romantic's pursuit of self-knowledge, truth, and beauty in a manner that does not avoid the complex blend of human experience, and in a form of sharply suggestive images that aspires to the evocative qualities of music. Baudelaire's most famous poem, "Correspondences," best typifies his fusion of ecstatic awareness with realistic details, and consummate artistic control of intricate melody:

> Some perfumes are as cool as babies' flesh,
> Mellow as the oboe, green as meadows,
> —And others, corrupt, rich, triumphant.
>
> Our spirits in the infinite expanse,
> Like amber, musk, myrrh, and frankincense,
> Sing the ecstasies of the soul and the sense.

SAMUEL BECKETT

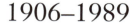

1906–1989

In the modern history of literature at least he is a unique moral figure, not a dreamer of rose-gardens but a cultivator of what will grow in the waste land, who can make us see the exhilarating design that thorns and yucca share with whatever will grow anywhere.
—Hugh Kenner, *A Reader's Guide to Samuel Beckett*

In announcing the arrival of the modern age, Matthew Arnold wrote, "the calm, the cheerfulness, the disinterested objectivity have disappeared; the dialogue of the mind with itself has commenced." Beckett is the master of the inner dialogue that shows an individual progressively stripped of sustaining illusions and clutter, King Lear–like, to the level of bare, unaccommodated man. In Beckett's world of essence and existence, comedy meets tragedy, and the goal of art seems to be the silence or stillness that invades and surrounds his works but never completely dominates them. As a native Irishman, Beckett is aligned with his countrymen SWIFT [41], STERNE [90], and JOYCE [7], and their comic genius; as a self-made Frenchman, Beckett is associated with existentialism and the theater of the absurd. Beckett, however, resists categorization into literary camps or clear lines of descent or affiliation. Instead, he is one of the 20th century's last dominating literary voices who managed a great shift in literary consciousness.

Like his fellow countryman and mentor James Joyce, Beckett defined himself in exile, but unlike Joyce, who managed to remain safely on the fringes of a modern world spinning out of control, Beckett was plunged into the maelstrom. He was born in Foxrock, outside of Dublin, of Protestant Anglo-Irish parents. His education at Portora Royal School (where Oscar Wilde had been a student) and at Trinity College, Dublin, where he received his degree in French and Italian, pointed him toward an academic career. Beckett gained an exchange lectureship at L'École normale supérieure in Paris in 1928, when he also met Joyce and assisted him in his labors on *Finnegans Wake*. Beckett returned to Trinity as a lecturer in French and a candidate for a master's degree, but found teaching uncongenial. In 1932 he left Ireland for good, except for short visits to his family. When World War II began, Beckett ended a visit to Ireland and returned to Paris, later stating, "I preferred France in war to Ireland in peace." During the war, Beckett joined the French underground in Paris and was forced to escape to unoccupied France in 1942, where he worked as a farm laborer until the war's end.

Beckett's literary work from 1927 until 1946 was in English. His early publications included a critical study of MARCEL PROUST [16], a collection of short stories (*More Pricks Than Kicks*), a volume of poems (*Echo's Bones*), and two novels (*Murphy* and *Watt*). In 1946, Beckett began a remarkable period of productivity that resulted in his most famous works. "I wrote all my work very fast—between 1946 and 1950," he later recalled. "Since then I haven't written anything. Or at least nothing that has seemed to me valid." During this period, Beckett completed a fictional trilogy (*Molloy, Malone Dies,* and *The Unnamable*) and the play *Waiting for Godot*, which brought him international attention. All were written in French, which Beckett found "easier to write without style," and then translated by the author into English.

Despite his dismissal of his later work, Beckett continued to publish important plays and fiction, including *Stories and Texts for Nothing* (1955), *Endgame* (1956), *Krapp's Last Tape* (1958), *How It Is* (1960), and *Happy Days* (1961), and a number of shorter works for radio, television, and film. His notorious reluctance to discuss himself and his works or to enter the debate over their meaning created a sense of mystery and puzzlement surrounding his intentions. Contrary to the modern role of the writer as celebrity, Beckett perfected his invisibility, which only a few other famous contemporaries, like J. D. Salinger and Thomas Pynchon, have duplicated. Beckett's reticence has not, however, prevented a staggering array of critical examinations of his works, making him one of the most analyzed of postwar writers. Critical preoccupation has been matched by widespread public awareness. Even those who have never read Beckett or seen his plays understand a reference to a "Beckett-like landscape" and "waiting for Godot" as shorthand to describe modern futility and angst.

In Beckett's work the atmosphere of futility and stagnation around which CHEKHOV [37] devised his stories and plays has become pervasive. The world is drained of meaning; human relationships are reduced to tensions between hope and despair in which consciousness itself is problematic. Beckett's protagonists, who lack the possibility of significant action, are locked in a futile search for the means of overcoming the tyranny of time, space, and awareness itself. Reversing the multiplicity of James Joyce, Beckett compresses his language and situations down to the level of the elemental forces without the possibility of escape from the basic absurdity of existence. Beckett's forte is the dramatic monologue in which the minds of his characters cycle through the comedy and terror of their own awareness without the means of answering their own questions.

Waiting for Godot gives dramatic form to the internalized preoccupations of Beckett's fiction. The nonspecific setting is symbolically suggestive of the modern waste land. The play's two protagonists, Vladimir and Estragon, engage in chatter derived equally from the music hall and metaphysics as they await the arrival of Godot, who never comes. What Godot represents is far less important than the defining condition of waiting that the play dramatizes. Beckett explores what is possible in a world in which nothing happens. In drama, which traditionally depends on an arrangement of significant action moving toward some climactic resolution, Beckett's conception is revolutionary and daring. Only a few other writers, such as KAFKA [31], have given voice to such essential questions without the need for the sustaining illusion of meaning and values. "I'm not interested in any system," Beckett said. "I can't see any trace of any system anywhere." At art's core is a fundamental comprehension of the world, but Beckett's art is based on the world's ultimate incomprehensibility. "I think anyone nowadays," Beckett remarked, "who pays the slightest attention to his own experience finds it the experience of a non-knower, a non-can-er."

From Beckett's perception that the world lacks meaning and that the self cannot make sense of the senseless, he offers a radical redefinition of art to reflect his discovery. Causality disappears, as does narrative perspective and the illusion of art as an ordered pattern that reflects significance. Beckett reduces his art to the key questions of who we are and what we can believe in the face of the impossibility of any belief. The effect is a remarkable series of challenges to our conception of the world and our capacity to accept the full implications of the mysteries of existence. If Beckett suggests that the perfect silence of incomprehensibility and the blank page is art's final inevitability, in his work there is also the sense of a fundamental discovery. As the nameless voice of thought itself concludes in *The Unnamable*, "You must go on, I can't go on, I'll go on."

VIRGINIA WOOLF

1882–1941

Her genius was intensely feminine and personal—private almost. To read one of her books was (if you liked it) to receive a letter from her, addressed specially to you.
—Christopher Isherwood, *Exhumations*

As one of the groundbreaking literary modernists of the 20th century, Virginia Woolf helped take the novel from the surface realism of external details to the deeper reaches of consciousness and the interior life. In her novels and essays, Virginia Woolf exerted a powerful influence in reshaping the possibilities of the novel and the role woman writers ought to play in creative life. At the core of the literary revolution Woolf helped create is her observation that "In or about December, 1910, human character changed." She may have been referring to the death of Edward VII, the true end of the Victorian period, and to the opening in London of the first postimpressionist exhibition to introduce the works of Matisse, Manet, Picasso, Van Gogh, Gauguin, and Cézanne to a reluctant British public. Both events announced a fundamentally altered view of reality. Woolf's novels and essays mark her exploration of that new reality and the search for the proper form to express it.

Virginia Woolf was born in London, the third child in a family of two boys and two girls. She was the daughter of the renowned Victorian critic, biographer, and scholar Sir Leslie Stephen, the author of the *History of English*

Thought in the Eighteenth Century and the editor of the *Dictionary of National Biography*. Her mother, Julia, was a famous beauty and hostess of a distinguished literary circle that gathered at the Stephenses' home. The Stephen children, Virginia, Vanessa, Thoby, and Adrian, were encouraged by both parents in intellectual pursuits, but it was her father's training that had the greatest impact on Virginia. During daily lessons with her father, she learned to read sensitively and to appreciate fine writing. As Woolf later recalled about her father, "As he lay back in his chair and spoke the words with closed eyes, we felt that he was speaking not merely the words of Tennyson or Wordsworth but what he himself felt and knew. Thus many of the great English poems now seem to me inescapable from my father. I hear in them not only his voice, but in some sort his teaching and belief."

Julia Stephen died when Virginia was 13, and this loss as well as her father's deep mourning contributed to the first of Woolf's several breakdowns. In 1904, her father's death resulted in a second breakdown and a suicide attempt. When Virginia recovered, she moved with her brothers and sister to a home of their own in bohemian Bloomsbury. There they were at the center of an eccentric and talented circle of artists, critics, and writers—including Lytton Strachey, Vita Sackville-West, E. M. Forster, and John Maynard Keynes—that would become famous as the Bloomsbury Group.

In 1912, Virginia married Leonard Woolf, a critic and political writer with whom she collaborated in establishing the Hogarth Press, the first publishers of Freud's works in English. The following year she completed her first novel, *The Voyage Out*, which she had been working on for six years. Her second novel, *Night and Day*, appeared in 1919. Both are traditional in form and content; however, in the collection of stories that became *Monday or Tuesday*, Woolf began to experiment with a less conventional form, using a more poetic, subjective style to render a character's stream of consciousness and the interior world of private thoughts and feelings. Her next novels, *Jacob's Room* (1922), *Mrs. Dalloway* (1925), and her masterpiece, *To the Lighthouse* (1927), are all written in Woolf's experimental style in which conventional plot is replaced by an emphasis on the inner, psychological states of her characters, and in which time and space reflect a deeply subjective vision. In *Mrs. Dalloway* the trauma of the post-World War I experience is examined on a single day as the title character prepares for an evening party while a shattered veteran moves toward his suicide. The past impinges on the present, and the relationships among dozens of characters are revealed in fragments of association connected by a web of metaphor and imagery. The result is a powerful and moving recreation of reality that is deepened and transfused with meaning and emotional resonance.

In *To the Lighthouse*, Woolf attempts an even grander orchestration of experimental effects in a three-part structure: an account of a single day in the life of the Ramsay family and their houseguests; a poetic reflection of the passing of 10 years; and the final description of the artist Lily Briscoe's attempt to finish a painting and resolve the enigma represented by Mrs. Ramsay. The effect is an elaborate pattern of meaning and relationships, and an exposure of the way the mind discovers them. Virginia Woolf succeeds in replacing what she regarded as the materialism of other novelists, the flat and insignificant data of experience, with a more resonant, poetic, inner experience of consciousness itself.

Woolf's later writing includes *Orlando* (1928), a mock biography of a character from Elizabethan times to the present in which the protagonist changes sexes to fit each age; *Flush* (1933), a biographical fantasy of the Brownings seen from the perspective of Elizabeth Barrett Browning's dog; *Roger Fry: A Biography* (1940), about the art critic; and the novels *The Waves* (1931), *The Years* (1937), and *Between the Acts* (1941). During the 1920s and 1930s, Woolf also wrote several volumes of reviews and criticism, including *The Common Reader* (1925) and *The Second Common Reader* (1932), *A Room of One's Own* (1929), and *Three Guineas* (1938), in which she expands on her philosophy of art and mounts a spirited campaign on behalf of women writers. Long suppressed and ignored, the feminine perspective, in Woolf's famous formula, needed "five hundred pounds a year and a room of one's own" to develop. For her advocacy of women's independence and unique contribution to literature, Woolf has been claimed as an important feminist and champion of women's rights.

In 1941, depressed over the outbreak of war and sensing the onset of another breakdown, Virginia Woolf drowned herself. In her distinguished career as a writer, she had met her father's challenge to make the highest use of her intellect and emotions, and she succeeded in converting an intensely private vision into enduring art. Few other writers have captured the elusive quality of inner life as well, or have made such an eloquent case for the centrality of a woman's perspective and its cultivation.

49

ALEXANDER POPE

1688–1744

In Pope I cannot read a line,
But with a sigh I wish it mine;
When he can in one couplet fix
More sense than I can do in six,
It gives me such a jealous fit,
I cry, "Pox take him and his wit!"

—Jonathan Swift, "Verses on the Death of Dr. Swift"

Alexander Pope has been called the quintessential writer of the neoclassical period in Europe. In his remarkable career, Pope set the standard for poetry and the moral and philosophical thinking that defined his age. Pope's is a poetry of statement rather than emotional self-expression. Its wide scope encompassed all the central issues of the day, in art, politics, and moral behavior, with wit that Pope defined as "Nature to advantage dressed,/What oft was thought but ne'er so well expressed." No other writer so exemplified the Augustan mind and period as Pope, and he has served, like SHAKESPEARE [1] and MILTON [8], as one of the giant poetic forces with which subsequent English poetry has had to contend.

Pope's emergence as the leading intellectual and artistic force of his age is even more remarkable in light of the obstacles he faced. Born in London of Catholic parents in the year of the Glorious Revolution that deposed the Catholic James II and brought the Protestant regime of William and Mary to power, Pope faced virulent anti-Catholic sentiment and laws. Catholics were forbidden to attend university, hold public office, own property, and even live within 10 miles of London. Pope was effectively banned from the patronage that supported most writers of the period, which forced him to become the first English writer since Shakespeare to earn his living from his pen. Plagued by ill health from infancy, Pope was deformed by tuberculosis of the spine. He never grew taller than four feet, six inches, and was unable to dress himself or stand unassisted until laced into stiff canvas garments. Throughout his life he endured chronic headaches, asthma, and other symptoms that made up, in his words, "this long disease, my life."

Pope was educated at home by tutors, and at the age of 12 moved with his family to a country home in Windsor Forest, where he completed a remarkable self-education. He taught himself ancient Greek, learned Italian and French, and mastered Latin and English poetry. His earliest writing before he was 16 was a tragedy and a fragmentary epic, which have not survived. In 1709, the publication of the *Pastorals* announced his arrival at the age of 21 as a major poetic voice that put him at the center of London literary life, which he dominated for nearly 40 years. He followed his initial success with one of the most astonishing decades of productivity and accomplishment in literary history, which included the *Essay on Criticism* (1711), *Windsor Forest* (1713), *The Rape of the Lock* (1714), and *Eloïsa to Abelard* (1717). His six-volume translation of Homer's *Iliad* (1715–20) secured his poetic reputation as the English Homer, and its sales secured his fortune. He followed its success with a translation of the *Odyssey* and an edition of Shakespeare's works.

After the death of his father in 1717, Pope moved with his mother to a villa at Twickenham, near Richmond along the Thames, which he turned into a model Augustan retreat that attracted a remarkable collection of the greatest figures of the age, anxious to pay their respects. His literary circle included such figures as SWIFT [41], John Gay, William Congreve, and John Arbuthnot. Beginning in 1727, Pope returned to original work that included the satirical *Dunciad* (1728–43), his indictment of the age's dullness and vulgarity, and the philosophical *Moral Essays* (1731–35), including *The Essay on Man* (1733), which, though unfinished, attempted to present a unified ethical system, echoing Milton, to "vindicate the ways of God to man." Pope was generous to his friends and revered by them, but his protracted acrimonious battles with his enemies earned him the epithet "the wasp of Twickenham." Despite the cruelty of some of his attacks, the overall character of Pope's massive canon is distinguished by its moral balance in which good sense and sympathy predominate.

Perhaps no single work captures Pope's amazing poetic virtuosity or his fundamental moral soundness better than *The Rape of the Lock*. The poem originated in Pope's intervention to stop a family feud that began when Lord Petre ungraciously cut a lock of hair from the head of Arabella Fermor without her permission. Pope's poem was intended to mend the ensuing breach between the pair through the delightful humor of elevating the incident to epic status, heroically inflating the trivial incident to point out the absurdity of taking something so minor so seriously. In the process, Pope produced one of the greatest mock-heroic poems ever written, comically echoing the epic devices of HOMER [3] and VIRGIL [9], including the arming of the hero, Belinda, at her dressing table; heroic combat at the card table; and the descent to the underworld into the Cave of Spleen. The poem's principle of good sense is provided by the worldly-wise Clarissa, who offers the poem's central truth:

> How vain are all these glories, all our pains,
> Unless good sense preserve what beauty gains;
> That men may say when we the front box grace,
> "Behold the first in virtue as in face!"
> Oh! if to dance all night, and dress all day,
> Charmed the smallpox, or chased old age away,
> Who would not scorn what housewife's cares produce,
> Or who would learn one earthly thing of use?
> To patch, nay ogle, might become a saint,
> Nor could it sure be such a sin to paint.
> But since, alas! frail beauty must decay,
> Curled or uncurled, since locks will turn to gray;
> Since painted, or not painted, all shall fade,
> And she who scorns a man must die a maid;
> What then remains but well our powers to use,
> An keep good humor still whate'er we lose?
> And trust me, dear, good humor can prevail
> When airs, and flights, and screams, and scolding fail.

Despite Clarissa's counsel, the battle to restore Belinda's sense and calm her hurt feelings is finally won only by the poet's considerable gift of permanently celebrating Belinda and her lock in art.

Pope's poetic skill is evident in his ability to achieve a naturalness and vitality within the constraints of the closed couplet—a series of two rhyming lines whose sense and grammatical structure conclude at the end of the second line—the poetic form that best reflected the Augustans' love of symmetry and order. His poetic genius rests in his ability to achieve surprising effects even in the regularity of his forms, and of distilling complex and ambitious thought into concisely ordered language. Despite the Romantics' opposition to the "artificial" style of Pope's poetic language, to reject it on behalf of a preferred "naturalness" is critically suspect. As W. H. AUDEN [103] observed,

"If Wordsworth had Pope in mind when he advised Poets to write 'in the language really used by men' he was singularly in error. Should one compare Pope at his best with any of the Romantics, including Wordsworth, at their best, it is Pope who writes as men normally speak to each other and the latter who go in for 'poetic' language." Within the bounds of Pope's challenging form, like JEAN RACINE [62] in neoclassical tragedy, he achieves an amazing range of dramatic effects, extending poetry's scope to consider the most central human and social questions.

FRANÇOIS RABELAIS

50

c. 1494–1553

Rabelais is so powerful and so disturbing a comic writer because he portrays human life as radically irrational, vitally unhinged, sublimely grotesque. He knows that to be alive is to be paradoxical and finally incomprehensible. Thus his moral instinct, which is strong and healthy, recognized the factitious element in authorized morality based only on reason, and reaches for an unauthorized alternative.

—Thomas M. Greene, *Rabelais: A Study in Comic Courage*

Rabelais, acknowledged as one of the greatest writers of world literature, is also one of the most challenging to categorize and summarize. His four-volume masterpiece that has come to be called *Gargantua and Pantagruel* defies reduction into any conventional literary genre. This comic monster fable has been viewed as a novel, a satire, a ribald collection of scatological jokes, and a serious moral inquiry into philosophy, politics, and education. *Gargantua and Pantagruel* is a result of an expansive comic vision so unique and unprecedented that it is difficult to trace its author's literary career along clear lines of influence and imitation. With Rabelais, comedy on a grand scale, as audacious and liberating as that of ARISTOPHANES [34], reasserted its hold on Western literature and would spawn the comic gigantism of such later talents as CERVANTES [11], SWIFT [41], STERNE [90], JOYCE [7], Thomas Pynchon, and others.

Because of his various careers and immense learning, Rabelais was a true Renaissance man, with all that the term implies. He was born in France near Chinon, in Touraine, at the end of the 15th century at a time when the revival of classical learning and the new attitudes of the Italian Renaissance were spreading throughout Europe. Rabelais was the son of a successful lawyer and became first a Franciscan and later a Benedictine monk. After leaving the monastery as a secular priest, he is thought to have studied law at Poitiers and medicine at the University of Paris. In 1530, he entered the University of Montpellier as a medical student and received his degree in two months. A learned humanist with interests in a great range of subjects, Rabelais found an intellectual mentor in Erasmus, whom he never met but of whom he wrote in an appreciatory letter, "What I am and what I am worth, I have received from you alone." In Lyons, the cultural capital of France at the time, Rabelais edited a number of Latin and Greek works for a humanist printer and became the private physician of Jean Du Bellay, the powerful bishop of Paris. He undertook several journeys with Du Bellay to Rome, and between 1532 and 1552 wrote the four volumes of his *Gargantua and Pantagruel* (a fifth volume appeared in 1562, but its authenticity has been questioned).

The genesis of Rabelais's masterpiece began in 1532, when an anonymous writer had commercial success with a book about the marvelous feats performed by the legendary giant Gargantua. Stories and jokes about Gargantua were part of the French folk tradition, and Rabelais attempted his own version, the story of Gargantua's son Pantagruel. Its success prompted Rabelais to publish a sequel, a longer version of the life of Gargantua. Twelve years later, a third book appeared, followed in 1552 by the "Fourth Book of the noble Pantagruel's Deeds and Sayings." Rabelais's masterpiece cannot be labeled a novel in any conventional sense. It is an episodic work, with an intermingling of fantasy and realism, lacking continuity and defying rules of time and space. It is best understood as a kind of literary compendium created by Rabelais in a form so expansive and various that it contains observations about life and his times ranging from the serious to the absurd, comprehending man's essential nobility as well as his all-too-human bestial nature. As giants, Rabelais's heroes provide a magnification of life akin to the comedy of caricature in which essential truths are exposed through exaggeration and excess.

Rabelais's targets in *Gargantua and Pantagruel* are the various enemies of human energy and freedom. Anything that restricts, limits, or diminishes is attacked in favor of expansion and vitality. The enormous appetites of Rabelais's giants serve his comedy but also his moral, which posits a utopian alternative to the world of ordinary men whose constriction and pettiness produce injustice and war. His fantastical reordering of life provides a place for the irrational, the ambiguous, and the paradoxical that define the human condition as much as its laws, logic, and reason. In Rabelais's distorted mirror, readers can distance themselves from the folly and pretense of their world with the corrective antidote of laughter, while at the same time experiencing a wider, more embracing conception of human life. As Thomas Greene observed in defining Rabelais's particular comic vision, "The comic sense of Rabelais, unlike Molière's, unlike most comic writers', does not repose on a judicious common sense, observing from the solid center of experience the eccentricities of deviation. . . . He writes rather from the fringe of nonsense. He knew the secret folly at the heart of the universe, the wild uncertainty, the abyss of lunacy that underlies our rational constructions. He embraces that lunacy, both within and without us, and builds his comedy upon it."

As a humanist, Rabelais struggled to achieve a liberation of the spirit in his art that was not bound by precedents or constrained by orthodoxy. In the riotous and profound creations of his imagination, he achieves just that. In his groundbreaking study of Rabelais, Mikhail Bakhtin writes, "His place in history among the creators of modern European writing, such as Dante, Boccaccio, Shakespeare, and Cervantes, is not subject to doubt. Rabelais not only determined the fate of French literature and of the French literary tongue, but influenced the fate of world literature as well (probably no less than Cervantes)." VICTOR HUGO [105], in examining the characteristics that separate the writer of genius from one who is merely great, identified the characteristic exaggeration and excessiveness of the genius. In this regard, Rabelais meets Hugo's test for literary greatness. At the core of Rabelais's importance and appeal is his daring comprehension of life as boundlessly various and full of unlimited possibilities.

FRANCESCO PETRARCH

51

1304–1374

In the world of the poets Petrarch reigned for centuries. He set the model of what a lyric poem should be—a brief outburst of passion, developing a single thought, symbol, or fancy, within a frame of fixed and arduous form. Even today the formula holds. No other poet in all time has wielded such an influence, so long and so far. . . . He helped to define and form the modern sensibility, in its appreciation of the beauty in nature, in its sense of the mystery and marvel in everyday reality, in its idealization of romantic love, in its refinement of self-scrutiny.

—Morris Bishop, *Petrarch and His World*

Commonly referred to as the first modern man, Petrarch saw himself as a bridge between the classical world and his own. "I am as if on the frontiers of two peoples," he observed, "looking forward and backward." By his own estimation, his greatest poetic achievement was his work in Latin, but posterity has valued most what he called the *Rerum vulgarium fragmenta* (Poetic fragments in the vernacular), his lyrical sequence in Italian for the woman he called Laura, in which he redefined love poetry in Western literature. In so many areas Petrarch is the great originator. He discovered important works by Cicero and edited Livy, producing the first scholarly edition of a classical writer. His scholarship helped restore classical learning in Europe and earned him the title the first writer of the Renaissance.

Petrarch can also be described as the first truly professional man of letters, who set the standard for the role of the poet in society. A confidante of popes and emperors, Petrarch cultivated his fame and was the first genuine literary celebrity in the modern sense. Fundamentally, however, Petrarch's most important legacy can be found in his poetry. Modern attitudes toward love and the poetic means by which they can be expressed are still essentially Petrarchan.

Petrarch was born in Arezzo, Italy, where his father had brought his family after being exiled from Florence in the same political crisis that drove Dante [2] from the city. In a sense, Petrarch was an exile all his life. Always regarding himself as a Florentine, he moved restlessly from place to place in southern France and throughout Italy. In 1312, his family relocated to Avignon, the seat of the papacy from 1309 to 1378. Petrarch studied law, first at Montpellier and then at Bologna, although he never completed his degree. After his father's death, Petrarch devoted himself exclusively to scholarship and literature, securing the first in a series of patrons to make this possible. The turning point of his emotional and poetic life occurred in 1327, when, at the church of St. Clare in Avignon, he first met the Laura of his poems. She had been married for two years at the time of their first encounter, and Petrarch's hopeless passion for her would dominate him for the next 21 years. After her death from the plague, allegedly on the anniversary of their first meeting, Petrarch continued to cultivate her memory in the sequence of love poems that she inspired, which he polished and reassembled until his own death.

The poetic convention of a series of lyrical poems describing the various stages of a love affair was not unique, with precedents in Catullus [82] and the troubadours of southern France, who in the 12th and 13th centuries addressed poems to unattainable women in the courtly love tradition. Dante, in *La Vita Nuova*, had earlier examined the stages in which the earthly Beatrice was transformed into a redeeming symbol of Christian salvation. Petrarch, however, refined the convention with new stylistic competence, codifying a new language of love and perfecting the verse form of the Petrarchan sonnet: a 14-line poem, divided into an eight-line octave that presents the theme or problem of the poem, followed by a six-line sestet that works out the resolution. His greatest innovation was in using his metrical and musical skill to fundamentally alter the love lyric to become an instrument of self-analysis and awareness. His poetic sequence captures the full emotional range of love (with the exception of the fulfillment of consummation) and has been called an autobiographical novel in verse, the true subject of which is not the beloved but the poet himself. In its final form, the sequence is comprised of 366 poems (317 of them sonnets), divided into two basic parts. The first concerns the living Laura and her effect on the poet, who is consumed with desire and alternates between hope and despair, exaltation and self-loathing. The second part is devoted to Laura's memory and her power to purify and redirect the poet toward the love of God. Few poets before or since Petrarch have been so candid in dissecting and displaying the self in the grip of emotional distress:

> And she for whom I wept and tuned my lyre
> Has gone, alas!—But left my lyre, my tears:
> Gone is that face, whose holy look endears;
> But in my heart, ere yet it did retire,
> Left the sweet radiance of its eyes, entire;—
> My heart? Ah, no! not mine! for to the spheres
> Of light she bore it captive, soaring high,
> In angel robe triumphant, and now stands
> Crown'd with the laurel wreath of chastity:
> Oh! could I throw aside these earthly bands
> That tie me down where wretched mortals sigh,—
> To join blest spirits in celestial lands!

(XLV)

Although the beloved is the cause of Petrarch's ecstasy and despair, the poems are essentially an expression of the poet's feelings and inner turmoil rather than a celebration of Laura. As critic James Harvey Robinson has observed, "Through him the inner world first receives recognition; he first notes, observes, analyzes, and sets forth its phenomena." Before Petrarch, introspection by religious mystics had been directed toward reaching fulfillment with God. Petrarch, however, uses introspection as a means for self-understanding, thus redefining the purpose and goal of poetry and artistic expression.

Petrarch's poetic style in describing the effects of love has entered modern culture with its full arsenal of conceits, attitudes, and mannerisms still in use on greeting cards and in pop songs, as well as in poetry. Hyperbole, metaphor, antithesis, and paradox are all woven together to capture the powerful effects of passion and the plight of the frustrated lover:

> Down my cheeks bitter tears incessant rain,
> And my heart struggles with convulsive sighs,
> When, Laura, upon you I turn my eyes,
> For whom the world's allurements I disdain.
> But when I see that gentle smile again,
> That modest, sweet, and tender smile, arise,
> It pours on every sense a blest surprise;
> Lost in delight is all my torturing pain.
> Too soon this heavenly transport sinks and dies:
> When all thy soothing charms my fate removes
> To that sole refuge its firm faith approves

My spirit from my ravish'd bosom flies,
And wing'd with fond remembrance follows you.

(XV)

SHAKESPEARE [1] was well aware of the Petrarchan tradition and comically
exploited it in his famous Sonnet 130:

> My mistress' eyes are nothing like the sun;
> Coral is far more red than her lips' red;
> If snow be white, why then her breasts are dun;
> If hairs be wires, black wires grow on her head.
> I have seen roses damasked, red and white,
> But no such roses see I in her cheeks;
> And in some perfumes is there more delight
> Than in the breath that from my mistress reeks.
> I love to hear her speak, yet well I know
> That music hath a far more pleasing sound;
> I grant I never saw a goddess go;
> My mistress, when she walks, treads on the ground:
> And yet, by heaven, I think my love as rare
> As any she belied with false compare.

If under the attack of Shakespeare's comic exaggeration Petrarch's language
of love now seems forced and in need of a realistic adjustment, the fault rests
more with Petrarch's many imitators overworking a rich vein of poetic inspiration till exhausted. The original, however, still exerts its powerful influence,
and Petrarch deserves his place as one of the great innovators in Western
literature.

EMILY DICKINSON

52

1830–1886

Her poetry is a magnificent personal confession, blasphemous and, in its self-revelation, its honesty, almost obscene. It comes out of the intellectual life towards which it feels no moral responsibility. Cotton Mather would have burned her for a witch.
— Allen Tate, "New England and Emily Dickinson"
in *The Recognition of Emily Dickinson*

The two giants of 19th-century American poetry who played the greatest role in redefining modern verse are WALT WHITMAN [39] and Emily Dickinson, a fact that would have stupefied their contemporaries. Whitman was considered a barbarous outsider with a strong taint of the outlandish and the obscene. Emily Dickinson was a recluse whose work was almost completely unknown to her contemporaries. Only seven of her poems were published during her lifetime, all anonymously. Yet the two poets' unique vision and opposite approach represent the poles between which modern poetry would swing—expansion and compression, engagement and detachment—and define a startling new poetic range.

    The details of Emily Dickinson's life are as mystifying as some of her poems. She was known in her Amherst, Massachusetts, community as "the myth," who retreated into the private world of her family. That she wrote at all was known only to her family and a small circle of close friends, although few suspected the extent and the quality of her poems. After she died, 1,775 poems were discovered in a locked box in her bureau. Although collections of her poetry were published in the 1890s, a definitive, complete edition did not appear until 1955. By that time Emily Dickinson was recognized as one of the world's greatest and most innovative poets. If her life was isolated and uneventful, her poems show a depth of turmoil and an exploration of essential questions rarely visited by other writers. Her dramatic conflicts and great events were played out internally in her art. In her words, "The soul should always stand ajar, ready to welcome the ecstatic experience."

Emily Dickinson was one of three children of Edward Dickinson, a prominent lawyer and the treasurer of Amherst College. Her mother was a chronic invalid who required nursing from Emily and her sister, Lavinia, throughout her life. The Amherst of Emily Dickinson's day was a rigidly pious and conservative village of some 500 families, over whom the church wielded the highest authority. In the Dickinson household, Edward Dickinson rivaled the church in his puritanical strictness. The rebel of the family was Emily's brother Austin, also a lawyer, who married a "worldly" New Yorker against his father's wishes and smuggled forbidden books to his sister, thus giving her access to a wider world.

As a young girl Emily was lively and outgoing. She was educated at the Amherst Academy and attended Mount Holyoke Female Seminary for a short time. During her teens, however, she began a gradual withdrawal from the world, and, except for occasional brief visits to Boston and Philadelphia, rarely ventured beyond her home. She gained a reputation as the village eccentric who always dressed in white and avoided company, even visitors to the family home. Her domestic routine included supervising the gardening, tending the greenhouse, and baking the bread, which her father regarded as Emily's particular talent. She read voraciously and corresponded with a small circle of friends. She resisted the Calvinist revivals that periodically swept Amherst and attracted her family. She stopped attending church and kept her own counsel about her religious faith, as well as about much else.

Some biographers speculate that Dickinson may have fallen in love with her father's law apprentice, Benjamin Newton, who, in 1848, was living with her family. A brilliant freethinker, Newton introduced Emily to a new world of ideas. He was too poor to marry and died of tuberculosis in 1853. Another suspected emotional attachment was with the Reverend Charles Wadsworth, whom Dickinson met in Philadelphia in 1854 while she was on her way to visit her father in Washington during his term in Congress. Although married, Wadsworth regularly visited the Dickinsons until 1862, when he accepted a position in California. Following his departure from her life, Dickinson produced a flood of poetry depicting personal crisis and emotional turbulence. A representative poem of the period displays her emotional torment:

I felt a Funeral, in my Brain,
And Mourners to and fro
Kept treading—treading—till it seemed
That Sense was breaking through—
And when they all were seated,
A Service, like a Drum—
Kept beating—beating—till I thought
My Mind was going numb—

The poem provides an instructive example of Dickinson's poetic characteristics. The basic pattern is borrowed from the rhymed quatrains of 19th-century Protestant hymns, but pushed to a unique expressiveness by rhythmic variations, unconventional rhymes, and the irregularity of Dickinson's thoughts and feelings. The emotional and intellectual weight she gives to her poems transforms her verses from deceptively simple quatrains into compressed, cosmic speculations on God, death, love, and nature. The simplest domestic detail is, in Dickinson's hands, arranged into the most intense engagement with the largest themes of existence. Her poetic voice modulates from the simple and naive to the complex and world-weary, but she plumbs truth in all its aspects of paradox and ambiguity with a lively, witty, and ironic intensity. Dickinson's poetic strategy elusive of indirection is explained in the following poem:

Tell all the Truth but tell it slant—
Success in Circuit lies
Too bright for our infirm Delight
The Truth's superb surprise

As Lightning to the Children eased
With explanation kind
The Truth must dazzle gradually
Or every man be blind—

Dickinson's poetry, crafted with a formal expressiveness, deals honestly and resolutely with a complex inner life, captured in all its dimensions. With Emily Dickinson, modern poetry can be said to have truly begun.

EDGAR ALLAN POE

53

1809–1849

He was an adventurer into the vaults and cellars and horrible underground passages of the human soul. He sounded the horror and the warning of his own doom.
—D. H. Lawrence, *Studies in Classic American Literature*

Poe has been called the evil genius of American literature, a *poète maudit* and worse, whose legend, compounded by Poe's own misrepresentations, his enemies' calumnies, and the sad facts of his life, has obscured a full appreciation of his achievement as one of America's most brilliant and original writers. In his native country, Poe's literary contributions have been consistently undervalued. Emerson rejected Poe the poet in the single phrase, "The jingle man"; HENRY JAMES [38] dismissed him with the sentence, "An enthusiasm for Poe is the mark of a decidedly primitive stage of reflection"; and T. S. ELIOT [19], in recognizing Poe's powerful intellect, rejects it by saying, "it seems to me the intellect of a highly gifted young person before puberty."

Poe's revival as a major force not only in American but also in world literature is due largely to his extraordinary impact on the French symbolists: on BAUDELAIRE [46], who called him "the most powerful writer of the age"; on Mallarmé, who regarded Poe as his "great master"; and on Valéry, who observed that "Poe is the only impeccable writer. He was never mistaken." Poe's true value lies somewhere between America's dismissal and France's adoration. He is one of the few literary figures to achieve distinction in poetry, fiction, and criticism whose primary literary contribution resides in his amazing innovations. Poe developed a new definition of art that would have a profound influence on literary modernism; turned the short story into a true art form; invented the detective story; expanded the possibilities of science fiction; and established the foundation for a new kind of fiction with a heightened psychological, emotional, and symbolic dimension.

That Poe achieved so much in so short a life filled with so many personal obstacles is also part of his legend. He was the son of itinerant actors, and his father abandoned his English-born mother when Poe was 18 months old. His mother died on tour in Richmond, Virginia, in 1811, and there Poe became the ward of the Allan family. John Allan, a prominent Scottish tobacco exporter, reared Poe in the style of a young Southern gentleman. Gambling debts caused Poe's removal from the University of Virginia within a year, and he resisted the pressure to join his foster father's business by running away to Boston. There he published *Tamerlaine and Other Poems* (1827) before enlisting in the army. John Allan agreed to send him to West Point, where he was quickly dismissed after an infraction of duty.

Between 1831 and 1835, Poe subsisted as a journalist. He lived in Baltimore with his aunt, Maria Poe Clemm, whose daughter, Virginia, he married in 1836 when she was not quite 14. During this period, Poe published his first short stories, which earned him a literary reputation that he used to secure editorial positions in Richmond and Philadelphia. Poe was a brilliant editor and a candid, perceptive, if occasionally intemperate, reviewer. He was the first critic to recognize NATHANIEL HAWTHORNE's [72] genius, and spoiled the mystery of *Barnaby Rudge*, by CHARLES DICKENS [6], by revealing the novel's secret after its first few installments. His productivity as a critic, poet, and fiction writer, however, was undermined by personal instability, alcohol, and his wife's tuberculosis, which took her life in 1847.

Poe's end has been shrouded in mystery and has contributed most to his legend. What is known is that in 1849 he proposed to his childhood sweetheart, Elmira Royster Shelton, a Richmond widow. On his way to Philadelphia to bring his aunt to his wedding, he disappeared (possibly on a drinking binge) and was found six days later, unconscious on the streets of Baltimore. He died in delirium a few days later. Poe's literary executor, R. W. Griswold, is responsible for distorting many of the facts about Poe, overemphasizing his faults and casting him in the role of the doomed and damned artist that has persisted ever since. Later writers have been drawn to Poe in an attempt to solve the riddle of his deep personal torments—his Oedipal relationship with his lost mother and his idealization of sexuality, focused on his relationship with his young wife. Like DOSTOEVSKY [14] and KAFKA [31], Poe offers many clues in his stories and poems of a complex artist who drew readily on his private obsessions as the basis for his art.

Although Poe has been one of the most heavily analyzed writers of all time, far less has been said about the way his poems and stories reveal not the tortured artist but instead a theory of art that has had such an important influence on later writing. Poe regarded all poetry as essentially an effective instrument whereby the poet produces an intense impression of emotion through the stimulation of a beautiful or melancholy subject. According to Poe, "a poem deserves its title only inasmuch as it excites, by elevating the soul." To achieve the desired effect, he emphasized the "unity of effect or impression" in a short lyric of less than 100 lines, to be read in a single sitting. In poems such as "The Raven," "Ulalume," "To Helen," "The City in the Sea," "Annabel Lee," and "The Bells," Poe attempts a synthesis of musical and visual effects in pursuit of the desired emotional stimulation. An example is the conclusion of "A Dream within a Dream," which combines Poe's characteristic musical tonality with the haunted contemplation of the poet whose heightened sensitivity leads to a chilling revelation:

> I stand amid the roar
> Of a surf-tormented shore,
> And I hold within my hand
> Grains of the golden sand—
> How few! yet how they creep
> While I weep—while I weep!
> O God! can I not grasp
> Them with a tighter clasp?
> O God! can I not save
> *One* from the pitiless wave?
> Is *all* that we see or seem
> But a dream within a dream?

Poe's emphasis on unity, brevity, and emotional response exerted a major influence on modern poetry, with its preference for the short lyric poem. Poe's insistence that the poem is sufficient as an entity in itself, neither a mirror to the poet's soul nor a didactic or moral argument, lies at the root of the art-for-art's-sake movement of the aesthetes in the 1890s, the strategies of the French symbolists, and New Criticism in the 20th century. In pursuit of heightened emotional states, Poe, according to Allen Tate, "discovered our great subject, the disintegration of personality."

In fiction, Poe adapted his poetic theories to narrative and helped raise the status of the short story from a loose and episodic sketch to a highly crafted unified whole. In his famous pronouncement, the short-story writer "having conceived with deliberate care, a certain unique or single effect to be wrought out he then invents such incidents—he then combines such events as may best aid him in establishing this preconceived effect. . . . In the whole composition there should be no word written, of which the tendency . . . is not to the one pre-established design."

As in his poetry, Poe's pursuit of beauty and an emotional response again led him to explore the symbolically suggestive and the states of deepest psychological pressure. In his tales of terror, Poe adapted popular Gothic elements of supernatural menace in the medieval castle and forest "not of Germany but of the soul." In such stories as "Ligeia," "The Masque of the Red Death," and "The Fall of the House of Usher," with their haunting exploration of extreme states, obsession, and guilt, Poe opened up new psychological territory in literature untouched by a narrow realism and concern for commonplace experience. In many of Poe's stories, such as "William Wilson," the narrator is unreliable, and the reader must become a detective, arriving at meaning through implication and nuance. In Poe's stories of actual detection, such as "The Purloined Letter" and "The Murders in the Rue Morgue," reason confronts its opposite as the irrational plays a major part in the puzzles Poe ingeniously unravels. The suggestiveness of his versions of the Gothic and detection would be developed by such writers as Dostoevsky and FAULKNER [15], as well as in popular literature of horror and crime, which can point to Poe as its modern originator.

Poe's work, like his life, is complex and enigmatic, as well as endlessly suggestive. If there is an uneven quality in his work, an occasional lapse in the high standard he set, and some truth to James Russell Lowell's caustic formula—"three-fifths of him genius and two-fifths sheer fudge"—few writers have asserted such an influence over so many areas of literature as Poe.

HENRY FIELDING

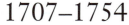

54

1707–1754

The genius of Cervantes was transfused into the novels of Fielding, who painted the characters, and ridiculed the follies of life with equal strength, humour and propriety.
    —Tobias Smollett, *Continuation of the Complete History of England*

If the English novel traces its origin to DANIEL DEFOE [85], its first undisputed masterpiece is surely Henry Fielding's *Tom Jones*. Although his rival and opposite, SAMUEL RICHARDSON [70], must receive considerable credit for refining the often primitive realism of Defoe into the unique artistic form that the novel became, Fielding supplied the comic strain and a synthesis of the epic and the dramatic, fused with the realism of ordinary life. Compared to the darker, meticulous intimacy of Richardson, Fielding offers expansive exuberance and a full portrait of human experience. "To take him up after Richardson," Coleridge observed, "is like emerging from a sick room heated by stoves into an open lawn, on a breezy day in May." Fielding's background, education, legal training, wide-ranging exposure to high and low life, and experience as a dramatist who came late to the novel provided the ideal conjunction of personal qualities and the cultural moment to establish the novel in England as a form to rival poetry and drama. The novel's eventual emergence as a dominant artistic medium owes much to Fielding's genius in harnessing his comic vision to its flexible and expansive form.

Different from those of other early practitioners of the novel, Fielding's background was not middle class but distinguished; he came from the privileged English class of the gentry and well-to-do professionals. He was educated first at home by private tutors, then at Eton (his classmates included William Pitt, the elder) and at the University of Leyden in the Netherlands. His first comedy, *Love in Several Masques*, was produced at London's Drury Lane in 1728, the year he began his university education. Despite his upper-class origins, his connection with the entire range of English society was established through years on the fringe of Grub Street as a playwright and journalist. In 1734, he married Charlotte Cradock, his model for the characters Sophia Western and Amelia, and in 1747, three years after she died, he wed her maid. His career as a dramatist, which included several successes, such as the burlesque *Tom Thumb* (1731) ended in 1737 with the passing of the Licensing Act, which restricted the number of authorized theaters, and was prompted by Fielding's attack on the government of prime minister Robert Walpole in his plays. The same year, Fielding entered the Middle Temple to study law, and his legal career, which required him to travel throughout the country, increased his knowledge of English life and added to his intimacy with clergymen, doctors, actors, writers, lawyers, the gentry, and the commercial and criminal classes. After 1748, Fielding became a London justice of the peace, which brought him into close association with the human suffering and moral issues reflected in his nonfiction writing.

The impetus for Fielding to take up fiction was provided in 1740 by the publication of Samuel Richardson's first novel, *Pamela, or Virtue Rewarded*. Told in a series of letters from the heroine, Pamela Andrews, Richardson's novel describes how the maid servant, Pamela, is beset by the rakish Mr. B., whose dishonorable intentions are finally conquered by a genuine love for the virtuous heroine. Fielding is thought to be the author of the pastiche *Shamela* (1741), in which a heroine's virtue is only a pretense to enflame her lover and manipulate an advantageous marriage. A similar attack on Richardson's sentimentality provides at least the initial ironic focus of Fielding's novel *Joseph Andrews* (1742). In Fielding's comic parody, Richardson's Pamela is now married to Squire Booby, and her brother, Joseph Andrews, has his virtue assaulted by Booby's sister. This comic reversal of Richardson's plot, however, becomes secondary to the story with the wider moral comedy of Parson Adams. Fielding, influenced by CERVANTES [11], presents in the simple, good-hearted, though slightly ridiculous curate an English echo of *Don Quixote*, as the social scene is measured against the idealistic good sense of Parson Adams. What began in *Shamela* as a satire on the narrow and hypocritical idea of virtue grows in *Joseph Andrews* into one of the English novel's first great social satires, in which Fielding's good humor and sympathy embrace a wider, comic conception of human nature as a blend of frailty and goodness, corruption and virtue. As announced in its preface, Fielding intended the novel to be an artistic departure "hitherto unattempted in our language." For his "comic romance" he provides a classical lineage from the epic and drama, but one that is different from prose romances or low comic burlesques:

> Now, a comic romance is a comic epic poem in prose, differing from comedy as the serious epic from tragedy, its action being more extended and comprehensive, containing a much larger circle of incidents, and introducing a greater variety of characters. It differs from the serious romance in its fable and action in this, that as in the one these are grave and solemn, so in the other they are light and ridiculous; it differs in its characters by introducing persons of inferior rank, and consequently of inferior manners, whereas the grave romance sets the highest before us; lastly, in its sentiments and diction, by preserving the ludicrous instead of the sublime.

With Fielding's classical background, the novel is shaped as a hybrid form that borrows elements from the epic and drama, incorporating both the epic's large vision of central cultural values and comedy's admission of ordinary characters and scenes. As Sheridan Baker has observed in a statement about *Tom Jones* that applies to all of Fielding's novels, "It universalizes the contemporary English scene, in part by putting behind it the learning of the ages. It makes the English novel thoroughly literate for the first time. It marries comedy and romance, by the grace of the classics, to produce a peculiarly fresh and ironic wisdom."

In *Jonathan Wild* (1743), Fielding takes up the story of the notorious criminal (executed in 1725) in an ironic paean to villainy. His comedy asserts the novel's moral decency indirectly, not through the example of the admirable like Parson Adams, but by exposing the pervasive moral iniquity of court and jail to his readers' scorn through ironic treatment. As in all of his novels, Fielding's comic vision presents a wide social portrait, held together by a core of good sense.

With *Tom Jones* (1749), Fielding's desire to write a comic epic is most masterfully fulfilled. His plot, which Coleridge called one of "the three most perfect plots ever planned" (the others are *Oedipus* and *The Alchemist*), launches his hero and heroine, the foundling and scapegrace Tom and the delightfully assertive Sophia, on a revealing journey through English society. Compared to Fielding's other novels, the scope of *Tom Jones* is panoramic, filled with portraits that serve both to document social life and to uncover universal principles of human behavior. All is controlled by the shaping presence of the book's narrator, whose compassionate sympathy insists on a moral standard that embraces man's weaknesses as well as his strengths, and accepts the world as it is, even as it is shown very much in need of the good sense that the novel supplies. As did Chaucer in his *Canterbury Tales*, Fielding incorporates into the novel the amplitude and comic vision that would become one of the novel's primary legacies for such writers as DICKENS [6] and JOYCE [7].

In Fielding's last novel, *Amelia* (1751), his comedy is darker and the characters are undiluted moral types, lacking the complexity of the characters in *Tom Jones*. The novel's social portraiture, however, is still strong, if less exuberant. Collectively, Fielding's novels represent one of the best sources of insight into English life and customs during his period. As Leslie Stephen argued in his *History of English Thought in the Eighteenth Century*, "a complete criticism of the English artistic literature of the eighteenth century would place Fielding at the centre, and measure the completeness of other representatives pretty much as they recede from or approach to his work." Fielding remains a central artistic figure who established the novel's tradition as a massive criticism of life.

JOSEPH CONRAD

1857–1924

It is agreed by most of the people I know that Conrad is a bad writer, just as it is agreed that T. S. Eliot is a good writer. If I knew that by grinding Mr. Eliot into a fine dry powder and sprinkling that powder on Mr. Conrad's grave, Mr. Conrad would shortly appear, looking very annoyed at the forced return and commence writing, I would leave for London early tomorrow morning with a sausage grinder.
—Ernest Hemingway, in the *Transatlantic Review*, 1924

Conrad's is one of the remarkable stories in literary history. Born Józef Teodor Konrad Nalecz Korzeniowski in a Polish town under Russian rule, Conrad's first career was as a merchant seaman. In 1895, at the age of 38 and after 21 years at sea, he began his literary career in England. He became one of the premier prose stylists in English, his adopted language, which he did not begin to learn until the age of 20. His books, based on his experience at sea in exotic locales, transform the adventure tale into a highly symbolic exploration of human psychology and community under the pressure of adversity and disintegration. Conrad succeeded in making himself into an influential literary artist whose innovations, particularly in fracturing narrative time and managing multiple perspectives, became pioneering elements in literary modernism. Few other writers have had the number and variety of experiences that Conrad had to form the background for their fiction. What is equally remarkable about Conrad is his continual experimentation to accomplish what he announced in his preface of the early *The Nigger of the "Narcissus"*: "My task which I am trying to achieve is, by the power of the written word, to make you hear, to make you feel—it is, before all, to make you *see.*"

The image of Conrad as an English literary icon, an admired colleague of HENRY JAMES [38], H. G. Wells, John Galsworthy, Arnold Bennett, and Ford Madox Ford, is far from his origin as the son of Polish patriots who went into political exile in northern Russia when Conrad was four. His father, Apollo Korzeniowski, was a poet, translator, and fervent Polish nationalist whose opposition to Russian rule led to his banishment. Conrad's mother died under the strain when he was seven, and his grieving father died four years later. The orphaned Conrad was reared by his maternal uncle, whom he surprised at the age of 15 by announcing his desire to go to sea, driven by a restless desire to see the world. He entered the French merchant marine at the age of 16 as an apprentice seaman and served for four years on voyages to the West Indies and South America. In Spain, he smuggled guns in the service of Don Carlos, the claimant to the Spanish throne, and engaged in shadowy activities that resulted in a mysterious chest wound, the result either of a duel over a woman (the story that Conrad later promulgated) or a suicide attempt.

When Conrad was 20, he joined the English merchant service, perfected his English, and rose through the ranks on a number of voyages to Australia, India, and Indonesia. He eventually gained a certificate as a ship captain in 1886, one of the first non-English seamen to do so, and received his first command in 1888. In 1890, between sea assignments, Conrad commanded a riverboat up the Congo River, an experience that would prove to be the decisive turning point in his career. Conrad's firsthand exposure to European colonial exploitation, which he later recalled as "the vilest scramble for loot that ever disfigured the history of human conscience and geographical exploration," changed him physically and emotionally. His health was permanently impaired, effectively ending his maritime career, and his experiences, profoundly dramatized in his masterpiece *Heart of Darkness* (1899), provided the impetus to become a full-time writer. He settled in Kent, in the southeast of England, where he lived for the rest of his life, married an Englishwoman, Jessie George, anglicized his name, and began to write fiction based on his considerable experiences at sea.

Conrad had begun his first novel, *Almayer's Folly* (1895), while he was still a captain, and he received encouragement from the novelist John Galsworthy, a passenger on one of his voyages. Over the next 17 years Conrad produced 16 books, including *Lord Jim* (1900), *Youth* (1902), *Nostromo* (1904), *The Secret Agent* (1907), and *Under Western Eyes* (1911). Despite the inherent appeal of Conrad's subjects—sea adventures and exotic locales—his books sold poorly, and his life as a writer was a long struggle of poor health and precarious finances—until the publication of *Chance* (1914) and *Victory* (1915) brought him his first considerable popular success and widespread recognition as one of England's foremost fiction writers.

Conrad is, however, one of the most uneven fictional masters. The pressure to publish and attain commercial success resulted in a number of weak efforts, alternating with some of the strongest in English fiction. His talent is best demonstrated in the novella and short story, forms in which he was able to sustain his desired unity of effects and symbolic suggestiveness most effectively. At its best, Conrad's fiction achieves a delicate balance between clearly documented experience and a wider universal resonance. The test of the sea and the remote, exotic locales reach levels of moral ambiguity and expose the deeply mysterious core of existence.

Conrad's greatest achievement is the short novel *Heart of Darkness*. Based on his own experiences in the Congo, the story is an amazing blend of sharply etched details and symbolic significance refracted by his storyteller, Marlow. The novel begins with the provocative statement, "'And this also,' said Marlow suddenly, 'has been one of the dark places of the earth.'" The unnamed narrator and the reader are then asked to decipher the connection between civilized London, where Marlow is on board a ship at anchor in the Thames, and the story of primitive degeneration that Marlow tells about the enigmatic figure of Kurtz in the Congo. Marlow's ruminative and allusive storytelling is a model for Conrad's own:

> The yarns of seamen have a direct simplicity, the whole meaning of which lies within the shell of a cracked nut. But Marlow was not typical (if his propensity to spin yarns be excepted), and to him the meaning of an episode was not inside like a kernel but outside, enveloping the tale which brought it out only as a glow brings out a haze, in the likeness of one of these misty halos that sometimes are made visible by the spectral illumination of moonshine.

Marlow's method of storytelling is to surround the story with suggestive meaning, as Conrad explains, "pushed a little (and only very little) beyond the actual facts of the case. . . . That somber theme had to be given a sinister resonance, a tonality of its own, a continued vibration that I hoped would hang in the air and dwell on the ear after the last note had been struck."

In his finest stories, *Heart of Darkness, The Nigger of the "Narcissus," The Secret Sharer, Lord Jim, Nostromo,* and *The Secret Agent,* Conrad achieves his desired effect of moral questioning through the complex interplay of situation and symbol; his stylistic brilliance and technique refuses to reduce experience to a simple kernel of truth. Instead Conrad achieves an intense exploration of some of life's most important questions: the nature of human evil, the complexity of experience, the difficulty of judging human actions, the paradoxes of identity, and the inability of society and politics to provide satisfactory solutions.

AUGUST STRINDBERG

56

1849–1912

His literary work is one long autobiography, whether it takes the form of confessional novels, misogynistic short stories, revolutionary verses, anguished letters, scientific treatises, theatrical manifestoes, or short plays, full-length works, double dramas, and trilogies. More than any other dramatist, who ever lived, Strindberg writes himself, and the self he continually exposes is that of alienated modern man, crawling between heaven and earth, desperately trying to pluck some absolutes from a forsaken universe.
—Robert Brustein, "August Strindberg" from *The Theatre of Revolt*

Perhaps no other modern writer, with the possible exception of FRANZ KAFKA [31], has so embodied the notion of art as the product of torment and neurosis as August Strindberg. A darker complement to his fellow Scandinavian and nemesis HENRIK IBSEN [36], Strindberg exerted a comparable influence on modern drama as a source for naturalism, expressionism, and various experimental modes on the modern stage. His importance has been recognized by such dramatists as GEORGE BERNARD SHAW [44], who donated his Nobel Prize money to efforts to translate Strindberg into English, and by EUGENE O'NEILL [59], who declared that "Strindberg was the precursor of all modernity in our present theater. . . . Strindberg still remains among the most modern of the moderns, the greatest interpreter in the theater of the characteristic spiritual conflicts which constitute the drama—the blood—of our lives today."

In an immense body of work that includes 58 plays, 15 novels, more than 100 short stories, three volumes of poetry, as well as historical works, scientific treatises and essays on chemistry, botany, politics, economics, philosophy, and religion, Strindberg's writing relentlessly pursues the author's personal demons and searches for answers in virtually every ideology, from spiritualism to the occult, from Darwinian determinism to Rousseauistic progressivism. Strindberg was a virulent misogynist and admirer of authoritarianism, as well as a supporter of women's suffrage and equal rights and a social democrat. His artistic genius encompasses all the contradictions in his thinking, achieving greatness in both groundbreaking realism and its anti-realistic opposite. Strindberg's art charts the unsteady shifts of a haunted and isolated mind sensitive to a driving need for affirmation and an awareness of the inadequacies of any consolation. In 1905, he wrote to his third wife, Harriet Bosse, a year after their divorce:

> My disharmonies lacerate me; my loneliness drives me out to seek other people, but after even the best of meetings I withdraw wounded and find myself inwardly worse. I feel shame without reason, remorse without having sinned, disgust with myself without knowing why. . . .
>
> I struggle upwards but go downwards. I want to see life as beautiful, but only nature is; I feel pity for people but can't respect them and can't love them, for I know from myself what they are. My only comfort now is in Buddha, who tells me in so many words that life is a phantasm, an inverted image, which we shall see righted only in another existence. My hope and my future are both on the other side; that is why I find life so difficult. Everything breaks and mocks. Everything should be viewed at a distance—everything!

Strindberg's revolt and restless search for sustaining absolutes began in Stockholm, Sweden, his birthplace. He was one of 12 children, the illegitimate son of his father's mistress, whom his father later married. His father, a shipping clerk, was bankrupt, and Strindberg grew up in severe poverty and neglect. Strindberg's opposition to authority was established from the start. After completing secondary school, he attended the University of Uppsala but despised formal studies and quarreled with his professors. He tried to become an actor and failed, but his stage experience convinced him to pursue a career as a playwright. His earliest plays dramatize the opposition between individual will and social conventions in stories derived from Swedish history. Strindberg's love affair and subsequent domestic life with a married woman, Siri von Essen, whom he later married, was the source for his naturalistic dramas, the greatest of which are *The Father* (1886), a modernized version of the Agamemnon story, and *Miss Julie* (1888), in which the battle for sexual mastery takes on profound, universal meaning.

Influenced by the notions of ZOLA [65] and the French naturalists, Strindberg's plays embody the concepts of determinism, the role of heredity, environment, and chance, while exploring the tensions of inner life and abnormal behavior. The preface to *Miss Julie*, one of the seminal documents in modern theatrical history, details many of Strindberg's premises for a new, psychologically realistic drama that breaks with theatrical conventions. *Miss Julie*, subtitled "A Naturalistic Tragedy," works out the ways in which an inner tragedy can be revealed despite the naturalistic denial of individual will. His conception of the "characterless character," which rejects simplified characterization in favor of ambiguity and complexity, has become one of the most important legacies for modern drama. "I do not believe, therefore, in simple stage characters," Strindberg declared, "and the summary judgments of authors—this man is stupid, that one brutal, this jealous, that stingy, and so forth—should be challenged by the naturalists who know the richness of the soul-complex and realize that vice has a reverse side very much like virtue." The multiplicity of identity and its fragmentation prepared the ground for his shift from naturalism to expressionism and more poetic and symbolic methods. At their core, all of Strindberg's plays, whether realistic or anti-realistic, attempt to embody the essential conflicts of life and a search to uncover universal motives.

During the 1890s Strindberg went to Paris, where he pursued his search for transcendence in alchemy and spiritualism. Paranoid, subject to violent hallucinations, and periodically hospitalized, Strindberg endured his so-called inferno crisis of self-doubt and guilt, followed by a remarkable burst of creativity that produced 29 plays, novels, poems, and critical essays. In these plays, Strindberg moved beyond his earlier naturalism and historical chronicles to redefine dramatic form, outlined in his prologue to *A Dream Play* (1902): "The writer has tried to imitate the disjointed but apparently logical form of a dream. Anything may happen; everything is possible and probable. Time and space do not exist. . . . The characters are split, doubled, and multiplied: they evaporate and are condensed, are diffused and concentrated. But a single consciousness holds sway over them all—that of the dreamer." Strindberg's expressionistic experiments in *A Dream Play*, *The Ghost Sonata* (1907), and other later plays replace conventional theatrical time and space with symbolic imagery and patterns of repetition around universal conflicts that open up modern drama for later experimental forms in the theater of the absurd and the theater of cruelty.

Strindberg's remarkable artistic development marks out the major boundaries of modern drama, derived from his intense self-analysis and the tormenting conditions of modern life. As Otto Reinert has observed:

> Strindberg's recurrent dramatic motifs define rather than explain the human situation: the ambiguities of childhood guilt, the uncertainty of identity, sex as the fatal mutual attraction of two hostile species whose

struggles serve some mindless life force, vampire figures that drain others of their vitality, endless household drudgery, disgust with physicality, the eternal return of the same sorrows and frustrations, myths of expiation of personal and collective sins. . . . He writes about souls that break under pressures from somewhere out of a dark chaos.

Few other dramatists have looked so unblinkingly at life or embodied their discoveries in as many different artistic patterns of meaning and expression.

D. H. LAWRENCE

57

1885–1930

Lawrence's special and characteristic gift was an extraordinary sensitiveness to what Wordsworth called "unknown modes of being." He was always intensely aware of the mystery of the world, and the mystery was always for him a numen, divine. Lawrence could never forget, as most of us almost continuously forget, the dark presence of the otherness that lies beyond the boundaries of man's conscious mind. This special sensibility was accompanied by a prodigious power of rendering the immediately experienced otherness in terms of literary art.

—Aldous Huxley, Introduction to *The Letters of D. H. Lawrence*

Along with JAMES JOYCE [7], D. H. Lawrence established the opposed boundaries for the novel in the 20th century. In contrast to Joyce's detachment in aesthetic patterns of myth and symbol, Lawrence is all engagement and exposure, a link with the romantics and the visionary quality of BLAKE [29], the sensuousness of KEATS [25], and the defiance of SHELLEY [77]. Both Lawrence and Joyce are haunted by the collapse of values in modern life, but Lawrence offers little of Joyce's alternative consolation in form and technique. As Stephen Spender explains, Lawrence was primarily interested in "the tension between art and life, not the complete resolution of the problems of life within the illusion of art. . . . For him literature is a kind of pointer to what is outside literature. . . .

211

This outsideness of reality is for Lawrence the waters of baptism in which man can be reborn."

Lawrence diagnoses the disintegration of modern society and man's relationship with the world as they reflect our deepest resources of human emotion and psychological well-being. No writer before Lawrence took the reader further in an exploration of our essential, especially our sexual, nature, nor dramatized as fully the consequences of the opposition between nature and society or reason and feeling. Lawrence is a forceful presence in almost every literary genre—the novel, short story, poetry, and criticism. In each, he offers imaginative engagement with some of the thorniest problems of modern experience.

Lawrence's sense of the modern dilemma had its basis in his background and biography. Lawrence was born in Nottinghamshire in England's coal mining region. His father was a miner; his mother, a former schoolteacher, came from a middle-class background. Their opposition of class and consciousness forms the basis of Lawrence's first important novel, *Sons and Lovers* (1913), which is the first of his works to examine the fundamental divisions in the relationships between men and women. Like Paul Morel in *Sons and Lovers*, Lawrence became the focus of his mother's desire for a more cultivated life at odds with their working-class realities. He was a good student and won a scholarship to attend Nottingham High School. After an interval as a clerk in a factory that manufactured artificial limbs, and then as a teacher, Lawrence enrolled in a two-year teaching certificate course at Nottingham University. In 1908, he spent three years as a teacher at a South London school.

Two years after his mother's death, in 1910, the most dramatic event in Lawrence's life occurred when he met Frieda von Richthofen Weekly, the wife of his former French teacher. They fell in love and eloped to the Continent, and were married in 1914 when Frieda's divorce was final. Their passionate, though contentious, partnership is the basis for much of Lawrence's writing on love relationships. The pair began a lifetime of movement around the globe, prompted by Lawrence's search for an ideal community and culture. In England during World War I, despite difficulties surrounding Frieda's German background, Lawrence wrote his most enduring books, following *Sons and Lovers* with *The Prussian Officer and Other Stories* (1914), *The Rainbow* (1915), and *Women in Love* (1916). An expurgated version of *The Rainbow* was condemned as obscene, and all copies were destroyed; *Women in Love* was not published until 1920. In 1919, Lawrence left England for Italy and subsequently traveled to Sicily, Ceylon, Australia, and finally to New Mexico and Mexico. He produced a series of travel books, essays, and a number of novels—*Aaron's Rod* (1922), *Kangaroo* (1923), and *The Plumed Serpent* (1926)—that reflected his search for an alternative to overly intellectualized modern industrialized society in primitive cultures that emphasized a closer relationship with nature. Lawrence's later books have been charged with a susceptibility to the charismatic leader and a sympathy to fascism, but their core beliefs are consistent with his central themes: the warping power of society and the regeneration of inner life through feelings. His plans to establish a utopian society in Mexico were halted by illness, first thought to be malaria, but discovered to be an advanced case of tuberculosis. Lawrence died of the disease in a sanitorium in the south of France in 1930. His final books included *Etruscan Places*, published in 1932, and *Lady Chatterley's Lover*, a synthesis of his themes on the relationship between men and women. It was issued in a number of limited and expurgated editions and remained unavailable in its definitive form until 1960, when its publication in England occasioned a notorious obscenity trial.

Lawrence courted controversy throughout his career and found it either in the sexual content of his books or in his abandoning the formalist detachment that marks much modern writing and facilitates critical attention and respect. In 1925, Lawrence wrote:

> A book should be a bandit or a rebel or a man in a crowd. People should either run for their lives or come under the colours, or say *how do you do?* I hate the actor-and-the-audience business. An author should be in among the crowd, kicking their shins or cheering on to some mischief or merriment. That rather cheap seat in the gods where one sits with fellows like Anatole France and benignly looks down on the foibles, follies, and frenzies of so-called fellow-men just annoys me. After all the world is not a stage—not to me: nor a theater: nor a show-house of any sort. . . . Whoever reads me will be in the thick of the scrimmage, and if he doesn't like it—if he wants a safe seat in the audience—let him read somebody else.

Lawrence's challenge, announced in all his books, is to see things with a radical freshness and clarity that overcomes conventional dualities between self and other, man and nature, subject and object. For Lawrence, the conventional patterns of art prohibited vitality and a relationship with experience that all his writing attempted to forge. From the redefinition of the autobiographical novel of development in *Sons and Lovers*, in which earlier treatment of psychological and emotional awareness seems pallid and shallow in comparison, to his longer studies of love relationships in modern society in *The Rainbow* and *Women in Love*, Lawrence crafted daring and unique responses to essential human questions, including the relationship between the head and the heart and the spirit and the flesh, as well as the moral imperatives that confront the individual without the traditional certainties of faith. His roles as polemicist and preacher often dominate his artistic vision, but few writers have equaled Lawrence's power of sensual perception or his ability to uncover universal significance beneath the surface. For the influential literary critic F. R. Leavis,

Lawrence represented the last figure in the great tradition of the English novel, whose moral vision allies him with JANE AUSTEN [20], GEORGE ELIOT [21], HENRY JAMES [38], and JOSEPH CONRAD [55]. Although Leavis's definition of that tradition can be excessively narrow and reductive, his appreciation of Lawrence's contribution is astute:

> What Lawrence offers is not a philosophy or an *oeuvre*—a body of literary art—but an experience, or, to fall back on the French again, an *expérience*, for the sense of "experiment" is needed too. In him the human spirit explored, with unsurpassed courage, resource and endurance, the representative, the radical and central problems of our time. Of course he went into dangerous places, and laid himself open to reprehension as setting dangerous examples and inciting to dangerous experiments. But if he earned reprehension, we owe him gratitude for earning it.

ROBERT BROWNING

58

1812–1889

In art, only Browning can make action and psychology one.

—Oscar Wilde, *Letters*

Robert Browning's reputation, like that of TENNYSON [81], plummeted with all things Victorian in the modernist reevaluation of 19th-century truths and habits of mind. Browning's reputation as a believer in Victorian progress, particularly in his later years, made him an inevitable target. But Browning also perfected the poetic technique of the dramatic monologue, which would become one of the principal legacies of modern poetry. In discovering a method to control romantic self-expression by dramatizing inner psychological states, Browning points the way toward "The Love Song of J. Alfred Prufrock" by T. S. ELIOT [19], and Ezra Pound's *Hugh Selwyn Mauberley*. *The Ring and the Book*, Browning's complex psychological novel in verse, is the forerunner of modern fiction's preoccupation with unreliable narrators and shifting narrative perspective. Rejecting explicit statement, Browning's poems work by indirection: the reader is expected to participate in uncovering the complex discrepancy between what a character says and what he reveals, and the even more difficult problem of what the poet intends. Browning's sacrifice of declamation for ambiguity has kept him modern, even at the cost of a large popular audience for his work, which gives him another link with the moderns. As Browning observed in 1868:

> I can have but little doubt that my writing has been, in the main, too hard for many I should have been pleased to communicate with; but I never designedly tried to puzzle people, as some of my critics have supposed. On the other hand, I never pretended to offer such literature as should be a substitute for a cigar, or a game of dominoes, to an idle man. So perhaps, on the whole, I get my deserts and something over—not a crowd, but a few I value more.

Browning did not invent the dramatic monologue or the poetic puzzle, but he did bring both to a new competence with a method and a style that have dominated poetic technique ever since.

Browning was born in London, the son of an official of the Bank of England. Educated in a London private school and at University College, London, Browning read widely and was supported by his parents in his desire to be a poet. At the age of 12, his first collection of poetry, *Incondita*, was regarded by his father as worthy of publication, but no publisher was found. Through a pirated volume, Browning came under the influence of SHELLEY [77], who was the primary inspiration for Browning's first published works, *Pauline* (1833), *Paracelsus* (1835), and *Sordello* (1840). All are monodramas dealing with geniuses who, despite their apparent external failure, ultimately attain spiritual success. These apprentice works show Browning developing his personal style, gradually effacing his own personality through dramatic personae, and correcting a tendency toward wordiness with the fragmented style of conversation and consciousness itself. The result often was incomprehensible to his first readers. It was said that when Douglas Jerrold, the editor of *Punch*, read *Sordello* when he was ill and understood none of it, he became panic-stricken, fearing that his illness had affected his mind.

Browning turned to the stage as a means of better demonstrating his dramatic method, but his characters' intense introspection and self-examination translated poorly in the theater, resulting in more reflection than action. Browning finally found an appropriate form for his skills in the dramatic monologue, which culminated in *Dramatic Lyrics* (1842) and *Dramatic Romances and Lyrics* (1845), Browning's first poetic triumphs. In such poems as "My Last Duchess," "Porphyria's Lover," "Soliloquy of the Spanish Cloister," and "The Bishop Orders His Tomb at St. Praxed's Church," Browning presents his characteristic method of using a single speaker to address a silent listener in a situation that reveals, often despite what is explicitly said, the speaker's values and personality. In "My Last Duchess," Browning's most famous poem, as the Duke of Ferrara negotiates for a new bride he exposes his murderous haughtiness: he prefers a portrait to the living presence of his last wife, whom he has put to death. In "The Bishop Orders His Tomb," Browning offers a revealing look at Renaissance values in the complex psychology of a worldly bishop more concerned with the immortality of art than his own soul. Both poems are remarkably subtle psychological portraits in which self-reflection is given vivid dramatic shape in language fitted to conversation but suggesting considerable complexity beneath the surface.

In 1845, Browning met Elizabeth Barrett, the invalid and reclusive poet, and the pair's courtship and secret marriage against her father's wishes form one of the most famous romantic stories of the 19th century. In 1846, the couple set out for Italy, their primary residence until Elizabeth Barrett Browning's death in 1861. At Casa Guidi, their villa in Florence, they entertained a stream of English and American visitors, and Browning began to absorb details of Italian history and customs that served as the background for many of his poems. His major work, *Men and Women* (1855), contains some of his greatest dramatic monologues, such as "Love Among the Ruins," "Fra Lippo Lippi," "Andrea del Sarto," and "Bishop Bloughram's Apology." All are highly polished explorations of intellectual and psychological themes, filled with erudition. Browning's intelligence moved so rapidly that occasionally his readers have difficulty following him, and Browning's reluctance to provide direct statement or clear narrative perspective adds to the obscurity. Even Henry James, no stranger to convolution and opacity, complained that "the idea, with Mr. Browning, always tumbles out into the world in some grotesque hind-foremost manner; it is like an unruly horse backing out of his stall, and stamping and plunging as he comes. His thought knows no simple stage—at the very moment of its birth it is a terribly complicated affair."

Perhaps the ultimate example of Browning's elusive manner is *The Ring and the Book* (1868–69), a 21,000-line poem in four volumes based on a 17th-century Roman murder trial. The story unfolds by implication from the often unreliable, limited testimony of nine speakers. The work achieves a dizzying yet illuminating relativity of perspective, recognizing that experience is never ultimately separate from how we see and who we are. Browning's poem is a tour de force of his mature method that integrates learning, ideas, and psychological truths into a complex dramatic structure.

After his wife's death in 1861, Browning returned to England and continued to write prolifically until his death. He was revered as a Victorian sage whose confident faith asserted itself in confrontation with the great issues of the day, despite the darker grotesqueries of much of his poetry. Along with Tennyson, Browning is one of the Victorian era's strongest currents in the literary stream that connects the romantics with the moderns. Browning in particular introduced the dramatic method that would shape modern poetry in the 20th century, challenging the reader to comprehend fully the shifting and various aspects of experience that the best of his poetry explores.

EUGENE O'NEILL

59

1888–1953

Life and death, good and evil, spirit and flesh, male and female, the all and the one. Anthony and Dionysius—O'Neill's is a world of these antithetical absolutes such as religion rather than philosophy conceives, a world of pluses and minuses; and his literary effort is an algebraic attempt to solve these equations.
  —Lionel Trilling, "Eugene O'Neill" in *After the Genteel Tradition*

The selection of the most significant and influential American playwright for *The Literary 100* was complicated by a number of worthy candidates, including ARTHUR MILLER [119], TENNESSEE WILLIAMS [113], and Edward Albee. The choice of Eugene O'Neill to head this ranking of American dramatists stems largely from the sense that he, as Tennessee Williams wrote, "gave birth to the American theater" and made possible the works of all the playwrights that followed him. As the great drama critic George Jean Nathan observed, "The truth about O'Neill is that he is the only American playwright who has what might be called 'size.' There is something relatively distinguished about even his failures; they sink not trivially but with a certain air of majesty, like a great ship, its flags flying, full of holes." In his considerable successes and occasional daring failures, O'Neill reinvigorated American drama, becoming its first great figure and transforming the commercialized, moribund American stage into an arena for the exploration of the most profound issues. "Most modern plays," O'Neill declared, "are concerned with the relation between man and man, but that does not interest me at all. I am interested only in the relation between man and God."

O'Neill came from a theatrical background that gave him an incentive to expose its shallowness and provide an alternative. Born in a hotel room in the heart of New York's theatrical district, O'Neill was the son of a matinee idol and one-time distinguished Shakespearean actor, James O'Neill, who made his reputation and fortune by endlessly touring in a melodrama based on Alexandre Dumas's *Count of Monte Cristo.* The commercial theater of the day, in which his father squandered his considerable acting talent, consisted of gratifying the lowest popular taste. O'Neill's break with stage conventions has its roots in his rebellion from his troubled family life; his domineering father, drug-addicted mother, and alcoholic elder brother were all in various ways products of the theater of the day. O'Neill's childhood was spent touring the United States with his parents and being irregularly educated at various boarding schools. He was suspended from Princeton after a year for a college prank and introduced to the bohemian world by his brother James, also an actor. Eugene O'Neill's aimless and dissipated youth is summarized by Jordan Y. Miller:

> At twenty, almost on a dare, he had married a girl he hardly knew, fathered a child he never saw until nearly twelve years later, went gold prospecting in Honduras, contracted malaria, and was divorced before he was twenty-two. He failed as a newspaper reporter, became intimate with all the more famous New York and Connecticut bordellos, to which he was guided by his brother James; evidence all of fast becoming a hopeless alcoholic; and, after attempting suicide, contracted a severe lung infection to place him in a Connecticut tuberculosis sanitarium at the age of twenty-four.

During his convalescence (1912 to 1913), O'Neill read widely and determined to become a dramatist. His first stage production, *Bound East for Cardiff,* based on his experience as a seaman, was done for the now famous Provincetown Players, the most influential company in the "little theater" movement, who performed on Cape Cod and in New York's Greenwich Village. It was followed by the successful *The Emperor Jones* and *Beyond the Horizon,* both in 1920, which established O'Neill as the dominating force in the American theater until 1934, when an unknown illness similar to Parkinson's disease made further writing increasingly difficult.

As a dramatist O'Neill displays an incredible range in his search for an expressive form that virtually catalogues the various methods of modern drama. To arrive at truth in the face of a breakdown of values and its crippling effect on the psyche, O'Neill experimented with symbolism, masks, interior monologues, choruses, and realistic and expressionistic styles. His early plays included "slice of life" dramas about the delusions and obsessions of ordinary characters adrift and deeply divided from their identities and sustaining values. Increasingly, his plays dramatized a tragic vision in the psychological explorations he undertook in naturalistic plays such as *"Anna Christie"* (1921) and *Desire Under the Elms* (1924), and in a series of expressionistic experiments, including *The Emperor Jones* (1920), *The Hairy Ape* (1920), and *The Great God Brown* (1926). In *Strange Interlude* (1928), O'Neill began dissecting character through interior monologue, a technique never before attempted onstage on such a scale.

O'Neill's work in the 1930s includes the monumental *Mourning Becomes Electra* trilogy, in which he transferred Aeschylus's story of the House of Atreus to post–Civil War New England, and derived much of its power and intensity from Freudian interpretation. O'Neill modulated the dark tragedy of his trilogy with a family comedy, *Ah, Wilderness* (1933), based on his happiest memories summering at his family's New London, Connecticut, home.

O'Neill then began a period of retirement from the theater. From 1934 until his death in 1953, only one new play, *The Iceman Cometh*, premiered in New York, in 1946. One of O'Neill's most powerful and pessimistic plays, it has been called a "nihilistic version of the Last Supper." Set in a New York City dive, the play centers on derelicts whose pipe dreams insulate them from facing the world and their pain. The play expresses O'Neill's lack of hope for the human condition; illusion alone is sustaining, and death is a final release and instrument of truth. The out-of-town failure in 1947 of *A Moon for the Misbegotten*, written in 1943, effectively ended O'Neill's theatrical activity, though not his writing career. He conceived a monumental 11-play cycle, *A Tale of Possessors Self-Possessed*, chronicling a family's history in America, and completed *A Touch of the Poet* and *More Stately Mansions*. In his later work, O'Neill returned to episodes in his early life and the naturalism of his first stage work. His greatest achievement in this method, and one of the landmark plays in modern theater, is *Long Day's Journey into Night*, a laceratingly revealing portrait of his family. The dynamics of the fictional Tyrones, covering a day in August 1912 when O'Neill learned he had tuberculosis, are stripped of plot contrivance and technical artifice, exposing human relations that are both moving and almost unbearably honest.

In his remarkable career, O'Neill embodied most of the ideas and conflicts of the first half of the 20th century, relentlessly pursuing his diagnosis of modern traumas with a determination that avoided easy consolation. The power of O'Neill's work derives from his ability to present his insights in multiple dramatic forms. He remains one of the great archetypal figures of modern art who wrung out of his own torment and the clarity of his vision dramatic versions of the human condition. As Sinclair Lewis observed, "Mr. Eugene

O'Neill, who has done nothing much in American drama save to transform it utterly, in ten or twelve years, from a false world of neat and competent trickery to a world of splendor and fear and greatness . . . he has seen life as not to be arranged in the study of a scholar but as a terrifying, magnificent, and often horrible thing akin to the tornado, the earthquake, the devastating fire."

CHARLOTTE BRONTË

1816–1855

She showed that abysses may exist inside a governess and eternities inside a manufacturer.
—G. K. Chesterton on Charlotte Brontë,
Twelve Types

EMILY BRONTË

1818–1848

She—
(How shall I sing her?)—whose soul
Knew no fellow for might,
Passion, vehemence, grief,
During, since Byron died.
—Matthew Arnold on Emily Brontë,
Haworth Churchyard

Charlotte and Emily Brontë are inseparably linked, not only by their remarkable achievements in revolutionizing the novel, but also by their incredible family saga. The sisters' personal and artistic development have fascinated readers as much as their literary work. Each woman reshaped great personal adversity into unique artistic visions of intense emotional engagement that few other authors can rival.

Charlotte and Emily Brontë were the third and fourth daughters in a family of six children. Their father, Patrick Brontë, was the vicar of the parish of Haworth in the West Riding region of Yorkshire, a picturesque but isolated community of virtually impassable roads and desolate moors. After their mother died in 1821, the children were reared by an aunt and their severe and puritanical father. After the two eldest Brontë daughters contracted tuberculosis at boarding school and died, Charlotte and Emily were brought home and, with their younger sister Anne and brother Branwell, were largely left to themselves. They filled their time together constructing elaborate fantasies involving the imaginary kingdoms of Gondal and Angria, which they populated with invented and historical figures. Charlotte's and Emily's first poems and stories, written in minuscule script on tiny homemade books, record the various lives and adventures in these invented kingdoms and form an essential key to the artistic vision of both novelists.

The siblings' imaginative play continued well beyond childhood, but economic pressure forced the Brontë children to leave their tight family circle and make their way in the world. Both Charlotte and Emily worked as teachers, and Anne became a governess. Branwell, whom the family hoped would succeed as a portrait painter, became instead a disgrace, succumbing to drink and opium. To keep the family together, the girls hatched a plan to open their own boarding school. To perfect their French, Charlotte and Emily left Yorkshire for a school in Brussels. Emily became so homesick that she almost immediately returned to Haworth, leaving Charlotte on her own to develop an emotional attachment with the school's owner, whose wife quickly stepped in and stopped the infatuation. Charlotte returned to Yorkshire, where she and her sisters collaborated on a volume of poetry and published it at their own expense under the pseudonyms of Currer, Ellis, and Acton Bell. Only two copies were sold. The sisters next turned to the commercial possibilities of the novel. Anne Brontë wrote *Agnes Grey*, based on her experiences as a governess; Emily transferred themes explored in her imaginary kingdom and the intensity found in her poetry to a Yorkshire setting in *Wuthering Heights*; and Charlotte adapted her experiences in Brussels into the realistic novel, *The Professor*. Anne and Emily's novels were accepted for publication, but Charlotte's book was rejected by several publishers. Encouraged by an editor, Charlotte recast some of the elements of her own childhood stories into *Jane Eyre*, which became a controversial literary success.

Jane Eyre, the story of a heroine, in Charlotte Brontë's words, "as plain and simple as myself," traces the title character's development in its first-person account from her troubled childhood to independence as a governess. Jane falls in love with her employer, Edward Rochester, whose secret blights their chance for happiness until the novel's sensational climax. The novel's first edition sold out in six weeks even though critics attacked it as both un-Christian and seditious. Jane's insistence on following the dictates of her own heart rather than custom and authority, and her willingness to forgive the rakish Mr. Rochester, delighted and shocked the Victorian audience. One reviewer charged that the book "might be written by a woman but not by a lady."

Charlotte Brontë's triumph, however, negatively affected the reception of Anne and Emily's novels. Most Victorian readers assumed that *Agnes Grey* and *Wuthering Heights* were the juvenile apprentice works of the author of *Jane Eyre*, and the novels were ignored. *Wuthering Heights*, therefore, has the distinction of being the only classic Victorian novel that was not a popular success. In the same year of Charlotte's great literary success, Branwell Brontë died, and at his funeral Emily caught a cold that developed into tuberculosis. She died at the end of the year. In the spring of 1849, Anne Brontë died. Charlotte wrote two other novels, *Shirley* and *Villette*, and in 1855 she married her father's curate. She lived for another year before dying of tuberculosis while pregnant. The irascible Patrick Brontë survived all of his children, living to the age of 84.

Given the unusual Brontë family history and the isolated artistic development of Charlotte and Emily, defined by little experience and much reading, it is not surprising that their two masterpieces—*Jane Eyre* and *Wuthering Heights*—are unique; in fundamental ways, they changed the form and possibilities of the novel. Both authors grafted onto the novel the emotional intensity previously reserved for lyrical poetry. The Brontës extend the novel, whose range had been defined by the realistic portrayal of social life and manners of JANE AUSTEN [20], to the interior of human nature and passion, and to the elemental heights and grandeur of myth and tragedy.

In *Jane Eyre* the conflict between love and duty is an interior drama within Jane's consciousness. Charlotte Brontë recasts the elements of Gothic romance—its dark secrets, presentiments, coincidences, and eerie atmospherics—into a moral and psychological journey of the soul to fulfillment. At the center of the novel's drama is an unconventional heroine, never seen in fiction before. Jane is plain; she is forced to earn her living in a society of limited possibilities. Her hard-fought reward of the heart is played out against her struggle toward independence and emotional equilibrium. It is not surprising that Jane and her creator have been cited as early feminist models. Called the first historian of the private consciousness, Charlotte Brontë has also been seen rightly as the ancestor of the 20th-century interior novelists such as MARCEL PROUST [16], JAMES JOYCE [7], and VIRGINIA WOOLF [48].

Wuthering Heights is one of the great literary masterworks whose precedents are classical tragedy and the works of SHAKESPEARE [1] rather than fiction. The story of Catherine Earnshaw, the orphan outcast Heathcliff, and their doomed love for each other presents a passionate relationship that attempts to defy the bounds of time and space. Catherine's and Heathcliff's story is so complex and intensely wrought that it must be reassembled by an outside narrator, Mr. Lockwood, who represents the reader as he is instructed in the meaning of a passion and love that defies any standard valuation. When Catherine Earnshaw declares, "I am Heathcliff," she means it literally. As both Catherine and Heathcliff test the limits of self locked into a struggle with time and circumstance, redefining any conventional notion of sin and redemption, the reader is left to wonder at the passionate welding of two wild souls, thus experiencing the same elements of pity and fear that Aristotle reserved for the working of great tragedy.

Charlotte and Emily Brontë crafted two of the most famous love stories in world literature while redefining the methods and the vision of the novel. It is not surprising that readers of both novels are equally fascinated by their authors and search to understand their origins and influences. The Brontës' accomplishments offer a strong lesson in the power of the imagination to dominate adversity. As literary artists, both extended the capacity of the novel to become an instrument of poetic intensity.

JEAN RACINE

1639–1699

There is in Racine a sort of intellectual Puritanism—or Jansenism—which, in the same way as moral Puritanism, distrusts everything that can cause us too much pleasure and regards a priori as suspect any proposition that flatters and suits us. . . . The fine gallantry, the noble fictions, and the becoming poses that have taken the place of the battle between man and woman, these he casts aside. He is unwearying in his efforts to undermine the idea of a paternal and reassuring providence, placed like a stage setting in front of the dead forces which govern the universe and the state of man. All the hallowed prejudices of the baroque, all its comforting illusions, all the themes of its resounding eloquence appear in his plays, only to be brilliantly disposed of.
    —Philip Butler, *Classicism and the Baroque in the Work of Racine*

Jean Racine's identification with neoclassical drama, a form that strikes most modern readers as overly conventional and stylized, has obscured his role as a literary revolutionary who restored tragedy and used drama to reveal profound depths of human emotions and psychology. Racine's drama is marked by a radical assault on the philosophy of his day, unconventional in its rejection of the baroque preference for tragicomedy with its happy ending and assumed providential will in which the good are rewarded and the bad are punished. With Racine, drama returns to the tragic vision of EURIPIDES [22] and examines the complexity of human nature unsupported by illusions of divine order or unqualified heroism. If MOLIÈRE [32] radically altered the history of dramatic comedy, Racine accomplished the same transformation of tragedy, synthesizing the classical and the modern.

Racine's plays are filled with the same divisions between the world and the spirit that marked his private and public lives and established his tragic vision. Born in a small provincial town northeast of Paris, Racine was orphaned at age four. He was brought up by nuns at the abbey of Port Royal, the center of Jansenism, an austere Catholic sect akin to Calvinism that emphasized predestination, personal holiness, and man's essentially corrupt nature. The theater was anathema to the Jansenists, and the conflict between their spiritual goals and more worldly attractions would dominate Racine's development throughout much of his life. Racine remained at Port Royal until he was 17, acquiring a solid education, particularly in ancient Greek, that made him well equipped to pursue a literary career. While a student at the University of Paris he achieved some acclaim for his poetry, and after a two-year interruption while training for the priesthood, he established himself among the court circle of Louis XIV as the age's preeminent tragedian.

Between 1664 and 1677, when he wrote 10 of his 12 plays, Racine displayed an unscrupulous ambition to outmaneuver his theatrical rivals, who included Pierre Corneille and Molière. The latter, at the height of his power, helped the young playwright with criticism and accepted two of Racine's early plays for production. Racine, however, gave one play to a rival company while Molière was performing it, and Racine persuaded his mistress, one of Molière's leading actresses, to quit Molière's troupe. Despite much theatrical and court intrigue, Racine managed to produce the seven plays that established his reputation as the master of French classical tragedy: *Andromache* (1667), *Brittanicus* (1668), *Berenice* (1670), *Bajazet* (1672), *Mithridates* (1673), *Iphigenia* (1674), and *Phèdre* (1677). After the production of *Phèdre*, Racine experienced a religious conversion that led him to abandon the theater and to reconcile with the Jansenists. A famous quip claimed that after his conversion "Racine loved God as he loved his mistresses." He obtained the position of royal historiographer and spent his last 22 years chronicling the activities of the king and his court. He wrote two religious plays, *Esther* (1689) and *Athalie* (1691), before falling from the king's favor in 1698, a year before he died.

The duality between Racine's life in the theater and his life of faith and devotion should be seen not simply as an internal division, but also as a possible reason that Racine, in an age of optimism, selected tragedy as a preferred form. In Jansenist thought, which Racine battled to absorb and overcome and finally incorporated into his tragedies, man was predestined for damnation or salvation. Racine echoes this in the Jansenist-inspired pessimism of his tragedies, in which his characters are beset either by malevolent gods or by an equally implacable impersonal fatality in working out their inevitable tragic conclusions. His conversion, in which he accepts God's grace as a means of achieving redemption, is the consolation that is absent from most of his plays. If his life reached a different conclusion than his tragedies, the same essentially tragic vision underlay both his artistic and religious thinking.

The rules and methods of neoclassical drama that Racine mastered insisted on the observation of the classical unities of time, place, and action. The plot should cover no more than a span of 12 to 24 hours in a single location, and all action must be consistent with the central situation. To reach the desired seriousness of purpose required for tragedy, the characters should be of noble rank; their language should reflect their high breeding and importance, and never descend to the crass or the common. Characters have no physical contact, and all violence takes place offstage. Almost as highly stylized as Japanese Noh drama, the neoclassical stage seems impossibly severe and formal, particularly when compared to the freedom of expression enjoyed by SHAKESPEARE [1] and the naturalism of modern dramatists, which spares the audience little. Racine, however, shows clearly how a great literary talent can make a virtue out of limitations, achieving unmatched intensity and psychological penetration within the prescribed neoclassical rules.

Racine is the master of artistic selection and economy of means. With action restricted offstage, Racine's drama is forced to locate interest within the characters, thus providing an interior view of motive and temperament. His plots, largely borrowed from classical and biblical sources, take as their themes the potentially damning effect of human passion in which love resembles hatred in its intensity and tendency toward self-destruction. In *Phèdre*, his masterpiece, the protagonist is locked in conflict with herself over her passion for her husband's son, Hippolytus. Phèdre knows that her fatal passion is wrong, that Hippolytus is unworthy, but she is incapable of forsaking either. As Bernard Weinberg points out in his survey of Racine's plays *The Art of Jean Racine*, it is in *Phèdre* that Racine finally solved the challenge of his demanding dramatic mode of expression:

> Where the action had seemed to be satisfactorily compounded, the emotion had sometimes remained divided among several main personages, it had at other times failed to become a truly tragic emotion. Where the protagonist had seemed to possess the necessary qualities and to produce the desired effect, his general effectiveness had been impaired or limited by the lack of a properly dramatic action. Only in *Phèdre* will Racine combine the lessons learned about both action and protagonist into a brilliantly successful synthesis.

The play more than justifies the neoclassical model and exposes Racine's great resources to achieve penetrating insights about human emotions and experience. If *Phèdre* is the pinnacle of Racine's achievement, his other attempts clearly show his skills as a craftsman, poet, and psychologist. If modern drama has drawn more on romantic and naturalistic sources for its inspiration, Racine remains a powerful force in defining a classical theater in the West and in achieving theater's dual goal of intensity and penetration.

ERNEST HEMINGWAY

63

1899–1961

He is a great writer. If I didn't think so I wouldn't have tried to kill him. . . . I was the
champ and when I read his stuff I knew he had something. So I dropped a heavy glass
skylight on his head at a drinking party. But you can't kill the guy. He's not human.
— F. Scott Fitzgerald, quoted in Jed Kiley,
Hemingway, A Title Fight in Ten Rounds

Through all the bluster, the style so easy to parody but so difficult to duplicate,
and the distractions of celebrity, Hemingway's excellence remains untouched
as one of this century's indispensable literary forces. Few other writers have
had Hemingway's impact on modern consciousness and literary sensibility.
In his time, as America's most famous writer, Hemingway was also America's
greatest literary export; his influences can be felt in every culture where his
books are read, and his works help to define modern themes, attitudes, and
a new fictional technique. A literary lightning rod, Hemingway continues
to attract admiration and censure as few other writers have done. We seem
to know his stances and poses so well, but the true nature of his work still
troubles and eludes us even as it continues to communicate important lessons
about the world and how it can be captured. His principal theme is war—as
a personal and symbolic experience, moral condition, and a steady state of
human existence. "I was trying to learn to write," Hemingway recalled about

his preoccupation, "commencing with the simplest things, and one of the simplest things and the most fundamental is violent death." No other writer has probed this fundamental truth so exhaustively nor has followed it so widely as a central condition of modern life, with its attendant code of heroic resistance to life's meaninglessness and destruction. As the character Brett Ashley states in *The Sun Also Rises*, "It's sort of what we have *instead* of God."

Born in Oak Park, Illinois, an affluent suburb of Chicago, Hemingway grew up with divided loyalties between his father, a doctor who introduced him to the joys and rituals of hunting and fishing, and his religious and musical mother. Much of his later imagination was stimulated by recollections of vacation trips to northern Michigan, the scene of some of his finest stories. His father would eventually take his own life, establishing at a private and personal level the theme of death that would haunt Hemingway throughout his career. After high school, anxious to participate in World War I, Hemingway instead secured a job as a reporter for the *Kansas City Star*. Within a year, however, Hemingway got into the war as an honorary lieutenant in the Red Cross, driving an ambulance on the Italian front. He was severely wounded in the knee while passing out chocolates to the troops. For Hemingway, the effects of war—actual combat, as well as more ritualized bullfighting and big game hunting—and its aftermath on a succession of wounded protagonists would form his characteristic subject. How one faced the ultimate test of existence was measured against a code of proper behavior that emerges in his stories and novels.

After the war, Hemingway returned home for a time before arriving in Paris as a foreign correspondent for the *Toronto Star*. There, in the midst of the expatriate community, whom GERTRUDE STEIN [125] named the Lost Generation, Hemingway began his writing career. His greatest achievements were his three major books written in the 1920s: a volume of short stories, *In Our Time* (1924), and the novels *The Sun Also Rises* (1926) and *A Farewell to Arms* (1929). Collectively they form a milestone in the history of literary technique and modern sensibility.

The stories of *In Our Time*, which can be read as a narrative sequence, introduce the characteristic Hemingway hero, Nick Adams. Nick is shown at various stages of his development attempting to cope with different traumas as the threat of death and destruction engulf him. Spare and specific, the famous Hemingway style emerges in force. "If a writer of prose knows enough about what he is writing about," Hemingway declared, "he may omit things he knows and the reader, if the writer is writing truly enough, will have a feeling of those things as strongly as though the writer had stated them. The dignity of movement of an iceberg is due to only one-eighth of it being above water."

Not since EDGAR ALLAN POE's [53] short fiction has a technique for the short story so dominated the form, as has Hemingway's method of suggestive indirection. In *The Sun Also Rises*, which explores futility in the postwar generation, Hemingway offers a variation on the theme *The Waste Land*, by T. S. ELIOT [19]. *A Farewell to Arms* more directly explores the war experience by presenting it as a universal condition: the two lovers make a separate peace that collapses when Catherine Barkley dies in childbirth, a result, in her words, of "a dirty trick." Nick Adams, Jake Barnes, and Frederic Henry are all variations on the typical Hemingway hero: wounded, alienated, and fundamentally alone, circulating around the same void and threat. They learn the proper method of dealing with both, of "grace under pressure," in Hemingway's famous phrase.

In ways that make it impossible to separate fully his art from his life, Hemingway translated his growing fame into exploits and adventures that reflected his fictional world. The Hemingway persona of legend was invented: hard-drinking, pugnacious, continually combative, a fan of bullfights, prizefights, big game hunting, and sport fishing. A synergistic relationship developed between the author and his works, between his autobiography and his fiction. In the 1930s, Hemingway resided mostly in Key West, Florida. Besides an additional collection of stories, *Winner Take Nothing* (1933) and the nonfiction works *Death in the Afternoon* (1932), and *Green Hills of Africa* (1935), he published only the weak novel *To Have and Have Not* (1937). During much of this period, the freshness and originality of Hemingway's writing dwindled, almost becoming parodies.

A rebirth began as a result of Hemingway's participation in the Spanish Civil War. Up to this point, the typical Hemingway hero was alienated and cut off from any sustaining connection to a larger world. In *For Whom the Bell Tolls* (1940), however, Hemingway worked toward a new stance of engagement. Larger issues of social and communal values begin to enter the Hemingway code. Robert Jordan, the protagonist, is committed to the republican cause in the Spanish Civil War even as he knows his actions in blowing up a strategic bridge will ultimately fail to make a difference. Despite some weaknesses, particularly in the sentimentality of the affair between Jordan and Maria, a young peasant girl, *For Whom the Bell Tolls* is an ambitious achievement, the last great book in Hemingway's career aside from the remarkable novella *The Old Man and the Sea* (1952), which was written in defiance of the prevailing notion that Hemingway's strengths had permanently declined.

During World War II, Hemingway's actual adventures in combat rival anything in his fiction. First searching out German submarines in his fishing boat, then covering the European theater as a newspaper and magazine correspondent, Hemingway participated on missions with the Royal Air Force and, after the invasion of Normandy, attached himself to an irregular unit that preceded Leclerc's French force in the liberation of Paris. After the war, Hemingway lived principally on a farm outside Havana, Cuba, with his fourth wife,

Mary Welsh. Plagued by ill health, Hemingway finally settled near Sun Valley, Idaho, where on July 2, 1961, he took his own life with his favorite shotgun.

Hemingway's life and literary career have been controversial from the start. His very public life has been viewed as a rather puerile celebration of maleness, and his work has been unfairly dismissed as excessively narrow in range and lacking in complexity. His proponents have been equally loud in his praise, linking Hemingway with MARK TWAIN [45] as one of the principal creators of a distinctively American voice. His presence, as a legend as much as a writer, is impossible to dismiss or to avoid in a study of modern American literature.

VLADIMIR NABOKOV

64

1899–1977

The power of the imagination is not apt soon to find another champion of such vigor. He was one of the last delegates of the nineteenth century; he takes with him the secret of an undiscourageable creativity, he leaves behind a resplendent oeuvre.
— John Updike, "Notes and Comment," *New Yorker,* 1977

One of the artistic giants of the 20th century, Nabokov was a major force in two different languages and cultural traditions. As a Russian writer, he is linked to the great figures of the Russian literary tradition that includes PUSH-KIN [18], TOLSTOY [4], DOSTOEVSKY [14], and GOGOL [93]. As an American writer, Nabokov wrote *Lolita,* which many consider the defining American novel of the postwar period, and which established him as America's dominant creative force. The legitimate heir to the European modernist tradition of PROUST [16], KAFKA [31], and JOYCE [7], Nabokov is a stylistic master who imaginatively reshaped artistic forms to reflect a unique sensibility.

The themes of exile and memory, and the ambiguous legacy of consciousness itself, haunt Nabokov's works and originate in his background. Born in St. Petersburg into an aristocratic family, Nabokov enjoyed a privileged youth that would be destroyed by the Russian Revolution. Nabokov's father was a professor of criminal law and a prominent leader of Russia's Constitutional-Democratic Party; his mother was the daughter of a landowner and philanthropist. A voracious reader who had access to his father's extensive library, Nabokov grew up trilingual, first learning English, then Russian and French. Nurses and tutors provided his earliest education prior to his attending one of St. Petersburg's most distinguished lycées. His first literary work was a collection of poems privately printed when he was 17.

During the Russian Revolution his family fled south to Yalta with few belongings other than the family jewels, and in 1919 Nabokov left Russia for the last time to attend Trinity College in Cambridge. There he studied Russian and French literature and played soccer. According to Nabokov, not once during his stay at Cambridge did he visit the university library, preferring an active social life.

In 1922, Nabokov's father was assassinated in Berlin by a Russian monarchist gunman. After graduating later that year, Nabokov rejoined his family in Berlin, among the Russian émigré community, where Nabokov was determined to become a writer. Between 1922 and 1940, when he arrived in America, he produced nine novels, 48 short stories, and essays, reviews, and translations. Fascinated with games and puzzles, he also composed chess problems and invented the Russian crossword puzzle. In 1925, he met and married his wife Véra, and in 1934 their only child, Dmitri, was born. Nabokov supported his family in Berlin and Paris with meager earnings from his writing, supplemented by teaching language and tennis lessons. Nabokov's major works in Russian include *The Defense* (1930), *Despair* (1936), *Invitation to a Beheading* (1938), and *The Gift* (published serially from 1937 to 1938), which Nabokov considered the best of his Russian novels.

After the outbreak of World War II, Nabokov arrived in the United States with only $100, but secured academic posts first at Stanford and then, from 1942 to 1948, at Wellesley College. He was also a part-time research fellow at the Museum of Comparative Zoology at Harvard, pursuing his lifelong passion for lepidopterology, the study of butterflies. Nabokov also continued his writing career first by translating and revising his earlier Russian novels, and, in 1947, with *Bend Sinister*, producing a succession of masterworks in English. In 1948, Nabokov began a 10-year appointment as a professor of comparative literature at Cornell University, and in 1955 burst on the international scene with the publication of *Lolita*. His best-known and, according to Nabokov, his best novel continues to generate controversy over its subject matter—the protagonist Humbert Humbert's tragic-comic passion for the nymphet Lolita—but it has been acclaimed the supreme novel of love in the 20th century. Nabokov's other important novels include *Pnin* (1957), *Pale Fire* (1962), and *Ada, or Ardor: A Family Chronicle* (1969). In 1959, Nabokov moved to Montreux, Switzerland, where he continued to write until his death, producing fiction and poetry, as well as a memoir, *Speak, Memory* (1966). When he died in 1977 he left an incomplete manuscript, *Original of Laura*.

Nabokov established his characteristic themes and techniques in his first Russian works. All but one of the nine novels he wrote prior to 1940 have a European setting, most often Berlin, and his characters are usually Russian émigrés. All of his fictions trace developments in an individual's consciousness either toward growth and integration or into decline through obsessions and self-delusions. "Being aware of being aware of being" is what Nabokov believed sets humans apart from other animals, and he put the mysterious workings of consciousness itself at the center of his work. Memories and the attraction of the past often stimulate the individual's attempt to fashion a working relationship between illusion and reality. Linear narrative sequence is often fragmented, to be reassembled by the reader. "I confess I do not believe in time," Nabokov declared. "I like to fold my magic carpet, after use, in such a way as to superimpose one part of the pattern upon another." It is also difficult to identify Nabokov's shaping hand and intentions in his fiction, since most of his novels come filtered through the consciousness of limited and unreliable narrators. Puzzles, which fascinated him, set the shape of many of his novels, with hints and clues detected through an elaborate pattern of motifs and allusions. Many readers find Nabokov a cold, detached gamesman whose central delight lies in manipulating and disappointing reader expectation: they read him as the master who refuses to be mastered. While it is certainly true that Nabokov's erudition and allusive quality can be daunting (in some cases even exasperating), there is an equally powerful sense of exhilaration in his absolute originality. "One of the functions of all my novels," he asserted, "is to prove that the novel in general does not exist." Each of his works, therefore, is meant to be unique, shaped by the novelist's contention that "great writers invent their own worlds."

Perhaps there is no better example of the character and the quality of Nabokov's remarkable imagination than his novel *Pale Fire*. The novel features a 999-line poem by the fictional American poet John Shade with commentary by Charles Kinbote, intended as a scholarly exegesis, equipped with an index. It is apparent from Kinbote's scholarship that he has misappropriated the poem and has interpreted it to suit his dementia as the deposed king of Zembla. The novel is a tour de force, a kind of eternal loop of meaning in which Nabokov demolishes the clear relationship between an author and his work and celebrates his assertion that "art at its greatest is fantastically deceitful and complex."

Nabokov's canon demonstrates that he is one of the imagination's greatest practitioners. A link between the giants of the 19th-century novel and the modernist innovators, Nabokov's work validates the power of the artist to create a new world.

ÉMILE ZOLA

65

1840–1902

Let us envy him: he honored his country and the world by an immense literary work and by a great deed. Envy him! His destiny and his heart made his lot that of the greatest: he was a moment of the conscience of man!
> —Anatole France, from his funeral oration on Zola, 1902

A provocative writer of enormous power and influence, Émile Zola uniquely shaped modern consciousness and the modern novel. His documentary style and controversial subjects opened up new ground for fiction, extending the novel's range into the working class and the darker truths of the human condition. Rising from destitution and obscurity, Zola ended his career as one of the most widely read contemporary authors in the world. A writer of seemingly inexhaustible energy in his drive to capture life truthfully, Zola rivals BALZAC [40] in sheer volume and comprehensiveness. In *L'Assommoir, Germinal, La Terre, Nana,* and *La Débâcle,* his experimental method codified literary naturalism and produced masterpieces of world literature that still move and instruct.

In a famous artistic pronouncement, Zola declared, "A literary work is a corner of nature seen through the temperament of the writer," and his temperament combined the pathologist with the sociologist, the romantic with the visionary. His considerable influence was dominant in France and

Germany, extended to Russia, helped shape modern drama through IBSEN [36] and STRINDBERG [56], and entered the English novel through George Moore and George Gissing, and the American novel through Frank Norris, Stephen Crane, THEODORE DREISER [110], and Upton Sinclair. His innovations and experiments created perhaps the single most powerful movement in modern literary consciousness, offering a new way of looking at the world.

Zola's daring assault on literary conventions was fueled by his identity as an outsider well-versed in the marginal lives of those in the substratum of society. Now buried in the Pantheon with the other immortals of French literature, Zola did not become a French citizen until age 22. His father, Francesco, was Italian, an engineer with plans for the fortification of Paris and the improvement of the water system in Aix-en-Provence, which he was working on when he died suddenly in 1847, leaving Zola and his French-born mother with little means of support. Zola's schooling began in Aix-en-Provence, where he was abused by his classmates for his insufficiently southern accent. He was befriended, however, by a schoolmate, the future artist Paul Cézanne, beginning a long relationship. In 1857, financial need drove Zola and his mother to Paris, where he twice failed the *baccalauréat*, the prerequisite examination for all university study. The period from 1860 to 1862 was the darkest and most desperate in Zola's life. He lived alone in an unheated room, staying in bed to keep warm and pawning his few belongings for food. He supported himself for a time as a clerk on the Paris docks. His rescue came when he was given a job in the shipping department of the publishers Hachette et Cie, which saved him from destitution and provided him with the literary contacts to begin his career as a writer.

Zola's early work was poetry, strongly influenced by the romanticism of VICTOR HUGO [105]. Louis Hachette encouraged his young employee to shift to prose, and Zola began a collection of short stories that became his first book, *Contes à ninon* (1864), and his first novel, *La Confession de Claude* (1865), while supplementing his income with journalistic work. Zola's two earliest books are autobiographical and sentimental. He followed these with several potboilers to make money. *Thérèse Raquin* (1867), the best known of Zola's early works, represented a breakthrough in subject matter and technique, and shows him tentatively working out of his theory of naturalism. Zola's grim and shocking tale of infidelity, murder, and suicide echoes the faithful realism of *Madame Bovary* by GUSTAVE FLAUBERT [30] but also considers the abnormal and extreme forces that drive individuals. As Zola explains in the preface to the book's second edition:

> In *Thérèse Raquin* I wanted to study temperaments and not characters. That's the essential point of the whole book. I chose people who were entirely dominated by their nerves and their blood, without free will, dragged into each action of their life by the fateful inevitability of their

flesh. Thérèse and Laurent are human beasts, nothing more. I tried to follow, step by step, the hidden work of passion in these beasts, the pressure of instinct, the mental breakdown that follows a nervous crisis.

Here Zola underscores the basic tenets of naturalism, with its emphasis on determinism and instinct as the prime motivation for human behavior. He also identifies his clinical approach, conceiving the novel as a kind of human experiment. "The novelist," he later wrote, "is part observer, part experimenter. As observer he collects the facts, sets the point of departure, establishes the solid ground on which the characters will walk. . . . Then the experimenter appears and institutes the experiment. I mean, causes the characters to move in a given story in order to show that the succession or order of facts will be such as is required by the determination of the phenomena under study." With the language of the scientist, Zola describes a new approach to the novel and role for the novelist, who "operates on characters" as "the chemist and physicist operates on inanimate bodies and the physiologist on living ones."

With his new experimental method, Zola next embarked on the massive and grandiose scheme of a proposed 20-novel cycle, comprising his epic saga *Les Rougon-Macquart, histoire naturelle et sociale d'une famille sous le Second Empire*. Although influenced by Balzac's *Human Comedy*, Zola intended to become the first novelist to systematically study a single historical period: France's Second Empire from the December 1851 coup to its fall in the Franco-Prussian War of 1870 to 1871. Unlike Balzac, Zola covered the entire social hierarchy in depth, particularly the working class, which Balzac often ignored. Like Balzac, Zola used recurring characters, but he also studied recurring characteristics, tracing the influence of heredity as well as environment on his characters through several generations. His ambitious and unprecedented plan took 25 years to accomplish, during which he conducted extensive research and from 1868 to 1893 wrote almost a novel a year. While some of the novels in his series are stronger than others, a few are indisputable masterpieces. The first is *L'Assommoir* (1877), which made Zola's reputation as one of the literary giants of the 19th century, and made him a rich man as well. The novel's title translates as "cudgel" or "club," and is the name of the cheap saloon that forms the locus for the novel's grim tale of working-class life. Before Zola, if workers appeared in fiction at all they were invariably caricatured and often sentimentalized. Zola takes his readers into an unfamiliar environment to reveal a tragedy that is grounded in its time and place yet retains a universality and sustained power. His other great novels all succeed on the same level, introducing aspects of contemporary life and events never treated as honestly before—miners in *Germinal*, country life in *La Terre*, prostitution in *Nana*, the Paris Commune in *La Débâcle*—while achieving genuine human drama through scrupulous documentation and sympathy.

Although often cloaked in the role of the objective narrative clinician, Zola possessed a strong reformer's zeal that entered his fiction and affected his experiments. "Don't forget," he observed, "that drama catches the public by the throat. Readers get angry, but they do not forget. Always give them, if not nightmares, at any rate excessive books which stick in their memory." To catch his readers, he challenged proprieties and courted controversy throughout his career. His famous letter, given the title "J'Accuse," alleging a political and military coverup in the treason case of Alfred Dreyfus, is the most famous example. Tried and convicted of libel, Zola spent a year in exile in England before returning to France when Dreyfus was exonerated. Zola died in an accident, asphyxiated by coal gas from a furnace. At his funeral, he was eulogized as one of the greatest moral and literary forces of the 19th century, which his fictional achievement more than justifies.

66

BEN JONSON

·1573–1637

Then Jonson came, instructed from the school,
To please in method, and invent by rule,
His studious patience and laborious art,
By regular approach, assail'd the heart.
Cold approbation gave the lingering bayes,
For those who durst not censure, scarce could praise.
A mortal born, he met the general doom,
But left, like Egypt's Kings, a lasting tomb.
 —Samuel Johnson, *Prologue at the Opening of the Drury Lane Theatre*

"What more difficult fate could there be for another writer, and what more crucial test, than to have his name perennially bracketed with that of the greatest writer who ever lived?" The distinguished critic Harry Levin posed this question about CHRISTOPHER MARLOWE [75], but it is equally applicable to Ben Jonson. Both writers have been overshadowed by the great SHAKESPEARE [1]; both deserve recognition for their considerable achievement and legacy. Without Shakespeare to contend with, Jonson would have unquestionably been deemed, as one of his contemporary eulogists asserted, the "Great Lord of Arts, and Father of the Age!" Actor, poet, playwright, scholar, critic, translator, Jonson is, in a sense, the first great man of English letters, one thoroughly devoted to the writer's craft and calling. In a writing career of more than 40 years (over twice as long as Shakespeare's) that produced over 60 plays, several collections of poetry, translations, criticism, and philosophical reflections, it was Jonson who mounted the case that English writers could incorporate and expand on the literary achievements of the giants of the classical tradition. In drama, Jonson became the only comparable non-Shakespearean alternative, offering the Elizabethan and world theater an opposing subject matter and method. The master of the urban, satirical comedy of manners, Jonson brought raw and unflattering contemporary life within dramatic range and harnessed disparate, rowdy Elizabethan life to the classically derived rules of dramatic construction that would shape neoclassical theatrical ideals for the next two centuries. Only Shakespeare and SHAW [44] have contributed more plays to the permanent national repertory. It was Jonson as well who insisted that drama was an esteemed form of poetry and, therefore, the noblest and profoundest human expression. More than any other English dramatist, Jonson helped to establish plays as literature, capable of the most serious inquiry into human nature and social life. If, as Jonson acknowledged, Shakespeare was the "Soule of the Age!" Jonson was its conscience and its unavoidable literary arbiter.

A comparison between Jonson and Shakespeare, though irresistible and often misleading, is still instructive in underscoring their different relationships to the theater and poetic practice. Born in 1572 or 1573, almost a decade after Shakespeare, Jonson was part of the next generation of Elizabethan and Jacobean dramatists who had Shakespeare's works and the drama that he pioneered to imitate, modify, and transform. Both Shakespeare and Jonson came from similar lower-middle-class backgrounds, but Shakespeare was a countryman, who drew extensively on his love for and familiarity with rural life, while Jonson was a Londoner, whose arena and references were predominantly urban. Jonson was the son of a minister who died a month before his birth. His widowed mother married a bricklayer, and Jonson was raised near Westminster where he enrolled at the prestigious Westminster School located in the precinct of the abbey. He studied under the age's greatest classicist and antiquarian, William Camden, whom Jonson would later credit for "All that I am in arts, all that I know." Camden would spark Jonson's lifelong devotion to classical literature, his love of scholarship, and his self-consciously academic approach to his writing and aspirations. Jonson, in contrast to Shakespeare's purported "little Latin and less Greek," would proudly assert that "he was better Versed & knew more in Greek and Latin, than all the Poets in England." It was at Westminster that Jonson was introduced to drama in annual performances mounted by its scholars. When he left Westminster, he did not, as might have been expected, matriculate at Oxford or Cambridge. Instead he apprenticed as a bricklayer, becoming a journeyman by 1598. The premature end of Jonson's formal education and his working-class background no doubt made him excessively proud and protective of his scholarly attainments and anxious that his writing should be measured against the revered classical standards. Jonson married unhappily, losing both his children to early illness, fought as a volunteer foot soldier against the Spanish in the Netherlands, and began his career as a playwright, like Shakespeare, after first acting in one of London's professional theater companies. He would never, however, like Shakespeare, become a full partner of any playing company as a resident actor or writer. He took instead an independent line to protect his scholarly and poetic aspirations to become more than a dramatic professional. Jonson would complain about "the lothed stage" that catered to popular tastes that were "not meant for thee, less, thou for them."

Jonson's debut as a playwright was inauspicious. In 1597 he completed a topical satire by Thomas Nashe, *The Isle of Dogs*, and was imprisoned for several weeks for sedition for acting in and co-authoring it. After his release, Jonson continued to collaborate on a number of plays (now lost) and produced his first solo effort, *The Case Is Altered* (1598), a comedy derived from Plautus. It was followed by *Everyman in His Humour* (1598) and *Everyman out of His Humour* (1599), performed by Shakespeare's company, the Lord Chamberlain's Men, which established Jonson as a coming playwright. Around the time of the debut of *Everyman in His Humour*, Jonson killed a young actor in a duel and was again imprisoned, avoiding execution by pleading the ancient benefit of clergy because he could read. When James I came to the throne in 1603, Jonson won favor and patronage as the chief author of court masques and entertainments, despite being imprisoned for supposed slights to the king and the Scots in 1605 for the comedy *Eastward Ho!* Following Jonson's failure with the tragedy *Sejanus*, which was hissed off the Globe stage in 1603, Jonson returned to stage comedy with *Volpone*, his first undisputed masterpiece, which was performed to great acclaim at the Globe in 1606. *Volpone* signaled a new kind of moral comedy and demonstrated Jonson's mature style and construction that joined his admired classical models to the popular traditions of English drama. *Volpone* initiated a string of comic masterworks, including *Epicoene* (1609), *The Alchemist* (1610), *Bartholomew Fair* (1614), and *The Devil Is an Ass* (1616).

Jonson articulated his break with the theater of his day in his prologue to the revised version of *Everyman in His Humour*, declaring his allegiance as a comic writer to "deedes, and language, such as men doe use," and to the presentation of an "Image of the times," embodied in ordinary characters and everyday circumstances—"with humane follies, not with crimes." He criticized contemporary dramatists for "all license of offence to God and man" for their improbable plots that relied on accidents, coincidences, and the stale contrivances of mistaken and concealed identities, for their indecorous mixture of comedy, pathos, and tragedy and violations of the unities of time, place, and action in language inappropriate to the speaker and marred by artificial sentiment and bombast. *Volpone* clearly shows Jonson's response. Instead of the conventional romantic intrigue that Shakespeare had relied on in his comedies, Jonson submits to comic ridicule the "ragged follies of the time." Blending the fortune-hunting plot and character types of Roman comedies with native allegorical elements of the morality play and the beast fable, Jonson ingeniously arranges variations on the theme of human greed. At the center of the play is Volpone, the fox, a Renaissance Venetian schemer, and Mosca (the fly), his servant, who extort riches from those courting Volpone's favor as the talented scoundrel pretends to be a dying man in need of an heir. What is striking about Jonson's arrangement here is his centering the play on a comic villain and his parasite. While Elizabethan tragedies featuring monstrous characters had been common since Marlowe's *Tamburlaine*, no Elizabethan comedies had ever dared such a complete capitulation to the villainous hero and his sidekick. *Volpone* presents a world inhabited exclusively by knaves, gulls, and the innocent victims of both. Jonson mounts his satiric argument here indirectly, not by opposing the vices and moral failings of his characters by the counterforces of good and virtue, but by multiplying and exaggerating through caricature greed, hypocrisy, and self-deception, and thereby shaming his audience into rejecting these false values by ridicule. Central to Jonson's strategy is the notion that the characters' greed will ensure their own downfall. As Volpone observes, "What a rare punishment / Is avarice to itself."

Playacting and self-deception also animate *The Alchemist*, considered by Samuel Taylor Coleridge, as one of "the three most perfect plots ever planned," along with *Oedipus* and *Tom Jones*. *The Alchemist*, as its title indicates, is a play about transformation. It is Jonson's *Midsummer Night's Dream* in which the confusion between appearance and actuality, desire and reality, is enacted, not in a fantastical forest outside Athens, but in a townhouse in London's Blackfriars. The agents of the play's many magical transformations are not fairies scrambling the affections of confused lovers but a trio of con artists fleecing the gullible and self-deluded. In its contemporary London setting, Jonson assembles a cross section of Elizabethan society—clerk, shopkeeper, country squire, rich widow, parson, nobleman, gamester, servant, charlatan, and prostitute. They are all frauds, either pretending to be what they are not or aspiring to become someone else. The play's gulls, including a law clerk who desires supremacy as a gambler, a country squire who has come to London "to learn to quarrel, and to live by his wits," a hypocritical clergyman, Tribulation Wholesome, and the voluptuarian Sir Epicure Mammon, are shown susceptible to the promise of the cozeners—a butler known as Face, a charlatan posing as an alchemist and necromancer named Subtle, and the prostitute Doll Common—because they are victims of their own delusions. The play offers an unrelentingly unflattering but undeniable examination of human nature in the grips of greed, vanity, and our preference for illusion over reality. With Jonson's broadest social canvas and its universally relevant theme of mankind's capacity for self-deception, *The Alchemist* is the playwright's most ambitious and profound play, which, more than any other of his dramas, helped to establish a new standard of dramatic construction and a realistic method and subject for the theater.

Jonson's plays were not always successful on the public stage, and, beginning in 1605, he began writing a series of masques—elaborately staged entertainments, incorporating spectacle, allegory, and philosophy—to entertain James I and his court. Jonson's royal favor was formalized in 1616 when he was appointed poet laureate with a substantial pension. In the same year, he published his collected *Works*, the first time an English writer had ever dared to be so presumptuous. The collection, to which Jonson continued to add until his death in 1637, displays the impressive range of Jonson's poetic skills. Included are succinct and direct elegies and epitaphs, melodic and lyrical songs, and classically inspired epigrams. Assimilating classical models with a sensibility in direct contact with his own age, Jonson laid the foundation for much of the 17th-century poetry that followed as practiced by Robert Herrick, Thomas Carew, Sir John Suckling, and others who proudly claimed kinship as "sons of Ben." Indeed, few writers in the 17th century, including JOHN DONNE [33], Andrew Marvell, JOHN MILTON [8], and John Dryden, could avoid the grandiose presence of Ben Jonson, a larger-than-life figure whose learning, combativeness, generosity, elegance, and bawdiness typify the contradictions as well as the richness of his age. In his dramatic and lyrical influence, in his establishing a new standard of competence and self-respect for the literary artist, Jonson is deservedly reckoned as one of English literature's fountainhead figures. As John Dryden observed, "Shakespeare was the Homer, or father of our dramatic poets; Jonson was the Virgil, the pattern of elaborate writing."

CAO XUEQIN

1715–1763

To show his scorn for contemporary Chinese writing, a scholar versed in traditional literature would often ask, "What has been produced in the last fifty years that could equal Dream of the Red Chamber?" *But one could also turn the tables on him and ask with equal expectation of a negative answer: "What work previous to* Dream *could equal it?"* . . . Dream *which embodies the supreme tragic experience in Chinese literature is also its supreme work of psychological realism.*

—C. T. Hsia, *The Classic Chinese Novel*

Few literary works in any country come closer to representing a national and cultural epic than Cao Xueqin's 18th-century Chinese novel *Dream of the Red Chamber* (also called *The Story of the Stone*). The greatest of all Chinese novels, *Dream of the Red Chamber* shifted the focus of the Chinese novel from morally irrelevant exploits of mythological heroes to the striving of a worldly and spiritual hero in a realistically conceived circle of social and psychological relationships. Like most Chinese novels, *Dream of the Red Chamber* is massive, with hundreds of characters and connected plots, but no other novel in China approaches it in depth and scope. Unique in the quality of its psychological realism, the novel has been called the only Chinese work of magnitude fully formed with the spirit of tragedy. In its range, seriousness of purpose, and comprehensive vision, *Dream of the Red Chamber* approaches the level of the epic as a storehouse of an entire culture's values and beliefs. As a work of art, it has remained the standard for fiction in China despite that nation's revolutionary change and turbulent history during the last 250 years.

· Details about the composition and the author of *Dream of the Red Chamber* are both scanty and controversial. Written by Cao Xueqin during the 1740s, the novel was published in 1791, nearly 30 years after his death, with only 80 of the novel's 120 chapters ascertained to be the work of Cao Xueqin. His manuscript circulated among his friends during his lifetime, and the version that exists today includes the commentary and corrections of another person with the pseudonym Red Inkstone, thought to be a close friend or relative of Cao Xueqin. The unfinished manuscript came into the hands of the writer Gao E, who, claiming to have worked from unfinished manuscripts, completed the story by adding its final 40 chapters. The degree of Gao E's invention and his reliance on primary sources are the basis for a continuing critical controversy. Because Red Inkstone's commentary establishes a link between the novel's characters and Cao Xueqin's autobiography, much critical attention has also been paid to uncovering and sifting the correspondences and trying to assemble a definite portrait of the author.

What is incontestable is that Cao Xueqin was a member of a prominent and prosperous family whose dramatic collapse provides one of the central themes of *Dream of the Red Chamber*. For three generations, Cao Xueqin's family had been bondservants to the Manchu emperors, holding the lucrative and powerful post of commissioner of the imperial textile mills in Nanjing. Managing a staff of as many as 3,000, Cao Xueqin's grandfather, himself a poet and a patron of letters, lived lavishly and entertained the emperor in his home at least four times, a sign of great distinction and plentiful means. In 1728, when Cao Xueqin was 13, the new emperor, Yongzheng, dismissed his father from his post, ordered his house raided, and confiscated most of his property. The family moved to Beijing, where Cao Xueqin lived in extreme poverty. Cao Xueqin was an accomplished painter, and the sale of his paintings is the only known source of his income, although he may also have worked as a private tutor or schoolmaster. Friends described him as short, plump, and dark, in marked contrast to the striking beauty of his central protagonist in *Dream*. The author also has been called a charming and witty conversationalist, of whom it was said that "wherever he was, he made it spring." One intimate has recorded a picture of Cao Xueqin, "discoursing of high, noble things while one hand hunts for lice." Encouraged by his friends to complete his masterpiece, Cao Xueqin made prodigious and heroic efforts under trying circumstances. He had no patron, and was uncertain how the finished novel would be received by the state, particularly because he broke with established traditional conventions, which the Chinese novel depended on for success.

Prior to *Dream*, Chinese novels impersonally reworked familiar stories of mythological heroes. Cao Xueqin expanded the traditional elements of romance with private experience based on his own family history. The first Chinese novel to use autobiographical material on such a grand scale, *Dream* became both a massive social panorama and a serious criticism of everyday life. The novel describes the intimate and complex family relationships of the Jai clan, a prosperous family that begins a dramatic decline. The novel's protagonist is Jai Baoyu, whose development and triangular relationship with Lin Daiyu and Xue Baochai form the core of the novel, but around which an ever-widening circle of relationships and characters emerge to place the story in a wider social context.

More than a single dramatic story, *Dream* is a multiple, complex panorama of an entire worldview, extending outward from the individual to the family, the community, and the culture at large. Simultaneously and intensely both private and public, the novel charts a search for the meaning of existence while revealing through a tragic awareness of the world the limits of individual will and possibilities, and the individual's power to corrupt and prevent fulfillment. Filled with allegorical and philosophical significance, the novel is sustained by a masterful realism that roots its many characters and episodes to the real world with psychological precision and skill. The culminating effect is a comprehensive view of the entire civilization and culture of imperial China, seen through the detailed exploration of everyday life. As the critic Andrew H. Plaks has argued, "As a result, the work stands in its own cultural milieu as the major works of Homer, Virgil, Murasaki, Dante, Milton, Cervantes, Goethe, and more recently Proust and Joyce, do in theirs: as an encyclopedic compendium of an entire tradition in a form that itself serves as a model against which to judge works of less imposing stature." It is Cao Xueqin's breadth of vision, allied with his remarkable skill for capturing the complexity of his world and characters, which finally makes *Dream of the Red Chamber* one of world literature's greatest achievements.

GIOVANNI BOCCACCIO

68

1313–1375

Boccaccio's works embrace medieval and classical literature, prose and poetry, epic and lyric, Latin and Italian, popular and "high" culture. He revived the pastoral romance, attempted a modern epic, established the vernacular ottava as the epic stanza in Italian, and then, later in life, renewed the classical epistle and eclogue in Latin, wrote biography, helped revive the study of Greek, and began formal Dante criticism. . . . The culmination of Boccaccio's literary experience is the Decameron, *which becomes perforce the touchstone for any consideration of his works. In it he proposes narration for its own sake, and in advocating amusement as much as improvement, his point of view becomes earthbound. The* Decameron *is Boccaccio's human comedy, "the luminous and fully human epic," that stands next to Dante's Divine Comedy.*

—Judith Powers Serafini-Sauli, *Giovanni Boccaccio*

Although Boccaccio willingly accepted his place as the third of the great Italian writers of the 14th century, a rank assigned to him by Petrarch [51], who placed himself second to Dante [2], the honor is in no sense a consolation prize. Boccaccio, the father of Italian prose and the master of the narrative, has exerted a powerful influence on Western literature. Like Dante and Petrarch, Boccaccio stood between medieval times and the modern era ushered in by the Renaissance. The realism of the *Decameron*, Boccaccio's masterpiece, by acknowledging the power of ordinary life and recognizable human characters helped establish a radical redefinition of literary form and content.

Boccaccio was the illegitimate son of a Florentine merchant-banker, a member of the growing middle class whose values Boccaccio reflected in his secular art. At age 14, he accompanied his father to Naples and began his training in commerce, intending to follow his father in business. There he was exposed to the world of culture and learning at the court of King Robert the Wise, an experience that helped convince him to pursue a literary career instead. In 1340, Boccaccio returned to Florence for its most tumultuous decade of the 14th century, an era that included the famine of 1346 and the plague of 1348, which reduced Florence's population of 100,000 by half. Boccaccio's early artistic efforts show him adjusting the medieval courtly forms as well as the classical learning that he began to master in Naples under the influence of Tuscan poetry and the middle-class mercantile world of Florence, which surrounded him.

Boccaccio's early writing is mixed: somewhat derivative, displaying his erudition and imitative skill, it also shows occasional flashes of originality and psychological insight. He tried his hand at almost all of the genres available to him, including the romance, pastoral, and allegory, and achieved greater originality with his short novel *Elegia di Madonna Fiametta* (c. 1344). Called the first psychological novel of modern literature, it is the story of an adulterous love affair between a Neapolitan noblewoman and a Florentine merchant, innovatively told in the first person from the perspective of the abandoned woman. Despite this innovation, nothing Boccaccio wrote previously anticipates the radical break from traditional literary form and originality that marks the *Decameron*, his masterwork, completed in 1353.

The 100 tales that make up the *Decameron* were not his exclusive creations, but are mostly reworked from the medieval storehouse of legends, fables, and jokes. Boccaccio's framing device, narrative skill, and approach, however, represented a major innovation. In the *Decameron* he attempts to elevate the previously modest genre of the novella into an art form rivaling the epic. He achieves his goal by linking a great variety of tales, characters, and situations within the narrative frame of 10 young people who flee the plague in Florence for refuge in a country villa. There they entertain themselves by telling stories on various themes over the course of 10 days. Each story is placed in a much larger context of association and contrast, allowing Boccaccio to extend the range of individual tales to embrace a variety of themes and concerns. The result is a narrative compendium that extends from the ribald to the tragic, from the serious to the sentimental. With the freedom to range widely, Boccaccio dramatizes seemingly every aspect of his society and its attitudes, from veniality to the impossible virtue of his most famous creation, patient Griselda.

What is striking about Boccaccio's narrative sequence is the almost exclusive secularism he portrays. While Dante portrayed love as damnable if it did not lead one to the greater love of God, Boccaccio presents love in all its manifestations as a universal human condition whose vicissitudes are impossible to resist and delightful to contemplate. Fate plays its part in the turn of the stories' plots, but in Boccaccio's hands, fate is not a divine agent. Characters themselves create their own dilemmas based on Boccaccio's perceptive sense of behavior and psychological motivation. The *Decameron* has rightly been called the mercantile epic because its situations and characters originate in the everyday world of contemporary society. Boccaccio's stories range from the bawdy, amorous intrigue and deception of Brother Alberto in his impersonation of the angel Gabriel to win a maid, to the hopeless but noble devotion of Federigo, who expends his fortune, as well as his most cherished possession, his pet falcon, in a futile attempt to win Monna Giovanna's affection. By eschewing the medieval preoccupation with the divine and the ideal, Boccaccio redirects literature toward the real. In place of instruction, he offers literature's capacity to delight as a new standard of purpose.

Commenting on the breakthrough that the *Decameron* represented, the 19th-century critic Francesco DeSanctis called it "not a revolution but a catastrophe." Boccaccio had achieved a transformation in literary form by asserting the power of prose fiction as an instrument directed at self and society. Before Boccaccio, vernacular prose was unsophisticated and unsuited to rival poetry as a literary medium. Boccaccio developed a new literary language as well as a new subject that would continue to exert its influence as the Middle Ages gave way to the modern. Chaucer comes first to mind as the writer who profited from Boccaccio's example, but almost all writers who followed Boccaccio were influenced by his work, either directly or by absorbing the cultural shift that he helped create.

After the *Decameron*, Boccaccio largely abandoned popular literature and comedy for scholarship. The great father of vernacular prose gave up Italian for Latin and renounced his earlier work as unworthy of his artistic aspirations. Despite his own negative valuation of his achievement in the *Decameron*, this is the work that assures Boccaccio's place as one of literature's great originators.

VOLTAIRE

69

1694–1778

Ecrasez l'infâme! ("Wipe out infamy!")

—Voltaire's motto and battle cry

With Voltaire, this book comes closest to violating its fundamental selection principle by including a literary figure whose reputation rests largely on his philosophy and the influence of his ideas rather than on his literary works. Although Voltaire, over a long career, produced plays, poetry, epics, essays, history, and fiction, there is little in his massive canon of some 30,000 pages, with the possible exception of *Candide*, that is an unqualified masterpiece. Voltaire is a curious literary giant—a great writer who, in the eyes of posterity, wrote no or few great individual works—yet few other writers so defined the age in which they lived. Voltaire towered over the Enlightenment of the 18th century as its guiding intellectual presence, and his influence continued long after his death as a shaping force in the American and French revolutions. Unlike other writers whose impact extended beyond the literary world, such as Plato, Rousseau, Freud, and Sartre, Voltaire deserves consideration as a literary artist, not solely as a thinker or philosopher. With Voltaire, literary creation was not only a vehicle for his ideas, though it is certainly possible to treat it as such. *Candide* alone, the one work of Voltaire's that continues to be read for pleasure and enlightenment, justifies his inclusion here. The scholar and critic H. N.

Brailsford contended that *Candide* "ranks in its own way with *Don Quixote* and *Faust*" as one of the world's great moral fables. If Voltaire's other literary creations are now consigned to the literary specialist and the cultural historian, *Candide* has earned Voltaire a distinguished place as a significant creative artist and continues to preserve his status as one of literature's giants.

Born François-Marie Arouet into a prosperous middle-class Parisian family, Voltaire's remarkable rise to become Europe's preeminent intellectual force spans the entire Enlightenment, from the reign of Louis XIV (1643–1714) to the years immediately preceding the French Revolution in the 1770s. As André Bellessort asserts, "We may say that the French Revolution began on 10 February 1778, the day that Voltaire entered Paris." A confidante of kings and emperors and an inspiration to revolutionaries, Voltaire was educated at the Jesuit Collège Louis-le-Grand in Paris and studied law for a short time. His first of many exiles occurred in 1716 for satirical works that attacked the regency of Phillippe d'Orléans; for 11 months in 1717 he was imprisoned in the Bastille for the same offense. During his prison term he wrote a tragedy, *Oedipus*, which became a great success, and he renamed himself Voltaire. The play made him famous; it also made him a target for controversy that continued throughout his life. A quarrel with the chevalier de Rohan over a Voltaire witticism at the nobleman's expense led to an assault by the chevalier's henchmen and a second imprisonment in the Bastille through the influence of the powerful Rohan family, followed by exile to England.

Voltaire's stay in England furthered the development of his political theories and philosophy of personal liberty. He met most of the leading English thinkers of the day and was impressed by English science and empiricism, as well as by the English political system that stood in marked contrast to the autocratic power of the church and state in France, where a French noble family like the Rohans could imprison a commoner for his opinions. When Voltaire returned to France, he wrote a history of Charles XII, regarded as the first modern historical study, and his first major philosophical work, *Lettres philosophiques* (1734). Controversy surrounding the book's publication caused Voltaire to flee Paris for Lorraine, where he lived for 15 years at the residence of his mistress, Madame du Châtelet, at Cirey. During this period, Voltaire continued to write voluminously, producing tragedies, satires, and philosophical and scientific works. Although many of his works are daring, he was not so much an original thinker as an extremely talented popularizer of the theories of democracy, religious tolerance, and intellectual freedom which he had absorbed from others, including John Locke and Isaac Newton. He helped spread their ideas throughout Europe.

After the death of Madame du Châtelet in 1749, Voltaire went to Prussia at the invitation of Frederick II before settling first in Geneva, and finally, for his last 20 years, at Ferney, in France near the Swiss border, where he wrote *Candide* in 1758. In his last year, Voltaire returned to Paris after a

28-year absence for a celebratory performance of his final tragedy, *Irene*, at the Comédie-Française, where he was lionized. He died a few weeks later, buried in secret against the wishes of the church, and was later reinterred in the Pantheon as an icon of the revolution.

Candide, which FLAUBERT [30]·called a summary of all of Voltaire's works, is a brilliant satire and synthesis of Voltaire's lifelong attack on falsity and hypocrisy. In its picaresque tale, the young, naive idealist Candide, whose mentor, Dr. Pangloss, convinces him to embrace the sanguine outlook of philosopher Gottfried Leibnitz, has a series of experiences that lead to his maturity and "cure" his early optimism. Voltaire attacks the notion that ours is the "best of all possible worlds," and that the worst kinds of evil can be explained away with the simple assertion of Providential benevolence, that "Whatever is, is Right," in the phrase of ALEXANDER POPE [49] from his "Essay on Man." Such a facile approach to human experience, used to justify a wide range of human misery and atrocities, is effectively demolished by Voltaire's plot, which tests optimism under increasingly more trying circumstances and exposes the dogmas and fanaticism that insulates the individual from dealing honestly with reality. His catalogue of human misery includes natural disasters, human ailments, war, religious persecution, and their accompanying social and personal ideologies of religious superstition, nationalism, and colonialism. Neither the idea of the progress of civilization nor the Rousseau-like faith in primitive innocence offers any consolation. In the end, Candide forms his own philosophy between the equally unworkable poles of optimism and pessimism. He is determined "to take care of his garden," offering the modest solution of meliorism based on human labor, cooperation, and an acceptance of the Manichaean duality of good and evil that forms the whole of human experience. Suspended between a limited, engaged activism and a tragic awareness of moral and social shortcomings, Candide reaches Voltaire's ideal and realizes that man and society, although far from perfect, are perfectible, at least in the hope that improvements can develop from truth.

In essence, *Candide* does synthesize Voltaire's entire career as an artist and thinker. His rallying cry, *Ecrasez l'infâme*, "Wipe out infamy!" which can be defined as dogmatism and intolerance, is his guiding principle. As he wrote, "Every individual who persecutes a man, his brother, because he does not agree with him, is a monster. . . . We should tolerate each other because we are all weak, inconsistent, subject to mutability and to error." Instead of illusion, Voltaire offered a relentless pursuit of the truth. As the cultural critic and historian Peter Gay summarized, "His empiricism made him hostile to political theorizing, but throughout his life he intervened in political controversies; he meddled whether he was asked to or not, and even, as sometimes happened, when he was earnestly begged to mind his own business. He always said demurely that he was only cultivating his garden, but privately he defined his garden as Europe." Thus, Voltaire remains an emblem of the artist as the world's conscience.

1689–1761

Erskine: "Surely, Sir, Richardson is very tedious."
Johnson: "Why, Sir, if you were to read Richardson for the story, your impatience would
be so much fretted that you would hang yourself. But you must read him for the
sentiment, and consider the story as only giving occasion to the sentiment."
—James Boswell, *Life of Johnson*

Burdened with the august title "Father of the English Novel," Samuel Richardson is today far more respected than read, to be encountered (and in the
views of some endured) only in college-level survey courses on the development of the novel or in graduate-level seminars rather than enjoyed like his
contemporary HENRY FIELDING [54] or his most devoted literary descendant,
JANE AUSTEN [20]. Few today have the stamina for Richardson's prolixity or
the patience for his moralism. As literary critic F. R. Leavis asserted, "It's no
use pretending that Richardson can ever be made a current classic again."
Yet Richardson's literary importance and influence are unavoidable. If DAN-
IEL DEFOE [85] is widely credited with first tapping into the English novel's
primary resource of realism, and Henry Fielding is mainly responsible for
establishing the affinity between the novel and the epic and drama, then Richardson played two equally crucial roles in establishing the novel in the Western literary tradition: He made the novel respectable as a vehicle for serious

moral and social exploration, and he began the process of turning the novel inward to delineate the private realms of the conscience and consciousness itself, showing how an individual perceives the world and the complex issues underlying motivation, judgment, and the emotions. Technically, Richardson's epistolary method—his surrender of authorial omniscience for a direct and immediate depiction of his characters' private thoughts and feelings—is an unmistakable influence on modern fiction, with Richardsonian elements detectable in writers as different as GOETHE [10], Jane Austen, STENDHAL [42], CHARLOTTE BRONTË [60], HENRY JAMES [38], JOSEPH CONRAD [55], JAMES JOYCE [7], VIRGINIA WOOLF [48], WILLIAM FAULKNER [15], and many others. Richardson decisively altered what the novel could do and how, and if as a novel reader you resist the prototypes—Pamela Andrews, Clarissa Harlowe, and Sir Charles Grandison—you cannot avoid Richardson's progeny: Elizabeth Bennett, Dorothea Brooke, Isabel Archer, Mrs. Dalloway, Molly Bloom . . .

Denis Diderot eulogized Richardson at his death in 1761 by ranking the Englishman with HOMER [3], EURIPIDES [22], and SOPHOCLES [13] as one who carried "the torch to the depths of the cave" of human nature. This is high praise indeed for a London printer who, at the age of 51, in his words, "slid into the writing of *Pamela*," with profits as much as pioneering on his mind. A self-educated, middle-class London businessman, respectable and prosperous but otherwise undistinguished, Richardson represented, in the words of critic R. F. Brissenden, "an affront to every conception of what an artist should be." Born in 1689, the son of a Derbyshire joiner, Richardson was pious and bookish and seemed ideally suited for the church, but his parents could not afford the requisite education. Instead, Richardson was apprenticed to a London printer, married his master's daughter, and managed through hard work and diligence to become one of the most prosperous publishers in London. Richardson's literary interests can be traced back to an early fondness for "epistolary correspondence." As a boy his letter-writing skills came to the attention of young women who commissioned him to embellish their love letters, providing him with direct access to the affairs of the heart from a woman's perspective that he would later draw on in his fiction. Richardson later obliged his fellow booksellers "with writing Indexes, Prefaces, & sometimes for their minor Authors, *honest* Dedications; abstracting, abridging, compiling, and giving his Opinion of Pieces offered them." Impressed by his literary ability, two colleagues in 1739 asked Richardson to compile a volume of model letters for the instruction of the newly literate. Richardson accepted the commission but insisted that the letters should teach not only how to write but "how to think and act justly and prudently in the common concerns of human life." While writing *Letters Written to and for Particular Friends*, or *Familiar Letters*, and working on a group of letters designed to advise handsome servant girls "how to avoid the Snares that might be laid against their Virtue," Richardson conceived of a didactic story based on an anecdote he had heard about a young servant who managed to resist the advances of her master until, won over by her virtue, he married her. "Little did I think," Richardson remarked concerning the origin of *Pamela* (1740–1741), "of making one, much less two volumes of it. But . . . I thought the story, if written in an easy and natural manner, suitably to the simplicity of it, might possibly introduce a new species of writing." The new species Richardson introduced was the novel of sensibility, adding to the realism of Daniel Defoe, a minute depiction of a mind and heart in operation. Nothing quite like the intimate immediacy and intensity had ever been achieved in the novel before as in the series of letters Pamela wrote to her parents concerning the assault, by her master, Mr. B., on her virtue. *Pamela*, which went through five editions in its first year, became an international sensation and the best-selling novel of the 18th century with its title character serving as the prototypical Cinderella figure in the novel tradition. Scenes from the novel decorated ladies' fans, and the book's popularity spawned sequels as well as attacks, most notably Fielding's *Shamela* and *Joseph Andrews* that comically ridiculed the moral seriousness of Richardson's contention, announced in the novel's subtitle, of "Virtue Rewarded."

Richardson's second novel, *Clarissa*, his masterpiece, is a symphonic orchestration of the plan for *Pamela* that occupied Richardson for nearly five years, from 1743 to 1748, when the last of the novel's seven volumes appeared. Instead of the reassuring notion of "Virtue Rewarded" in *Pamela*, *Clarissa*, which tells of the "Distresses that may attend the Misconduct both of Parents and Children in Relation to Marriage," aims at a darker, tragic outcome and a more sophisticated and challenging portrait of human nature, social behavior, and virtue's costs. Clarissa Harlowe is the youngest daughter in a merchant family that wishes her to marry their rich, elderly neighbor, Mr. Solmes, to advance their interests. She is also pursued by the aristocratic rake, Robert Lovelace, whom her family opposes as a libertine but to whom Clarissa is attracted. Desperate to avoid a forced marriage with Solmes, Clarissa reluctantly accepts Lovelace's assistance to escape her family's campaign to compel her submission but is tricked by him into virtual imprisonment in a brothel. There Lovelace duels with Clarissa in a long series of stratagems to gain her sexual compliance, finally drugging and raping her. Convinced that "once subdued, always subdued," Lovelace is surprised by Clarissa's continued resistance, and his marriage proposal guiltily offered in compensation for his act is adamantly rejected. Clarissa eventually manages to escape from him and, under the strain of her experiences, dies, with her family and Lovelace's repentance coming too late to save her. Lovelace is ultimately killed in a duel with Clarissa's cousin.

Compared to the Cinderella-like wish fulfillment of *Pamela* in which the heroine's rectitude rehabilitates her rakish pursuer, *Clarissa* offers a far more realistic challenge to the concept of "Virtue Rewarded" that must accommodate Clarissa's disobedience of her parents, elopement with a libertine whom she equally desires, her rape, and her eventual demise unalloyed by much poetic justice. Here Virtue is its only reward with little earthly consolation. Moreover, compared to *Pamela*, the social observation in *Clarissa* is far more acute, and Richardson's psychological exploration is more complex and challenging. Clarissa's self-awareness is brought to the forefront of the drama as she is pressed by adversity to hold onto her principles in a complex world of mixed and disguised motives. As in *Pamela*, Richardson's epistolary method achieves a closeness of view and immediacy through his strategy of writing "to the moment," with the correspondent direct dealing with experiences as they occur, as Richardson declares in his Preface, "while the hearts of the writers must be supposed to be wholly engaged in their subjects." However, *Pamela* is close to a monologue in which almost all of the letters are written by the heroine to her parents, with Pamela's naiveté crucial for the unfolding action. In *Clarissa*, Richardson widens his focus and drama by including multiple correspondents. The reader, therefore, gains access to both Clarissa and Lovelace's thoughts and feelings, as well as a multidimensional perspective on their circumstances through contrasting viewpoints. By strategically cutting from one correspondent to another, Richardson aids verisimilitude by advancing the story more plausibly from several points of view. He also fully exploits dramatic irony by contrasting one character's knowledge with another's, while orchestrating a fuller social context to the ongoing crises. The overall effect is an enhancement of both breadth and depth over the earlier achievement in *Pamela*, while involving the reader actively in the complex issues of right behavior and self-awareness that the novel raises. At a daunting length of nearly 1 million words, *Clarissa* is both one of the world's longest and greatest novels, best showing Richardson's skill in sustaining an intense and unified story with believable human characters in crises beyond what had ever been attempted before or rarely exceeded subsequently.

Having mastered portraits of female virtue, Richardson was urged by friends to offer a complementary depiction of a good man. He responded with his final novel, *The History of Sir Charles Grandison* (1753–1754). Although lacking the vitality and originality of *Pamela* and the dramatic unity and tragic intensity of *Clarissa*, the novel is animated by its opening situation—the entry of the beautiful and accomplished Harriet Byron into London society. Abducted by an unscrupulous nobleman, Harriet is rescued by the impossibly virtuous Sir Charles Grandison. The couple falls in love, but Grandison's obligation to another complicates their happiness until the final pages. Harriet Byron's progress both into society and in love, the subjects that would be taken up by countless subsequent novelists, no doubt helps to explain why Jane Austen valued *Sir Charles Grandison* above any other novel. Despite its tortuous length and priggish title character, it, like Richardson's previous books, pioneered the creation of dramatized consciousness, opening up the psychological dimension that the novel is ideally suited to display.

After *Sir Charles Grandison*, Richardson wrote little more of importance, confessing in 1755 "an unconquerable Aversion to the Pen," after such great labor. His publishing business continued to prosper, and he was elected master of the Stationers' Company, law printer to the king, and granted the commission to print the journals of the House of Commons. He died following a stroke in 1761.

Readers without the patience to contend with Richardson's many pages and sentimentality, who might be tempted by the more fast-paced social comedy of Fielding, should keep in mind the view of Samuel Johnson. Fielding offered manners, Johnson insisted, but Richardson provided human nature itself. "Characters of manners are very entertaining," Johnson observes, "but they are to be understood by a more superficial observer, than characters of nature, where a man must dive into the recesses of the human heart." Comparing England's two greatest 18th-century novelists, Johnson insisted "there was as great a difference between them as between a man who knew how a watch was made and a man who could tell the hour by looking on the dial-plate."

71

EDMUND SPENSER

1552?–1599

Sweet Spenser, moving through his clouded heaven,
With the moon's beauty, and the moon's soft pace,
I call him Brother, Englishman, and Friend!
          —William Wordsworth, *The Prelude*, Book III

Among the recognized earliest giants of English literature—CHAUCER [5], Spenser, SHAKESPEARE [1], and MILTON [8]—Spenser, the greatest nondramatic writer of the English Renaissance, has fared the worst in our own time. Shakespeare's grip on our imagination persists; Chaucer still sustains us with his subjects and artistry; and Milton commands respect, if not devotion. Spenser, however, is another matter. Despite producing in *The Faerie Queene* the first great English epic, despite his renown as the "English Virgil" and one of the truly great metrists among English poets, Spenser has, like Samuel Richardson, been relegated to mainly academic interest by the specialist. Critic Graham Hough has asserted that "Spenser has been the most neglected of all our great poets." There are many reasons why Spenser is far less valued today than he has been in previous centuries. As Hough argues, "In entering Spenser's world we enter a foreign country; we must learn a different language and a different set of conventions; and this we often fail to see. We expect Spenser to satisfy more of our 20th-century expectations than he does, and feel a sense of failure and disappointment when this turns out not to be case." We also have a diminished appreciation of the kind of poetry Spenser produced. Modern readers have privileged the lyric at the expense of the long narrative poetry that Spenser provides. We are more likely to go to the novel or films for our narratives. We are also resistant to Spenser's didacticism, staunch moralism, and allegorical method. However, Spenser merits our effort in appreciating his achievement on his own terms. Few others match Spenser for extending the boundaries and capacity of poetic expression and his influence on the English literary tradition is enormous. Milton regarded "our sage and serious" Spenser as "a better teacher than Scotus or Aquinas." According to Dryden "the Soul of Chaucer was transfus'd into his Body." Spenser was POPE's [49] "mistress," WORDSWORTH's [23] "inspiration," and haunts the lines and music of KEATS [25], SHELLEY [77], YEATS [17], ELIOT [19], and countless others. Spenser is one of the great nourishers of the English poetic tradition who more than deserves his place here as one of the greatest of literary artists.

In many ways, Spenser's career is the archetypal success story of the Elizabethan period, showing the rise of someone of low origins to become the most famous poet of his era who managed to raise the status of poetry as he rose in the ranks of privilege and power. Spenser was born around 1552. He would describe London as his "kindly Nurse," while claiming connection with the wealthy gentry family of the Spencers in Northamptonshire. His father was possibly John Spenser, a Lancashire cloth weaver who had moved to London. This may explain why Spenser attended the Merchant Taylors' School, one of the great humanistic schools of the English Renaissance that was founded in 1561. Its headmaster was the renowned scholar Richard Mulcaster, who taught Hebrew, Greek, and Latin but advocated strenuously on behalf of the potential power and richness of English, declaring that "I do not think that anie language . . . is better able to utter all arguments, either with more pith, or greater planesse, than our *English* tung is" and "I honor Latin but I worship *English*." Spenser, no doubt, caught Mulcaster's enthusiasm and would later carry on his master's work, raising the expressive power of English to rival and surpass classical and European languages. Spenser's first published work appeared during his student days in 1569, translations of poems by PETRARCH [51] and others.

He went on to Pembroke College, Cambridge, as a "sizar," a scholarship student, earning his B.A. in 1573 and his M.A. in 1576. Using his degrees to gain court preferment and patronage, Spenser secured a place in the household of the powerful earl of Leicester and an acquaintance with his nephew, Sir Philip Sidney, who, like Spenser, was committed to improving the quality of English poetry and prose. Spenser's contribution was the groundbreaking collection, *The Shepheardes Calender,* published anonymously in 1579 with a dedication to Sidney. Regarded by literary historians as a turning point in English verse, *The Shepheardes Calendar*—eclogues in the manner of VIRGIL [9], combining pastoral sentiment with references to contemporary religious and political issues—is monumental both in subject matter, scope, and especially verse forms. Providing an astounding demonstration of what could be done in English verse, Spenser uses as many as 13 different meters, several for the first time in English, in an extraordinary display of his poetic skills, very much announcing the arrival of a new poetry for the Elizabethan age.

For whatever reason, neither service with Leicester nor the success of *The Shepheardes Calender* led Spenser to a distinguished court position in London. Instead, in 1780, he departed for Ireland as the secretary of Arthur Grey, the newly appointed Lord Deputy of Ireland. Spenser would spend most of the rest of his life in Ireland in a succession of administrative posts, including clerk in the Court of Chancery (1581), clerk of the Council of Munster (1584), and justice of the County of Cork (1594). As a reward for services rendered, in 1586 he was granted the 3,000-acre estate of Kilcolman and its castle, and its landscape would inspire much of his finest poetry. Highly critical of the often unruly Irish, Spenser had no such qualms about their land and would write in *A View of the Present State of Ireland* (1596): "It is a moste bewtifull and sweete Countrie as anye is under heaven."

It was in Ireland that Spenser commenced work on his monumental *The Faerie Queene*, intended as the first sustained poetic work in English since Chaucer and the first truly English epic, combining both the nationalist spirit of Virgil's *Aeneid* and the religious and moral seriousness of DANTE's [2] *Divine Comedy*. Describing the plan for his poem to his fellow Irish landholder, Sir Walter Raleigh, Spenser set out through a "continued Allegory, or dark conceit," to "fashion a gentleman or noble person in virtuous and gentle discipline" by exhibiting the qualities such a person should have. Combining elements of the "courtesy book" such as Castiglione's *Courtier* that outlined the necessities for a respectable courtier with a structure borrowed from Italian romantic epics such as Ariosto's *Orlando Furios* (1516) and allegorical narratives like Tasso's *Jerusalem Delivered* (1575), along with native stories of King Arthur and his questing knights from Mallory and others, Spenser intended to fashion a grand epic poem of Elizabethan and Protestant beliefs and values. Each of the intended 12 first books of *The Faerie Queene* would be devoted to an example of "private morall vertues." Another section of the poem, perhaps of equal length but never written, was to cover the public or "polliticke" virtues. Each book in this vast structure was to concentrate on a single habit of character, represented by one or more exemplary knights, unified by two repeated characters: Arthur, the mythical founder of the Round Table, who was to appear as a wandering knight in each of the books, and Gloriana, the Faerie Queene, representing Elizabeth, who was to frame the action of the poem by holding an annual feast in which she assigned her knights quests, each described in one book of the epic. Spenser managed to complete only six books of his massive plan, dealing with holiness, temperance, chastity, friendship, justice, and courtesy. A seventh and uncompleted book, called "The Mutabilitie Cantos," concerns constancy.

Even unfinished, only Chaucer's *Canterbury Tales* is its rival in scale and ambition in English poetry up to this time. The poem's opening announces Spenser's Virgilian intentions, to set aside the pastoral for the epic:

> Lo I the man, whose Muse whilome did maske,
>   As time her taught, in lowly Shepheards weeds,
>   Am now enforst a far unfitter taske,
>   For trumpets sterne to change mine Oaten reeds,
>   And sing of Knights and Ladies gentle deeds;
>   Whose praises have slept in silence long,
>   Me, all too meane, the sacred Muse areeds
>   To blazon broad emongst her learned throng:
> Fierce warres and faithfull loves shall moralize my song.

Narrated in a succession of these nine-line "Spenserian stanzas," *The Faerie Queene* proceeds with the stories of the Red Cross Knight (who emerges as St. George, patron saint of England), Sir Guyon, the female knight Britomart, and Sir Artegal, the Knight of Justice. Each book works on multiple levels, combining often rousing interlocking romances with political and moral commentary delivered in allegorical terms, all presented with Spenser's characteristic sensuous vividness and metrical skill. With *The Faerie Queene*, Spenser raises the status of both the English poet as the custodian of a nation's values and of English poetry to delight, instruct, and inspire.

Returning to England for an extended visit in 1589, Spenser brought with him the first three books of *The Faerie Queene*. Raleigh introduced Spenser to Elizabeth who heard him read from his work. Returning to Kilcolman, Spenser married Elizabeth Boyle in 1594. To celebrate their courtship and marriage, Spenser produced the impressive sonnet sequence, *Amoretti*, and what has been called the greatest marriage poem ever written, *Epithalamion*. The six completed books of *The Faerie Queene* were published in 1596, capping Spenser's reputation as the most accomplished and famous poet of his age. Spenser had gained both wealth and fame, but prosperity would not last. In 1598 the earl of Tyrone mounted a rebellion that spread throughout Ireland. Kilcolman was overrun and burned, and Spenser with his family sought refuge in Cork, from which he was sent with papers for the Privy Council in London. Shortly after arriving, he died in Westminster in 1599 to be buried beside Chaucer at Westminster Abbey. An observer, William Camden, records that at his funeral, "his herse being attended by poets, and mournful elegies and poems, with the pens that wrote them thrown into his tomb."

Spenser left his fellow poets a rich legacy that has been drawn on ever since. Neither poetry nor the poet in England had ever reached the heights that Spenser had taken both. The so-called Heroic Paramour of Faerie Land had ventured farther in verse than any of his contemporaries, announcing to his fellow poets and readers that the native language could become a boundlessly expressive tool.

NATHANIEL HAWTHORNE

72

1804–1864

There is a certain tragic phase of humanity which, in our opinion, was never more power-fully embodied than by Hawthorne. We mean the tragicalness of human thought in its own unbiassed, native, and profounder workings. We think that into no recorded mind has the intense feeling of the visible truth ever entered more deeply than into this man's. By visible truth we mean the apprehension of the absolute condition of present things as they strike the eye of the man who fears them not, though they do their worst to him. . . .

There is the grand truth about Nathaniel Hawthorne. He says no! in thunder; but the devil himself cannot make him say yes.

—Herman Melville, *Letters*

Few writers were so contrary as Nathaniel Hawthorne in refusing to live according to the conventional notion of the background and experiences of a great novelist. A solitary figure whose literary apprenticeship consisted of 12 years spent in his room in his family's home in Salem, Massachusetts, Hawthorne could report with only slight exaggeration that "I doubt whether I have ever really talked with half a dozen persons in my life, men or women." For Hawthorne, writing was not the social art of Dickens [6] or Trollope [107], whom he admired, but a private exploration of moral and spiritual values lurking deeply beneath the surface of things. As the American poet and critic James Russell Lowell observed, "Had he been born without the poetic imagination, he would have written treatises on the Origin of Evil."

With *The Scarlet Letter*, America's first great literary classic, Hawthorne set the prototype for what has become a particular genre of American fiction: romances heavily freighted with existential themes. HERMAN MELVILLE [24] saw Hawthorne as a fellow "diver" whose allegorical imagination helped Melville find the direction he would take in *Moby-Dick*. The mid-19th century saw the emergence of a distinctly American variety of poetry and fiction, and Hawthorne is one of the prime originators of that native voice.

The Hathorne family (Hawthorne added the w after leaving college) could trace its ancestry to a member of John Winthrop's Massachusetts Bay Colony who moved to Salem in 1636. An ancestor was a judge in the Salem witchcraft trials; according to family legend, one of the victims placed a curse on Judge Hathorne and all his descendants before her execution. Hawthorne's father was a ship's captain, and his mother was the daughter of Richard Manning, a blacksmith who became the proprietor and manager of the Boston and Salem Stage Company. When Nathaniel was only four, his father died in Surinam of yellow fever, and the family was absorbed into the large Manning clan. Nathaniel's childhood was spent between Salem and Maine, where the Mannings owned property, and he felt somewhat lost in the practical bustle of the large family. At 17, the sensitive Hawthorne decided to become a writer: "I do not want to be a doctor and live by men's diseases, nor a minister to live by their sins, nor a lawyer and live by their quarrels. So, I don't see that there is anything left for me but to be an author."

In 1821, Hawthorne matriculated at Bowdoin College. Among his classmates were Henry Wadsworth Longfellow and Franklin Pierce. He later recalled, "I was an idle student, negligent of college rules and the Procrustean details of academic life, rather choosing to nurse my own fancies than to dig into Greek roots and be numbered among the learned Thebans." After graduating, Hawthorne returned to Salem, where, from 1825 to 1837, he lived a reclusive life, reading voraciously, particularly in the history of colonial New England, and emerging from his room only for evening walks and occasional walking trips around Massachusetts. During this period Hawthorne published his first novel, *Fanshawe* (1828), at his own expense, and his first stories and sketches began to appear anonymously in various magazines. The best of Hawthorne's early stories—"The Gentle Boy," "Young Goodman Brown," "The Minister's Black Veil," and "My Kinsman, Major Molineux"—explore the nature of sin and guilt and the end of innocence set against the background of New England's colonial past. Hawthorne's imagination displays the ability to reach the symbolic and the allegorical through the suggestive experience of the Puritan past and the simple style and characterization of the folktale.

Hawthorne emerged from his seclusion in Salem when he became engaged to Sophia Peabody, whom he married in 1842, and secured a position at the

Boston Custom House. Prior to his marriage he spent seven months at the socialist cooperative Brook Farm before settling in Concord at the Old Manse, Ralph Waldo Emerson's ancestral home. A second collection of stories, *Mosses from an Old Manse*, was published in 1846 (the first, *Twice-Told Tales*, had appeared in 1837). Discouraging sales sent Hawthorne back to Salem as a surveyor in the custom house, a position he lost in the political defeat of the Democrats in 1848. In 1850, he published *The Scarlet Letter*, which became a best-seller and established his reputation as one of America's most important writers.

In *The Scarlet Letter* Hawthorne takes up his characteristic themes of sin and repentance, played out in a striking symbolic tableau drawn from Boston's Puritan past. The adultery of Hester Prynne and Reverend Dimmesdale and the retribution pursued by Chillingworth provide Hawthorne with the occasion to examine the psychological results of sin and the various ways individuals express their moral identity. There had never been anything quite like Hawthorne's symbolic drama in American fiction before, with its rich evocation of internal states cast in a historical setting that is both sharply imagined and symbolically suggestive. It is not surprising that the younger Herman Melville, who met Hawthorne in the Berkshires as he was writing his whaling tale, seized upon Hawthorne as his mentor. Their friendship was sustained largely by the more aggressive and expansive Melville during sessions of "ontological heroics," in Melville's phrase, in which Hawthorne's "sympathetic silences" suggest his usefulness as an audience for the more voluble Melville. Unfortunately, in Melville's effusive correspondence we have only one side of their relationship; Hawthorne's replies have not survived.

Hawthorne followed the success of *The Scarlet Letter* with the very different *The House of the Seven Gables* (1851), a novel with a contemporary setting and a moral, announced by Hawthorne in this preface: "The truth, namely, that the wrong-doing of one generation lives into the successive ones, and divesting itself of every temporary advantage, becomes a pure and uncontrollable mischief." The family saga of Salem's Pyncheon clan shows Hawthorne widening his moral exploration to embrace "the folly of tumbling down an avalanche of ill-gotten gold, or real estate, on the heads of an unfortunate posterity," as the past works out its consequences on the present. In 1852, Hawthorne published *The Blithedale Romance*, based on his experiences at Brook Farm, and managed a final collection of stories, *The Snow-Image*, and *The Marble Faun* (1860), his last novel.

The election of his college friend Franklin Pierce as U.S. president in 1852 exposed Hawthorne to the larger world of politics and current events. Hawthorne wrote the campaign biography of Pierce and was awarded the consulship of Liverpool, England, where he served diligently during Pierce's single term in office. Hawthorne spent seven years in Europe, traveling in France and Italy after leaving his post, before returning with his family to Concord. He died on a New England excursion with Pierce in 1864.

Hawthorne's genius is unique in American letters, uneven in its creations but unfaltering in its moral seriousness. In his short study of Hawthorne, HENRY JAMES [38] wrote, "He combined in a singular degree the spontaneity of the imagination with a haunting care for moral problems. Man's conscience was his theme but he saw it in the light of a creative fancy which added, out of his own substance, an interest, and, I may almost say, an importance." The novelist Anthony Trollope, very different in style from James, though granting that "there never surely was a powerful, active, continually effective mind less round, more lop-sided than that of Nathaniel Hawthorne," stated that "when you have studied him, [Hawthorne] will be very precious to you. He will have plunged you into melancholy, he will have overshadowed you with black forebodings, he will almost have crushed you with imaginary sorrows; but he will have enabled you to feel yourself an inch taller during the process."

BERTOLT BRECHT

73

1898–1956

Nowadays, anyone who wishes to combat lies and ignorance and to write the truth must overcome at least five difficulties. He must have the courage to write the truth when truth is everywhere opposed; the keenness to recognize it, although it is everywhere concealed; the skill to manipulate it as a weapon; the judgment to select those in whose hands it will be effective; and the cunning to spread the truth among such persons. These are formidable problems for writers living under Fascism, but they exist also for those writers who have fled or been exiled; they exist even for writers working in countries where civil liberty prevails.

—Bertolt Brecht, "Writing the Truth: Five Difficulties"

It is one thing to be an important and influential literary artist; it is another to become an adjective. Bertolt Brecht joins a select group of writers who have given us Shakespearean, Dickensian, Shavian, Kafkaesque, and Orwellian. "Brechtian" or "brechtisch" has become, in the words of critic Ronald Speirs, "an established part of cultural vocabulary, referring not only to a method of staging plays, but also to a style of expression, a way of thinking, a way of looking at the world even." As both playwright and dramatic theorist, Bertolt Brecht's influence on the modern stage is immense. Aristotelian describes the accepted dramatic conventions in operation for the last 2,500 years; Brechtian indicates its challenge—a radical reconception of theater's essential principles.

Rejecting the mimetic tradition that had dominated Western art, Brecht famously declared, "Art is not a mirror held up to reality, but a hammer with which to shape it." Brecht widened the focus of drama from the concerns of an individual to the historical, social, and economic context surrounding identity, motive, and action. Embracing the role of artist as provocateur and reformer, Brecht mounted a sustained critique of the historical moment and modern life while the universal principles he uncovered have sustained his work with a persistent relevance. "Brecht's importance," argues literary critic Martin Esslin, ". . . transcends his significance as a dramatist, poet, or amusing personality. He is above all an epitome of his times: most of the cross-currents and contradictions, moral and political dilemmas, artistic and literary trends of our times are focused and exemplified in Brecht's life and its vicissitudes." An oversized figure of great contradictions and contentiousness, Brecht remains a force to be reckoned with whose writing challenges the very foundations of our understanding of the way of the world and the purposes of art.

Eugen Berthold Friedrich Brecht was born in 1898 in the Bavarian city of Augsburg. He would later rename himself less grandly Bertolt or Bert Brecht as a challenge to his bourgeois background. His father, the business manager of a paper mill, was a Catholic; his mother, a Protestant. Raised in his mother's Lutheran faith, Brecht, despite a future antichurch stance, would claim that the book that influenced him most was the Bible. His first play, published in a school journal, was in fact titled *Die Bibel* (The Bible), about a young girl trapped by the religious wars of the 17th century. Religious conflict would be a recurrent theme in his work, prompted no doubt by his early family experience. An indifferent and at times rebellious student, Brecht excelled at writing and published his first poems and reviews as a teenager in local newspapers. After completing his secondary education in 1917, to evade the draft during World War I, Brecht studied medicine at the University of Munich but was conscripted in 1918 to serve as a corpsman in his hometown's military hospital. There he witnessed firsthand the terrible cost of war, which reinforced a lifelong pacifistic view. Following Germany's defeat, Brecht supported himself in Munich as a freelance writer and cabaret performer, singing witty, ribald ballads to his own guitar accompaniment. He responded to the postwar social chaos, including the turbulent formation of the Weimar Republic and the brutal suppression of the 1918–1919 socialist revolution, with his first major dramatic works and a commitment to socialism and the German communist party.

Baal, written in 1918 and first performed in 1923, concerns a poet who murders his best friend in a fit of jealousy. In 22 loosely connected scenes, the play shows the influence of Georg Büchner's groundbreaking 19th-century drama *Woyzeck* and the German expressionists. Although the play's nihilism would be subsequently mitigated by Brecht's growing Marxist faith, *Baal* contains core elements of the mature Brecht in its dialectical form and his welding together of multiple sources with an intense poetic lyricism. His next play, which was performed to acclaim in Munich in 1922, *Trommeln in der Nacht* (Drums in the night), is a bitter drama about a war veteran who learns that his fiancée has been seduced by a war profiteer and that the ideals he fought for have been betrayed. Praised for his stark and sobering assessment of postwar reality and his innovative dramatic techniques, Brecht moved to Berlin in 1924 where he served as a play reader for the great German director Max Reinhardt, while continuing his theatrical experimentation in such plays as *In the Jungle of the Cities* and *A Man's a Man*. He achieved his greatest popular success in 1928 with *The Threepenny Opera*, an adaptation of English writer John Gay's 1728 *The Beggar's Opera*, written in collaboration with composer Kurt Weill. The first of Brecht's plays to employ music and song to interrupt and comment on the action, *The Threepenny Opera* was a direct assault on audience's expectations and complacency as the world of thieves and beggars becomes a distorted mirror to satirize bourgeois values. Combining social and moral instruction with rollicking entertainment, the play demonstrates the methods that Brecht would later codify in his conception of the "*episches*," or epic drama.

Initially conceived in articles and notebooks during the 1920s and worked out in several essays in the early 1930s, Brecht's formulation of a new theory of drama would become a crucial contribution to modern theater. "No other twentieth-century writer," drama historian Marvin Carlson has argued, "has influenced the theatre both as a dramatist and theorist as profoundly as Bertolt Brecht." Rejecting the assumptions of realism and naturalism that had dominated the European theater after Ibsen, Brecht opposed the realistic "theater of illusion" that encouraged an audience's emotional involvement and identification through verisimilitude by a different kind of drama designed to provoke thought and action. Traditional Aristotelian or "dramatic theater," in Brecht's view, was restrictive and falsifying. Brecht's alternative was a drama derived from the epic: the narrative form in which each episode is significant, not only for what it contributes to the whole, but in itself. The epic further differs from drama by dealing with past events rather than with the imaginary "present" of the drama, which unfolds before an audience as if it were happening for the first time. In his epic theater, Brecht wanted the audience to see the action as something that has happened and is now being reenacted on a stage. The deliberate distancing of the audience from the onstage experience is encapsulated in the key Brechtian term, *verfremdung*, "to make strange," or the so-called alienation principle. Contrary to the theater of verisimilitude that draws the audience into the illusion of life enacted on stage, Brecht endorsed techniques of dramatic structure, staging, and acting to maintain the audience's critical distance and judgment, to "make strange" habitual ways of seeing experience and thereby open up new possibilities and perceptions.

After Hitler came to power in 1933, Brecht's socialist and anti-Nazi writings, including such plays as *Saint Joan of the Stockyards* and *The Mother*, marked him for liquidation. The playwright began what would become 15 years of exile from Germany, "Changing more countries than shoes," as he ruefully observed. His first stop with his wife and children was Austria, then Czechoslovakia, Switzerland, France, Denmark, Sweden, Finland, and, finally, via the Trans-Siberian Railroad, the United States in 1941, where he remained for the duration. Despite these dislocations, the continual threat of the war catching up to him, and enormous family and financial pressures, Brecht managed to complete his greatest work during these exile years. Ironically, Brecht's years out of Germany, freed from political and theatrical responsibilities that had formerly absorbed him, gave him both the time to devote himself exclusively to his writing and the distance that widened his perspective. In 1938 Brecht completed his first version of *Leben des Galilei* (*Life of Galileo*; first performed, 1943). His only major play about a historical figure, *Galileo* is a chronicle drama initially conceived to dramatize, in the playwright's words, "Galileo's heroic struggle for his modern scientific conviction." It became, through successive revisions and reevaluation, a much more ambiguous and complex drama dealing with the crisis of conscience that led to the scientist's recantation of his beliefs under pressure from the church. The play explores the responsibilities of the scientist and the conflict between truth and survival under an authoritarian regime. Blurring easy distinction of victim and victimizer, hero and villain, the play provocatively explores questions regarding science's ultimate responsibility and whether survival or principle matters most. Survival, its costs and consequences, would again be the theme of Brecht's next play and his masterpiece, *Mutter Courage und Ihre Kinder* (*Mother Courage and Her Children*, 1941), one of the most powerful antiwar dramas ever written. Set during the 17th-century Thirty Years' War, the play follows the experiences of canteen woman Anna Fierling, nicknamed Mother Courage, as she tries to make her living selling her wares from her cart to the soldiers. One of the stage's great paradoxes, Mother Courage is a woman of enormous strength, cunning, and resilience in the face of the war's toll that gradually takes the lives of her three children. However, her trade that depends on the war and her cupidity make her a collaborator in the destruction of her family. The play makes explicit the conjunction between war and capitalism with greed and exploitation warping Mother Courage into a "hyena of the battlefield." *Mother Courage* fully justifies the techniques of the epic drama by creating a stage experience that is simultaneously a moving human story, a brilliant meditation on the nature of war and commerce, and a terrifying modern fable.

The elements of fable are further displayed in Brecht's final major works—*Der gute Mensch von Szechuan* (*The Good Person of Setzuan*, 1943) and *Der kaukasische Kreidekreis* (*The Caucasian Chalk Circle*, 1948). Both draw on stylized, antirealistic elements of the Asian theater, reinforcing Brecht's conception of the epic drama. *The Good Person of Setzuan* is set, in Brecht's words, in a "half Europeanized" China, both ancient and modern, familiar and strange, to achieve the distancing alienation effects he desired. It concerns the gods' search for a single good person to justify humanity's continuation. Their sole candidate is the good-hearted, poor prostitute Shen Te, who is rewarded with enough money to set up a small tobacco shop. Beset by parasites who take advantage of her, Shen Te is compelled to invent and impersonate a ruthless male cousin, Shui Ta, to drive the hard bargains that her good nature resists. In Brecht's ethical fable, good and evil are shown as mutually dependent, with evil necessary for survival in a world of parasites and gulls. *The Caucasian Chalk Circle* is set in Soviet Georgia in the aftermath of World War II and concerns a dispute among the peasants about how best to restore their ravaged lands. It, like *The Good Person of Setzuan*, poses a central moral question: How is justice possible? Both plays push Brecht's stage innovations to their logical conclusions, turning the theater into an arena where the largest human questions could be debated.

In 1947, Brecht returned to Europe after being called to testify before the House Committee on Un-American Activities about his communist affiliations. In 1948, he settled in East Berlin as the artistic director of his own theater and a troupe of actors known as the Berliner Ensemble. Brecht oversaw productions of his own works and mounted innovative interpretations of plays by MOLIÈRE [32], SHAKESPEARE [1], SOPHOCLES [13], and others, while battling once again with an authoritarian regime that sought to curtail his freedom of expression. He died in 1956 of a heart attack during rehearsals of *Galileo*. In addition to adding several plays to the world drama repertory, Brecht as dramatic theorist and practitioner helped to liberate and enrich modern literature. With Brecht whatever could be imagined, whatever paradoxes embedded in the human condition, could be staged and given a hearing.

WALLACE STEVENS

74

1879–1955

Stevens' place is therefore clearly in the tradition of existentialist romanticism. The fertile fact or sensation is primary; everything including the existence or non-existence of God, follows from that. The only order worth looking for is the order of chaos itself.
—William Burney, *Wallace Stevens*

Wallace Stevens deserves to join the select company of WILLIAM BUTLER YEATS [17], T. S. ELIOT [19], RAINER MARIA RILKE [78], ROBERT FROST [86], and PABLO NERUDA [102] as the 20th century's greatest poetic masters. Stevens has been called the "dandy of American letters," but his stylistic brilliance, drolleries, and occasional buffooneries should not obscure the fact that he is a poet of great speculative genius. If his poems lack the monumental qualities of Yeats's and Eliot's work, they are no less concerned with some of the essential questions of modern art in how the world can be imagined, the relationship between art and life, and a description of human consciousness itself.

In a sense, Stevens synthesizes all the major strains in poetry since the romantics, including the French symbolists and aesthetics of the 1890s, into the dominant strain of modern poetry through his restless and continual search for meaning in an otherwise valueless world. His deeply philosophical contemplations are rooted in concrete images of great visual and symbolic suggestiveness in a style that is both expressive and dazzling in its virtuosity.

As critic Edmund Wilson observed, "His gift for combining words is baffling and fantastic but sure; even when you do not know what he is saying, you know that he is saying it well." Another writer described Stevens's poetic style as "never soft or merely pretty, always hard as a diamond and regally controlled." Both opinions suggest Stevens's qualities as a daring and assured literary performer, and efforts to penetrate his surface brilliance are repaid by confronting a mind of great magnitude engaged with some of life's most disturbing, perennial questions.

No other modern poet seems as cast against type as Wallace Stevens, the antithesis of the literary bohemian and alienated outsider. Stevens was born in Reading, Pennsylvania; his father and mother were both schoolteachers, although his father became an attorney. In 1897 Stevens enrolled at Harvard as a nondegree student. There he became president of the Harvard *Advocate* and got to know the philosopher George Santayana, whose theories of the imagination resonated with the young Stevens. In 1900, Stevens left Harvard, working as a journalist while completing his law degree in New York. He was admitted to the bar in 1904 and entered the insurance business in 1908, joining the Hartford Accident and Indemnity Company in 1916, where he remained until his death, becoming vice president of the company in 1934. Unlike other writers for whom business was an anathema to the creative process, Stevens thrived in the dual role of corporate executive and poet, dictating both business correspondence and his poetry to his secretary. In Hartford, where he lived with his wife and daughter, Stevens was detached from the contemporary literary scene but developed friendships with the poets William Carlos Williams and Marianne Moore. Stevens's poetic development, however, was largely shaped by himself alone, unaffiliated with any particular school or movement. *Harmonium*, his first collection of poetry, appeared in 1923, followed by *Ideas of Order* (1936), *The Man with the Blue Guitar* (1937), *Parts of a World* (1942), *The Necessary Angel* (a collection of prose essays) and *The Auroras of Autumn* (both in 1951), and his *Collected Poems* in 1955, the year he died of cancer.

Stevens's characteristic subjects are epistemological and aesthetic, concerned with the opposition between reality and the imagination, how things truly are and what we perceive them to be. In an early poem, "Anecdote of the Jar," Stevens juxtaposes the creative act, the means of ordering experience, with nature itself, establishing the possibilities and the limitations of both. Upon a hill, the poet asserts grandly, "I placed a jar in Tennessee," and the "slovenly wilderness" found some order for the first time. The jar now dominated the landscape, which had become "no longer wild":

> It took dominion everywhere,
> The jar was gray and bare,
> It did not give of bird or bush,
> Like nothing else in Tennessee.

Despite the jar's power of dominion over the wilderness, it is still "gray and bare," an artifact barren of natural life. With his characteristic method of juxtaposing opposites, Stevens suggests the dependency of nature on our perception to establish any meaning and value, as well as the imagination's limitations. For Stevens, the poet's role was to trace "the resemblances between things," which he explores in an essay "The Realm of Resemblances":

> Take, for example, a beach extending as far as the eye can reach bordered on the one hand, by trees and, on the other, by the sea. The sky is cloudless and the sun is red. In what sense do the objects in this scene resemble each other? There is enough green in the sea to relate it to the palms. There is enough sky reflected in the water to create a resemblance, in some sense, between them. The sand is yellow between the green and the blue. In short, the light alone creates a unity not only in the recedings of distance, where differences become invisible, but also in the contacts of closer sight. So, too, sufficiently generalized, each man resembles all other men, each woman resembles all other women, this year resembles last year. The beginning of time will, no doubt, resemble the end of time. One world is said to resemble another.

Poetry, too, the essay suggests, unites the disparate through metaphor, the creative tracing of perceived resemblances. Stevens's theory establishes his characteristic dialectical method that attempts to work out the relationship between things and their meaning. In one of his best-known and bitterest poems, "The Emperor of Ice-Cream," he contrasts two modes of being: the fact of death and a hedonistic avoidance of it. A woman has died, and some appropriate recognition is called for:

> Let the wenches dawdle in such dress
> As they are used to wear, and let the boys
> Bring flowers in last month's newspapers.
> Let be be finale of seem.
> The only emperor is the emperor of ice-cream.

Undercutting the paltry and stale celebration is the fact of death, which is confronted directly in the poem's second stanza. The poet urges that the woman's face be covered with a sheet on which she "embroidered fantails once." However, the facts cannot be so artfully concealed:

> If her horny feet protrude, they come
> To show how cold she is, and dumb.
> Let the lamp affix its beam.
> The only emperor is the emperor of ice-cream.

With his characteristic sharply realized images and at times playful epigrammatic style, Stevens packs his poem with reverberations and meaning. The first stanza's indulgence in illusion and avoidance of reality stands in opposition to the second stanza's revelation about the facts of death, and the poem traces the resemblances between the two states, both affirming and denying the truth of each stanza's last line. The poem's loaded line, "Let be be finale of seem," functions as a kind of credo of all of Stevens's poetry in which being—simple physicality—is the goad and challenge of seeming—the imagination's search for order and understanding.

For Stevens, temporal social and political issues recede in importance beside the larger theme of how the mind conceives its own world, and the poet's wrestling with this fundamental question produced some of the most challenging and satisfying poetry written in the 20th century.

CHRISTOPHER MARLOWE

75

1564–1595

It was Marlowe who first wedded the harmonies of the great organ of blank verse which peals through the centuries in the music of Shakespeare. It was Marlowe who first captured the majestic rhythms of our tongue, and whose "mighty line" is the most resounding note in England's literature. . . . He stands foremost and apart as the poet who gave us, with a rare measure of richness, the literary form which is the highest achievement of expression.
　　　　　　　　—Henry Irving, speech unveiling a statue, Canterbury, 1891

For a period of roughly six years from 1587 to 1593, Christopher Marlowe dominated the Elizabethan stage, establishing the themes and methods that would produce one of the greatest creative explosions in literary history and setting the direction that subsequent English dramatists would follow. There was simply nothing like the power and emotional and intellectual expressiveness on the English stage before Marlowe, and drama would never be the same after him. According to Swinburne, Marlowe was "the father of English tragedy and the creator of English blank verse" as well as "the most daring and inspired pioneer in all our poetic literature, the first English poet whose powers may be called sublime." T. S. Eliot [19] described Marlowe as "the most thoughtful, the most blasphemous (and, therefore, probably the most Christian) of his contemporaries," and asserted that the trajectory of Marlowe's development, abruptly halted in 1593 with his death at the age of 29, was toward "intense and serious and indubitably great poetry." Literary history is rife with intriguing what-if scenarios, and what would have happened had Marlowe survived the brawl in Deptford that claimed his life is surely one of these. (If SHAKESPEARE [1] had died at 29, none of the plays that we value as undisputed masterpieces would have been written.) Equally fascinating is the manner of his going and what we know and do not know about Marlowe's meteoric career that is as suspenseful and as riveting as any of his plays.

Christopher Marlowe was born in Canterbury, two months before fellow playwright William Shakespeare in 1564. Both men came from the rising middle stratum of Elizabethan society, from the world of trade and the yeomanry. Like Shakespeare's father, who was a glover, Marlowe's father was a successful shoemaker, but Marlowe, unlike Shakespeare, gained a scholarship to attend Cambridge University to prepare for a clerical career. Marlowe received his B.A. degree in 1584 and his M.A. in 1587, but only after Queen Elizabeth's Privy Council interceded on his behalf when university officials, suspecting Marlowe's Catholic sympathies, balked at granting his degree. Their suspicions were aroused by Marlowe's travels to Rheims in France, a prominent center for English Roman Catholic expatriates and, it was feared, conspirators against the English Crown. The letter from the Privy Council on Marlowe's behalf asserted that "in all his accions he had behaved him selfe orderlie and discreetlie wherebie he had done her Majestie good service." What exactly was the service that Marlowe provided is unknown, but his clandestine activities, possibly as a spy and informer, would continue to shadow Marlowe, as would a reputation for unorthodox and subversive ideas, as he rejected ordination, the approved purpose of his college education, and began to make his name as a poet and playwright in London.

At Cambridge Marlowe began writing verse by translating the Roman poets OVID [26] and Lucan, substituting for their elegiac meter of a hexameter line followed by a pentameter rhymed pentameter couplets, a form that would be imitated by Dryden, POPE [49], and other English poets. Marlowe's classicism stands behind what was probably his first play, *Dido Queen of Carthage*, derived from VIRGIL's [9] *Aeneid*. His first produced play is *Tamburlaine the Great*, performed in two parts by the Admiral's Men around 1587. Marlowe's assault on the dramatic conventions of his day is clearly announced in the play's prologue in which he contemptuously dismisses the prevailing "jygging vaines of riming mother wits" and the "conceits clownage keepes in pay." With an unprecedented verbal power in some of the most eloquent poetry in English drama, Marlowe puts at center stage the larger-than-life Tartar conqueror who threatens "the world with high astounding terms." The play depicts Tamburlaine's rise from shepherd to bandit to conqueror of much of Central Asia and Eastern Europe through his wit, brute force, and driving ambition. In his protagonist, Marlowe pioneered a new breed of hero for the Elizabethan stage: the master of his own destiny who succeeds by the strength of his will, claiming authority by his own human powers. The play also dramatizes the cost of such ambition, setting a new focus and standard for drama that would dominate the Elizabethan period and tragedy ever since. *Tamburlaine* also introduced the expressive power of what BEN JONSON [66] called "Marlowe's mighty line"—iambic pentameter—whose sweeping and captivating cadences are evident in the speech in which Tamburlaine offers a self-justification:

> Nature that fram'd us of foure Elements,
> Warring within our breasts for regiment,
> Doth teach us all to have aspiring minds:
> Our soules, whose faculties can comprehend
> The wondrous Architecture of the world:
> And measure every wandring planets course:
> Still climing after knowledge infinite,
> And always moving as the restless Spheares,
> Wils us to weare our selves and never rest,
> Untill we reach the ripest fruit of all,
> That perfect blisse and sole felicitie,
> The sweet fruition of an earthly crowne.

The matching of a larger-than-life hero-villain in a succession of sensational scenes with a flexible, resonant poetic language created a stage sensation, and at the age of 23 Marlowe became the most celebrated and imitated of Elizabethan playwrights.

It is not possible to date with certainty the works that followed, but during the next five years Marlowe produced the narrative poem *Hero and Leander*, two history plays, *The Massacre at Paris* and *Edward II*, and two tragedies, *The Jew of Malta* and *Dr. Faustus*. Barabas, the title character of *The Jew of Malta*, is one of drama's great antiheroes who rejects conversion to Christianity to protect his wealth and then embarks on a bloody campaign of revenge and domination. If Tamburlaine is driven by an ambition for power, Barabas is ruled by greed and destroyed by it. The play shows Marlowe trying to fuse elements of the medieval morality play with blood-and-thunder melodrama and a psychological drama in which Barabas is both a typical figure of evil and a recognizable and even sympathetic personality. The play's challenge to the audience's expectations is even more on display in *Dr. Faustus*. Like Oedipus, Faustus, who bargains away salvation for knowledge and power, has become a resonating tragic archetype, epitomizing the doomed but daring overreacher whose rebellion and defeat enact a struggle for transcendence against the gravitational pull of the human condition. Faustus's bargain with the devil, his ambitious rise and terrifying fall, encapsulates and typifies the dilemma of a thoroughly modern tragic hero. His final words reach an intensity and sublimity equaled on the English stage only by Shakespeare as Faustus mounts the ultimate existential battle to comprehend the limits and the nature of the human condition in the last grip of mortality and morality. The chorus, Marlowe's borrowing from classical drama that helps to frame the play's tragic dimension, is given the final word on Faustus's fall and its lesson:

> Cut is the branch that might have grown full straight,
> And burnèd is Apollo's laurel bough
> That sometime grew within this learnèd man.
> Faustus is gone. Regard his hellish fall,
> Whose fiendful fortune may exhort the wise
> Only to wonder at unlawful things,
> Whose deepness does entice such forward wits
> To practice more than heavenly power permits.

Dr. Faustus, Marlowe's masterpiece, and the greatest non-Shakespearean English tragedy, synthesizes the allegorical religious drama of salvation and damnation with the classical tragedy of the hubris of the exceptional hero who tests the limits of existence and humanity's deepest aspirations and darkest fears.

The violence and rebellion Marlowe put on stage dogged the playwright's life as well. In 1589 Marlowe was arrested and jailed for a fortnight over his involvement in a fatal brawl. The homicide would be ruled "in self-defence" and "not by felony." For a time Marlowe shared quarters with playwright Thomas Kyd, and, in 1593, when Kyd was arrested for sedition, the authorities discovered documents in his rooms containing "vile hereticall Conceiptes Denyinge the Deity of Jhesus Christ our Savior." Kyd insisted that the papers belonged to Marlowe, and the Privy Council issued an arrest warrant. Before it could be executed, however, Marlowe was killed in the house of Mrs. Eleanor Bull in Deptford, where the writer had spent the day with companions eating and drinking, in a scuffle ostensibly about who should pay the bill. An inquest ruled Marlowe's death accidental, but conspiracy theories have persisted that Marlowe was assassinated for political or religious reasons or in connection with his espionage activities. The manner of Marlowe's early death at age 29, as well as the details and rumors of a contentious and possibly shadowy secret life, has helped burnish the legend of a doomed literary artist of great genius who embodies baffling contradictions. Was Marlowe an Elizabethan apologist or an apostate? A scholar and intellectual, Marlowe was nevertheless a habitué of the seedy underworld of Elizabethan informers, spies, and tavern brawlers. He was the praised servant of the authoritarian, theocratic Elizabethan state but also a radical freethinker and deemed by some a dangerous religious skeptic. Marlowe's plays exalt daring rebels even as they work out their inevitable punishment for transgressions of accepted limits. At the core of Marlowe's life and works, therefore, are some of the fundamental contradictions of the Elizabethan (and the modern) age in the contention between the religious and the secular, the individual and the community, restraint versus liberation, power versus morality, ambition versus responsibility.

GABRIEL GARCÍA MÁRQUEZ

76

1928–

Face to face with a reality that overwhelms us, one which over man's perception of time must have seemed a utopia, tellers of tales who, like me, are capable of believing anything, feel entitled to believe that it is not yet too late to undertake the creation of a minor utopia: a new and limitless utopia for life wherein no one can decide for others how they are to die, where love really can be true and happiness possible, where the lineal generations of one hundred years of solitude will have at last and for ever a second chance on earth.
— Gabriel García Márquez, Nobel address, 1982

If various critics are correct that the literary history of the second half of the 20th century is defined by the remarkable imaginative power of Latin American writers, at the peak of their achievement is certainly the still-evolving oeuvre of Gabriel García Márquez. When García Márquez's masterpiece, *One Hundred Years of Solitude*, appeared in 1967, it represented not only a synthesis of Hispanic literary tradition and international modernist themes and techniques, but also that rarest of all modern literary achievement: a critical and popular success that is both sophisticated and complex, accessible and enthralling. Popular demand for the novel resulted in almost weekly reprintings after it first appeared, and it has been translated into more than 25 foreign languages. *One Hundred Years of Solitude* made García Márquez an international figure and became the best-known work by a Latin American author, prompting a worldwide explosion of

283

interest in Latin American writing and culture. García Márquez merits comparison with the greatest literary modernists, including FRANZ KAFKA [31], WILLIAM FAULKNER [15], ERNEST HEMINGWAY [63], ALBERT CAMUS [99], and JORGE LUIS BORGES [98], whose influence is strongly felt in García Márquez's work, as well as such modern giants as JAMES JOYCE [7] and THOMAS MANN [35], whose imaginative reach and wide scope he rivals. For his achievement, García Márquez was awarded the Nobel Prize in Literature in 1982.

García Márquez's themes as well as his essential techniques are rooted in his background. Born in Aracataca, a small town on Colombia's Caribbean coast, García Márquez was the eldest of 12 children and spent his first eight years in the home of his maternal grandparents. He credits his grandmother with his interest in local myths and legends as well as the manner of his storytelling, which combines the marvelous with simple, precise realism. His grandfather, a participant in the civil wars in Colombia during the 1890s, inspired some of García Márquez's greatest fictional characters. About his grandfather's death when he was eight, García Márquez has observed, "Nothing interesting has happened to me since."

In 1946, García Márquez completed high school in Zipaquirá, near Bogotá, and studied law briefly at the National University of Colombia. From 1950 to 1965 he worked as a journalist in Colombia, France, Venezuela, the United States, and Mexico. His 1955 series of articles about the ordeal of a Colombian sailor, which was critical of the Colombian navy, caused the newspaper to be shut down and García Márquez to lose his job as a foreign correspondent in Paris. After the Cuban revolution, he joined Prensa Latina, the Cuban news agency, and worked in Bogotá, New York City, and Mexico City, where he also worked for a public relations firm and wrote film scripts. Before he wrote *One Hundred Years of Solitude*, García Márquez published four books that earned some prizes and critical attention but gained limited popularity: the novels *Leaf Storm* (1955) and *The Evil Hour* (1962); a novella, *No One Writes to the Colonel* (1961); and a collection of short stories, *Big Mama's Funeral* (1962). All show traces of his characteristic themes of social decay and political repression and the development of his mature style. His early influences are noticeably derived from Kafka in his interest in irrational and nightmarish visions; from Faulkner in his complex narrative structure and universalized regional landscape; and from Hemingway in his spare realism. These various elements find a masterful synthesis in *One Hundred Years of Solitude*, García Márquez's massive social and family chronicle, which he claimed he had conceived in his youth before he possessed the necessary skill to achieve his vision. In Mexico City in 1965, suffering from a severe case of writer's block, García Márquez solved the problem of composition with visionary clarity while he and his family were driving along the Mexico City–Acapulco highway. Suddenly, the entire shape and words of the novel were revealed to him. "It was so ripe in me," he later recalled, "that I could have dictated the first chapter, word by word, to a typist." He spent the next 18 months composing the novel, as his wife secretly pawned valuables to meet living expenses that eventually resulted in a $10,000 debt.

One Hundred Years of Solitude interweaves individuals, family, community, nation, and race into a vast epic. The novel traces the history of the fictional village of Macondo from its founding to its decline and destruction a century later by a hurricane. Macondo's story is also the chronicle of the Buendía family over several generations, as the "original sins" of incest and violence committed by the head of the family dynasty, José Arcadio, and his wife Ursula, recur in succeeding generations. On the historical level, Macondo's story and that of the Buendías also reflect the pattern of Latin American history in general, and Colombia's in particular, since the overthrow of Spanish rule. Finally, on the mythical level, the novel is a record of the village's movement from paradise in its early days to its ultimate corruption and decline through recurrent patterns of human behavior in a cycle of sin and guilt, violence and retribution. In García Márquez's handling, the real and the fantastic coexist and reinforce the novel's captivating specificity and universal meaning. The result is a richly absorbing fictional universe in which elements of traditional Hispanic literature and modernist techniques support one another and in which oppositions, such as reality and fantasy, history and myth, reason and irrationality, come together in an astonishing complex.

One Hundred Years of Solitude is such a distinctive masterpiece that there is a tendency to compare García Márquez's subsequent work to it exclusively. Although certain themes and techniques recur, García Márquez does not repeat himself; rather, he continually surpasses our expectations in the diversity and richness of his imagination. The novelist Mario Vargas Llosa has said of García Márquez: "Political or literary opinions, judgments of people, things or countries, projects and ambitions, everything is expressed in the form of anecdotes. His intelligence, his culture, and his sensitivity display a curious stamp of the specific, the concrete, the anti-intellectual, and the anti-abstract. Upon contact with this personality, life becomes a cascade of anecdotes." These anecdotes have taken the shape of a second collection of short stories, *The Incredible and Sad Tale of Innocent Eréndira and Her Heartless Grandmother* (1972); *The Autumn of the Patriarch* (1975), a fictional study of corruption and totalitarianism; *Chronicle of a Death Foretold* (1981), a fictional treatment of an actual murder case in Colombia; *Love in the Time of Cholera* (1985), the story of a lifelong love affair described in a series of flashbacks; and *The General in His Labyrinth* (1989), which imagines the last months in the life of Simón Bolívar. All these works form chapters in the history of Latin American consciousness while pursuing central themes of historical and social change, expressed not through social protest—although García Márquez's political commitment has remained strong—but through the inner reform identified by a powerful imagination engaged with the deepest questions of the human condition.

PERCY BYSSHE SHELLEY

77

1792–1822

Shelley, lyric lord of England's lordliest singers, here first heard
Ring from lips of poets crowned and dead the Promethean word
Whence his soul took fire, and power to out-soar the sunward-soaring bird.
                    —Algernon C. Swinburne, "Eton: An Ode"

Of all the English romantic poets, Shelley is the easiest to disdain as well as to admire. In one view, he represents the paradigm of romantic self-absorption, whose emoting easily slides into sentimental posturing. Such lines as the following represent what has been called his emotional slither that the moderns later rejected:

> Woe is me!
> The winged words on which my soul would pierce
> Into the height of Love's rare Universe,
> Are chains of lead around its flight of fire—
> I pant, I sink, I tremble, I expire!
>
> *—(Epipsychidion)*

For such writers as T. S. ELIOT [19], Shelley was a poet of adolescence whose lapses of taste, sentimentality, and delusion deny him greatness. According to William Hazlitt, Shelley's poetry is "a passionate dream, a straining after impossibilities, a record of fond conjectures, a confused embodying of vague abstractions—a fever of the soul, thirsting and craving after what it cannot have, indulging its love of power and novelty at the expense of truth and nature, associating ideas by contraries, and wasting great powers by their application to unattainable objects." Many others, including WORDSWORTH [23] and YEATS [17], however, have admired Shelley for his pure lyricism and also for his political and social themes, which cast him as the avatar of personal liberation and the challenger of all limits that restrict and repress individual transcendence. As such, he is one of literature's greatest figures. His engagement and insistence on the power of poetry to restore the world have challenged succeeding generations of writers in the continuing debate between the demands of self and society, resistance and accommodation, lyrical expressiveness and dramatic presentation.

Shelley's short but contentious literary career is divisible into three fairly distinct, though at times overlapping, stages. The son of a Sussex country squire, Shelley was educated at Eton and Oxford, although he was expelled after only a year at college for the polemical "The Necessity of Atheism," which announced his defiance of orthodoxy. The first phase of Shelley's work, from his 1810 departure from Oxford to 1814, when he left England, is marked by a radical liberalism and a search for a political solution to the perceived repression and stultifying conservatism of England. The culmination of his early development is the philosophical poem "Queen Mab" (1813), which catalogues of Shelley's rants against kings, priests, statesmen, marriage, commerce, and Christianity. The years between 1814 and 1819 represent the second stage, in which Shelley gradually abandoned his faith in a political solution for more personally focused poetry of man's inner nature. These are the years when Shelley's failed marriage to Harriet Westbrook led to his elopement with Mary Wollstonecraft Godwin and his self-exile to Switzerland and Italy. The third phase, between 1819 and his death in 1822 by drowning while sailing off the Italian coast, is the period of his greatest poetic achievement. Shelley's work in this period asserts the power of the imagination to transform experience and reveals the progressive darkening of his worldview and his preoccupation with death and the hopelessness of human life. He produced the philosophical verse drama *Prometheus Unbound* (1820); *Epipsychidion* (1821), a daring moral attack on marriage; and the elegy *Adonais* (1821), on the occasion of KEATS's [25] death. In his longer works and his lyrics, Shelley is faithful to his vision of poetry contained in his essay "A Defence of Poetry," published posthumously in 1840. In it Shelley concludes:

It is impossible to read the compositions of the most celebrated writers of the present day without being startled with the electric life which burns writing their words. They measure the circumference and sound the depths of human nature with a comprehensive and all-penetrating spirit, and they are themselves perhaps the most sincerely astonished at its manifestations, for it is less their spirit than the spirit of the age. Poets are the hierophants of an unapprehended inspiration, the mirrors of the gigantic shadows which futurity casts upon the present, the words which express what they understand not; the trumpets which sing to battle, and feel now what they inspire; the influence which is moved not, but moves. Poets are the unacknowledged legislators of the World.

Shelley reflects the spirit of his age in its revolutionary change, which he was determined to play a role in shaping. Characteristically, his poetry sets the individual at the center of the conflict, suspended between the drive for transcendence and an awareness of the limitations that life imposes. Few other poets have exposed so much of themselves in this battle, revealing the full range of emotions present as the self attempts to answer its feelings of angst. At his worst, Shelley seems to indulge his pain with a luxuriant sentimentality, but at his best, as in the brilliant "Ode to the West Wind" or "The Skylark" and "Stanzas Written in Dejection," he embodies his emotions and ideas in concrete and suggestive language that opens up complex experience instead of closing it down in bathos. Like BLAKE [29], Shelley is concerned with redeeming the world and the individual through the power of the imagination to break the bonds that diminish what is possible. His lyrical drama *Prometheus Unbound* explores the mythical figure of Prometheus, chained and punished for eternity for providing man with fire, which is symbolic of man's creativity and imagination. In embracing this power, Shelley suggests the ways in which resistance can be transformed into liberation. In many ways, Shelley anticipates the existentialism of CAMUS [99] and his *Myth of Sisyphus*, and the current of much modern thought. In the lyrical "Ode to the West Wind," Shelley contemplates the symbolic force of nature as both a "Destroyer and Preserver," and the poet who functions in the same way. A meditation on the West Wind's power, the poem traces how this force can be transformed into the poet's instrument:

> Make me thy lyre, even as the forest is;
> What if my leaves are falling like its own!
> The tumult of thy mighty harmonies
>
> Will take from both a deep, autumnal tone,
> Sweet though in sadness. Be thou, Spirit fierce,
> My spirit! Be thou me, impetuous one!
>
> Drive my dead thoughts over the universe
> Like withered leaves to quicken a new birth!
> And, by the incantation of this verse,

Scatter, as from an unextinguished hearth
Ashes and sparks, my words among mankind!
Be through my lips to unawakened Earth
The trumpet of prophecy! O Wind,
If Winter comes, can Spring be far behind?

    The poem brings together Shelley's political, philosophical, and imaginative aspirations in a forceful and revealing manner that is uniquely his own. His self-exposure, easily parodied and patronized, is both risky and admirable. His revelations, which often exceed the bounds of custom and taste, still reach a level of the heroic for their daringness and originality.

RAINER MARIA RILKE

78

1875–1926

Rainer Maria Rilke was poorly suited for this age. This great lyric poet did nothing but perfect the German poem for the first time. He was not a peak of this age, he was one of the pinnacles on which the destiny of the spirit strides across ages. . . . He belongs in the context of centuries of German poetry, not in the context of the day.
—Robert Musil, "Address at the Memorial Service for Rilke in Berlin," 1927

Rainer Maria Rilke can be included among a select group of poets—CHARLES BAUDELAIRE [46], Paul Valéry, T. S. ELIOT [19], ROBERT FROST [86], and W. B. YEATS [17]—who revolutionized modern lyric poetry. Very much the poet as restless searcher for the answers to the great mysteries of the universe and human existence, Rilke managed to leave behind messages from his inward journeying, offering in his poetry an unprecedented access to a questing mind in dialogue with itself and the world. Anticipating the existentialists who would follow him, Rilke surveyed the human condition unsupported by traditional sources of consolation and belief. Cut off from previous systems of order and coherence, he set out to create his own, bringing together the great contradictions—subject/object, man/nature, spirit/flesh, past/present, beauty/suffering, life/death—in a new synthesis. In search of a new philosophy to understand the modern world, Rilke pioneered a new poetic language to communicate his discoveries. To comprehend all aspects of modern life in his

290

poetry, Rilke mounted a revolution in German prosody comparable to that undertaken by GOETHE [10] and others at the end of the 18th century in which a new authenticity and intimacy replaced the stylized feelings and decorous language of conventional verse. Rilke would push these innovations even farther, propelling German poetry into accommodating the experimentation and vision of the European modernists. Fiercely committed to his poetic mission, Rilke is one of the great exemplars of artistic integrity and vision. As critic C. M. Bowra observed, "Where others have found a unifying principle for themselves in religion or morality or the search for truth, Rilke found his in the search for impressions and the hope these could be turned into poetry. . . . For him Art was what mattered most in life." SHELLEY [77] famously declared poets the "unacknowledged legislators of the world." Rilke set out to prove Shelley's point.

Born in Prague, then a part of the Austro-Hungarian Empire, Rilke, who was called René until 1897, was the only child of German-speaking parents who separated when he was 11. His father, Joseph, was a career military officer who became an Austrian railroad official after a chronic throat problem obliged him to resign his commission. His mother, Phia, was a poet and an eccentric, who dressed her son in girls' clothes to compensate for the loss of a baby daughter. Rilke's father wanted his son to achieve the glorious military career he had been forced to abandon and to that end sent him to military school, which added to the boy's unhappiness. In 1891, after four years at two different military academies, Rilke withdrew from his second school because of chronic illness that may have been psychosomatic. He entered a German preparatory school and then studied at Charles University in Prague. Although his uncle expected him to take over his law practice, Rilke was determined to pursue a literary career and while still at the university published his first three volumes of poetry, *Life and Songs* (1894), *Sacrifice to the Lares* (1895), and *Crowned by Dreams* (1896), all of which are early efforts of sentimental intensity and lyricism, drawing on the German folk song tradition and the lyrics of HEINRICH HEINE [123] and others.

In 1896 Rilke left Prague for Munich, where he thrived within its artistic and literary community. There, he met and fell in love with Lou Andreas-Salomé, a Russian intellectual whose circle included Friedrich Nietzsche, Gerhart Hauptmann, Franz Wedekind, and Arthur Schnitzler. Fifteen years his senior, Andreas-Salomé became a lifelong influence on Rilke and, as the poet's mistress, companion, and teacher, helped to inform his maturing sensibilities as a writer. She would provide Rilke with an enhanced self-confidence while helping him to rid his poetry of its previous sentimentality and self-indulgence and opening up for him new influences from her intellectual and artistic circle. Rilke traveled to Berlin and Florence with Lou and her professor husband, and, in 1899, he accompanied the Andreases to Russia, which he later said "was in a certain sense the foundation of my ways of experiencing and absorbing the world." There, Rilke met Tolstoy [4] and the painter Leonid Pasternak (the father of Boris Pasternak) and became fascinated by Russian mysticism and religious faith, as well as the Russian landscape and the simple life of the peasants. Soon after his return from Russia in 1900, Rilke began writing the poems that became *The Book of Hours* (1906), a spiritual exploration in three books (*Of the Monastic Life, Of Pilgrimage,* and *Of Poverty and Death*). Resembling the prayers of a Christian mystic, the poems radically invert the traditional Christian message. As critic Hester Pickman summarizes, in Rilke's reworking of Christian spirituality, "God is not light but darkness—not a father, but a son, not the creator but the created. He and not man is our neighbor for men are infinitely far from each other. They must seek God, not where one or two are gathered in His name, but alone." God in Rilke's cosmogony is less a personal deity than a life force, and the essential subject of *The Book of Hours* is the necessity and the perils of tapping into it in the poet's own inner life. *The Book of Hours* would establish Rilke's essential poetic and visionary mission in the search for a sustaining spiritual and psychological basis for understanding the world.

After a second trip to Russia in 1900, Rilke spent two years at the artists' colony at Worpswede in Saxony, where he met and married the sculptor Clara Westhoff; the couple's daughter, Ruth, was born in 1901. Rilke, whose poetic vocation was paramount, was unsuited to married life, and in 1902 he separated from Westhoff, although the couple would maintain a relationship that lasted throughout Rilke's remaining years. Rilke spent the next 14 years in Paris, apart from occasional visits to Italy, Denmark, and Sweden. In Paris, Rilke began a biographical monograph of the sculptor Auguste Rodin, with whom he lived and worked as a private secretary for a time, and whose friendship helped to overcome the isolation Rilke felt as an émigré. Rilke's difficulties in Paris resulted in his only novel, the semiautobiographical *The Notebooks of Malte Laurids Brigge,* begun in 1904 and published in 1910. A diary chronicle of a sensitive soul experiencing loneliness and depression amid the cosmopolites of a modern city, *Notebooks* can be compared to Joyce's [7] *A Portrait of the Artist as a Young Man,* as both novels explore the challenges faced by the artist. Rilke's time in Paris and the influence of Rodin and the painter Paul Cézanne would result in important alterations in his poetic style and technique. Both artists taught Rilke the value of objective observation, which is evident in the so-called Thing-Poems in Rilke's collection, *New Poems* (1907). In describing concrete common objects, Rilke's new works show him turning away from his previous subjective and private impressionism to a presentation anchored by the details and reality of ordinary life. Rilke's new objective style would open up German lyric poetry to subjects never previously considered in a style that replicated the methods of modernist and imagist poets like Ezra Pound. Rilke, however, would regard this new style as incomplete and insufficient, failing to release the "secret of living things" that he longed to explore.

After the publication of *Notebooks*, an exhausted Rilke went to Egypt and Spain to gain inspiration for what would become his final poetic phase; he also occupied himself by translating French, Spanish, Italian, and English poets. From 1911 to 1912 he stayed at the Castle Duino on the Adriatic Sea near Trieste, the home of the Princess Marie of Thurn and Taxis-Hohenlohe. There, Rilke composed a 15-poem cycle, *The Life of the Virgin Mary*, a celebration of Marian sensitivity and strength inspired by the Spanish artist Ribadaniera. The image of the "great angel" had always been a recurring theme in Rilke's work and immediately appears in the first line of his greatest work, the *Duino Elegies* (1923), begun on January 21, 1912, with the supplication, "Who, if I cried out, would hear me among the angels' hierarchy?" For Rilke, the angel, an imagined being of perfect consciousness, became a personal symbol for the perfection of life in all its forms to which he aspired. Grappling with this angel and all it represented would occupy Rilke for the next ten years as he struggled to complete the sequence of ten long poems that became the *Duino Elegies*. During his stay at Duino, Rilke wrote the first and second elegies, the beginning of the third, and parts of the sixth, ninth, and tenth. After traveling in Spain, he returned to Paris in 1913 and completed the third elegy. In 1914 he went to Munich, where he embarked upon a turbulent two-year affair with the painter Lou Albert-Lasard and in 1915 finished the fourth elegy. When World War I began, Rilke, considered an enemy alien in France, could not return to Paris, and his property there was confiscated and sold at auction. He was drafted in 1916 and after basic training was given a job as a desk clerk in the War Archives Office in Vienna. Influential friends helped secure his discharge in June 1916, and he returned to Munich, unable to write and traumatized by his military service, which was a painful reminder of his youthful experiences at the military academies. In 1919 Rilke went to Switzerland to lecture in Zurich and to try to complete the *Duino Elegies*. In an attempt to find affordable lodgings, he moved from town to town until 1922, when a patron, Werner Reinhart, purchased the Chateau de Muzot near Sierre and allowed him to live there rent free. Rilke completed the *Duino Elegies* there and almost immediately afterward produced *Sonnets to Orpheus*, a two-part sequence of 55 sonnets written as a memorial for the young daughter of a friend. Both poems orchestrate Rilke's evolving philosophy and represent his singular contribution to modern poetry.

The *Duino Elegies* have been described by author Colin Wilson as possibly "the greatest set of poems of modern times," having a comparable influence in German-speaking countries "as *The Waste Land* has in England and America." Like Eliot's poem, the *Duino Elegies* survey the wreckage of modern life while questing for answers to life's purpose, enduring values, and the role of the poet as mediator of those values. Beginning in the first elegy with a confession of poetical and emotional bankruptcy, Rilke moves through the elegies diagnosing their causes. Limited by time, passions, and the flesh, humanity is condemned to a suffering in which endurance seems to provide the only legitimate response. By the seventh elegy, however, Rilke's lament turns to celebration of the possibility of a creative existence that transcends all existential limitations. "The lesson of the seventh elegy," argues critic E. M. Butler, "is that the only real world is with us, and that life is one long transformation. Rilke had at last found the formula for his cosmic vision and a connecting link between himself and the angel." By actively confronting existence in all its aspects, Rilke manages to turn from despair to joy. In the ninth elegy he declares the poet's mission to praise and extol the simplest things of existence:

> Praise this world to the angel, not the unsayable one,
> you can't impress *him* with glorious emotion; in the universe
> where he feels more powerfully, you are a novice. So show him
> something simple which formed over generations,
> lives as our own, near our hand and within our gaze.
> Tell him of Things. He will stand astonished . . .
> Show him how happy a Thing can be, how innocent and ours,
> Serves as a Thing, or dies into a Thing—

Despite arriving at an affirmation of life's purpose and the role of the poet in harmonizing the paradoxes of existence, a tragic awareness permeates the *Duino Elegies*. *Sonnets to Orpheus* by contrast offers a comic vision with its tone of joyful, ecstatic celebration of life and poetic power. One of the greatest sonnet sequences and a brilliantly innovative use of poetic tradition, *Sonnets to Orpheus* is simultaneously didactic, reflective, and impassioned, bringing Rilke's lifelong poetic quest for answers to life's most vexing mysteries to a glorious and resounding fulfillment.

During his final years Rilke became ill with what was eventually diagnosed as leukemia; however he continued to write individual poems. In December 1926, after pricking his finger on the thorn of a rose, Rilke developed an infection and died soon after at a sanatorium in Valmont. Rilke has gone on to become one of the most translated of modern world poets and an inspiration to many. As critic Stuart Holroyd argues, the "poetry which Rilke wrote to express and extend his experience . . . is one of the most successful attempts a modern man has made to orientate himself within his chaotic world."

ROBERT MUSIL

79

1880–1942

In the last analysis, War and Peace, Remembrance of Things Past, Ulysses, *and* The Magic Mountain *remain statements about life.* The Man Without Qualities *is more than this. It is an open rather than a closed system of thought, a search on the border of the impossible for new directions of moral development. The basic moral question is how to live; this question is at the center of the work. The author's conception of his novel as a bridge being built out into space is a moral one; the ideal at the other end of the bridge is the right life. No other work of literature goes further in laying bare for its readers the moral dilemmas of life in western civilization of the twentieth century. No other novel makes its readers aware to the same extent of these moral conflicts within themselves.*
—Burton Pike, *Robert Musil: An Introduction to His Work*

Of all the legitimate giants of the modern novel, Robert Musil is the least read or appreciated. Musil died in obscurity in the midst of World War II, having failed, unlike his rival THOMAS MANN [35], to secure support and a reception for his books in America, and leaving his monumental magnum opus, *The Man Without Qualities*, unfinished. At nearly 1,600 pages, the novel has been called the supreme example in Western literature of the novel of ideas and a compendium of contemporary uncertainty. Formidable as it is in length and complexity, *The Man Without Qualities* (published in Germany, 1930–42, and in translation, 1953–60) is every bit as much a landmark in modern thought and

295

artistic conception as JOYCE's [7] *Ulysses*, PROUST's [16] *Remembrance of Things Past*, and Mann's *The Magic Mountain*, entitling Musil to comparison with the very greatest of literary artists. With a highly praised English translation that appeared in 1995, Musil's masterpiece is likely to reach a wider audience and generate greater appreciation for his considerable achievement.

Robert Musil was born in Austria into a family with a heritage of professional success in the army, civil service, and science, which Musil followed until he broke away from his family's expectations to pursue his writing. His father was an engineer at a machine factory who eventually became the chair of mechanical engineering at the Technical University of Brünn. Musil's mother was as temperamental and emotional as his father was withdrawn and inhibited. Seven years after their marriage, she formed a romantic attachment to a teacher who moved in with the Musils the year Robert was born and became a permanent member of the family for the next 40 years. Excluded from this unorthodox triangular relationship, Musil was a brooding and rebellious child who was sent away from home in 1892, at the age of 12, to prepare for a career in the military. In 1894, Musil attended the senior military academy at Mährisch-Weisskirchen, the same school that the poet RAINER MARIA RILKE [78] had earlier attended in misery. Appalled by its filth and the psychological debasement of the cadets, who were treated more like prisoners than students, Musil called the school "the devil's anus." The experience remained a bitter memory, to be exorcised in his first novel, *Young Törless*.

Close to receiving his commission, Musil abandoned an army career for training as an engineer at the University of Brünn from 1898 to 1901. After earning his degree, completing a year of compulsory military service, and working in an engineering laboratory in Stuttgart, out of boredom Musil began to write *Young Törless*, a novel about a sensitive adolescent coming to terms with himself and society. In 1903, at the age of 23, Musil shifted yet again, giving up engineering to study philosophy, psychology, and mathematics at the University of Berlin, where he remained for five years. Although he seriously considered a career as a philosophy professor, Musil was persuaded by the recognition he received with the publication of *Young Törless* to pursue a career as a writer instead.

In 1911, Musil published two short stories in the volume *Unions* and married Martha Marcovaldi, who would become his valued companion and essential support in arranging the details of everyday life that he ignored to concentrate on his writing. During World War I, Musil served in the Austrian army both at the front and as the editor of a military newspaper. From 1918 to 1922, Musil held military posts as a liaison press officer with the Austrian Foreign Ministry and as a scientific adviser to the War Office, while publishing the play *Enthusiasts* (1920). After 1922, he subsisted as a freelance writer of essays, criticism, and journal and newspaper articles, producing a second collection of short stories, *Three Women* (1924) and the play, *Vinzenz and the*

Girl Friend of Important Men (1924). From then until his death, Musil devoted himself exclusively to his second and final novel, *The Man Without Qualities*, supported in part by Musil societies in Berlin and Vienna formed to assist his literary efforts.

After the Nazis came to power in Germany, Musil moved to Vienna, where he remained until 1938, when Germany annexed Austria. Exiled in Switzerland, Musil lost his German Jewish publisher, any additional royalties from his works, and his charitable support from Germany and Austria. Continual fruitless appeals for support from various relief organizations kept him from completing his great novel. On April 15, 1942, after a morning spent working on his novel, Musil suffered a fatal cerebral hemorrhage. Only a handful of mourners attended his funeral. In a 1940 letter he wrote: "I have always kept some slight distance from the main road of success. I am not the kind of author who tells his readers what they want to hear because they know it anyway. My attitude and my work tend rather towards the severe, and my readers have gradually come to me, not I to them." Musil's self-assessment has proven prophetic. Despite his lack of popular or great critical success during his lifetime, his reputation as one of this century's greatest artists has grown steadily, and his masterpiece, *The Man Without Qualities*, has been recognized as one of the touchstones of modern consciousness.

An encyclopedic panorama of prewar Austria, *The Man Without Qualities* is set during the months leading up to August 1914. The novel's protagonist is Ulrich, an intelligent veteran of three careers—army, engineering, and mathematics—who at the age of 32 takes a sabbatical to reassess his life. His ensuing search for answers about how one should live becomes an outward and inward journey of self-awareness and a social satire that reveals the moral and political decline of the Austro-Hungarian empire and the cultural crisis that led to World War I. The novel replaces dramatic action with the internal states of mind and emotions of characters forced to make sense of their world. Fragmented and limited, Musil's characters fall short of the integration and unity that the book as a whole strives to provide in its massive criticism of life. Ulrich's search for solutions to his and his society's dilemma turns increasingly inward toward mysticism, and the completion possible through love to unite the disjunction between the self and the world. The novel breaks off at this point, but clearly suggests that historical events will finally triumph, destroying any possibility for a utopian solution. Ulrich's fate is fundamentally beyond his control, and in his novel Musil has diagnosed, as powerfully as any novelist has ever done, the testing ground of modern identity.

80

HORACE

65–8 B.C.

Ovid succeeded in writing the greatest poem in the Latin language. . . . Propertius wrote the most original and artistic poetry in Latin. . . . Lucretius wrote the most intelligent and most ingenious poem in Latin. Virgil wrote the most imaginative, the most passionate, the most haunting, and the most spiritual poem in ancient literature. Where does that leave Horace? Is he not, after all, the genial, plump don with a flair for sherry and an infinite capacity for platitudes, and common sense, and taking pains? No, I compare him with Homer, Dante, Shakespeare, and Goethe. My criteria are: breadth of vision and sympathies; maddening facility with language and verification; sheer guts; irony that has outgrown egotism; capacity for change; willingness to confront the tragedies of history without casting oneself (or anybody) in a permanent tragic role; not looking backward too much and not pretending to be able to look forward very far; courage to be free; finally, a deep charity for what sustains what is, for other beings, for oneself.

—W. R. Johnson, foreword to *The Essential Horace*

Few other poets, as both practitioner and theorist, have had a greater impact on literature than Horace. Regarded as the greatest Roman lyric poet, Horace helped to establish the lyric in the Western poetic tradition over the epic as the dominant and privileged genre for private and public expression. It is his *Ars poetica* that set the standards for poetry that would govern literary criticism for nearly 2,000 years, formalizing the concepts that would define neoclassicism.

Yet one of the preeminent romantic poets, William Wordsworth, also claimed kinship, stating that "He is my great favorite"; while the modern poet W. H. AUDEN [103] called Horace one of the poets without whom "I couldn't have managed / even my weakest lines." Subsequent poets have been shaped by the extraordinary poetic craftsmanship of Horace's verses and his ability to turn poetry into a capacious and flexible form for intimate self-expression and the sanest and most salutary reflections on the world and human nature. *Horatian* has become the accepted descriptive term for a distinctive combination of formal perfection, elegance, succinctness, and moral and emotional clarity. English-language imitators and translators include Sir Philip Sidney, BEN JONSON [66], Andrew Marvell, JOHN MILTON [8], John Dryden, JONATHAN SWIFT [41], ALEXANDER POPE [49], Samuel Johnson, ALFRED TENNYSON [81], Ezra Pound, Robert Lowell, and many more. No other ancient writer has formed a more intimate bond with his readers. "If Virgil has been the most revered of Latin poets," literary historian Moses Hadas has argued, "Horace has been the most beloved." This sentiment is shared by critic Grant Showerman who has asserted that "No poet speaks from the page with greater directness, no poet establishes so easily and so completely the personal relation with the reader, no poet is remembered so much as if he were a friend in the flesh."

Horace's eminence is particularly impressive when weighed against the challenges he faced from his background and the age his life spanned that included the death throes of the Roman republic, the assassination of Julius Caesar, the civil wars that followed, and the establishment of the Roman Empire under Augustus. Quintus Horatius Flaccus was born in 65 B.C., the son of a former slave in the Apulian provincial town of Venusia, in southeast Italy. Horace's father amassed sufficient wealth to have his son educated in Rome, and Horace acknowledged his great debt to his beloved father:

> If my nature is to have few and middling faults . . .
> if no one can reproach me with greed or meanness . . .
> my father was the cause. Low-born, and not rich in land,
> he would not have me sent to Flavius's day school,
> where hulking centurions' hulking louts of sons,
> with pack and tablets hung on their left arms,
> went clutching their eight brass pennies on the ides;
> but dared to take his son to Rome and teach him
> whatever studies the greatest knight or senator
> would teach his sons.
>
> (*Satires* 1.6 65–78)

It was Horace's father who recognized his son's abilities and made it possible for him to become, in the words of scholar David Armstrong, "one of the most successful arrivistes in Roman social history." Horace was at school in Rome when Julius Caesar defied the Senate, crossed the Rubicon, and assumed control of the state in 48 B.C. At 19, Horace traveled to Athens to continue his studies in both Greek philosophy and poetry. Following Caesar's assassination in 44 B.C., Horace welcomed the conspirators' arrival in Athens and accepted an appointment as a junior officer in Brutus's army. Participating in the defeat at Philippi at the hands of the triumvirate of Octavian, Antony, and Lepidus, Horace returned to Rome under a general amnesty to find his father's property confiscated. To support himself Horace managed to secure a position as a treasury clerk. It was during this period that he began to write poetry that attracted the attention of others, including Virgil, who introduced Horace to Gaius Maecenas, the wealthy literary patron and influential adviser to Octavian. After defeating his former ally Marc Antony, Octavian, assuming the honorific Augustus, now reigned supreme as Rome's first emperor. Maecenas would become Horace's lifelong friend and sponsor, making possible Horace's movement among Rome's imperial circles and giving the poet a retreat in the Sabine hills that allowed Horace to devote himself exclusively to his writing. Dividing his time between activities in Rome and his retreat contributed to the characteristic dualities in Horace's works between the city and the country, public and private, the enduring certainties of nature and the vagaries of fortune and mortality.

Horace's first publication in 35 B.C. was a collection of *Satires* in hexameters, a mixed literary genre popularized by the Latin poet Lucilius that included dialogues, anecdotes, and autobiographical and philosophical reflections. Horace's critiques of political, social, and moral failures in friends, acquaintances, and society are handled with a characteristic deftness of wit and verbal skill in which style matches sense in Horace's urging moderation and balance in everything: "There is measure in all things," Horace observes. "There are, finally, certain boundaries beyond or this side of which the right cannot stand." A second volume of *Satires*, published after Horace had acquired his Sabine farm in 31 B.C., celebrates the Epicurean delights of country life. The *Epodes*, a volume of love lyrics and political and satirical verses, appeared in 29 B.C. In contrast to the informal conversational tone and hexameter form of the *Satires*, the volume's stylistic variety and complexity express Horace's major poetic innovation—introducing into Latin verse the methods and meter of Greek lyric poets such as Sappho, Archilochus, Alcaeus, and Pindar. Horace would devote the next seven years adapting Greek verse forms into some of the most polished and expressive Latin poetry ever written. His masterwork, the *Odes*, a three-book sequence of 88 lyrics, was published in 23 B.C. CATULLUS [82] had earlier imitated Greek models, but no Latin poet had ever imitated the complex musicality of Greek verse on such a scale. The *Odes*, Horace's meditations on love, friendship, and mortality, has been described by David Armstrong as "the most profoundly finished, variegated, and learned books in the whole of Roman poetry." Scholar Maurice Bowra goes even farther, asserting that the *Odes* "cover a wider range of experience and present it in a more satisfying form than almost any other comparable book written by man."

Horace's amazing linguistic versatility and beautiful lyrical effects in meter, word choice, and placement in the *Odes* are mainly lost in translation. For the non-Latinist, as VIRGINIA WOOLF [48] said about JANE AUSTEN [20], it is difficult to catch Horace in the act of greatness. His considerable artistry mainly disappears under the demands of English's noninflected syntactical coherence. For scholar Harold Mattingly, the epitome of the "fantastically difficult" is "making ropes out of sand or translating the *Odes* of Horace in English." Poets and translators have faced the challenge for centuries. No less a poet than John Milton attempted to preserve the Latin meter and word order of the Horatian original in his translation of "Ode I.5," the so-called Pyrrha Ode:

> What slender Youth bedew'd with liquid odours
> Courts thee on Roses in some pleasant Cave,
>   Pyrrha for whom bind'st thou
>   In wreaths thy golden Hair,
> Plain in thy neatness; O how oft shall he
> On Faith and changed Gods complain: and Seas
>   Rough with black winds and storms
>   Unwonted shall admire:
> Who now enjoys thee credulous, all Gold,
> Who always vacant, always amiable
>   Hopes thee; of flattering gales
>   Unmindfull. Hapless they
> To whom thou untry'd seem'st fair. Me in my vow'd
> Picture the sacred wall declares t'have hung
>   My dank and dropping weeds
>   To the stern God of Sea.

If the complex and beautiful musicality of the *Odes* is difficult to replicate in English, the non-Latinist can still profit from their sense and overall impact. Without knowing the source, many of us still can quote Horace from *Carpe diem* to *Dulce et decorum est pro patria mori*. As critic Moses Stephen Slaughter has observed, "His thought, never very original or very intense, has long since become absorbed in the common thought of the world." Horace's poems range widely over multiple topics with each lyric placed with care, proceeding through juxtaposition of contrasting subjects and moods. The *Odes* are one of the first examples of the poetic sequence in which individual lyrics are orchestrated into a much more expansive whole, as meaning and significance accumulate through counterpoint and contrast. Horace considers the pleasures of wine and country delights, the pangs of mortality, the pains and joys of love, and the value of poetry. Experience is surveyed with a critical detachment that achieves a balanced view of the mixed nature of human experience. In contrast to the emotional extremes of Catullus or the passionate intensity of SAPPHO [88], Horace offers what has been called the "poetry of common experience," capturing a multiplicity of responses to existence, while not excluding from poetic consideration the ordinary and mundane. With Horace, the range of poetic experience expands dramatically. "It is in the 'middle range' of human experience that Horace is supreme," scholar David Armstrong asserts, "and his limitations are, perhaps, one reason for his continued popularity. We have all felt what Horace feels more than what Catullus or Hopkins feels, whether this is to our credit or not."

Horace, in retirement on his Sabine farm, closed his career with a series of *Epistles*, verse letters on various subjects, including the seminal treatise on poetry, the *Ars poetica*, one of the foundation texts of literary criticism. In it, Horace enumerates both the purpose of poetry—mixing "the useful with the sweet"—and the rules that should govern poetic and dramatic construction. Along with Aristotle's *Poetics*, Horace's *Ars poetica* set the classical benchmarks with which subsequent writers and critics have had to contend. Horace died suddenly at the age of 56 in 8 B.C., having risen from being a freedman's son to become the acknowledged poet laureate of Augustan Rome. In his writing Horace achieved even more: the artistic immortality that he confidently predicted in the *Odes*:

> I have built a monument more lasting than bronze,
> that looms about royal deserted pyramids,
> that no eroding rain nor raving wind
> can ever crumble, nor the unnumbered
> series of years, the flight of generations.
> I shall not wholly die. . . .

ALFRED, LORD TENNYSON

81

1809–1892

Tennyson is a great poet, for reasons that are perfectly clear. He had three qualities which are seldom found together except in the greatest poets: abundance, variety, and complete competence. We therefore cannot appreciate his works unless we read a good deal of it. We may not admire his aims; but whatever he sets out to do, he succeeds in doing, with a mastery that gives us the sense of confidence that is one of the major pleasures of poetry. . . . He had the finest ear of any English poet since Milton.

—T. S. Eliot, Introduction to Tennyson's *Poems*

To see Tennyson's literary achievement clearly, one must first contend with the modern period's rejection of all things Victorian. Tennyson was the greatest literary voice of his age and one of the most famous and popular poets of all time. Like WORDSWORTH [23], Tennyson became an institution, the exalted literary spokesman for the Victorian era. Like ALEXANDER POPE [49], he has been unfairly judged by the generations that followed as an embodiment of all that needed to be changed. "To care for his poetry is to be old-fashioned," A. C. Bradley observed in 1914, "and to belittle him is to be in the movement." Samuel Butler provides a typical rejection of the past centered on Tennyson: "Talking it over, we agreed that Blake was no good because he learnt Italian at sixty in order to study Dante, and we knew Dante was no good because he was fond of Virgil, and Virgil was no good because Tennyson ran him, and as for Tennyson—well, Tennyson goes without saying." In 1922, THOMAS HARDY [43] felt the need to qualify a quotation from Tennyson with the aside, "if one may quote Tennyson in this century," and summarized the decay of Tennyson as a literary icon in the following verse:

> The bower we shrined in Tennyson, Gentlemen,
> Is roof-wrecked; damps there drip upon
> Sagged seats, the creeper-nails are rust;
> The spider is sole denizen.

Although there is much in Tennyson that deserves to be criticized, there is much also that commands our attention and respect. If the modern age cannot rise to Tennyson's affirmations, the quality of his doubt and the sheer power of his imagination to grapple with some of the most profound aspects of human experience show that he is still able to communicate with an audience. Tennyson is one of the figures linking the romantics with the moderns, serving both as an influential author against whom to react and one with whom to reckon, both as a target and an abiding poetic presence.

Tennyson was a poet first and nothing else. He looked the part. "Six feet high, broad-chested, strong-limbed," a friend described him in college, "his face Shakespearean, with deep eyelids, his forehead ample, crowned with dark wavy hair, his head finely poised, his hand the admiration of sculptors, long fingers with square tips, soft as a child's but of great size and strength. What struck one most about him was the union of strength and refinement." He was the third of 11 children who grew up in a vicarage in Lincolnshire. His father, given to fits of drunken rage, was a disappointed clergyman and scholar, and Tennyson's childhood alternated between the joys of country idylls and family fellowship and an almost suicidal depression caused by his unpredictable father. A precocious literary talent, Tennyson wrote poetry from the age of five. In 1828, he joined a circle of talented young men at Cambridge who formed a discussion group called the Apostles, through which he became the intimate friend of Arthur Henry Hallam, the central figure in his life, whose sudden death in 1833 became the occasion for Tennyson's greatest poem, *In Memoriam*. His first important volume of poetry, *Poems, Chiefly Lyrical* (1830), marked his arrival as an important new literary voice. Within two years of his departure from the university, the Cambridge Union debated the question "Tennyson or Milton, which the greater poet?"

In 1832, Tennyson followed up his initial success with a collection of poems, but some stinging criticism caused a 10-year silence before he published again. From the misleading modern perspective that sees Tennyson as a spokesman for Victorian sentiment and orthodoxy, it is surprising to note how much his contemporaries actually rejected his poetry as irregular and daringly experimental. He challenged conventional standards of meter with an organic sense of form fitted to the demands of voice and situation; experimented with the dramatic monologue that ROBERT BROWNING [58] would perfect; and explored themes, such as the effects of industrialism and biological evolution, that would transform Victorian life and shake its faith. In the best of his poetry—"The Lotus-Eaters," "Ulysses," and "The Two Voices"—Tennyson juxtaposes the contrary positions of the intoxication of art versus action, self and duty, life and death in an imaginatively expressive dialectic. In such poems as "Mariana" and "The Lady of Shalott," sound, idea, and image are fused in a complexity that recalls the great works of KEATS [25] and anticipates the modern imagists such as Ezra Pound and T. S. ELIOT [19]. Although Tennyson would be publicly admired for his faith and affirmation, it is the quality of his doubt and his ability to realize the forces in opposition to belief that give his poems their tension, energy, and edge.

Perhaps the best example of this is his masterpiece *In Memoriam* (1850), written over a 17-year period as Tennyson attempted to cope with the death of his friend Arthur Hallam. His elegy is a sequence of 131 separate lyrics on the sudden and lamentable passing of a young man bound for greatness. Tennyson's doubts battle with faith in an impressive blending of personal and larger public themes. The work contains the Virgilian melancholy for which Tennyson was famous, but it also modulates a variety of emotions derived from the depth of his loss and his meditation on the world. The conflict between hoped-for consolation and forces in opposition are displayed in the following famous lines:

> Man, her last work, who seem'd so fair,
>   Such splendid purpose in his eyes,
>   Who roll'd the psalm to wintry skies,
> Who built him fanes of fruitless prayer,
> Who trusted God was love indeed
>   And love Creation's final law—
>   Tho' Nature, red in tooth and claw
> With rapine, shriek'd against his creed—

The eventual faith that the poem affirms mirrored the events in Tennyson's life as he emerged from a long, dark period of soul-searching. *In Memoriam* solidified Tennyson's status as the age's greatest poetic voice. His success allowed him to marry Emily Sellwood in 1850 after a 17-year courtship, and earned him the post of poet laureate and his eventual elevation to lord in 1883. The second half of Tennyson's long life was tranquil and domestic, and he embarked on writing the monumental *Idylls of the King* over three decades, beginning in 1859. His epic intentions, derived from his version of the Arthurian legend, were to detail the rise and fall of a civilization, expressed in the tension between ideals of duty and self-interest, which leads to social collapse, fragmentation, and disintegration. *Idylls of the King* was hugely admired by the Victorians, but its achievement is mixed. Overbalanced by the weight of Tennyson's monumental intention, the work is filled with impressive passages but also marred by slack, overly pretty language.

In all of Tennyson's poetry there is a great deal to admire as well as censure—though perhaps not enough to justify such dismissals as W. H. AUDEN's [103] statement that "he had the finest ear, perhaps of any English poet; he was also undoubtedly the stupidest; there was little about melancholia that he didn't know; there was little else that he did," or SHAW's [44] comment that "Brahms is just like Tennyson, an extraordinary musician, with the brains of a third-rate village policeman."

Tennyson himself acknowledged the cycle of literary reputation. "Modern fame is nothing," he observed. "I'd rather have an acre of land. I shall go down, down! I'm up now. Action and reaction." The reaction against the Victorians in general and Tennyson in particular has shifted once again to a more balanced appreciation of both. Tennyson remains an important poetic force whose establishment as a classic is secure, despite overpraise and undervaluation.

82

CATULLUS

c. 84–c. 54 B.C.

It was Catullus who taught Europe and America how to sing tender songs of love, to phrase bitter words of hate; who "pointed the way to a more exact prosody and a richer versification"; who showed us how to flash on the mental retina whole pictures in a single word; who left an imperishable imprint of a throbbing heart which will always appeal to every other soul of man.

—Karl P. Harrington, *Catullus and His Influence*

Catullus, one of the greatest lyric poets in literature, revolutionized Roman and Western poetry, replacing the heroic and epic style and subject with a subjective, emotional personal voice. His direct, conversational tone and inward reflection provide a link backward to the lyrical mastery of SAPPHO [88], and forward to the poetic revolution of the English romantic poets in the 19th century.

Gaius Valerius Catullus was born in Verona in the province of Cisalpine Gaul during the last violent century of the Roman Republic. His family was wealthy and prominent enough to host Julius Caesar. Except for a visit to Asia Minor as a member of the entourage of the governor of Bithynia, where he visited the grave of his brother, Catullus divided his time between his home province and Rome. It is likely that in 62 B.C. the 22-year-old Catullus met Clodia, the wife of Metellus Celer, governor of Cisalpine Gaul and the sister of the political adventurer Publius Clodius. Their affair, a heartbreaking one for Catullus, is dissected in the series of poems that represent his most enduring work. Clodia was beautiful and unscrupulous, and gossip suggests that she was both the lover of her brother and the poisoner of her husband. Our sense of Clodia, however, is largely provided by Cicero, who attacked her in his defense of one of her lovers on a charge of attempted poisoning. Whatever Clodia's true nature, it is clear that their tempestuous relationship provided Catullus with material for a full and complex poetic analysis of love and its consequences.

Catullus was a member of a group of so-called New Poets (whose works, except for Catullus's, have not survived). The New Poets consciously broke from the main tradition of Roman poetry, derived from heroic Greek poetry. In place of the high seriousness of the epic and tragedy and their public themes, best represented by the works of VIRGIL [9], Catullus and the New Poets restored the lyric tradition inherited from Sappho and the Alexandrian Greek poets of the fourth and third centuries B.C. Highly personal and subjective, Catullus's intimate and elegant verse is crafted with a direct and conversational voice, charting the range of the poet's emotions.

That any of Catullus's verse survived at all depended upon the chance discovery around 1300 of a manuscript containing 116 poems. The manuscript, now lost but fortunately copied, provides us with an astonishing demonstration of his range and poetic achievement. The poems comprise Catullus's imitations of the Greek poets, including a translation of one of Sappho's lyrics, a marriage hymn, poems on Greek mythological themes, personal attacks on contemporary politicians, and lighthearted verses to amuse his friends. The 25 poems describing his love affair with Clodia, however, whom he names Lesbia, best represent his genius and poetic power. One of the earliest lyrical poetic sequences, the poems reveal the stages of the affair from idealism to cynical scorn and illustrate Catullus's ability to capture complex and contrary emotions in diverse and expressive lyrical forms.

Catullus's chronicle of his feelings begins with the ennobling and transforming power of love:

> He seems to me to equal to a god, he, if it may be,
> Seems to surpass the very gods, who sitting opposite you
> Again and again gazes at you and hears you sweetly laughing.
>
> Such a thing takes away all my senses, alas!
> For whenever I see you, Lesbia,
> At once no sound of voice remains within my mouth,
> But my tongue falters . . .

(LI)

The joy of possession is undercut by growing feelings of doubt that the couple's love can survive:

> You promise to me, my life, that this love of ours
> Shall be happy and last for ever between us.
> Oh great gods, grant that she may be able to keep
> This promise truly, and that she may say it sincerely,
> So that it may be our lot to extend through all our life,
> This eternal compact of hallowed friendship.
>
> (CIX)

Lesbia's inconstancy provokes the poet's jealousy and self-recriminations that his love has been misspent on an unworthy partner, prompting a cry of pain and self-pity:

> Poor Catullus, 'tis time you should cease your folly,
> And account as lost what you see is lost.
> Once the days shone bright on you, when you used to go
> So often where my mistress led, she who was loved by me
> As none will ever be loved.
>   . . .
> Now she desires no more—pursue not her who flies,
> Nor live in misery, but with resolved mind endure, be firm.
> Farewell, my mistress; now Catullus is firm;
> He will not seek you nor ask you against your will.
> But you will be sorry, when your nightly favors are no more desired.
> Ah, poor wretch! What life is left for you?
>
> (VIII)

Catullus battles his conflicting feelings to a conclusion in which he offers Lesbia a contemptuous and heartbreaking farewell:

> Bid her live and be happy with her lovers,
> Three hundred of whom she holds at once in her embrance,
> Not loving one of them really, but again and again
> Draining the strength of all.
> And let her not look to find my love, as before;
> My love, which by her fault has dropped,
> Like a flower on the meadow's edge,
> When it has been touched by the plough passing by.
>
> (XI)

Few poets have exposed themselves as fully as Catullus and have recorded the dramatic arc of a love affair so directly and brilliantly. His influence is evident in the works of such different Roman poets as HORACE [80] and Virgil, and in the confessional revelations of the romantic poets and their modern descendants. Literature can credit Catullus for reviving the lyric as a means for probing the depths of human passion and temperament.

GEORGE GORDON BYRON, LORD BYRON

83

1788–1824

If they had said the sun or the moon had gone out of the heavens, it could not have struck me with the idea of a more awful and dreary blank in the creation than the words: Byron is dead.

—Jane Welsh Carlyle, in a letter to Thomas Carlyle

Jane Carlyle's shock at the early death of Byron, one of many such testimonies in the memoirs of his contemporaries, reveals Byron's powerful influence. He is not so much a great literary genius as a literary phenomenon, whose life and legend are inextricably linked to his work as English literature's first great celebrity superstar. "I awoke one morning and found myself famous," Byron stated, describing the impact when the first cantos of *Childe Harold* were published. Later, with characteristic dismissal, he measured his global impact:

> Even I,—albeit I'm sure I did not know it,
> Nor sought of foolscap subjects to be king,—
> Was reckon'd, a considerable time,
> The grand Napoleon of the realms of rhyme.

> (*Don Juan*, Canto XI)

No other figure in the early 19th century came as close to dominating the spirit and the imagination of his age as Byron. The "Byronic hero," with his outlaw stance and emotional excesses, attained mythical stature throughout the world. Byron's influence is found in references from such diverse writers as JANE AUSTEN [20] and MARK TWAIN [45]. The greatness of PUSHKIN [18] has its source in Byron, and Byron's influence is evident in such characters as Heathcliff in *Wuthering Heights* (EMILY BRONTË [61]), Mr. Rochester in *Jane Eyre* (CHARLOTTE BRONTË [60]), and Ahab in *Moby-Dick* (HERMAN MELVILLE [24].) Byron, for good or ill, defined the role and appeal of the romantic artist, as well as a distinctive attitude toward life marked by total engagement. As the writer and critic Paul West has observed:

> If he is great, he is so for reasons not primarily poetic. But we do not always want to be reading "great" poets: and our main pleasure in reading Byron is the contact with a singular personality. It is not a silly pleasure either: it reminds us that all poems, sooner or later, return us to persons and, in Byron's case, return us to ourselves with illumination and no little shock after we have seen our own weaknesses, poses, aspirations, and manias writ large in his essentially human yet effectually exaggerative temperament.

Byron's singular personality and history are inseparable from his poetry. He was, in effect, his own greatest creation. His verse was an accompaniment to his operatic private and public life in which, as Matthew Arnold observed, "thousands counted every groan,/And Europe made his woe her own." His father, the aristocratic "Mad Jack" Byron, married Byron's mother, a descendant of an old Scottish family, for her money, and she left him when he squandered it. Byron was born lame with a club foot, and his early years were spent in poverty in Aberdeen, Scotland. When his father and grandfather died, Byron inherited their title and embarked on a colorful youth of profligacy and sensual pleasures. Educated at Harrow and Trinity College, Cambridge, Byron was the model of misspent youth with the means to develop and indulge a host of vices, including an affair with his half-sister. He wrote continually, usually in the early morning after an evening's debauch. His first published volume, *Hours of Idleness* (1807), suggests his attitude toward writing as that of an aristocratic dabbler, and also shows his preference for the satirical and neoclassical verse forms of ALEXANDER POPE [49], which put him at odds with other romantic poets of the period.

At the age of 21, Byron embarked on a two-year grand tour, customary for young gentlemen, which took him to Portugal, Spain, Albania, Greece, and Constantinople. His exposure to exotic scenery and cultures formed the basis for the travelogue-cum-confession *Childe Harold*, the first two cantos of which appeared in 1812 to thunderous acclaim. The poem's appeal stemmed from its colorful, foreign settings united to the remarkably fresh, unusual perspective of the passionate, melancholy Harold. Forever fused in the public's mind as a reflection of Byron himself, Harold is the first embodiment of the temperament and attitude of the alienated Byronic hero that would be featured in a string of verse narratives, including *The Giaour* (1813), *The Bride of Abydos* (1813), and *The Corsair* (1814), which were phenomenal best-sellers throughout Europe and America and made Byron the most famous literary celebrity in Europe. In many ways Byron's hero, and by inference Byron himself, was an embodiment of GOETHE's [10] Werther, excessively sensitive and full of angst, combined with the characteristics of the swashbuckling adventures of a romance novel, setting a type that has persisted in fiction and film.

From 1812 to 1816, Byron indulged in a series of notorious love affairs, including one with Lady Caroline Lamb, the beautiful, impulsive, and indiscreet wife of British statesman William Lamb, Viscount Melbourne, as well as a marriage of sorts with Annabella Milbanke, who left him after a year. The scandal over their relationship caused Byron to leave England permanently, and his later work would satirize English hypocrisy as well as the dullness and unctuous sanctity of the literary establishment that attacked him. In Italy and Switzerland, Byron continued to generate notoriety and scandal. In 1817 Byron spent the summer on Lake Geneva in the company of PERCY BYSSHE SHELLEY [77] and Mary Wollstonecraft Shelley, when Byron's initiating a ghost story competition resulted in her conception of *Frankenstein*. Byron continued to expand *Childe Harold* and write other important works, such as *Manfred* (1817) and *The Vision of Judgment* (1822), his satirical demolition of the English poet Robert Southey, who became the principal target in Byron's attack on the English literary and political establishment. During his years in exile, Byron perfected his characteristic ottava-rima stanza, which he used with distinction in *Beppo* (1818), a satire on Venetian manners, and his most important poem, the monumental *Don Juan*, which he began in 1818 and continued to expand until his death. The poem describes the adventures of the Spaniard Juan, who travels across Europe to Greece, Constantinople, the court of Catherine the Great (where he is the empress's lover), and to England. The narrative offered Byron a flexible vehicle to express every element of his complex personality as well as to satirize contemporary subjects from social conditions in England, and conventional attitudes toward love, marriage, religion, and politics. Toward the end of Canto VIII, the poet announces the intention of his comic epic:

> Reader! I have kept my word,—at least so far
>   As the first Canto promised. You have now
> Had sketches of love, tempests, travel, war—
>   All very accurate, you must allow,
> And *epic*, if plain truth should prove no bar;

> For I have drawn much less with a long bow
> Than my forerunners. Carelessly I sing,
>   But Phoebus lends me now and then a string.

If his poem rarely reaches the profundity of other great poems, *Don Juan* possesses all the energy and vitality of Byron himself. The Byron legend of the oversized adventure culminated in his death, when Byron succumbed to fever before he was able to join the fight on behalf of Greek independence from the Turks. If Byron finally failed to achieve the heroism in action that he desired, his art established the measure of the man: complex, contradictory, and self-aggrandizing, yet daring and provoking as few other writers have ever attempted in life or art. In Canto XV of *Don Juan*, Byron modestly presents his own testimony:

> I perched upon a humbler promontory,
>   Amidst life's infinite variety:
> With no great care for what is nickname'd glory,
>   But speculating as I cast mine eye
> On what may suit or may not suit my story,
>   And never straining hard to versify,
> I rattle on exactly as I'd talk
> With anybody in a ride or walk.

That Byron revealed so much of himself and his world to an audience entranced with his version of both, asserts his stature as one of literature's most fascinating presences.

F. SCOTT FITZGERALD

84

1896–1940

His talent was as natural as the pattern that was made by the dust on a butterfly's wings. At one time he understood it not more than the butterfly did and he did not know when it was brushed or marred. Later he became conscious of his damaged wings and of their construction and he learned to think and could not fly any more because the love of flight was gone and he could only remember it when it had been effortless.
—Ernest Hemingway, *A Moveable Feast*

Along with Hemingway [63] and Faulkner [15], F. Scott Fitzgerald defined American literature in the important period between the two world wars of the 20th century. Like Hemingway as well, Fitzgerald's legend—the close relationship between his life and his art—continues to adhere to and at times to obscure his achievement, which includes *The Great Gatsby*, arguably America's greatest novel. As Lionel Trilling remarked, "Fitzgerald was perhaps the last notable writer to affirm the Romantic fantasy, descended from the Renaissance, of personal ambition and heroism, of life committed to, or thrown away for, some ideal of self."

Fitzgerald's romantic search for affirmation and transcendence is the quintessential drive in American literature that establishes him as a central literary figure. Perhaps no other literary career is as sad or as tortured as Fitzgerald's. Although he has been attacked by Glenway Wescott as the representative of a "group or cult of juvenile crying-drunks," there is still a poignancy about Fitzgerald's failures that forms the tragic core of his novels and stories. If, as Fitzgerald asserted, "the test of a first-rate intelligence is the ability to hold two opposed ideas in the mind, at the same time, and still retain the ability to function," he faced throughout his life and career the conflict between a transcendent dream and the awareness of its destruction and impossibility. Few other writers have captured their times with the same degree of satiric as well as mythic power of universal relevance. Unlike Fitzgerald's fictional hero, Jay Gatsby, who dutifully and systematically invented himself, Fitzgerald took a more casual, less deliberate approach to his own development, though both seem equally lit by the same overriding dreams.

Francis Scott Key Fitzgerald was born in St. Paul, Minnesota, a descendant of two colonial American families, the Scotts and the Keys. He was named for his most famous ancestor, the author of "The Star-Spangled Banner." His father, an unsuccessful businessman, had come to Minnesota from his native Maryland after the Civil War. Fitzgerald's mother was the oldest daughter of an Irish immigrant who amassed a fortune as a wholesale grocer. The Fitzgeralds largely lived on the financial sufferance of her family, establishing in young Fitzgerald an awareness at a young age of the possibilities of wealth and its denial.

Fitzgerald was indulged by his mother and encouraged to believe that his desires were paramount. In 1911, he was sent to a Roman Catholic academy in New Jersey, and in 1913 he proceeded to Princeton, largely, as he recalled, to participate in the Triangle Club, a dramatic group for which he wrote the lyrics for their yearly musical-comedy productions. His enjoyment of Princeton's extracurricular pursuits imperiled his academic progress, putting him in danger of flunking out. He left the school due to illness halfway through his junior year. Having secured a commission as a second lieutenant in the army, to counter the tedium of camp life Fitzgerald began the novel that would become *This Side of Paradise*. In 1918, while he was stationed in Alabama, he met the coquettish Zelda Sayre, with whom he fell in love. Marriage, however, would be possible only if Fitzgerald could find the financial means that Zelda required, so after his discharge in 1919 he began to work in New York City for an advertising agency while submitting stories to magazines. Scribner's, which had first rejected his novel, finally accepted the rewritten manuscript. Its publication, along with the sale of a story to the *Saturday Evening Post*, allowed Fitzgerald to marry Zelda in 1920.

Few writers had such sudden and spectacular success as the young Fitzgerald. His first two novels, *This Side of Paradise* (1920) and *The Beautiful and Damned* (1922) were sensational best-sellers. He added to his reputation with two collections of stories, *Flappers and Philosophers* (1920) and *Tales of the Jazz Age* (1922), which gave the name to the period and its social liberation that Fitzgerald captured in his novels and stories. Success made possible an extravagant lifestyle, but also heightened expectations for sustained commercial success, and Fitzgerald squandered his talent on magazine stories certain to sell, while other more thoughtful and serious work was ignored or fared badly. His masterpiece, *The Great Gatsby* (1925), never achieved the popularity of his breakthrough first novels. This period, which Scott and Zelda spent at home and abroad, has become legend, with the battling Fitzgeralds notorious for their sybaritic lifestyle. Fitzgerald managed only one additional completed novel, *Tender Is the Night* (1934). He sustained his professional career partially by writing movie scripts in Hollywood, while his personal life collapsed from alcoholism and his wife's mental deterioration. (Zelda Fitzgerald was later diagnosed with schizophrenia and institutionalized.)

Fitzgerald's despair during this period is brilliantly captured in the posthumously published collection of essays, letters, and fragments, *The Crack-Up* (1945). In 1940, Fitzgerald died of a heart attack in Hollywood, leaving a final novel, *The Last Tycoon* (1941), unfinished. Zelda Fitzgerald died in a fire in 1948 that destroyed the mental institution where she had long been a patient. At the end of his life Fitzgerald was convinced of his failure both personally and professionally. It was only after his death that a gradual reassessment of his writing secured his place as a classic American writer and the distinctive chronicler of his time.

Fitzgerald's reputation today rests largely on the achievement of a handful of his best stories, *The Great Gatsby*, *Tender Is the Night*, and the promising hints of *The Last Tycoon*. His first two novels and many of the stories are interesting primarily for their sociological evidence, capturing as few other books have the feeling and the attitudes of the age. The exuberance of youth and its impossible, fleeting glamor attracted Fitzgerald and formed the core of his tragic sense of dreams deferred and betrayed. This is what makes *The Great Gatsby* a masterpiece. Jay Gatsby, an emblem of the American success story, sets out to recapture the past and the paradise he has associated with his first love, Daisy Buchanan. He is cheated by a dream that is shown to be unworthy of him, and Fitzgerald raises Gatsby's fall to the level of a central American myth. The novel ends with one of the most suggestive, lyrical passages in literature:

> Gatsby believed in the green light, the orgiastic future that year by year recedes before us. It eludes us then, but that's no matter—tomorrow we will run faster, stretch out our arms farther. . . . And one fine morning—
>
> So we beat on, boats against the current, borne back ceaselessly into the past.

In *The Great Gatsby*, Fitzgerald achieved what would elude him for the rest of his career: a comedy and satire of contemporary manners that possesses the most profound personal and social truths. As war is Hemingway's continual subject, Fitzgerald's is the American dream and its betrayal, a subject that unites his personal life, his career, and his books into a thematic whole. Fitzgerald remains the principal chronicler of the seductive power of wealth and fame. No other American writer has put himself so centrally in the heart of the American psyche.

85

DANIEL DEFOE

1660?–1731

He belongs, indeed, to the school of the great plain writers, whose work is founded upon a knowledge of what is most persistent, though not most seductive, in human nature. . . . He is of the school of Crabbe and Gissing and not merely of a fellow-pupil in the same stern place of learning, but its founder and master.

—Virginia Woolf, *The Common Reader*

Although Daniel Defoe lacks the artistic excellence of most of the writers in this ranking, he claims a place as the originator of the novel in English. His *Robinson Crusoe* is the first true English novel, and its manner and style are every bit as revolutionary as the rediscovery of perspective in Renaissance painting. The quintessential representative man of the 18th century, Defoe, out of the experience of his middle-class background, helped shape a startling new art form that located interest in the ordinary details of life and characters who reflected his readers. Instead of the earlier prose romances involving idealized characters, fantastical adventures, and exotic locations, Defoe offered the pleasurable recognition of the familiar and set the novel on the realistic course that has sustained it ever since. When JAMES JOYCE [7] was asked to deliver a lecture on English literature, he chose for his subjects Daniel Defoe and WILLIAM BLAKE [29]. In Joyce's mind, the two authors, Defoe the realist and Blake the symbolist visionary, represented the opposite boundaries of literature that he combined in his own work. Defoe established the claim of reality as one of fiction's essential resources, and for this discovery alone he is entitled to inclusion here as one of the greatest literary figures.

Defoe came to fiction writing late in a varied career; he first worked as a businessman and then as a journalist. His father was a London tallow chandler and a religious dissenter named Foe (Defoe added the aristocratic prefix in middle age) who expected his son to become a minister. Barred by his non-conformist religion from a university education, Defoe studied at a dissenters' academy on the outskirts of London. In 1684, he married the daughter of a prosperous cooper and became a trader in a variety of commodities, including hosiery, wine, and tobacco. Commerce would continue to fascinate him throughout his life and provide him with a broad view of English life and customs. His interests, however, were too varied to be restricted to business alone. In 1685, he took part in Monmouth's rebellion against James II, but through a pardon, probably the result of a large cash payment, avoided transportation or execution when captured. In 1692, war with the French resulted in financial losses when ships in which he had an interest were captured, and Defoe was bankrupt. In a scheme to pay off his creditors, he started a successful brick and tile factory.

During the 1690s, Defoe began his long and prolific career as a writer, first as the author of a number of political pamphlets. The most famous, *The True-Born Englishman*, was a long poem that ridiculed anti-Dutch sentiment among the English and attracted the attention of the Whig leaders of King William's government. However, his pamphlet *The Shortest Way with the Dissenters* (1702), in defense of religious freedom, led to his imprisonment for seditious libel in Newgate Prison. His punishment included being forced to stand in the pillory on several occasions.

At age 43 Defoe found himself bankrupt a second time. He was eventually released through the intercession of Robert Harley, the speaker of the House of Commons and secretary of state and later prime minister, who employed Defoe as a political agent to gather intelligence throughout England and Scotland—a kind of domestic spy. In 1704, while undertaking his government work, Defoe edited and wrote for his most famous periodical, the *Review*, which he continued to publish until 1713. Defoe produced a continual stream of journalism, eventually becoming associated with 26 different periodicals, writing on current and foreign affairs, religious controversies, and the political conflict between the Tories and the Whigs.

In 1719, at age 59, while still busy with daily and weekly journalism as well as pamphlets on current affairs, Defoe launched a new career as a fiction writer. Beginning with *Robinson Crusoe*, Defoe wrote a succession of novels taking the forms of fictional biographies, memoirs, and autobiographies, including two Crusoe sequels, *Captain Singleton* (1720), *Moll Flanders* (1722), *A Journal of the Plague Year* (1722), *Colonel Jack* (1722), and *Roxana* (1724). He concluded his remarkably productive writing life with two guidebooks, *A Tour Thro' the Whole Island of Great Britain* (1726) and *The Complete English Tradesman* (1727), a manual for young merchants and shopkeepers on how to succeed in business.

Defoe's literary reputation rests primarily on *Robinson Crusoe* and *Moll Flanders*. In both Defoe shows his genius as a storyteller, not in his ability to create a complex plot, but in his skill in fascinating his reader with the ordinary details of life. In his fiction Defoe exploited his talents as a journalist to involve his reader in the factual appeal of a fascinating story. *Robinson Crusoe* is based on the real-life experiences of seaman Alexander Selkirk, whose four years on a deserted island Defoe reworked into his fictional account. Here is the perfect material for an expected romantic treatment: the possibility for fantastic adventures in a remote and exotic faraway place. Instead of romance, however, Defoe offers the attraction of ordinary life as the practical Crusoe sets about domesticating the wilds. Until Friday arrives on the scene in the last quarter of the novel, very little happens in *Robinson Crusoe*. There are no monsters and very few cannibals, but much discussion about how Crusoe can make a proper tea set and with industry and ingenuity raise his standard of living. Crusoe is not a warrior knight of the prose romance but an earnest, industrious, conventional fellow, and one of the continuing delights of the novel is the readers' ability to see themselves reflected in Crusoe's domestic challenges.

The same attraction of real life is present in Defoe's account of the life and times of Moll Flanders. Far from a romance novel's idealized heroine, Moll is no Guinevere but closer to Chaucer's Wife of Bath. For Moll, a prostitute, love is a business transaction, and her adventures resemble those of the middle class in its struggle for survival and respectability, but which are understood not in terms of ideals and morals but in pounds and pence. With the convincing texture of the customs of real life, Defoe shows Moll making her way by her wits and practical resilience, much like Crusoe. After each encounter in love and trade, she calculates her profits or losses and moves on to her next opportunity. Exciting things happen in the novel, such as Moll marrying her brother, but such exceptional situations prove the rule of the ordinary, which predominates.

Both novels indicate a fundamental shift in art to the radical notion that ordinary experience merited literary and artistic attention, and that the stories of ordinary characters—not kings, knights, or paragons—could entertain readers. Defoe, a member of the new middle class, had discovered a fictional formula to attract the attention of a growing class of readers who were interested in the appeal of the particular. They saw their own world reflected in a new art form that became the novel. Occasionally crude and makeshift, Defoe's novels rarely reach beyond the compelling episode to a dramatic plot and are frequently marred by inconsistency, suggesting that he was making it up as he went along, rather than outlining a plot beforehand. Still, Defoe, started the novel on its course to rival drama and poetry as a significant reflection of human experience.

ROBERT FROST

86

1874–1963

For Frost there must always be in poetry the reconciliation between the cadence, the rhythm, of the spoken sentence and the cadence, the rhythm, of the meter. Lacking this reconciliation of these two elements in sound, the intended poem, as such, has failed. Achieving it, the poem combines manner and matter with its own subtle music which is as natural as it is unmistakable.

— Lawrance Thompson, *Fire and Ice, The Art and Thought of Robert Frost*

SEAMUS HEANEY [117], in a thoughtful assessment of the achievement of Robert Frost, has written that among major poets in English in the 20th century, Frost "is the one who takes the most punishment." Arguably the most beloved and popular poet in his day, Frost has met critical resistance, some of the causes of which Heaney summarizes: "His immense popular acclaim during his own lifetime; his apotheosis into an idol mutually acceptable to his own and his country's self-esteem, and greatly inflationary of both; his constantly resourceful acclimatization of himself to this condition, as writer and performer—it all generated a critical resistance and fed a punitive strain which is never far to seek in literary circles anyhow." Many think they know Frost better than they do. Relegated to the role of the good gray poet of New England, a repository of Yankee common sense and natural scenes, Frost's image has been smoothed and sandblasted of its depths and edges. A refreshing reassessment was ventured by

322

the distinguished critic Lionel Trilling at a 1959 banquet on the occasion of the poet's 85th birthday, who startled his audience by insisting that he found Frost "a terrifying poet," not a poet of reassuring consolation but a visionary probing our darkest recesses, anxieties, and fears. Focusing on the dark aspects of his works, the shadows and complexities that intrude on his apparent straightforward scenes and regular verse forms, helps us to see Frost in full: as one of the greatest of American poets. Fellow poet and critic Randall Jarrell insisted that Frost must be included with the dominating American poets of the 20th century, with T. S. ELIOT [19] and WALLACE STEVENS [74], because, "No other [poet of his time] has written so well about the actions of ordinary men: his wonderful dramatic monologues or dramatic scenes come out of a knowledge of people that few poets have had, and they are written in verse that uses, sometimes with absolute mastery, the rhythms of actual speech."

The initial contradiction surrounding Robert Frost is that this quintessential New England poet was born in San Francisco, California. He was 11 years old when his father, a hard-drinking journalist and politician, died, and his family relocated to Lawrence, Massachusetts, where his paternal grandparents lived. His mother taught school, and Frost graduated from Lawrence High School in 1892, co-valedictorian with Elinor White, whom he would marry three years later. After graduation, Frost briefly attended Dartmouth College before working as a grammar school teacher, in a mill, and as a newspaper reporter. His first verses appeared in his high school newspaper, and, in 1894, his first poem, "My Butterfly: An Elegy," appeared in the New York magazine *The Independent.* Mainly rejections followed, and Frost, having married in 1895, studied at Harvard as a special student until 1899 when he purchased a poultry farm in Methuen, Massachusetts. In 1900, Frost and his family moved to his grandfather's farm in Derry, New Hampshire, which Frost inherited after his grandfather's death in 1901. Frustrated by a lack of success in interesting publishers in his poems, Frost sold the Derry farm and moved his family to England, where he could "write and be poor without further scandal in the family." Living on a farm in Buckinghamshire, he struggled to hone his distinct poetic voice. Writing home to a former classmate, John T. Bartlett, following the publication in England of his first major collection, *A Boy's Will* (1913), Frost confidently declared, "I am one of the few artists writing. I am one of the few who have a theory of their own upon which all their work down to the least accent is done. I expect to do something to the present state of literature in America." He delivered on his assertion with his second collection, *North of Boston* (1914), regarded by many as one of the milestone volumes in the history of English poetry. Some of Frost's most anthologized and popular poems are included. "Mending Wall" is a meditation on the conflict between individualism and community based on the annual spring ritual of repairing the stone walls that divide New England farms, which includes perhaps his most repeated line: "Good fences make good neighbors." "Death of a Hired Man" is a dramatic narrative in which a wife pleads the case of an old, unreliable laborer to her husband. "After Apple-Picking" celebrates the values of hard work and its tragic insufficiency, while "Home Burial," in which a couple tries to deal with the death of their child, reflects the death of Frost's first child in 1900. Anchored by the specificity of place and managing a distinctive musicality from colloquial directness, *North of Boston* marked the arrival of a distinctive and original poetic voice. As the impresario of the modernist revolution in verse, Ezra Pound, declared, Frost's poetry "has the tang of the New Hampshire woods, and it has just this utter sincerity. It is not post-Miltonic or post-Swinburnian or post-Kiplonian. This man has the good sense to speak naturally and to paint the thing, the thing as he sees it."

Returning to the United States in 1915, Frost and his family moved onto a farm in Franconia, New Hampshire, while his first two collections were published in America. Frost's third book, *Mountain Interval*, appeared in 1916, featuring some of his finest poems, including "Birches" and "The Road Not Taken." The Pulitzer Prize–winning *New Hampshire* followed in 1923, which includes "Fire and Ice" and what has been called his perfect lyric and the most explicated poem in all American literature, "Stopping by Woods on a Snowy Evening," in which the speaker is drawn to a wood filling up with snow on "the darkest evening of the year." The poem ends suggestively suspended between the magnetic attraction of the woods, "lovely, dark and deep," and his responsibility to others, and "miles to go before I sleep." Frost regarded this deceptively simple, endlessly suggestive poem as his "best bid for remembrance."

Frost continued from strength to strength in the volumes *West-Running Brook* (1928) and *A Further Range* (1936). In the first, Frost demonstrates his power in the short lyric in such poems as "Spring Pools," "On Going Unnoticed," "Bereft," "Tree at My Window," and "Acquainted with the Night," in which he manages to probe deeply psychologically and emotionally charged states of mind and feeling, anchored by the familiar and the ordinary. In *A Further Range*, Frost combines an increasing social conscience in responding to the events of the Great Depression ("A Lone Striker," "Build Soil," "To a Thinker," and "Two Tramps in Mud Time") with darkly lyrical meditations confronting what he called the background of "hugeness and confusion shading away . . . into black and utter chaos" ("Desert Places," "A Leaf-Treader," "Neither Out Far Nor in Deep," and "Design"). The last is one of Frost's most striking poems and one of the most unusual sonnets in the language in which the poet contemplates a moth in the grip of a white spider on a white flower and concludes with the questions:

> What had that flower to do with being white,
> The wayside blue and innocent heal-all?
> What brought the kindred spider to that height,
> Then steered the white moth thither in the night?

> What but design of darkness to appall?—
> If design govern in a thing so small.

Frost manages the most profound examination of free will, fate, order and randomness, violence and beauty, characteristically in focusing on "a thing so small." In the fatal meeting of spider and moth, Frost unlocks a double terror: either their encounter is accidental and no design governs existence or the principle of design is death dealing. Few poets have a comparable ability to anchor the most far-reaching abstractions in the tactile details of ordinary life.

There is a critical consensus that Frost's work during the 1940s and 1950s grew more abstract and more sententious. Other important poems would be written, including "The Silken Tent," and "Carpe Diem," but increasingly the later volumes—*A Witness Tree* (1942), *A Masque of Reason* (1945), *Steeple Bush* (1947), *How Not to Be King* (1951), and *In the Clearing* (1962)—disappoint compared to the earlier work. Ironically, as Frost's artistic powers diminished, the recognition for his achievement increased, culminating in his being selected by John F. Kennedy to read a poem at his inauguration. Frost recited "The Gift Outright," from *A Witness Tree* when his failing eyesight prevented him from reading the new poem he had composed for the occasion. Robert Frost died two years later, less than a month after being awarded the Bollingen Prize for poetry.

In every important way Frost had delivered on his declaration to contribute something unique to literature that he asserted his friend John Bartlett in 1913:

> To be perfectly frank with you I am one of the most notable craftsmen of
> my time . . . I am possibly the only person going who works on any but
> a worn out theory (principle I had better say) of versification. . . . I alone
> of English writers have consciously set myself to make music out of what
> I may call the sound of sense. Now it is possible to have sense without
> the sound of sense (as in much prose that is supposed to pass muster but
> makes very dull reading) and the sound of sense without sense (as in *Alice
> in Wonderland* which makes anything but dull reading). The best place to
> get the abstract sounds of sense is from voices behind a door that cuts off
> the words. . . . It is the abstract vitality of our speech. It is pure sound—
> pure form. One who concerns himself with it more than the subject is
> an artist. . . . But if one is to be a poet one must learn to get cadences by
> skillfully breaking the sounds of sense with all their irregularity of accent
> across the regular beats of the metre.

Frost revitalized poetics in the 20th century both by orchestrating the music of ordinary speech and exposing so authentically the ongoing drama of ordinary life.

87

WALTER SCOTT

1771–1832

His works (taken together) are almost like a new edition of human nature. This is indeed to be an author!

—William Hazlitt, *English Literature*

It is no doubt difficult, in the face of a steady decline of critical and reader interest in the works of Sir Walter Scott, to convince the modern reader of Scott's enormous influence in shaping not only English but world literature in the 19th century. He dominated the first half of the century like no other figure except BYRON [83], with an influence so great that MARK TWAIN [45] blamed him for the Civil War by teaching the South the code of chivalry, which resulted in a bloodbath. Having invented the historical novel and liberated the novel form to admit the past, regional characteristics, and diverse characters from different classes, Scott left his mark on writers as different as ALEXANDER PUSHKIN [18], STENDHAL [42], James Fenimore Cooper, LEO TOLSTOY [4], and CHARLES DICKENS [6]. In their appearance and cost alone, his novels set a standard that dictated the form and distribution of the genre for almost a century. It is not likely that Scott's power as a writer can still move a modern audience, as it did his contemporaries. If the novel has largely left Scott behind, with only occasional film or television versions of his stories to remind us of his work, his impact still claims attention as one of the pioneering forces of the novel and literary sensibility.

Any consideration of Scott must begin with his Scottish background, the source of his imaginative power and the origin of his characteristics as a man and a writer. Born in Edinburgh into a prosperous middle-class family, Scott could trace his heritage for many generations, back through the clan history of the Scottish Borderers. At the age of two an attack of infantile paralysis left him permanently lame, and he was sent to his grandfather's farm to restore his health. There, he was exposed to the Scottish past through ballads and stories that shaped his own storytelling ability and his antiquarian interests. Educated in Edinburgh, Scott was trained in the law at the University of Edinburgh and admitted to the bar in 1792. It was clear, however, that his main interest lay in literature, which he pursued with a gentleman's avocation, first as an editor and translator.

His first published works were translations of the German Sturm und Drang poet Gottfried Bürger, whose Gothic elements and ballad form would influence Scott's own poetry. His first major work was *The Minstrelsy of the Scottish Border* (1802), a collection of border ballads accompanied by lengthy annotation. The work pointed Scott to his main subject, Scottish history and tradition, which he exploited in *The Lay of the Last Minstrel* (1805), a narrative poem set in the Scottish border during the medieval era. The poem was a phenomenal best-seller and convinced Scott to become a professional writer. He followed up his success with the equally popular narrative poems *Marmion* (1808), which dealt with 16th-century Scottish history and the disastrous Battle of Flodden, and *The Lady of the Lake* (1810), which had a Highlands setting. The poems established Scott as the most famous and best-selling poet in Great Britain.

Today, Scott's poetry has little more than historical interest. As he did with all his writing, Scott approached his poetry as a craftsman with an eye on narrative interest rather than intensity and expressiveness, and a characteristic dismissal of any profundity or great polish. In his daughter's famous reply that she had not read *The Lady of the Lake*, she explained, "Papa says there's nothing so bad for young people as reading bad poetry." The poetry is more interesting today as a preliminary stage toward his novels, on which his literary reputation depends. After the comparative failure of the long, complex poem *Rokeby* (1813), Scott recognized that his novelty and inspiration were flagging, and he was not likely to be able to compete with the intensity and exotic appeal of Byron, so he turned to the novel, a far less respectable form at the time.

Scott took up a fragment of a novel he had written 10 years before that dealt with the Jacobite rebellion of 1745. This became *Waverley*, the first of about 30 novels that he wrote from 1814 to 1831, the year before his death, in a literary production that is almost unmatched. In *Waverley*, Scott's great innovation is contained in the novel's subtitle, "'Tis Sixty Years Since." By setting his novel in the recent past, bringing customs and historical events to life, Scott extended the range of the novel, capturing history with the same immediacy and detail that earlier novels had brought to contemporary, ordinary life and customs. Published anonymously to add interest, and no doubt to protect his reputation as a poet, Scott became the "Great Unknown" (though his identity as the author of the Waverley novels was common knowledge) and the "Wizard of the North," who legitimized the novel and extended its audience through the tremendous popularity of his books. Scott set the standard for the novel against which subsequent novelists in the 19th century would have to measure their own achievement. As JANE AUSTEN [20] wrote in a letter in 1814: "Walter Scott has no business to write novels, especially good ones— It is not fair. —He has Fame and Profit enough as a Poet, and should not be taking the bread out of other people's mouths.—I do not like him and do not mean to like *Waverley* if I can help it—but I fear I must."

What strikes a current reader of Scott's novels is his remarkable ability to bring Scottish customs and dialect to life. The important books in the Waverley series—*Waverley, Old Mortality, Rob Roy, The Heart of Midlothian,* and *Redgauntlet*—are all deserving of attention for the animated quality of their historical imagination that sets individuals in the larger context of the pressures and great events of the times. Too often, however, Scott's books are marred by hasty construction and his reluctance to plan or revise his work. "I never could lay down a plan—"Scott declared, "or, having laid it down, I never could adhere to it. . . . I only tried to make that which I was actually writing diverting and interesting, leaving the rest to fate." To maintain reader interest, Scott moved beyond his Scottish background to medieval Britain and France, and often depended more on formula than inspiration for dramatic effects. His driving need to create a great ancestral home at Abbotsford forced him to produce continuously to fund his venture. The financial collapse of his publisher also pressured him to pay off creditors, to whom he felt he had a moral, if not legal, obligation. As a novelist who literally wrote himself to death, his decline through overwork became a powerful admonitory emblem for Dickens and other subsequent writers.

Any final valuation of Scott's literary achievement, beyond the still viable appeal of his best books, must reside primarily in his groundbreaking innovation and influence on other novelists. After Scott, the novel became a much wider instrument of truth. If he lacks the technical perfection and subtlety of other great masters, he locates in the past and the power of regional characteristics some of the central recourses of the novelist's art. The Wessex of THOMAS HARDY [43], Yoknapatawpha County of FAULKNER [15], and the creative power of a particular place and time can all be traced to Scott's example, as can the creation of the novel as the preeminent modern literary medium.

SAPPHO

c. 620 B.C.–550 B.C.

...ure poetess with marvellous ...ot only haunts the dawn ...t glint from vases and ... . I for one have ...d all question and ...t poet who ever ...o a poet, but ...t who ever ...art and

influence

Although only ... from these samples that Sappho, who ... deserves her place in literature as one of lyr... ...gures. Sappho's creative brilliance and the unmiti... ...onal intensity of her lyrics have inspired ancient and m... ...ke to use such adjectives as "incandescent" when describing ... ...try, and she is rightly considered the most famous, as well as the most in...resting, figure in the canon of the nine Grecian lyric poets. Adding to her significance is the fact that she was a woman author, an incredible rarity in the ancient world. Thus, she can be regarded as the first woman author and the founder of women's literature.

Facts are scanty and uncertain concerning Sappho's life. *Psappha*, as she would have been called in Aeolic, her native dialect, was born to an aristocratic family on the Greek island of Lesbos in either Eressos or Mytilene, the island's main city and the one most closely associated with her. Lesbos, a brilliant cultural center in Sappho's day, was less misogynous than many Greek city-states; Lesbian women mixed freely with men, were highly educated, and formed clubs for the cultivation of poetry and music. Sappho's father, whose name is sometimes given as Skamandronymous, is believed to have been a wine merchant, as was her eldest brother. Another brother is said to have held the prestigious position of wine pourer for the Mytileneans at the city's town hall. Sappho had a daughter, Cleïs, named after her mother, according to ancient Greek tradition; some sources record the child's father as Cercylas, a wealthy merchant to whom Sappho was probably married and who died when she was about 35. Sappho lived mainly in Mytilene, but it is recorded that she was briefly exiled to Sicily, probably because of her family's political activities. She is reputed to have been dark-haired and small in an era when the feminine ideal was tall and fair-haired. Sappho's lovers may have included the poet Alcaeus, and, according to some traditions, she threw herself off a cliff because of her unrequited love for a man named Phaon. The story of Sappho and Phaon was related by OVID [26] and is generally considered among scholars to be apocryphal. Although Sappho was satirized in Greek comedies as having a voracious appetite for men, the traditional view is that her sexual preference was for women, and she has achieved immortal status as the patron and muse of lesbian lovers. Sappho may well have had female lovers, and her poetry is regarded as homoerotic. However, it was a convention of the time for women to praise the beauty of other women in romantic fashion, and translations of Sappho's poetry from ancient Greek, while suggestive, are often indefinite concerning the sex of the love object.

Lyric poetry, which evolved to describe any short poem expressing a subjective experience regardless of meter or rhyme scheme, experienced its initial flowering between 700 and 500 B.C. and reflected a reworking of traditional values, such as the oral tradition, between 700 and 600 B.C. The first known Greek lyric poet was Archilochus (c. 680–c. 645 B.C.), who wrote in the Ionic dialect and has been credited as the creator of lyric verses called epodes and the rhythmic trochaic meter, both influential in the development of lyric poetry. Unlike the Greek epic—long, narrative poems about heroes and important events of an often-romanticized past—and choral poetry, written for many voices and sung on public occasions such as weddings, lyric poetry is an example of monody—poetry written for a single voice and performed to the accompaniment of a lyre. It is characterized by its short length, variety of meter, and personal emotions and perceptions about such subjects as love, friends, and enemies, as well as individual experiences of war. These would be performed for small, private audiences at dinners and other intimate get-togethers.

Like the work of Archilochus, Sappho's poetry had a subversive element, in that it challenges the heroic and patriotic ethos of the epic and insists on the validity and relevance of individual consciousness and experience. She composed her poetry for her daughter and her circle of friends and disciples, mostly, but not exclusively, young women. Sappho wrote in the Aeolic dialect in many meters, one of which has been called, after her, the Sapphic stanza. While some of Sappho's works are ritualistic and religious poems, the principal subject of her poetry is love, with all its physical and romantic passion, joy, sorrow, jealousy, frustration, and longing. Her verse is a classic example of the candidly personal love lyric and is written with a direct simplicity, a perfect control of meter, and the use of powerful and memorable imagery. Sappho may have also composed and performed choral poetry, such as epithalamiums, songs or poems celebrating marriages that usually tell of the happenings of the wedding day. Her most complete poem in the surviving fragments of her work is "Hymn to Aphrodite," which consists of seven stanzas. Praised by Dionysius of Halicarnassus, a Greek historian of the Roman period, for its "elegance and smoothness of construction," it is an invocation to the goddess to intercede on behalf of the poet in her relationship, as the translation indicates, with a woman:

> Thorned in splendor; beauteous child of mighty
> Zeus, wile-weaving, immortal Aphrodite,
> smile again; your frowning so affrays me
>   woe overweighs me.

> Come to me now, if ever in the olden days
> you did hear me from afar, and from the
> golden halls of your father fly with all speeding
>   unto my pleading.

> Down through mid-ether from Love's highest regions
> swan-drawn in car convoyed by lovely legions
> of bright-hued doves beclouding with their pinions
>   Earth's broad dominions.

> Quickly you came; and, Blessed One, with
> smiling countenance immortal, my heavy heart
> beguiling, asked the cause of my pitiful condition—
>   why my petition:

What most I craved in brain-bewildering yearning;
whom would I win, so winsome in her spurning;
"Who is she, Sappho, so evilly requiting?
    fond love with slighting?

"She who flees you soon shall turn pursuing,
cold to your love now, weary with wooing,
gifts once scorned with greater gifts reclaiming
    unto her shaming."

Come thus again; from cruel cares deliver;
of all that my heart will graciously be giver—
greatest of gifts, your loving self and tender
    to be my defender.

In the third and second centuries B.C., Aristophanes of Byzantium and Aristarchus of Samothrace collected and edited Sappho's poetry in nine books, according to meter. By the fifth century A.D., when scholars began to transcribe works from papyrus scrolls to books, Sappho's poetry was omitted and largely forgotten. Her works were not collected and arranged until the 1890s; the first modern anthology of her poetry was published by the Oxford University Press in 1925. Recognition of Sappho and her work may have arrived late, but her influence was felt as early as the Roman period, in the poems of CATULLUS [82], Ovid, and HORACE [80]. Further evidence of her influence can be found in the works of such later poets as Thomas Campion, Philip Sidney, BYRON [83], TENNYSON [81], Swinburne, and Ezra Pound. There are numerous references to Sappho in literature: The French poet Christine de Pisan praised Sappho in her 1405 biographical catalogue of great women, *The Book of the City of Ladies*; Byron, in *Childe Harold's Pilgrimage*, wrote of the poet's "breast imbued with such immortal fire"; and BAUDELAIRE [46] mentions her in *Les Fleurs du Mal*. J. D. Salinger's story, "Raise High the Roof Beam, Carpenters" takes its title from a line of Sappho's poem, "Dearest Earth's Offspring and Heaven's": "Raise high the roof beam, carpenters. Like Ares comes the bridegroom, taller far than a tall man."

The Greek poet Odysseas Elytis, in one of his *Mikra Epsilon*, describes Sappho as a poet "that did prove to be equally capable of subjugating a roseflower, interpreting a wave or a nightingale, and saying 'I love you,' to fill the globe with emotion." Referred to in antiquity as simply "the Poetess," as HOMER [3] is known as "the Poet," Sappho reminds us through her verses of the deeply personal and enduring nature of love.

KĀLIDĀSA

c. 340–400

Wouldst thou the young year's blossoms and the fruits of its decline,
And all by which the soul is charmed, enraptured, feasted, fed?
Wouldst thou the earth and heaven itself in one sole name combine?
I name thee, O Sakuntala, and all at once is said.

—Johann Wolfgang von Goethe

Sanskrit poet and dramatist Kālidāsa is commonly viewed as India's national laureate, the writer who best embodies in literary forms Indian consciousness. Seven of his works survive: three plays, two narrative poems, and two lyrics. All are characterized by a delicate and expressive power that captures both emotional nuances and the beauties of nature. Yet Kālidāsa's importance as a writer goes beyond his verbal mastery and sensitivity. As critic Arthur W. Ryder has asserted, "Poetical fluency is not rare; intellectual grasp is not very uncommon: but the combination has not been found perhaps more than a dozen times since the world began. Because he possessed this harmonious combination, Kālidāsa ranks not with Anacreon and Horace and Shelley, but with Sophocles, Virgil, Milton." In 1789, *Śakuntalā*, Kālidāsa's dramatic masterpiece, became the first work in Sanskrit to be translated into a modern European language. It was widely read and admired, and Kālidāsa was proclaimed by his translator, Sir William Jones, "the Shakespeare of India." GOETHE [10]

333

recognized in Kālidāsa the poet's "highest function as the representative of the most natural condition, of the most beautiful way of life, of the purest moral effort, of the worthiest majesty, of the most sincere contemplation."

Facts surrounding Kālidāsa's life are almost nonexistent, and speculation has depended on gleaning details from his work and assessing the various legends that have surrounded him. One has it that he was born into a Brahman family but abandoned as a baby and reared as a lowly ox-driver. In his youth, he was dressed in the clothes of a courtier to play a trick on a haughty princess. Smitten by his beauty and graceful manners, the princess desired to marry him. After he revealed the truth about his identity, the incensed princess eventually forgave the deception and urged him to gain the accomplishments that his looks and manners demanded by praying for learning and poetic skill from the goddess Kali. His prayer was granted, and the former ox-driver took the name Kālidāsa, or servant of Kali, in appreciation. From his writing it is clear that Kālidāsa was both well educated and well traveled throughout India. We know that he spent at least part of his life in the city of Ujjain, in west-central India. Tradition has it that Kālidāsa was one of the "nine gems"—poets, scientists, and artisans—of the court of King Vikramaditya of Ujjain (also known as Chandragupta II), the great patron of learning and the arts whose reign (c. 380–415) marked one of the great flowerings of Indian culture. Another legend holds that when the king's daughter married the crown prince of a neighboring state, Kālidāsa accompanied the bride as the king's ambassador. The poet's intimate familiarity with court life revealed in his works gives substance to the suggestion that he served at court in some capacity. Kālidāsa's works, according to K. Krishnamoorthy, indicate that he "lived in times of peace, when the leisured class would pursue the fine arts, free from threats of invasion from without or from conflicts within." This suggests that Kālidāsa lived and worked sometime between the fourth and fifth centuries.

In whatever capacity he served during this period of Indian cultural renaissance, Kālidāsa worked in the established traditions of Indian court poetry and drama. His surviving poetic works include the lyric poem, *Ritusamhara* (The cycle of the seasons), in which the six Indian seasons are chronicled from a lover's perspective. Love's fulfillment is contrasted with its heartbreak in the elegiac *Meghadūta* (The cloud messenger), in which a cloud serves to bridge the gap between parted lovers. These poems are thought to be Kālidāsa's earliest works, which possibly secured his position as a court poet. Two longer narrative poems—*Raghuvamśa* (Dynasty of Raghu) and *Kumārasambhava* (Birth of the war god)—likely followed. Both celebrate ideal virtues of legendary Indian kings and heroes and may have been written to inspire and guide the rulers of Kālidāsa's day. His three surviving plays are *Mālavikā and Agnimitra*, a conventionally comic harem intrigue; *Vikramorvaśī* (Urvaśī won by valor) about a mortal's love for a divine maiden, and *Abhijñānaśākuntala* (Śakuntalā and the Ring of Recollection, commonly referred to as *Śakuntalā*).

Textual evidence supports the assumption that *Mālavikā and Agnimitra* is an early, apprentice work; while *Vikramorvaśī* may have been written in the poet's decline. *Śakuntalā* is his most accomplished drama, written at the height of his poetic skill and in full mastery of the procedures and aesthetic potentialities of Sanskrit drama.

The classical drama of India grew out of both Hindu religious temple ceremonies and popular folk entertainments combining dance, acrobatics, mime, and singing. The chief treatise on Indian drama and the most important source for establishing Sanskrit theatrical traditions is the *Natyasastra* (The science of dramaturgy) attributed to the sage Bharata, written c. 200 B.C.–200 A.D. According to it, drama originated when Indra, king of the gods, asked Brahma, the creator of the universe, to devise an art form to be seen, heard, and understood by all men. Brahma considered the four Vedas, the sacred books of Indian wisdom, and selected one component from each—the spoken word from the Rig-Veda, song from the Sama-Veda, mime from the Yajur-Veda, and emotion from the Atharva-Veda—and combined them to form drama. Brahma requested that Indra compose plays based on the fifth, Natya-Veda, and have the gods enact them, but, since Indra did not consider it appropriate for gods to act, priests were selected to serve, and Bharata was summoned to be instructed in the art of the drama from Brahma himself. Bharata then recorded the divine rules of dancing, acting, and stage production that define Sanskrit drama in the *Natyastra*, the most extensive book of ancient dramaturgy in the world, covering acting, theater architecture, costuming, makeup, dance, music, play construction, the organization of theater companies, and many more topics.

Unlike Western drama, Sanskrit dramas are not classified into categories of comedy, tragedy, and tragicomedy, and neither action nor character or thematic development is as important as achieving an appropriate *rasa*, variously translated as mood, sentiment, or aesthetic delight. Human experience, according to Indian dramaturgy, is divided into eight basic sentiments or *rasas*—the erotic, the comic, pathos, rage, heroism, terror, odiousness, and the marvelous. These sentiments are aroused in the audience by actors' representations of the corresponding eight states of emotions or feelings. Every play has a predominant emotion, producing a corresponding *rasa* through the artful combination of words, action, movement, costume, makeup, music, etc. Since the goal of all Hindu plays is to provide a sense of harmony and serenity, all must end happily, with death and violence occurring offstage, and right and wrong clearly differentiated. However, replicating the unity among all things, plays could intermingle the exalted and the commonplace, poetry and prose, the learned language of Sanskrit (spoken by Gods, kings, and sages) and the everyday speech, called Pakrit (spoken by peasants, soldiers, servants, women, and children). Of the prescribed 10 categories of plays, the most important were the *nataka*, based on mythology or history and involving an exemplary hero, such as a king and royal sage, dealing with the sentiments of love and heroism, and the *prakarana* in which its plots and characters are entirely imaginary. A Brahman, merchant, or minister could serve as the hero; a courtesan as the heroine, and love was its dominant sentiment. Plays of between one and 10 acts would be mounted on specially built stages for each performance before a largely aristocratic audience. No scenery was used, but place and situation would be established by narration or pantomime. Both men and women acted with costume, makeup, gesture, and movement strictly refined and stylized. Characters of many social ranks and types could appear, but the hero was almost always a ruler or an aristocrat, often paired with a clown who served as comic relief. The basic human emotions (*bhavas*) that could be portrayed on stage were identified and represented by a set number of approved movements, hand gestures, and facial expressions. A Sanskrit drama was, therefore, an elaborate blend of rigidly codified emotions, character types, costumes, makeup, gesture, movement, situations, and music, all orchestrated to arouse the appropriate audience response. A theater of elevated principles, Sanskrit drama's goal was to edify and inspire through the idealization of the characters, their values, and the actions represented.

The great achievement of *Śakuntalā* is Kālidāsa's remarkable ability to achieve an expressive lyric power of great subtlety within the drama's tightly prescribed conventions. Based on an ancient Hindu legend recounted in book one of the *Mahabharata* about a charm that causes a lover to forget his beloved, its story becomes the vehicle for Kālidāsa to explore love in multiple aspects and under the most testing circumstances. In the first of the play's seven acts, King Dusyanta on a hunt enters a forest that is the residence of the sage Kanva and his stepdaughter, Śakuntalā. Falling in love with her, Dusyanta remains with her until duties demand his return to the court. Before leaving, Dusyanta gives her a ring as a token of their union. Distracted by her lover's parting and neglecting her duties in the hermitage, Śakuntalā ignores the arrival of the ill-tempered, self-important sage Durvāsas. Feeling slighted by Śakuntalā for not performing the expected rites of hospitality to suit him, Durvāsas places a curse on Śakuntalā making the king forget her until he sees the ring again.

Pregnant with the king's child, Śakuntalā sets off for court, but while worshipping at a river shrine during the journey, she loses the ring, and, when she presents herself before Dusyanta at court, he has no memory of her and dismisses her from his presence. Devastated and angered by the king's rejection, Śakuntalā prays for the earth to open and receive her. In response a light in the shape of a woman carries her off into heaven. When the ring is eventually recovered, Dusyanta's memory returns, and he is stricken with remorse. His contrition causes the nymph who had rescued Śakuntalā to pity him, and she sends the chariot of the god Indra down to earth to convey the king to heaven to be reunited with Śakuntalā. In heaven, Dusyanta encounters a young boy who is revealed to be his son, Bharata (considered the forefather of the Indian nation). Dusyanta is finally reunited with Śakuntalā who, having learned of the curse, readily forgives him. The gods send husband, wife, and son back to earth for a life of happiness together.

In keeping with the fundamental principle of Sanskrit drama that subordinates plot and characterization to a dominant emotion or sympathy, *Śakuntalā* displays the full gamut of human love with each act presenting obstacles that explore the nature of love and test its intensity, depth, and breadth. Beginning with infatuation, the love between Śakuntalā and Dusyanta is enflamed into an intense physical passion that then must be refined by the effects of the curse. The lovers are separated, and, when she is unrecognized by her lover, Śakuntalā experiences betrayal and is desolated by love's denial. Recovering his memory, Dusyanta experiences guilt, remorse, and despair over his lost love, yet his devotion sustains him to face the supernatural challenge in heaven. Proving his kingly courage and his duty as hero and lover, Dusyanta is shown worthy of his reward in recovering son and wife, as love culminates in the bliss of marriage and family. In this way, *Śakuntalā* demonstrates not just passion achieved and denied, not just love's raptures and torments, but centrally important cultural values of duty, spiritual reverence, and the ennobling power of love. One of the preeminent dramas of love in world literature, *Śakuntalā* remains a masterpiece of a culture's consciousness and a standard by which a nation's literature has for centuries been judged.

LAURENCE STERNE

90

1713–1768

For indeed if Tristram Shandy *as we have it did not exist, we should have to say that that achievement also, twenty years after* Pamela, *was not to be imagined. To see what Sterne's achievement really was, is I believe only in these last years possible, in a mind made aware by* The Magic Mountain, Ulysses, *and* The Remembrance of Things Past.
　　　　—Benjamin H. Lehman, "Of Time, Personality, and the Author"

It is intriguing to speculate how Laurence Sterne, his contemporaries, and later critics would have greeted his inclusion in this book. Sterne certainly would have felt a sense of vindication. After all, he asserted "I wrote, not to be *fed* but to be *famous.*" One suspects that he would also have delighted in being a subversive presence in a ranking of literature's most august figures. Although *Tristram Shandy* brought Sterne notoriety and acclaim, it has remained one of literature's great oddities. To hostile critics, who included such contemporaries as Samuel Richardson [70], Horace Walpole, and Oliver Goldsmith and later readers such as Coleridge and Thackeray [94], *Tristram Shandy* was little more than an amalgam of obscenity mixed with sentimentality, imbedded in an artistic form that was both impenetrable and perverse. "Nothing odd will do long," Samuel Johnson noted. "*Tristram Shandy* did not last."

　　Dr. Johnson, however, was incorrect; the book and its author have persisted. As the form of the novel has developed, particularly in the 20th century,

Sterne and *Tristram Shandy* have proven to be far from a dead-end siding but instead on the novel's main track. The novel's self-reflectivity, its challenge to a willing suspension of disbelief, its complicated tension between life and artifice—all elements of the novel since *Don Quixote*—are in Sterne given a remarkable airing. His subversive challenge is a central element in the modern novel and his principal literary legacy.

Sterne's radical undermining of the novel's conventions is remarkable, coming so early in the genre's development and from such an unlikely source. *Tristram Shandy* burst on the scene when Sterne was 46, after he had spent 21 years as a minor cleric and dilettante offering few hints that he was capable of the originality and daringness of his masterpiece.

Sterne was born in Clonmel, Ireland, the son of an army subaltern who moved from garrison to garrison. When his father died in 1731, Sterne was left penniless but was sent to Jesus College, Cambridge, through the generosity of a cousin. He was an unremarkable student but read widely and was a member of a lively set of collegiate wits called the Demoniacs. While at university he suffered his first serious bout with tuberculosis, which would plague him throughout his life. With the help of his uncle, the precentor and canon of York Cathedral, Sterne was ordained in 1738, becoming the vicar of Sutton-in-the-Forest, near York, where he served until 1759. He married Elizabeth Lumley in 1741 after a two-year courtship, but the marriage was not happy. She became insane in 1758, the year before Sterne began writing his comic masterpiece, *Tristram Shandy*. Up to this point Sterne's life had been unexceptional; he was a cultivated amateur who took up painting and music and wrote sermons, some political pieces for the Yorkshire newspapers, and a satire on ecclesiastical misconduct at York, *The History of a Good Warm Watch Coat*. He was clever, with a variety of artistic and intellectual interests, but there was little to suggest the imaginative resources that he would bring to play in his novel. The first two volumes of *Tristram Shandy* appeared, after first being rejected by a publisher, in York in 1759 and London in 1760. They created an immediate sensation, and Sterne found himself a literary celebrity at home and abroad. Seven additional volumes of his novel would appear until 1767, the year before he died, with a plan for more volumes to come that were never written. Ill health sent him abroad in 1762, and he lived for a time in Toulouse, France. His reflections on his travels in France and Italy were collected in *A Sentimental Journey* (1768). He also published volumes of sermons by "Mr Yorick," Sterne's parson in *Tristram Shandy*. A love affair with Mrs. Eliza Draper was the occasion for a journal account of their relationship, which was not published until 1904. Sterne died of pleurisy, in debt, in a London lodging house.

The full title of Sterne's comic masterpiece, *The Life and Opinions of Tristram Shandy, Gentleman*, is the first of Sterne's continual reversals and jokes. Readers have pointed out that despite its title, the book gives us very little of the life and nothing of the opinions of its nominal hero, whose birth does not even occur until volume four, near the novel's midpoint. The arrangement gives the reader a clue that the novel will challenge whatever conventional expectations are brought to it. Sterne's fundamental premise is that the patterning of life in the novel is deceptive, the result of artifice that the narrator of the book frankly admits. Life is not necessarily best captured in a linear sequence of dramatic incidents rounded off to a pleasing moral interpretation, but is instead fragmentary and shifting, a complex of associations and influences pointing forward and backward in time. To understand Shandy's life, one must begin not with birth but with conception, and the various occurrences that conspired to make the man, including how he was named, formed, and injured. In *Tristram Shandy*, however, very little happens that is conventionally dramatic, and the narrative stubbornly resists an arrangement of events into a clearly defined plot. Instead there is a digression on digressions, and pages of scholarly babble to impede the novel's forward progress. The novel concerns the Shandy family, notably Walter Shandy, Tristram's father; Tristram's uncle Toby, a retired soldier whose hobby is the science of attacking fortifications; and Corporal Trim, Toby's servant. Within their restricted world is a plenitude of contradictions and ambiguities, the stuff of both farce and sentiment.

The novel and Tristram's history begin with the comedy of his conception. As in a modern metafiction, Sterne's book is a novel about the writing of a novel in which the details of Tristram's life compete with the challenges and distortions of being converted into language and print. Sterne constantly reminds the reader that the novel is not life but an approximation of it translated into text. There is a black page for the death of Yorick and a blank page for the reader's own description of Widow Wadman, as well as a graph to indicate the narrative design. These visual jokes underscore the novel's deeper conception that life is far more complex than most novels suggest, and that literary experience is inevitably shaped by the artist and his medium. The dislocation of time and the concentration on the larger meanings embedded in the most trivial details of life contain a similar notion of the flux and suggestiveness of life that PROUST [16] would develop in his masterpiece, *Remembrance of Things Past*. There is also a great deal of the erudition of JOYCE [7] and a reworking of the sheer data of experience. As its core, *Tristram Shandy* shares with the work of these modernist masters the notion that life resists reduction to set formulas of perception, and that the imagination, in all its multiplicity, orders experience. Compared to the orderliness of the 18th-century mind, Sterne has a high tolerance for the absurd. Unlike the savage indignation of SWIFT [41] or the bitterly absurd world of BECKETT [47], Sterne's sense of the chaotic untidiness of life and human experience is finally affirming. Although he removed all the consoling illusions of the novel and broke it up into its parts with a perversity that still shocks and surprises, Sterne manages to delight with the life he uncovers and his dazzling performance.

FEDERICO GARCÍA LORCA

91

1898–1936

There has always seemed to be a doubt in the minds of Spaniards that their native meters were subtle enough, flexible enough to bear modern stresses. But Lorca, aided by the light of twentieth century thought, discovered in the old forms the very essence of today. Reality, immediacy; by the vividness of the image invoking the mind to start awake. This peculiarly modern mechanic Lorca found ready to his hand. He took up the old tradition, and in a more congenial age worked with it, as the others had not been able to do, until he forced it—without borrowing—to carry on as it had come to him, intact through the ages, warm, unencumbered by draperies of imitative derivation—the world again under our eyes.
—William Carlos Williams, "Federico García Lorca," in *Selected Essays of William Carlos Williams*

In a tragically foreshortened life that echoes the remarkably intense and rapid artistic development of JOHN KEATS [25], Spanish poet and playwright Federico García Lorca has claimed the world's attention as Spain's most distinctive and important literary voice since CERVANTES [11]. In his poetry and plays, Lorca opened up Spanish literature to accommodate elements of literary modernism without losing any of the forces of tradition and regionalism, from which he derived so much strength. His artistic achievement surpasses narrow political and ideological functions to reach a wider, universal resonance, making him one of the 20th century's greatest voices. Through his intense analysis of himself and his world, Lorca formed the basis for a redefinition of Spanish identity and consciousness while grappling with the widest possible themes.

So much of Lorca's inspiration and artistic power are derived from his background and the influence of his native Andalusia, with its rich blend of Arabian, gypsy, and rural Spanish tradition. Born in a small village west of Granada, Lorca was the son of a prosperous farmer and a former schoolteacher who encouraged her precocious son in his reading and musical ability. An accomplished pianist and guitarist, Lorca began to study law at the University of Granada but left for Madrid in 1919. He lived at the Residencia de Estudi-antes of the University of Madrid for 10 years, where he read widely, wrote, and improvised music and poetry at the center of a group of young intellectu-als and artists, among them the poets Gerardo Diego and Rafael Alberti, Luis Buñuel, who would become the great Spanish film director, and the artist Salvador Dali. He also met such international figures as the authors François Mauriac and H. G. Wells, and the composer Igor Stravinsky, and was exposed to avant-garde music and painting, dadaism and surrealism. Lorca absorbed modern techniques while preserving traditional poetic forms, performing his poetry like a troubadour in cafés and night-clubs. In 1921, he published *Poems*. He achieved his first theatrical success with *Mariana Pineda* in 1927, and with the first edition of *Gypsy Ballads* in 1928, Lorca became famous.

In 1929, seeking relief for severe depression and emotional distress, the causes of which have never been fully revealed, Lorca went to New York City, where he studied briefly at Columbia University. His experience in an urban, foreign culture, so contrary to his Andalusian background, produced an emotional crisis and self-exploration of his identity and homosexuality in the nightmarish visions of the poetic sequence, *Poet in New York*, published posthumously in 1940. In 1930, when he returned to Spain, Lorca dedicated himself increasingly to the theater, forming the traveling theatrical company La Barraca, which was subsidized by the republican government, and per-formed classical and modern plays for a largely peasant audience. He wrote a series of farces and the three rural tragedies upon which he established his theatrical reputation: *Blood Wedding* (1933), *Yerma* (1934), and *The House of Bernarda Alba*, published posthumously in 1945. In 1936, the fascists led by Francisco Franco revolted, setting off the Spanish Civil War. Lorca's homo-sexuality, literary reputation, and connections with the republican government made him a target in the purges of Franco's troops. He sought protection in the house of a friend near Granada but was arrested and executed by a firing squad at the age of 38. Lorca had become a martyr to the doomed republican cause: as PABLO NERUDA [102] lamented, "Those who in shooting him wanted to hit the heart of his people made the right choice."

Like any writer who dies early, in his artistic prime, the question of what might have been lingers over Lorca's achievement. Ironically, his tragic death helped to spread his reputation internationally and has contributed to his wide influence. What Lorca accomplished as an artist, however, more than deserves the attention that he has received as a casualty of the Spanish civil war and as a chronicler of those forces opposed to human fulfillment and vitality. His remarkable artistic growth developed from his earliest poetry of adolescent longing to his more mature achievement of the *Gypsy Ballads*, in which a highly personal style emerges with a fusion of traditional poetic elements and striking modern images. In the breathtaking sequence of *Poet in New York*, Lorca abandons traditional poetic forms for a succession of surreal images capturing the chaotic nightmare of modern, urban life and his anguish as he confronts it. When Lorca returned to Spain he returned to traditional metrical forms and Spanish subjects as well, producing his poetic masterpiece, "Lament for Ignacio Majías," an elegy for a famous bullfighter who died in the ring. Lorca's lament faces the physical reality of death without any compensating consolation other than the integrity of the bullfighter's heroic and dignified confrontation with his ultimate fate.

Lorca's plays are filled with the same intensity, daring imagery, and preoccupations that mark his poetry, forming a unique poetic drama. Based on rural themes, his dramas explore psychological and social forces, particularly on women, whose erotic and natural life force conflicts with society's restraints. Endorsing the social function of drama to reform and revitalize society, Lorca wrote that "a theater that is sensitive and well oriented in all of its branches, from tragedy to vaudeville, can in a few years change the sensibility of a people; and a shattered theater, in which hoofs substitute for wings, can debase and benumb an entire nation." Full of the lyrical power of his poetry, Lorca's plays both indict the repressive moral codes that prevent self-fulfillment and reveal the power of passion that is humanly and symbolically expressed. At his best, Lorca achieves the effects of poetic drama that YEATS [17] and T. S. ELIOT [19] struggled with mixed results to produce, creating a rich blend of folk tradition, contemporary social analysis, and deeply personal exploration of universal themes.

Lorca's poetic and dramatic gifts integrate traditional elements and modern expression so that each reinforces and enriches the other. By doing so, Lorca established himself as one of the seminal figures in the Spanish literary tradition who speaks as well and as strongly across cultures and other national traditions, exposing the ways in which intensely local cultural elements can reach a level of universality.

OSCAR WILDE

92

1854–1900

I think his tragedy is rather like Humpty Dumpty's, quite as tragic and quite as impossible to put right.

—Constance Wilde in a letter to her brother, 1897

In *De Profundis*, Oscar Wilde provides his own succinct summary of his achievement:

> The Gods had given me almost everything. I had genius, a distinguished name, high social position, brilliancy, intellectual daring: I made art a philosophy, and philosophy an art: I altered the minds of men and the colours of things: there was nothing I said or did that did not make people wonder: I took the drama, the most objective form known to art, and made it as personal a mode of expression as the lyric or the sonnet, at the same time I widened its range and enriched its characterisation: drama, novel, poem in rhyme, poem in prose, subtle or fantastic dialogue, whatever I touched I made beautiful in a new mode of beauty: to truth itself I gave what is false no less than what is true as its rightful province, and showed that the false and the true are merely forms of intellectual existence. I treated art as the supreme reality, and life as a mere mode of fiction: I awoke the imagination of my century so that it created myth and

344

legend around me: I summed up all systems in a phrase and all existence in an epigram.

This is not the full story, however. Wilde wrote this confident assertion of his contribution to art and culture while serving a two-year sentence at hard labor in Reading Gaol, in a whitewashed cell 13 feet by 7 feet, for his homosexuality. What the gods provided, they also took away, and Oscar Wilde's meteoric ascension to notoriety also included his tragic fall from grace.

Perhaps no other writer except BYRON [83] matched Wilde's fame or bitter fate as an artist whose own life was his greatest creation. In a career so entangled with his own personality and legend, it is inevitable that what Wilde actually produced would become relegated to auxiliary importance. Wilde himself famously declared, "I have put my genius into my life; I have put only my talent into my works." Wilde's excellence as a poet, short story writer, novelist, playwright, and essayist is clear, but not sufficient alone to secure his ranking here. He is selected as the key representative figure of the aesthetic movement, whose life and work changed the direction and purpose of art. Wilde put the integrity and autonomy of the artist's vision at the core of artistic expression, ignoring the claims of any narrow moral standard and conventionality. By doing so, Wilde extended the boundaries of literature and redefined the role and responsibility of the artist.

Paradox, the cornerstone of Wilde's art, is also the defining element in his life, beginning with his Irish background. Oscar Fingal O'Flahertie Wills Wilde was born in Dublin. His father, who was knighted in 1864, was a famous surgeon and eye specialist who treated Queen Victoria and founded a hospital for the treatment of eye and ear diseases. Wilde's mother was the Irish daughter of a solicitor with literary and Irish nationalist inclinations. She was best known as a writer of poems and patriotic tracts, published under the name "Speranza." In 1848, when one of her articles called for an Irish revolt, the newspaper it appeared in was suppressed, and Gavin Duffy, a leader of the Young Ireland party, was prosecuted for sedition and high treason as its alleged author. At his trial, Wilde's mother rose in court to claim authorship and became a national hero. His mother's second son, Oscar Wilde was his mother's favorite, and she expected great things from him. At the age of 10 Wilde was sent to Portora Royal School in Enniskillen. He was tall, awkward, and dreamy, disliked sports, and was a voracious reader. In 1871, he entered Trinity College, Dublin, studying classics, and in 1874 he went on to Magdalen College, Oxford. This was the first, by his own estimation, of two turning points in his life; the second was when he was sent to prison.

At Oxford, Wilde was strongly influenced by two of his professors, John Ruskin and Walter Pater. From Ruskin, Wilde became aware of the disjunction between art and contemporary English life and the need to connect the two. From Pater, whose *Studies in the History of the Renaissance* (1873) stressed the cultivation and intensification of private experience and response to beauty as a primary aim, Wilde discovered aesthetic beliefs and a way of life. He embarked on a kind of promotional pilgrimage in a quest for beauty and self-realization as an artist that took the guise of flamboyant dress, the self-conscious attitudes of the idle poseur and dandy, and outrageous statements, such as "Oh, would that I could live up to my blue china!"

In 1878, after graduating, he went down to London, declaring, "I'll be a poet, a writer, a dramatist. Somehow or other I'll be famous, and if not famous I'll be notorious." He quickly became associated with the aesthetic movement, a loose collection of artists and attitudes that challenged Victorian conventionality, valued art for art's sake, and held beauty, not morality, as art's standard. The aesthetic movement's principal legacy, particularly to literary modernism, was its emphasis on craftsmanship and a defiance of any wider public or ethical role for art or the artist. As Wilde asserted in "The Decay of Lying," "Art takes life as part of her rough material, recreates it, and refashions it in fresh forms, is absolutely indifferent to fact, invents, imagines, dreams, and keeps between herself and reality the impenetrable barrier of beautiful style, of decorative or ideal treatment."

In the early 1880s, Wilde's notoriety as the representative figure of the aesthetic movement stemmed from his outrageous dress and witty conversation rather than anything he had written. As the model for the character of Reginald Bunthorne in Gilbert and Sullivan's opera *Patience*, famous for recommending a walk "down Piccadilly with a poppy or a lily in your mediaeval hand," Wilde was sent on a lecture tour of America by the play's producers to generate publicity for their New York opening. Wilde's fame increased primarily due to his inexhaustible supply of witty maxims and daring inversions of conventional truths. Characteristic examples include: "The only way to get rid of a temptation is to yield to it" (*The Picture of Dorian Gray*); "Experience is the name everyone gives to their mistakes" (*Lady Windermere's Fan*); and "To lose one parent . . . may be regarded as a misfortune; to lose both looks like carelessness" (*The Importance of Being Earnest*).

In 1884, Wilde married Constance Lloyd, the daughter of an Irish barrister, with whom he had two sons. Paradoxically, given the scandal that was soon to break over his homosexuality, Wilde loved his wife and adored his children. At the age of 30, Wilde had produced only one volume of poems and several unsuccessful plays. To secure an income he became a book reviewer and drama critic and the editor for the *Woman's World*, for which he wrote short stories. His most popular stories, some of which have remained children's classics, were published in the 1888 collection *The Happy Prince and Other Tales*, and in 1890 Wilde serialized the novel *The Picture of Dorian Gray*. Critical essays followed, and in 1892, with the production of *Lady Windermere's Fan*, Wilde began a series of four society comedies, concluding with his comic masterpiece, *The Importance of Being Earnest*, in 1895. Wilde's poetic drama, *Salomé*, written in French and intended for Sarah Bernhardt, was banned on the stage in London but was published with the sensual illustrations of Aubrey Beardsley in 1894.

At the height of his career, while producing his best work, Wilde's intimacy with Lord Alfred Douglas, the third son of the eighth marquis of Queensberry, resulted in one of the most famous trials of the 19th century. The marquis, infuriated by Wilde's relationship with his son, left a card at Wilde's club addressed "to Oscar Wilde posing as a somdomite [sic]." Wilde sued the marquis for libel; the marquis was acquitted. The testimony from stolen letters and male prostitutes offered in the marquis's defense resulted in Wilde being charged with sodomy, which led to his conviction and sentencing to two years of hard labor. Wilde's world had collapsed, but the experience produced two of his greatest works: *De Profundis*, his letter written in Reading Gaol to Lord Douglas, and his greatest poem, *The Ballad of Reading Gaol* (1898), which concerns the execution of a murderer.

Released from prison in 1897, Wilde immediately and permanently left England for France, where he died in Paris in 1900. Despite, or possibly because of, his pathetic and shabby end, Wilde subsequently has been all but canonized as a martyr for sexual and artistic freedom. His plays, fiction, and essays continue to be read and performed. His lasting impact and influence, however, originate from attitudes that changed the fundamental relationship between art and its audience. Wilde considered art not a mirror but a veil in which the artist uncovered beauty and universal truths through the imagination. For Wilde, "Truth in Art is the unity of a thing with itself—the outward rendered expressive of the inward: the soul made incarnate: the body instinct with spirit." Contrary to the realism and documentary impulse of the naturalists, Wilde led readers toward the spiritual and symbolic, an alternative force of artificiality and formal design that would help shape modern expression.

NIKOLAI GOGOL

93

1809–1852

Steady Pushkin, matter-of-fact Tolstoy, restrained Chekhov have all had their moments of irrational insight which simultaneously blurred the sentence and disclosed the secret meaning worth the sudden focal shift. But with Gogol this shifting is the very basis of his art, so that whenever he tried to write in the round hand of literary tradition and to treat rational ideas in a logical way, he lost all trace of talent. When, as in his immortal The Overcoat, *he really let himself go and pottered happily on the brink of his private abyss, he became the greatest artist that Russia has yet produced.*
—Vladimir Nabokov, *Lectures on Russian Literature*

Nikolai Gogol and ALEXANDER PUSHKIN [18] are commonly regarded as the twin progenitors of modern Russian literature. If Pushkin is Russia's founding poet and soul, Gogol, Russia's greatest comic writer, is its sense of humor and its storyteller, the acknowledged fountainhead of the Russian drama, short story, and novel. Moreover, Pushkin's translucent clarity and Gogol's grotesquery have long served as the contrasting poles of the Russian literary sensibility and approach. Allied to the Pushkin camp are writers such as Lermontov, Turgenev, and TOLSTOY [4]; while DOSTOEVSKY [14], Andrey Bely, NABOKOV [64], and others are counted among Gogol's direct literary descendants. Initiating Russia's golden age of prose fiction, Gogol has been claimed both as the father of Russian naturalism, for his opening up of significant aspects of

Russian life and experience for literary treatment, and Russia's first great prose symbolist and fantasist. Few writers have contributed as much to their national literature and consciousness or puzzled critics and biographers more. As critic Victor Erlich has observed, "We are still far from agreement as to the nature of his genius, the meaning of his bizarre art, and his still weirder life."

Nikolai Vasil'evich Gogol was born in a small Ukrainian town, the first surviving child of a minor landowning family. His mother instilled in him a strong spiritual belief in the certainty of both heaven and hell, while his father, who wrote Ukrainian folk comedies, introduced his son to the beauty of the surrounding countryside and its legends, songs, and stories. After an undistinguished school career, Gogol left home for St. Petersburg in 1828, simultaneously seeking distinction as a civil servant, an actor, and a writer. Hating the mind-numbing clerical position he was offered and with his acting skills rejected, Gogol eventually concentrated on making his mark with writing. One of his first publications was a long poem, printed at his own expense. It was savaged by the critics, and the humiliated Gogol bought and burned all remaining copies before departing for Germany in disgrace. He achieved his first success, absorbing the influence of German romanticism and the fairy tale, in a collection of comic folktales set in his native Ukraine. *Evenings on a Farm Near Dikanka* (1831) displays Gogol's characteristic idiosyncratic style that combines elements of realism, fantasy, comedy, social satire, and the grotesque, in which dreams and magic coexist with the mundane. Gogol's stories brought him to the attention of Pushkin, and their ensuing association would significantly shape Gogol's future literary career.

In 1834, with no academic qualifications, Gogol managed to secure an appointment as a lecturer in history at St. Petersburg University. One of his students, the future writer Turgenev, has recorded Gogol's considerable shortcomings as a teacher, in which his aspiration fell short of his ability and his assumed role as a scholar clashed with the reality of Gogol's actual attainments, themes that Gogol would take up in his subsequent writing as he increasingly shifted his attention from his native Ukraine to the more cosmopolitan milieu of St. Petersburg. The stories in *Arabesques* (1835)—"Nevski Prospect," "Portrait," and "Diary of a Madman" (in which a minor civil servant records his delusions that he is the king of Spain)—show for one of the first times in Russian literature the lives of the petty strivers in a depersonalized, dreamlike Russian city. Two subsequent "St. Petersburg Tales" followed, both among the greatest short stories in world literature. "The Nose" (1836) dramatizes the mysterious disappearance and eventual return of a vain, ambitious bureaucrat's nose. "The Overcoat" (1842), deemed by many the greatest short story in Russian, concerns the efforts of an impoverished clerk, Akaky Akakyvitch, to claim self-esteem by purchasing a new overcoat. When it is stolen, his appeals for assistance go unheeded, and he subsequently dies, returning as a ghost haunting the Important Personage who rejected Akaky's demands in life. Both stories suffuse the mundane with the fantastical, joining psychological projections with social criticism. In each, Gogol opens up both a milieu, exposing the comic and tragic lives of insignificant characters previously ignored in Russian literature, along with a symbolic and dreamlike method that would have an important impact on subsequent Russian literature. This debt has been acknowledged in a famous remark widely attributed to Dostoevsky: "We all came out from under Gogol's 'Overcoat.'"

Following his dismissal from his university post in 1835, Gogol produced what Vladimir Nabokov has called "the greatest play ever written in Russian (and never surpassed since)." *The Inspector General*, produced in St. Petersburg in 1836 and based on a story idea suggested by Pushkin, concerns what happens when the corrupt officials of a small provincial town believe that a penniless young civil servant is the august government inspector they believe is visiting their province incognito. With its provocatively unflattering epigraph, "If your face is crooked, don't blame the mirror," the play shows the accidental imposter Khlestakov bribed, feted, and pursuing the seduction of both the mayor's wife and daughter before departing shortly before the town's residents learn of their mistake and await the actual arrival of the real government inspector. Russian drama before *The Inspector General* was for the most part imitative of foreign models. Gogol, however, took up a distinctively Russian subject while challenging audience expectations about what a comedy could be. Gone are the standard idealized characters and romance plot as well as the expected poetic justice in which virtue is rewarded and vice punished. Instead, Gogol places at the center of his comedy recognizable mixed human characters in unflattering situations that turn his comedy into a substantive critique of Russian life and human nature. *The Inspector General* brought within comic range for the first time the ways in which Russian society and government work, in all their petty corruption and ineptitude, while embodying in his characters key national traits—archetypes that continue to serve the Russian imagination and collective consciousness. Critic Thomas Seltzer has asserted that "There is no other single work in the modern literature of any language that carries with it the wealth of associations which the *Inspector-General* does to the educated Russian. The Germans have their *Faust*; but *Faust* is a tragedy with a cosmic philosophic theme. In England it takes nearly all that is implied in the comprehensive name of Shakespeare to give the same sense of bigness that a Russian gets from the mention of the *Revizor* (the Inspector General)."

Criticism of the play as a slander on the Russian character and society drove Gogol into exile to Rome where he remained for most of the next 12 years, writing his masterpiece *Dead Souls* (1842). Again from a story idea suggested by Pushkin, Gogol's novel is based on a curious loophole in the Russian tax law under serfdom. Every 10 years landowners were required to supply a census of their "souls," or male serfs, and pay a poll tax on the numbers provided. If serfs died before the next census, the landowner was still financially liable for the valuation based on the original number. If a swindler purchased these "dead souls" (at a discount to relieve a landowner's tax burden), he could then use these "holdings" as collateral to secure a mortgage, becoming in effect a person of landed wealth based on his title to no longer existent but still precious souls. "I began to write with no definite plan in mind," Gogol recalled, "without knowing exactly what my hero was to represent. I only thought that this odd project . . . would lead to the creation of diverse personalities and my own inclination toward the comic would bring on amusing situations that I could alternate with pathos." Such an ironic situation gave Gogol a ready, sardonic means with which to survey and criticize Russian customs and behavior, with the grotesque trading in dead souls commenting on an institution that treated living humans as chattel and even more devilishly calling into question who were in fact the deader souls, the departed serfs or the living gentry, enclosed by a stifling conventionality. Chichikov, the novel's rogue hero, encounters a rich gallery of grotesque characters that have subsequently served as embodiments of essential Russian comic traits. The novel eventually collapses in a Kafkaesque world of threat, confusion, and absurdity that creates a withering exposé of contemporary Russian society. Uncovered as a fraud, Chichikov departs hastily, allowing Gogol a final and famous comparison between Russia and his careening carriage:

> Rus, are you not similar in your headlong motion to one of those nimble *troikas* that none can overtake? The flying road turns into smoke under you, bridges thunder and pass, all falls back and is left behind! The witness of your course stops as if struck by some divine miracle: is this not lightning that dropped from the sky? And what does this awesome motion mean? . . . Rus, whither are you speeding so?

Gogol would spend the rest of his life formulating answers to those questions, as he moved from chronicling the eccentricities and contradictions of Russian life to preaching about its correction. He long labored on a sequel to *Dead Souls* that would show Russia's path to moral regeneration but twice burned the results, and only fragments have survived. In 1847, Gogol published *Selected Passages from Correspondence with Friends*, a collection of reactionary didactic and moralistic letters that shocked his supporters who considered Gogol a champion of liberal reform. Gogol's preaching on behalf of the established church, government, and the status quo under serfdom elicited from critic Vissarion Belinsky the "Letter to Gogol," one of the most famous rebuttals in Russian literature. In it Belinsky accused the writer of becoming "an apostle of the knout, of obscurantism, of mystical demagoguery." Dismayed by the firestorm his book had created, Gogol again left Russia. After a desultory pilgrimage to Jerusalem, Gogol came under the influence of a fanatical Russian priest who urged the writer to abandon literature and purify his soul. In 1852, after burning the almost completed second part of *Dead Souls*, in an act of spiritual mortification Gogol literally fasted himself to death. He died at the age of 42 with the last words, "Dai lestnitsu!" (Give me a ladder!). Like his works that combine the most disparate elements—realism, fantasy, serious social criticism, and madcap verbal foolery—Gogol remains defiantly a mass of irresolvable contradictions. His superb eye for the revealing trivial detail and manic humor coexists with a deep religiosity and existential terrors. Despite baffling his countrymen through most of his life, in death, many still claimed kinship, providing the Russians with a look at themselves in his remarkable, grotesque mirror. Thousands attended his funeral, prompting a passerby to ask, "Who is this man who has so many relatives at his funeral?" A mourner responded, "This is Nikolai Gogol, and all of Russia is his relative."

WILLIAM MAKEPEACE THACKERAY

94

1811–1863

I approve of Mr. Thackeray. This may sound presumptuous perhaps, but I mean that I have long recognized in his writings genuine talent, such as I admired, such as I wondered at and delighted in. No author seems to distinguish so exquisitely as he does dross from ore, the real from the counterfeit.

—Charlotte Brontë in a letter to W. S. Williams, 1847

In 1848, after a long and often disappointing search for a profession and a voice, Thackeray could gloat to his mother that he had suddenly "become a sort of great man . . . . all but at the top of the tree: indeed there if truth were known and having a great fight up there with Dickens." The reason for this long-awaited feeling of satisfaction was the success of his serialized novel, *Vanity Fair.* Thackeray's success came during one of the most remarkable periods in the history of the novel, a time which saw, over several months, not only the publication of *Vanity Fair* but also *Jane Eyre* by CHARLOTTE BRONTË [60], *Wuthering Heights* by EMILY BRONTË [61], and *Dombey and Son* and *David Copperfield* by CHARLES DICKENS [6]. The period was a watershed for the Victorian novel, and Thackeray had managed with a single blow to assert himself as Dickens's chief rival for recognition as the age's greatest novelist, and in the process to have as great an impact on the development of the novel as JOYCE [7] would with the publication of *Ulysses* in the 20th century.

The subtitle of *Vanity Fair*, "A Novel Without a Hero," marked Thackeray's book as a radical departure from other novels. It offered readers of the time a portrait of English life and society stripped of the idealization they had come to expect from the novel. The characters who are the likely candidates for romantic treatment, Amelia Sedley and George Osborne, are paired with realistic opposites, Becky Sharp and William Dobbin, and exposed as inadequate. George's expected redemption from cad to hero is cut short on the battlefield of Waterloo in the first third of the book. Marriage, the climactic goal of most previous novels, is only the starting point for Thackeray's massive study of domestic realism and criticism of society. The novel's standard for realism, the destruction of make-believe, pointed fiction toward the serious purpose of GEORGE ELIOT [21] and GUSTAVE FLAUBERT [30] as an instrument of truth. Dickens, influenced by Thackeray's example, worked out his own synthesis between the ideal and the real in his fictional formula, which he announced in the preface to *Bleak House* as the "romantic side of familiar things."

Among the great Victorian novelists, Thackeray today is probably the least read. His massive social panoramas have not found favor measured against the controlled focus promulgated by Flaubert and HENRY JAMES [38]. His novels also are tied closely to his age, which grows increasingly remote from ours. The surface details require more and more documentation to understand, and his values of class and race become increasingly awkward. Despite his shortcomings, Thackeray is one of the world's great literary artists, whose basic theme is the expansion of human sympathy, and tolerance unsupported by falsehood and simplification.

Events in Thackeray's biography prevented his assuming the role of the complacent gentleman he was raised to become—and the snob that he satirized. He was born in Calcutta, India, the only son of a distinguished member of the India civil service. He was brought up in luxury like a young prince, but only until age five, when he was sent to England for his schooling. Like the trauma Dickens faced when he was sent to work at the blacking factory, Thackeray's school miseries left an indelible imprint on his imagination. He began to see life as a dichotomy between the warmth of the home circle and the brutality and indifference of the outside world. In his public schooling at Charterhouse (which he referred to as Slaughterhouse), the world was further divided between knaves and dupes, victimizers and their victims (in which he clearly was among the latter), which formed the principal contrast in his satirical writing before *Vanity Fair*. Thackeray attended Cambridge for two years before embarking on the gentleman's alternative education, European travel, which took him to Germany and France. Gambling and business failure cost Thackeray most of his father's legacy and stripped him of the means to pursue a life of idleness and amusement. After his marriage to Isabella Shaw in 1836, he was forced to earn a living and support a family. After unsuccessfully trying his hand as an artist, which included his rejected bid to become Dickens's illustrator for *The Pickwick Papers*, Thackeray began a period of "writing for his life." He produced assorted journalism, sketches, and stories under such pseudonyms as Michael Angelo Titmarsh, Yellowplush, Ikey Solomon, Fitzboodle, and Mr. Snob. His fictional works during the period included *The Luck of Barry Lyndon* (1844) and *The Snobs of England* (1847), harsh portraits of human weakness and cynical ambition.

Domestically, Thackeray began to experience a change of values after suffering through the death of his second daughter and his wife's six-year drift into insanity, which, in 1846, proved incurable and required the permanent care of an attendant. He was bereft of a happy, domestic center, and the experience matured him. His earlier high spirits and cynicism were abandoned, and he began to see the world as one composed of fellow sufferers worthy of sympathy as well as satire. It is this mood that informs *Vanity Fair* and makes the novel a full account of human experience, rather than just another in a series of snob portraits.

Thackeray wrote three major novels after *Vanity Fair*. The first, *Pendennis*, appeared in installments from 1848 to 1850. *Henry Esmond* (1852), Thackeray's attempt to show his critics that he was capable of producing a novel with an elaborate plot and structure, is a historical work that features a remarkable reconstruction of the 18th century. *The Newcomes* (1853 to 1855), an ambitious return to the mode of *Vanity Fair*, contains his richest social panorama and most complex characterizations, but it is a book without a central focus of interest or dramatic movement. During Thackeray's last decade he was a literary celebrity and editor of the *Cornhill* magazine, very much the tastemaker and Victorian icon. His final novels, however, show a slackening of concentration and focus, eclipsed by the work of novelists like George Eliot and ANTHONY TROLLOPE [107], who built upon the realistic foundation that Thackeray had developed.

Vanity Fair, however, remains one of the essential novels of world literature in its range and nuanced portrait of life and society. Its story begins in the Regency period when the novel's two heroines, Amelia Sedley and Becky Sharp, leave school. The plot follows their divergent courses through the marriage market, in which Becky announces her rebellion from the conventional role of the passive, submissive heroine by throwing her presentation copy of Samuel Johnson's *Dictionary of the English Language* out of the coach window and audaciously and treasonously declaring, *"Vive la France! Vive l'Empereur! Vive Bonaparte!"* With fascinated horror, the reader follows Becky's campaign against opponents easily bested by flattery and subterfuge. Amelia's story takes her in the opposite direction. Beginning with all the possibilities of the conventional heroine, she marries the shallow George Osborne and maintains a long widowhood dedicated to his false image while claiming fealty from the ever-dependable, noble, but dull Dobbin. When the Regency gives way to the Victorian period, an era of domestic sentimentality, Becky Sharp has a much harder time surviving. Her eventual ruin is paralleled by Amelia's final recognition of George's betrayal and Dobbin's worthiness. The novel's conclusion is one of muted happiness, with Thackeray's dual vision of sympathy and criticism firmly in place:

> Here it is—the summit, the end—the last page of the third volume. Good-bye, colonel—God bless you, honest William!—Farewell, dear Amelia—Grow green again, tender little parasite, round the rugged oak to which you cling! . . Ah! *Vanitas Vanitatum!* Which of us is happy in this world? Which of us has his desire? or, having it, is satisfied?—Come, children, let us shut up the box and puppets, for our play is played out.

Thus the showman of the fair closes the performance, having taken his characters from adolescence to maturity, from the Regency to the Victorian period, and having instructed his readers in the absorbing fascination of ordinary life. Thackeray's genius rests in his ability to create a new standard for the novel in which truth in all its complexity is predominant over make-believe.

CHINUA ACHEBE

1930–

Literature, whether handed down by word of mouth or in print, gives us a second handle on reality, enabling us to encounter in the safe manageable dimensions of make-believe the very same threats to integrity that may assail the psyche in real life; and at the same time proving through the self-discovery which it imparts, a veritable weapon for coping with these threats whether they are found within our problematic and incoherent selves or in the world around us. What better preparation can a people desire as they begin their journey into the strange, revolutionary world of modernization?

—Chinua Achebe, *Hopes and Impediments*

Nigerian writer Chinua Achebe has managed what only a handful of literary figures such as DANTE [2], CERVANTES [11], PUSHKIN [18], and GOETHE [10] have achieved: recognition as a progenitor of a national literature. However, in Achebe's case, it can be claimed that he is responsible for originating the modern literary history of an entire continent. From his first and greatest work, *Things Fall Apart* (1958), Achebe has pioneered the postcolonial African novel and initiated an indigenous imaginative repossession of the African past and cultural identity. *Things Fall Apart* has achieved canonical status as the most widely read and influential work by an African writer and an essential modern classic that provides an alternative to the Western ethnocentric distortions of African experience that Achebe found so inadequate. As Achebe reflected on his artistic mission, "I had to tell Europe that the arrogance on which she sought to excuse her pillage of Africa, i.e., that Africa was a Primordial Void, was sheer humbug; that Africa had a history, a religion, a civilization and displayed it to challenge the stereotype and the cliché. Actually it was not to Europe alone that I spoke. I spoke also to that part of ourselves that had come to accept Europe's opinion of us." In an ongoing act of creative repossession and assessment, Achebe, over a distinguished career, has given voice to a past and a people with an intellectual and artistic seriousness that refuses to idealize or simplify the legacy that has created a complex African identity and history. Achebe has been no less clear-eyed and critical of Africa's postcolonial experience. When he was awarded the Man Booker International Prize in 2007 for "contribution to fiction on the world stage," one of the judges, writer Nadine Gordimer praised Achebe as the "father of modern African literature as an integral part of world literature" for his early work. "He has gone on to achieve," Gordimer asserted, "what one of his characters brilliantly defines as the writer's purpose: 'a new-found utterance' for the capture of life's complexity. This fiction is an original synthesis of the psychological novel, the Joycean Stream of Consciousness, the postmodern breaking of sequence—thereby outdating any prescriptivity. A joy and an illumination to read."

Born in 1930 in the village of Ogidi in eastern Nigeria, Chinua Achebe was the son of one of his clan's first Christian converts and an Anglican church leader. Named Albert Chinualumogu Achebe, after Queen Victoria's consort, Achebe grew up balanced between the two conflicting worlds of traditional Ibo tribal life and the new European/Christian beliefs and values that he would chronicle in *Things Fall Apart*. "When I was growing up," Achebe has observed, "I remember we tended to look down on the others. We were called in our language 'the people of the church' or 'the association of God' . . . The others were called . . . the heathen or even 'the people of nothing.' . . . We lived at the crossroads of cultures. We still do today. . . . On one arm of the cross we sang hymns and read the Bible night and day. On the other my father's brother and his family, blinded by heathenism, offered food to idols. . . . What I do remember was a fascination for the ritual and the life on the other arm of the crossroads. And I believe two things were in my favour—that curiosity, and the little distance imposed between me and it by the accident of my birth." Educated first at a local mission school before attending a secondary school in Umuahia, Achebe was among the first group of students to attend the newly founded University College, Ibadan, administered by the University of London. Initially studying science and medicine, Achebe changed to literary studies and received his B.A. in English in 1953. He then went to work for the Nigerian Broadcasting Service as a broadcaster and producer for the next 12 years, while writing with "his left hand," determined to correct the picture of Africa by Western writers he had read as a student. As Achebe recalled the origin of his first novel that had begun to form in his mind while an undergraduate, "I was quite certain that I was going to try my hand at writing, and one of the things that set me thinking was Joyce Cary's novel set in Nigeria, *Mr. Johnson*, which was praised so much, and it was clear to me that this was a most superficial picture of—not only of the country, but even of the Nigerian character, and so I thought if this was famous, then perhaps someone ought to try and look at this from the inside." To counter the simplifications and distortions of the African experience and identity he found in writers like Joyce Cary, JOSEPH CONRAD [55], and Graham Greene, Achebe was determined to "teach my readers that their past—with all its imperfections—was not one long night of savagery from which the first Europeans acting on God's behalf delivered them." Central, therefore, to Achebe's intentions in *Things Fall Apart* is the restoration of an awareness of a rich, complex precolonial cultural history destroyed through the assimilation of Western beliefs and customs. Yet Achebe's assessment of the past resists a simplified nostalgia for a lost way of life that casts the Africans in the blameless victim's role and the Europeans as soulless victimizers. *Things Fall Apart* instead offers a searching analysis of the crucial encounter between two imperfect conflicting value systems, each with strengths and weaknesses that collectively form a destructive dynamic that creates the novel's tragedy. The first two-thirds of the novel details traditional Ibo life around the end of the 19th century before the arrival of Western missionaries and colonial administrators and taps into the rich poetry of Achebe's native vernacular language and customs, establishing a complex and coherent community that belies any suggestion of primitivism. The novel also presents the cracks both in its practices and values and in one of the society's strongest representatives who will contribute to its destruction by his inability to adapt to change. The novel's protagonist, Okonkwo, is a man of tremendous strength and pride whose refusal to compromise and adapt to the encroaching European influences leads him to murder and suicide. *Things Fall Apart* links the disintegration and destruction of an individual and his society, dramatizing the causes of both. Through Okonkwo's destruction, Achebe produces a compelling modern tragedy convincing both in its psychological penetration and cultural sophistication. Appearing two years before Nigerian independence during a period of national and cultural self-definition and assessment, *Things Fall Apart* became a foundation document for Nigerian and wider African understanding of its colonial past and postcolonial challenges. Eventually translated into 50 foreign languages, the novel has become one of the most read and influential modern novels worldwide, and Achebe has become the most translated African author of all time.

Continuing his examination of Nigerian history in his second novel, *No Longer at Ease* (1960), Achebe treats Okonkwo's grandson, Obi, in the 1950s in the period immediately preceding Nigerian independence. Educated in Britain and pursuing an affluent, modern lifestyle in Lagos, Obi, like his grandfather before him, struggles to reconcile his tribal heritage with the forces of change coming with self-rule. As critic Eustace Palmer argues, *No Longer at Ease* deals with the plight of a new Nigerian generation, "who, having been exposed to education in the western world and therefore largely cut off from their roots in traditional society, discover, on their return, that the demands of tradition are still strong, and are hopelessly caught in the clash between the old and the new." Adrift and untethered to sustaining values, Obi forsakes his former principles and succumbs to the growing corruption that he previously despised. Again, as in *Things Fall Apart*, Obi's personal dilemma becomes symptomatic of a wider cultural and national crisis connecting the African colonial past with its postcolonial prospects.

Achebe's third novel, *Arrow of Gold* (1964) looks at another Nigerian colonial generation during the 1920s. Its protagonist is a tribal priest, Ezeulu, who, like both Okonkwo before him and Obi after him, struggles to find a balance between the old and the new under the pressure of Western influences that undermine his society's foundations. A novel pitting the individual against the responsibilities of his community, *Arrow of Gold* is a rich exploration of power, belief, and the complex interplay among public, political, and religious motives. Achebe's fourth novel, *A Man of the People* (1966), set in an unnamed postindependent African country with clear resemblances to Nigeria, transfers the village power dynamic to a national level, exposing the limitations of leadership in the midst of corruption fueled by a material acquisitiveness unrestrained by traditional moral values. The title character, Chief Nanga, a senior government minister, and his political colleagues have created, a "fat-dripping, gummy, eat-and-let-eat regime," and the novel looks at its working from the perspective of Odili, a village schoolteacher, who finds himself swept up in and compromised by the corruption surrounding him.

The novel ends with an army coup that topples the corrupt political regime, anticipating the actual events that took place in Nigeria in the same month the novel was published when an Igbo army general seized control of the government in an anticorruption drive. Six months later a counter-coup plunged the country into a three-year civil war in which eastern Nigeria attempted and failed to establish the independent nation of Biafra. During the period, Achebe went on fund-raising missions to Europe and the United States on behalf of the Biafran cause. After the war ended in 1970, he became a visiting professor at universities in the United States before returning to Nigeria in 1976 to teach at the University of Nigeria in Nsukka. His publications during this period included *Beware, Soul Brother* (1971), a collection of poems, *Girls at War* (1972), a short story collection, and collections of essays, *Morning Yet on Creation Day* (1975) and *The Trouble with Nigeria* (1983). In 1987, after a 21-year break from writing long fiction, Achebe published *Anthills of the Savannah*. Set two years after the military has replaced the corrupt civilian regime in *A Man of the People*, the novel traces the careers of three childhood friends who gain influential government posts. When one fails in his bid to be named president for life, he precipitates a violent conflict that destroys all three. Again, Achebe is concerned with the ways in which power corrupts and the anarchy that is unloosed when a society forsakes its past and communal responsibility.

Paralyzed from the waist down in an automobile accident in Nigeria in 1990, Achebe continues to write, publishing the collection of essays, *Home and Exile*, in 2000. Over a distinguished career Chinua Achebe has allowed non-African access into the complex dynamic of a colonial African past and postcolonial present, forever altering assumptions about African identity while challenging Africans and non-Africans to a greater understanding of the complex interaction between history, culture, politics, and the individual.

CHIKAMATSU MONZAEMON

96

1653–1725

Chikamatsu's plays offer . . . a vivid picture of a unique age in Japan, and have a special importance among the dramas of the world in that they constitute the first mature tragedies written about the common man.

—Donald Keene, introduction to *Major Plays of Chikamatsu*

Japan's greatest dramatist, Chikamatsu Monzaemon, is the author of the first plays of lasting value for both the Kabuki and Bunraku (puppet) theaters. Commonly referred to as the Shakespeare of Japan, Chikamatsu, like SHAKE-SPEARE [1], with consummate dramatic and poetic skill, raised the stature of a disreputable popular art form to an expressive and serious medium for the exploration of great psychological and social truths. It can be argued that the two figures who exerted the greatest influence on the development of Japanese drama were ZEAMI MOTOKIYO [101] in the medieval Noh theater and Chikamatsu who introduced the world of ordinary experience as a subject for Japanese dramatic art. As literary historian Donald Keene has observed, Chikamatsu "created a new genre of Japanese theater, the *sewamono*, or plays about contemporary life. The Noh plays invariably dealt with the distant past, and Kabuki plays that in fact treated recent events always masked them by pretending that the story was set in the world of some centuries earlier. . . . [Chikamatsu] seems to have been insisting that tragedy was possible even in such peaceful, humdrum times, and he emphasizes his point by choosing quite ordinary people for the heroes and heroines of various plays." Like Lady MURASAKI [12] whose 11th-century narrative masterpiece, *The Tale of Genji*, anticipates the realistic development of the novel by nearly 800 years, Chikamatsu's dramas are the earliest example of a realistic middle-class drama that would not appear in the West for another 150 years. None of Shakespeare's tragic heroes resemble in social rank or background the majority of his audience. Lower- and middle-class individuals were fine for comedy, but tragedy, as Aristotle maintained, depended on individuals of high rank. Chikamatsu would alter that restriction by exploring characters from the lower orders—merchants, clerks, and prostitutes—engaged in ordinary activities, and gaining for them through his great artistry an unprecedented tragic dignity. What makes his achievement even more remarkable is that the realism that Chikamatsu pioneered was performed in Japan's puppet theater.

Born Sugimori Nobumori in 1653, it is believed, in the province of Echizen, Chikamatsu was a member of a samurai family who came to live in Kyoto after his father, for reasons unknown, lost his position as a retainer of the daimyo (feudal lord) of Echizen and became a *ronin*, or masterless samurai. Facts about his youth are scanty, but from the evidence of his plays, his familiarity with Chinese philosophical writings and Japanese Buddhist texts suggests he received a good education, possibly by priests at the temple from which he took his pseudonym, Chikamatsu. In an autobiographical account written shortly before his death, Chikamatsu summarized his development: "I was born into a hereditary family of samurai but left the martial profession. I served in personal attendance on the nobility but never obtained the least court rank. I drifted in the marketplace but learned nothing of trade." Chikamatsu's failures would be compensated by a breadth of experience, taking in 17th-century Japan's three major, nonpeasant social ranks—samurai, nobility, and merchants. It was likely during Chikamatsu's service as a page among the nobility who would have patronized the dramatic arts that Chikamatsu had his initial exposure to the new theater that was flourishing in 17th-century Japan. Chikamatsu would pursue a theatrical career during the second great flowering of Japanese drama following the development of Noh in the 15th century that produced the other enduring Japanese dramatic forms—the puppet theater (later called Bunraku) and Kabuki.

The first mention of puppetry in Japan dates from the eighth century, and throughout the Heian period (794–1185) puppet performers traveled the country with their "stage," a rectangular box open at the front, carried on their backs. In the 17th century, a new dramatic art form evolved from the fusion of puppetry with the recitation of storytellers, accompanied by music. The popularity of the puppet theater, called *jōruri* after the term used to designate the narrator or chanter, coincided during the 17th century with the rise of Kabuki. A woman dancer named Okuni is credited with performing the first Japanese plays of contemporary urban life, brief playlets interspersed by singing and dance that developed into multiscene narrative plays of Kabuki in which elements of Noh drama were adapted for a wider, socially diverse audience, serving less a religious function than a secular one. The great popularity of the new dramatic forms stemmed from their contemporary relevance, initiating a realistic element in Japanese drama that reflected Japan's emerging class of merchants, traders, and artisans. In Western terms, Noh drama corresponds to the medieval miracle and morality plays, while Kabuki and the puppet theater resemble Elizabethan drama's wider interest in actuality.

Chikamatsu's career as a dramatist began in 1683, at the age of 30, when he wrote the puppet play, *The Soga Successors*, which was selected by Takemoto Gidayū (1651–1714), the period's most celebrated chanter of the puppet theater, to open his new theater in Osaka in 1684. The chanter functioned as a narrator and commentator on the action who also provided speech for the puppets. The puppets in Chikamatsu's day were each operated by one man who remained visible to the spectators. A successful performance relied on an ideal balance of three elements—the play's text delivered by the chanter, the musical accompaniment, and the puppets. Chikamatsu's first major play was the heroic drama, *Kagekiyo Victorious* (1684), which, due to its superior dramatic construction, expressive language, and considerable literary merits unprecedented in the puppet theater up to that point, is regarded by scholar Donald Keene as "so important a work that it is considered the first 'new' puppet play." Despite Chikamatsu's notoriety as a playwright for the puppet theater, between 1684 and 1695 he also produced many Kabuki plays, mainly for Sakata Tōjūrō, the leading actor of the day, a collaboration that was so successful that for the next decade (1695–1705) Chikamatsu wrote mainly for Kabuki. When Sakata Tōjūrō retired from the stage in 1705, Chikamatsu returned exclusively to the puppet theater until his death in 1725. Various conjectures have been advanced to explain his decision to devote his artistic maturity to the puppet theater. He may have been convinced that no actor of comparable skills would follow Sakata Tōjūrō or he may have grown frustrated by the Kabuki "star" system that privileged the actor over a play's text. His decision, however it was reached, presented the playwright with an enormous challenge, particularly one like Chikamatsu whose plays show an ambition to display a full range of complex human emotions and situations. Live actors have the ability to alter expressions and show change and development; puppets come in types—hero, villain, and clown—with their identities firmly set in wood.

Chikamatsu's approximately 130 plays fall into two general categories: historical plays and domestic dramas. He began his dramatic career writing plays on historical themes, adapted from various chronicles or from Noh plays. His works served to instruct the emerging merchant class who patronized the puppet and Kabuki theaters in Osaka on the events of Japan's past, as Shakespeare's history plays made the English past understandable to Elizabethan audiences.

His most popular historical play is *The Battles of Coxinga*, first performed in 1715. It concerns the exploits of a semilegendary hero who participated in the battles surrounding the fall of China's Ming dynasty. Chikamatsu presents a series of exciting vignettes from Coxinga's career, mixing nationalistic, sensational, and poetic elements that insured theatrical success. Often bombastic in style with larger-than-life characters and extraordinary incidents, Chikamatsu's history plays balance the elevated with the recognizably human. Asserting his intention in an interview that was published after his death, Chikamatsu declared "Art is something which lies in the slender margin between the real and the unreal . . . and entertainment lies between the two."

In his domestic plays, Chikamatsu would create a sensation by locating his drama not in the heroic past but in the familiar milieu of his audience. In 1703, the actual suicides in Osaka of Tokubei, a shop assistant, and Ohatsu, a prostitute, had generated a considerable scandal, and the incident inspired Chikamatsu's groundbreaking play, *The Love Suicides at Sonezaki*, the first of his domestic plays. The actual deaths were generally regarded as sordid and far from edifying, with one account sternly condemning the lovers for having "polluted the woods of Sonezaki." Chikamatsu's play explores what motivated these lovers' deaths, devising a set of believable social circumstances with which the lovers must contend. Chikamatsu set out to elevate their actions to the level of the tragic, ennobling the lovers by the strength and purity of their commitment to one another. The audience extends its sympathy for the lovers even though Tokubei, in marked contrast to any previous conventional stage hero, is a lowly young clerk "with the firm of Hirano," trading in soy sauce. "Chikamatsu created in Tokubei," critic Donald Keene has asserted, "a hero of a kind not found in Western drama before the 20th century." Rather than a paragon of virtue or strength, Tokubei is a mixed character, initially characterized by his gullibility and only eventually rising to the tragic occasion. Pressed by realistic circumstances involving money that cannot be repaid and intractable family obligations, suicide becomes the lovers' only option. The growing sympathy that the audience feels for Tokubei and Ohatsu is enhanced by Chikamatsu masterfully exploiting the conventions of the puppet theater by having the lovers journey to the place where they are to die narrated with exquisite lyricism:

> Farewell to this world, and to the night farewell.
> We who walk the road to death, to what should we be likened?
> To the frost by the road that leads to the graveyard,
> Vanishing with each step we take ahead:
> How sad is this dream of a dream!

After Tokubei confesses his sins and Ohatsu bids farewell to her family, she begs him to "kill me quickly!" Then in excruciatingly realistic detail, the narrator relates how Tokubei "tries to steady his weakening resolve, but still he trembles, and when he thrusts, the point misses. Twice or thrice the flashing blade deflects this way and that until a cry tells it has struck her throat." Determined to "draw our last breaths together," Tokubei kills himself, and the play concludes with the narrator's elegy:

> No one is there to tell the tale, but the wind that blows through Sonezaki Wood transmits it, and high and low alike gather to pray for these lovers who beyond a doubt will in the future attain Buddhahood. They have become models of true love.

The Love Suicides at Sonezaki created a popular sensation and a vogue. Chikamatsu would follow it with several other love-suicide plays, including *The Love Suicides at Amijima*, written in 1721. Again, Chikamatsu features an ordinary protagonist, an owner of a stationery shop in Osaka, torn between his wife and his courtesan lover. The play's emotional intensity and brilliant characterization have caused some to consider *The Love Suicides at Amijima* the greatest single work written for the traditional Japanese stage. The poetic immediacy and dramatic impact of Chikamatsu's domestic dramas featuring double suicides in a contemporary, recognizable setting prompted imitations on stage and in life. The genre became so popular (and tempting) that the authorities considered it a social threat, banning all plays with the word *shin* (suicide) in the title. Such a reaction is a testimony to the power and persuasiveness of the theatrical experience that Chikamatsu pioneered. It can be argued that modern Japanese literature begins with the psychological and social realities that Chikamatsu first explored on stage.

RALPH ELLISON

97

1914–1994

No one has made more unrelenting statements of the dehumanizing pressures that have been put upon the Negro. And Invisible Man *is, I should say, the most powerful artistic representation we have of the Negro under these dehumanizing conditions; and at the same time, a statement of the human triumph over those conditions.*
                    —Robert Penn Warren, "The Unity of Experience"

Ralph Ellison, author of only one completed novel, is still a seminal literary figure in the second half of the 20th century. Through his mastery of European modernist techniques joined to the American folk tradition, Ellison captured in *Invisible Man* the black experience in ways that refused reduction to the narrowly sociological minority perspective, and instead created in the theme of race in America a centrally important human myth that continues to assert its power. Throughout his career, Ellison resisted the marginalization of his voice to that of protest or victimization, and wrote a novel that has earned him comparison with such writers as DOSTOEVSKY [14], JOYCE [7], and FAULKNER [15]. Ellison's influence on African-American and white writers has been profound. His nameless protagonist has become the prototype for characters in a host of novels by such writers as Joseph Heller, Ken Kesey, Kurt Vonnegut, and Thomas Pynchon, while Ellison's writing about American democracy and the role of the literary artist has set the context for the debate over this important topic, which continues among critics and writers alike. Very much the pioneer (perhaps as a result of his southwestern background) Ralph Ellison celebrates American possibilities and promises delivered and broken, opening up new territory for the imagination.

Ralph Waldo Ellison was born in Oklahoma City, where his parents, originally from the South, had settled. All four of Ellison's grandparents had been slaves, and Oklahoma, which had no tradition of slavery, offered the possibility of a better, less segregated life. As Ellison observed, in Oklahoma "there was a sense that you had to determine your own fate, and that you had a chance to do it." His father died when Ellison was three, and his mother supported her two sons by working as a domestic servant. Encouraged by his mother and other teachers, Ellison read voraciously—especially frontier literature, English classics, and the writers of the Harlem Renaissance. He also absorbed the area's rich oral tradition. His first artistic expression, however, was in music. Ellison received private lessons in trumpet and symphonic composition from the conductor of the Oklahoma City Orchestra in exchange for cutting the conductor's lawn. Ellison also was strongly influenced by the Oklahoma City jazz scene. In 1933, he won a scholarship to attend Tuskegee Institute, in Tuskegee, Alabama, to study music, and reached the school by riding as a hobo on freight trains. In school, working part time in the college library, Ellison first read modernist writers such as James Joyce, GERTRUDE STEIN [125], and ERNEST HEMINGWAY [63] and was greatly impressed by T. S. ELIOT's [19] *The Waste Land*. Ellison recalled being "moved and intrigued" by the poem and wondered "why I had never read anything of equal intensity and sensibility by an American Negro writer." After three years at Tuskegee, Ellison left for New York City to earn money for his senior year and also to study sculpture. He would stay there for most of the rest of his life.

On Ellison's first day in New York he met by accident the poet Langston Hughes, who introduced Ellison to RICHARD WRIGHT [111]. Wright became an important friend and mentor who encouraged Ellison's writing. During his long literary apprenticeship, Ellison supported himself by working as a waiter, barman, and freelance photographer. When his mother died in 1937, he attended her funeral in Dayton, Ohio, staying on with his brother to shoot quail and sell them to General Motors officials to support themselves. Back in New York, Ellison began to write book reviews for Wright's *New Challenge*, and his first short story, based on his hoboing experiences, was accepted by the magazine, but it folded before the story was published. The experience, however, had convinced Ellison to give up music for writing. From 1938 to 1942 he worked for the Federal Writers Project, collecting an oral history of the black experience in New York through dozens of interviews. After unsuccessfully trying to enlist in the U.S. Navy band, Ellison served in the merchant marine as a cook until 1945, working on his writing during voyages and layovers.

After meeting his future wife, whom he would marry in 1946, and while working on a novel involving a black American pilot in a prison camp, Ellison went to a friend's Vermont farm to recover from a kidney infection. As he later recalled, "creatures from Afro-American fables—Jack-the-Rabbit and Jack-the-Bear—blended in my mind with figures of myth and history." While "images of incest and murder, dissolution and rebirth whirled in my head," Ellison sat at a typewriter and suddenly typed, "I am an invisible man," the words that became the first sentence of his masterpiece, "and I gasped at the range of implication." The novel would take Ellison seven years to complete. When it appeared in 1952, *Invisible Man* was acclaimed by one reviewer as "one of the best novels yet written by an American Negro . . . concerned with themes which are . . . universal rather than racial," though some critics attacked its obscurity and its "vicious distortion of Negro life." Despite these criticisms, the novel quickly was regarded as a literary classic of the first magnitude.

Ellison's life after *Invisible Man* was a series of academic appointments with essays and excerpts from his long-awaited second novel occasionally appearing. The essays have been collected in *Shadow and Act* (1964) and *Going to the Territory* (1986). His second novel, monumental in length and already heavily freighted with its own legend, including the accidental burning of a large section of the manuscript in a Berkshire house fire, remained unfinished at the time of his death. John F. Callahan, the executor of Ellison's literary estate has arranged for publication Ellison's *Collected Essays* (1995) and a collection of short stories, *Flying Home and Other Stories* (1995). In 1999, a version of Ellison's long-anticipated second novel was published with Callahan's supplied title, *Juneteenth*, a reference to the date celebrating the Emancipation. The book, a composite of fragments arranged by Callahan into a narrative that Ellison never finally resolved, is an often brilliant series of imagined scenes in the life of a white-skinned boy named Bliss who is raised by a black preacher, Alonzo Hickman. Bliss has turned away from the culture that formed him to become a racist United States senator named Adam Sunraider. Shot by an assassin on the Senate floor, Sunraider—in the hospital, in the company of Hickman—revisits his past. Although by necessity only a collection of brilliant parts, *Juneteenth* provides convincing testimony of Ellison's power to create remarkable scenes and characters while confronting America's rich and troubling collective racial identity and heritage.

At New York University during the 1970s, Ellison used the course he taught, Literature and Democracy, as the occasion for extended riffs on subjects ranging from TWAIN [45], Hemingway, and Faulkner, to jazz composition, and the best method for getting on and off a slow-moving freight train. All discussions circled back to essential notions of what it meant to be American and how the complexity and contradictions of American life could best be captured in art. He rarely spoke of his own work. In 1980, when his appointment as the Albert Schweitzer Professor of Humanities ended, he responded to a question about what he would be doing next. "Writing," he said. "After all, I'm supposed to be a novelist."

It may well be that additional posthumous material will add additional luster to Ellison's considerable stature as a great writer of an American classic. Remarkable in a novel so sharply drawn out of Ellison's own experiences and the historical moment, little about *Invisible Man* seems dated, now almost 50 years after its publication. From his underground cellar illuminated by 1,369 lightbulbs to assure his visibility, Ellison's unnamed narrator recounts his adventures as a black man in America. From his high school graduation, in which he is blindfolded and forced to fight in a boxing ring before delivering his valedictory address on humility, the Invisible Man endures external definitions and attempts to co-opt him—at school, then by the political Brotherhood, and finally by black nationalists. Betrayed by all in scenes of surrealistic brilliance, he eventually retreats into the illumination of self-knowledge. His experiences produce limited victories but are fundamentally liberating. This defines Ellison's strategy as a writer: he confronts at the deepest level the complexity of experience, and by naming it, masters it. As Ellison states through his nameless protagonist at the end of his remarkable American odyssey, "Who knows but that, on the lower frequencies, I speak for you?"

98

JORGE LUIS BORGES

1899–1986

And which is Borges, which his double? . . . there is the Borges who plays with the notion that all our works are products of the same universal Will so that one author impersonally authors everything (thus the labors of that provincial librarian are not in vain), and the Borges whose particular mark is both idiosyncratic and indelible. The political skeptic and the fierce opponent of Perón: are they the same man? . . . Is this impish dilettante the same man who leaves us so uneasily amazed?

—William H. Gass, "Imaginary Borges and His Books,"
in *Fiction and the Figures of Life*

Jorge Luis Borges's identifying image is the labyrinth. His fictions are puzzles that are both playful and disorienting. Another image associated with Borges is the mirror, in which his words reflect both the world and themselves as the imagination becomes lost and liberated in its own self-conjuring. Borges the fabulist sparked a radical redefinition of fiction's means and ends, and he is, along with KAFKA [31], one of the 20th century's supreme ironists. The first internationally prominent Latin American writer, Borges's influence is evident in the subsequent flowering of Latin American "magical realism" and the rise to world prominence of the second generation of Latin American artists, including GABRIEL GARCÍA MÁRQUEZ [76], José Donoso, Julio Cortázar, Carlos Fuentes, and Mario Vargas Llosa. Beyond Latin America, Borges influenced the French new novelists, such as Alain Robbe-Grillet, Marguerite Duras, and Michel Butor, as well as the post–World War II American generation of anti-realists, such as John Barth, John Hawkes, and Donald Barthelme. Borges's world of experience and the imagination is no less problematic or terrifying than that of SAMUEL BECKETT [47], but Borges's fictional world is filled with an amazing display of metaphysical juggling and magical illusions. At their core, his stories force the reader to radically reconceptualize fiction, the imagination, and experience.

Two other settings—the garden and the library—dominate the Borgesian landscape. Both are reflections of Borges's background and biography. Born in Buenos Aires, Argentina, Borges was the son of a distinguished but not wealthy family who could trace its origins to the conquistadores. Of his childhood, he observed, "For years I believed I had been brought up in a suburb of Buenos Aires, a suburb of dangerous streets and conspicuous sunsets. What is certain is that I was brought up in a garden, behind lanceolate iron railings, and in a library of unlimited English books." Borges's father was half English, a lawyer and a man of letters whose literary example and library introduced his son to the world of literature. "If I were asked to name the chief event in my life," Borges later recalled, "I should say my father's library. In fact, sometimes I think I have never strayed outside that library." Borges, who mastered English before Spanish, learned from his father "the power of poetry . . . the fact that words are not only a means of communication but also magic symbols and music."

His father's deteriorating eyesight made further legal work impossible, so the family planned to spend an extended period in Europe, sightseeing and seeking treatment for his father's condition. "We were so ignorant about universal history," Borges recalled, "and especially about the immediate future, that we traveled in 1914 and got stuck in Switzerland." For the duration of World War I, Borges attended a French school, and after the war the family moved to Spain. There Borges associated with a group of experimental poets, the ultraists, a variant of the French symbolists and imagists. In 1921, when the family returned to Argentina, Borges headed an Argentinean ultraist group and acquired a reputation as a leading avant-garde poet and essayist.

In 1937, when his father's declining health forced his son to secure a permanent job, Borges gained through friends a position at a municipal library in Buenos Aires. He spent his time cataloging the library's collection, but his colleagues discouraged him from too much effort, feeling it would expose their incompetence and the redundancy of their labor. Borges found the work and surroundings dreary and the company contemptible. "Ironically," he remembered, "at the time I was a quite well-known writer—except at the library. I remember a fellow employee's once noting in an encyclopedia the name of a certain Jorge Luis Borges—a fact that set him wondering at the coincidence of our identical names and birthdates."

During the 1930s, Borges moved away from poetry and his earlier avant-garde style and began to experiment with combining two previously separate literary genres, the essay and fiction. His first collection, *A Universal History of Infamy*, (1935) contained brief biographical sketches that incorporated features of short fiction. In 1938, Borges suffered a head injury and blood poisoning from an accident on a poorly lit stairway. To counteract his fear that he had lost his capacity for reasoned and lucid argument, he began the story "Pierre Menard, Author of *Don Quixote*," his first mature achievement in his new elliptical, metaphysical style. Borges imagined a literary artist who sets himself the impossible goal of composing a perfect replica of CERVANTES's [11] masterpiece. Menard succeeds in writing a few chapters in which the scholarly narrator deciphers a completely different meaning in the identical texts, with Menard's "almost infinitely richer." Paradox and absurdity residing in the imagination and the systems of language and literature would become hallmarks of Borges's subsequent work. In 1941, his first collection of short stories, *The Garden of Forking Paths*, appeared. Borges's biographer, Emir Rodriguez Monegal, called it "perhaps the single most important book of prose fiction written in Spanish in this century." *Ficciones* followed in 1944, adding six new stories to the earlier collection, and became the author's most significant book. Later collections include *The Aleph* (1949), *Other Inquisitions* (1952), *The Book of Imaginary Beings* (1957), *Dr. Brodie's Report* (1970), and *The Book of Sand* (1975).

Borges's opposition to the military dictatorship of Juan Perón in the early 1940s resulted in the loss of his librarian's post and a humiliating offer of a government job as chicken inspector, which he immediately declined. With Perón's fall in 1955, Borges regained a prominent place in his country's intellectual life as the director of the national library, a member of the Argentine Academy of Letters, and a professor of English literature at the University of Buenos Aires. By the mid-1950s, his deteriorating eyesight, the same congenital condition that afflicted his father, resulted in near total blindness. He lived in the company of his widowed mother, who read to him and assisted in his literary work. Borges married for the first time at the age of 68, to a childhood sweetheart whom he divorced three years later. A few weeks before his death, he married his secretary and former student. Despite his blindness, Borges traveled the world to lecture and sustained a growing international reputation as one of the century's most influential literary voices.

Borges's achievement rests on his ability to replace a narrow verisimilitude in fiction, constrained by consistency and probability, with a wider realm that incorporates mind play and fantasy. The inconceivable is given shape in Borges's imagination. Readily accepting the artifice of the storyteller, Borges achieves a continual double focus, reflecting experience as well as the paradoxes that emerge from reflecting the world in language and reading. Eschewing the novel for the compact form of short fiction, Borges explained:

The composition of vast books is a laborious and impoverishing extravagance. To go on for five hundred pages developing an idea whose perfect oral exposition is possible in a few minutes! A better course of procedure is to pretend that these books already exist, and then to offer a résumé, a commentary. . . . I have preferred to write notes upon imaginary books.

Borges's commentary examines the absurd from a variety of perspectives, including the distrust of language as a means of depicting reality, the inadequacy of reason to comprehend the universe, and the failure of moral and philosophical systems to provide meaning. Many of his stories take the form of quests for knowledge or salvation that are frustrated by his skepticism and characteristic method of elaborating an idea to its logical extreme. Borges's fiction is ultimately liberating in its expression of the imagination's resources. Liberating as well is Borges's transcendence of fictional realism through fantasy, one of the defining conditions of literary fiction in the second half of the 20th century, and one that Borges helped initiate.

99

ALBERT CAMUS

1913–1960

His obstinate humanism, narrow and pure, austere and sensual, waged an uncertain war against the massive and formless events of the time. But on the other hand through his dogged rejections he reaffirmed, at the heart of our epoch, against the Machiavellians and against the Idol of realism, the existence of the moral issue.

—Jean-Paul Sartre, "Tribute to Albert Camus"

Albert Camus intellectually and artistically dominated the post–World War II period in literature. In a career foreshortened by his death in an automobile accident at the age of 46, Camus became the most influential French voice worldwide since VOLTAIRE [69]. Like BECKETT [47], Camus diagnosed an absurd world, but only Camus managed to develop an affirming response of reengagement based on the acceptance of existential meaninglessness. His intellectual vigor and stylistic brilliance are evident in his novels, short stories, essays, and plays; these works are intimately connected to his philosophical quest, but are not simply vehicles for his ideas. All of Camus's works have a sensuous and experiential quality that combines thought and feeling into significant artistic forms.

The uniqueness of Camus's thinking and expression derives from his background and an intimate acquaintance with human suffering. He was born in Mondavi, Algeria. His father was killed in the first battle of the Marne in

1914, when Camus was one year old. His deaf mother supported her family as a housecleaner, bringing up her family in a tiny apartment in the working-class section of Algiers. In his first book, *Betwixt and Between*, a collection of childhood reminiscences and travel sketches, Camus recalls his childhood:

> I think of a child who lived in that poor section, that section, that house. There were only two floors and the stairs weren't lighted. Even now, after many long years, he could find his way there in complete darkness. . . . His body is impregnated with that house. His legs preserve the exact measure of the height of the steps. His hand the instinctive, never vanquished horror of the banisters. Because of the roaches.

Camus won a scholarship to a good high school, but his studies and hopes for an academic career were interrupted by an attack of tuberculosis, the illness that would recur throughout his life. He held a variety of jobs in Algiers in the 1930s, read widely, and acted and wrote for an amateur theatrical company that he founded, the Workers' Theater. In 1938, Camus became a reporter for the *Alger Républicain*. His first literary works show the recurrent themes that dominate his writing in the pathos between the sensuous joy derived from the North African landscape and man's essential isolation and loneliness.

In 1942, Camus left Algiers for Paris, where he joined the French resistance and helped edit the underground journal *Combat*. During the war, Camus formed a friendship with Jean-Paul Sartre and published his most influential books, *The Stranger* and *The Myth of Sisyphus*, and the play *Caligula*, which collectively defined existentialist philosophy and dominated postwar thinking.

From its deadpan opening line, "Mother died today," *The Stranger* creates a modern landscape of absurdity. Meursault, the narrator and the archetype for the modern antihero, is governed by sensation alone and displays no feelings at the death of his mother. His detachment and nonconformity eventually lead to his death. In the company of his friend Raymond, Meursault encounters two Arabs on a beach who are in pursuit of Raymond. When his friend puts a revolver in his hand, Meursault kills one of the pursuers, motivated more by the heat and the sun's glare than his friend's plight. At his trial, Meursault is judged less for his crime than for his alienation and refusal to conform to society's rules—"an inhuman monster wholly without moral sense." Sentenced to death, Meursault in his final hours tries to understand his relationship to the world that has condemned him. He gradually realizes the inherent absurdity of his situation and the ultimate truth of the human condition in the "benign indifference of the universe." This knowledge provides a form of liberation that allows Meursault to face his death and accept his fate.

The Myth of Sisyphus is a lengthy essay that distills many of the existential themes of *The Stranger*. The absurd is represented by the connection between the human condition and the plight of Sisyphus, condemned in Hades to push a stone up a mountain for eternity. By accepting his fate and the essential meaninglessness of his labor, Sisyphus manages a kind of triumph. Camus asserts, "The struggle itself toward the heights is enough to fill a man's heart. One must imagine Sisyphus happy." For Camus, man's dignity and heroism begin with fully confronting the world's indifference and hostility and still persisting in the face of overwhelming obstacles.

Caligula, generally regarded as Camus's greatest play, reimagines the infamous Roman emperor as an actor whose life is a masquerade and whose cruelty becomes a form of self-definition. If life is without meaning, as Caligula realizes, then power is unbounded by any controls or limits. Caligula's madness and self-destruction, however, result not from his challenge to the cosmos but from his crimes against mankind. "If his truth is the denial of the gods," Camus writes, "his error is the denial of men. He has not understood that you cannot destroy everything without destroying yourself." For Camus, realization of the universe's meaninglessness marks the beginning of morality and man's duty, not their end.

Camus's later works further develop the existential and moral themes of these three central works. His other plays are *The Misunderstanding* (1944). *The State of Siege* (1948), and *The Just Assassins* (1950). His essay "The Rebel" (1951), which outlines an ethical rather than political rebellion, prompted his split from Sartre, who adhered to a more ideological stance in the existential dilemma that both writers popularized internationally. Camus's novel *The Plague* (1947), concerning the effects of an epidemic in the North African city of Oran, shows a shift of emphasis from the fate of the individual to that of the community. As the disease advances, the city is closed to the outside world and gripped by a sense of exile and isolation. The tragedy, however, forces a growing interdependence and solidarity among the inhabitants. Doing one's job becomes the way to meet the challenge of absurd extinction, and Camus describes resistance to the forces that destroy happiness and value as the means for triumphing over suffering and death.

Camus's philosophy, derived from his own experience with suffering and absurdity, embraced a solution to man's predicament based on a hard-fought struggle to reach meaning. Camus regarded his happiest times as those spent working on a newspaper and acting and directing in the theater, both collective activities and antidotes to man's isolation and loneliness. The ultimate irony of Camus's life is the absurdity of his death in a traffic accident. The works that he left are some of literature's strongest and most artistic confrontations with such senseless events and their existential implications.

LUIGI PIRANDELLO

100

1867–1936

Pirandello's plays grew from his own torment . . . but through his genius they come to speak for the tormented and, potentially, to all the tormented, that is, to all men. And they will speak with particular immediacy until the present crisis of mankind—a crisis which trembles, feverishly or ever so gently, through all his plays—is past.
   —Eric Bentley, introduction to *Naked Masks: Five Plays by Luigi Pirandello*

Luigi Pirandello, the greatest Italian playwright of the 20th century, is deservedly ranked among such great modernist innovators as FRANZ KAFKA [31], MARCEL PROUST [16], JAMES JOYCE [7], ROBERT MUSIL [79], and VIRGINIA WOOLF [48] who pioneered new forms and a radical shift of focus for modern literature. As important in the development of modern drama as James Joyce is to modern fiction and T. S. ELIOT [19] is to modern poetry, Pirandello renewed the philosophical dimension of drama with disturbing uncertainties and discontinuities that undermine fundamental concepts of identity and reality. Among 20th-century dramatists, only BERTOLT BRECHT [73] and SAMUEL BECKETT [47] are his rivals in influence, and Pirandello's imprint in both form and content are unmistakable in the works of both playwrights, as well as in the drama of Eugene Ionesco, Jean Anouilh, Jean Genet, Jean-Paul Sartre, EUGENE O'NEILL [59], HAROLD PINTER [115], Tom Stoppard, Edward Albee, and many more. Pirandello, who called his plays "naked masks" for a "theater of mirrors," challenged the realistic and naturalistic drama pioneered by IBSEN [36] and STRINDBERG [56], exposing the conventions of the stage as metaphors to test basic assumptions of existence and knowledge. Dissolving the barrier dividing playwright, player, and audience, Pirandello revolutionized European stage practice that has liberated and problematized drama and, by extension, modern art and philosophy ever since. British playwright Tom Stoppard has asserted the "impossibility" of any contemporary Western playwright producing "a play that is totally unlike Beckett, Pirandello, [or] Kafka." Rejecting a drama of entertaining diversion, Pirandello directs his audience's attention to the psychological reality beneath the masks of social appearance and to the theatricality of behavior. By doing so, Pirandello challenges accepted distinctions between art and life, reality and illusion, sanity and madness. *Pirandellismo* or "Pirandellism" has come to stand for the application of Macbeth's assertion that "all the world is a stage." Offering a self-reflective double focus, Pirandello's stage becomes an embodiment of Einstein's theory of relativity, a demonstration of the concept that certainties are delusions and what we see and understand depends on a point of view that is often unreliable. If Einstein assaulted our construct of time and space, Pirandello has done something quite similar to our understanding of identity and reality, to our awareness of the gap between being and seeming.

Luigi Pirandello was born in Girgenti, Sicily, in 1867. His father was a wealthy owner of a sulfur-mining business. "I am the son of Chaos," Pirandello wrote, "and not allegorically but literally, because I was born in a country spot called by the people around *Cávusu*, a dialectal corruption of the authentic Greek word *Xáos*." Expected to enter the family firm, Pirandello was appalled by the conditions in the mines in which men were "turned into animals by the mean, ferocious fight for gain" and chose instead academic and artistic pursuits. Producing his first play with siblings and friends at the age of 12, Pirandello attended universities in Palermo, Rome, and finally Bonn, where he earned a doctorate in linguistics with a dissertation on the dialect of his hometown. Settling in Rome to establish himself as a literary figure, Pirandello agreed in 1894 to an arranged marriage to Antonietta Portulano, the daughter of one of his father's business associates. To support his wife and three children, Pirandello became a literature teacher at a woman's college where he worked for 24 years. Having produced short stories, poems, novels, essays, and several plays that he was unable to get produced, Pirandello achieved his first major success with *Il fu Mattia Pascal* (The Late Mattia Pascal). The novel dramatizes what happens when the title character is mistakenly reported as dead and he, a failure in life, decides to remain so, giving him the opportunity of creating a new identity, freed from previous constraints and liabilities. Anticipated freedom and autonomy, however, elude him, and the novel considers the themes of the problematic nature of identity and the self's dependency on others to provide shape and meaning, themes that Pirandello would continue to explore in his subsequent fiction and plays. His literary success was overshadowed by the failure of his father's mining business in a flood. Pirandello's fortune and his wife's dowry were lost, and the resulting stress and anxiety led to Antonietta's mental collapse that manifested itself in worsening fits of compulsive jealousy and delusions. Enduring constant accusations and abuse from his mentally unstable wife, Pirandello refused to have her committed until 1919, finding refuge in his study and his writing that reflected his tormented domestic life and his fascination, prompted by his wife's condition, with the conflict between truth and illusion and the borderline between sanity and insanity.

His early writing was strongly influenced by the Italian naturalist movement that advocated a truthful reflection of reality. Pirandello, however, came to believe that truth could neither be apprehended objectively nor scientifically, and that reality itself was a problematic concept. Experience, in Pirandello's developing view, is chaotic, in constant flux, in which individuals impose ideas, concepts, and systems of beliefs to make sense of it. Identity itself is not intrinsic but multiple, constructed out of the roles and conditions circumstances impose on individuals. Pirandello's evolving aesthetic principles are outlined in the important essay *L'umorismo* (On Humor), published in 1908. In his theory of humorism, which serves as a key to his art, the comic writer exploits the opposition between appearance and reality. Comedy derives from the perception of this opposition, which leads both to a compassionate understanding of a character's fictive situation and a deeper insight into actuality. Pirandello's art is at its core epistemological, concerned with the problem of knowing and the embodiment of crucial philosophical ideas in a compelling human drama. "My works are born from live images which are the perennial source of art," Pirandello insisted, "but these images pass through a veil of concepts which have taken hold of me. My works of art are never concepts trying to express themselves through images. On the contrary. They are images, often very vivid images of life, which, fostered by the labors of my mind, assume universal significance quite on their own, through the formal unity of art."

By the outbreak of World War I, Pirandello had established his reputation as a narrative master. During the war years he would increasingly devote himself to playwriting. "My taste for the narrative form had vanished," Pirandello recalled. "I could no longer limit myself to story telling, while there was action all around me . . . The words would not remain on the written page: they had to explode into the air, to be spoken or cried out." Pirandello asserted that "the war had revealed the theater" to him. "When passions were let loose, I had my characters suffer those passions onstage." His plays reflected the crisis of confidence produced by the war, dramatizing the breakdown of absolutes and collapse of coherence. In 1917 Pirandello completed *Così è (se vi pare)* translated as *Right You Are (If You Think So)*, the first of his theatrical considerations of relativity. The play concerns a community's attempt to learn the truth surrounding a family's relationships and behavior, complicated by the assertions by the husband and the mother-in-law that each is mad and cannot be believed. Circumstances frustrate all certainty, and the drama makes clear that the truth about another is impossible because each person perceives reality according to his or her limited vantage point and biases.

Following *Right You Are (If You Think So)* Pirandello wrote three plays— *The Pleasure of Honesty* (1918), *The Rules of the Game* (1919), and *All As It Should Be* (1920)—that further present the unstable nature of identity and the conflict between reality and illusion. These themes would have their greatest expression in *Six Characters in Search of an Author* (1921). There is in the history of the modern theater perhaps no more shocking moment than the opening of *Six Characters* in which the audience, expecting to be entertained by an illusion of real life, confronts a bare stage and a group of actors preparing to rehearse. Six characters interrupt the rehearsal—a Father, Mother, Stepdaughter, Son, adolescent Boy, and young Girl—who claim to be characters created by an author who has abandoned their story. They seek from the actors the means for self-expression. The audience, initially dealing with the notion of actors playing actors in a play that appears spontaneous, must now adjust to the more radical premise of actors playing characters who become actors in a dramatic version of their lives. The play's startling opening and premise were so shocking when the play was first performed in Rome in 1921 that the audience rioted. Catcalls and jeering led to punches. *Six Characters* would be subsequently performed internationally to great acclaim and acknowledgment as a watershed drama with its innovative treatment of philosophical themes and dazzling experimentation with dramatic structure.

Pirandello's next play, *Enrico IV (Henry IV)* (1922), continues the themes of role-playing, self-expression, and the illusive concept of reality. Suffering under the delusion that he is the 11th-century Holy Roman Emperor, the title character has been supplied with a royal entourage to help him live his mad fantasy. Unknown to his accomplices, however, he has regained his sanity but has decided to continue the fantasy as compensation for his life's disappointments. Violently provoked by attempts to "cure" him, he asserts the truth but must resume his masquerade to save himself after killing another. The play becomes a dizzying hall of mirrors in which the distinction between history and the present and sanity and insanity is investigated, while Pirandello poses the question of how an "authentic" life is possible.

In 1924 Pirandello joined the Italian Fascist Party and, benefiting from state support, founded the Teatro d'Arte di Roma, serving as its director until 1928. Critics remain divided over whether Pirandello fully subscribed to fascism or only supported the government as an expedient for getting his plays produced. Asked why he was a Fascist, Pirandello, the radical skeptic of all systems of order to make sense of the chaos of existence, declared "I am a Fascist because I am an Italian," a statement that could be interpreted as patriotic enthusiasm or resignation. Pirandello's later plays, including *Ciascuno a suo modo* (*Each in His Own Way*) (1924) and *Questa sera si recita a soggetto* (*Tonight We Improvise*) (1930), forming a trilogy with *Six Characters* on the connection between theatrical life and human existence and understanding, continued to explore the dominant themes of his work: the interplay between reality and illusion, role playing, and the paradoxical concepts of sanity and madness. In 1934, Pirandello received the Nobel Prize in literature. He died two years later, frustrated by his failure to establish a national theater in Rome and disillusioned with the Fascist state. His dying instructions were to stage-manage his own burial, dropping the masks that had defined his own life performance: "Dead, let me not be clothed. Let me be placed, naked in a sheet. No flowers on the bed, no lighted candle. . . . The cart, the horse, the driver, *e basta!*"

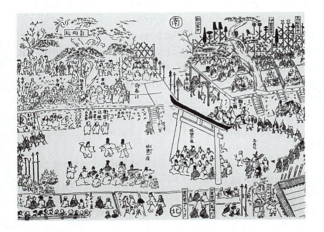

Zeami's plays concentrate attention on the essential nature of an individual's experience; the goal of their aesthetic is the lyric exfoliation of identity.
—Thomas Blenham Hare, *Zeami's Style: The Noh Plays of Zeami Motokiyo*

Zeami Motokiyo is one of the founders and the principal codifiers of Noh, the classical theater of Japan, the world's oldest, continuous professional theater. As the greatest playwright, critic, and actor of his age, Zeami combines, by Western standards, the stature of SHAKESPEARE [1], Aristotle, and the English actor Edmund Kean in the history of Japan's classical drama. Given the traditional nature of Japanese drama, Zeami's plays remain a major part of the Noh repertory since their creation 600 years ago. In the West, Noh drama has exerted its influence, particularly in modern drama, in the works of W. B. YEATS [17] and in the poetry of Ezra Pound. Zeami's theories of performance and the art of Noh helped shape an alternative to realism in literary art by demonstrating means of rendering the symbolic and universal intensely, purified by economy and technical perfection.

The origin of Noh has many parallels with that of ancient Greek drama. Both arose out of religious rites; both combined music and dance and included a chorus; and both evolved solo parts and dialogue involving masked male actors. As Greek and Western drama moved closer to realistic representation, however, Noh retained its highly stylized and ritualized form in its attempt to reveal *yugen*, a complex term denoting beauty, mystery, and depth—literally, an object concealed from view. Like Zen, a philosophy very much a part of Noh, the drama's aesthetics proceed from the fundamental notion that outward reality is an illusion, and that inner truth is reached through contemplation of the essence beneath the surface of things. Noh derives its power and beauty from its concentration: all its elements—music, verse, costumes, and motion—unite to produce a single, clarified impression of some primary human relation or emotion. Whereas Western drama depends on conflict, little happens in a Noh play. The action that determines the play's present situation occurs in the past, and a pair of actors, the principal figure, or the *shite*, and the *waki*, or companion, embody the emotion that the play dramatizes. The characters represent a part of the human psyche, magnified in time and space and revealed through speech and gesture. To produce Noh's desired goal of illumination the actors must be able to reveal profound significance with an economy of method.

Zeami was the eldest son of Kannami, a distinguished actor who is credited along with his son as the founder of Noh. In 1374, after Kannami's troupe performed for the 17-year-old shogun Ashikaga Yoshimitsu, the shogun, captivated by Zeami's beauty and charm as an actor, became the patron of his father's troupe. The effect on Noh was to change its primary religious purpose to that of entertainment, in which aristocratic taste and values would become increasingly important. The rural and folk elements out of which Noh was derived were refined to reflect the spirit and beliefs of the samurai culture of Noh's upper-class patrons. When Kannami died in 1384, Zeami, at age 22, assumed leadership of the troupe. In 1400, Zeami wrote the first of his treatises on Noh, *Fushikaden*. The first work of its kind in Japanese history, it formulates an aesthetic of the theater, including the training necessary for an actor; categorizes types of Noh plays and characters; and lists the philosophical principles that form the core of Noh.

Fushikaden and the treatises that followed were not meant for a wide audience, but instead as lessons for Zeami's fellow professionals. They also reveal the values Zeami considered essential in his plays and performance. He makes clear that a play's text must be viewed, like an opera's libretto, as only a single part of a much more complex work that includes music and movement. The play depends on the intricate skill of the actor, whose lifelong training eventually leads to mastery of the tradition and the possibilities of the form. Describing the stages of the actor's craft, Zeami writes that around the age of 25 the actor's skills will sharpen, but he warns:

> People will be generous with praise, and you may come to think of yourself as a really accomplished actor. This is very dangerous. . . . Your achievement at this time is not true artistic excellence. It is born of youth

and the novelty the spectators see in you. Anyone with a discriminating eye will recognize this fact. . . . Nearly everyone becomes enthralled with this temporary achievement and fails to realize it will disappear. . . . Ponder this long and hard. If you really have a grasp of your level of achievement at this stage, that achievement will not disappear throughout your life. If you overestimate your level of achievement, even the level once attained will fade away. Think this over carefully.

The *Fushikaden* and Zeami's treatises, in the absence of other factual sources, offer a possible insight into Zeami's own development as an actor and playwright and the evolution of his thinking about his art. His works display a dedicated craftsman whose religious and moral principles shape the refined technique of Noh.

With Yoshimitsu's death in 1408, Zeami's preeminence began a long, slow decline as Yoshimitsu's sons gradually withdrew the privileges Zeami and his troupe had received. In 1432, Motomasa, Zeami's eldest son, who had succeeded to the leadership of the troupe, suddenly died. It has been speculated that he may have been assassinated on the orders of the shogun Yoshinori, who also exiled Zeami to Sado Island in the Sea of Japan in 1434. The exact reason for Zeami's exile is unclear. The source of Motomasa's death and Zeami's banishment may have been an artistic dispute with the shogun, but it might also have been because father and son were suspected of being spies committed to his overthrow. Tradition, however, asserts that before his death in 1443, Zeami was pardoned and allowed to return to the mainland.

Over his long career as an actor and theorist of Noh, Zeami produced 30 to 40 classics of Noh drama, the best of which are *The Well-Curb* and *The Lady Aoi*. The plays represent a considerable portion of the repertory of 250 plays that are still performed. In a traditional and conventional art form like Noh theater, it is somewhat misleading and inappropriate to stress an individual's unique contribution to such a collective and formalized art. Within the constraints of the tradition that Zeami helped define and perfect, however, a personal voice and particular vision are still evident. One distinction of Zeami's work, compared to other plays in the classical repertory, is his formal unity of dramatic effects; another is the deepened exploration of the individual's emotions and humanistic concerns. Zeami's plays trace the complex nature of human identity and the profound recesses of the human psyche.

Noh continues to be an important art form in Japan and provides one of the best windows through which Westerners can glimpse Japanese thought and culture. Zeami's place in Noh drama remains the epitome of achievement, setting the standard by which the art is judged.

PABLO NERUDA

1904–1973

We all know that he has sung in praise of everything—love, birds, stones, southern rains, the rough Pacific Ocean, the Araucan pine, cactus, spoons, onions, salmon-bellied eels, everything he ever saw and touched with his poet's eyes and feelings. And also human beings, our national heroes and our Araucanian forefathers, the miner, the railroader, the baker, workers of all kinds, the great epics of our time. He has written moving verses for his Party, poetry of love for his people, and poetry of fire against the enemy.
> —Luis Corvalán, "Pablo's Examples," from *El Siglo*

Pablo Neruda's poetry and politics have made him the writer with perhaps the greatest influence in contemporary Latin America. In his native Chile, Neruda has been lionized as a national hero, revered by a wide popular audience as the celebrator of the common life, and the creator of a national identity. A shanty-town in Santiago, Chile's capital, bears his name, with unpaved streets named after the poet's books. Beyond Chile, Neruda is undoubtedly the most trans-lated Latin American poet of all time, making him one of the region's defining voices in Latin American poetry, as GABRIEL GARCÍA MÁRQUEZ [76] is in fiction, and a source of inspiration and influence worldwide. In a remarkable career that produced more than 30 books of poetry, Neruda's poetic development reflects both a personal odyssey and the history of poetic expression in the 20th century. Few other poets have been so versatile or multidimensional. From the intensely subjective love lyrics, to his epic poem of Latin American history and politics, to his odes on everyday objects, Neruda refracted seemingly every aspect of his world into powerful forms of exploration and meaning.

Neruda was born Ricardo Eliecer Neftalí Reyes Basoalto in Parral, a small village in Chile's central valley. His mother died of tuberculosis a month after he was born; his father, a train engineer, remarried and moved his family south to the remote city of Temuco, a lushly forested setting of almost constant rain. The images that predominate in Neruda's poetry—the rain, sea, and forest— derive from his first 15 years spent in Temuco. The headmistress at Neruda's school was the poet Gabriela Mistral, who in 1945 would win the first Nobel Prize in literature given to a Latin American. The coincidence of this meeting between two future Nobel laureates in a remote corner of Chile is striking. Under Mistral's tutelage, Neruda was first exposed to the Russian novelists and French symbolists, notably among the latter the poetry of Verlaine.

In 1921, after finishing his secondary studies, Neruda went to Santiago to study at the University of Chile. He planned to become a French teacher, but he had already achieved his first literary success by winning a local poetry competition. Discouraged from pursuing literature by his father, he persisted and adopted the pseudonym Pablo Neruda, taking his surname from the 19th-century Czech author Jan Neruda, a leader of the Eastern European symbolists. Dressed in a cape and a wide-brimmed hat he inherited from his father, Neruda was the picture of the romantic, struggling poet wandering the streets of Santiago. His first major work, *Twenty Love Poems and a Song of Despair*, appeared in 1924 to wide acclaim. Nothing quite like Neruda's clear and intense poems of longing and sensual love had ever been achieved in Spanish poetry. His early poetry, greatly influenced by Latin American modernism and French surrealism, broke with traditional verse forms. Neruda's free verse was crafted of sharply defined images and a succession of often unrelated metaphors with the haunted quality of a dream state. He achieved a balance between subjectivity and sensuality, and his striking personal style opened up Latin American poetry to modernist techniques without losing its distinctive feel for place and identity. A characteristic example is this excerpt from "*Cuerpo de Mujer*" (Body of a Woman):

> Body of a woman, white hills, white thighs,
> you resemble a world in your pose of surrender.
> My rough peasant's body wildly digs in you
> and makes the son leap from the depth of the earth.
>
> I was only like a tunnel. The birds fled from me,
> and night overcame me with its powerful invasion.

In order to survive I forged you like a weapon,
like an arrow in my bow, like a stone in my sling.

By the age of 23, Neruda had a wide and enthusiastic following. His admirers recited his poems and imitated his dress. His fame helped him secure a diplomatic posting as consul first to Burma, then to Ceylon, Java, and Singapore. The experience darkened Neruda's poetry, which increasingly displayed themes of tragic isolation in a disintegrating world. This phase of Neruda's development culminated in the landmark cycle of poems *Residence on Earth* (1935), considered by critics to be his most important work and a high point of Latin American poetry. In 1930, Neruda married Maria Antonieta Hagenaar, an Indonesian woman of Dutch background, and in 1934 he was appointed consul to Barcelona and then Madrid, where his only daughter was born. In Spain, Neruda associated with a wide circle of Spanish writers, especially FEDERICO GARCÍA LORCA [91], but their productive interchange was ended in 1936 by the outbreak of the Spanish civil war. Neruda's anguish and despair at the defeat of the republicans is expressed in his volume, *Spain in My Heart* (1937).

Neruda's experience in Spain formed his political and social conscience and his commitment to Communist activism. Increasingly drawn to historical and political themes, he reflected his interest in a new epic and documentary manner and a renewed absorption with the history of his native country and Latin America, which would reach its fullest expression in *General Song* (1950). Neruda's epic is the culmination of a decade of intense political activity and immersion in Latin American affairs. Neruda was elected a Communist party senator in 1945, but his opposition to the ruling Chilean government of González Videla forced him to go underground, where he sought refuge in the homes of various supporters from different social classes to avoid arrest. In 1949, he crossed the Andes on horseback to begin a period of exile. In *General Song*, Neruda reflects his political and ideological analysis in a history of Latin America's victimization, first as a colony of Spain and later by foreign powers allied to dictators who betray their own people. The poem, which works out the means for liberation in the collective power of the people, blends history, ideology, and subjectivity on an epic scale never before attempted by a Latin American poet.

On Neruda's return to Chile after the government relented in prosecuting him as a subversive, his style shifted from the grandiloquence of *General Song* to simple poems celebrating the material objects of daily life. His *Odas*, odes to common life and its humble details—onions, coffee cups, and a dictionary—show Neruda repopulating his world with basic elements that give life meaning and value. In his "Ode to a Lemon," Neruda shows the transformative power of his imagination to elevate the simplest object into a magical and powerful symbol:

. . .
So, while the hand
holds the cut half of lemon,
half a world on a plate,
a universe of gold overflows
a
cup yellow
with miracles,
one of the nipples
fragrant from the
breast of the earth
the ray of light that made fruit,
the little fire of a planet.

His later years were marked by worldwide travel and increasing international recognition, culminating in his being awarded the Nobel Prize in literature in 1971. He remained active in politics and was a strong supporter of the government of Salvador Allende. Stricken with cancer, Neruda died at his home when the military leaders who toppled Salvador Allende refused to allow an ambulance to reach him. The death of Neruda, which coincided with the deaths of Allende and the democracy movement in Chile, provides a chilling, symbolic conclusion to the career of a poet dedicated to the spirit of liberation against the many forces in opposition.

Over his lifetime Neruda recorded a remarkable odyssey of self-discovery and engagement with deeply personal and publicly important questions, distilled into poetry of consummate craftsmanship and power. Through his many shifting styles Neruda never lost touch with an audience for whom his poetry deeply resonated.

W. H. AUDEN

103

1907–1973

It is hard to think of another writer in English the progress of whose lustra—*those five-year periods by which the Romans marked out life's phases or stages—would seem to matter so much. It is not only that he is our foremost poet, but that his career has been full of the ambivalences and paradoxes that have marked the moral history of the past 40 years.*
—John Hollander, "Auden at Sixty," *Atlantic Monthly,* July 1967

Presented with the National Medal for Literature in 1967, Auden was praised as a poet who "has illuminated our lives and times with grace, wit, and vitality. His work, branded by the moral and ideological fires of our age, breathes with eloquence, perception, and intellectual power." Arguably the most important English-speaking poet born in the 20th century, Auden represents at times a slippery, protean figure who evades description: British or American? Marxist or Christian? Satirist or romantic? Traditionalist or experimenter? Serious or playful? Summarizing the contradictions of Auden, fellow poet Randall Jarrell observed, "We never step twice into the same Auden." Auden is as multiple as the era he has named—the Auden generation—writers who succeeded the first great modernists such as YEATS [17], Pound, ELIOT [19], JOYCE [7], LAWRENCE [57], and WOOLF [48] and chronicled the ideological, cultural, and psychological conflicts between the wars. Auden provides us with an understanding of the inner tensions and motives of a pivotal period in modern life. If one of the principal legacies of the modernist revolution in literature was a retreat by the artist to the order and ideal consolation of art, Auden's poetry shows an alternative direction toward engagement and exposure. As fellow poet Dana Gioia explains, "Auden's extraordinary intelligence never detaches itself from emotions. He analyzes what he feels—which are often contradictory impulses—with imaginative brilliance and penetrating candor. The honesty is sometimes astonishing." Over a long career, through the social crises of the 1930s, the war years, and the aftermath, Auden remained committed to poetry's central mission. "In so far as poetry . . . can be said to have an ulterior purpose," he declared, "it is by telling the truth, to disenchant and disintoxicate." Embracing that claim, Auden produced memorable and unavoidable modern poetry.

Wystan Hugh Auden was born in York and raised in a heavily industrialized area of northern England. From his physician father, Auden gained his initial fascination with natural science; his mother, a strict Anglican, stimulated an interest in music and spirituality. Intending to study science and engineering at Oxford, Auden shifted his field of study to English due to a growing fascination with poetry. Auden claimed that his poetic vocation was prompted suddenly when, at the age of 15, he was asked by a classmate if he wrote poetry. Having never before thought of doing so, he immediately became determined, as he declared to his English tutor at Oxford, to become "a great poet." At Oxford Auden became a central member of a group of young writers that included Stephen Spender, Christopher Isherwood, C. Day Lewis, and Louis MacNeice, who would be collectively labeled the Oxford Group and later the Auden generation. Coming of age following the events of World War I and absorbing its impact in the postwar world, they were committed to bringing new techniques and attitudes into English poetry. Auden and the others were very much influenced by the poetry of T. S. Eliot, whose watershed poem, *The Waste Land*, was published in 1922. Other influences on Auden's early work came from Gerard Manley Hopkins, Wilfred Owen, and the 16th-century poet John Skelton. Auden collected his earliest poems in a privately printed first book, *Poems*, in 1928. After completing his undergraduate degree in the same year, Auden moved to Berlin with his friend Isherwood, whose *Berlin Stories* chronicle the bohemian lifestyle of Weimar Germany that engaged both men. Auden's reflection of his time in Germany was the verse play, *Paid on Both Sides*, one of the first works in English to incorporate German expressionist and Brechtian techniques. T. S. Eliot would accept the play for publication in his magazine *Criterion*. Returning to England in 1930, Auden supported himself with various teaching jobs as a revised version of *Poems* appeared in 1930, followed by his second volume, *The Orators*, in 1932. Taking direct aim at the postwar stagnation of British life and institutions, Auden's poems created a sensation and established him as the major poet of his generation. It was asserted that the poems offered proof that "the country is not going to the dogs after all." Critic John Hayward declared *The Orators* "the most valuable contribution to English poetry since *The Waste Land*," in which Auden in luminous images, memorable lines, and musical phrasing captured the thoughts and feelings of the times. Dylan Thomas carried around a copy of the volume until it fell to pieces.

Increasingly, in the works that followed, Auden moved from an interior landscape of thought and feelings to a more direct confrontation with politics and the historical moment allied with a more disciplined formal style. His next collection, *Look, Stranger!* (1936) opens with these dedicatory lines: "Since the external disorder, and extravagant lies, / . . . What can truth treasure, or heart bless, / But a narrow strictness?" Auden here announces his break with modernist poetic techniques by restoring traditional meter, while incorporating in intimate and private moments the impact of political and social forces antithetical to human freedom and relationships. Reflecting the impact of the Great Depression and the rise of fascism, Auden's work expressed his increasingly socialist views, but he resisted the charge that his poetry had become either doctrinaire or propagandistic. "Poetry is not concerned with telling people what to do," he insisted, "but with extending our knowledge of good and evil, perhaps making the necessity for action more urgent and its nature more clear, but only leading us to the point where it is possible for us to make a rational and moral choice." Among his important works during the second half of the 1930s are "Spain," based on his experiences there during the civil war, and "In Time of War," Auden's sonnet sequence based on his travels in China.

In 1939 Auden left England for America, becoming an American citizen in 1946. At the time of his departure, he was the preeminent English poet of his day and was decried for abandoning his country at the outset of the war. Auden defended his action by insisting that he was attempting to break free from the demands imposed on him by his fame. Settling in New York City with Chester Kallman, who would become his longtime companion, Auden would write that "For the first time, I am leading a life which remotely approximates to the way I think I ought to live." His first book after his move was *Another Time* (1940), a pivotal volume containing some of his most anthologized and greatest poems, including "September 1, 1939," "Musée des Beaux Arts," "Lullaby," and "In Memory of W. B. Yeats." In the first, Auden reflects on the impact of the outbreak of World War II from the vantage point of a New York bar, "Uncertain and afraid / As the clever hopes expire / Of a low dishonest decade." Considering the causes and effects of the war to come, the poem has some of Auden's most memorable lines such as "Those to whom evil is done / Do evil in return" and "We must love one another or die." In "Musée des Beaux Arts," Auden considers Brueghel's painting *Icarus* as a kind of visual parable on the human tragedy:

> About suffering they were never wrong,
> The Old Masters: how well they understood

> In human position; how it takes place
> While someone else is eating or opening a window or just walking dully
>   along.

"Lullaby" is one of Auden's most beautiful and evocative love poems and meditations that manages, despite its range of allusions and turns of phrase and idea, an emotionality that compels without ever descending into sentimentality. It opens:

> Lay your sleeping head, my love,
> Human on my faithless arm;
> Time and fever burns away
> Individual beauty from
> Thoughtful children, and the grave
> Proves the child ephemeral:
> But in my arms till break of day
> Let the living creature lie,
> Mortal, guilty, but to me
> The entirely beautiful.

His elegy to Yeats contains one of Auden's most quoted phrases, "For poetry makes nothing happen," as well as a memorable concluding epitaph that equally applies to Auden himself:

> In the deserts of the heart
> Let the healing fountain start,
> In the prison of his days
> Teach the free men how to praise.

During the war years, Auden experienced something of a spiritual awakening that led him back to the orthodoxy of Anglo-Catholicism, and his work became increasingly dominated by his Christian belief and an existential search for redemption. Technically, lyrics gave way to longer, more ruminative works, including *The Double Man* (1941), *The Sea and the Mirror* (1944), *For the Time Being* (1944), and *The Age of Anxiety* (1947), for which Auden won the Pulitzer Prize. Regarded by some at the time as an artistic decline into the sententious and a betrayal of his former activist political and social views, Auden's later works have increasingly been reassessed positively as evidence of his continuing creative growth. Important later works include the collection *Nones* (1951), which includes the much-anthologized "In Praise of Limestone," and the first poems of the magnificent *Horae Canonicae* sequence that appeared in full in *The Shield of Achilles* (1955). His last works, less overtly Christian in content, continue to offer meditations on existence and the sources of transcendence, and include *Homage to Clio* (1960), *About the House* (1965), *City without Walls* (1969), *Epistle to a Godson* (1972), and the posthumously published *Thank You, Fog: Last Poems* (1974). Auden returned to England to accept a professorship at Oxford in 1956. From 1958 he divided his time between Oxford and a home in Austria. He died in Vienna in 1973 following a final poetry reading.

Like Yeats, whom Auden greatly admired, there is a sense both of completion in Auden's long and productive career as well as a continual development in which the poet persisted in his search for the appropriate language to bring to life his and his age's deepest anxieties, dreams, and desires. Allow another great master poet a final word on Auden's achievement. According to SEAMUS HEANEY [117], "Auden was an epoch-making poet on public themes, the register of a new sensibility, a great sonneteer, a writer of perfect light verse, a prospector of literature at its most illiterate roots and a dandy of lexicography at its most extravagant reaches."

RABINDRANATH TAGORE

104

1861–1941

Flowers and rivers, the blowing of conch-shells, the heavy rain of the Indian July, or the parching heat, are images of the moods of that heart in union or in separation; and a man sitting in a boat upon a river playing upon a lute, like one of those figures full of mysterious meaning in a Chinese picture, is God Himself. A whole people, a whole civilization, immeasurably strange to us, seems to have been taken up into this imagination; and yet we are not moved because of its strangeness, but because we have met our own image, as though we had walked in Rossetti's Willow Wood, or heard, perhaps for the first time in literature, our voice as in a dream.

—W. B. Yeats, *"Gitanjali"*

Only a few literary giants, such as DANTE [2], SHAKESPEARE [1], PUSHKIN [18], and GOETHE [10], have had as comparable an impact on a people's language, literature, and cultural identity as Rabindranath Tagore, the preeminent figure in Bengali literature. Tagore's influence extends into the artistic achievement of other Indian languages, and in the West, Tagore is the most respected of all Indian literary artists. A prodigious and varied writer, Tagore's canon includes over 1,000 poems, 10 novels, more than 100 short stories, more than 50 plays, and more than 2,000 songs (including the national anthems of both India and Bangladesh), and several volumes of essays on literary, social, religious, and political topics, as well as translations. Tagore is both the preserver of Indian literary tradition and the creator of new forms in the synthesis of classical, modern, vernacular, and European elements. A philosopher and a founder of two important schools, Tagore was both directly and indirectly involved in Indian's transformation from British colony to sovereign nation, which his writing and example helped inspire. A writer of seemingly boundless energy and curiosity, Tagore is rightfully regarded, along with Gandhi, as one of the central figures of modern India.

Born in Calcutta in the heart of British India, Tagore was the youngest of 14 children in a distinguished family whose members each would play a role in the Bengali Renaissance, the formulation of a national identity and literature under the pressure of traditional and Western forces. Rabindranath's grandfather was a merchant prince who was received by Queen Victoria in London. Debendranath, Rabindranath's father, was a revered religious figure and a leader of the Brahmo Samaj, a Hindu social reform group. Rabindranath grew up in a literary, multicultural household in which, as critic Mary M. Lago observed:

> Goethe was read in German and de Maupassant in French, *Sakuntala* in Sanskrit, and *Macbeth* in English; poetry was written, upon models supplied by Keats, Shelley, and the Vaishnava lyrics then being compiled and appearing in Bengali periodicals; plays and songs were composed and performed. There were experiments in the writing of Bengali novels that drew on Bengali history as Scott had drawn on the history of England and Scotland; the French short story writers of the nineteenth century were the models for experiments in writing short fiction in Bengali. Journals were edited and secret patriotic societies organized. Friends, associates, and tutors came and went, all against a background of traditional Bengali life; the inner rooms were the women's world; the boys were invested at the proper age with the sacred thread of the Brahmins, the spiritual life of the household was grounded in the *Upanishads.*

Formally educated in a series of schools on the English pattern, whose rigidity he rebelled against, and at home by private tutors and his brothers, Rabindranath later attended University College, London, in 1878 to study law, though be returned to India in 1880 to resume his family's intellectual activities. After marrying in 1883, Rabindranath was sent to manage his family's East Bengal estates. His exposure there to the life of the Bengali peasant provided him with a rich source of material for his writing, and their songs and stories formed the basis of his own creations in "the most productive period of my literary life, when, owing to great good fortune, I was young and less well known."

In 1898, to spare his children the kind of regimented schooling he had resisted, Tagore decided to educate them himself and opened his own school, financed and maintained by the sale of his wife's jewelry and his own continual writing. During India's nationalist struggles in the early years of the 20th century, Rabindranath was an advocate of nonviolent noncooperation more than a decade before Gandhi's rise to prominence. By 1907, however, dispirited by the growing tension between Hindus and Muslims and the terrorist attacks of the nationalist extremists, Tagore withdrew from direct political involvement to concentrate on his literary and educational activities. He would never be forgiven by the nationalists for his perceived abandonment of their cause, though few contributed as much as Tagore to the formulation of a distinct Indian national identity or to the exposure of colonial abuses.

In 1912, at the age of 51, after playing an important role in turning the vernacular Bengali language into an expressive literary medium, Tagore gained worldwide attention with the English translation of *Gitanjali: Song-Offerings*, which featured an appreciatory introduction by W. B. YEATS [17]. A year later, Tagore received the Nobel Prize for literature, and his years as an international literary celebrity began. During his last 30 years Tagore made nine foreign trips, which took him to England, Europe, North and South America, and the Far and Middle East, where he used his position to speak out against colonial oppression, human rights abuses, and destructive nationalism. In his travels and in his writing Tagore spoke in favor of international cooperation and pursued a political synthesis between the East and the West, between sustaining tradition and modern reform and revitalization.

Although Tagore achieved mastery in almost every literary genre, an appreciation of his achievement should begin with his poetry. Unlike Bengali prose, Bengali poetry has a rich tradition of lyrical and narrative forms that Tagore respected but also transformed with modernist techniques and elements such as a spare, direct style infused with suggestive imagery. For Tagore, the lyric and the associated song form the core of his writing, collected in 54 separate volumes with six additional collections published posthumously. All reveal his ability to shape language for various purposes, fusing a highly personal voice with sharply drawn images, reflections on actual life, and metaphysical ideas. In the West, an insufficient knowledge of Tagore's traditions and the subtlety of his effects, which resist translation, have led to a misreading of his works as romantic and loosely mystical, which a full appreciation of his canon belies.

In prose, Tagore is more obviously a distinctive innovator. Short fiction in the Bengali vernacular or in any other Indian language did not exist in any significant form before Tagore adapted the genre from European models to reflect Indian themes. His earliest stories, written during the 1890s, are based on his experiences of rural life, including the beauty of the agricultural landscape and the emotional and psychological lives of his characters, who endure various forms of oppression derived from social, political, and traditional forces. Tagore's novels expand the theme of social and psychological restriction, especially for women, and his social critique and subtle presentation of character set a new standard for the Bengali novel.

Tagore's greatest achievement beyond the excellence of individual works is in creating artistic possibility out of his national language and culture. By expanding tradition with borrowed elements from other cultures and turning his artistic attention to the concerns of his own people, Tagore helped develop Bengali literature and spread its distinctiveness around the world. As the Bengali poet Jibananda Das has observed in predicting the future of Bengali literature after Tagore, "As the English poets who, age after age, revolve about the centrality of Shakespeare, constantly extended themselves toward creation of a perfect circle, our poets, too, revolving around Rabindranath, will do the same."

VICTOR HUGO

105

1802–1885

[Hugo's poetry] is often no more than a grand parade, a sort of triumph, of vocables. . . . What is perhaps a more damning reproach than any is that his work is saturate in his own remarkable personality. . . . It is a proof of the commanding genius that was his that in spite of [these objections] he held in enchantment the hearts and minds of men for over sixty years. He is, indeed, a literature in himself.

—W. E. Henley, in the *Athenaeum*

No other figure more dominated his age, nation, and literature, or has more confounded later evaluation than Victor Hugo. The undisputed leader of French romanticism, Hugo asserted his influence in every available genre: poetry, drama, fiction, literary criticism, and religious and political essays. More a phenomenon and a force than a conventional literary figure, Hugo, through his long life, embodied the history and the spirit of France during most of the 19th century. Despite his near deification by his countrymen, Hugo's lasting achievements in his works are much more qualified successes. English readers know him for his two great novels, *Notre Dame of Paris* and *Les Misérables*, works of enormous power and force often marred by melodrama and slack construction. His poetry and plays are important today primarily for their romantic spirit and their considerable impact on French and world literature, which followed Hugo's towering example. It was fashionable during

Hugo's time and immediately following his death to depreciate his genius and his life as insufficient to his own claims of importance, but few other writers have ever made themselves so indispensable to so many readers. If Hugo's power to move readers has passed with his era, his role in shaping that era is still relevant.

Hugo's assault on literary supremacy began early. His background reflects the political tensions that he absorbed throughout his life. Hugo's father was one of Napoleon's generals; his mother, an unreconstructed royalist. Their differences and incompatibility were the major feature of Hugo's childhood and the source of the divisions that saw him shift political allegiance throughout his life from the empire, to the monarchy, to the republic. His father encouraged his son to study law, but his mother fostered his interest in literature. At age 14, Hugo declared, "I must be Chateaubriand or nothing," and mounted a determined campaign to become France's preeminent literary figure. When in 1820 he finally met the great writer, Hugo's literary nemesis referred to him as *l'enfant sublime.*

Hugo's poetry and drama made him the leader in the French romantic movement, which he helped define in his preface to his play *Cromwell* (1827), and most defiantly with the production of his play *Hernani* (1830). The drama, described by one reviewer as not only a play but a cause, was a landmark in the battle between classical and romantic form, with its first audiences divided between Hugo's proponents, the Hugolaters, and his equally vociferous opponents, who decried his challenge to the classical unities and form of the neo-classical playwright JEAN RACINE [62]. Today, the play, featuring the wellborn outlaw Hernani who rebels against society and is tragical betrayed by those in power, reads like an extravagant romantic melodrama—as one critic recognized, like the libretta of an opera. For Hugo and his admirers it represented a revolutionary overthrowing of conventional poetic forms and the liberation of the imagination for a new display of the emotions. The same free expression of emotions is evident in Hugo's lyrics, which share with the English romantics a similar meditative quality directed by the contemplation of nature and the poet's internal states in search of expansion and wholeness. In Hugo's poetry, nature provides a veil that the poet penetrates for a deeper, universal meaning, mediated by the poet's imagination and emotions.

Throughout his life, despite a complicated marriage, a succession of mistresses, and disappointment with his children, Hugo wrote his 100 lines of poetry or 20 pages of prose daily in a remarkable variety of forms. His energy and ego were unbounded, and his sense of his own leadership of the spirit of France extended beyond literature into politics. He had shifted his political views under the Restoration and the republic, opening himself to a charge of opportunism. As the dramatist Victorien Sardou bitterly commented, "It is not a crime to change one's opinions. . . . What is despicable is that this transformation of our beliefs should coincide with that of our interests. This is constantly the case with Victor Hugo." His self-interest even extended to his 19-year, partially self-imposed exile in the Channel Islands during the reign of Napoleon III, in which Hugo's prestige was considerably enhanced as France's outspoken champion of democracy. In his old age Hugo had become an institution, the living embodiment of French art and national spirit. When he died, it seemed that the entire era embodied by his massive output had passed.

For the English reader, his two classic novels, *Notre Dame of Paris* (1831), the story of the hunchback bell-ringer Quasimodo and his love for the gypsy dancing girl Esmeralda during the reign of Louis XI, and *Les Misérables* (1862), the epic pursuit of the criminal Jean Valjean, condemned for stealing a loaf of bread for his sister's starving family, by police inspector Javert, continue to exert their power to move audiences in film and stage adaptations. Both show Hugo's considerable strength in evoking their periods with vivid intensity. Our sense of medieval Paris is largely derived from Hugo's portrait in *Notre Dame of Paris*, and it has been argued that Paris's preservation of its architectural past can be traced to Hugo. In *Les Misérables*, Hugo transforms a moving indictment of human laws as a force of oppression into a panorama of human liberation. Both novels succeed less as convincing dramas than as symbolic and mythical experiences in which the particular and the specific are raised to the level of the universal and the archetypal.

Victor Hugo remains a grandiose literary figure whose life and works exceed the reach of almost any other writer. Treated as a god in his lifetime, it is inevitable that he should be later revealed as mortal. Yet no other writer has exerted such a hold on a critical and mass audience. André Gide, in his famous retort to the question of who was the supreme French poet, remarked, "Victor Hugo, hélas!" Hugo's legacy is contained both in Gide's assertion and his qualification that indicates a limited yet unavoidable literary force.

TANIZAKI JUN'ICHIRŌ

106

1886–1965

No one would turn to Tanizaki for wisdom as to how a man should live his life, nor for a permanent analysis of the evils of modern society, but anyone seeking the special pleasure of literature and an echo in even his most bizarre works of eternal human concerns could hardly find a superior writer.

—Donald Keene, *Dawn to the West*

Among the great modern Japanese novelists—Natsume Sōseki, KAWABATA YASUNARI [109], and Tanizaki Jun'ichirō—vying for placement here, Natsume is undoubtedly the initial dominant figure of modern Japanese literature, whose reputation is greatest among Japanese readers themselves, and whose likeness appears on the 1,000-yen note. Kawabata received the first Nobel Prize for literature given to a Japanese writer. Tanizaki's stature, in comparison, is far more ambiguous and controversial. Of these three, he is perhaps the best-known outside of Japan, but in his native country Tanizaki has something of the reputation of BYRON [83] in England—morally unsavory and suspected of lacking intellectual substance. The position of Tanizaki in this ranking, however, stems from my agreement with scholar Donald Keene's assessment offered in his survey of modern Japanese literature that "if any one writer of the period will stand the test of time and be accepted as a figure of world stature, it will be Tanizaki." Few other writers in any language have probed

402

the dark recesses of human passion and desire so deeply, nor has any Japanese writer drawn so much from the conflicting attractions of Western and Japanese traditions. In a canon that is fetish-laden with the preoccupation of his own obsessions, Tanizaki delights in what embarrasses or is ignored by other writers and readers. At his best, however, he offers far more than a confession, whether we like what he reveals or not.

Born in Tokyo, Tanizaki grew up in a family crippled by financial distress. His father was an unsuccessful businessman who failed at every venture he undertook. Tanizaki's mother was a great beauty, her son's inspiration for the ideal of Japanese womanhood that haunts his writing. A precocious and talented student, Tanizaki was introduced by a teacher to the classics of the East and West. In 1901, when he graduated from elementary school, his father was anxious that he should go to work to help support the family, but a teacher persuaded him to allow Tanizaki to continue his education at middle school. A version of this incident is dramatized in Tanizaki's first story published in 1903, "Shumpu Shuu Roku" (Account of spring breezes and autumn rain).

Tanizaki financed his education by serving as a *shosei*, a houseboy and tutor in the family of a restaurant owner, an experience he bitterly resented. In 1908, he enrolled in the Tokyo Imperial University but neglected his studies and largely ignored his family's financial distress to pursue his writing and indulge in flamboyant sexual experimentation, a lifestyle from which his early writing is drawn. He began to publish his work in 1909, rejecting the prevailing fashion of naturalism for an interest in private desires and unusual characters and events. His story "Shisei" (The tattooer), a haunting tale of an artist enslaved by a girl he has helped transform by tattooing a spider on her back, established his reputation and taste for the perverse and the sinister. (Tanizaki's first short story collection, was published in 1911 under the same title.) Nicknamed the Diabolist, Tanizaki shocked readers with his sexual candor, indulgence in the abnormal, and defense of masochism and other deviance. His work during this "bad period" would embarrass Tanizaki in maturity, and much of his writing from it has not been collected or reprinted. In 1916, he commented on the relationship between his life and his art during this time:

For me art came first and life second. At first I strove to make my life accord, insofar as possible, with my art, or else to subordinate it to my art. At the time I was writing "The Tattooer," "Until One Is Deserted," and *Jotaro*, this seemed possible. And I managed to carry on my pathological life of the senses in the greatest secrecy. When eventually I began to feel that there was a gap between my life and art that could not be overlooked, I planned how I might, at the very least, make as advantageous use of my life as possible for my art. I intended to devote the major part of my life to efforts to make my art complete.

Tanizaki's overall reputation has been negatively shaped by his early dissolute lifestyle, his overriding hedonism, and indulgences that included his highly publicized mistreatment of his wife. Despite his excesses and the artistic weakness of many of his efforts at this time, his early work remains an important indicator of his probing of hidden motivations that he discovered in himself and which would resurface in his later masterpieces.

Tanizaki was equally extreme in his noninterest in politics and current Japanese cultural issues, indulging instead in his exorbitant taste for everything Western. He moved to Yokohama to enjoy its large foreign enclave, dressed in brown suits and played the guitar, ate roast turkey and kidney pie, and seemed to obliterate from himself any traces of Japanese customs and the past. As Tanizaki admitted, "I discovered that, as a modern Japanese, there were fierce artistic desires burning within me that could not be satisfied when I was surrounded by Japanese. Unfortunately for me, I could no longer find anything in present-day Japan, the land of my birth, which answered my craving for beauty."

A turning point, however, occurred as a result of the great earthquake of 1923 that devastated Tokyo. Tanizaki, away from the city when it hit, greeted the news with a perverse joy. He later recalled thinking, "Now Tokyo will become a decent place!" He hoped the city would be rebuilt along modern, Western lines more to his taste, with Western customs finally replacing Japanese ways. While living temporarily in the Kansai region near Kyoto, in the heart of traditional Japan, however, Tanizaki began to reassess his earlier enthusiasm for the West and his rejection of Japanese tradition. He would remain in the area for the next 20 years, and his rediscovery of the Japanese past and customs would be reflected in his mature works, through their more complex blend of past influences with modern ideas and concerns.

Tanizaki produced his best work under the pressure to absorb and express his infatuation with Japanese culture and his own past. *Tade kuu Mushi* (*Some Prefer Nettles*) (1929), regarded by many as Tanizaki's finest work, describes a protagonist like the author, whose attraction to the West is slowly replaced by the enduring values he remembers from childhood. Tanizaki's own immersion in that world is perhaps most comprehensively expressed in the novel *Sasmeyuki* (*The Makioka Sisters*) (1948). Written during World War II, the novel was first suppressed for not contributing to the war effort. Instead of praising Japan's military and extolling the superiority of its heroic traditions, Tanizaki offered a detailed reconstruction of commonplace prewar life in the efforts of a traditional Japanese family to find a husband for one of three sisters. Their traditional values, sustained despite the onslaught of change from the West, lend the work an air of nostalgic appreciation for a vanished world. Tanizaki retreated to that world in a number of historical novels based on Japan's past, as well as reflections of his own childhood and two separate modern translations of the classic, *The Tale of Genji*, by Lady MURASAKI [12].

Tanizaki continued to write provocatively up to his death, reexamining his preoccupation with sexual themes and the subconscious in novels such as *Kagi* (*The Key*) (1957), *Yume no ukihashi* (*The Bridge of Dreams*) (1959), and *Fūten Rōjin Nikki* (*Diary of a Mad Old Man*) (1962). In these novels Tanizaki continues to haunt the shadowy region of human desires and obsessions in search of an ideal of beauty. Tanizaki offers a remarkable amalgam of Lady Murasaki, EDGAR ALLAN POE [53], and OSCAR WILDE [92], whom he considered among his strongest influences, in his delicate evocation of Japanese tradition with dark grotesqueries and mannered artistic control. Like Wilde, Tanizaki continually asserts the power of his artistic vision as an alternative to a world indifferent to or destructive of both beauty and truth.

ANTHONY TROLLOPE

107

1815–1882

His first, his inestimable merit was a complete appreciation of the usual.
—Henry James, *Partial Portraits*

The inclusion of Anthony Trollope in this ranking of literary excellence would likely have gratified but certainly surprised him. Trollope claimed only the distinction of "persevering diligence in my profession"; he saw himself not as a genius but as a craftsman. Author of 65 books (of which 47 were novels), Trollope wrote more good novels than any other English Victorian novelist, but a charge of greatness may seem too extreme, beyond the reach of Trollope's intentions and his conscious restriction to the world of ordinary life in his novels. Yet, like the realism of JANE AUSTEN [20], Trollope's art is the basis for a compelling moral and social drama that few writers have bettered.

Overshadowed in his lifetime by the towering Victorian figures of DICKENS [6], THACKERAY [94], and GEORGE ELIOT [21], Trollope has emerged over the last 50 years with more of his canon back in print to meet the demand of a growing audience. Although the full depth of his achievement still has not been critically explored, future generations will turn to Trollope for the clearest insights into the life of the Victorians, as we now turn to Austen for our view of the Regency period. Trollope's novels are of more than just historical interest, however: there are some genuine masterpieces as well. To appreciate Trollope's contribution to literature requires a critical standard different from that usually applied to literary modernism; the skills acquired in reading HENRY JAMES [38], WILLIAM FAULKNER [15], and JAMES JOYCE [7] are not those that best serve Trollope's novels. Trollope's goal was clarity: he avoided symbolic patterns and a self-conscious style. Learning to read Trollope for what he offers, rather than what he does not, can uncover excellence in quality as well as quantity.

Trollope's remarkable skill in imagination and storytelling stemmed from inclination, heredity, and necessity. His father was an unsuccessful London barrister who turned to farming, crippling his family with debt. Trollope was the youngest of four sons and was educated as a day student at Harrow and Winchester, prestigious boys' boarding schools, but failed to win a scholarship to Oxford. "Something of the disgrace of my school-days has clung to me all through life," he later recalled. Awkward and disadvantaged by his family's financial disarray, Trollope asserted that he had been "flogged oftener than any human being alive." Bankruptcy drove the family to Belgium for a life of shabby gentility, supported mainly by the writing efforts of Trollope's mother, Frances, who produced novels and a celebrated travel book, *Domestic Manners of the Americans* (1832), after a visit to America. Trollope's schooling ended at the age of 19, when he began a distinguished career as a postal civil servant. From 1841 to 1851 Trollope was transferred to Ireland, a personal and professional turning point, in which he married, took up fox hunting ("one of the great joys of my life"), and began to write, at the age of 29.

Trollope's early work included two novels with an Irish setting, a historical novel, and an attempt at a play. He would find his true subject, however, when, in 1851, he went to the south of England to help regularize country mail delivery. While widely observing country life on horseback, he visited the cathedral town of Salisbury and conceived the story of *The Warden*, the first in his series of ecclesiastical novels of country life that became the popular *Chronicles of Barsetshire* (1855–67). The series offers a faithful rendering of the complexity of English social customs, centering on the machinations and foibles of the clergy and gentry families in Barset, his imaginary county. With superb portraits of the professional and landed classes, the series avoids idealization and any stronger dramatic stimulus beyond the probability of ordinary life. To produce his book while professionally engaged at the post office in positions of increasing responsibility, Trollope devised a systematic plan at variance with any typical notions of the inspiration and excesses of genius. In his *Autobiography*, he revealed:

> When I have commenced a new book, I have always prepared a diary, divided it into weeks, and carried it on for the period which I have allowed myself the completion of the work. In this I have entered, day by day, the number of pages I have written, so that if at any time I have slipped

into idleness for a day or two, the record of that idleness has been there, staring me in the face, and demanding of me increased labor, so that the deficiency might be supplied. . . . I have prided myself on completing my work exactly within the proposed dimensions. But I have prided myself especially in completing it within the proposed time,—and I have always done so. . . . A small daily task, if it be really daily, will beat the labors of a spasmodic Hercules. It is the tortoise that always catches the hare.

Trollope paid a servant extra to wake him each morning at 5:30 with his morning coffee, after which he wrote for three hours before going to work. Trollope was relentless, writing in railway carriages on journeys and in hotel rooms, tapping his amazing imagination to produce the allotted 10 pages a day.

In 1867, Trollope retired from the post office with the design of the famous red column postal box his legacy to posterity. He intended to enter politics, declaring, "I have always thought to sit in the British Parliament should be the highest object of ambition to every educated Englishman." Trollope failed in an election bid, but his experience and interest in politics prompted the six Palliser novels (1864–80). During the 1870s, Trollope experimented with different styles and subjects, but interest in his work waned, and his revelation in his *Autobiography* of his workmanlike approach and clear financial accounting of the à70,000 he earned from his writing did nothing to enhance his reputation as a writer of literature rather than a hack. After his death, his books were dismissed, along with everything else Victorian, by the Edwardians and Georgians, to whom Trollope was a complacent chronicler of a hypocritical age who concentrated excessively on the surface of life and missed its depth.

Trollope's reputation was slowly revised in the second half of the 20th century as readers grew to appreciate his abilities. His strengths as a novelist are quiet ones and cumulative; each novel paints an intimate portrait of life as it is truly lived. Like Dickens did in his later novels, Trollope wrote of social panoramas. His concern is not the unwinding of a single individual life but life in society, three-dimensional portraits of multiple characters in many changing situations. Like CHAUCER [5], Trollope numbered the classes of people, chronicling the nuance of behavior and the sense of how humans act, which much modern fiction often ignores. A list of a dozen of his finest books might include, in order of excellence: *The Last Chronicle of Barset, Orley Farm, Barchester Towers, Phineas Redux, Doctor Thorne, The Way We Live Now, The Eustace Diamonds, Harry Hotspur, The Small House at Allington, Mr. Scarborough's Family, The Duke's Children,* and *The Claverings.* Other titles or arrangements of merit are certainly possible, but at his best, Trollope excelled at capturing the world truthfully and in establishing a compelling, realistic standard for the novel.

FLANNERY O'CONNOR

108

1925–1964

What we can know for sure is that Flannery O'Connor created a remarkable art, unique in its time. Unlike any Southern writer before her, she wrote in praise of ice in the blood.
—Josephine Hendin, *The World of Flannery O'Connor*

No other writer who has come out of the American southern tradition, with the exception of WILLIAM FAULKNER [15], has exerted such a major influence on 20th-century American literature as Flannery O'Connor. Her unique blend of irony, black comedy, and traditional belief can be traced in the works of such diverse writers as John Hawkes, Cynthia Ozick, and Cormac McCarthy. No other American writer besides HERMAN MELVILLE [24] has used fiction to explore existential themes so fiercely and deeply. O'Connor's novels and short stories, filled with stark, brutal comedy, disturbing violence, and grotesque characters, dramatize the difficulty and necessity of spiritual belief and redemption in a world increasingly devoid of meaning and transcendence. "My subject in fiction," O'Connor observed, "is the action of grace in territory held largely by the devil. I have also found that what I write is read by an audience which puts little stock either in grace or the devil." A Catholic southerner, O'Connor labored with patience and determination to express her uncompromising moral vision, resisting demands that her fiction should conform to popular standards. She once declared that she could "wait a hundred years for readers."

409

Born in Savannah, Georgia, Mary Flannery O'Connor was the only child of Edward and Regina Cline O'Connor. As a child she was precocious and independent, preferring the company of adults to other children. Besides reading and writing, her passion was raising chickens. The star of her collection was a chicken that could walk backwards, and Pathé News photographed O'Connor, age five, and her chicken for the newsreels. O'Connor liked to say that this was the high point of her life and the rest was anticlimactic. When O'Connor was 12, her father became terminally ill with lupus erythematosus, the same illness that would later afflict his daughter. After his death, she and her mother moved to Regina O'Connor's family home in Milledgeville, Georgia, where Flannery attended Peabody High School and Georgia State College for Women, graduating in 1945. Her family was devoutly Catholic in the predominantly Protestant South, which no doubt contributed to the religious themes in her works and cultivated in her the sense of being both a member of her Southern community but also critically distant from it.

O'Connor went on to do graduate work at the University of Iowa, where she studied at the Iowa Writer's Workshop. She perfected her craft and in 1946 sold her first short story, "The Geranium," to *Accent* magazine. During her second year at Iowa, she won the Rinehart-Iowa prize for fiction on the basis of the draft of what would become her first novel, *Wise Blood*. The novel tells the story of a fanatically religious backwoodsman who, after rejecting the fundamentalist faith in which he was raised, creates his own religion—the Church of Christ Without Christ—to attack that faith. His subsequent desperate search for salvation leads to violence and disaster. When O'Connor's editor at Holt, Rinehart found the novel too bizarre and tried to redirect her into more conventional channels, she resisted and changed publishers.

In December 1950, O'Connor was diagnosed with lupus, which, although incurable, was controllable with medications that had been developed since her father's death. It would be a year, however, before O'Connor was again mobile. Once her health had stabilized, she moved with her mother to a dairy farm called Andalusia near Milledgeville. The two women divided the household labor, and O'Connor once again raised birds, now adding peacocks to her flock, a bird that her readers have associated with her. O'Connor's return to the South, which she loved and where she felt she belonged, put her again in touch with the characteristic scenes and themes of her fiction. A steady flow of stories followed, all marked by superb craftsmanship and disturbing black comedy, in which O'Connor makes full use of the grotesque and violent dislocation of ordinary experience. *Wise Blood* was published in 1953. Two years later a collection of short stories, *A Good Man Is Hard to Find*, appeared. Her second novel, *The Violent Bear It Away*, was published in 1959.

In 1963, O'Connor's health declined. She continued to write, however, producing two of her most admired stories, "Judgement Day" and "Parker's Back." O'Connor died at age 39 of kidney failure. The following year, her last collection of short stories, *Everything That Rises Must Converge*, was published, and in 1969 *Mystery and Manners*, a collection of her articles, talks, and essays, appeared to critical acclaim. Despite her relatively small body of work—two novels and two collections of short stories—her writing established her direct lineage with American writers such as NATHANIEL HAWTHORNE [72] and Melville in the depth of her spiritual vision, and with EDGAR ALLAN POE [53] and ERNEST HEMINGWAY [63] in exerting such influential mastery over the short story form.

At the core of O'Connor's artistry is the struggle to achieve significance and meaning in a world of disbelief that undermines relationships and defines individuals not as spiritual beings but as animals and automatons. To awaken her readers to larger possibilities of the spirit, O'Connor arranges a grotesque and often violent disruption of the ordinary and the expected. She contended that "mine is a comic art, but that does not detract from its seriousness," and she argued, "A serious fiction writer describes an action only to reveal a mystery."

Convinced of the redemptive power of fiction, O'Connor saw her role as comparable to the Old Testament prophets whose task was to "recall people to known but ignored truths." She wrote that "in the novelist's case, prophecy is a matter of seeing near things with their extensions of meaning and thus of seeing far things close up. The prophet is a realist of distances, and it is this kind of realism that you find in the best modern instances of the grotesque." In one of her most acclaimed short stories, "A Good Man Is Hard to Find," a southern family's complacency and self-centered blindness are shattered through the agency of a homicidal maniac called the Misfit. Seen by the author as an agent of the Devil, the Misfit nonetheless prompts a redemptive act on the part of the family's self-centered grandmother and provides her appropriate epitaph: "She would of been a good woman . . . if it had been somebody there to shoot her every minute of her life." The story is a paradigm of O'Connor's craft and vision, in which scenes and dialogue are sharply rendered with grotesque comedy that elucidates some of life's most fundamental questions.

O'Connor wrote, "If the writer believes that our life is and will remain essentially mysterious . . . then what he sees on the surface will be of no interest to him and only as he can go through it and into an experience of mystery itself. His kind of fiction will always be pushing its own limits outward toward the limits of mystery. . . . Such a writer will be interested in what we don't understand rather than in what we do. He will be interested in possibility rather than in probability. He will be interested in characters who are forced out to meet evil and grace and who act on a trust beyond themselves." Subversive and disturbing, her works embody writing's highest aspiration: to give shape to what is most essential and inescapable about our existence.

KAWABATA YASUNARI

*Mr. Kawabata, as everyone knows, is a great stylist, but I believe he is finally without a
style. Because style for the novelist means the will to interpret the world and discover the
key to it. To arrange the world, separate it, and bring it out of chaos and angst into the
narrow framework of form, the novelist has no other tool than style. . . . What is . . . a
work of art, like Kawabata's masterpiece, which is perfection in itself, but has abandoned
the will to interpret the world so entirely? It fears no chaos, no angst. But its fearlessness
is like the fearlessness of a silk string suspended before the void. It is the extreme opposite
of the plastic will of the Greek sculptors who committed themselves to the permanence of
marble; it is in sharp contrast to the fear that the harmonic Greek sculpture fights with
its whole body.*

—Mishima Yukio, "The Eternal Traveler"

In 1968 Kawabata Yasunari became the first Japanese writer awarded the
Nobel Prize in literature. In its citation the Swedish Academy praised Kawabata's narrative mastery, which "with great sensibility, expresses the essence of
the Japanese mind." Regarded widely by his countrymen as the most Japanese
of modern Japanese writers, a celebrator and preserver of the Japanese artistic
traditions, Kawabata is also credited with infusing into the Japanese literary
sensibility elements derived from European modernism. Kawabata's unique
blend of tradition and experimentation has made him one of the essential,

founding figures of modern Japanese literature. Moreover, the impact of modernism—its psychic displacement, deracination, and emphasis on the isolated individual—on traditional sources of sustaining values forms Kawabata's central theme and establishes his persistent relevance to a worldwide audience.

Kawabata's preoccupations in his work can be traced to the losses he experienced in childhood. Born in Osaka in 1899, Kawabata was the second child of a bookish physician who died when his son was two. Kawabata's mother died a year later. Kawabata was separated from his older sister and sent to live with his grandparents in a farming village on the outskirts of Osaka, with further family disruption and loss following him. His grandmother died when he was seven and his sister when he was nine. He cared for his aging, blind grandfather, his last surviving relative, until his death when Kawabata was 15. Death became so much a part of Kawabata's experience that he became known as the "master of funerals." In response, Kawabata developed a lifelong habit of retreat into a trancelike detachment. He also became a voracious reader, particularly of Japanese classic texts, especially MURASAKI SHIKIBU's [12] *The Tale of Genji*, which would become a principal influence on his subsequent writing. Following his grandfather's death, Kawabata lived in his school's dormitory, experienced intense loneliness, but marshaled his thoughts and feelings into his first poems, essays, and short fiction.

At university in Tokyo, Kawabata cofounded a literary magazine, came to the attention of an influential editor who provided him with an outlet for his writing, and increasingly became associated with a group of young writers who advocated a "new perception" in literature to challenge the predominant naturalism of contemporary mainstream Japanese writing. Kawabata and the so-called neoperceptionists promoted new expressive methods derived from European symbolists, surrealists, and writers such as JAMES JOYCE [7] and T. S. ELIOT [19] in which mood and image trumped linear plot development and narrative logic. Kawabata's contributions to the movement were radically truncated short stories averaging two or three pages in length. "Many men of literature write poetry when they are young," Kawabata recalled, "but, instead of poetry, I wrote these palm-of-the-hand stories." Kawabata's evolving aesthetic combined the compression, elimination of transitions, presentation through image, and interior monologues of Western writers like James Joyce with Japanese *renga*, traditional linked-verse poetry in which a longer poem evolves by successive additions that responds to the verse that came before, linked by association, repetition, and contrast. Characteristically, Kawabata's innovation in fiction was both to enrich traditional Japanese literary forms with borrowed European modernists elements, while at the same time calling upon those same traditional elements to extend and restore their expressive powers. Kawabata, perhaps more than any other modern Japanese writer, significantly annexed to prose fiction the lyricism, compression, and intensity of Japanese poetry.

Kawabata's fiction also shares with much Japanese poetry a quest for beauty and transcendence along with a tragic awareness of the forces inimical to both. His first major literary success came in 1926 with the short story "Izu no odoriko" ("The Izu Dancer"), based on Kawabata's own travels around the Izu Peninsula during his student days in search of consolation for the many losses and disappointments of his youth. In the story, still the most popular and widely read of his works in Japan, a wandering student meets a group of traveling performers and becomes infatuated with their beautiful dancing girl. He learns that she is far younger than she has been made up to appear, but instead of disappointment, the realization produces in the student a relief that the sexual tension he had experienced has been replaced by a refined idealization of her innocence and purity that sustains him. The story sounds Kawabata's characteristic note of melancholy, loss, and a search for the means to overcome the intractable in nature and human experience. This theme dominates Kawabata's first extended narrative, *Yukiguni* (*Snow Country*), published in parts in 1937 and expanded into its final version in 1948. Alternatingly spare and direct and complexly elusive, *Snow Country* describes three visits by the wealthy, middle-class Tokyo resident Shimamura to a hot-spring resort in a snowy northern mountain province of Japan over a period of nearly three years. Cut off from modern Japan by snowfalls of as much as 15 feet and its rugged mountain scenery, "snow country" represents a retreat into a revivifying natural, pristine setting and a way of reconnecting with traditional Japanese customs and values by Shimamura, who is described as living "a life of idleness," who "tended to lose any sense of purpose, and he frequently went out into the mountains to recover something of it." Allied (and contrasted) to the purifying association of the regenerating quality of snow country is the well-known, somewhat tawdry sexual allure provided by the hot-spring geishas to gratify unaccompanied male visitors. Unlike city geishas whose accomplishments as singers, dancers, and great beauties ennoble, hot-spring geishas are closer in association to common prostitutes, doomed to fade with their looks. At its core, therefore, *Snow Country* considers the role and nature of beauty, its necessity and sacrifice, embodied in the landscape and in particular in the woman, Komako, whom Shimamura meets. Their doomed relationship brilliantly encapsulates Kawabata's meditation on the fleetingness and tragic insufficiency of youth, beauty, and relationships and the forces antithetical to them. Designed with the associational and symbolic logic of an extended poem, *Snow Country* has long maintained its preeminence as a Japanese classic. Its evocative opening lines, "As the train emerged from the long border tunnel, they were in the snow country. The earth turned white under the night sky. The train stopped at a signaling station," have been committed to memory by college applicants in Japan to demonstrate their qualification for higher education.

During the war years, Kawabata increasingly withdrew from society and the transformation of Japanese life that the war and the forces of modernization produced. Increasingly, he focused on the Japanese past, and his work began to reflect the impact of modern life on Japanese traditions and the attendant conflicts produced in the individual and the community. *Sembazura* (*Thousand Cranes*), published serially in 1949 and in book form in 1952, explores sin and guilt measured against decay in the tradition of the Japanese tea ceremony. *Meijin* (*The Master of Go*, 1954) uses a match of the traditional Japanese game of *go* to dramatize the changes in values as a traditionally trained master is eventually bested by a challenger representing rationality and an approach to the game antithetical to its spirit.

Kawabata's most accomplished treatment of the theme of the passing of the old guard is *Yana no oto* (*The Sound of the Mountain*, 1954), a work writer and critic Kenkichi Yamamoto has described as the "very summit of postwar Japanese literature." Set in Japan during the early 1950s, the novel dramatizes the struggles of an aging businessman, Shingo, who retreats from the pressures of family into the sustaining memories of his past. In Shingo, Kawabata creates his most fully drawn protagonist, who, like his creator, is both drawn to the beautiful and is aware of the forces of time, death, and present actuality that prevent fulfillment. Beautifully modulated between sharp family scenes and the interior landscape of memories and dreams, *The Sound of the Mountain* forms a kind of capstone to Kawabata's mature style, preoccupations, and literary achievement. Several important works followed, including *Mizuumi* (*The Lake*, 1955), *Koto* (*The Old Capital*, 1962), and *Utsukushisa to Kanashimi* (*Beauty and Sadness*, 1965). Honored at home and increasingly recognized and translated abroad, Kawabata maintained his engagement in the contemporary literary scene, serving for 17 years as president of Japan's PEN Club and vice president of PEN International. It was largely through his efforts that PEN's international congress was held in Japan in 1957, focusing important worldwide attention on Japanese literary achievement and stimulating translations. A powerful influence on the next generation of Japanese writers, Kawabata was an early champion of such writers as Ibuse Masuji and Mishima Yukio. It was Mishima's suicide—an act of seppuku at the Tokyo headquarters of Japan's Self-Defense Forces—in 1970 that may have contributed to Kawabata's death. Writing about his protégé only a few days before his own death, Kawabata declared, "I am not free for a single moment from the grief and sorrow I feel over Mishima's deplorable death." In April 1972, Kawabata was found dead, apparently having taken his own life by gas poisoning. No suicide note was found, and friends have clung to the belief that his death was accidental.

Called by Mishima the "Eternal Traveler," Kawabata has left a series of compelling reports from a lifetime of wandering, a lifetime in search of beauty and truth in the face of loss and the forces antithetical to rootedness and fulfillment. As a recorder of the ache of desire and the poetry beneath the quotidian, just beyond our grasp, Kawabata is an essential traveling companion.

THEODORE DREISER

110

1871–1945

At a time when the one quality which so many American writers have in common is their utter harmlessness, Dreiser makes painful reading. The others you can take up without being involved in the least. They are "literature"—beautiful, stylish literature. You are left free to think not of the book you are reading but of the author, and not even of the whole man behind the author, but just of his cleverness, his sensibility, his style. Dreiser gets under your skin and you can't wait to get him out again; he stupefies with reality.
  —Alfred Kazin, from the introduction to *The Stature of Theodore Dreiser*

Admiration for Theodore Dreiser as a literary pioneer has been grudging at best. Dreiser has been castigated for his ponderous, inelegant style and crude manner. The experience of reading his novels was described by the critic T. K. Whipple as "being pursued over endless wastes of soft sand. The experience, however instructive, is too painful to be sought out by normal humanity." For Dreiser, such dismissals missed the point: "To sit up and criticize me for saying 'vest' instead of 'waistcoat,' to talk about my splitting the infinitive and using vulgar commonplaces here and there, when the tragedy of a man's life is being displayed, is silly. More it is ridiculous, it makes me feel that American criticism is the joke that English authorities maintain it to be." Despite such condescension and even censorship of his works, Dreiser persisted in pursuit of a greater truthfulness in the novel and the integrity of his subject matter. As the author John Dos Passos argued, "It was the ponderous battering ram of his novels that opened the way through the genteel reticences of American 19th-century fiction for what seemed to me to be a truthful description of people's lives. Without Dreiser's treading out a path for naturalism none of us would have had a chance to publish even." In Dreiser's penetration of the workings of American society and its sensibility, he exerted a more profound influence on American realism than perhaps any other novelist. The first important writer in American literature from a non–Anglo Saxon, lower-class background, Dreiser fundamentally liberated American literature to pursue the widest and most ignored truths and to capture modern American experience in all its complexity and contradictions.

Dreiser's relentless search for a theory of existence, which he explored in all his writing, originated from his own experience. Perhaps more than any other writer, Dreiser confined his attention to that experience at the expense of all other considerations such as style and technique. He was born in Terre Haute, Indiana. His father was an immigrant German workman whom Dreiser described as fanatically religious, honest, hardworking, but a continual failure, lacking the will to succeed and crippled by a fear of religious punishment. Dreiser's illiterate mother came from a small Mennonite sect in rural Pennsylvania, and her affection for her son was Dreiser's principal consolation during a childhood of continual poverty and disappointment. The family moved constantly throughout Indiana and finally settled in the crowded West Side of Chicago. Dreiser's work reflects his own background, and in that respect he was one of the first American novelists to celebrate and anatomize the modern American city and the effects of urbanization on the individual. He was a brooding youth, slow to develop mentally, whose education was drawn primarily from his experience. During his teenage years he worked a succession of jobs—in a Chicago restaurant, for a laundry, as a bill collector for a furniture store, in a real estate office, and for a hardware company as a stockboy. In his early 20s, Dreiser began to work in Chicago and on the East Coast as a newspaper reporter. "I was an Ishmael, a wanderer," Dreiser recalled. He turned to fiction to capture his experience of America while searching for a social theory to help explain his life and the world around him. During the 1890s, the dominate social theory was Social Darwinism, the attempt to explain society under the rubric of biological evolution and determinism. The notion that an individual's biological and instinctual drives determine actions, that the struggle for sex, wealth, and power is won by the strongest, and that society is imposed on the individual to coerce and repress basic needs helped shape Dreiser's outlook and gave his fiction its philosophical basis. Knowing little of literary movements such as French naturalism, Dreiser arrived at his own realistic and naturalistic conclusions inductively through his experiences—experiences he was determined to record faithfully without recoiling from or sugarcoating the commonplace or sordid.

Dreiser's first novel, *Sister Carrie* (1900), one of the seminal texts of American realism, is the story of a sensitive young girl, Caroline Meeber, who escapes poverty by trading on her only valuable commodity, her sexual allure. Starting in a sweatshop, Carrie becomes the mistress of a wealthy salesman and then has a relationship with a bar owner, whose life is destroyed by their romance. Carrie eventually finds a means of income on the stage but is always restless for something better. She eventually manages to achieve some insights into her limitations and the superficiality of her life and commercial success, while the reader gains insights into the hereditary and environmental forces that have determined her actions. The novel's sexual candor, along with its unflinching portrayal of basic instinctual needs and modern urban life, is a radical departure from the more genteel realism that dominated American fiction at the end of the 19th century. Dreiser's refusal to compromise his vision for popular considerations caused *Sister Carrie* to be ignored, virtually suppressed by its own publisher until the publication of Dreiser's second novel, in 1911. During the 11-year silence, Dreiser subsisted on journalistic work, refusing to temper his subject and treatment for commercial reasons while awaiting an audience for his fiction. *Jennie Gerhardt* is a variation on the theme of *Sister Carrie*, with a similar realistic depiction of the instinctual and deterministic forces underlying social and human relationships. Dreiser's integrity and singleness of purpose are heroic and far more worthy of critical respect than the scorn his novels have received for their poor construction and bad grammar.

Dreiser followed his first two stories about flawed women and economic struggle with novels dramatizing American success stories. The character of Frank Cowperwood, in the trilogy *The Financier* (1912), *The Titan* (1914), and *The Stoic* (1947), and Eugene Witla in *The "Genius"* (1915), provide the masculine alternative to Caroline Meeber and Jennie Gerhardt. Both men, driven by basic instincts, relentlessly pursue wealth, power, and beauty, Dreiser's perceived origin of human motivation. As Cowperwood discovers:

> So far as he could see, force governed this world—hard, cold force and quickness of brain. If one had force, plenty of it, quickness of wit and subtlety, there was no need for anything else. Some people might be pretending to be guided by other principles—ethical and religious for instance; they might actually be so guided—he could not tell. If they were, they were following false or silly standards. In those directions lay failure. To get what you could and hold it fast . . . that was the thing to do.

The social successes claimed by both forceful and talented protagonists are contrasted with the failure of the weak, vacuous Clyde Griffiths in Dreiser's masterpiece, *An American Tragedy* (1925). Based on an actual murder case, the novel, through a scrupulous accretion of details and trivial events, follows

Griffiths's fall, lost in the false dream of prosperity and happiness that American culture advertises. Driven to pursue wealth and its expected rewards, Griffiths finds a job in a factory in upstate New York and becomes involved with a wealthy woman, Sondra Finchley, whom he sees as a way out of his straitened circumstances. However, he also begins an affair with Roberta Alden, another factory worker, who becomes pregnant. Desperate to silence Roberta and her demands that he marry her, he takes her into the country, where she drowns in a boating accident. Dreiser leaves Griffiths's complicity in Roberta's death purposely ambiguous, since Griffith's inadequacies and social forces conspire to prevent individual choice and will. The tragedy of the novel's title is ironic, with social and biological determinants replacing the hero's freedom of choice to claim his destiny. The novel is a culmination and synthesis of all Dreiser's important themes about social order and the human condition, and is one of the touchstones of 20th-century American fiction.

Following *An American Tragedy*, Dreiser's work and interests were increasingly dominated by politics, causes, and his communist sympathies—the search for absolutes that his earlier fiction had resisted as irrelevant. Dreiser's greatness is based not on the answers he discovered but instead on his clear-eyed questioning of American experience. As Philip L. Gerber has observed, "Dreiser was the first American to portray with truth and power our modern world of commerce and mechanization, the first to portray the dismal depersonalization of the individual which results from urbanization and intensifying societal pressure to conform, the first to draw us frankly and grimly as a nation of status-seekers."

RICHARD WRIGHT

111

1908–1960

In this country there were good Negro writers before Wright arrived on the scene—and my respects to all the good ones—but it seems to me that Richard Wright wanted more and dared more. He was sometimes too passionate. . . . But at least Wright wanted and demanded as much as any novelist, any artist, should want: He wanted to be tested in terms of his talent, and not in terms of his race or his Mississippi upbringing. Rather, he had the feeling that his vision of American life, and his ability to project it eloquently, justified his being considered among the best of American writers.
—Ralph Ellison, "Remembering Richard Wright"

For sheer visceral power along with his groundbreaking achievement in giving voice to the black experience in America, Richard Wright deserves inclusion here. Neither a great craftsman nor a stylistic innovator, Wright has few peers in the force and impact of his work. His reputation as one of the most influential writers in the 20th century is based principally on two great works: his novel *Native Son* (1940), which gained for the first time a worldwide audience for a black writer, and the autobiographical *Black Boy* (1945), Wright's moving attempt to expose past wounds and fashion an identity. Torment and anguish fueled Wright's imagination, driving him for consolation to communism and existentialism, which at times negatively affected his work. The power of his imagination, however, remains intact, despite lapses of craft and reduction to

420

dogma and propaganda. As Wright observed, "The Negro is America's metaphor," and he pioneered its study and articulation.

A rebel and outsider from the start, Wright was born on a cotton plantation near Natchez, Mississippi, in the Jim Crow South that defined black life as second-class and inconsequential. His father was a sharecropper who deserted his wife and family when Wright was five years old. His mother, working as a cook and housemaid, attempted to raise Wright, but he was shunted from place to place to be brought up by various relatives who introduced him to a cycle of abuse and violence that would fill his later writing. His grandmother, a stern evangelical Christian, offered a severe form of spiritualism that forbade most recreation and nonreligious books. Largely self-educated, Wright ended his formal schooling in the ninth grade. At age 17 he moved to Memphis, where his intellectual awakening was stimulated by an editorial that attacked the editor and critic H. L. Mencken. Wright was determined to find out what could have so enraged southern whites to attack such a man, and, barred by color from access to the public library, forged a note to gain access to Mencken's works: "Dear Madam: Will you please let this nigger boy have some books by H. L. Mencken?" Mencken's essays provided Wright with the artistic stance of the muckraker, with its assault on conventionality and irreverence that would eventually lead him to the naturalist tradition of THEODORE DREISER [110] and Sinclair Lewis. From Mencken, Wright discovered his characteristic attitude of attack; from the naturalists Wright derived his method, his realism, and his interest in the effects of heredity and environment on the individual.

In 1927, Wright and his family participated in the Great Migration of rural blacks to northern cities. In Chicago for the next decade, Wright worked as a porter, dishwasher, postal clerk, and insurance salesman while attempting to understand the social breakdown of the Great Depression. The communists offered a possible solution, and Wright joined the party in 1932, remaining a difficult and contentious loyalist until finally being expelled from the party in 1944. Wright's literary apprenticeship consisted of journalism, poetry, and fiction for party publications, and in 1937 he moved to New York as the Harlem editor of the *Daily Worker*. The decade Wright spent in New York until his permanent residence in Paris in 1947 produced his finest literary work. His collection of stories, *Uncle Tom's Children*, appeared in 1938, and *Native Son* in 1940. *Native Son* was a bestseller: it secured Wright's international reputation and added to the canon of American literature for the first time a significant new voice and subject matter. *Black Boy*, the first major attempt to analyze modern life in the South from a black perspective, was published in 1945. Wright's first marriage failed, but his relationship with Ellen Poplar, a Jewish woman from Brooklyn, developed during this period and produced two daughters.

After Wright moved to Paris with the assistance of GERTRUDE STEIN [125], a prolonged creative silence followed as he struggled for an alternative to the communist ideology that had failed him. He found it in existentialism. Wright explored exile and rootlessness as a permanent condition in the novels *The Outsider* (1953), *Savage Holiday* (1954), and *The Long Dream* (1958). Wright's power as a writer suffered a decline: the quality of felt experience that had been his great strength now became formulaic. Driven to discover the philosophical or ideological means to exorcise the demons of his past, Wright distanced himself from the source of his greatness as a writer in his honest probing of his experience as a black man in America.

There is perhaps no better example of the power and the shortcomings of Richard Wright than his achievement in *Native Son*. The novel, set in Chicago's South Side ghetto, centers on Wright's most famous creation, Bigger Thomas, who embraces the role of the outlaw and murderer in defiance of the conventional role he is expected to assume as a dutiful black. "We black and they white. They got things and we ain't," Bigger reflects. "They do things and we can't. It's just like living in jail. Half the time I feel like I'm on the outside of the world peeping in through a knot-hole in the fence." The ultimate outsider and dangerously repressed, Bigger asserts his individuality in crime and vengeance against a social system that has reduced him to nothingness. His murders of Mary Dalton, a white woman, and of his girlfriend are destructive but perversely heroic assertions of self. Defined almost exclusively in the negative, Bigger moves in the direction of what he can believe. Rejecting both religion and politics, Bigger is left only with his acceptance of his own existential self—as he says, "What I killed for, *I am!*"

The novel touches a raw nerve by daring to present Bigger as a product of social conditions that refuse to acknowledge him and grant his selfhood. The power of the novel to evoke the moral horror of being black in America is weakened considerably by the communist ideological strain in the conclusion. Nonetheless, Wright had found his target. As James Baldwin wrote of *Native Son*, "no American Negro exists who does not have his private Bigger Thomas living in his skull." According to critic Irving Howe, "The day *Native Son* appeared, American culture was changed forever. No matter how much qualifying the book might later need, it made impossible a repetition of the old lies. In all its crudeness, melodrama and claustrophobia of vision, Richard Wright's novel brought out into the open, as no one ever had before, the hatred, fear and violence that have crippled and may yet destroy our culture."

The daring honesty of Wright's vision made possible the next generation of black writers, such as James Baldwin, Ralph Ellison [97], and Amiri Baraka, in the debate over American culture. No one before Wright had probed so deeply into the racial trauma of American life, and few who followed him have achieved his imaginative power.

GÜNTER GRASS

1927–

But it is not Grass's enormous success that matters most, nor the fact that he has put German literature back on the market. It is the power of that bawling voice to drown the siren-song of smooth oblivion, to make the Germans—as no writer did before—face up to their monstrous past.

—George Steiner, "The Nerve of Günter Grass"

At the epicenter of World War II, the 20th century's defining tragedy, Günter Grass has achieved literary greatness through his constant posing of difficult questions and avoidance of easy answers. Few other writers in the post–World War II era have so persistently courted controversy. Coming to the world's attention in 1959 with the publication of his first novel, *The Tin Drum*, Grass has become the world's best-known living German writer. Vocal in Germany's national debate over its past and its future, Grass has also made German issues internationally relevant. The winner of the Nobel Prize in literature in 1999, he has become as much a spokesman for modern consciousness as the conscience of his nation. In Germany every new work by Grass is an event, the occasion for redefining and disputing ideological and artistic assumptions. He remains a continual target, contemptuously dismissed by conservatives as "Pornograss" or as *der Schnauzbart* (the mustache). Grass has also enraged the left with equal vigor. Elsewhere Grass's reputation has grown as few other modern writers can hope to emulate, as a challenging, provocative artist whose works claim center stage in the drama of modern ideas. With the richness and depth of the greatest modernist masters, Grass has avoided both the solipsism of the aesthete and the narrowness of the ideologue, joining the private and the public, the personal and the historical, into a grand artistic synthesis.

The locus of Grass's inspiration is his native Danzig (now the Polish city of Gdańsk), his childhood under Hitler, and his experience of war. Grass's father was a German grocer; his mother was Kashubian, a Slavic ethnicity indigenous to the rural areas around Danzig, with its own language and culture. Grass was five years old when the Nazis took control of the city (later, the liberation of the Germanic population of Danzig would be the pretext for Hitler's invasion of Poland in 1939 which touched off World War II). As Grass recalled, "At the age of ten, I was a member of the Hitler Cubs; when I was fourteen, I was enrolled in the Hitler Youth. At fifteen, I called myself an Air Force auxiliary. At seventeen, I was in the armored infantry." Grass left Danzig as a soldier in 1944. (He provoked a firestorm of criticism when he revealed in 2006 in a memoir, *Peeling the Onion*, that he had actually served in the Waffen S.S., the notorious military wing of Himmler's elite corps, which had been absorbed into the regular German army.) Serving in a tank division in rearguard action against the Russians, Grass was wounded and captured by American troops and was one of the first Germans to be marched through Dachau to confront the enormity of the Nazi holocaust. A patriotic and a self-styled "dutiful youth," Grass confessed, "I myself was thinking right up to the end in 1945 that our war was the right war." Grass's reassessment of his own and Germany's past has caused him to suspect all absolutes and simple solutions. "I have no ideology, no *Weltanschauung*," he has written. "The last one I had fell apart when I was seventeen years old."

After the war, Grass worked on farms, in a potash mine, and as a stonemason's apprentice before enrolling in 1948 at the Düsseldorf Academy of Art as a student of painting and sculpture, supporting himself as a drummer in a jazz band. In 1952, he moved to Berlin to work as a sculptor and graphic designer; in 1954, he married his first wife, Anna, a Swiss ballet dancer, with whom he had five children. Grass's initial literary efforts were poetry and plays. In 1955, Anna submitted a selection of her husband's poems to a radio contest, and they won him third prize. This brought Grass to the attention of Group 47, a forum of young German writers dedicated to reclaiming German literature after the Nazis.

In 1956, Grass moved his family to Paris, where he worked on his first novel, *The Tin Drum*, which appeared to great acclaim in 1959. *Cat and Mouse* (1961) and *Dog Years* (1963) complete Grass's "Danzig Trilogy." In his later work Grass has shifted his concern to include Germany's present as well as its past, reflecting his involvement in politics and his active campaigning for the Social Democratic Party and his friend Willy Brandt. The novel *Local*

Anaesthetic (1969) is set in contemporary Germany and concerns the ambiguity of social protest in the new German consumer state. *From the Diary of a Snail* (1972) is Grass's fictional memoir of his campaigning, and *The Flounder* (1977) treats the relationship between the sexes from the Stone Age to the present with Rabelaisian gusto.

Grass's recent work has increasingly melded fiction, history, and autobiography, with Grass continuing to take on centrally important themes in his exploration of the consciousness of modern Germany. One of his more recent novels, *Ein Weites Feld* (*Too Far Afield*, 1995) examines the controversial subject of German unification seen against the larger background of German history. Grass does not paint the situation in black and white. Instead, the novel approaches unification from the perspective of the East Germans, whose rapid absorption into the Federal Republic left them no opportunity to maintain an independent political or cultural identity. Yet Grass avoids taking sides, instead spreading before the reader the multiple complexities and ironies of this most recent chapter of German history. As in his previous novels, Grass fixes his gaze on hypocrisy and cowardice while fully recognizing the pressures and dilemmas that human beings always face. A novel, *Crabwalk*, appeared in 2002, preceded by a story sequence, *My Century* (1999).

Despite the ever-evolving Grass canon, which shows no diminution of his gusto for taking on large topics or risks, his literary reputation rests primarily on the spectacular triumph of his first novel, *The Tin Drum*, which has become both a German and a world literary classic, the defining masterpiece of the Nazi experience from a German viewpoint. Grass's rich and ambiguous novel unfolds from the perspective of Oskar Matzerath, confined in a mental hospital for the criminally insane, charged with a murder he did not commit. Oskar tells the story of his life covering the years before, during, and after World War II. The ultimate outsider, Oskar wills himself to stop growing at the age of three to avoid joining the adult world of betrayal and corruption. He is also the prototypical artist who expresses himself in his drumming and his piercing scream that shatters glass. Oskar's picaresque adventures take him across a nightmarish landscape that reflects the causes and effects of the Nazis at a deeply psychological and mythical level. The ambiguity of who or what Oskar is intended to be—a reflection of Hitler himself or his alternative—gives the novel a disturbing and multilayered quality that resists simple formulation. The novel's tragcomic, and at times scatological and obscene, images are some of the most unforgettable in modern fiction.

The complex theme of the perversion of Germany under the Nazis recur in the concluding novels of Grass's trilogy. In *Cat and Mouse*, this theme takes the form of the fascination Heini Pilenz has for Joachim Mahlke, who becomes an ironic savior figure through the experience of the war. *Dog Years* is a dense and complex novel that incorporates myth, legend, history, politics, and fantasy. Focused by the protean Eduard Amsel, Grass examines the role of the artist as seer and creator, and asserts the artist's responsibility to tell the full truth in a cautionary and visionary tale of modern Germany.

In all of Grass's work, experience is refracted into dense levels of meaning, alternatively shocking and touching by embracing the complexity of modern experience. His fictional world is as richly and symbolically patterned as that of JOYCE [7] and GARCÍA MÁRQUEZ [76]. Like these authors, he draws on tradition and private experience to refashion a modern, expansive myth for our times.

TENNESSEE WILLIAMS

113

1911–1983

Like William Faulkner, Williams created a world which was manifestly his own. His South is coterminous but not identical to the real South (though the supposed reality of the South, composed as it is, of fragments of myth, fiction and self-sustaining deceits, is itself suspect). It is a world on the turn, a culture caught at a moment of precarious balance. It was not for nothing that he was drawn to the work of Chekhov. And what is true of the public world is no less true of the private one, of characters who are themselves caught precisely at the moment when personal dreams and myths are under pressure and when the reality of mortality and the fact of physical decline become undeniable. The shock of that change is registered in his work in the form of neurotic recoil. And that moment of recoil is central to his work.
—C. W. E. Bigsby, *A Critical Introduction to Twentieth-Century American Drama*

A towering figure of post–World War II theater, Tennessee Williams changed the direction of the American stage from what he termed "the exhausted theatre of realistic conventions," to a new and poetic language- and character-focused drama that unflinchingly yet compassionately explored the deepest recesses of individual emotional experience. The themes and emotions explored in his plays, together with his gallery of memorable characters, reinforce Williams's view of what drama should be and provide an understanding of why he was such an influential playwright: "It is not the essential dignity but the essential ambiguity of man that I think needs to be stated."

Williams's difficult childhood contributed to his understanding of the ambiguity of human behavior and engendered within him a capacity for compassion and empathy that he would draw upon when creating characters caught up in emotionally destructive moral and social conditions. Thomas Lanier Williams was born in Columbus, Mississippi, the eldest son of Cornelius Williams, a boisterous traveling shoe salesman, who relocated the family to St. Louis, Missouri, when Tennessee was eight. There, Williams's overprotective mother, Edwina, a physically fragile clergyman's daughter and former southern belle, took refuge in memories of the past to cope with her far from genteel life and marriage to a man with whom she had little in common. Williams's beloved older sister, Rose, later diagnosed with schizophrenia and institutionalized, coped with her parents' arguments by closeting herself away with her collection of glass animals. Williams would later use his mother and sister as prototypes for Amanda Wingfield and her shy, delicate daughter, Laura, in his first successful Broadway play, *The Glass Menagerie*. Williams, a precocious, sensitive, shy, and sickly child, was often bullied at school and refused to participate in sports, which disappointed his father. The birth of a younger brother, Dakin, together with his mother's frequent illnesses, added to his insecurity and sense of a hostile world. Williams coped with an uncongenial home and school life by reading voraciously and engaging in imaginative play with Rose. He began to write after his mother gave him an old typewriter for his 11th birthday and continued to write with only intermittent interruptions for the rest of his life. By the time he was 16, he had published his first story.

At the University of Missouri, Williams won prizes for verse and fiction, discovered the plays of STRINDBERG [56], and wrote a few dramatic pieces of his own. However, after failing ROTC because of his physical limitations, his father refused to support him any longer, and he was forced to drop out of college. He returned to St. Louis and, like his discontented character, Tom Wingfield, the narrator and brother of Laura in *The Glass Menagerie*, went to work for a shoe company, a tedious job he later referred to as a "season in hell." The job contributed to Williams's nervous breakdown two years later, in 1935. He recuperated at his maternal grandparents' home in Memphis and began to write again. He briefly attended Washington University in St. Louis and then transferred to the State University of Iowa, from which he graduated in 1938 with a degree in playwriting. After graduation, Williams took to the road, living the life of an itinerant writer and working at a variety of jobs. In Chicago he tried to join the WPA Writers Project, but his work was considered by the group to be lacking in "social content." In 1939 he won a $100 award from the Group Theatre for a collection of four one-act plays, called *American Blues*, and acquired an agent, Audrey Wood, who had been one of the judges. Through Wood's support, Williams received several foundation grants and began to establish himself in New York as a serious, promising young writer. His first full-length play, *Battle of Angels*, was produced in Boston in 1940 and closed after a disastrous opening night. An exploration of religion, sexuality, and repressed passions set in the South, topped off by a final lynching scene featuring an elaborate smoke effect, the play horrified theatergoers and was banned. *Orpheus Descending* (1957), Williams's revision of *Battle of Angels*, proved to be a similar critical and commercial failure; however, a film adaptation, *The Fugitive Kind* (1960), with a screenplay by Williams, was more successful.

After the failure of *Battle of Angels*, a dejected Williams returned to New York, where he supported himself by working as a theater usher, elevator operator, and waiter. Rejected for military service during World War II, Williams went to work as a screenwriter for MGM Studios in 1943. After writing a script for a film starring Lana Turner, he turned down the next project, a movie starring child actress Margaret O'Brien, and instead submitted an outline for a film titled "The Gentleman Caller," based on his early short story, "Portrait of a Girl in Glass." Williams's idea was rejected and, although he was kept under contract, the studio implied that his services were no longer required. Williams used the time away from his office to develop his scenario and turn it into a stage play he titled *The Glass Menagerie*. Audrey Wood submitted the play to actor-producer Eddie Dowling, who directed and appeared in it, playing the role of Tom Wingfield. *The Glass Menagerie* opened in Chicago on December 26, 1944, and garnered much attention due to the return to the stage of renowned actress Laurette Taylor in the role of Amanda Wingfield. The following March, the play moved to New York, where it was a resounding success and won the New York Drama Critics Circle Award less than two weeks after its opening.

The Glass Menagerie, like much of Williams's drama, is an exercise in illusion and reality and is Williams's most autobiographical play. The action revolves around the anticipation experienced by Amanda and Laura Wingfield when they learn that Tom has invited Jim O'Connor, the "gentleman caller" of Williams's original scenario, to dinner. Tom is unaware that his mother plans to present him as a prospective suitor for Laura. After Jim reveals that he is soon to be married, Laura and Amanda's hopes are dashed, the emotionally fragile Laura retreats farther into seclusion with her "glass menagerie," and Tom, after a heated confrontation with his mother, leaves home. The pathos and poetry of *The Glass Menagerie* heralded a new, more fluid kind of drama, which Williams called "plastic theater," a concept he may have borrowed from the abstract expressionist painter and teacher Hans Hoffman, who had used the term "plastic space" to describe his art. Although Williams was influenced by the realism of CHEKHOV [37], he was dedicated to creating drama that would incorporate many theatrical styles and the use of different media and poetic language to create a more authentic and vivid dramatic expression on stage.

Williams followed the success of *The Glass Menagerie* with *You Touched Me!* (1945), a sex farce starring rising young actor Montgomery Clift, that was unfavorably compared to *Menagerie*. In 1946, while Williams was living in New Orleans, his short play *27 Wagons Full of Cotton* was published. After a sojourn in Nantucket, Williams returned to New Orleans to live with his beloved 90-year-old grandfather, the Reverend Dakin; the two eventually traveled to Key West, where Williams would later settle with his partner, Frank Merlo. In 1947, *A Streetcar Named Desire* opened on Broadway and *Summer and Smoke* premiered in Dallas and moved to New York the following year. Based on Williams's short story, "The Yellow Bird," *Summer and Smoke* concerns a prudish minister's daughter who is hopelessly in love with an attractive, philandering doctor, loses him to a younger woman, and afterward seeks solace in affairs with traveling salesmen. Although a fine drama, which would enjoy a well-received revival in 1952, *Summer and Smoke* was compared unfavorably to *Streetcar* at the time. *A Streetcar Named Desire*, with its heightened naturalism and portrayal of fragility, sexual violence, and shattered illusions rising up from the deepest recesses of the human heart, mind, and soul, is perhaps Williams's greatest play. Set in the working-class French Quarter of New Orleans, the play is revolutionary in the history of drama for its depiction of sexuality and its exploration of the uneasy relationships between men and women. *Streetcar* is Williams's most widely successful drama and its frequent revivals worldwide attest to the fact that it is one of the most popular American plays. It had the longest Broadway run of any of Williams's plays and won for him the Pulitzer Prize and the Drama Critics' Circle Award. In 1951, the play was turned into an acclaimed motion picture, with Marlon Brando repeating his stage role as the unrefined, brutish Stanley Kowalski and Vivien Leigh as Blanche DuBois, an aging, emotionally fragile Southern belle and teacher-turned-prostitute.

Williams's visit to Italy in the late 1940s resulted in two Italian-centered works. *The Roman Spring of Mrs. Stone* (1950), a novel set in Rome, concerns the love affair between a retired actress in her 50s and a young count who eventually abandons her for a young, glamorous Hollywood starlet. The novel was adapted for the screen twice, in 1961 and 2003. In 1951, *The Rose Tattoo*, a play with Dionysian farcical elements, set in a Sicilian community on the Gulf Coast, opened on Broadway. The play deals with a passionate and earthy seamstress, recently widowed, who refuses to believe the truth about her husband's unfaithfulness; she eventually develops a love relationship with a man who is a truck driver like her husband and also like him wears a rose tattoo on his chest. *Camino Real* (1953), a play with expressionistic qualities set in an unspecified Latin American country, concerns the boundaries between dreams and reality. In *Cat on a Hot Tin Roof* (1955), Maggie, the central character, tries desperately to emotionally and sexually reconcile with her husband, the hard-drinking, cynical, sexually confused younger son of a wealthy Mississippi family. The play won for Williams his third New York Drama Critics' Circle Award and second Pulitzer Prize. *Baby Doll* (1956) was an Elia Kazan film featuring a screenplay by Williams taken from *27 Wagons Full of Cotton* and a second early one-act play, *The Long Stay Cut Short*. Notorious in its day, the film was repeatedly condemned by the Catholic archbishop of New York and censored by the Catholic Legion of Decency because of its plot centering on an infantile, sexually provocative 19-year-old virgin who marries a lecherous much older man. The late 1950s and early 1960s saw the productions of *Suddenly Last Summer* (1958), a one-act play with gothic overtones that is considered Williams's most shocking drama for its depiction of homosexuality and cannibalism; *Sweet Bird of Youth* (1959), in which an aging movie star is caught in a love triangle with an opportunistic young actor; *Period of Adjustment* (1960), a domestic comedy; and *Night of the Iguana* (1961), Williams's last major theatrical success. Set on the west coast of Mexico in 1940, the play concerns a psychologically troubled defrocked minister-turned-tour guide, who must come to terms with his situation.

The 1960s and 1970s were troubled decades for Williams. *The Milk Train Doesn't Stop Here Anymore* debuted on Broadway in 1963 and was not well received; the same year, Frank Merlo died, leaving Williams inconsolable. He became addicted to alcohol and prescription medications and tried to seek solace in religion, converting to Catholicism in 1969. After three months in a hospital psychiatric unit, where he suffered three grand mal seizures and two heart attacks, Williams recovered from his addictions and returned to writing. However, his critical reputation had begun to wane, and he was castigated by critics for abandoning his previous dramatic themes and "voice" in favor of plays that were bolder, more experimental in the use of stagecraft, and built around the artist as protagonist. Williams's later works also included collections of short stories, poetry, and essays; a novel; and an autobiography, *Memoirs* (1975). One of his most successful later plays is *Vieux Carré*, set in a New Orleans boardinghouse populated by artists, which opened on Broadway in 1977. Despite critical skewering, Williams continued to be popular with audiences and was publicly recognized as one of the great figures in American literature. He was the frequent recipient of academic honors for his work, and in 1980 his play *Will Mr. Merriwether Return from Memphis?* debuted at the newly opened Tennessee Williams Fine Arts Center in Key West. Three years later, Williams choked to death in a New York City hotel suite after swallowing a plastic medicine cap. Despite his written wish to be buried at sea in the Gulf of Mexico, where his favorite poet, Hart Crane, had committed suicide, his estranged brother, Dakin, buried him in the family plot in St. Louis. After his death, there was revived critical interest in his lesser-known and later works, the most recent of which was a production of *And Tell Sad Stories of the Death of Queens*, which premiered at the Kennedy Center in Washington, D.C., in 2004.

If WILLIAM FAULKNER [15] is the most influential figure in the novel during the Southern literary renaissance, Tennessee Williams, although a latecomer to the period, is its most significant playwright. But his works, while rich in Southern sensibilities, articulate much more than a sentimental and nostalgic regional perspective. ARTHUR MILLER [119], one of many playwrights influenced by Williams, has characterized his dramas as the first to express "an eloquence and amplitude of feeling" in the American theater. Poetry and emotion inform Williams's dramatic world; there, grotesqueness and beauty, brutality and fragility, guilt and expiation exist side by side and then collide to make us confront essential and universal truths about the myths and realities that inform the human condition.

LI BO

114

701–762

Bo, the poet unrivaled,
In fancy's realm you soar alone. . . .
Now on the north of the Wei River
I see the trees under the vernal sky
While you wander beneath the sunset clouds
Far down in Chiang-tung.
When shall we by a cask of wine once more
Argue minutely about poetry.

—Du Fu, "To Li Bo on a Spring Day"

One of China's greatest poets and certainly its most notorious, Li Bo has traditionally been linked to his contemporary Du Fu [28] as the complementary halves of the Chinese sensibility. Translator David Hinton summarizes the dichotomy as follows: "Li Bo [is] the Taoist (intuitive, amoral, detached), and Tu [Du] Fu the Confucian (cerebral, moral, socially engaged)." While such a distinction is a simplification, it does underscore crucial elements that Li Bo added to the Chinese literary tradition. In a Western context, Du Fu is Apollonian; Li Bo is Dionysian. If Du Fu represents classical balance and grounded certitude, Li Bo embodies a romantic sensibility in his ecstatic flights celebrating the sublimity of nature, the irrational and magical, in his seeking

433

illumination and transcendence on the open road, in the wilds, or through intoxication. If classical Chinese poetry is defined by its rules and customs, by skillful conformity to the poetic conventions, Li Bo injects individuality and eccentricity into the process. His poetry is purposefully shocking in attitude and style, and his works represent such a radical innovation that the Chinese literary scholar Stephen Owen subtitles his chapter on Li Bo in his *The Great Age of Chinese Poetry* "A New Concept of Genius." Owen argues that "Beside his preeminence as a poet, Li Bo left this one great legacy to future poets: an interest in personal and poetic identity. Mere excellence was no longer sufficient; the poet had to be both excellent and unique. Thus, later critics admonished aspiring poets to imitate Du Fu rather than Li Bo. . . . The rationale for directing young poets away from the model of Li Bo was that Li's art was perfectly natural, uncontrollable, almost divinely inspired. But the real reason that Li Bo was inimitable was that Li Bo's poetry primarily concerned Li Bo: its goal was to embody a unique personality, either through the persona of the poem or through an implied creator behind the poem." With Li Bo the Chinese poetic paradigm begins an important shift away from proficiency in the proscribed manner to a new liberating expressiveness encompassing exceptional circumstances and a unique personality.

Li Bo's background and poetic development reinforce his reputation for eccentricity and outsider status. Little is known for sure about his birthplace or background. It is believed that he was born in Turkestan, a descendant of a Chinese nobleman named Li Gao who had been exiled to Central Asia. Living on the trading routes between China and the West, his family may have turned to trading for its livelihood. When Li Bo was a child, his father moved his family back to China, to Chengdu, in Sichuan Province. Li Bo would promote his Central Asian background as a mark of difference, while also claiming a family connection to the founder of the Tang dynasty, Li Yuan, as well as the Daoist philosopher Laozi (whose family name was Li). Despite such a pedigree (real or invented), Li Bo rejected the conventional route for advancement for a young man of ambition, intelligence, and literary talent through the imperial examination. Instead he spent several years as a Daoist recluse in the mountains near his home. An accomplished swordsman, Li Bo also served for a time as a kind of avenging knight, defending the helpless in several duels. As David Hinton observes, both activities "are emblematic of Li Bo's temperament: a deep and quiet spirituality on the one hand, and on the other, a swaggering brashness."

Around 724, Li Bo left his home province in the west to journey down the Yangtze River into eastern China, beginning the wandering life that he would follow for most of his career. By 730, he had settled in Yumen, Hebei Province, where he married into a socially prominent local family. By 740, after his wife and perhaps a son had died, Li Bo resumed his wanderings, possibly to advance his ambitions as a poet. Through the support of a Daoist master

Wu Yun, who had befriended him, Li Bo was summoned to the imperial court of Emperor Xuanzong at Changan, the Tang dynasty capital. There, another famous Taoist He Zhizhang exclaimed after reading one of Li's poems, "You do not belong to this world. You are an immortal banished from Heaven!" From then on, Li Bo was referred to as the "Banished Immortal." Impressed with his brashness and poetic abilities, the emperor appointed Li to the Hanlin Academy for priests, doctors, poets, and entertainers serving the emperor. Li Bo's duties included drafting imperial documents and likely producing poetry that was performed at court occasions. Surviving anecdotes about Li Bo's time at court stress his habitual drinking, outlandish behavior, and lack of proper respect for courtly protocol. In one of the most famous stories about the poet's rowdiness, he supposedly justified his drunken rudeness with the famous quip, "Wine makes its own manners." Making enemies as well as wearing out the patience of admirers, Li Bo managed to keep his place at court for only three years before he was dismissed. For the next 10 years Li Bo traveled from place to place throughout China, surviving by his reputation as a poet and eccentric.

In the scramble for power during the An Lushan rebellion of 755, Li Bo entered the service of a member of the royal family, Prince Yong, who tried unsuccessfully to establish an independent regime in the south. After Yong's defeat and execution, Li Bo was arrested as a traitor and sentenced to death. He gained his release due to the intercession of a soldier whom Li had assisted years before who was now the commander in chief of the imperial army. Banished, the poet resumed his wandering, petitioning for a pardon that he finally received in 759 and vainly hoping for a government position that was finally awarded to him in 762. Before the news could reach him, however, he had died. Legend has it that he drowned after leaning too far over the edge of a boat in a drunken effort to embrace the reflection of the Moon on the water.

The majority of the several thousand poems Li Bo is said to have written have been lost. A large number of those that have survived are in the *yuefu* ballad style that reworks themes drawn from the folk song tradition. As critic Burton Wilson points out, Li Bo's "distinction lies in the fact that he brought an unparalleled grace and eloquence to his treatment of the traditional themes, a flow and a grandeur that left his work far above the level of mere imitations of the past." His contemporaries found his reworking of established subjects and methods shocking in their violations of the accepted rules and in the new elements that Li Bo added such as inventing outlandish dramatic situations and impersonating fictional perspectives that were unprecedented in Chinese poetry. Moreover, Li Bo resisted the conventions that called for a resolution of the tensions raised by the poems through moralizing or an expected regularity of meter and diction. One of his most popular and provocative poems is "The Road to Shu Is Hard," which begins indecorously with a shriek: "A-eee! Shee-yew! Sheeeeee! So dangerous! So high! / The road to Shu is hard, harder than climbing the sky." The difficult ascent is matched stylistically by irregular meter and broken syntax that reflect the traveler's laboring and exhausted condition. As Stephen Owen observes, "There had never been anything like it in Chinese poetry." Li Bo's violations of expectations and custom prompted one contemporary to describe his works as "strangeness on top of strangeness." Part of this strangeness was self-induced through alcohol. Du Fu famously memorialized his friend in his poem "The Eight Immortals of the Winecup":

> As for Li Bo, give him a jugful,
> He will write one hundred poems.
> He drowses in a wine shop
> On a market street of Chang'an;
> And though the emperor calls
> He couldn't stagger aboard the royal barge.
> "Please your Majesty," says he,
> "I am a god of wine."

For Li Bo, his indulgence provided a means of breaking down the barriers of subjectivity and circumstance that grounded the flight of his imagination. As he writes in "Drinking Alone in the Moonlight":

> I have ten million sources of sorrow,
> But only three hundred cups of wine,
> My sorrows are many and the cups are few,
> But pouring a cup keeps sorrow away.
> And I know that I have the sage in my cup,
> For in my cups my heart always smiles. . . .
> The thing to do is drink good wine;
> Go out with the moon and get drunk on a tower.

It is Li Bo's exuberant appetite for experience and his ability that appealed to the Beat Generation in the 1950s; while his poetic method of argument through image provided a model for the modernist poetic revolution of the 20th century led by Ezra Pound and T. S. ELIOT [19]. Pound's translation of Li Bo's "The River Merchant's Wife: A Letter," has been called by fellow poet Kenneth Rexroth, "one of the dozen or so major poems to be written in America in the twentieth century":

> While my hair was still cut straight across my forehead
> I played about the front gate, pulling flowers.
> You came by on bamboo stilts, playing horse,
> You walked about my seat, playing with blue plums.

And we went on living in the village of Chokan:
Two small people, without dislike or suspicion.

At fourteen I married My Lord you.
I never laughed, being bashful.
Lowering my head, I looked at the wall.
Called to, a thousand times, I never looked back.

At fifteen I stopped scowling,
I desired my dust to be mingled with yours
Forever and forever and forever.
Why should I climb the look out?

At sixteen you departed,
You went into far Ku-to-yen, by the river of swirling eddies,
And you have been gone five months.
The monkeys make sorrowful noise overhead.

You dragged your feet when you went out.
By the gate now, the moss is grown, the different mosses,
Too deep to clear them away!
The leaves fall early this autumn, in wind.
The paired butterflies are already yellow with August
Over the grass in the West garden;
They hurt me. I grow older.
If you are coming down through the narrows of the river Kiang,
Please let me know beforehand,
And I will come out to meet you
      As far as Cho-fu-Sa.

The poem captures the essence of Li Bo's work: fleeting images, complex and contrary emotional states, and an expressive style that remains contemporaneous and powerful.

115

HAROLD PINTER

1930–

Man's existential fear, not as an abstraction, not as a surreal phantasmagoria, but as something real, ordinary and acceptable as an everyday occurrence—here we have the core of Pinter's work as a dramatist.

—Martin Esslin, *Pinter the Playwright*

Harold Pinter is unrivaled as the most innovative and influential English dramatist during the second half of the 20th century. Nobel Committee chair, Per Wästberg, in announcing Pinter's selection as the 2005 literature laureate, declared the playwright "the renewer of English drama in the twentieth century." Only the greatest dramatists pioneer a new form and vocabulary for the theater, and Pinter's originality, innovation, and pervasiveness are evident in the various coinages that have entered contemporary parlance. "Pinterland" stands for the enclosed, ostensibly secure rooms and ordinary spaces inhabited by Pinter's unexceptional characters in which apparent normality is disrupted by an intruder or shattered by the eruption of inner compulsions. The "Pinter pause" refers to the dramatist's frequent reliance on what is not said to reveal his characters' identities and motives. Their silences and non sequiturs produce the typical "Pinter moment," and the often inconclusive outcome of his so-called comedies of menace with their trademark fusion of reality and the absurd is encapsulated in the catchall "Pinteresque." No English dramatist in this or the past century has so forcefully expressed, in Wästberg's words, "the abyss under chat, the unwillingness to communicate other than superficially, the need to rule and mislead, the suffocating sensation of accidents bubbling under the quotidian, the nervous perception that a dangerous story has been censored."

Harold Pinter was born in Hackney, in East London, in 1930, the son of a Jewish tailor. "It was a working-class area—" Pinter recalled, "some big, run-down Victorian houses, and a soap factory with a terrible smell, and a lot of railway yards. And shops. It had a lot of shops." At the outbreak of the war, he was evacuated to Cornwell and to the London suburbs. Back home in 1944, Pinter experienced the blitz firsthand: "There were times when I would open our back door and find our garden in flames. Our house never burned, but we had to evacuate several times." Pinter's wartime experiences, as well as the anti-Semitism he encountered—the sense of threat and dislocation—help explain the themes of vulnerability and menace that stalk his works. Attending Hackney Downs Grammar School, Pinter excelled at sports (football, cricket, and track) and got his first acting experience playing Macbeth and Romeo in school productions. After leaving school in 1947, he worked at a variety of odd jobs as a dishwasher, waiter, and salesman. Called for National Service at 18, Pinter declared himself a conscientious objector. Tribunals twice refused Pinter's application for objector status, but instead of being jailed for his refusal to serve, a sympathetic judge merely fined him. He studied acting for a short time at the Royal Academy of Dramatic Art and later at the Central School of Speech and Drama. Securing acting jobs, Pinter toured Ireland in a Shakespearean company and worked in provincial repertory theaters throughout England. In 1957, at the insistence of a friend, Pinter attempted his first play, *The Room*, in which a middle-aged couple's complacent domestic routine is violently and mysteriously shattered. The play foreshadows many of the themes and motifs of Pinter's subsequent dramas, most directly in the play's title. "Two people in a room—I am dealing a good deal with this image of two people in a room," Pinter later summarized. "The curtain goes up on the stage, and I see it as a very potent question: What is going to happen to these two people in the room? Is someone going to open a door and come in?" *The Room* also features Pinter's trademark realistically depicted domestic routine that is gradually supercharged with menace and mystery. The hallmarks of Pinter's dramatic method would also be established in its mixture of tragedy and farce, the spot-on accuracy of its dialogue, in all its trivialities, cross talk, and avoidance of true communication, and a deliberate elimination of exposition and explicit motivation for his characters.

First produced by the drama department of Bristol University, *The Room* received a favorable review from Harold Hobson, the distinguished drama critic of the *Sunday Times*. This would lead to Pinter's first professional production of *The Birthday Party* in 1958. Set in a dingy, seaside boardinghouse, the play concerns the psychological deterioration of a boarder named Stanley, prompted by the arrival of two sinister strangers. Why Stanley is a target and by whom is never answered. However, by eliminating conventional dramatic exposition and resolution, Pinter achieves a tension and resonance that tap into powerful anxieties of uncertainty and threat. Initially, Pinter's realistic working-class characters and settings associated him with the so-called kitchen sink school of realism associated with dramatists such as John Osborne and Shelagh Delaney. "I'd say what goes on in my plays is realistic," Pinter has said, "but what I'm doing is not realistic." His often illogical action and existential themes suggest a closer affinity to the theater of the absurd. It is actually the fusion of both—realism and absurdity—that characterizes Pinter's originality and his singular contribution to modern drama. Disrupting audience expectations of coherent dramatic action and clear motivation, Pinter manages a maximum emotional and intellectual impact with minimal means. "By stripping his characters and drama to bare essentials," critic Evelyn Schreiber summarizes, "Pinter reaches unconscious levels, capturing the essence of human thought and, consequently, a basis of human interaction that often goes unrecognized."

The Caretaker (1960), Pinter's second full-length play and his first major public success, concerns a tramp, Davies, who is given shelter in the home of two brothers—Aston and Mick—who quarrel over the prospect of giving Davies the job as caretaker of the house. Pinter's recurrent themes of the problems of communication and language and the struggle for dominance and power are expressed in a drama that is by turns comic, absurd, malevolent, enigmatic, and moving. As in Pinter's best work, the play operates simultaneously on the realistic and symbolic levels as the three characters and their circumstances are both individualized and representative of archetypes and universals. This same mixture gives Pinter's third full-length play, *The Homecoming*, a tremendous power and unsettling energy. Set in a North London sitting room, the play concerns the homecoming of the eldest son, Teddy, a professor of philosophy at an American college, after an absence of six years. Having told his family nothing about his marriage or his three sons in America, Teddy has brought his English wife, Ruth, whom he had married before leaving, to meet his family for the first time. They are Max, a retired butcher; Teddy's two brothers, the contentious, self-assured Lenny and the slow-witted, brawny Joey; and Max's brother Sam, a hire-car driver. The opening scene of verbal sparring among the house's occupants sets the tone in its rapidly unsettling alterations from commonplace domestic routine to brutal attack. Furthermore nothing quite makes sense regarding this homecoming. Anxious that Ruth meet his family, whom he assures her are "very warm people, really," Teddy makes no effort to wake them or announce their arrival. Ruth, who initially complains of being tired, refuses to go upstairs to bed with her husband, insisting on going for a walk instead. Teddy's first encounter with Lenny betrays no sign that either brother is pleased or surprised at seeing the other after such an absence. Going to bed, Teddy neglects to mention Ruth, who must identify herself when she returns. Lenny ignores the news, and instead they battle for dominance, culminating with Ruth's refusal to comply with Lenny's order to return a glass he has given her, saying "If you take the glass . . . I'll take you." Act one violates virtually every sanctity of family life by revealing the compulsions and aggression uniting this family unit. The home becomes a winner-take-all war zone in which the mundane spontaneously combusts with verbal and physical violence, while mutuality is expressed by assertions of dominance and control. None of the characters conforms to expected behavior patterns. The aging patriarch Max insists on his virility with masculine aggression, while assuming the family's maternal role as homemaker and cook; Ruth is both passive and something of a sexual predator; the long-absent Teddy is greeted by matter-of-fact indifference. Act two escalates the assault on conventions while suffusing the play's naturalism with a poetic and archetypal resonance. The interactions among the six characters culminate in Teddy's abrupt insistence that he and Ruth must depart, and Ruth's decision to stay, complacently agreeing to Lenny's proposal, endorsed by the others, that she be put to work as a prostitute, along with "her obligations this end." The play ends with one of the most disturbing tableaux in modern drama in which familial dynamics, gender assumptions, and sexual dominance are fused in a bizarre family portrait: Teddy has left with Ruth's dismissive farewell—"Don't be a stranger." She is now enshrined in Max's chair, maternally caressing Joey's head in her lap as Max collapses before her, begging a kiss and asserting "I'm not an old man," and Lenny watches.

The Birthday Party, The Caretaker, and The Homecoming established Pinter as Britain's preeminent contemporary dramatist. His three important full-length plays during the 1970s are Old Times (1971), No Man's Land (1975), and Betrayal (1978). In Old Times a married couple's relationship is tested by the arrival of Anna, the wife's former roommate and lover. In No Man's Land the themes of The Caretaker are reworked in a more fashionable setting, as Hirst brings home a shabby poet after a pub encounter, and a combat for dominance and control is played out with the household's two servants. Hirst resorts for refuge either in the idyllic memories preserved in his photo album or an alcoholic stasis, a no-man's-land "Which never moves, which never changes, which never grows older, but which remains forever, icy and silent." Betrayal dramatizes the course of an extramarital affair in reverse chronological order from its end to its origin. Since the 1970s, Pinter has steadily supplemented his work as a dramatist with directing, acting, screenwriting, and poetry. His more recent plays include Family Voices (1981), Moonlight (1993), Ashes to Ashes (1996), Celebrations (2000), and War (2003). Most are marked by increasing formal experiments and a much greater engagement with political issues. Pinter has said that he has probably written his last play and intends to focus on "the very very worrying" political state of affairs. "I've written 29 plays. Isn't that enough? It's enough for me. I've found other forms now." Pinter's legacy is secure. No contemporary dramatist has done more to alter audience expectations about the theatrical experience and dramatic possibilities.

1931–

Toni Morrison is unquestionably the great inheritor of the giant figures of the early twentieth century—Proust, Joyce, Woolf, and Faulkner; she is the proof that what they wrought is still going strong. Time, consciousness, history, the inside story: All this is at the heart of her fiction, even if it seems sea-changed. . . . If Proust, Joyce, Woolf, and Faulkner speak to us of the heart's secrets and the dimensions of the self, Toni Morrison dares to go still further inside, to a time and a place before we were individuated, to the red heart that fuels humankind and signals our connectedness to one another.
—Arnold Weinstein, *Recovering Your Story*

A case can be made that Toni Morrison is the world's most important living novelist. When she was awarded the 1993 Nobel Prize in literature, she became the eighth woman laureate in literature, the 10th American and the first African American to be so honored. This is a remarkable achievement for a writer who did not publish her first novel until she was 39. So far, seven novels have followed, each a richly textured and complex chapter in her ongoing imaginative exploration of race, gender, and identity. Although Morrison's verbal mastery and symphonic narratives have invited comparison to such modernist writers as PROUST [16], JOYCE [7], WOOLF [48], and FAULKNER [15], Morrison herself has traced the inspiration for her themes and style to her African-American heritage and its rich repository of potent stories, personalities, vernacular, and visionary power. She has unapologetically identified herself as a "black woman novelist," rejecting any limitations associated with such a label by asserting that "The range of emotions and perceptions I have had access to as a black person and a female person are greater than those of people who are neither. . . . My world did not shrink because I was a black female author. It just got bigger." It is a testament to Morrison's genius that her reflection of black American experience and particularly the black woman's experience has resonated so widely. She is one of contemporary literature's great exceptions: a demanding and serious writer who challenges her readers but has still managed to attract a large, worldwide audience. Her books, intensely focused on essentials of place, race, and gender, reveal the transformative power of literature to reach universals through the particular.

Born Chloe Anthony Wofford in Lorain, Ohio, a small steel-mill town west of Cleveland, Morrison was the second of four children of parents who were part of the great northern migration of southern blacks seeking greater social, political, educational, and economic opportunities. Her mother's parents came from Alabama via Kentucky where her grandfather had worked as a coal miner. Her father, a former Georgia sharecropper who supported his family as a shipyard welder, was, according to Morrison, "a racist" who, based on his experiences, felt he was justified in despising all whites. Although her mother was more hopeful about the benefits of integration and improved race relations, both taught their daughter to rely on and draw sustenance from the black community—its heritage, folklore, and expressions. "In Lorain, Ohio," Morrison recollected, "when I was a child, I went to school with and heard the stories of Mexicans, Italians and Greeks, and I listened. I remember their language, and a lot of it is marvelous. But when I think of things my mother or father or aunts used to say, it seems the most striking thing in the world. That's what I try to get into my fiction." Her family struggled through the Great Depression, depending on relief and once being burnt out of their home by an irate landlord. As writer Jean Strouse has observed, Morrison "comes from a long line of people who did what they had to do to survive. It is their stories she tells in her novels—tales of the suffering and richness, the eloquence and tragedies of the black American experience." Describing her background, Morrison has stated, "I am from the Midwest so I have a special affection for it. My beginnings are always there. . . . No matter what I write, I begin there. . . . It's the matrix for me . . . Ohio also offers an escape from stereotyped black settings. It is neither plantation nor ghetto." In addition to the importance of place on her development as a writer, another crucial influence was the element of the supernatural Morrison absorbed from her grandmother's dream interpretations and her father's ghost stories that formed a significant part of the family's entertainment. Both forecast the unique blend of the uncanny and the everyday that suffuses Morrison's fiction.

Graduating from public schools in 1949, Morrison attended Howard University where she majored in English and classics and renamed herself Toni, a nickname she acquired in college. After earning a B.A. degree in 1953, Morrison added a Master's degree from Cornell University where she wrote a thesis on the fiction of William Faulkner and Virginia Woolf. After working as an English instructor for two years at Texas Southern University, in 1957 Morrison returned to Howard to teach. There she met and married Jamaican architect Harold Morrison. They would divorce in 1965, when Morrison found herself a single mother of two sons. She began writing as an outlet and relief from the pressures of her marriage and motherhood by joining an informal writers' group that met monthly to exchange stories. After exhausting the writing she had done in high school, Morrison, now 30, began a new story of someone she had known in Lorain, an African-American girl who had prayed to God for blue eyes. She would eventually expand this story into her first novel.

Morrison resigned her teaching appointment to become a textbook editor in Syracuse, New York. Alone in the evenings, after putting her children to bed, Morrison took up writing again as a means of staying in touch with her past and her Ohio community when, as she explained, she "had no one to talk to." In 1967 she took a position as a trade book editor at Random House in New York City. She would remain there for the next 17 years as a senior editor nurturing the careers of such writers as Amiri Baraka, Angela Davis, Toni Cade Bambara, and Gayl Jones. Her first novel, *The Bluest Eye*, was published in 1970. A second novel, *Sula* (1974), about the intersecting lives and relationship of two black girls in the 1920s and 1930s, was mentally composed during Morrison's daily commute on the subway from her home in Queens to her office in Manhattan. Both books were praised for their poetic prose, emotional intensity, and unique interpretation of the African-American experience through a previously neglected female perspective, but neither was a popular success, and both books were out of print when Morrison published her breakthrough novel, *Song of Solomon* (1977), which established Morrison's reputation as a preeminent voice in contemporary fiction worldwide. It won the National Book Critics' Circle Award and the American Academy and Institute of Arts and Letters Award; it was also the first novel by a black writer to be selected as a Book-of-the-Month Club main selection since Richard Wright's *Native Son* in 1940. *Song of Solomon* shows Morrison extending her range as a novelist, employing for the first time a male protagonist, whom critic Margaret Wade-Lewis has called "undoubtedly one of the most effective renderings of a male character by a woman writer in American literature." Milkman Dead's quest to find a family legacy and to decipher his racial identity is a complex and compelling interweaving of myth and history that draws equally on black folklore and classical archetypes. As novelist Reynolds Price observed in his review, "Here the depths of the younger work are still evident, but now they thrust outward, into wider fields, for longer intervals, encompassing many more lives. The result is a long prose tale that surveys nearly a century of American history as it impinges upon a single family." He goes on to assert that "Few Americans know, and can say, more than she has in this wise and spacious novel."

The widening of Morrison's scope is further evident in her next novel, *Tar Baby* (1981), in which she continues an imaginative search for identity in the confrontation between blacks and whites, but here in a global setting that encompasses the entire African diaspora. *Tar Baby* became a best seller and prompted *Newsweek* to do a cover story on the writer. Ironically, Morrison felt at the time that she had exhausted her subject and its expression. "I would not write another novel to either make a living or because I was able to," she later recalled. "If it was not an overwhelming compulsion or I didn't feel absolutely driven by the ideas I wanted to explore, I wouldn't do it. And I was content not to ever be driven that way again." The compulsion came eventually as a result of Morrison's editorial work on Middleton Harris's documentary collection of black life in America, *The Black Book*. Morrison became fascinated by a historical incident from a newspaper clipping contained in it entitled "A Visit to the Slave Mother Who Killed Her Child." A journalist reports on a runaway slave from Kentucky, Margaret Garner, who in 1855 tried to kill her children rather than to allow them to be returned to slavery. Successful in killing one, Margaret Garner would provide the historical access point for her next novel and what many consider her masterpiece as Morrison explored imaginatively the conditions that could have led to such a horrific act and its consequences on the survivors. If *Song of Solomon* and *Tar Baby* dramatize the importance of recovering the past to make us fully human, *Beloved* (1987) concerns the tyranny and toxicity of the past and the most painful legacy of the black experience, the crippling impact of slavery. Morrison's protagonist, Sethe, along with her daughter Denver, live alone in a house outside Cincinnati in the 1870s and are literally haunted by the spirit of Sethe's murdered daughter who comes back to life demanding to be served. In masterful orchestration of fragmented chronology and perspectives, Sethe's painful memories gradually surface and the process of her recovery and the exorcism of the past are dramatized. "I certainly thought I knew as much about slavery as anybody," Morrison told an interviewer. "But it was the interior life I needed to find out about." *Beloved* probes the interior, psychic world of slavery from the formerly neglected perspective of slave, wives, and mothers. In the process, *Beloved* offers one of the most humanly compelling and intellectually and emotionally complex explorations of the legacy of slavery that has ever been attempted. With its vision, which has been aptly described as "encompassing both a private and a national heritage," and its masterful orchestration, *Beloved* invites comparison with the greatest American novels, one of the unavoidable and essential 20th-century American texts.

The three novels that have followed *Beloved* continue Morrison's ambi-tious exploration of the complex intersection of race, gender, and identity as refracted in American and African-American history. *Jazz* (1992), set in Harlem in the 1920s, explores a tragic romantic triangle involving Violet, her husband Joe, and Dorcas, a young woman who bewitches him. "He fell for an 18-year-old girl," the novel begins, "with one of those deep down, spooky loves that made him feel so sad and happy he shot her just to keep the feeling going." Told in a series of flashbacks, *Jazz* arranges the perspectives of each into a bravura verbal performance. According to one reviewer, "You do not read this book; you listen to it." *Paradise* (1998), completing the tril-ogy begun with *Beloved*, explores the tensions that divide the all-black town of Ruby, Oklahoma, prompted by an all-women convent on the outskirts of the town. Racial solidarity collides with gender empowerment in a haunting moral parable that reexamines the biblical concepts of redemption, salvation, sacrifice, and love. The last is explicitly the focus of Morrison's most recent novel, *Love* (2003), in which two women—Heed and Christine—battle over the memory and legacy of the long-deceased Bill Cosey, former owner of "the best and best-known vacation spot for colored folk on the East Coast." Through a series of retrospectives, the mystery of Cosey's death and his role in these and other women's lives are revealed. Critic Adam Langer has called it "a compact meditation on the aftermath of the civil rights movement, a chill-ing ghost story about a friendship destroyed by the whims of a wealthy and respected patriarch, an epic saga about the generation gap, a concise reflec-tion on the African-American experience in the twentieth century." Langer's words capture Morrison's greatness as a writer with a rare ability to tap into the latent power of the past and consciousness itself in such a way that we are reintroduced to ourselves and our heritage.

117

SEAMUS HEANEY

Here is the great paradox of poetry and of the imaginative arts in general. Faced with the brutality of the historical onslaught, they are practically useless. Yet they verify our singularity, they strike and stake out the ore of self which lies at the base of every individuated life. In one sense the efficacy of poetry is nil—no lyric has ever stopped a tank. In another sense, it is unlimited. It is like the writing in the sand in the face of which accusers and the accused are left speechless and renewed.

—Seamus Heaney, "The Government of the Tongue"

In "Under Ben Bulben," W. B. YEATS [17] in his poetic last will and testament lays down a challenge to those writers who would follow him:

> Irish poets, earn your trade,
> Sing whatever is well made . . .
> Sing the peasantry, and then
> Hard-riding country gentlemen,
> The holiness of monks, and after
> Porter-drinkers' randy laughter;
> Sing the lords and ladies gay
> That were beaten into the clay
> Through seven heroic centuries;

Cast your mind on other days
That we in coming days may be
Still the indomitable Irishry.

Seamus Heaney has responded to Yeats's charge by singing both "whatever is well made" and the "Irish peasantry." The main divergence between the greatest 20th-century poet in English and its finest living poet is their identifications: Yeats with the Protestant Ascendancy ("hard-riding country gentlemen") and Heaney with the Catholic laboring class of his background. Conflict, however, or what Heaney has called "the brutality of the historical onslaught," is central to both poets. Each has crafted memorable and important poetry out of the exigencies of the Irish past, its politics, and its ongoing search for identity and values. One of Yeats's most important collections is called *Responsibilities*. The word underscores a shared concern in both poets' attempts to reconcile the opposition between the permanence of art and the historical moment, between the poet's responsibility to his craft and vision and to political, historical, and social realities. Heaney's ongoing engagement with these issues has made him a centrally important modern writer who has managed to transform the personal, local, and at times unimaginable present into timeless and universal art.

Seamus Heaney was born in 1939, the year Yeats died. He was the eldest of nine children, raised on a family farm in County Derry, a Catholic in predominantly Protestant Northern Ireland. Although his family was part of the Catholic majority in their local area, living peaceably with their Protestant neighbors, Heaney was from an early age aware of what he has called the "split culture of Ulster," with Catholics deprived of equal rights, divided between "the marks of English influence and the lure of the native experience, between 'the demesne' [representing British and Loyalist power and privilege] and the bog." This sectarian divide and its impact in the formation of modern Irish identity and politics would shape both Heaney's career and development as a writer. At the age of 11, Heaney left home as a scholarship boarder at Derry's St. Columb's College. Taking advantage of legislative changes that increased educational opportunities for Catholics in Northern Ireland, Heaney, in his words, "emerged from a hidden, a buried life and entered the realm of education." In 1957 he went on to Queen's University, Belfast, where he studied literature and began his encounter with the works of poets such as ROBERT FROST [86], Ted Hughes, and Patrick Kavanagh who drew on the particulars of place and their native backgrounds to anchor their work. "I learned that my local County Derry experience," Heaney later recalled, "which I had considered archaic and irrelevant to 'the modern world' was to be trusted. They taught me that trust and helped me to articulate it." After receiving a degree in English in 1961 and his teaching certificate in 1962, Heaney taught at a secondary school for a year before becoming a lecturer in English at St. Joseph's College of Education in Belfast, a position he held from 1963 to 1966.

Heaney's first collection, *Death of a Naturalist*, appeared in 1966, the same year he returned to Queen's University as a faculty member.

The poem that opens *Death of a Naturalist*, "Digging," qualifies as a kind of manifesto and poetic credo. Reflecting the continuity and disjunction between himself and memories of his grandfather cutting turf and his father using his spade to harvest potatoes, the speaker observes that "I've no spade to follow men like them," but concludes that his pen will be his tool and "I'll dig with it."

Heaney would state that "Digging" was the first poem he wrote "where I thought my feelings had got into words, or to put it more accurately, where I thought my *feel* had got into words. . . . This was the first place where I felt I had done more than make an arrangement of words. I felt I had let down a shaft into real life." The poems in *Death of a Naturalist* would be shaped by the experiences and landscape of his rural upbringing. With titles such as "The Barn," "Blackberry-Picking," and "Churning Day," they are precise evocations of the poet's past and native ground and a search for an understanding of the observer's relationship with that world that is often shown as more disturbing and problematic than initially suspected. Heaney's early poems represent a vivid recovery of the past and its traditions, as well as a nuanced meditation about their meaning. "Bogland," the closing poem from Heaney's second collection, *Door into the Dark* (1969), indicates that the act of digging into layer and layer of accumulated history is a centrally important metaphor for Heaney's understanding Irish consciousness, landscape, and the mission of the Irish poet. Contrasted with the horizontal dimension of the American frontier, Ireland's mythic direction is vertical: "Our pioneers keep striking / Inwards and downward." Heaney's implied poetic mission is to take on that internal journey in search of the continuity and dialogue between past and present, the local and the universal.

If Heaney's initial poetry is characterized by a Keatsian sensuousness and lyrical evocation of private memories and pastoral experiences, he would find himself more and more compelled to confront wider public issues as the repression of the civil rights movement in Northern Ireland spawned escalating and seemingly unending violence beginning in the late sixties. In his third collection, *Wintering Out* (1972), and particularly in *North* (1975), Heaney's focus shifts from the natural, rural world to the harsh and deadly realities of the bigotry and sectarian violence that were crippling Northern Ireland. "From the moment the problems of poetry moved from being simply a matter of achieving the satisfactory verbal icon to being a search for images and symbols adequate to our predicament," Heaney asserted, ". . . I felt it imperative to discover a field of force which, without abandoning fidelity to the processes and experiences of poetry . . . it would be possible to encompass the perspectives of a humane reason and at the same time to grant the religious intensity of the violence its deplorable authenticity and complexity." *North*, written with an intention, in Heaney's words, "to take the English lyric and make it eat stuff that it had never eaten before," has been praised by critic Helen Vendler as "one of the crucial poetic interventions of the twentieth century, ranking with *Prufrock* and *Harmonium* and *North of Boston* in its key role in the history of modern poetry." Poems, such as "Funeral Rites," "Punishment," "Act of Union," "A Constable Calls," and "Exposure," are simultaneously intensely local and universally resonant in their attempt to come to grips with the meaning and significance of the past and a lethal contemporary world.

At the height of the Troubles in 1972, Heaney and his family crossed the border to live outside Dublin where Heaney joined the faculty of Caryfort Teaching Training College, eventually accepting visiting professorships at Harvard and Oxford. Increasingly recognized worldwide as one of the most important contemporary poets, Heaney would continue to confront his responsibilities as a poet and the effectiveness (or futility) of poetry itself in the face of realities he left behind in Northern Ireland. As critic Andrew Murphy has observed, "Heaney ranks as one of a handful of writers who have genuinely struggled to bring their work into some kind of fruitful relationship with the contemporary political situation and its historical antecedents." Heaney's engagement with these issues is evident in the title work of *Station Island* (1984), a poetic sequence in which the speaker, on a pilgrimage of atonement, confronts various figures from his past searching for self-renewal and a direction forward from his survivor's guilt. JAMES JOYCE [7], the archetypal Irish exile who rebelled against the nets of family, religion, and nationality claiming his allegiance and threatening to co-opt his art, becomes the speaker's final guide and provides a last word in his quest for an answer to questions of the efficacy of art and the responsibilities of the artist. "The main thing," the spirit urges, "is to write for the joy of it."

Joyce's advice "to swim out on your own and fill the element with signatures on your own frequency," becomes a testament to artistic integrity and the liberating power of the imagination that would frame the next significant stage in Heaney's work in which the paralysis and guilt experienced in confronting the pressing realities of Northern Ireland are modulated by a renewed faith in the power of poetry and the imagination to reconcile differences and discover sustaining truths. Subsequent volumes—*The Haw Lantern* (1987), *Seeing Things* (1991), *The Spirit Level* (1996), *Electric Light* (2001), *District and Circle* (2006)—have added to Heaney's reputation as a poet of consequence. Awarded the Nobel Prize in literature in 1995, joining Yeats as the second Irish poet so honored, Heaney was praised by the Nobel judges for his creation of "works of lyrical beauty and ethical depths which exalt everyday miracles and the living past." Sustaining a long and productive career as poet, essayist, and translator is Heaney's commitment to the poetic enterprise and the transformative power of his art. "You write books of poems because that is a fulfillment," Heaney has stated, "a making; it's a making sense of your life and it gives achievement, but it also gives you a sense of growth."

GEORGE ORWELL

118

1903–1950

Every line of serious work that I have written since 1936 has been written, directly or indirectly, against totalitarianism and for democratic Socialism, as I understand it. It seems to me nonsense, in a period like our own, to think that one can avoid writing of such subjects. Everyone writes of them in one guise or another. It is simply a question of which side one takes and what approach one follows.

—George Orwell, *Why I Write*

George Orwell wrote the sentences quoted above in 1947, between the publications of *Animal Farm* (1945) and *Nineteen Eighty-Four* (1949), two indisputable classics of 20th-century literature and the novels for which he is most celebrated. A writer of great intellectual integrity, Orwell was, first and foremost, a moralist who, through his works, asked that readers share his concerns about the great political and social issues and ideologies of the 1930s and 1940s and to respond to these issues with thoughtful, honest individualism.

George Orwell was born Eric Arthur Blair in Motihari, Bengal (now Bihar), in colonial India, the second child and only son of Richard and Ida Blair. His father was a low-level administrator in the Opium Department of the Government of India. In 1905 Orwell's mother returned to England with her children and settled in Henley-on-Thames; his father left India for England in 1911, when he retired. Orwell, later a self-confirmed Democratic Socialist, described his family as "lower-upper-middle-class," a reflection of his ambivalence toward the Blairs' place in English society as colonial servants of the British imperialist ruling class together with their modest middle-class economic status. As a child, Orwell compensated for the emotional distance of his parents together with a sense of isolation caused in part by the five-year age gap between himself and his older sister by exploring the English countryside and developing a love of nature that would last into adulthood and prompt him later to write, "By retaining one's childhood love of such things as trees, fishes, butterflies . . . one makes a peaceful word a little more probable." For Orwell, the period before the two world wars seemed a time of tranquility and sanity in England, and he would draw upon it for such novels as *Coming Up for Air.* In 1911 he was sent to St. Cyprian's, an exclusive preparatory school in Eastbourne, which had accepted him at half-fees because of his academic promise. During his five years at St. Cyprian's, Orwell did well academically, but he detested the class-and-money consciousness and misuse of power and prestige evident at the school. His long essay, "Such, Such Were the Joys," written in the 1940s and published posthumously in 1953, is an unsparing account of the snobbish English preparatory school system and Orwell's feelings of failure to conform within it. He went on to Eton College in 1917 on a scholarship; there, although he did not exert himself academically, he thrived in the school's freer intellectual atmosphere and emphasis on individual development, which he expressed through cynicism and outspokenness toward the imperialist values with which he was raised. His best academic efforts were in French, in which he was taught briefly by Aldous Huxley, and was encouraged by his tutor to forgo the customary weekly essay and instead compose fables, short stories, and accounts of his likes and dislikes. He also read a great deal of fiction, most prominently the works of Galsworthy, SHAW [44], Wells, and Samuel Butler.

Orwell graduated from Eton in 1921, but, unlike most of his classmates, he did not go on to Oxford or Cambridge. Instead, he applied for and won a post as a policeman with the Indian Imperial Police in Burma. There, he found the life of a bureaucratic British *sahib* stifling after the free-spirited intellectual atmosphere at Eton. In 1927 he returned to England on medical leave, possibly due to an early bout of tuberculosis and resigned his post without any explanation to his superiors. He announced to his parents his intention to become a writer, a decision based in part on his need to find a social and psychological identity apart from the class pressures he had experienced while growing up and working in colonial India. However, his literary sensibilities, formed at Eton, had not evolved during his years in Burma, and he had not yet been exposed to the modernist writers who reshaped literature during the second and third decades of the 20th century. His early work, therefore, reflected the Victorian and Edwardian writers with whom he was familiar.

In 1928, Orwell moved to London and immersed himself in the underground world of the poor in the East End, an anti-imperialist, proto-socialist exercise, in which, as he later wrote, he intended "to get right down among the oppressed, to be one of them and on their side against their tyrants." He next spent 18 penniless months in Paris, where he had several articles published in Parisian magazines on the subjects that would come to dominate his interests: Burma, popular culture, and social, economic, and political oppression and power. He also wrote two novels and some short stories, the manuscripts of which he destroyed after they were rejected, and he was forced to take a job as a dishwasher in a Paris hotel. When he returned to England late in 1929, he continued to write, and a distinct narrative voice began to emerge in two articles about Burma published in *Adelphi* magazine in 1931, "The Spike" and "A Hanging," both of which successfully combined reportage with imaginative writing. From 1931 to 1936, Orwell worked at a variety of occupations to supplement his writing, including as a teacher at private schools and a clerk in a used bookstore.

Orwell's experiences in Paris and London and his predilection for acerbic social criticism formed the basis for his first long work, *Down and Out in Paris and London*, which was completed in 1930 but went through several revisions and rejections before it was finally accepted by the publisher Victor Gollancz. Orwell insisted that the book be published under a pseudonym and suggested four possible names: P. S. Burton, Kenneth Miles, H. Lewis, and George Orwell. He preferred the last name on the list, and Gollancz decided to use it. Published in 1933, *Down and Out in Paris and London* was a moderate success and earned a second and third printing. Orwell next produced three novels in rapid succession: *Burmese Days* (1934); *A Clergyman's Daughter* (1935), set in a fourth-rate private school; and *Keep the Aspidistra Flying* (1936), which focuses on the advertising industry. All three novels feature Orwell's views on the realities of social and economic inequity and feature protagonists who question class divisions and the values of money and position. *Burmese Days* was published first by Harper's in New York, after Victor Gollancz, despite his socialist leanings, rejected the novel, worried that it would offend British colonials in Burma and India.

Orwell's next work was commissioned by Gollancz, who wanted him to write about the plight of northern English industrial workers. The result was *The Road to Wigan Pier* (1937), a critical study of coal miners in Yorkshire and Lancashire, the second half of which includes Orwell's commitment to socialist aims and ideals. In 1936 Orwell married Eileen O'Shaughnessy and for the next four years rented a general store in Wallington, which he managed when he was not writing. Earlier in 1936, Orwell had gone to Spain as a journalist to cover the Spanish civil war and almost immediately joined an anti-fascist combat militia in Catalonia, organized by the Workers' Party of Marxist Unity (POUM). Eileen, who had gone with him, worked behind the lines. Orwell's six months in Spain produced *Homage to Catalonia* (1938), a personal chronicle of the drudgery of war, his disillusionment caused by the struggle between his personal ideals and self-serving party power politics, and his faith in the potential of the common citizenry. The threat of totalitarianism, together with the themes of propaganda and political deception that Orwell explored in *Homage to Catalonia*, would later form the basis for *Animal Farm* and *Nineteen Eighty-Four*. Orwell's health suffered during his six months in Spain; he had been wounded in the neck and suffered permanent damage to one of his vocal cords, and a tubercular hemorrhage forced him to spend five months in a sanatorium. During his recovery in Morocco, he wrote *Coming Up for Air*, which was published in 1939. In the novel, Orwell, through his protagonist, acknowledges the moral and cultural strength that can result from a stable and secure childhood but warns of a complacency stemming from nostalgia for the past that is unaware of a potential totalitarian "hate-world, slogan-world."

During World War II, Orwell abandoned his earlier antiwar stance in favor of intense patriotism. Turned down for military service several times because of his precarious health and his past association with the POUM in Spain, he joined the Home Guard and the BBC, where he prepared cultural talks to be broadcast to Asia. Orwell attempted to reconcile his conservative and radical beliefs in his 1941 pamphlet, *The Lion and the Unicorn: Socialism and the English Genius*, developed from his 1940 essay, "My Country Right or Left." In it, Orwell links socialism to patriotism and English history and points to a common and continuous English cultural heritage that transcends ideology, especially during times of national crisis. In 1943, disappointed by the BBC's caveat against covering such issues as Asian self-rule and the fate of British colonialism, Orwell resigned and took a position as literary editor of the *Tribune* newspaper.

In four months between 1943 and 1944, Orwell wrote the first of two novels that would become highly acclaimed and seal his literary reputation. Written as a fable, *Animal Farm* is a bitter anti-Soviet, satirical allegory set in a barnyard. The novel concerns the revolution of the animals against their abusive human masters that occurs after the death of Old Major, an elderly boar representing Karl Marx. Representing the communist party are the pigs, two of whom, Napoleon (Stalin) and Snowball (Trotsky), assume leadership and create a self-sufficient cooperative society. Napoleon, who uses propaganda as a tool to control the other animals, carries out a massive purge, which results in the slaughter of Snowball and his supporters. Ultimately the original tenets of the revolution are forgotten as the pigs become indistinguishable from the vicious humans they sought to depose. The theme of *Animal Farm* is perhaps best illustrated by the last of the Seven Commandments of the Rebellion, "All animals are equal," which, by the end of the novel, becomes "All animals are equal but some animals are more equal than others."

According to Orwell, *Animal Farm* represented the first time he had consciously fused "political purpose and artistic purpose into one whole." The novel was turned down by several publishers in England because of its anti-Stalin and anti-Soviet position at a time when Russia was an ally. An American publisher rejected *Animal Farm* with the explanation that Americans were not in the mood for animal stories. Orwell considered publishing the short novel as a two-shilling pamphlet until it was finally accepted by a British publisher, which held it for publication until 1945. It came out in the United States the following year. *Animal Farm* was a great success and was immediately hailed as a modern classic. Orwell followed it with *Critical Essays* (1946), a collection on popular culture that was published in the United States as *Dickens, Dali, and Others*. The same year, Orwell, whose wife had died in 1945, rented a house in Jura, in the Outer Hebrides. There, he wrote the majority of a novel he had originally entitled *The Last Man in Europe*, and which would be retitled as *Nineteen Eighty-Four*. Orwell finished the first draft in 1947, but an attack of tuberculosis forced him into a sanatorium for seven months and he was not able to complete the novel until 1948. It was published the following year and was a best seller in Britain and the United States.

Set in the near future in a world that has been divided into three super-states engaged in perpetual war with one another, *Nineteen Eighty-Four* takes place in Oceania, which is ruled by a collectivist oligarchy that has brutally eliminated everything associated with a free society: intellectual expression, individual autonomy, friendship, free speech, and the consciousness of a personal and cultural past and present. Presiding over the behavior of Oceania's citizenry—the Inner Party (the ruling elite), the Outer Party (the party functionaries), and the proles (the vast underclass of laborers)—is Big Brother, a figurehead who may or may not be an actual person, but whose images are everywhere. Citizens are bombarded with "doublethink" and "newspeak," which include the central party slogans "War is Peace," "Freedom is Slavery," and "Ignorance is Strength." The novel records the brief rebellion and downfall of its protagonist, Winston Smith, an Outer Party member, who rewrites history for the Ministry of Truth, a governing body involved in falsification. Smith's forbidden love affair with a coworker, Julia, and the couple's misplaced trust in Mr. Charrington, a kindly antique shop owner who is in reality a member of the Thought Police, and O'Brien, a Ministry of Truth functionary, leads to Winston's physical and mental torture, his betrayal of Julia, and his "successful" reeducation in party principles: "But it was all right, everything was all right, the struggle was finished. He had won the victory over himself. He loved Big Brother."

Nineteen Eighty-Four is a magnification of all that Orwell witnessed (and wrote about) throughout his life regarding totalitarianism and the deleterious manipulation effected by governments on its citizens. It is very much a novel of the postwar and early cold war eras—but Orwell's warning to abandon complacency in favor of vigilance toward those who hold political power has remained strikingly relevant.

Orwell was remarried in 1949 to editorial assistant Sonia Brownell. The following year he died of tuberculosis in London. His influence has endured into the 21st century; no writer of the previous century approached the excesses and abuses of power with such inventiveness. Orwell's novels, especially *Nineteen Eighty-Four*, together with his essays and other works of nonfiction, produced in a comparatively short span of time, are deftly written explications and uneasy prognostications of an uncertain present and future culled from a faithful perception of his own experience as an Englishman of his time. Orwell was, as critic V. S. Pritchett described him after his death, the "conscience of his generation."

ARTHUR MILLER

119

1915–2005

Arthur Miller was the last of the great titans of the American stage. He brought to the English-speaking theatre a poetic urgency and tragic sweep that had been absent since the Elizabethan era. I have no doubt that plays like Death of a Salesman, The Crucible, *and* A View from the Bridge *will always stand with the masterpieces of Ibsen, Shakespeare and Sophocles.*

—Nicholas Hytner, director of the Royal National Theatre,
quoted in *The Guardian*

British playwright David Hare greeted the news of Arthur Miller's death in 2005 by observing that "He was one of the playwrights who made the 20th century the American century. When you think about American theatre it's Miller, Tennessee Williams, O'Neill—and now we've lost them all." If O'NEILL [59] is the soul of American theater and WILLIAMS [113] its passion, Miller is undoubtedly its conscience. His plays helped to establish American drama as a decisive and crucial arena for addressing the core questions of American identity and social and moral values, while pioneering modes of expression that liberated American theater. "Arthur's special achievement," Hare added, "was to make political and social plays which belonged on Broadway and yet were also powered to reach out into America and way beyond." In a succession of intense and profound dramatic meditations and explorations, including *All My Sons, Death of a Salesman, The Crucible, A View from the Bridge,* and *After the Fall,* Miller embraced the role of the playwright as social conscience and reformer who could help change America and the world, by, as he put it, "grabbing people and shaking them by the back of the neck." As drama historian C. W. E. Bigsby has asserted, "No other American dramatist has so directly engaged the anxieties and fears, the myths and dreams of a people desperate to believe in a freedom from which they see ever less evidence. No other American writer has so successfully touched a nerve of the national consciousness. But Miller is claimed with equal avidity by the international community. . . . Miller may have been moved to write by specific circumstances but the plays which resulted transcended those circumstances as they did national boundaries."

Miller's subjects, themes, and dramatic mission reflect his life experiences, shaped principally by the Great Depression, which he regarded as a "moral catastrophe," rivaled, in his view, only by the Civil War in its profound impact on American life. Miller was born in 1915, in New York City. His father, who had emigrated from Austria at the age of six, was a successful coat manufacturer, prosperous enough to afford a chauffeur and a large apartment overlooking Central Park. For Miller's family, an embodiment of the American dream that holds that hard work and drive are rewarded, the stock market crash of 1929 changed everything. The business was lost, and the family was forced to move to considerably reduced circumstances in the Flatbush section of Brooklyn to a small frame house that later served as the model for the Lomans' residence in *Death of a Salesman.* Miller's father never fully recovered from his business failure, and his mother was often depressed and embittered by the family's decline and poverty, though both continued to live in hope of better times ahead. For Miller, the Depression exposed the hollowness and fragility of the American dream of material success and the social injustice inherent in an economic system that created so many blameless casualties. The paradoxes of American success—its stimulation of both dreams and guilt when unrealized or lost, as well as the conflict it creates between self-interest and social responsibility—would become dominant themes in Miller's work. "Arthur Miller," critic Leonard Moss has asserted, "has focused upon a single subject—the struggle . . . of the individual attempting to gain his 'rightful' position in his society and in his family."

As a high school student, Miller was more interested in sports than studies. "Until the age of seventeen I can safely say that I never read a book weightier than *Tom Swift* and *Rover Boys,*" Miller recalled, "and only verged on literature with some of Dickens. . . . I passed through the public school system unscathed." After graduating from high school in 1932, Miller went to work in an auto parts warehouse in Manhattan. It was during his subway commute to and from his job that Miller began reading, discovering both the power of serious literature to change the way one sees the world and his vocation: "A book that changed my life was *The Brothers Karamazov* which I picked up, I don't know how or why, and all at once believed I was born to be a writer." In 1934 Miller was accepted as a journalism student at the University of Michigan. There he found a campus engaged by the social issues of the day: "the place was full of speeches, meetings and leaflets. It was jumping with Issues. . . . It was, in short, the testing ground for all my prejudices, my beliefs and my ignorance, and it helped to lay out the boundaries of my life." At Michigan, Miller wrote his first play, despite having seen only two plays years before, to compete for prize money he needed for tuition. Failing in his first attempt, he would eventually twice win the Avery Hopwood Award for playwrighting. Winning "made me confident I could go ahead from there. It left me with the belief that the ability to write plays is born into one, and that it is a kind of sport of the mind." Miller became convinced that "with the exception of a doctor saving a life, writing a worthy play was the most important thing a human could do." Two years after graduating in 1938, having moved back to Brooklyn and married his college sweetheart, Miller had completed six plays, all but one of them rejected by producers. *The Man Who Had All the Luck*, a play examining the ambiguities of success and the money ethic, managed a run of only four performances on Broadway in 1944. While working at the Brooklyn Navy Yard, Miller tried his hand at radio scripts and attempted one more play. "I laid myself a wager," he wrote in his autobiography. "I would hold back this play until I was as sure as I could be that every page was integral to the whole and would work; then, if my judgment of it proved wrong, I would leave the theater behind and write in other forms." The play was *All My Sons* (1947) about a successful manufacturer who sells defective aircraft parts and is made to face the consequences of his crime and his responsibilities. It is Miller's version of an IBSEN [36] problem play linking a family drama to wider social issues. Named one of the top 10 plays of 1947, *All My Sons* won the Tony Award and the New York Drama Critics' Circle Award over Eugene O'Neill's *The Iceman Cometh*. The play's success allowed Miller to buy property in rural Connecticut where he built a small studio and began work on *Death of a Salesman*, arguably the greatest play ever written by an American.

Chronicling the last 24 hours of the aging and failing traveling salesman Willy Loman who is betrayed by the American dream, *Death of a Salesman* (1949) achieves its striking power and persistence from a remarkably intimate and unflinching portrait of a family riven by their collective dreams and trapped by their unspoken secrets. Critical debate over whether Willy lacks the stature or self-knowledge to qualify as a true tragic hero seems beside the point in performance as few other modern dramas have so powerfully elicited pity and terror in their audiences. Willy Loman's fall has become one of the core American myths, dramatizing the consequences for the prototypical

American dreamer. Willy's friend Charley offers the salesman's eulogy that brilliantly summarizes both Willy's heroism and its tragic cost:

> Nobody dast blame this man. You don't understand: Willy was a sales-
> man. And for a salesman, there is no rock bottom to the life. He don't put
> a bolt to a nut, he don't tell you the law or give you medicine. He's a man
> way out there in the blue, riding on a smile and a shoeshine. And when
> they start not smiling back—that's an earthquake. And then you get a
> couple of spots on your hat, and you're finished. Nobody dast blame this
> man. A salesman is got to dream, boy. It comes with the territory.

All My Sons and *Death of a Salesman* firmly established Miller's preeminence as a dramatist and a social critic, earning both great praise and censure
for his critique of American life and values. *Death of a Salesman* in particular
was attacked by conservatives as "a time bomb expertly placed under the edifice
of Americanism," and, in the ensuing Red Scare that gripped America in the
1950s, Miller was frequently branded that "pinko playwright." Subpoenaed to
appear as a witness before the House Committee on Un-American Activities,
Miller refused to give the names of writers he had seen at a communist writer's meeting in 1947. Charged with contempt of Congress and fined, Miller
appealed to the Supreme Court, which acquitted him in 1958. The betrayal
of America's most cherished principles of personal liberty and the protections
of conscience that Miller experienced during this period would be reflected in
his next play, *The Crucible* (1953), which refracts the present through the lens
of the 17th-century Salem witch trials. The hysteria that grips the community
forces a moral and ethical testing for the play's protagonist, John Proctor, who
ultimately chooses death and integrity over "naming names" and capitulation
to a falsehood. Declaring that "I will have my life," John initially agrees to
save himself by falsely confessing his allegiance to Satan to the delight of his
accusers, but changes his mind when he is asked to name others and hand over
his signed confession for public display. Asked to explain why, John answers:
"Because it is my name! Because I cannot have another in my life! Because
I lie and sign myself to lies! Because I am not worth the dust on the feet of
them that hang! How may I live without my name? I have given you my soul;
leave me my name!" John's assertion of personal integrity in the face of death
becomes the play's great tragic turning point. It is, in Miller's words, "that
moment of commitment . . . that moment when, in my eyes, a man differenti-
ates himself from every other man. . . . the less capable a man is of walking
away from the central conflict of the play, the closer he approaches a tragic
existence. In turn, this implies that the closer a man approaches tragedy the
more intense is his concentration upon the fixed point of his commitment."
Managing a universal relevance in dealing with its issues of autonomy versus
conformity and the conflict between the individual and the community, *The*

Crucible has transcended both its historical era and 1950s relevance to become one of the most performed American plays worldwide.

Miller's other important play of the 1950s was *A View from the Bridge* (1956; revised 1957), a return to his familiar Brooklyn setting and a family drama in which longshoreman Eddie Carbone's self-deception about his incestuous feelings for his niece leads to betrayal and the ruin of himself and his family. In 1956 Miller divorced his first wife, Mary Slattery, to marry actress Marilyn Monroe. During their four-year marriage, Miller created nothing for the stage but produced his first film script, *The Misfits* (1960), starring his wife. After an absence of nine years, Miller returned to Broadway with *After the Fall* (1964), his most personal and innovative play in which the protagonist's inner torment is externalized in a despairing review of his past and his own culpability. Two additional plays—*Incident at Vichy* (1964), Miller's consideration of the Holocaust, and *The Price* (1968), in which two brothers assess their life choices as they meet in the attic of their New York brownstone to arrange the sale of the family furniture to an antique dealer—appeared on Broadway. Miller, however, grew increasingly dissatisfied with the limitations of Broadway, stating that "I had been backed into a corner, really . . . I didn't know who I was talking to." His later plays, including *The Archbishop's Ceiling* (1977), *The American Clock* (1980), *Playing for Time* (1985), *The Ride Down Mt. Morgan* (1991), *Broken Glass* (1994), and *Resurrection Blues* (2002), premiered at various venues in the United States and abroad, expressing the playwright's ongoing search for a wider and sympathetic audience for his works that continued to engage the thorniest moral, political, and existential questions.

Over his long career, Miller was consistently a passionate moralist, often as hard on himself for failing to live up to his principles as he was on his fellow Americans and mankind. His plays show a restless search for a moral center, testing the cherished values of democracy and freedom against the reality of history and our personal and collective failures to live up to our best selves. In what could serve well as his own epitaph Miller wrote, "Maybe all one can do is hope to end up with the right regrets."

DORIS LESSING

120

1919–

Clearly Lessing has not yet concluded her career-long investigation of her major topics. She has probably not exhausted the subject of evolution, any more than she has finished with the dialogue between the private and the public, identity and role, self and other, inner self and outer self, child and parent, mortality and spirituality, or among the individual, the collective, and the whole. After writing fiction for forty years, she is still engaged with the themes and concerns mapped out in her first novels and stories. Her work may be regarded as an extended dialogue on the important topics of the times. In the magnitude of her interests and her dialogic inclusivity, which makes impossible a final formulation of her thought, she is a major recorder and interpreter of the human condition in the twentieth century.
—Jean Pickering, *Understanding Doris Lessing*

An ambitious and restless intelligence in the service of a relentless and abiding inquiry into the human condition, together with a genius for portraying people and events in precise, concrete, and sometimes alarming detail, characterizes Doris Lessing's works and makes her one of the most important writers of the 20th century. The prolific author of novels and more than 50 short stories, Lessing was awarded the Nobel Prize in literature in 2007. In her long and varied literary career, she has produced everything from realistic works set in Africa and England that primarily focus on colonial culture, the relationships between men and women, the inner lives of women, and women's place in modern society to a daring multivolume science-fiction epic set in another galaxy.

Doris Lessing was born in 1919, in Kermanshah, Persia (now Iran), the elder of two children of Alfred Cook Tayler, a bank clerk who had lost a leg as the result of a wound suffered in the battle of Passchendaele during World War I. "I knew him," Lessing later wrote, "when his best years were over." Lessing's mother, Emily, was a nurse who had met Tayler while he was convalescing in a London hospital. Like Martha Quest, her main character in the series, *Children of Violence*, Lessing grew up in Africa. In the mid-1920s, Alfred Tayler had moved his family to a large farm he had purchased in Rhodesia (now Zimbabwe), then a British colony. Lessing, who later described the family's thatched farmhouse as "a living thing, responsive to every mood of the weather," memorialized it in a poem, "The House at Night," and in the novel *Martha Quest*. The Taylers' farm failed to prosper for the 20 years the family owned it, but Lessing benefited from the experience of living in Africa in the independence of mind and gift for observation that were shaped in great part by her childhood experiences roaming the veldt alone, sometimes with a rifle to shoot game for family meals. Sent to the Dominican convent school in Salisbury (now Harare), Lessing, although an avid reader, disliked the rigidity of formal education and left school at 14, apparently because of an eye infection. She worked as an au pair in Salisbury for two years and then returned to the farm to write. At the same time she read extensively the works of the great 19th-century European novelists. In 1938 she went back to Salisbury, where she worked as a telephone operator and a secretary. The following year she married Frank Wisdom, a civil servant. The couple had two children and divorced in 1943. The same year, Lessing published her first poems and stories in local journals. She became involved in radical politics and, in 1945, married Gottfried Lessing, a German communist, with whom she had a son. After moving to London in 1949, Lessing was declared a Prohibited Immigrant and barred from Rhodesia until the advent of black majority rule, in 1980. She wrote an article on the subject, "Being Prohibited," for the *New Statesman* in 1956, in which she referred to herself as being in a "select company of people deported, prohibited and banned." Gottfried Lessing immigrated to East Germany, where he became the commissar of trade and ambassador to Uganda. He was accidentally killed in 1979, during the revolt against Idi Amin. Since 1949, Lessing has lived with her son, Peter Lessing, in various residences in London.

Lessing's first novel, *The Grass Is Singing*, was written before she left Rhodesia and published in 1950. The title comes from a passage in ELIOT's [19] *The Waste Land*, which pictures a decayed hole among the mountains, where the grass is singing over tumbled graves, and ends with the threatening image of "the jungle crouched, humped in silence. . . . then spoke the thunder." One of the few novels about Africa at the time, *The Grass Is Singing* is set in Rhodesia and tells the story of Mary Turner, a white farmer's wife, and her black male servant, and the violent conclusion to their relationship. A complex and candid presentation of apartheid and the status of women in a colonial culture, the novel presages the psychological insight and political and social consciousness Lessing would bring to her later works. She followed her debut novel with *This Was the Old Chief's Country* (1951), a volume of ten short stories that are Rhodesian in theme and setting; *Martha Quest* (1952), the first novel in Lessing's five-volume *Children of Violence* series; and *Five* (1953), a group of five novelettes, for which she received the Somerset Maugham Award in 1954.

During the 1950s and 1960s, Lessing completed the *Children of Violence* quintet: besides *Martha Quest*, these include *A Proper Marriage* (1954), *A Ripple from the Storm* (1958), *Landlocked* (1965), and *The Four-Gated City* (1969). The novels, each of which reflects the times in which they were written, trace the history and maturation of the protagonist, Martha Quest, from her childhood in Rhodesia through her developing social conscience regarding racism and inequality, her involvement with communism and rejection of ideology, her experiences as a wife and mother, and her struggle to attain personal freedom. The last novel ends in 1997, after Martha has immigrated to England and a nuclear accident has destroyed civilization. There is an "Appendix" of documents by the main characters that describe the postapocalyptic utopian society they have founded, a harkening back to a daydream that haunts Martha in the first novel of "a noble city, set foursquare and colonnaded along its falling, flower-boarded terraces" with "the blue-eyed, fair-skinned children of the North playing hand in hand with the bronze-skinned, dark-eyed children of the South." Lessing disputed critics' observations that there were autobiographical parallels in the series, especially with the first novel. Instead, she preferred to characterize *Children of Violence* objectively as a "study of the individual conscience in its relations with the collective."

In the years Lessing was working on *Children of Violence*, she published two additional novels: *Retreat to Innocence* (1956), Lessing's first full-length novel to be set in England, and *The Golden Notebook* (1962), which is considered to be her masterpiece. A massive and intense novel employing an intricate and self-conscious interior structure, *The Golden Notebook* demands from its reader both an objective consideration of its fragmented construction and a visceral response to each of its parts. The story of Anna Freeman Wulf, a blocked writer, the novel is divided into five sections, four of which contain subsections called "The Notebooks," framed by a short, realistic novel, "Free Women," presented in segments. In between are transcriptions of the notebooks in which Anna records aspects of her past and present. The final "Golden Notebook" is a culmination of what has been written before and records Anna's breakdown and her movement from destruction toward control, from fragmentation to unity, reassembling her past and psyche, as she refuses the role of victim (in love, politics, and art) and accepts the conditions of her past and present circumstances. In doing so, she breaks the spell that has incapacitated and silenced her. At once a self-reflective text, a feminist manifesto, and an exploration of contemporary and colonial British culture, *The Golden Notebook* explores, as a *New Statesman* reviewer observed, what it means to be "free and responsible, a woman in relation to men and other women, and to struggle to come to terms with one's self about these things and about writing and politics."

During the early 1970s, Lessing produced three novels, two of which, *Briefing for a Descent into Hell* (1971) and *The Memoirs of a Survivor* (1974) show the influence of the British psychologist R. D. Laing and the mystical principles of Sufi Islam. Both novels expand upon and reflect the self-actu-alization and introspective themes present in *The Golden Notebook*. A more traditional narrative characterizes *The Summer before the Dark* (1973), a novel concerning a middle-aged woman's inner struggle to accept the inevitability of aging. Lessing, ever a courageous writer, completely shifted genres in the late 1970s with *Re: Colonized Planet 5—Shikasta* (1979), the first in what would become an epic five-volume science-fiction series, *Canopus in Argos: Archives*, a cosmic view of human history from the perspective of a distant galaxy. The four subsequent novels in the quintet are *The Marriages between Zones Three, Four, and Five* (1980), *The Sirian Experiments* (1980), *The Making of the Repre-sentative for Planet 8* (1982), and *Documents Relating to the Sentimental Agents in the Volyen Empire* (1983). Readers and reviewers variously greeted Lessing's science-fiction series with admiration for her audacious achievement and dis-appointment that she had seemingly abandoned her role as realistic observer and chronicler of self and society.

Lessing resumed that role in the 1980s with three novels, *The Diaries of Jane Somers* (1984), *The Good Terrorist* (1985), and *The Fifth Child* (1988). These later works, like the earlier novels, reflect the times in which they were composed and explore the tensions that persist between the individual and, in the latter work, the family, in relation to the larger collective. Lessing's later works display a more ironic expression of this ongoing theme, which suggests that the author, mirroring Martha Quest and Anna Wulf, has moved forward, in her own inner journey, toward a detachment and wisdom that has developed through her years as observer and analyst of human relationships. During her long career, Lessing has demonstrated a profound lack of literary com-placency, becoming in the process an artist firmly placed, in her own words, outside "that cage of associations and labels that every established writer has to learn to live inside."

E. M. FORSTER

121

1879–1970

Forster's world seemed a comedy, neatly layered and staged in a garden whose trim privet hedges were delicate with gossamer conventions. About its lawns he rolled thunderstorms in teacups, most lightly, beautifully.

— T. E. Lawrence, in the *Spectator*, 1927

Despite E. M. Forster's distinction as one of the 20th century's fictional masters, he is one of the century's most problematic figures. As Lionel Trilling perceptively observed in his pioneering critical study of the novelist, "He is sometimes irritating in his refusal to be great." A self-confessed victim of sloth and procrastination, Forster largely abandoned fiction for nearly 50 years after the success of *A Passage to India*, an indisputable modern masterpiece. As the clever cliché asserts, he became more and more famous with every book that he did not write. His diffidence, playfulness, and elusiveness contributed to critic I. A. Richards's judgment in 1927 that Forster is "the most puzzling figure in contemporary English letters." Forster embodied great contradictions and paradoxes in his novels, short stories, and essays, and battled them ultimately into a creative silence.

A lament for what Forster did not write, however, should not obscure an appreciation for what he did produce. Even though Forster himself insisted, "I am quite sure I am not a great novelist," his achievement, despite his limitations, justifies his ranking here for tackling some of life's most intransigent issues. As Cyril Connolly argued, "'Only connect . . .', the motto of *Howards End*, might be the lesson of all his work." Forster's genius rests in his struggle to unite the irreconcilable differences between the frenzied modern world and the stability and order of the Victorian era in which he was born, between thought and feeling, the inner and outer world.

Edward Morgan Forster was the only surviving child of Edward Forster, an architect, who died of tuberculosis when Forster was not yet two years old. His mother came from a poor middle-class family who, on the sudden death of her drawing-master father, was left with no financial support. She was taken in by Marianne Thornton, a scion of the famous Clapham Sect of social reformers, and prepared for a career as a governess. She eventually married Miss Thornton's nephew, Edward Forster. Their son, the future novelist, was deeply imbued with the values of middle-class Victorian life, with its moral earnestness and proprieties, as well as the disjunction that he increasingly detected between the head and heart. He identified a fear of feelings as the characteristic defect of the English middle-class. This would become a central theme in his fiction.

Forster spent his childhood in a country house called Rooksnest in Hertfordshire, the model for the house in *Howards End*. Precocious and overprotected, at the age of 14 Forster was sent as a day student to Tonbridge School, the model for Sawston School in *The Longest Journey*. The novelist later recalled this period as "the unhappiest time of my life," which further divided Forster's experience between a sensitive and valued inner life and a hostile, alienating public world. Classical studies at Cambridge followed in 1897, and in 1901, during his fourth year studying history, he was elected to membership in the intellectual society of the Cambridge Apostles, whose members included Bertrand Russell, Alfred North Whitehead, and figures of the future Bloomsbury Group, such as John Maynard Keynes, Roger Fry, Lytton Strachey, and Leonard Woolf. Forster was nicknamed by Lytton Strachey "the taupe," or mole, as Leonard Woolf explained, "because of his faint physical resemblance to a mole, but principally because he seemed intellectually and emotionally to travel underground and every now and again pop up unexpectedly with some subtle observation or delicate quip which somehow or other he had found in the depths of the earth or of his own soul." Forster was energized by the group's heterodoxy, its opposition to philistine values outside the members' own elite, and its homosexual sympathies.

After graduation, a legacy from his great-aunt Marianne Thornton left Forster free to travel. In the company of his mother he embarked on an extended trip to Italy, beginning a pattern of foreign travel that would continue throughout his writing career. Italy was a personally transforming experience. It was also the source for his first important literary work, which exposed the tensions in his own identity that he began to explore through fiction. Forster's first important short story, "The Story of a Panic," dramatizes the visitation of the Great God Pan to a 14-year-old English adolescent on an Italian holiday. For his elders, the experience results in shock and horror, but for the boy it is a joyous release of his inner self. The story duplicates Forster's own epiphany, through which he determined to become a writer and to base his work on his own private experience with the world.

Back in England in 1902, Forster taught a weekly Latin class at the Working Men's College in London, and in 1905 tutored the children of Elizabeth, Countess von Arnim in Germany. His first novel, *Where Angels Fear to Tread*, was published in 1905. It was followed by *The Longest Journey* (1907), *A Room with a View* (1908), and his first major success, *Howards End* (1910). In 1912, Forster visited India for the first time and began to collect material for *A Passage to India*. During World War I, Forster worked for the Red Cross in Alexandria, Egypt. In 1921, he made his second visit to India as the private secretary to the maharajah of Dewas. This job afforded him the final source material for *A Passage to India*, which was published to great acclaim in 1924. On the basis of it alone, Forster earned his place as a major 20th-century novelist, but at the age of 46, with exactly half of his lifetime ahead of him, he wrote no more novels. Instead he produced biographies, essays, literary journalism, and a famous series of lectures that was published as *Aspects of the Novel* (1927). He also partially completed the libretto for Benjamin Britten's opera *Billy Budd*. Elected as an honorary fellow at King's College in 1945, he returned to Cambridge, where be remained until his death, dividing his time among Cambridge, a country house (designed by his father), and a pied-à-terre in London.

Forster had by then reached the stature of a liberal sage and the conscience for civilization. He invariably answered repeated inquiries about the status of any forthcoming novel by asserting that he had nothing further to say and confessing his inability to capture the postwar world, so different from the vanished world of his novels. "It is impossible," Forster wrote in *Howards End*, "to see modern life steadily and see it whole." *Maurice*, a final novel with an explicit homosexual subject, which Forster wrote in 1913, was published posthumously.

Forster's strengths as a novelist are derived from the continuity between his books and the comic tradition of the novel, perfected by JANE AUSTEN [20] in the comedy of social manners. Unlike HENRY JAMES [38], VIRGINIA WOOLF [48], or JAMES JOYCE [7], Forster was not a stylistic innovator: he employed techniques closer to those of the great Victorians. An ever-present narrative voice comments on the action of his stories, and is not hidden by dramatic masks or fragmented by complex and shifting narrative perspectives. All of Forster's novels launch his characters on a revealing journey to a new and radically different environment or culture, which tests their original conception of the world and forces a new understanding that reveals a deeper and more complex sense of the individual and of human possibilities. Examples include the opportunity for reassessment that confronts the conventional Mrs. Moore and her son's intended, the earnest Adela Quested, on their arrival in India. British, Hindu, and Muslim cultures collide, producing absurd, ironic, and eventually tragic misunderstandings. Another is the juxtaposition, in *Howards End*, between the cultured, intellectual sensibility of the two Schlegel sisters, Margaret and Helen, and the plodding, self-satisfied practicality of the bourgeois Wilcox family, in which witty social satire as well as profound questions of human nature are explored in the testing of values that the novel arranges. Forster's novels focus on opposition, particularly between one's private self and a hostile, repressive outer world, often expressed as a sexual scandal that illuminates the gap between instinct and morality, private demands and public obligations.

Forster often fails to dramatize heterosexual love convincingly, and his thematic design sometimes predominates over felt experience in his books, but his successes as a social satirist, moralist, and psychological analyst are sufficient compensation. In his autobiography, Christopher Isherwood records a novelist friend's remark that "Forster's the only one who understands what the modern novel ought to be. . . . Our frightful mistake was that we believed in tragedy . . . tragedy is quite impossible nowadays. . . . We ought to aim at being essentially comic writers." Forster's comic battle to connect the deeply private inner self with an antagonistic public world to reform both constitutes an important and central challenge for the contemporary novelist.

ISAAC BASHEVIS SINGER

1904–1991

Singer is not an innovator. He uses traditional forms—fable, folktale, and sermon—because he regards himself as a storyteller. When he is writing well—that is, most of the time!—he is able to relate the most extraordinary, unbelievable events in a matter-of-fact tone. He never loses grip of the tension between the daily occurrences and the "miracle." Indeed he sees the miracle in the newspaper, the divine in the material experience.
—Irving Malin, *Isaac Bashevis Singer*

In one sense Isaac Bashevis Singer's death in 1991 represented the end of a tradition and culture. Writing in Yiddish, a language then close to extinction, about life in the vanished world of Polish shtetls, Singer seems the end of a line, a traditional storyteller of a departed world. In another sense, however, the elegiac note is muted by Singer's gaining a wide international audience of readers in translation, which culminated in his 1978 Nobel Prize for literature. Intensely local, shaped by an increasingly remote tradition, Singer's imagination still communicates across cultural differences in a language of universality and myth. No other writer has seemed so able, in the words of WILLIAM BLAKE [29], "To see a world in a grain of sand / And a heaven in a wild flower."

Singer's art is rich from the compound of his cultural experience and his many dimensions, contained in his statement on accepting the 1974 National Book Award in fiction: "I am happy to call myself a Jewish writer, a Yiddish

471

writer, an American writer." Consequently, Singer's literary achievement seems as capable of affecting the future as commemorating the past. As the English poet Ted Hughes observed, "His powerful, wise, deep, full-face paragraphs make almost every other modern fiction seem by comparison labored, shallow, overloaded with alien and undigested junk, too fancy, fuddled, not quite squared up to life."

Singer's artistic development is inextricably linked to his formative years in Poland prior to his immigration to America in 1935. He was born in Leoncin, Poland, the third child of Pinchos-Mendel Singer, an impoverished rabbi, and Bathsheva (née Zylberman), the daughter of a rabbi. Raised in an Orthodox Jewish tradition, Singer inherited a mystical and visionary streak from his father, and his rationalism and worldliness from his mother. The conflict would define both his life and his art. For Singer's family, the Orthodox religious tradition was under attack by worldly concerns, and Singer's older brother, Israel Joshua, broke with the family's values to become a "worldly man"—an artist, writer, and a soldier in the czar's army. "In my family, of course," Singer recalled, "my brother had gone first, and I went after him. For my parents, this was a tragedy."

It was Singer's brother who in 1914 gave him his first secular book, *Crime and Punishment*, by FEODOR DOSTOEVSKY [14]. Singer was thus introduced to an alternative world beyond his family's isolated spiritual existence. He considered his childhood years in Warsaw his most important. "Between 1908 and 1917," Singer observed, "I keep going back to 10 Krochmalna Street in my writing. I remember every little corner and every person there. I say to myself that just as other people are digging gold which God has created billions of years ago, my literary gold mine is this street."

Between 1918 and 1920, Singer began to write poems and stories in Hebrew and became a Hebrew teacher in Bilgoray. In 1921, he enrolled in a rabbinical seminary in Warsaw but left after only a year. In the 1920s, Singer published his first Yiddish stories while working as a proofreader for a Yiddish literary magazine and translating modern fiction into Yiddish. Finally, in 1935, with the publication of his first book, *Satan in Goray*, Singer immigrated to New York City. "When I came to America," Singer recalled, "I had a feeling of catastrophe. I ran from one catastrophe in Poland and I found another one when I came here." In America, the crisis that confronted Singer resulted from his sense of being lost in a language and culture he did not understand. For the next eight years he wrote no fiction, publishing only articles and sketches in the Yiddish newspaper the *Forward*. Singer saw himself as a has-been or ex-writer, "a writer who had lost both the power and the appetite for writing."

He met his future wife Alma in 1937, and persuaded her to marry him in 1940. A German Jew, Alma could speak no Yiddish, and Singer could not prove to her that he was a writer who could make a living through his writing. In 1943, Singer published four new stories in a Yiddish reissue of *Satan in*

Goray, and between 1945 and 1948 *The Family Moskat* appeared serially in the *Forward.* It was issued in book form in Yiddish and English in 1950. In 1953, his story "Gimpel the Fool," translated by Saul Bellow in the *Partisan Review,* exposed Singer's work to a non-Jewish, international audience. A succession of novels, nonfiction, and stories followed, all first serialized in the *Forward* and then translated into English under Singer's close supervision. Important titles with the date of their English translation include *The Magician of Lublin* (1960), *The Slave* (1962), *In My Father's Court* (1966), *The Manor* (1967), *The Estate* (1969), *A Friend of Kafka and Other Stories* (1970), *Enemies, A Love Story* (1972), *A Crown of Feathers and Other Stories* (1973), for which he won the National Book Award, and *Shosha* (1978). Singer's canon also includes children's books, such as *When Shlemiel Went to Warsaw and Other Stories* (1968) and *A Day of Pleasure* (1970), and plays, most notably *The Mirror* (1973).

Singer rediscovered his artistic voice by recreating, in *The Family Moskat,* the world of his childhood at the point of contemporary Jewish history when the traditions and certainty of shtetl life faced dissolution from the forces of change. The threat comes both from external sources, such as Nazi tyranny, and internally as individuals turn away from the spiritual to embrace the worldly. Often this conflict is shaped by a generational battle, as children refuse to follow the old ways of their parents. The necessity of assimilation and its cost to identity and belief are at the core of Singer's concerns, animated by his excellence as a storyteller. His style is marked by a blend of the realistic, the supernatural, and the mystical. As Singer has observed, "I am a realist. Even when I write about demons, they are not just general demons, they are demons of particular towns and they speak the language of the people."

Neither a self-conscious stylistic innovator nor a technical one, Singer anchors his stories in his past and experience, but with a realism that is wide enough to embrace both the material and the spiritual worlds. The rare combination of felt experience, entertaining storytelling, and a unique depiction of the world as beautiful, troubling, and finally, irreducibly mysterious, has made him one of the most popular writers of the postwar era, as well as one of the most respected.

HEINRICH HEINE

123

1797–1856

The spirit of the world
Beholding the absurdity of men—
Their vaunts, their feats—let a sardonic smile
For one short moment wander o'er his lips.
That smile was Heine! for its earthly hour
The strange guest sparkled; now 'tis pass'd away.
                    —Matthew Arnold, from "Heine's Grave"

Heinrich Heine is Germany's greatest 19th-century poet and is, in the words of his biographer Jeffrey L. Sammons, "the most read and *heard* poet ever to have written in the German language." There are thousands of musical versions of his works, and, as Sammons suggests, "among the poets of the world only the biblical psalmist has been set to music more often." Best known for his lyric poetry, Heine was also the author of witty and subversive prose works, travel books, political journalism, and caustic satires that made him a lightning rod figure among his contemporaries and succeeding generations. Frequently censored for his liberal views and attacks on orthodoxy, Heine was a hero to many European intellectuals but scorned in his native Germany as a traitor to the cause of German nationalism and reviled for his Jewish background. Hostility to Heine in Germany culminated under the Nazis when he was retroactively stripped of his German citizenship, with the author of arguably the most famous and popular poem in German, "Die Lorelei," officially listed as "an unknown poet." A figure of multiple dimensions and contradictions, Heinrich Heine has retained his hold on readers, both through the beauty and wit of his writing and the provocations he offers that challenge conventional responses and unexamined beliefs. There is precious little of the conformist in Heine, and the continued vitality and relevance of his writing stem from a sense in his work of continual reassessment. For Matthew Arnold, who would honor him in both poetry and prose, Heine became a symbol of the modern spirit, engaged in a lifelong, passionate battle with forces of repression, a crusader for liberation and transcendence.

Heinrich Heine was born in Düsseldorf, Germany, which was then occupied by France and which later became part of Prussia after Napoleon's defeat at Waterloo in 1815. Heine would later write about the disposition of the city during his boyhood in the autobiographical section of *Ideas: The Book of Le Grand*, included in *Book of Songs* (1827). He was the eldest of four children in a family of assimilated German Jews; his father, Samson, was a textile dealer, and his mother, Betty, came from a distinguished family of court Jews, the van Gelderns. Although Heine learned some Hebrew as a child, he was educated at Catholic schools in a former Franciscan monastery. After Samson Heine's bankruptcy in 1819, Heinrich went to live with his great-uncle, Salomon Heine, a wealthy Hamburg banker. While there, he fell in love with Salomon's daughter, Amalie, the inspiration for his early lyrics, "Youthful Sorrows." The poems in the "Home-Coming Cycle" (1826) were inspired by her younger sister, Therese, whom Heine later, and unsuccessfully, courted. Heine failed in the business his great-uncle financed for him and was sent to the University of Bonn, where he studied law and attended lectures on history and literature, some of which were taught by the critic August Wilhelm Schlegel. In 1820 he transferred to the University of Göttingen, which at the time was known more for the rowdiness of its students than for its academics. He found his law studies boring, joined a fraternity that expelled him, probably because of his Jewishness, and was suspended from the school for six months for dueling. He next entered the University of Berlin, where he studied with Hegel, whom he admired but would also later satirize in *The Town of Lucca* (1831). Heine's sojourn in cosmopolitan Berlin allowed him to pursue his literary and artistic interests, and he attended the prominent salon of Rahel Varnhagen, a writer and convert from Judaism, and her husband, Karl, a writer and diplomat.

Heine's first book of poetry, *Poems*, was published in 1822. Two romantic verse plays followed: *Tragedies with a Lyrical Intermezzo* (1823), including *Almansor*, which concerns the oppression of the Moors in medieval Spain; and *William Ratcliff*, set in Scotland and written in the currently fashionable form of fate-tragedy. A three-week walking tour of the Harz Mountains in 1824 inspired his first major prose work, *The Harz Journey* (1826), a compilation of travel sketches and verses that would later become the first of four volumes of *Pictures of Travel* (1826–31). Heine received his law degree from the University of Göttingen in 1825 and the same year was baptized into the Lutheran Church. The main reason for Heine's conversion was his disinclination to practice law and his desire to become a university teacher, a profession from which Jews were barred in Germany. However, despite his claim that conversion was his "ticket of admission into European culture," Heine was unable to secure a teaching position in Germany and elsewhere in Europe, and he wrestled with issues of his religious and cultural identity for most of his life. He found a job as editor of a periodical in Munich, but lived mainly in Hamburg or traveled, with financial assistance from his great-uncle or his publisher.

The *Book of Songs*, a collection that includes Heine's lyrics written since his teens, contains 236 poems, among them his finest romantic-ironic poems, including "Belshazzar," "The Two Grenadiers," and the "Pilgrimage to Kevlaar." Almost all are variations on the dominating theme of love, mostly unrequited and unsettling. Typically, his lyrics are deceptively simple, employing clearly defined situations, diction, and well-known metrical patterns taken from traditional ballads. Drawing on familiar and established romantic motifs, Heine characteristically adds a turn or ironic twist to the proceedings that undermines or complicates the reader's expectations, adding an unsettling perspective or injecting a note of discord or distancing in which the emotions on display begin to reflect wider themes, including the contradictions of love and the ambiguous role of the poet and poetry itself. This persistent self-reflectiveness in Heine's poetry turns his love lyrics into much more profound and wide-ranging meditations on human experience and nature. In his most famous poem, "Die Lorelei," a lovely maiden combing her golden hair and singing on the Rhine shore leads a boatman to his doom when he is "seized by turbulent love" and no longer "marks where the cliff is," an "age-old tale" that confounds the poet. In "My Beauty, My Love, You Have Bound Me," again love is seductive, unavoidable, and fatal:

> My beauty, my love, you have bound me
> As only you can do.
> Wrap your arms and legs around me,
> And your agile body too.
>
> And now in mighty embraces
> Entwining and holding on
> The most beautiful serpent faces
> The happiest Laocoon.

Love for Heine is never straightforward, never unalloyed, always presented with elements that complicate simple consolation and contentment. Despite darker undercurrents in his verse, Heine's musicality and mastery of the lyrical conventions secured him an audience. While not an immediate best seller, *The Book of Songs* sold steadily and was reprinted 13 times during Heine's lifetime.

Heine's later poems would increasingly deal directly with the political upheavals of his times. Writing to a friend, he complained that "poesy is, after all, only a beautiful irrelevancy," and his work both in verse and prose began to take up bolder themes dealing with social issues and the fate of the individual in the political rather than the amatory sphere. An example is his poem, "The Silesian Weavers," that treats their poverty and despair as a social and moral indictment. It concludes:

> "The loom is creaking, the shuttle flies;
> Nor night nor day do we close our eyes.
> Old Germany, your shroud's on our loom,
> And in it we weave the threefold doom.
>   We weave; we weave!"

In 1831, unable to support himself by his writing, disillusioned with growing German xenophobia and repression, and inspired by the Revolution of 1830 in France, which resulted in a constitutional monarchy, Heine immigrated to Paris, where he would settle permanently. There, he worked as a correspondent for German newspapers and journals from about 1836 to 1848. Heine's clever and insightful essays on the German romantic poets and German thought from Luther through Hegel comprised the collection *On the History of Religion and Philosophy in Germany* and *The Romantic School*, which appeared in 1835. Later that year, Heine's works, together with those of the so-called Young German school of writers, were officially banned in Germany. In 1841 Heine married Eugenie Mirat, an uneducated Frenchwoman with whom he had been living since 1834 and who he referred to as "Mathilde" in his poetry. Heine's work during this period includes *Atta Troll: A Midsummer Night's Dream*, written in 1842 and published in 1847; it is a long romantic and humorous poem that satirizes, among other topics, German political poets. After revisiting Germany in 1843 and establishing a friendship with Karl Marx, Heine produced a fictionalized account of his visit to his native land, *Germany: A Winter's Tale*, and a new collection of poetry, *New Poems*, both in 1844.

In 1848, the year of the great European revolutions, Heine suffered a physical collapse that resulted in a spinal paralysis that left him bedridden for the last eight years of his life. A major collection of poems, *Romanzero*, was published in 1851 and demonstrated the tender and delicate lyricism and wit for which Heine is renowned. The collection includes ballads, lyrical cycles, and short songs, as well as the poet's famous "Hebrew Melodies." Heine's later works include a ballet libretto for *Der Docktor Faust* (1852), an essay titled

"The Gods in Exile" (1853), the mocking and ribald *Last Poems and Thoughts* (published posthumously in 1869), the *Confessions*, and much of the *Memoirs*. Heine's last poem, "Die Passion Blume," which describes a dead man conversing with Death as he lies in a tomb, was written a week before his death in February 1856. He is buried at Montmartre and provided his own eulogy:

> I know not if I deserve that a laurel-wreath should one day be laid on my coffin. Poetry, dearly as I have loved it, has always been to me but a divine plaything. I have never attached any great value to poetical fame; and I trouble myself very little whether people praise my verses or blame them. But lay on my coffin a sword; for I was a brave soldier in the Liberation War of humanity.

124

LU XUN

Lu Xun was the major leader in the Chinese cultural revolution. He was not only a great writer but a great thinker and a great revolutionist. . . . Lu Xun breached and stormed the enemy citadel; on the cultural front he was the bravest and most correct, the firmest, the most loyal and the most ardent national hero, a hero without parallel in our history. The road he took was the very road of China's new national culture.
—Mao Zedong, "The Culture of New Democracy"

Considered the founder of modern Chinese literature, Lu Xun holds a place in contemporary Chinese art and culture virtually unrivaled by any other writer. Regarded as a national hero and canonized by the Chinese Communist Party, Lu Xun has been revered as the intellectual source of the Chinese Revolution who prepared the ideological ground for Mao Zedong. Despite attempts to co-opt Lu Xun for narrower political purposes, he remains a central figure in the transition of Chinese thought and consciousness to modern awareness, as important in the formation of modern expression as Du Fu [28] and Li Bo [114] have been in classical Chinese poetry and Cao Xueqin [67] in the Chinese novel. Thoroughly rooted in traditional culture, Lu Xun incorporated Western ideas and techniques into a new synthesis to reflect contemporary concerns and a new cultural identity. The development of a new Chinese literature begins with Lu Xun, whose unique literary skills and imaginative gifts continue to challenge his

479

successors. His literary repossession of the Chinese cultural tradition dominates efforts by others to refashion a modern, national Chinese literature.

Lu Xun's development as a literary artist reflects the turbulent history and events of modern China. Born into a declining gentry family in Shaoxing, Lu Xun, whose real name was Zhou Shuren, received a traditional education appropriate for the Confucian scholar-official tradition of his forebears. In 1893, his grandfather was imprisoned due to a scandal over the official civil service examinations. This event marked a significant decline in his family's fortune and Lu Xun's prospects. "Is there anyone whose family sinks from prosperity to poverty?" Lu Xun wrote in his autobiographical preface to his first story collection. "I think in the process one can probably come to understand what the real world is like." Contrary to the usual method of securing a successful career—the civil service examination based on mastery of classical texts—Lu Xun took a different path. He first attended a modern school in Nanjing, and in 1902 he went to Japan on a government scholarship, where he studied first in Tokyo and later at a medical school in Sendai. Like many in his generation interested in modern thought, he sought a wider, less traditional education abroad. A year after his arrival in Japan, Lu Xun cut off his long pigtail, a symbol of submission to the Qing dynasty, and in 1906 abandoned his medical study for a literary career. In a famous anecdote, Lu Xun recalls the circumstance, while viewing news slides during the Russo-Japanese War of 1904–05, that triggered his decision:

> One day in a slide I suddenly came face to face with many Chinese on the mainland, and I had not seen any for a long time. In the center of the group there was one who was bound while many others stood around him. They were all strong in physique but callous in appearance. According to commentary, the one who was bound was a spy who had worked for the Russians and was just about to have his head cut off by the Japanese military as a warning to others, while the people standing around him had come to watch the spectacle.
>
> Before the term was over I had left for Tokyo, because after seeing these slides I felt that medical service was not such an important thing after all. People from an ignorant and weak country, no matter how physically healthy and strong they may be, could only serve to be made examples of, or become onlookers of utterly meaningless spectacles. Such a condition was more deplorable than dying of illness. Therefore our first important task was to change their spirit, and at the time I considered the best medium for achieving this end was literature. I was thus determined to promote a literary movement.

In Japan, Lu Xun founded a journal, wrote literary essays, and translated Western fiction as a means of rejuvenating his country's spiritual and cultural identity. Returning to China in 1909, he taught in a variety of schools, and finally earned literary acclaim in 1918 when he published his most famous short story, "Diary of a Madman." The story appeared in the journal *Xinqingnian* (New youth) that would initiate the May Fourth Movement, the intellectual revolution sparked by Chinese opposition to the terms of the Treaty of Versailles. Although Lu Xun remained apart from the movement, its repudiation of classical Chinese literature is reflected in his short story, regarded as China's first modern short story due to its use of the vernacular and its critique of traditional Chinese culture. Narrated in 13 diary entries, the story details the increasingly paranoid dementia of the protagonist, whose heightened sensitivity reveals a vision of China as a society that feeds on itself. Parodying the self-enclosed world of Chinese scholarship and tradition bound by precedent, the story provides a searing social indictment artfully presented in a multilayered, subjective narrative.

Between 1918 and 1926, Lu Xun wrote all but one of the 25 short stories upon which his literary reputation largely depends, collected in two volumes, *Call to Arms* (1923) and *Wandering* (1926). His collected works include 16 volumes of essays, collections of personal reminiscences, prose poetry, and historical tales, classical poems, and several volumes of scholarly research on Chinese fiction (his *Outline History of Chinese Fiction* and companion compilations of classical fiction are regarded as standard works), as well as translations of Russian, East European, and Japanese writers.

In 1927, Lu Xun settled in Shanghai and was regarded as the preeminent figure in the New Literature movement, the effort to modernize traditional literary forms and themes, and increasingly became a political activist. As the founding member of the League of Left-Wing Writers, established in 1930, he became a spokesperson for the left. In the years preceding his death, Lu Xun was frustrated by the internal squabbles within the revolutionary faction that he played a significant part in inspiring through the devastating indictment of traditional Chinese life in his fiction. After his death in 1936, Lu Xun, through the support of Mao Zedong, who considered him an exemplar of the revolution and one of its ideological fountainheads, was virtually deified as one of the fundamental instigators of reform and revolutionary change which gripped China throughout the 20th century.

Lu Xun's literary innovations are as sweeping as the political and cultural revolution that they helped to launch. Lu Xun mounted a radical redefinition of the form and content of Chinese literature. Choosing fiction over the preferred forms of the prose essay and poetry of traditional literature, he depicted Chinese life and consciousness in a society that had atrophied and been paralyzed by its history, social hierarchy, and narrow materialism. "As for why I wrote fiction," Lu Xun explained in 1933, "I still uphold the principle of 'enlightenment' of more than a decade ago. I think it must 'serve life' and furthermore reform life. Thus my subjects were often taken from the unfortunate people in this sick society; my aim was to expose the disease so as to draw attention to its cure."

Despite Lu Xun's clearly reformist purpose, his stories are far from the simple propaganda of social realism. Instead, their strength comes from an amazing technical virtuosity and innovation that transforms traditional literary forms and imbues them with elements borrowed from Western modernist sources. His 25 stories demonstrate continual experimentation and formal innovation, from character portraits ("Kong Yiji" and "Tomorrow"), satire ("Storm in a Teacup," "A Happy Family," "Soap," and "Divorce"), monologues ("The Story of Hair"), studies of abnormal psychology ("The Lamp That Was Kept Alight" and "Brothers"), to autobiography ("My Old Home"). In each, Lu Xun's didacticism is balanced with a subjective awareness of himself and society that reaches a complexity far beyond most social protest literature. One of his greatest stories, "The True Story of Ah Q," masterfully blends humor and pathos in an insightful attack on the old Chinese order. In "Upstairs in a Wineshop," Lu Xun explores the psychic effect on characters imprisoned by a past that has lost all meaning. The narrator's friend, once hopeful about the future, finds himself back in his hometown caring for the family graves. To set his mother's mind at ease, he must rebury his younger brother in a new grave, but finds nothing left of his brother's corpse. Still he follows the old forms, according reverence to a body that no longer exists, a prisoner of the past and the paralysis of tradition and family. In stories such as these Lu Xun's greatness as a writer is evident in his dramatizing the curious, limbo state between the traditional world and the modern, and the corresponding human cost that results in the absence of a sustaining source of moral, social, and spiritual values.

Lu Xun's desired goals of breaking China out of its cultural paralysis and revivifying Chinese consciousness and identity remain central aims in modern Chinese literature, whose writers continue to look to him as an initiator and paradigm.

GERTRUDE STEIN

125

1874–1946

Eschewing Joyce's concern with myth and historical cycles and Proust's obsession with memory, Miss Stein is primarily concerned with the concept of the continuous and ongoing present.

—Michael Hoffman, *The Development of Abstraction in the Writings of Gertrude Stein*

Gertrude Stein represents a special case: an important writer whom few read. If she is remembered at all today, it is likely to be for her portrait by Picasso; the term "the Lost Generation," which she coined; the line "rose is a rose is a rose is a rose"; a Paris address, 27 rue de Fleurus; or her relationship with Alice B. Toklas. Of her portraits, short stories, novels, poems, operas, plays, essays, art criticism, lectures, autobiographies, and diaries, only two works have endured: *Three Lives* and *The Autobiography of Alice B. Toklas*. As Richard Kostelanetz has argued, however, "if claims for Stein are based upon *Three Lives* and *Alice Toklas*, she is a minor modernist; but if our sense of her reputation is founded upon *Geography and Plays*, *Making of Americans*, 'Stanzas in Meditation' and other works in that vein, then Stein becomes the greatest experimental writer in American literature, an inventor whose achievements are, indicatively, scarcely understood, even today, more than four decades after her death."

At the center of the avant-garde in literature, art, music, and drama, the influence Stein exerted on modernism has been acknowledged by writers as diverse as Ford Madox Ford, E. M. FORSTER [121], JAMES JOYCE [7], Sherwood Anderson, ERNEST HEMINGWAY [63], and Thornton Wilder. She was a primary influence on the French New Novelists and the writers of Beat Generation. Stein regarded herself as "the creative literary mind of the century," urging her readers and critics to "Think of the Bible and Homer, think of Shakespeare and think of me." With an assault on conventional literature and the means of its creation, Stein destroyed mimesis, representation, plot, causal sequence, characterization, even the referential quality of language itself. The result is a liberation and a challenge that has intimidated and bored as well as inspired. As Clifton Fadiman scornfully remarked, "Miss Stein was a past master in making nothing happen very slowly." Despite her abstruseness, Gertrude Stein was a force in the creation of modern literature, entitled to inclusion here as one of the principal reshapers of the tools and forms of the literary artist and one of the leading innovators in modernist writing.

The youngest of seven children, Gertrude Stein was born in Allegheny, Pennsylvania. Her father, a restless and often unsuccessful businessman, moved his family to Vienna when Gertrude was one year old. They would shift to Paris, back to Baltimore, and finally to Oakland, California, where Stein's father's investments in real estate and the stock market secured their fortune. Raised by governesses and tutors, Stein was emotionally neglected by both her parents. She formed her primary bond with her older brother Leo, whom she followed to Harvard and Johns Hopkins. Enrolled at the Harvard Annex, which would later be renamed Radcliffe College, Stein was an idiosyncratic student, talented but phlegmatic. Under the mentorship of the philosopher William James, Stein intended to become a physician and psychologist, but failed her medical school courses after the first two years and eventually followed her brother to London, then Paris. Nothing about Gertrude Stein was conventional, neither her appearance nor her sexuality, but she concealed her lesbianism at the time.

In Paris, Leo Stein intended to become an artist but showed more talent as a shrewd collector. Stein again followed her brother; they cultivated their enthusiasm for Paul Cézanne, Henri Matisse, and Pablo Picasso. Their apartment at 27 rue de Fleurus became one of the most famous salons in history, representing ground zero of the modernist explosion. Stein's writings attempted to duplicate what she saw the great modern painters achieving in their art. Her first published book, *Three Lives* (1909), examines the life histories of three working-class American women in mundane details that eliminate linear sequence and climaxes. Tone and texture are delivered through a pattern of repetition that suggests the equal importance of every element, like a Cézanne painting. Stein's revolutionary approach found few readers but many admirers. The most important was Alice B. Toklas, a Californian drawn to Paris, who met Stein in 1908 and after Gertrude's estrangement from her brother became her principal companion, secretary, housekeeper, and lover for the next 39 years, until Stein's death. In 1911, Stein completed her massive *The Making of Americans* and her volume of "cubist" poetry, *Tender Buttons*, published in 1914. During the war Stein and Toklas left Paris for Spain, but returned in 1916 when Stein learned to drive and volunteered for the American Fund for French Wounded, delivering supplies by truck.

After the war, Stein's apartment became the essential stopover for American expatriates, including Ernest Hemingway and F. SCOTT FITZGERALD [84]. Stein encouraged Hemingway to give up poetry for prose and quit his journalism for creative writing. Hemingway acknowledged learning from Stein the rhythm of prose and the value of repetition. He used her now-famous statement, "You are all a lost generation," as the epigraph for *The Sun Also Rises*.

Stein's impact throughout the postwar period stemmed from her reputation as "the Sibyl of Montparnasse" rather than from her works, which met with little publishing success. Her most popular and accessible book, *The Autobiography of Alice B. Toklas* (1933), however, established Stein's popular reputation as a sage and prophet of modernism. The book's popularity resulted in a contract to publish her work regularly and a triumphal lecture tour of America, which included tea at the White House with Eleanor Roosevelt. Stein and Toklas remained in occupied France during World War II, relatively unaffected by the occupation; Stein became something of an apologist for the Vichy government, and her massive ego viewed much of the horror of the war as essentially issues of her own convenience. After the war, the couple settled in Paris and found Stein's valuable art collection remarkably intact. Stein made speaking tours of American army bases in occupied Germany and lectured in Brussels before dying after an operation for cancer in 1946.

Despite Stein's arrogance and proclamation of her own genius (she allegedly asserted that there have been "only three originative Jews—Christ, Spinoza, and Gertrude Stein"), her work is important because it takes modernism to its logical extreme. If the literary patterns of the past have lost their capacity to create meaning, the modernist artist must remake language, stripped of past practices, into something daring and new. As Harold Bloom has observed, "The greatest master of dissociative rhetoric in modern writing is Gertrude Stein." By dissociative rhetoric, Bloom means "to break down preconceived patterns in our response, so as to prepare us for discourse that will touch upon the possibilities of transcendence." To achieve the revolution her art intended, Stein strips language of its referents into pure sound and rhythm, while her portraits explore the ultimate mystery of identity itself. Credited with the invention of "literary cubism," Gertrude Stein did more than lead a literary movement. Her genius rests in her fundamental reconceptualization of language and literature that continues to dominate modern consciousness.

HONORABLE MENTIONS

What follows is an additional listing of 100 important writers who deserve consideration when assembling a ranking of the most influential literary artists of all time and their principal works.

Shmuel Yosef Agnon (1888–1970)   Israeli novelist and short story writer. *A Guest for the Night, The Day before Yesterday.*

Edward Albee (1928–   )   American dramatist. *Who's Afraid of Virginia Woolf, The Zoo Story, A Delicate Balance.*

Yehuda Amichai (1924–2000)   Israeli poet and one of the most respected and influential chroniclers of Israelis' post-Holocaust and post-liberation experience. *Now and Other Days, Not of This Time, Not of This Place, The World Is a Room.*

Matthew Arnold (1822–1888)   English poet and critic. "Dover Beach," "Isolation: To Marguerite," "The Scholar Gypsy," "Thyrsis."

Miguel Angel Asturias (1899–1974)   Guatemalan novelist, the first Latin American writer to receive the Nobel Prize in literature. *Mr. President.*

Margaret Atwood (1939–   )   Canadian novelist and poet and Canada's most celebrated literary figure. *The Circle Game, The Handmaid's Tale, The Robber Bride, Lady Oracle, The Edible Woman.*

Isaac Babel (1894–1941)   Russian short story writer and playwright. *The Odessa Tales, Red Cavalry, Sunset, Maria.*

James Baldwin (1924–1987)   American author and influential writer on race in America during the 1950s and '60s. *Go Tell It on the Mountain, Giovanni's Room, The Fire Next Time, Another Country.*

Amiri Baraka (formerly LeRoi Jones) (1934–) American playwright and poet, the major voice of the black arts movement of the 1960s. *The Toilet, The Slave, Dutchman.*

Saul Bellow (1915–2005) American novelist and Nobel Prize winner. *The Adventures of Augie March, Herzog, Seize the Day.*

Elizabeth Bishop (1911–1979) American poet and one of the 20th century's most important poetic voices. *North and South—A Cold Spring.*

Heinrich Böll (1917–1985) German novelist and short story writer who, along with Günter Grass, dominated German postwar literature. *Group Portrait with Lady, The Clown, The Lost Honor of Katharina Blum.*

Joseph Brodsky (1940–1996) Regarded as the greatest Russian poet of his generation and winner of the 1987 Nobel Prize in literature. *A Part of Speech, To Urania, Less Than One, On Grief and Reason.*

Gwendolyn Brooks (1917–2000) American poet, the first black poet to win the Pulitzer Prize. *A Street in Bronzeville, The Bean Eaters, Annie Allen.*

Georg Büchner (1813–1837) Innovative and groundbreaking German dramatist. *Woyzeck, Danton's Death.*

Mikhail Bulgakov (1891–1940) Russian writer considered by many to be the most important Russian writer of the 20th century. *The Master and Margarita.*

Robert Burns (1759–1796) Scottish poet. *Poems, Chiefly in the Scottish Dialect,* "Flow Gently, Sweet Afton," "My Heart's in the Highlands," "Auld Lang Synge," "Comin' Thro' the Rye."

Pedro Calderón de la Barca (1600–1681) Spanish dramatist and last important figure of Spain's golden age. *Life Is a Dream.*

Aimé Césaire (1913–2008) West Indian poet associated with the concept of Négritude, the uniqueness of black experience. *Return to My Native Land, A Season in the Congo.*

Kate Chopin (1851–1904) American novelist and short story writer as well as an early feminist. *The Awakening, Bayou Folk, A Night in Acadie.*

Samuel Taylor Coleridge (1772–1834) English poet and essayist whose collaboration with Wordsworth helped launched English romanticism. "Kubla Khan," "The Rime of the Ancient Mariner," "Dejection: An Ode."

Pierre Corneille (1606–1684)   French dramatist and master of French classical tragedy and the grand style. *Le Cid, Médée, Horace, Cinna.*

Stephen Crane (1871–1900)   One of America's foremost realistic writers, credited with pioneering both naturalism and impressionism in American fiction. *Maggie: A Girl of the Streets, The Red Badge of Courage, "The Open Boat," "The Bride Comes to Yellow Sky."*

Rubén Darío (1862–1916)   Nicaraguan poet and leader of the Spanish-American modernist literary movement. *Songs of Life and Hope.*

Denis Diderot (1713–1784)   French philosopher, critic, novelist, and dramatist. *Rameau's Nephew, Jacques the Fatalist, Natural Son.*

Birago Diop (1906–1992)   Senegalese poet and dramatist noted for his adaptations of African folktales and oral tradition. *The Tales of Amadou Koumba.*

Alfred Döblin (1878–1957)   German novelist, playwright, poet, and essayist, regarded as one of the most important German prose writers in the 20th century. *Berlin Alexanderplatz.*

José Donoso (1924–1996)   Chilean writer, one of the central figures in the resurgence of Latin American literature. *The Obscene Bird of Night, A House in the Country.*

John Dos Passos (1896–1970)   American novelist. *U.S.A., Manhattan Transfer.*

Arthur Conan Doyle (1859–1930)   Scottish-born master of detective fiction and the creator of one of the most familiar and popular of all fictional characters, Sherlock Holmes. *A Study in Scarlet, The Sign of Four, The Hound of the Baskervilles.*

John Dryden (1631–1700)   English poet, dramatist, and critic. *All for Love, Absalom and Achitophel, MacFlecknoe.*

Alexandre Dumas (1802–1870)   French master storyteller. *The Three Musketeers, The Count of Monte Cristo.*

Ford Madox Ford (1873–1939)   English novelist, poet, and critic, influential figure of 20th-century modernism. *The Good Soldier, Parade's End.*

Brian Friel (1929–   )   Irish playwright and short story writer. *Philadelphia, Here I Come!, Faith Healer, Translations, Dancing at Lughnasa.*

Carlos Fuentes (1928–   )   Mexican novelist, short story writer, and critic, one of the chief proponents of magical realism. *The Death of Artemio Cruz, Terra Nostra.*

Ghalib (1797–1869)   Preeminent poet of the North Indian language of Urdu. *Ghazal* lyrics, *Bouquet of Flowers.*

André Gide (1869–1951)   French writer and leader of French liberal thought, whose partially autobiographical works challenged moral standards and accepted literary conventions. Awarded the Nobel Prize in 1947. *The Immoralist, The Counterfeiters.*

Allen Ginsberg (1926–1997)   American poet and leading figure of the Beat Generation. *Howl, Kaddish.*

Ivan Goncharov (1812–1891)   Russian writer who helped establish the realistic tradition in Russian fiction with his authentic treatment of ordinary Russian life. *A Common Story, Oblomov, The Precipice.*

Nadine Gordimer (1923–   )   South African novelist and short story writer who was awarded the Nobel Prize in literature in 1991. *A Guest of Honour, The Conservationist, Burger's Daughter.*

Knut Hamsun (1859–1952)   Norwegian novelist, dramatist, and poet who was awarded the Nobel Prize in literature in 1920. *Hunger, Growth of the Soil.*

Gerard Manley Hopkins (1844–1889)   English priest and poet whose daring poetic techniques had a major influence on poetry in the 20th century. "The Wreck of the *Deutschland*," "God's Grandeur," "The Windhover."

Langston Hughes (1902–1967)   American poet and the best-known black writer of the first half of the 20th century, whose career spanned the Harlem Renaissance of the 1920s to the black arts movement of the 1960s. *Montage of a Dream Deferred, The Weary Blues.*

Zora Neale Hurston (1901?–1960)   American novelist, short story writer, and folklorist. *Their Eyes Were Watching God, Tell My Horse.*

Sor Juana Inés de la Cruz (c. 1651–1695)   Mexican poet, playwright, and essayist. *Muse's Flood, Love, the Greater Labyrinth, A Woman of Genius, Divine Narcissus.*

Eugène Ionesco (1912–1994)   Romanian-born French dramatist who helped pioneer the theater of the absurd. *The Bald Soprano, Rhinoceros.*

Jack Kerouac (1922–1969) American novelist and influential figure of the Beat Generation. *On the Road, The Dharma Bums.*

Milan Kundera (1929–) Czech-born novelist, short story writer, poet, essayist, and playwright. *The Unbearable Lightness of Being.*

Marie de la Vergne, comtesse de La Fayette (1634–1692) French novelist and author of the first great French novel, *The Princess of Cleves.*

Giacomo Leopardi (1798–1837) Italian poet, scholar, and one of the most formidable linguists, thinkers, and writers of his time, considered the most outstanding Italian poet of the 19th century. *Canti.*

Mikhail Lermontov (1814–1841) Russian poet and novelist. After Pushkin, considered the greatest Russian poet of the 19th century. *The Demon, A Hero of Our Time.*

Lucretius (99 B.C.–55 B.C.) Roman writer regarded as one of the great philosopher-poets for his didactic epic on Epicurean philosophy. *De rerum natura (On the Nature of Things).*

Joaquim Maria Machado de Assis (1839–1908) Brazilian novelist, poet, and short story writer. *Epitaph of a Small Winner, Philosopher or Dog?, Dom Casmurro.*

Naguib Mahfouz (1911–2006) Egyptian writer and the foremost modern novelist in Arabic. Received the 1988 Nobel Prize in literature. *Cairo Trilogy, Midaq Alley, Miramar.*

Norman Mailer (1923–2007) American novelist. *The Naked and the Dead, An American Dream, The Executioner's Song.*

Stéphane Mallarmé (1842–1898) French poet and chief precursor of the symbolists. *Hérodiade, The Afternoon of a Faun.*

Sir Thomas Malory (?–1471) English author of *Le Morte d'Arthur.*

Alessandro Manzoni (1785–1873) Author of the first great Italian novel, distinguished by its psychological insight, use of common people as protagonists, and the introduction of spoken Italian as a medium for literary expression. *The Betrothed.*

Marguerite de Navarre (1492–1549) Queen consort of Navarre, sister of King Francis I of France, and the author of *Heptaméron*, a collection of tales in the manner of Boccaccio.

Andrew Marvell (1621–1678)   English poet and one of the masters of the lyric in the 17th century. "To His Coy Mistress," "The Garden," "The Mower's Song."

Matsuo Bashō (1644–1694)   Japanese poet who perfected the haiku form, considered one of the most important figures of classical Japanese literature. *Narrow Road to the Interior.*

Guy de Maupassant (1850–1893)   French short story writer and novelist. *One Life,* "The Necklace."

Gabriela Mistral (1889–1957)   Chilean poet, the first Spanish-American writer to win the Nobel Prize in literature. *Desolation, Tenderness.*

V. S. Naipaul (1932–   )   Trinidadian writer. *A House for Mr. Biswas, A Bend in the River, The Enigma of Arrival.*

Natsume Sōseki (1867–1916)   Japanese novelist and one of the first important Japanese fiction writers of the modern period. *Sanshirō, Kokoro.*

Ōe Kenzaburo (1935–   )   Japanese fiction writer and winner of the 1994 Nobel Prize in literature. *The Silent Cry, The Story of the Wonders of the Forest, Flaming Green Tree.*

Petronius (?–A.D. 66)   Roman satirist whose work *Petroni arbitri satyricon* is an early forerunner of the novel in its vivid study of the customs of the times.

Pindar (518?–c. 438 B.C.)   Greek poet who is regarded as the greatest Greek lyric poet. *Odes.*

Plautus (254 B.C.–184 B.C.)   Roman playwright and an influential master of comic drama. *Amphitruo, The Pot of Gold, The Menaechmus Brothers, The Braggart Soldier.*

Ezra Pound (1885–1972)   American poet and critic, one of the most influential figures in shaping literary modernism. *Personae, Hugh Selwyn Mauberley, Cantos.*

Propertius (55 B.C.–16 B.C.)   Roman elegiac poet. *Cynthia.*

Thomas Pynchon (1937–   )   American novelist. *V, Gravity's Rainbow, Mason & Dixon.*

Arthur Rimbaud (1854–1891)   French poet who anticipated the methods of the symbolists and much of modern poetry. *Les Illuminations, Le Bâteau ivre (The Drunken Boat), Une Saison en enfer (A Season in Hell).*

Pierre de Ronsard (1524–1585)   One of France's greatest poets, author of numerous lyrics, sonnets, and the unfinished epic *La Franciade.*

Jean-Jacques Rousseau (1712–1778)   Swiss-French philosopher, political theorist, and novelist. *Julie, ou La Nouvelle Héloïse, Émile, Confessions, The Social Contract.*

Sa'di (1184–1291)   Persian poet, one of the greatest of the Sufi writers. *Gulistan.*

J. D. Salinger (1919–)   American novelist and short story writer. *The Catcher in the Rye, Franny and Zooey, Nine Stories.*

Jean-Paul Sartre (1905–1980)   French philosopher, playwright, and novelist, leading proponent of existentialism. *No Exit, The Fleas, The Age of Reason, Nausea.*

Friedrich von Schiller (1759–1805)   German dramatist, poet, and historian, one of Germany's greatest literary figures. *The Robbers, Don Carlos, Wallenstein.*

Léopold Sédar Senghor (1906–)   Senegalese poet and statesman, one of the foremost modern writers in French, associated with the concept of Négritude, an assertion of black cultural values. *Songs of Shadow, Black Offerings.*

Richard Brinsley Sheridan (1751–1816)   Dublin-born English playwright of witty and sophisticated comedies of manners. *The Rivals, The School for Scandal,* and *The Critic.*

Alexander (Aleksandr) Solzhenitsyn (1918–2008)   Russian writer and winner of Nobel Prize in literature in 1970. *One Day in the Life of Ivan Denisovich, Cancer Ward, August 1914.*

Wole Soyinka (1934–)   Nigerian playwright, poet, and novelist. *The Invention, The Lion and the Jewel, The Interpreters.*

John Steinbeck (1902–1968)   American novelist awarded the Nobel Prize in literature in 1962. *Cannery Row, East of Eden, The Grapes of Wrath, Of Mice and Men.*

Tom Stoppard (1937–)   British playwright. *Rosencrantz and Guildenstern Are Dead, Travesties, The Real Thing.*

John Millington Synge (1871–1909)   Irish playwright, essayist, and poet and one of the major contributors to the Irish literary renaissance and the creation of an Irish national drama. *Riders to the Sea, The Playboy of the Western World, The Aran Islands.*

Tawfiq Al-Hakim (1898–1989)   Egyptian dramatist, inventor and master of the Arabic literary drama. *The Sultan's Dilemma, A Thousand and One Nights, The Tree Climber.*

Edward Taylor (1642–1729)   America's first great poet who wrote his devotional and inventive poems as a Puritan minister. *God's Determinations Touching His Elect* and *Preparatory Meditations.*

Terence (c. 185 B.C.–159 B.C.)   Roman playwright and a much imitated master stylist. *The Brothers, The Eunuch, A Mother-in-Law, Phormio.*

Dylan Thomas (1914–1953)   Welsh poet and important voice in 20th-century poetry. *The Map of Love, Under Milk Wood.*

J. R. R. Tolkien (1892–1973)   English philologist and master of fantasy fiction. *The Hobbit, The Lord of the Rings.*

Ivan Turgenev (1818–1883)   Russian novelist, dramatist, and short story writer, one of the pivotal figures in 19th-century Russian literature. *Fathers and Sons, A Sportsman's Sketches, A Month in the Country.*

Paul Valéry (1871–1945)   French poet and critic, a symbolist and one of the greatest French poets of the 20th century. *La Jeune Parque.*

Lope de Vega (1562–1635)   Spanish dramatist and the founder of Spanish drama. *The King, the Greatest Alcade; Peribáñez.*

Paul Verlaine (1844–1896)   French poet and one of the first symbolists. *Stories Without Words, The Damned Poets.*

François Villon (1431–1463?)   France's earliest great poet. *The Legacy, Grand Testament.*

Derek Walcott (1930–   )   West Indian poet and playwright who received the Nobel Prize in literature in 1992. *Dream on Monkey Mountain, Omeros, In a Green Night.*

Edith Wharton (1862–1937)   American novelist and short story writer. *The House of Mirth, Ethan Frome, The Age of Innocence.*

Thornton Wilder (1897–1975)   American playwright and novelist. *The Bridge of San Luis Rey, Our Town, The Skin of Our Teeth.*

William Carlos Williams (1883–1963)   American poet, one of the most important poetic voices of the 20th century. *Paterson, In the American Grain.*

SELECT BIBLIOGRAPHY

Chinua Achebe
Ezenwa-Ohaeto. *Chinua Achebe: A Biography*. Bloomington: Indiana University Press, 1997.
Innes, Catherine Lynette. *Chinua Achebe*. New York: Cambridge University Press, 1990.

Aeschylus
Herrington, John. *Aeschylus*. New Haven, Conn.: Yale University Press, 1986.
Murray, Gilbert. *Aeschylus: The Creator of Tragedy*. Oxford: Clarendon Press, 1940.

Aristophanes
Dover, K. J. *Aristophanic Comedy*. London: Batsford, 1972.
McLeish, Kenneth. *The Theater of Aristophanes*. New York: Taplinger, 1980.

W. H. Auden
Carpenter, Humphrey. *W. H. Auden: A Biography*. Boston: Houghton Mifflin, 1981.
Hecht, Anthony. *The Hidden Law: The Poetry of W. H. Auden*. Cambridge, Mass.: Harvard University Press, 1993.

Jane Austen
Litz, A. Walton. *Jane Austen: A Study of Her Artistic Development*. New York: Oxford University Press, 1965.
Tomalin, Claire. *Jane Austen: A Life*. New York: Knopf, 1997.

Honoré de Balzac
Marceau, Felicien. *Balzac and His World*. New York: Orion Press, 1966.
Robb, Graham. *Balzac: A Life*. New York: W. W. Norton, 1994.

Charles Baudelaire

Richardson, Joanna. *Baudelaire*. New York: St. Martin's, 1994.

Turnell, Martin. *Baudelaire: A Study of His Poetry*. New York: New Directions, 1972.

Samuel Beckett

Kenner, Hugh. *Reader's Guide to Samuel Beckett*. New York: Farrar, Straus, 1973.

Knowlson, James. *Damned to Fame: The Life of Samuel Beckett*. New York: Simon & Schuster, 1996.

William Blake

Ackroyd, Peter. *Blake: A Biography*. New York: Knopf, 1996.

Frye, Northrop. *Fearful Symmetry*. Princeton, N.J.: Princeton University Press, 1974.

Giovanni Boccaccio

Bergin, Thomas G. *Boccaccio*. New York: Viking Press, 1981.

Serafini-Sauli, Judith P. *Giovanni Boccaccio*. Boston: Twayne Publishers, 1982.

Jorge Luis Borges

Stabb, Martin S. *Borges Revisited*. New York: Twayne Publishers, 1991.

Woodall, James. *Borges: A Life*. New York: Basic Books, 1997.

Bertolt Brecht

Esslin, Martin. *Brecht: The Man and His Works*. Garden City, N.Y.: Doubleday, 1971.

Völker, Klaus. *Brecht: A Biography*. New York: Seabury Press, 1978.

Charlotte and Emily Brontë

Barker, Juliet. *The Brontës*. New York: St. Martin's, 1995.

Gordon, Felicia. *A Preface to the Brontës*. New York: Longman, 1989.

Robert Browning

Jack, Ian. *Browning's Major Poetry*. Oxford: Clarendon Press, 1973.

Ryals, Clyde de L. *The Life of Robert Browning*. Cambridge, Mass.: Blackwell, 1996.

Lord Byron

Marchand, Leslie. *Byron: A Biography*. New York: Knopf, 1957.

McGann, Jerome J. *Fiery Dust: Byron's Poetic Development*. Chicago: University of Chicago Press, 1968.

Albert Camus

Brée, Germaine. *Camus.* New Brunswick, N.J.: Rutgers University Press, 1972.

Todd, Olivier. *Albert Camus: A Life.* New York: Knopf, 1997.

Cao Xueqin

Plaks, Andrew. *Archetype and Allegory in the "Dream of the Red Chamber."* Princeton, N.J.: Princeton University Press, 1976.

Yu, Anthony C. *Rereading the Stone: Desire and the Making of Fiction in "Dream of the Red Chamber."* Princeton, N.J.: Princeton University Press, 1997.

Catullus

Quinn, Kenneth. *Catullus: An Interpretation.* London: Batsford, 1972.

Small, Stuart G. P. *Catullus: A Reader's Guide to the Poems.* Lanham, Md.: University Press of America, 1983.

Miguel de Cervantes Saavedra

Canavaggio, Jean. *Cervantes.* New York: W. W. Norton, 1990.

McKendrick, Melveena. *Cervantes.* Boston: Little, Brown, 1980.

Geoffrey Chaucer

Donaldson, E. Talbot. *Chaucer's Poetry.* New York: John Wiley, 1975.

Pearsall, Derek. *The Life of Geoffrey Chaucer: A Critical Biography.* Oxford: Blackwell, 1992.

Anton Chekhov

Rayfield, Donald. *Anton Chekhov: A Life.* New York: Henry Holt, 1997.

Senelick, Laurence. *Anton Chekhov.* London: Macmillan, 1985.

Chikamatsu Monzaemon

Gerstle, Andrew C. *Circles of Fantasy: Convention in the Plays of Chikamatsu.* Cambridge: Harvard University Press, 1986.

Keene, Donald. *The Major Plays of Chikamatsu.* New York: Columbia University Press, 1990.

Joseph Conrad

Karl, Frederick R. *Joseph Conrad: The Three Lives.* New York: Farrar, Straus, 1979.

Watt, Ian. *Conrad and the Nineteenth Century.* Berkeley: University of California Press, 1979.

Dante Alighieri

Auerbach, Erich. *Dante, Poet of the Secular World*. Chicago: University of Chicago Press, 1961.

Bergin, Thomas G. *Dante*. Boston: Houghton Mifflin, 1965.

Daniel Defoe

Backscheider, Paula R. *Daniel Defoe: His Life*. Baltimore: Johns Hopkins University Press, 1989.

Sutherland, James. *Daniel Defoe: A Critical Study*. Boston: Houghton Mifflin, 1971.

Charles Dickens

Johnson, Edgar. *Charles Dickens, His Tragedy and Triumph*. New York: Viking Press, 1977.

Monod, Sylvère. *Dickens, the Novelist*. Norman: University of Oklahoma Press, 1968.

Emily Dickinson

Sewall, Richard B. *The Life of Emily Dickinson*. New York: Farrar, Straus, 1974.

Stocks, Kenneth. *Emily Dickinson and the Modern Consciousness*. New York: St. Martin's, 1988.

John Donne

Bald, R. C. *John Donne: A Life*. New York: Oxford University Press, 1970.

Carey, John. *John Donne: Life, Mind, and Art*. New York: Oxford University Press, 1981.

Feodor Dostoevsky

Frank, Joseph. *Dostoevsky*. Princeton, N.J.: Princeton University Press, 1976–1997.

Hingley, Ronald. *Dostoyevsky, His Life and Work*. New York: Scribner, 1978.

Theodore Dreiser

Lingeman, Richard. *Theodore Dreiser*. 2 vols. New York: Putnam, 1986–90.

Moers, Ellen. *Two Dreisers*. New York: Viking Press, 1969.

Du Fu

Chou, Eva Shan. *Reconsidering Du Fu*. New York: Cambridge University Press, 1995.

Davis, A. R. *Du Fu*. New York: Twayne Publishers, 1971.

George Eliot
Karl, Frederick. *George Eliot, Voice of a Century: A Biography*. New York: W. W. Norton, 1995.
Purkis, John Arthur. *A Preface to George Eliot*. London: Longman, 1985.

T. S. Eliot
Ackroyd, Peter. *T. S. Eliot: A Life*. New York: Simon & Schuster, 1984.
Williamson, George. *Reader's Guide to T. S. Eliot*. London: Thames and Hudson, 1960.

Ralph Ellison
Busby, Mark. *Ralph Ellison*. Boston: Twayne Publishers, 1991.
O'Meally, Robert G. *The Craft of Ralph Ellison*. Cambridge, Mass.: Harvard University Press, 1980.

Euripides
Murray, Gilbert. *Euripides and His Age*. New York: Oxford University Press, 1947.
Webster, T. B. L. *The Tragedies of Euripides*. London: Methuen, 1967.

William Faulkner
Blotner, Joseph. *Faulkner*. New York: Random House, 1974.
Minter, David. *William Faulkner: His Life and Work*. Baltimore: Johns Hopkins University Press, 1980.

Henry Fielding
Battestin, Martin C. *Henry Fielding: A Life*. New York: Routledge, 1989.
Dircks, Richard J. *Henry Fielding*. Boston: Twayne Publishers, 1983.

F. Scott Fitzgerald
Meyers, Jeffrey. *Scott Fitzgerald: A Biography*. New York: HarperCollins, 1994.
Miller, James E. *F. Scott Fitzgerald: His Art and Technique*. New York: New York University Press, 1964.

Gustave Flaubert
Buck, Stratton. *Gustave Flaubert*. Boston: Twayne Publishers, 1966.
Lottman, Herbert R. *Flaubert: A Biography*. Boston: Little, Brown, 1989.

E. M. Forster
Beaumann, Nicols. *E. M. Forster: A Biography*. New York: Knopf, 1994.
Furbank, P. N. *E. M. Forster: A Life*. New York: Harcourt, Brace, 1978.

Robert Frost

Pritchard, William. *Frost: A Literary Life Reconsidered.* New York: Oxford University Press, 1984.

Thompson, Lawrance. *Robert Frost.* New York: Holt Rinehart, 1966–1976.

Federico García Lorca

Gibson, Ian. *Federico García Lorca: A Life.* New York: Pantheon Books, 1989.

Honig, Edwin. *García Lorca.* New York: Octagon Books, 1981.

Gabriel García Márquez

Bell-Villada, Gene H. *García Márquez: The Man and His Work.* Chapel Hill: University of North Carolina Press, 1990.

Williams, Raymond L. *Gabriel García Márquez.* Boston: Twayne Publishers, 1984.

Johann Wolfgang von Goethe

Gray, Ronald. *Goethe: A Critical Introduction.* London: Cambridge University Press, 1967.

Boyle, Nicholas. *Goethe.* New York: Oxford University Press, 1991.

Nikolai Gogol

Maguire, Robert A. *Exploring Gogol.* Stanford, Calif.: Stanford University Press, 1994.

Setchkarev, Vsevolod. *Gogol: His Life and Works.* New York: New York University Press, 1965.

Günter Grass

Hollington, Michael. *Günter Grass: The Writer in a Pluralistic Society.* Boston: M. Boyars, 1980.

Lawson, Richard H. *Günter Grass.* New York: F. Ungar, 1985.

Thomas Hardy

Millgate, Michael. *Thomas Hardy.* New York: Random House, 1982.

Howe, Irving. *Thomas Hardy.* New York: Macmillan, 1967.

Nathaniel Hawthorne

Martin, Terence. *Nathaniel Hawthorne.* Boston: Twayne Publishers, 1983.

Mellow, James R. *Nathaniel Hawthorne in His Times.* Boston: Houghton Mifflin, 1980.

Seamus Heaney

Collins, Floyd. *Seamus Heaney: The Crisis of Identity*. Newark, N.J.: University of Delaware Press, 2003.

Vendler, Helen. *Seamus Heaney*. Cambridge, Mass.: Harvard University Press, 1998.

Heinrich Heine

Phelan, Anthony. *Reading Heinrich Heine*. Cambridge: Cambridge University Press, 2007.

Sammons, Jeffrey L. *Heinrich Heine: A Modern Biography*. Princeton, N.J.: Princeton University Press, 1980.

Ernest Hemingway

Baker, Carlos. *Ernest Hemingway: A Life Story*. New York: Scribner, 1969.

Young, Philip. *Ernest Hemingway: A Reconsideration*. University Park: Pennsylvania State University Press, 1966.

Homer

Camps, W. A. *An Introduction to Homer*. New York: Oxford University Press, 1980.

Clarke, Howard. *Homer's Readers*. Newark, N.J.: University of Delaware Press, 1981.

Horace

Levi, Peter. *Horace: A Life*. New York: Routledge, 1998.

McNeill, Randall L. *Horace: Image, Identity, and Audience*. Baltimore: Johns Hopkins University Press, 2001.

Victor Hugo

Houston, John Porter. *Victor Hugo*. Boston: Twayne Publishers, 1988.

Robb, Graham. *Victor Hugo*. New York: W. W. Norton, 1997.

Henrik Ibsen

Meyer, Michael. *Ibsen: A Biography*. Garden City, N.Y.: Doubleday, 1971.

Thomas, David. *Henrik Ibsen*. New York: Grove Press, 1984.

Henry James

Edel, Leon. *Henry James: A Life*. New York: Harper and Row, 1985.

Poole, Adrian. *Henry James*. New York: St. Martin's, 1991.

Ben Jonson

Kay, W. David. *Ben Jonson: A Literary Life*. New York: St. Martin's Press, 1995.

Riggs, David. *Ben Jonson: A Life*. Cambridge, Mass.: Harvard University Press, 1989.

James Joyce

Beja, Morris. *James Joyce: A Literary Life*. Columbus: Ohio State University Press, 1992.

Ellmann, Richard. *James Joyce*. New York: Oxford University Press, 1982.

Franz Kafka

Hayman, Ronald. *Kafka: A Biography*. New York: Oxford University Press, 1982.

Lawson, Richard H. *Franz Kafka*. New York: F. Ungar, 1987.

Kālidāsa

Miller, Barbara Stoler, ed. *Theater of Memory: The Plays of Kālidāsa*. New York: Columbia University Press, 1984.

Sabnis, S. A. *Kālidāsa, His Style and His Times*. Bombay: N. M. Tripathi, 1966.

Kawabata Yasunari

Gessel, Van C. *Three Modern Novelists: Soseki, Tanizaki, Kawabata*. New York: Kodansha International, 1993.

Miyoshi, Masao. *Accomplices of Silence: The Modern Japanese Novel*. Berkeley: University of California Press, 1974.

John Keats

Bate, Walter Jackson. *John Keats*. Cambridge, Mass.: Harvard University Press, 1963.

Wasserman, Earl. *The Finer Tone*. Westport, Conn.: Greenwood Press, 1983.

D. H. Lawrence

Hobsbaum, Philip. *Reader's Guide to D. H. Lawrence*. London: Thames and Hudson, 1981.

Moore, Harry T. *The Priest of Love: A Life of D. H. Lawrence*. New York: Farrar, Straus, 1974.

Doris Lessing

Pickering, Jean. *Understanding Doris Lessing*. Columbia: University of South Carolina Press, 1990.

Whittaker, Ruth. *Doris Lessing*. New York: St. Martin's Press, 1988.

Li Bo

Varsano, Paula M. *Tracking the Banished Immortal.* Honolulu: University of Hawaii Press, 2003.

Waley, Arthur. *The Poetry and Career of Li Bo.* New York: Macmillan, 1950.

Lu Xun

Lee, Leo Ou-Gan. *Voices from the Iron House: A Study of Lu Xun.* Bloomington: Indiana University Press, 1974.

Lyell, William A. *Lu Hsün's Vision of Reality.* Berkeley: University of California Press, 1976.

Thomas Mann

Hayman, Ronald. *Thomas Mann: A Biography.* New York: Scribner, 1995.

Reed, T. J. *Thomas Mann: The Uses of Tradition.* New York: Oxford University Press, 1996.

Christopher Marlowe

Kocher, Paul H. *Christopher Marlowe: A Study of His Thought, Learning, and Character.* Chapel Hill: University of North Carolina Press, 1946.

Levin, Harry. *The Overreacher: A Study of Christopher Marlowe.* Boston: Beacon Press, 1964.

Herman Melville

Miller, James F., Jr. *A Reader's Guide to Herman Melville.* New York: Octagon Books, 1973.

Robertson-Lorant, Laurie. *Melville: A Biography.* New York: Clarkson Potter, 1995.

Arthur Miller

Bigsby, Christopher. *Arthur Miller: A Critical Study.* New York: Cambridge University Press, 2005.

Miller, Arthur. *Timebends: A Life.* New York: Grove Press, 1987.

John Milton

Miller, David M. *John Milton: Poetry.* Boston: Twayne Publishers, 1978.

Parker, William Riley. *Milton: A Biography.* New York: Oxford University Press, 1968.

Molière

Howard, W. D. *Molière, A Playwright and His Audience.* New York: Cambridge University Press, 1982.

Walker, Hallam. *Molière.* Boston: Twayne Publishers, 1990.

Toni Morrison

David, Ron. *Toni Morrison Explained: A Reader's Road Map to the Novels.* New York: Random House, 2000.

Peach, Linden. *Toni Morrison.* New York: St. Martin's Press, 2000.

Murasaki Shikibu

Bowring, Richard. *Murasaki Shikibu: "The Tale of Genji."* New York: Cambridge University Press, 1988.

Field, Norma. *The Splendor of Longing in "The Tale of Genji."* Princeton, N.J.: Princeton University Press, 1987.

Robert Musil

Bangerter, Lowell A. *Robert Musil.* New York: Continuum, 1989.

Pike, Burton. *Robert Musil: An Introduction to His Work.* Ithaca, N.Y.: Cornell University Press, 1961.

Vladimir Nabokov

Boyd, Brian. *Vladimir Nabokov.* 2 vols. Princeton, N.J.: Princeton University Press, 1990–91.

Rampton, David. *Vladimir Nabokov.* New York: St. Martin's, 1993.

Pablo Neruda

Costa, René de. *The Poetry of Pablo Neruda.* Cambridge, Mass.: Harvard University Press, 1978.

Teitelboim, Volodia. *Neruda: An Intimate Biography.* Austin: University of Texas Press, 1991.

Flannery O'Connor

Orvell, Miles. *Flannery O'Connor: An Introduction.* Jackson: University Press of Mississippi, 1991.

Whitt, Margaret Earley. *Understanding Flannery O'Connor.* Columbia: University of South Carolina Press, 1995.

Eugene O'Neill

Berlin, Normand. *Eugene O'Neill.* New York: Grove Press, 1982.

Sheaffer, Louis. *O'Neill.* 2 vols. Boston: Little, Brown, 1968–73.

George Orwell

Myers, Valerie. *George Orwell.* New York: St. Martin's Press, 1991.

Shelden, Michael. *George Orwell: The Authorized Biography.* New York: HarperCollins, 1991.

Ovid

Brooks, Otis. *Ovid As an Epic Poet.* Cambridge: Cambridge University Press, 1970.

Mack, Sara. *Ovid.* New Haven, Conn.: Yale University Press, 1988.

Petrarch

Bergin, Thomas G. *Petrarch.* Boston: Twayne Publishers, 1970.

Bishop, Morris. *Petrarch and His World.* Bloomington: Indiana University Press, 1963.

Harold Pinter

Billington, Michael. *The Life and Work of Harold Pinter.* London: Faber and Faber, 1996.

Thompson, David T. *Pinter, the Player's Playwright.* London: Macmillan, 1985.

Luigi Pirandello

Bassabesem, Fiora A. *Understanding Luigi Pirandello.* Columbia: University of South Carolina Press, 1997.

Giudice, Gaspar. *Pirandello: A Biography.* New York: Oxford University Press, 1975.

Edgar Allan Poe

Hoffman, Daniel. *Poe Poe Poe Poe Poe Poe Poe.* Garden City, N.Y.: Doubleday, 1972.

Silverman, Kenneth. *Edgar A. Poe: Mournful and Never-Ending Remembrance.* New York: HarperCollins, 1991.

Alexander Pope

Mack, Maynard. *Pope: A Life.* New York: W. W. Norton, 1986.

Rogers, Pat. *Introduction to Pope.* London: Methuen, 1975.

Marcel Proust

Painter, George. *Proust.* New York: Random House, 1978.

Shattuck, Roger. *Proust.* New York: Viking Press, 1974.

Alexander Pushkin

Bayley, John. *Pushkin: A Comparative Commentary.* Cambridge: Cambridge University Press, 1971.

Edmonds, Robin. *Pushkin: The Man and His Age.* New York: St. Martin's, 1995.

François Rabelais

Frame, Donald M. *François Rabelais: A Study.* New York: Harcourt, Brace, 1977.

Greene, Thomas M. *Rabelais: A Study in Comic Courage.* Englewood Cliffs, N.J.: Prentice-Hall, 1970.

Jean Racine

Maskell, David. *Racine: A Theatrical Reading.* New York: Oxford University Press, 1991.

Weinberg, Bernard. *The Art of Jean Racine.* Chicago: University of Chicago Press, 1963.

Samuel Richardson

Brophy, Elizabeth Bergen. *Samuel Richardson: The Triumph of Craft.* Knoxville: University of Tennessee Press, 1974.

Flynn, Carol Houlihan. *Samuel Richardson, a Man of Letters.* Princeton, N.J.: Princeton University Press, 1982.

Rainer Maria Rilke

Prater, Donald. *A Ringing Glass: The Life of Rainer Maria Rilke.* Oxford: Clarendon Press, 1986.

Ryan, Judith. *Rilke, Modernism and Poetic Tradition.* New York: Cambridge University Press, 1999.

Sappho

Greene, Ellen, ed. *Reading Sappho: Contemporary Approaches.* Berkeley: University of California Press, 1996.

Wilson, Lyn Hatherly. *Sappho's Sweetbitter Songs.* New York: Routledge, 1996.

Walter Scott

Cockshut, A. O. J. *The Achievement of Walter Scott.* London: Colliers, 1969.

Johnson, Edgar. *Sir Walter Scott: The Great Unknown.* New York: Macmillan, 1970.

William Shakespeare

Bradbrook, M. C. *Shakespeare: The Poet in His World.* New York: Columbia University Press, 1978.

Honan, Park. *Shakespeare: A Life.* New York: Oxford University Press, 1998.

George Bernard Shaw

Bentley, Eric. *Bernard Shaw: A Reconsideration.* New York: W. W. Norton, 1976.

Holroyd, Michael. *Bernard Shaw*. 4 vols. New York: Random House, 1988–92.

Percy Bysshe Shelley
Holmes, Richard. *Shelley: The Pursuit*. New York: Dutton, 1975.
Reiman, Donald. *Percy Bysshe Shelley*. Boston: Twayne Publishers, 1990.

Isaac Bashevis Singer
Friedman, Lawrence S. *Understanding Isaac Bashevis Singer*. Columbia: University of South Carolina Press, 1988.
Hadda, Janet. *Isaac Bashevis Singer: A Life*. New York: Oxford University Press, 1997.

Sophocles
Knox, Bernard M. W. *The Heroic Temper: Studies in Sophoclean Tragedy*. Berkeley: University of California Press, 1964.
Scodel, Ruth. *Sophocles*. Boston: Twayne Publishers, 1984.

Edmund Spenser
Oram, William A. *Edmund Spenser*. New York: Twayne Publishers, 1997.
Waller, Gary. *Edmund Spenser: A Literary Life*. New York: St. Martin's Press, 1994.

Gertrude Stein
Bowers, Jane P. *Gertrude Stein*. New York: St. Martin's, 1993.
Mellow, James R. *Charmed Circle: Gertrude Stein and Company*. Boston: Houghton Mifflin, 1974.

Stendhal
Keates, Jonathan. *Stendhal*. New York: Carroll & Graf, 1997.
Talbot, Emile J. *Stendhal Revisited*. New York: Twayne Publishers, 1993.

Laurence Sterne
Cash, Arthur H. *Laurence Sterne*. 2 vols. New York: Methuen, 1975–86.
Kraft, Elizabeth. *Laurence Sterne Revisited*. New York: Twayne Publishers, 1996.

Wallace Stevens
Newcomb, John T. *Wallace Stevens and Literary Canons*. Jackson: University Press of Mississippi, 1992.
Richardson, Joan. *Wallace Stevens*. 2 vols. New York: Beech Tree Books, 1986–88.

August Strindberg

Meyer, Michael. *August Strindberg*. New York: Random House, 1985.

Sprinchorn, Evert. *Strindberg As Dramatist*. New Haven, Conn.: Yale University Press, 1982.

Jonathan Swift

Ehrenpreis, Irvin. *Swift, the Man, His Works, and the Age*. 2 vols. Cambridge, Mass.: Harvard University Press, 1962–83.

Nokes, David. *Jonathan Swift, a Hypocrite Reversed*. New York: Oxford University Press, 1985.

Rabindranath Tagore

Chatterjee, Bhabatosh. *Rabindranath Tagore and Modern Sensibility*. Delhi: Oxford University Press, 1996.

Kripalani, Krisna. *Rabindranath Tagore: A Biography*. New York: Oxford University Press, 1962.

Tanizaki Jun'ichirō

Gessel, Van C. *Three Modern Novelists: Soseki, Tanizaki, Kawabata*. New York: Kodansha International, 1993.

Ito, Kenneth K. *Visions of Desire: Tanizaki's Fictional Worlds*. Stanford, Calif.: Stanford University Press, 1991.

Alfred, Lord Tennyson

Martin, Robert B. *Tennyson: The Unquiet Heart*. New York: Oxford University Press, 1980.

Ricks, Christopher B. *Tennyson*. Berkeley: University of California Press, 1989.

William Makepeace Thackeray

Colby, Robert A. *Thackeray's Canvass of Humanity*. Columbus: Ohio State University Press, 1979.

Ray, Gordon N. *Thackeray*. 2 vols. New York: McGraw-Hill, 1955–58.

Leo Tolstoy

Christian, R. F. *Tolstoy: A Critical Introduction*. London: Cambridge University Press, 1969.

Wilson, A. N. *Tolstoy*. New York: W. W. Norton, 1988.

Anthony Trollope

Hall, N. John. *Trollope: A Biography*. New York: Oxford University Press, 1991.

Harvey, Geoffrey. *The Art of Anthony Trollope*. New York: St. Martin's, 1980.

Mark Twain

Gerber, John C. *Mark Twain*. Boston: Twayne Publishers, 1988.

Kaplan, Justin. *Mr. Clemens and Mark Twain: A Biography*. New York: Simon & Schuster, 1966.

Virgil

Knight, W. F. Jackson. *Roman Vergil*. New York: Barnes and Noble, 1971.

Otis, Brooks. *Virgil: A Study in Civilized Poetry*. Oxford: Clarendon Press, 1964.

Voltaire

Aldridge A. Owen. *Voltaire and the Century of Light*. Princeton, N.J.: Princeton University Press, 1975.

Mason, Haydon. *Voltaire*. London: Hutchinson, 1975.

Walt Whitman

Allen, Gay Wilson. *The Solitary Singer: A Critical Biography of Walt Whitman*. New York: Macmillan, 1955.

Miller, Edwin H. *Walt Whitman's Poetry: A Psychological Journey*. Boston: Houghton Mifflin, 1968.

Oscar Wilde

Ellmann, Richard. *Oscar Wilde*. New York: Knopf, 1988.

Gillespie, Michael Patrick. *Oscar Wilde: Life, Work and Criticism*. Fredericton, New Brunswick: York Press, 1990.

Tennessee Williams

Griffin, Alice. *Understanding Tennessee Williams*. Columbia: University of South Carolina, 1995.

Hayman, Ronald. *Tennessee Williams: Everyone Else Is an Audience*. New Haven: Yale University Press, 1993.

Virginia Woolf

Bell, Quentin. *Virginia Woolf*. New York: Harcourt, Brace, 1972.

Gordon, Lyndall. *Virginia Woolf: A Writer's Life*. New York: W. W. Norton, 1984.

William Wordsworth

Moorman, Mary. *William Wordsworth: A Biography*. 2 vols. Oxford: Clarendon Press, 1957–65.

Woodring, Carl. *Wordsworth*. Cambridge, Mass.: Harvard University Press, 1965.

Richard Wright

Fabre, Michel. *The World of Richard Wright.* Jackson: University of Mississippi Press, 1985.

Webb, Constance. *Richard Wright: A Biography.* New York: Putnam, 1968.

William Butler Yeats

Foster, R. F. *W. B. Yeats: A Life.* New York: Oxford University Press, 1997.

Unterecker, John. *A Reader's Guide to W. B. Yeats.* New York: Octagon Books, 1971.

Zeami Motokiyo

Hare, Thomas Blenman. *Zeami's Style: The Noh Plays of Zeami Motokiyo.* Stanford, Calif.: Stanford University Press, 1986.

Seking, Masaru. *Zeami and His Theories of Noh Drama.* Gerrards Cross, Eng.: C. Smythe, 1985.

Émile Zola

Berg, William J., and Laurey K. Martin. *Emile Zola Revisited.* New York: Twayne Publishers, 1992.

Brown, Frederick. *Zola: A Life.* New York: Farrar, Straus, 1995.

INDEX

Z